Against the Odds

DISADVANTAGED STUDENTS
WHO SUCCEED IN SCHOOL

OECD

This work is published on the responsibility of the Secretary-General of the OECD. The opinions expressed and arguments employed herein do not necessarily reflect the official views of the Organisation or of the governments of its member countries.

Please cite this publication as:
OECD (2011), *Against the Odds: Disadvantaged Students Who Succeed in School*, OECD Publishing.
http://dx.doi.org/10.1787/9789264090873-en

ISBN 978-92-64-08995-2 (print)
ISBN 978-92-64-09087-3 (PDF)

The statistical data for Israel are supplied by and under the responsibility of the relevant Israeli authorities. The use of such data by the OECD is without prejudice to the status of the Golan Heights, East Jerusalem and Israeli settlements in the West Bank under the terms of international law.

Photo credits:
Getty Images © Ariel Skelley
Getty Images © Geostock
Getty Images © Jack Hollingsworth
Stocklib Image Bank © Yuri Arcurs

Corrigenda to OECD publications may be found on line at: *www.oecd.org/publishing/corrigenda*.
PISA™, OECD/PISA™ and the PISA logo are trademaks of the Organisation for Economic Co-operation and Development (OECD). All use of OECD trademarks is prohibited without written permission from the OECD.

© OECD 2011

You can copy, download or print OECD content for your own use, and you can include excerpts from OECD publications, databases and multimedia products in your own documents, presentations, blogs, websites and teaching materials, provided that suitable acknowledgment of OECD as source and copyright owner is given. All requests for public or commercial use and translation rights should be submitted to *rights@oecd.org*. Requests for permission to photocopy portions of this material for public or commercial use shall be addressed directly to the Copyright Clearance Center (CCC) at *info@copyright.com* or the Centre français d'exploitation du droit de copie (CFC) at *contact@cfcopies.com*.

Foreword

Most of the students who perform poorly in PISA share a challenging socio-economic background. Some of their socio-economically disadvantaged peers, however, excel in PISA and beat the odds working against them. This report focuses on resilient students; those who succeed at school despite a disadvantaged background. These individuals show what is possible and provide students, parents, policy makers and other education stakeholders with insights into the drivers of skills and competencies among socio-economically disadvantaged students.

While the prevalence of resilience is not the same across educational systems, it is possible to identify substantial numbers of resilient students in practically all OECD countries. Using a comparable definition, in Australia, Canada, Finland, Japan, Korea, New Zealand and Portugal, close to one-half of disadvantaged students exceed an internationally comparable performance benchmark and can be considered successful from a global perspective. In other countries, the proportion is more modest.

The evidence from PISA shows that many disadvantaged students do not enjoy as many opportunities to learn science at school as their more advantaged peers. On average, across OECD countries, disadvantaged students spent 20% less time learning science at school than their more advantaged peers. Among disadvantaged students in countries like France, Germany and the Netherlands, resilient students spend over one hour and 45 minutes more learning science at school than disadvantaged low achievers. The evidence in PISA suggests that investing into learning time is even more important for disadvantaged students. Opportunities to learn science at school, measured in courses and hours, allow some disadvantaged students to close the performance gap with their more advantaged peers.

Positive approaches to learning are naturally associated with better performance for all students. High levels of self-confidence or interest in science across disadvantaged students are good predictors of student resilience. However, the evidence from PISA shows that the association between performance and positive approaches to learning is stronger for more advantaged students than for disadvantaged students. In some cases, like in Germany, this association simply disappears among disadvantaged students; in other cases, such as in New Zealand, it is halved. This evidence suggests that from an equity perspective, targeting disadvantaged students when implementing policies aimed at fostering positive approaches to learning among students is necessary to avoid widening the performance gap between disadvantaged students and their more advantaged peers.

This publication was prepared at the OECD Directorate for Education under the direction of Andreas Schleicher with advice from the PISA Analysis and Dissemination Group of the PISA Governing Board. The report was completed with the support of the countries participating in PISA, the experts and institutions working within the framework of the PISA Consortium and the OECD. The initial draft was prepared by Luke Miller and Gayle Christensen, from the Urban Institute, who conceptualised the report, performed preliminary analyses and drafted the initial chapters. Francesca Borgonovi, Maciej Jakubowski and Pablo Zoido, from the OECD, conceptualised and wrote Chapter 4 and edited and wrote the report in its final form.

Soojin Park and Simone Bloem, from the OECD, provided analytical and editorial assistance. Niccolina Clements, Juliet Evans and Elisabeth Villoutreix provided administrative and editorial input for the report. Fung Kwan Tam did the layout design. The development of the report was steered by the PISA Governing Board, which is chaired by Lorna Bertrand (United Kingdom).

The report is published on the responsibility of the Secretary-General of the OECD.

Lorna Bertrand
Chair of the PISA Governing Board

Barbara Ischinger
Director for Education, OECD

Table of Contents

EXECUTIVE SUMMARY 11

CHAPTER 1 PISA AS A STUDY OF STUDENT RESILIENCE 13

Introduction 14
Socio-economic background and academic success 14
Student resilience 16
The Programme for International Student Assessment (PISA) as a study of student resilience 16
Structure of the report 18

CHAPTER 2 DEFINING AND CHARACTERISING STUDENT RESILIENCE IN PISA 21

Introduction 22
Defining resilient and disadvantaged low-achieving students using PISA 22
- An international perspective 23
- Comparing the shares of resilient students across countries 24
- A within-country perspective 24

Similarities and differences of resilient students across countries 25
Student resilience across science, reading and mathematics 28
Student resilience among specific demographic groups within countries 28
- Gender 29
- Immigrant background 30
- Language spoken at home 31

Conclusion 32

CHAPTER 3 A PROFILE OF STUDENT RESILIENCE 35

Introduction 36
Students' attitudes and behaviours and the learning environment at school:
Definitions and overview 36
The analysis: A brief description of the models presented in this chapter 39
Student approaches to learning 39
- Student motivation to learn science 39
- Student engagement with science activities outside of school 43
- Student confidence in their science ability 46
- Student perspectives towards science-related careers 49

Student engagement in science courses at school and time spent learning 52
Learning environment at school 55
Combined effects of student and school factors on student resilience 61
Conclusion 65

CHAPTER 4 CLOSING THE GAP? ENHANCING THE PERFORMANCE OF SOCIO-ECONOMICALLY DISADVANTAGED STUDENTS 67

Introduction 68
Models of student resilience 68
Student approaches to learning 69
- Improved performance 69
- Closing the gap 70

Hours spent and courses taken to learn science 72
- Improved performance 72
- Closing the gap 73

Learning environment at school 75
- Improved performance 75
- Closing the gap 75

Conclusion 75

CHAPTER 5 CONCLUSIONS AND POLICY IMPLICATIONS 79

Introduction 80
Findings and implications for educational policy and practice 81

REFERENCES 83

ANNEXES 87
Annex A1: Defining and characterising student resilience in PISA 87
Annex A2: A profile of student resilience 100
Annex A3: Closing the gap? Enhancing the performance of socio-economically disadvantaged students 149
Annex A4: Conclusions and policy implications 160
Annex A5: Technical notes 179

BOXES

Box 1.1	Key features of PISA 2006	15
Box 3.1	Interpreting the PISA indices on students' approaches to learning	37
Box 3.2	Interpreting the data from schools and their relationship to student performance	38
Box 3.3	Interpreting predictive models on the likelihood of being resilient	40
Box A5.1	General interest in science	186
Box A5.2	Instrumental motivation to learn science	186
Box A5.3	Participation in science-related activities	187
Box A5.4	Self-efficacy	188
Box A5.5	Self-concept	188
Box A5.6	School preparation for science careers	189

Box A5.7	Information on science-related careers	189
Box A5.8	Attendance in compulsory science courses at school	191
Box A5.9	Number of regular science learning hours	191
Box A5.10	Public and private schools	192
Box A5.11	School competition	192
Box A5.12	Academic selection in student admission policies	193
Box A5.13	School activities to promote science learning	193
Box A5.14	School's educational resources	194
Box A5.15	Understanding logistic regression and interpreting odds ratios	197

FIGURES

Figure 1.1	A map of PISA countries and economies	17
Figure 2.1	Shares of resilient and disadvantaged low achievers among disadvantaged students, by country	24
Figure 2.2	PISA index of economic, social and cultural status for system average, resilient and disadvantaged low achievers	26
Figure 2.3	Performance in PISA science, system average, resilient and disadvantaged low achievers	26
Figure 2.4	Percentage of resilient and disadvantaged low achievers above and below the basic level of proficiency	27
Figure 2.5	Overlap of resilience in different subject domains	28
Figure 2.6	Percentage of male students among disadvantaged students and resilient students	29
Figure 2.7	Percentage of native students among disadvantaged students and resilient students	30
Figure 2.8	Percentage of students who speak the test language at home among disadvantaged students and resilient students	32
Figure 3.1	Internal and external motivation to learn science	41
Figure 3.2	Engagement in science-related activities	45
Figure 3.3	Student self-confidence in their science ability	47
Figure 3.4	Students' perspectives towards science related careers	50
Figure 3.5	Student engagement in science courses at school	53
Figure 3.6	Hours in science regular lessons at school	54
Figure 3.7	Schools' competition, and management	57
Figure 3.8	Schools' academic selectivity	58
Figure 3.9	School resources and science promotion activities	60
Figure 3.10	Combined model	62
Figure 4.1a	Association between student approaches to learning and performance in science	70
Figure 4.1b	Differential effect for disadvantaged students of student approaches to learning	71
Figure 4.2a	Association between students' participation in science courses and student performance in science	73
Figure 4.2b	Differential effect for disadvantaged students of students' participation in science courses	74

TABLE OF CONTENTS

Figure 4.3a   Association between school characteristics and student performance in science 76
Figure 4.3b   Differential effect for disadvantaged students of school characteristics 77
Figure A5.1   Within-country relative definition of resilient and disadvantaged students in comparison to
               the internationally comparable definition 182

TABLES

Table A1.1   Shares of resilient and disadvantaged low achievers among all students, by country and gender 88
Table A1.2   PISA index of economic, social and cultural status for system average, resilient and
              disadvantaged low achievers 89
Table A1.3   Differences in the components of the economic, social and cultural status index 90
Table A1.4   Performance in PISA science, system average, resilient and disadvantaged low achievers 93
Table A1.5   Percentage of resilient students and disadvantaged low achievers above and below the basic level of proficiency ... 94
Table A1.6   Overlap of student resilience by subject 95
Table A1.7   Percentage of male students among resilient, low achievers and all disadvantaged students 97
Table A1.8   Percentage of native students among disadvantaged students and resilient students 98
Table A1.9   Percentage of students who speak the test language at home among disadvantaged students
              and resilient students 99
Table A2.1   Correlations among key indices 100
Table A2.1a   Interest in science (underlying percentages), by student group 101
Table A2.1b   Interest in science (underlying percentages), by student group 103
Table A2.1c   Interest in science (underlying percentages), by student group 104
Table A2.2a   Instrumental interest in science (underlying percentages), by student group 105
Table A2.2b   Instrumental motivation by student group 107
Table A2.2c   Relationship between being resilient and PISA index of instrumental motivation in science learning 108
Table A2.3a   Engagement in science-related activities outside school (underlying percentages), by student group 109
Table A2.3b   Engagement in science-related activities outside school, by student group 111
Table A2.3c   Relationship between being resilient and PISA index of science activities outside the school 112
Table A2.4a   Science self-efficacy (underlying percentages), by student group 113
Table A2.4b   Science self-efficacy by student group 115
Table A2.4c   Relationship between being resilient and PISA index of science efficacy 116
Table A2.5a   Science self-concept (underlying percentages), by student group 117
Table A2.5b   Science self-concept by student group 119
Table A2.5c   Relationship between being resilient and PISA index of science self-concept 120
Table A2.6a   Science-related careers (underlying percentages), by student group 121
Table A2.6b   Science-related careers by country and student group 122
Table A2.6c   Relationship between being resilient and PISA index of school preparation for science career 123

Table A2.7a	Students' information on science-related careers (underlying percentages), by student group	124
Table A2.7b	Students' information on science-related careers by student group	125
Table A2.7c	Relationship between being resilient and PISA index of student information on science careers	126
Table A2.8a	Share of students who took general science compulsory courses this or last year, by student group	127
Table A2.8b	Relationship between being resilient and taking general science compulsory courses	128
Table A2.9a	Number of attended compulsory courses in general science, physics, biology and chemistry, by student group	129
Table A2.9b	Relationship between being resilient and number of attended compulsory courses in general science, physics, biology and chemistry	130
Table A2.10a	Number of hours students report spending in regular lessons at school learning science	131
Table A2.10b	Relationship between being resilient and hours spent in regular lessons at school learning science	132
Table A2.11a	Share of students in private schools	133
Table A2.11b	Relationship between being resilient and being in private schools	134
Table A2.12a	Share of students in schools which compete with other schools	135
Table A2.12b	Relationship between being resilient and being in schools which compete with other schools	136
Table A2.13a	Share of students in schools which select students based on academic record	137
Table A2.13b	Relationship between being resilient and being in schools which select based on academic record	138
Table A2.14a	Quality of educational resources (underlying percentages), by student group	139
Table A2.14b	Quality of school educational resources, by student group	141
Table A2.14c	Relationship between being resilient and index of the quality of school educational resources	142
Table A2.15a	School activities to promote the learning of science (underlying percentages), by student group	143
Table A2.15b	School activities to promote the learning of science, by student group	145
Table A2.15c	Relationship between being resilient and index of school activities to promote the learning of science	146
Table A2.16	Combined model	147
Table A3.1a	Approaches to learning among disadvantaged and non-disadvantaged students	149
Table A3.1b	Approaches to learning, overall performance effect and differential effect for disadvantaged students	152
Table A3.2a	Number of science courses and learning hours among disadvantaged and non-disadvantaged students	154
Table A3.2b	Courses and hours, overall performance effect and differential effect for disadvantaged students	155
Table A3.3a	Learning environment at school among disadvantaged and non-disadvantaged students	156
Table A3.3b	Learning environment at school, overall performance effect and differential effect for disadvantaged students	158
Table A4.1	Missing data analysis and agreement analysis for parental occupation by country and ESCS tertile	160
Table A4.2	Missing data analysis and agreement analysis for parental education by country and ESCS tertile	160
Table A4.3	Difference in means test results on matched sample for selected variables	161
Table A4.4	Difference in means test results on alternative definition for selected variables	163
Table A4.5	Country means of student approaches to learning	166

TABLE OF CONTENTS

Table A4.6	School policies, descriptive statistics	168
Table A4.7	Odds ratios for the background model used in Chapter 3	169
Table A4.8	Regression coefficients for the background model used in Chapter 4	171
Table A4.9	Percentage of students with missing information on the socio-economic status in the original PISA sample by country	175
Table A4.10	Share of students with missing information on a variable (Percentage of observations in the analytical sample)	176
Table A4.11	Weighted percentage of resilient students and comparison group	178

Executive Summary

School success is possible for socio-economically disadvantaged students; in fact, resilient students are a common feature in some educational systems.

The proportion of disadvantaged students that are successful varies considerably across educational systems. In some education systems, like in Australia, Canada, Finland, Japan, Korea, New Zealand and Portugal close to half of disadvantaged students exceed an internationally comparable benchmark and can be considered successful from an international perspective.

A within-country perspective is best suited for analysing policies, school and student characteristics associated with student resilience. When looking at disadvantaged students that are succesful within countries, resilient students' performance is high even when compared to their more advantaged peers. On average, most resilient students in OECD countries are strong performers, achieving proficiency Level 4 in the PISA science scale (which has 6 Levels). Students performing at Levels 5 and 6 are considered top performers. In partner countries and economies the vast majority of resilient students achieve at least Level 2, the baseline level, in the PISA science scale. Thus, it is possible to find disadvantaged students, who despite the odds against them, become resilient and succeed at school. These young people show that it is possible for disadvantaged students to excel in PISA.

Taking more science courses benefits disadvantaged students even more than it does their more advantaged peers. Therefore, exposing disadvantaged students to science learning at school might help close performance gaps.

Disadvantaged students in many countries spend little time learning science in regular lessons at school. On average, across OECD countries, disadvantaged students spent 20% less time learning science at school than their more advantaged peers. While relatively advantaged students spend more than three hours on regular science lessons at school per week, disadvantaged students spend about two hours and a half. For example, in Belgium, Luxembourg, the Netherlands, the Slovak Republic and Switzerland disadvantaged students spend less than two hours a week in regular lessons at schools learning science.

Among disadvantaged students, resilient students – who beat the odds and succeed at school – spend more time learning science at school than disadvantaged low achievers. Differences are especially pronounced in France, Germany, and the Netherlands, where resilient students spend at least one hour and 45 minutes more than disadvantaged low achievers learning science at school per week. In the Netherlands, on average disadvantaged low achievers spend less than one hour and 15 minutes a week learning science at school, the lowest average across OECD countries.

In general, time spent learning science is one of the correlates of better performance that benefits the most disadvantaged students. An extra hour of regular science classes increases the likelihood of being resilient in all OECD countries (except Denmark, Iceland, Portugal, and Mexico). Across OECD countries, on average, the odds of being resilient for disadvantaged students who spend an extra hour a week learning science at school are 1.27 times greater than the odds of disadvantaged students who do not have that opportunity to learn science at school, after accounting for a host of student and school background factors, approaches to learning and school policies.

How to get more disadvantaged students further exposed to science at school varies across countries. For example, in some countries, it may mean ensuring that more disadvantaged students participate in compulsory science courses. In countries like Australia, Germany, the Netherlands, the United Kingdom, Sweden or the United States, with large relative differences (more than 8 percentage points) between the proportion of disadvantaged and more advantaged students taking compulsory courses in science, the differences in performance between those taking science courses and those that do not are also large. For example, in the United States across the board attending a science course is associated with a relatively modest increase in performance of about 15 score points on the PISA science scale, but for disadvantaged students that advantage almost triples, to more than 40 score points. In Australia, the odds of being resilient for disadvantaged students who take part in compulsory science course are four times greater than the odds of being resilient for disadvantaged students who do not take part on these courses, even after accounting for student and school background factors.

If science is important to success later in life and the betterment of society, then disadvantaged students need to be exposed to science in school. All else equal, policies geared to this goal will help improve equity in educational outcomes and boost average performance.

Positive approaches to learning are also key predictors of student resilience, but policies to help bridge the performance gap in this area need to target disadvantaged students.

Focusing on disadvantaged students, the evidence in PISA reveals that resilient students are engaged and confident learners who enjoy learning science and display a series of positive attitudes towards learning science. Resilient students are more motivated, more engaged and more self-confident than their disadvantaged low-achieving peers. For example, across OECD countries, on average, self-confident disadvantaged students are 1.95 times more likely to be resilient than disadvantaged students who are not so self-confident, even after accounting for a host of student and school background factors, including how many hours they spend learning science at school per week.

Yet, an analysis of the relationship between these factors and performance in a broader context suggests that correlates of achievement such as self-confidence, engagement and other approaches to learning are less beneficial for disadvantaged students than for their more advantaged peers. For example, among more advantaged students in the United Kingdom those who express a high level of instrumental motivation and are interested to learn science achieve more than 20 PISA score points than those who are less motivated and interested in science. This positive relation is only half as strong for disadvantaged students. In Germany, the positive association between performance and a high level of instrumental motivation to learn science that is apparent for advantaged students disappears among disadvantaged students. In New Zealand high self-concept means an increase of almost 40 PISA score points among relatively advantaged students, however this positive relation is half as strong among disadvantaged students.

It is therefore possible that policies aimed at raising student attitudes or engagement with science will not help bridge and may even widen the achievement gap between disadvantaged students and their more advantaged peers. From an equity perspective, targeted policies to disadvantaged students aimed at fostering positive approaches to learning, such as building student confidence are better suited than untargeted policies in these areas. More advantaged students probably enjoy a supportive household environment that makes their confidence and other positive approaches to learning more effective. The evidence shows disadvantaged students do not enjoy this extra boost on positive approaches to learning.

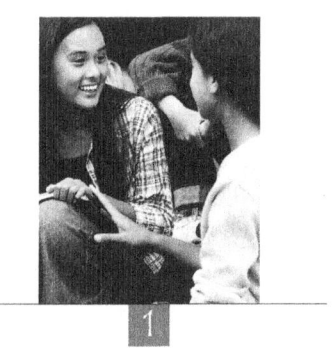

PISA as a Study of Student Resilience

INTRODUCTION

Educating children and youth is a global imperative: ensuring the academic success of all students is necessary to meet the growing demands of a dynamic global economy and to promote individuals' wellbeing and quality of life. Academic achievement can also promote social mobility. Students who are equipped with greater skills and knowledge are more likely to enter careers that can help them exit a cycle of deprivation and low aspirations by improving their economic and social conditions (Hout and Beller, 2006). Education can improve not only an individual's life chances, but also the conditions of future generations: better educated parents generally have children who are healthier, who perform better at school and who have better labour market outcomes.

At present, many children struggle to master basic literacy and numeracy skills, especially students who face challenging economic and social circumstances. Nevertheless, there are some socio-economically disadvantaged students who are able to overcome their personal challenges and perform well at school. Here the focus is on this too often overlooked group of students: those disadvantaged students who are resilient – *i.e.* students who come from a relatively disadvantaged socio-economic background and yet exhibit relatively high levels of achievement. Resilient students may be a small minority, but they may also be crucial to our understanding of the characteristics and contexts that make a positive difference in the lives of vulnerable populations.

This report explores the factors and conditions that could help more students succeed at school despite challenging socio-economic backgrounds. It does this by studying resilient students and what sets them apart from their less successful peers. Understanding how educational systems can support disadvantaged students and help them "beat the odds" to succeed in school is a central challenge facing education policymakers, school administrators and teachers today.

The Programme for International Student Assessment (PISA), conducted by the Organisation for Economic Co-operation and Development (OECD), offers an opportunity to study resilient students across many countries. The assessment examines how well 15-year-old students are able to use the knowledge and skills they have gained to solve standardised tasks in reading, mathematics and science as they approach the end of secondary school. It also collects contextual information about the students, their families and their schools (Box 1.1). In 2006, 57 countries and more than 400 000 students participated in PISA.

SOCIO-ECONOMIC BACKGROUND AND ACADEMIC SUCCESS

The relationship between socio-economic background and student achievement is well documented and indicates that students from more advantaged backgrounds perform better at school. Since the publication in the 1960s of the landmark Coleman Report on equality and educational opportunity (Coleman *et al.*, 1966), numerous international and country-specific studies have reported a significant association between students' socio-economic background and their achievement at school (notable examples include Baker, Goesling and Letendre, 2002; and Crane, 1996). Recent evidence shows that the situation has not changed much over the past half century, with socio-economic background still one of the strongest correlates of academic performance (Sirin, 2005; OECD, 2001; OECD, 2004; OECD 2007a).

One of the key findings of the Coleman report was that school-level inputs were only weakly associated with student outcomes. More recent studies however suggest that schools do have a role to play in promoting student achievement (examples include Fuller and Clarke, 1994; Goldhaber and Brewer, 1997; Hanushek, 1986; and Wößmann, 2003). Notable examples of school-level factors that have a positive effect on achievement are smaller class sizes, teacher quality and peers' success (Hanushek *et al.*, 2002; Rivkin *et al.*, 2005).

Box 1.1 **Key features of PISA 2006**

Content

- Although the main focus of PISA 2006 was science, the survey also covered reading and mathematics. PISA considers students' knowledge in these areas not in isolation, but in relation to their ability to reflect on their knowledge and experience and to apply them to real world issues. The emphasis is on the mastery of processes, the understanding of concepts and the ability to function in various situations within each assessment area.

- The PISA 2006 survey also, for the first time, sought information on students' attitudes to science by including questions on attitudes within the test itself, rather than only through a complementary questionnaire.

Methods

- Around 400 000 students were randomly selected to participate in PISA 2006, representing about 20 million 15-year-olds in the schools of the 57 participating countries.

- Each participating student spent two hours carrying out pencil-and-paper tasks. In three countries, some students were given additional questions via computer.

- PISA contained tasks requiring students to construct their own answers as well as multiple-choice questions. These were typically organised in units based on a written passage or graphic, of the kind that students might encounter in real life.

- Students also answered a questionnaire that took about 30 minutes to complete and focused on their personal background, their learning habits and their attitudes to science, as well as on their engagement and motivation.

- School principals completed a questionnaire about their school that included demographic characteristics as well as an assessment of the quality of the learning environment at school.

Outcomes

- A profile of knowledge and skills among 15-year-olds in 2006, consisting of a detailed profile for science, and an update for reading and mathematics.

- Contextual indicators relating performance results to student and school characteristics.

- An assessment of students' attitudes to science.

- A knowledge base for policy analysis and research.

- Trend data on changes in student knowledge and skills in reading and mathematics.

Future assessments

- The PISA 2009 survey will return to reading as the major assessment area, while PISA 2012 will focus on mathematics and PISA 2015 once again on science.

- Future tests will also assess students' capacity to read and understand electronic texts – reflecting the importance of information and computer technologies in modern societies.

PISA AS A STUDY OF STUDENT RESILIENCE

STUDENT RESILIENCE

Hundreds of research studies spanning four decades have chronicled the association between socio-economic background and student outcomes, but only a few have looked specifically at students who, despite coming from disadvantaged backgrounds, exhibit high levels of academic achievement (Finn and Rock, 1997; Rouse, 2001; Waxman and Huang, 1996). The educational research literature calls these students resilient because they overcome adversity to achieve academic success.

Resilience has been the subject of study in both the psychology and education fields. Several definitions of resilience have been proposed in the psychological literature. Although definitions vary widely depending on the specific context of empirical and theoretical studies, resilience generally involves the study of individuals who succeed despite encountering significant adversity (Luthar et al., 2000). The lack of consensus on a definition of resilience is matched by the lack of consensus on *i)* the roots of resilience, *ii)* the factors associated with resilience, *iii)* whether resilience is the result of the interaction between individuals and the context in which they operate and *iv)* whether resilience can be promoted through concerted effort. While the exact definition of resilience also varies in the educational literature, both theoretical and empirical studies on student resilience examine disadvantaged students who, despite their background, exhibit high academic performance. Often these studies use relative outcomes on achievement tests to identify resilient students (examples include Connell et al., 1994; Lee et al., 1991; Rouse, 2001; Waxman and Huang, 1996). Others use achievement in combination with other characteristics, such as daily homework and motivation (see for example Finn and Rock, 1997; Padron et al., 2000).

Both theoretical explorations and empirical analyses of resilience in the education literature have explored a wide range of school and student characteristics which may contribute to students beating the odds (for a good overview of the theoretical literature see Masten, 1994). Empirical studies indicate that resilient students may approach learning differently from other students: they generally put more effort in their studies and have a higher level of homework completion (Finn and Rock, 1997; Lee et al., 1991). They display greater preparation and participation in class work and come to class on time more frequently (Finn and Rock, 1997). They make better use of their time both during and after school hours (Lee et al., 1991), they participate more in extracurricular activities (Catterall, 1998) and they display greater engagement in academic activities (Catterall, 1998; Borman and Overman, 2004). Psychologically, resilient students tend to have a higher sense of self-esteem (Connell et al., 1994; Borman and Overman, 2004), higher self-efficacy (Borman and Overman, 2004; Shumow et al., 1999) and a greater sense of control over success and failure in school than their non-resilient counterparts (Connell et al., 1994). Resilient students come from disadvantaged families by definition, but they tend to enjoy greater than average parental involvement (Shumow et al., 1999; Connell et al., 1994) and watch television less (Catterall, 1998), a possible indication of greater parental supervision.

Findings from the studies reported above describe the features of resilient students using country-specific data, mostly from the United States, and thus may not be informative in settings that differ because of culture, institutions, economic development or educational systems. A cross-country analysis of student resilience can illuminate the stability of relationships across different settings and whether the key features associated with being a resilient student differ across countries.

THE PROGRAMME FOR INTERNATIONAL STUDENT ASSESSMENT (PISA) AS A STUDY OF STUDENT RESILIENCE

PISA is particularly suited for a cross-country investigation of student resilience: no other survey on academic achievement has the same breadth in terms of geographical coverage while containing rich information on the socio-economic circumstances of surveyed populations. In the 2006 cycle, nationally representative samples of 15-year-old students from all 30 OECD countries and 27 partner countries took part in the

PISA assessment (see Figure 1.1). This report uses data from all PISA 2006 participating countries except Liechtenstein and Qatar.[1] The PISA survey and assessments are specifically designed and tested to ensure comparability across countries. Most importantly for this study, PISA includes two key variables that enable the identification of resilient students: an index summarising the socio-economic background of individual students and measurements of students' literacy skills in science, mathematics and reading.

Figure 1.1
A map of PISA countries and economies

OECD countries*

Australia	Korea
Austria	Luxembourg
Belgium	Mexico
Canada	Netherlands
Czech Republic	New Zealand
Denmark	Norway
Finland	Poland
France	Portugal
Germany	Slovak Republic
Greece	Spain
Hungary	Sweden
Iceland	Switzerland
Ireland	Turkey
Italy	United Kingdom
Japan	United States

Partner countries and economies in PISA 2006

Argentina	Liechtenstein
Azerbaijan	Lithuania
Brazil	Macao-China
Bulgaria	Montenegro
Chile	Qatar
Colombia	Romania
Croatia	Russian Federation
Estonia	Serbia
Hong Kong-China	Slovenia
Indonesia	Chinese Taipei
Israel	Thailand
Jordan	Tunisia
Kyrgyzstan	Uruguay
Latvia	

Partner countries and economies in previous PISA surveys or in PISA 2009

Albania	Moldova
Costa Rica	Netherlands-Antilles
Dominican Republic	Panama
Georgia	Peru
Himachal Pradesh-India	Shanghai-China
Kazakhstan	Singapore
Macedonia	Tamil Nadu-India
Malaysia	Trinidad and Tobago
Malta	United Arab Emirates
Mauritius	Viet Nam
Miranda-Venezuela	

These are the countries that were members of the OECD at the time of the PISA 2006 main data collection in 2006

The PISA index of economic, social and cultural status is a comprehensive measure of socio-economic background. The indicator captures students' family and home characteristics that describe their socio-economic background. It includes information about parental occupational status and highest educational level, as well as information on home possessions, such as computers, books and access to the Internet (for additional information see OECD, 2007, Annex A1). Index values are standardised such that the mean is equal to zero and the standard deviation equals one across all students in OECD countries. Therefore, a negative value on the economic, social and cultural status index means that the student's socio-economic background is below that of the OECD average student. The more socio-economically disadvantaged students are the lower are the values on the economic, social and cultural status index.

The assessment component of the PISA survey evaluates students' ability to apply their knowledge and skills to real-life situations. It covers three domain areas: reading, mathematics and science. In 2006, the PISA assessment focused on science and gathered a rich set of information on factors potentially related to academic success in this particular subject. Consequently, this report emphasises science literacy both in defining resilient students and in considering which approaches to learning may be particularly associated with resilience. The report also compares resilience in science to resilience in reading and mathematics. PISA assesses students' science literacy by testing their ability to perform scientific tasks in a variety of situations. In 2006, a large portion of the tasks were designed to measure students' performance in relation to science competencies and scientific knowledge (for more information see OECD, 2007, Chapter 2). Students' performance on these tasks was used to create standardised scales, constructed such that the average OECD student score was 500 points with a standard deviation of 100 points. This means that about two-thirds of students in the OECD countries scored between 400 and 600 points.

PISA also collects data on many of the variables the literature suggests may be important in understanding and promoting student resilience, such as students' approaches to learning, motivation and self-concept. By exploring the association between performance and such variables, this report seeks to provide policymakers with insights as to the policies and programs that are likely to foster academic success among their most challenging student populations. PISA includes many, but not all, the variables that have been shown to be associated with resilience in previous research. Important factors that are not included in PISA are student participation during class time, information on teachers' characteristics and information on specific policies and programmes which countries or schools may have implemented to promote resilience among disadvantaged students. Furthermore, using PISA, it is only possible to define resilience in terms of achievement in the PISA assessment - other outcome variables such as course grades, truancy, grade repetition and dropout rates are not available at the level of the individual student.

A final limitation of the report is that the PISA data only allow for the construction of a descriptive picture of resilience at a single point of time. As such, findings in this report cannot be interpreted through causal lenses (*i.e.* specific student approaches to learning cause resilience). Rather this report highlights important associations between variables (*i.e.* specific student approaches to learning are associated with or correlated with or related to resilience). In this way, the analysis provides new information and insights into patterns of and differences in student resilience across participating countries. As part of PISA 2006, 16 countries implemented an additional parent questionnaire. While the role of parents in resilience is important, this report however does not include any information from these data. The parent data for students from disadvantaged socio-economic backgrounds is limited and any analysis would have relied on an insufficient number of observations.

STRUCTURE OF THE REPORT

The rest of this report is organised as follows.

Chapter 2 presents two complementary approaches used to report on student resilience. The chapter also identifies as a suitable comparison group: those students who are also disadvantaged but do not achieve academic success and analyses those features that characterise resilient and disadvantaged low-achieving students. The first approach builds on an international benchmark of resilience, comparing students of similar socio-economic background across countries. An international perspective, however, provides limited analytical power to draw insights for policies aimed at fostering resilience. The second approach tackles this limitation by providing a country-specific definition. This definition provides no internationally comparable data on the extent of resilience across countries, but it does deliver important insights on policy levers that are associated with more resilience in different educational systems. Thus, the rest of the report builds on this second approach to draw insights for policy for all of the countries and economies participating in PISA.

Chapter 3 explores the within-country association of student and school characteristics with resilience. The chapter compares resilient students to their disadvantaged low-achieving peers in terms of these characteristics and predicts the probability that disadvantaged students will be resilient depending on their characteristics and the environment in their schools.

Chapter 4 extends the analysis presented in Chapter 3 and attempts to capture the association between student and school characteristics with performance. The chapter looks at the varying relationships between student and school variables and performance and addresses the question of which student and school characteristics might help disadvantaged students close the performance gap with more advantaged students.

Chapter 5 summarises the key findings from this analysis and highlights several implications for educational policy and practice. The analysis focuses on the proximate outcomes through which policies and programmes may improve performance of socio-economically disadvantaged students and help them beat the odds.

Note

1. The exclusion of these two countries reflects data limitations. In the case of Liechtenstein, the sample was too small to produce reliable indicators for resilient students. In the case of Qatar, data on student socio-economic background were not sufficiently reliable to carry out a rigorous analysis of resilience.

Defining and Characterising Student Resilience in PISA

INTRODUCTION

Resilient students come from disadvantaged backgrounds yet exhibit high levels of school success. This chapter answers a question central to this report from a PISA perspective: What does it mean to "beat the odds" and how does this differ across countries?

To address these questions, the chapter presents two different complementary approaches.

First, it discusses resilience from an international perspective. A global perspective is useful to address questions such as to what extent different systems vary in terms of the proportion of students from a disadvantaged socio-economic background that are able to perform at the relatively high levels in PISA. It is possible to tackle this question using an internationally comparable definition of resiliency that takes into account how socio-economic background is related to achievement across countries.

Second, what factors are associated with student resilience within countries? The relationship between resiliency and individual or school level factors is best analysed within the specific context of each educational system. This report presents results from analyses that use a country-specific definition of resilience that is suitable for addressing these issues.

The chapter defines resilient students to be those who, despite being socio-economically disadvantaged compared to other students in their own country, are high achievers in the PISA science assessment. To address the different questions outlined above, the chapter compares these students to students in other countries, for international comparisons, and to other students in their country for drawing insights on policies aimed at fostering high performance among disadvantaged students.

As a comparison group for resilient students, the chapter also identifies disadvantaged low achievers, a group of students that share a similar socio-economic background to resilient students but whose members are among the lowest performers in the PISA science assessment, be it internationally or in their country.

The chapter first presents measures of the share of resilient students across countries that are internationally comparable and then explores potential within-country differences between resilient students and disadvantaged low achievers in terms of three individual student characteristics: gender, immigrant background and language spoken at home.

Although it focuses on resilient students and disadvantaged low achievers defined using information on students' performance in science, the chapter also reports briefly on the findings when resilience is based on mathematics or reading performance. It also considers whether students resilient in relation to science are also resilient in reading and mathematics.

DEFINING RESILIENT AND DISADVANTAGED LOW-ACHIEVING STUDENTS USING PISA

Chapter 1 identified resilient students as those students who "beat the odds". As previously discussed, there is no one commonly-used definition of resilience. The definitions developed and applied in this report were chosen after careful consideration of the many definitions used elsewhere. Within the context of PISA, two distinct and complementary perspectives are possible for identifying resilient students. Each responds best to a particular concern. The report identifies disadvantaged low achievers as the comparison group for resilient students. The definitions of disadvantaged low achievers are therefore always complementary to the resilience definitions.

This chapter develops two operational definitions and empirical approaches to student resilience. From an international perspective, countries are interested in knowing the proportion of internationally successful disadvantaged students different educational systems are able to produce. In this case, success should be defined in the same way for all countries allowing direct cross-country comparisons. This chapter develops first a definition of resilience that is appropriate for this purpose, namely to compare the share of resilient students across countries. Some systems may be able to produce a larger share of resilient students among their disadvantaged students and their experience may yield insights for other countries. A low proportion of disadvantaged but internationally successful students may point to areas for improvement. These countries may need to carefully analyse policies and resources related to the performance of disadvantaged students, which are analysed in Chapters 3 and 4.

From a within-country perspective, policy makers and stakeholders want to know more about how to foster resilience within their educational system. They are interested in the policy levers that may help increase the performance of socio-economically disadvantaged students. In this case, the performance of disadvantaged students relative to their peers from more advanced socio-economic backgrounds is a more valid indicator of success at school. Looking at relative performance means that successful disadvantaged students in one country may be seen as poor performing in other contexts and therefore relative performance within a system is not useful for comparisons across systems. Although this definition is not used to compare the share of resilient student across countries, it is more helpful when searching for policies and resources related to better performance among disadvantaged students within the context of national educational systems.

Both approaches use two measures: the PISA index of economic, social and cultural status to characterise socio-economic disadvantage and the PISA science scale to characterise academic achievement. Both definitions share the same approach to socio-economic disadvantage: they focus on the context closest to the student and the educational system they experience. The key difference is on performance: the first approach focuses on an international benchmark whereas the second uses a country-specific one.

An international perspective

With this definition, a resilient student is the one who outperforms her or his colleagues sharing the same socio-economic background. In this case, the level of performance above which a student can be called resilient is established as the top third of performers across all countries, after accounting for their socio-economic background. In other words, these are students from all countries who outperformed their peers with the same socio-economic background. The share of resilient students in a country is then calculated as the percentage of high performers among students in a bottom third of socio-economic background in each country (see Annex A5 for details on this definition).

The relation between socio-economic background and performance is established using data from all countries. Therefore, students with the same socio-economic background and the same performance have equal probability of being resilient regardless of the performance of other students in their country. For example, Ana, a student in country A, is resilient if her background is among the bottom third in country A and her performance is on the top third across countries among those students whose background is similar to Ana's, irrespective of their country. In this sense, this definition is mixed because it sets an international benchmark for performance and a national benchmark for socio-economic background. Because it compares equals across countries, using an international benchmark on performance and adjusting for a student background, this definition of resilience yields measures of the extent of resilience at the system level that are comparable across countries.[1]

Within an international perspective, disadvantaged low achievers are students who share the same socio-economic background as resilient students, *i.e.* fall in the bottom third of their country's distribution of socio-economic background, but whose performance is in the bottom third of the student performance after adjusting for socio-economic background.

Comparing the shares of resilient students across countries

Figure 2.1 presents the proportion of resilient and disadvantaged low achievers among disadvantaged low achievers across countries using an internationally comparable definition. One hundred percent in this case represents the bottom third of the student population in each country in terms of socio-economic background.

Figure 2.1
Shares of resilient and disadvantaged low achievers among disadvantaged students, by country

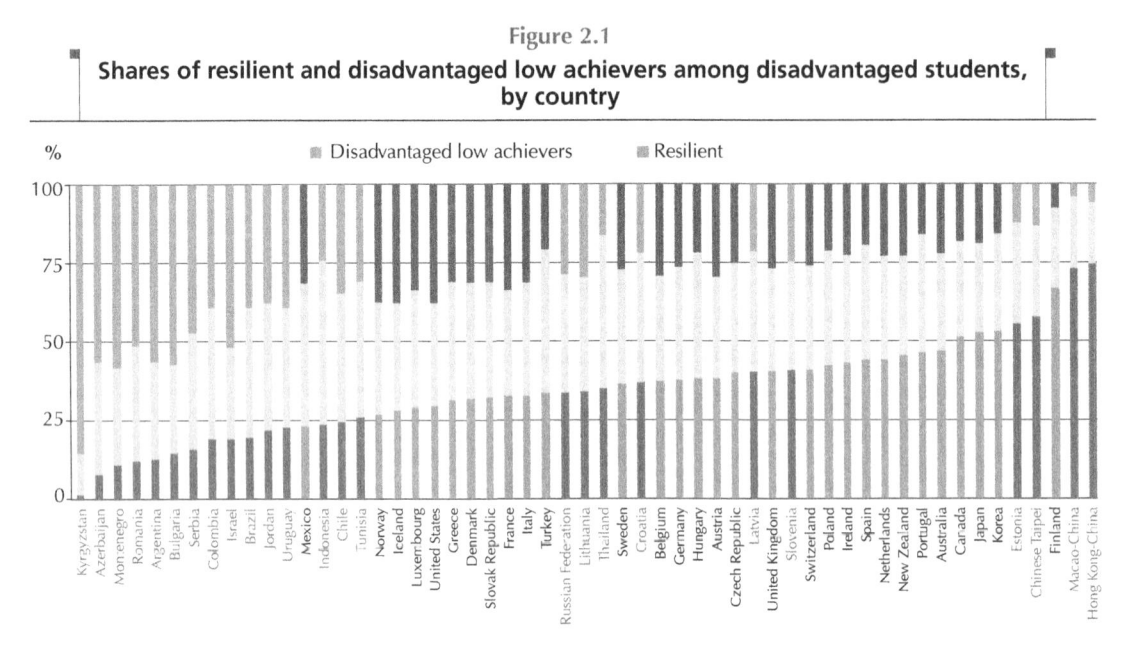

Source: *OECD PISA 2006 Database.*

Some countries have noticeably high shares of resilient students, while others have only few high performing students among disadvantaged ones. Student resilience is more common in OECD countries like Canada, Finland, Japan, and Korea, and among partner countries and economies in Chinese Taipei, Estonia, Hong Kong-China and Macao-China where more than half of disadvantaged students are among top third of performers in all countries after accounting for socio-economic background (Table A1.1). In partner countries and economies the share of resilient students is generally much lower, with only few resilient students in Azerbaijan, Kyrgyzstan, Montenegro and Romania. Students in these countries are rarely outperforming their peers in other countries sharing the same socio-economic background.

Figure 2.1 also shows that there is a close relationship between the shares of resilient and disadvantaged low achievers. The countries with the highest shares of resilient students tend to display also the lowest shares of disadvantaged low achievers. In Canada, Finland, Japan, and Korea, and in the partner countries and economies Chinese Taipei, Estonia, Hong Kong-China and Macao-China, the share of disadvantaged low achievers among disadvantaged students is always below 20%. In Portugal and Spain and partner country Thailand, however, these shares are equally low. The figure also shows examples of countries with relatively low levels of resilient students and low levels of disadvantaged low achievers among disadvantaged students (Table A1.1).

A within-country perspective

For the second perspective, a within-country approach is necessary. With an international perspective in some countries the number of resilient students is extremely small, leaving no room for any analysis of how resilience associates with student or school characteristics. The within-country perspective defines resilient students as those who fall in both the bottom third of their country's socio-economic background distribution and the top third of their country's performance distribution on the PISA science assessment scale.[2]

This definition allows the examination of factors helping to beat the odds in each country by comparing within-country relationships across countries in order to draw inferences about how to foster resiliency within countries. The data presented in the report enable each country's school leaders to see how student characteristics are associated with resilience within their country's educational context and to look to other countries to see if there are consistent patterns across countries, for example in the relationships of resilience to student approaches to learning as potential levers for increasing the prevalence of resilient students. This requires country-specific cut-points for both socio-economic disadvantage and academic achievement.[3]

Within a country-specific approach disadvantaged low achievers are students who share the same socio-economic background as resilient students but whose scores fall in the bottom third of their country's PISA science assessment score distribution. To the extent that socio-economic background predicts academic performance, disadvantaged low achievers represent how one might expect disadvantaged students to score on the science assessment.

SIMILARITIES AND DIFFERENCES OF RESILIENT STUDENTS ACROSS COUNTRIES

Even within the country-specific perspective, resilient students (and disadvantaged low achievers) share a set of common characteristics across countries, notably in terms of their socio-economic background and performance relative to other students and peers in their country.

In terms of socio-economic background, across OECD countries, resilient students and disadvantaged low achievers share a disadvantaged socio-economic background that is well below the average background within their country. The results presented in Figure 2.2 and Table A1.2 highlight the differences and similarities between resilient students, disadvantaged low achievers and the average student in the country in terms of socio-economic background. The average socio-economic background of resilient students is between three quarters and one full standard deviation below the national average (except in Portugal and Mexico where they are 1.2 standard deviations below). Disadvantaged low achievers are about a standard deviation below the national average in terms of socio-economic background (except in Turkey, Portugal and Mexico where they are more than 1.4 standard deviations below the national average). The same pattern can be observed in partner countries and economies. Figure 2.2 also shows that across all OECD countries, resilient students on average have a somewhat more advantaged socio-economic background than disadvantaged low achievers. In general, however, the relative advantage of resilient students compared to disadvantaged low achievers is less than a fourth of a standard deviation, ranging from a third of a standard deviation in Germany and Luxembourg to a little more than one tenth of a standard deviation in Finland and Japan. The same holds true for partner countries and economies. Additional analysis reveals these differences are driven primarily by group differences in the educational resources, cultural possessions, number of books and parental education components of the index not the wealth and parental occupation components (Table A1.3).

In terms of performance, resilient students in OECD countries perform between three quarters and one full standard deviation better than the average student in the same country (Figure 2.3). The difference is smallest in Mexico and Turkey, where the average resilient student scores less than 75 points, or two thirds of a standard deviation, above the average student (Table A1.4). It is largest in Austria, New Zealand, the United Kingdom and the United States where the average resilient student scores close to a standard deviation, 100 score points, better than the average student. In general, the average disadvantaged low achiever performs about a standard deviation below the average student.

DEFINING AND CHARACTERISING STUDENT RESILIENCE IN PISA

Figure 2.2
PISA index of economic, social and cultural status for system average, resilient and disadvantaged low achievers

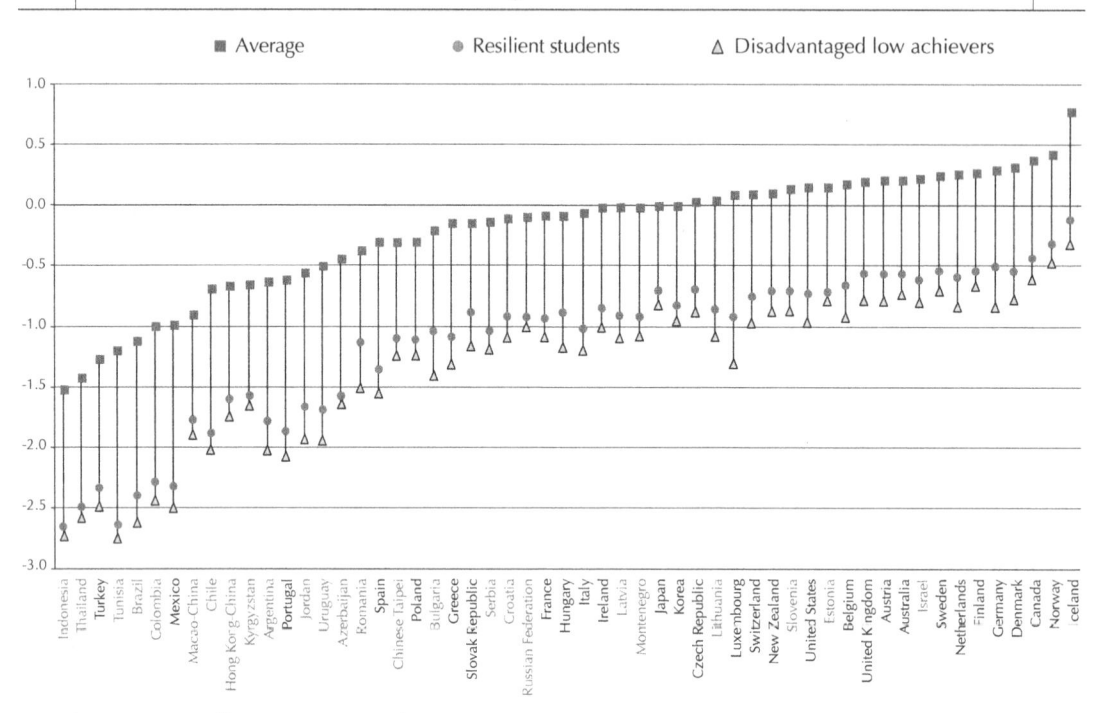

Note: Countries are sorted by system average performance
Source: *OECD PISA 2006 Database.*

Figure 2.3
Performance in PISA science, system average, resilient and disadvantaged low achievers

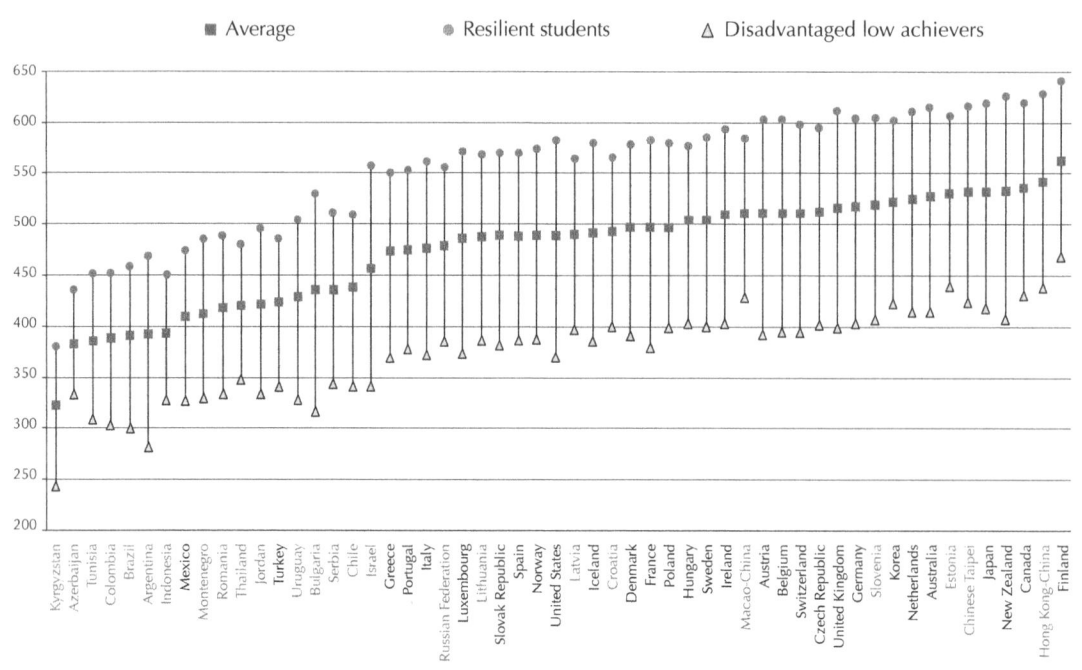

Source: *OECD PISA 2006 Database.*

© OECD 2011 *Against the Odds: Disadvantaged Students Who Succeed in School*

DEFINING AND CHARACTERISING STUDENT RESILIENCE IN PISA

An alternative measure of performance is provided by proficiency levels. PISA developed six proficiency levels to describe the science competencies students have at different levels of performance. The PISA Science Expert Group identified Level 2 as the baseline level of proficiency, this being the point at which students start to exhibit a level of basic scientific skills that will allow them to effectively participate in real-life situations related to science (see OECD, 2009b for a description of the proficiency levels).

Because performance varies across countries and because students are defined as resilient if they perform among the top third of students in their country, in some countries being resilient implies being able to tackle the most difficult questions in the PISA assessment while in other countries resilient students are not able to successfully complete even some of the simplest tasks.

In general, however, the vast majority of resilient students achieve Level 2 or above whereas more than 25% of disadvantaged low achievers perform below Level 2 in all countries except Finland, Estonia, Hong Kong-China and Macao China. In most OECD countries the majority of resilient students in fact achieve proficiency Level 4 (Figure 2.4 and Table A1.5). In partner countries and economies, the majority of resilient students achieve at least Level 2. This indicates that in many countries a large fraction of disadvantaged students do not have even basic science literacy skills.

Figure 2.4
Percentage of resilient and disadvantaged low achievers above and below the basic level of proficiency

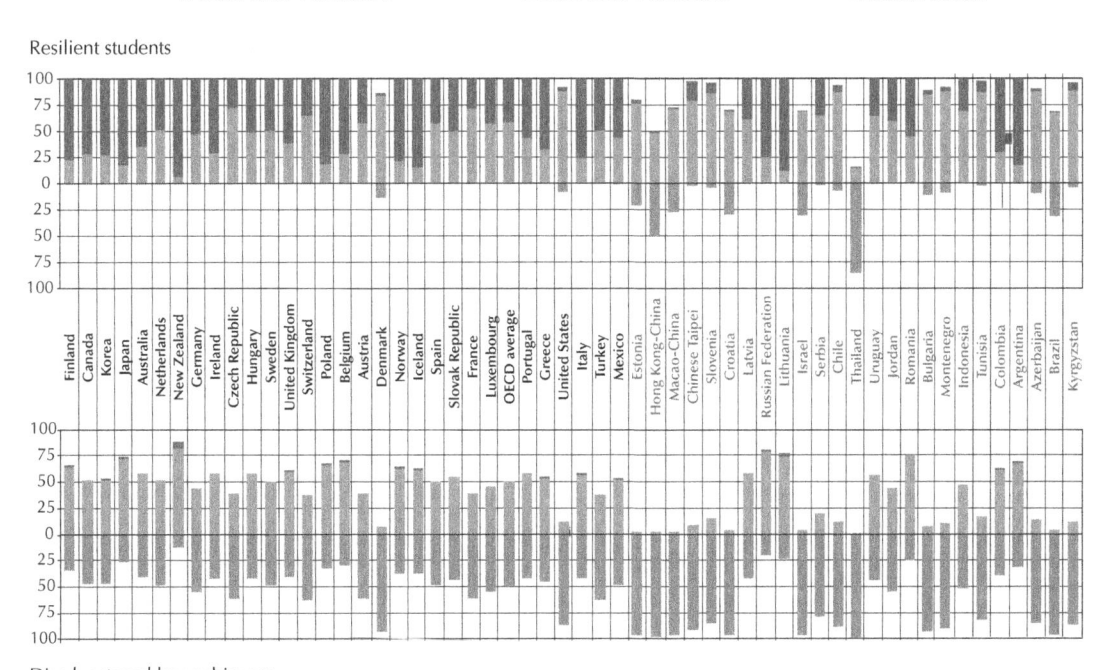

■ From level 4 to level 6   ■ From level 2 to level 3   ■ Below Level 2

Source: *OECD PISA 2006 Database*.

This section and most of the report draws country-specific conclusions on resilience but it does not compare the proportions of resilient students across countries. Because of the country-specific nature of these analyses, it is possible to compare country experiences of factors that are associated with resilience while it could be misleading to draw conclusions on the prevalence of resilience across countries.[4]

DEFINING AND CHARACTERISING STUDENT RESILIENCE IN PISA

The rest of this chapter and Chapter 3 compare the characteristics of different groups of disadvantaged students within countries. Analysing how these within-country comparisons vary across countries can lead to new insights into what factors may help some disadvantaged students to overcome social and economic barriers and succeed at school.

STUDENT RESILIENCE ACROSS SCIENCE, READING AND MATHEMATICS

PISA 2006 focused on science. This report uses the PISA 2006 science assessment to identify resilient students. However, PISA also tests students in reading and mathematics. It is possible, therefore, to define resilience in terms of reading and mathematics. The sections that follow report results first in terms of science resilience and then comment on the results for each of mathematics and reading resilience.

Do students who exhibit resilience in one domain – science – also exhibit resilience in the other domains? Figure 2.5 shows the proportion of students resilient in science who are also resilient in mathematics and reading. Among OECD countries, between 44 and 59% of those students resilient in science are also resilient in mathematics and reading. The percentages are somewhat lower in partner countries and economies, ranging from 27% to 56% (Table A1.5).

Figure 2.5
Overlap of resilience in different subject domains

- Resilient in science
- Resilient in science and reading
- Resilient in science and mathematics
- Resilient in science, mathematics and reading

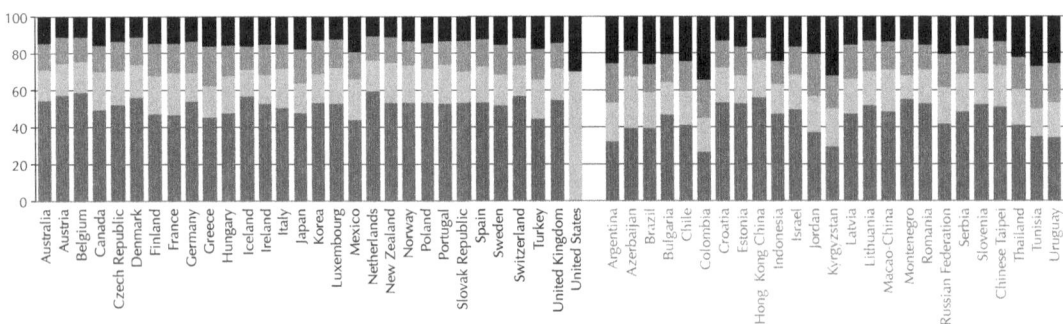

Source: *OECD PISA 2006 Database.*

The proportion of students resilient in both science and one of the other assessment domains (either reading or mathematics) is also shown in Table A1.6. This evidence indicates that the vast majority of students who are resilient with respect to science are also resilient in at least one if not both of the other domains. Among OECD countries, the proportion of students who are resilient in science only ranges from 11% in Austria, Belgium, Denmark, the Netherlands and New Zealand to 19% in Mexico.[5] The percentages are somewhat higher in partner countries and economies, ranging from less than 12% in Hong Kong-China to almost 35% in Colombia (Table A1.6). These results suggest that resilience in science is not a domain-specific characteristic but rather there is something about these students or the schools they attend that lead them to overcome their social disadvantage and excel at school in multiple subject domains.[6]

STUDENT RESILIENCE AMONG SPECIFIC DEMOGRAPHIC GROUPS WITHIN COUNTRIES

Previous sections of this chapter developed a working definition of resilience among school age students and presented an empirical approach to identify two particular groups of disadvantaged students: resilient students and disadvantaged low achievers. This section describes some key demographic characteristics of resilient students and disadvantaged low achievers within each country: gender, immigrant background and language spoken at home.

Gender

Overall, male students are not over-represented among resilient students in science, nor among low achievers or disadvantaged students in general (Figure 2.6). This finding is in line with previous research indicating no gender differences in the prevalence of academic resilience (examples include Catterall, 1998 and Martin and Marsh, 2006). But some exceptions exist, Chile among other countries – where males are over-represented among resilient students and under-represented among disadvantaged low achievers – and Turkey and Jordan – where males are under-represented among resilient students and over-represented among disadvantaged students.

Figure 2.6
Percentage of male students among disadvantaged students and resilient students

- ■ Percentage of males among disadvantaged students
- ● Percentage of males among resilient students
- △ Percentage of males among disadvantaged low achievers

Source: *OECD PISA 2006 Database.*

Across OECD countries, the difference in the proportion of males among resilient, and low achievers or disadvantaged students is very small, on average less than 2 percentage points. Exceptions include Greece and Turkey, where male students are relatively under-represented among resilient students by more than 5 percentage points and Luxembourg and the United Kingdom where male students are over-represented by more than 5 percentage points. The differences between low achievers and disadvantaged students in general are even smaller, less than one percentage point on average. The pattern is similar among partner countries and economies, except in Chile, where males are over-represented by more than 10 percentage points and Jordan where males are under-represented among resilient students by more than 10 percentage points. Among partner countries and economies differences are also smaller between low achievers and disadvantaged students in general than between resilient students and disadvantaged students (Table A1.7).

While there are no overall gender differences in science, weak gender differences can be found in mathematics. When mathematics is used to define resilient students, male students are over-represented among resilient students and under-represented among disadvantaged low achievers (except in the

OECD countries of France, Greece and Iceland and in the partner countries of Jordan, Lithuania and Thailand where the pattern is reversed). The differences in the proportions of male students among resilient and all disadvantaged students exceed 5 percentage points in 14 OECD countries and 11 partner countries and economies. The differences in the proportions of male students among disadvantaged low-achieving and all disadvantaged students are smaller and exceed 5 percentage points only in Jordan (Table A1.7).

Gender differences are starkest when reading assessment scores are used to define resilience. In this case male students are under-represented among resilient students and over-represented among disadvantaged low achievers in all countries. The difference in the proportions of male students among resilient and all disadvantaged students exceeds 10 percentage points in 21 OECD countries and 18 partner countries and economies. Again for disadvantaged low achievers the gap is smaller; the difference in the proportions of male students between disadvantaged low achievers and all disadvantaged students exceeds 10 percentage points in 2 OECD countries and 3 partner countries and economies (Table A1.7).

Immigrant background

Many OECD and partner countries and economies are experiencing record levels of immigration. For countries that have a substantial number of immigrant students (see OECD, 2007a for minimum standards for inclusion), this section examines the prevalence of immigrant and native students among all disadvantaged students as well as among resilient and disadvantaged low-achieving students. Students with an immigrant background are defined as those students who were themselves born outside the country (first-generation immigrants) or whose parents were born outside the country (second-generation immigrants).

Figure 2.7
Percentage of native students among disadvantaged students and resilient students

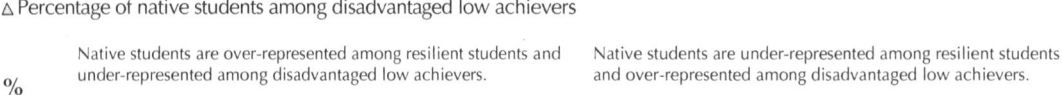

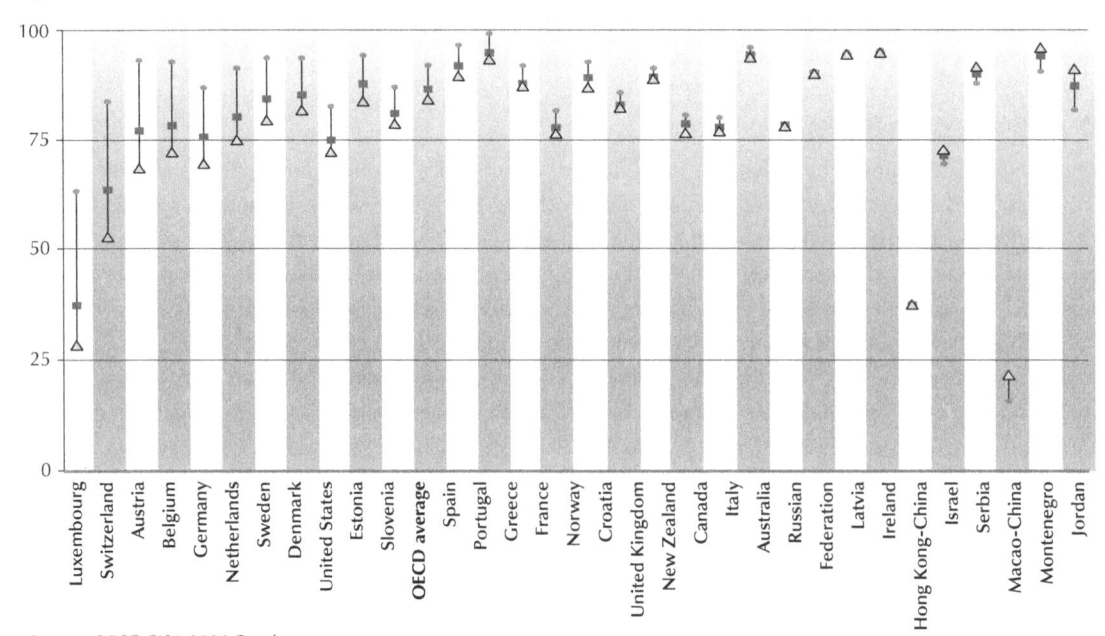

■ Percentage of native students among disadvantaged students ● Percentage of native students among resilient students
△ Percentage of native students among disadvantaged low achievers

Source: *OECD PISA 2006 Database.*

When looking at students with an immigrant background across countries it is important to recognise that these students come from a wide range of countries and might differ along several dimensions. For example, in Australia the largest three immigrant groups are from the United Kingdom, New Zealand and China; in Belgium the most common origin countries are France, Turkey and the Netherlands; and in the United States the largest group of immigrants is from Mexico – outnumbering the next largest group by seven to one (OECD, 2006). In Australia, native students and students with an immigrant background exhibit similar levels of achievement while in many other countries there are large and significant differences in achievement between these students (Christensen and Segeritz, 2008).

As a general rule, native students tend to be over-represented among resilient students than students with an immigrant background. The gap is not very large but native students tend to be over-represented among resilient students, particularly so in Austria, Belgium, Germany, Luxembourg, the Netherlands and Switzerland where the difference in the proportions of native students among resilient students and among all disadvantaged students is over 10% percentage points (Table A1.8). In no OECD country are native students over-represented among disadvantaged low achievers. Among partner countries and economies the pattern is generally similar but weaker in that the differences are smaller. While studies have shown that students with an immigrant background tend to possess higher levels of motivation than native students (see OECD, 2006 or Christensen and Segeritz, 2008 for an overview), it appears that in many countries only a small fraction of students with an immigrant background beat the odds. These findings highlight one of the challenges facing many of the countries participating in PISA.

The pattern is generally similar when performance on the mathematics or reading assessments is used to define resilience. Native students continue to be over-represented among resilient students in OECD countries (except in Australia for both reading and mathematics). Differences in the proportions of native students among resilient and all disadvantaged students exceed 10 percentage points in four countries on the basis of reading (Austria, Belgium, Luxembourg and Switzerland) and in five countries in the case of mathematics (the same four countries plus Germany). Differences in the proportions of native students among disadvantaged low achievers and all disadvantaged students are smaller than for science, with the largest differences in the same set of countries identified with respect to resilient students. No clear patterns are found among the partner countries and economies (Table A1.8).

Language spoken at home

Frequently as a result of immigration (and in some cases history), a growing numbers of students speak a language at home other than the test language. This presents challenges as many schools and school systems struggle to provide for the needs of this group of students.

Speaking the language of the test (*i.e.* the language of instruction) at home provides a small advantage to students in terms of resilience. As shown in Figure 2.8, in no OECD country, students who speak the language of the test are significantly under-represented among resilient students in those countries where there is sufficient data available to do the analysis. There are only three countries (Austria, Germany and Switzerland) where the proportion of students who speak the test language at home among resilient students in science is more than 10 percentage points higher than the proportion for disadvantaged students generally (Table A1.9). The pattern is very similar in partner countries and economies but the differences are somewhat smaller. In most countries, there is a relative under-representation of students that speak the language at home among low achievers, but again the size of the difference is rather small and it only exceeds 10 percentage points in Switzerland. Similar patterns are identified using either reading or mathematics assessment scores. The differences tend to be slightly smaller on average than those found using science scores (Table A1.9).

DEFINING AND CHARACTERISING STUDENT RESILIENCE IN PISA

Figure 2.8
Percentage of students who speak the test language at home among disadvantaged students and resilient students

- ■ Percentage of students who speak the test language at home among disadvantaged students
- ● Percentage of students who speak the test language at home among resilient students
- △ Percentage of students who speak the test language at home among diadvantaged low achievers

Students who speak the test language at home are over-represented among resilient students and under-represented among disadvantaged low achievers

Students who speak the test language at home are under-represented among resilient students and under-presented among disadvantaged low achievers

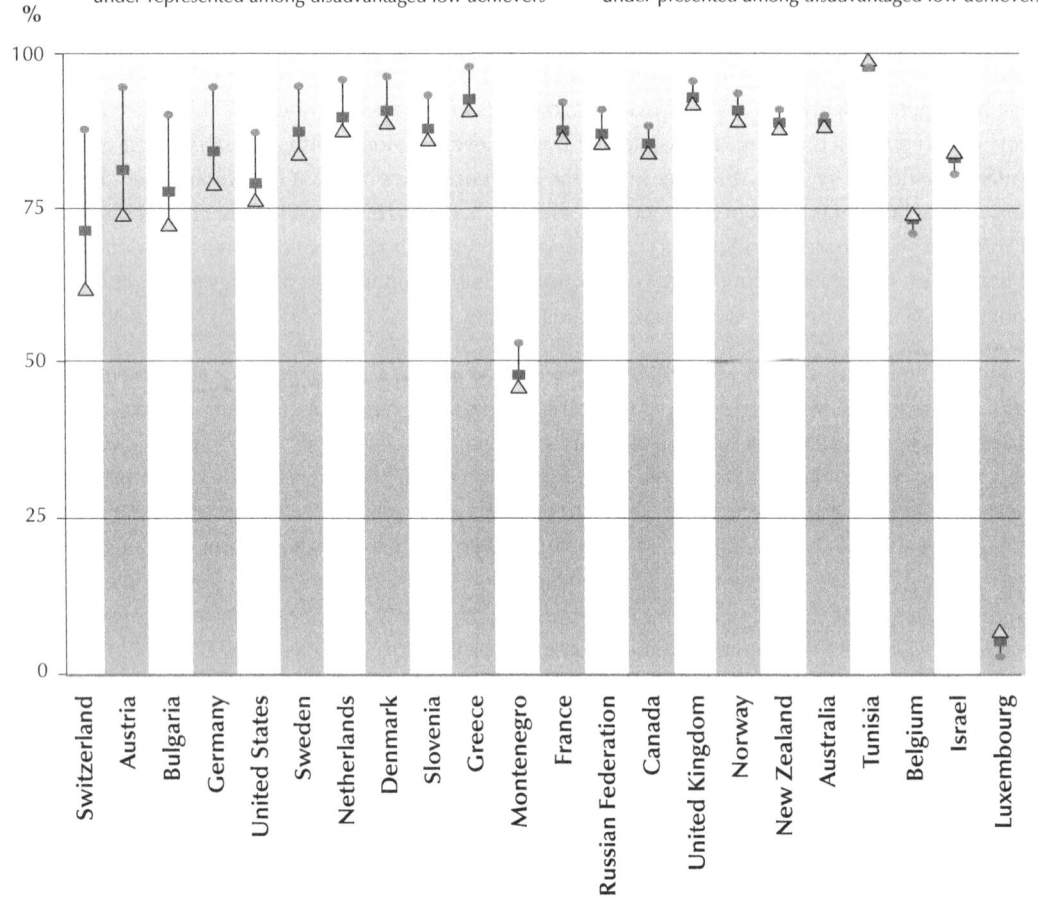

Source: OECD PISA 2006 Database.

CONCLUSION

This chapter defined and empirically characterised resilience among socio-economically disadvantaged students. It is possible to characterise relatively disadvantaged students who beat the odds and achieve academic excellence relative to their peers. These findings show that resilient and disadvantaged low achievers share some common characteristics. While comparing the prevalence of resilient students across countries is problematic with this definition, it is possible and useful to draw conclusions across countries from within-country group comparisons. Several key findings emerge from the analyses presented in the chapter.

- In all participating countries, it is possible to identify a group of students that does well despite their relatively disadvantaged socio-economic background. The report categorises these students as resilient. By comparison, disadvantaged low achievers share a similar background but perform poorly. Practically all resilient students exhibit a proficiency level in science that is above the baseline level of competency in PISA 2006.

- In most countries the vast majority of students who are resilient in science would be categorised as resilient if their performance in mathematics and/or in reading had been considered instead. Resilience does not appear to be a domain-specific characteristic but rather a general feature of some disadvantaged students, their communities or the schools they attend that help them overcome their social disadvantage and become high performers.

- In general, there is no gender gap in resilience for science (there is a gap for reading but it is small). In almost all countries, male and female students are equally represented among resilient students, disadvantaged low achievers and disadvantaged students more generally. Notable exceptions include the partner country Chile, where males are over-represented among resilient students (and under-represented among disadvantaged low achievers) and Turkey, where males are under-represented among resilient students (and over-represented among disadvantaged students).

- Language and immigrant background appear to be associated with resilience only marginally and only in few countries. Results suggest that native students and students who speak the language of the test at home are over-represented to a marked degree among resilient students (and under-represented among disadvantaged low achievers) most notably in Austria, Germany and Switzerland.

Findings presented in this chapter show that some students from disadvantaged backgrounds are beating the odds and are thriving in school. Understanding more about these students and the approaches to learning and school characteristics that are associated with resilience could help policymakers and school leaders foster resilience among a greater number of students. The next chapters of this report focus on these issues.

Notes

1. An international cut-point for socio-economic disadvantage would identify almost all students in some countries as disadvantaged students and all students in other countries as advantaged. No country would describe their student population in such terms. Similarly a single international cut-point for academic achievement may leave some countries and economies with no resilient students and therefore no analytical power to study what makes these students different.

2. The decision to divide the socio-economic background and science score distributions into thirds was driven partly by theoretical considerations and partly by statistical requirements. The variables which comprise the background index and the test items that comprise the assessment score were chosen for their theoretical ability to discriminate among differing levels of socio-economic background and academic performance. Other cut-points could have been applied to these indices such as choosing different cut-points (e.g., the 25th and 75th percentiles) or choosing specific proficiency levels to indicate high achievement. However, if proficiency levels or if the 25th and 75th percentiles are used rather than the 33rd and 67th percentiles as cut-points the resultant groups of disadvantaged students would have been too small in some countries to allow the precise measurement of mean differences. Dividing the distributions into thirds to distinguish groups of students with different levels of socio-economic background and different levels of performance balanced the theoretical need for distinction with the statistical need for large enough sample sizes.

3. Because each of the groups identified is country-specific, it is not possible to compare across countries the shares of resilient students calculated using this definition. Disadvantaged students in one country, for example, would not necessarily be defined as disadvantaged in another. The proportion of resilient students within each country change when different cut-off points are used but the ranking of countries of countries does not change substantially. Obviously, less stringent requirements, such as lower performance or higher socio-economic background limits, result in higher proportions of resilient students. This fact highlights that cross-country comparisons of the proportion of resilient students may be misleading and that the interpretation of these proportions as representing the prevalence of resilience in each country may be misleading. For information and to clarify the size of the sample on which the analysis in this report is carried out and the proportions of resilient students and disadvantaged low achievers, see Table A5.11.

4. Table A5.11 in Annex A5 includes a description of the relative sample sizes for each of these groups. For reference, the proportion of resilient, average achievers and low achievers among disadvantaged students are presented for each country. However, given the country-specific definition used in this report, they are a potentially misleading indication of the prevalence of resilience across countries.

5. Please note data for the United States are only available in science and mathematics making the comparison across the three domains impossible and that is why it was not included in this discussion.

6. The results are similar but less marked if one looks at resilience defined using mathematics or reading, but this evidence is not reported on this report.

A Profile of Student Resilience

A PROFILE OF STUDENT RESILIENCE

INTRODUCTION

Chapter 2 characterised resilience and contrasted it with low performance among disadvantaged students. It also explored differences in the main individual background characteristics between these two groups of disadvantaged students: resilient and disadvantaged low achievers.

This chapter extends this analysis to student approaches to learning and school factors that may be related to performance. In particular, the chapter examines whether differences in student approaches to learning, in student engagement in science courses and time spent learning science and learning environments at school, may help to explain performance differences between resilient and disadvantaged low achievers. Chapter 4 extends this analysis to all students and explores the factors that may help disadvantaged students close the achievement gap with more advantaged students.

The chapter is structured on the basis of three themes – approaches to learning, engagement in science courses, and learning environments at school – that may be associated with disadvantaged students being resilient. For each domain, the chapter first provides a brief description of the indicators available from PISA. These are generally in the form of indices based on the responses of students and the principals at their schools. It then explores the differences between resilient students and disadvantaged low achievers, both on the overall indices and on each of the single items used in the construction of the indices. Thirdly, the chapter analyses whether the indicators are associated with the probability that disadvantaged students will be resilient.[1]

With respect to students' approaches to learning, the chapter identifies four broad areas that the literature suggests are particularly associated with academic success among disadvantaged students: *i)* motivation to learn science, *ii)* engagement in science activities outside the school, *iii)* confidence in science abilities and *iv)* perspectives towards science-related careers. With respect to engagement in science courses, the second domain, the chapter examines *i)* the number of science courses students take and *ii)* the amount of time they spend learning science at school. And with respect to the learning environment at school, the third domain, the chapter considers school factors that are commonly believed to be associated with performance, in particular: *i)* school management, competition and admittance policies and *ii)* school resources.

The chapter concludes by developing a model which includes measures of all three areas (approaches to learning, hours spent and courses taken, and learning environment at school), aimed at evaluating whether the relationships found for each factor separately are robust to the inclusion of full information on students' circumstances.

STUDENTS' ATTITUDES AND BEHAVIOURS AND THE LEARNING ENVIRONMENT AT SCHOOL: DEFINITIONS AND OVERVIEW

As discussed in Chapter 1, empirical studies indicate that student approaches to learning, such as their motivation, engagement and confidence, as well as learning time are strongly associated with academic success. For example, students with greater motivation to learn, who have greater confidence in their abilities and who exert greater effort on their coursework tend to have higher achievement scores than students with less motivation and confidence and who put less effort into learning (Deci *et al.*,1991; Eccles *et al.*, 1998; OECD, 2003a; OECD, 2003b; OECD, 2009a).

The chapter identifies ten indices that describe students' approaches to learning and engagement in science courses: *i)* motivation to learn science, *ii)* engagement in science activities outside the school, *iii)* confidence in science abilities, *iv)* perspectives towards science-related careers, *v)* the number of science courses students take and *vi)* the amount of time they spend learning science at school. These indices are constructed using information on a subset of the measures included in the PISA student and school questionnaires that could potentially characterise how students approach science learning, the hours spent and the courses taken to learn science. The full array of constructs included within PISA was considered for this analysis with the selected indices chosen because the literature highlighted their relative importance in explaining the academic performance of resilient students. Details on the methods used to construct these indices can be found in the PISA 2006 Technical Report (OECD, 2009b).

Box 3.1. **Interpreting the PISA indices on students' approaches to learning**

The OECD constructed a set of indices to describe students' approaches to learning for which the average OECD student (*e.g.*, the student with an average level of interest) was given an index value of zero and about two-thirds of the OECD student population were between the values of -1 and 1 (*i.e.* the index has a standard deviation of 1). Therefore, if a student group has a negative mean index value, this does not necessarily imply that the student group responded negatively to the underlying questions. Rather, students in this group responded less positively than students on average across OECD countries. (The standardisation procedure on the indices was carried out using the full student population in OECD countries not just resilient and disadvantaged low achievers.) Likewise positive mean index values indicate that students in that group responded more positively on average than the average student among OECD countries. While every effort was made to make these indices comparable across countries, cultural differences may be reflected in results on the association between students' approaches to learning and academic success and therefore care should be taken when interpreting findings across countries (OECD, 2009b).

The number and type of courses in which students decide to enrol reflect both the way they approach learning as well as the school's learning environment. While in some cases students are required to take certain courses, in most circumstances students have the possibility to choose whether to take one course or the other. In this report, the measures capturing the number of courses and the time spent in regular classes are based on student reports. There are therefore certain limitations to the use of these data and the results presented below should be analysed with these caveats in mind. Still, these measures approximate an important element in how students approach and engage in learning at school, namely how they use their time there.

The PISA 2006 indices for the learning environment at school are based on school principals' reports and answers to the school questionnaire. They cover a broad range of issues, including the management and funding of the school, admittance policies and the quality and use of school resources. In particular, the report looks at five school learning environment variables: *i)* private/public management, *ii)* school competition, *iii)* admittance policies, *iv)* school resources and *v)* school activities to promote science learning. The report also uses some school variables that were produced by aggregating the answers of the students in the same school, such as the average socio-economic intake of the school. Annex A5 provides detailed definitions for each of these variables. The PISA 2006 report and the technical publications provide a full description of how these indices were constructed (OECD, 2007a, 2007b and 2009b).

PISA data on the learning environment at school present some limitations and this report can only address these issues up to a point. There are important contextual factors that international comparative surveys cannot capture. For example, PISA does not examine processes over time and the responses of the school principals refer to the circumstances that students might have faced for a relatively short period of time. Box 3.2 presents in more detail the limitations of these measures.

A PROFILE OF STUDENT RESILIENCE

Except for courses and hours, all variables characterising students' approaches to learning are standardised to have a mean of zero and a standard deviation of 1 across OECD students. Negative values on these indices therefore indicate that the mean student group index value is below the average index value among OECD students. (See Box 3.1 for detailed information on how to interpret the indices and Annex A5 for a detailed description of these measures.)

Box 3.2. Interpreting the data from schools and their relationship to student performance

Several limitations of the information collected from principals should be taken into account in the interpretation of the data. On average, only 300 principals were surveyed in each OECD country and in seven countries fewer than 170 principals were surveyed. Although principals are able to provide information about their schools, generalising from a single source of information for each school (and then matching that information with students' reports) is not straightforward. Most importantly, students' performance usually relates to the work of many teachers in various subject areas.

The learning environment in which 15-year-olds find themselves and which PISA examines may only be partially indicative of the learning environment that shaped their educational experiences earlier in their schooling career, particularly in education systems where students progress through different types of educational institutions at the lower secondary and upper secondary levels. To the extent that the current learning environment of 15-year-olds differs from that of their earlier school years, the contextual data collected by PISA is an imperfect proxy for the cumulative learning environments of students and their association with learning outcomes is therefore likely to be underestimated.

The definition of the school in which students are taught is not straightforward in some countries, because 15-year-olds may be in different school types that vary in the level of education provided or the programme destination. Because of the manner in which students were sampled, the within-school variation includes variation between classes as well as variation between students.

The study of school resources requires precision that might not be easily captured in surveys, especially surveys with time restrictions that affect what can be requested of respondents. For example, a principal may not have accurate data on such matters as class sizes in specific subjects, nor the time or resources to gather such data. Moreover, it is important to associate specific resources with specific students rather than school averages to ascertain how a change in one type of resource might impact student performance.

The combination of these restrictions limits the ability of PISA to provide direct statistical estimates of the relationships of school resources with educational outcomes. Caution is therefore required in interpreting the school resource indicators bearing in mind that there are potential measurement problems and omitted variables. However, despite these caveats, the information from the school questionnaire can be instructive as it provides important insights into the ways in which national and sub-national authorities implement their educational objectives.

In using results from non-experimental data on school performance such as the PISA database, it is also important to bear in mind the distinction between school effects and the effects of schooling, particularly when interpreting the modest association between factors such as school resources,

...

> ...
> policies and institutional characteristics and student performance. The effect of schooling is the influence on performance of not being schooled versus being schooled, which can have significant impact not only on knowledge but also on fundamental cognition.
>
> School effects are education researchers' shorthand way of referring to the effect on academic performance of attending one school or another, usually schools that differ in resources or policies or institutional characteristics. Where schools and school systems do not vary in fundamental ways, the school effect can be modest. Nevertheless, modest school effects should not be confused with a lack of an effect by schooling.
>
> Where data based on reports from school principals or parents are presented in this report, it has been weighted so that it reflects the number of 15-year-olds enrolled in each school.

THE ANALYSIS: A BRIEF DESCRIPTION OF THE MODELS PRESENTED IN THIS CHAPTER

This chapter focuses on comparisons across disadvantaged students, namely between resilient students and disadvantaged low achievers. The goal is to provide an answer to these two questions: How are resilient and disadvantaged low achievers different in terms of the variables described above? And which of these factors are associated with the likelihood that a disadvantaged student will beat the odds? To address these questions, the chapter presents three perspectives, proceeding from general and simple comparison to more complex models that adjust for student and school characteristics. Annex A5 discusses all the details for each of these models.

First, the chapter presents the difference in raw measures as collected in the PISA student and school questionnaires. These can give a precise idea of what different groups of students responded on average to different questions. They provide a rough approximation to differences among both groups. Here the chapter reports simply the proportion of resilient and disadvantaged low achievers that responded a certain way to a particular question.

Second, the chapter explores differences in a range of PISA indices constructed to aggregate these answers along a broad set of issues. These differences are a good way to summarise the raw answers of students and school principals. They provide insights into how different these students are but they fail to account for factors other than the ones measured by these indices that may help explain those differences. Here the chapter looks at the difference in the average index for each of the two groups of students, resilient and disadvantaged low achievers.

Third, the chapter presents predictive models on the likelihood of being resilient. Box 3.3 describes how to interpret these results. These models go from a simple model including only the measure of interest to more complex models that adjust for student and school socio-economic and demographic characteristics.

STUDENT APPROACHES TO LEARNING

Student motivation to learn science

Students who are more motivated to learn science achieve higher levels of performance than students with less motivation (Deci and Ryan, 1985; OECD, 2007a; Wigfield *et al.*, 1998). In particular, disadvantaged students who are motivated are significantly more likely to be resilient than disadvantaged students who are not motivated (Connell *et al.*, 1994; Martin, 2002).

Two PISA indices characterise student motivation to learn science. The index of general interest in science is an indicator of students' internal motivation. Students' views of the importance of science for future academic and professional pursuits constitute the elements of the index of instrumental motivation to learn science, which captures students' external motivation.

A PROFILE OF STUDENT RESILIENCE

> **Box 3.3. Interpreting predictive models on the likelihood of being resilient**
>
> The results for these predictive models are presented in terms of odds ratios. The odds ratios reported here compare the probability of being resilient for two groups of students. These two groups are identified by a one unit increase in the variable measuring the factor of interest. For variables such as gender or private school, a one unit increase is the difference between male and female or private and public schools. For the PISA indices, a unit difference is taken from the mean and represents a standard deviation increase in the index.
>
> Odds ratios over one indicate that higher values of a particular factor are associated with a greater likelihood that a disadvantaged student will be resilient, while odds ratios below one are suggestive of a negative relationship between the factor and resilience. For example, if the estimated odds ratio for private is 2.0, this implies that students at private schools are two times more likely to be resilient than students at public schools.
>
> By comparing estimates of the relationship between different factors and resilience obtained in the simple model and those adjusting for individual and school characteristics, the chapter examines to which extend the estimated relationships are explained by differences in individual characteristics and the schools which students attend.

The index of general interest in science combines students' responses on the extent to which they are interested or very interested in: topics in physics, topics in chemistry, the biology of plants, human biology, topics in astronomy, topics in geology, ways scientists design experiments and what is required for scientific explanations. Annex A5 includes the actual questions addressed to students.

Resilient students tend to show more interest in science topics than disadvantaged low achievers. While around 60% of resilient students in OECD countries report being interested in chemistry, astronomy and physics, less than 40% of disadvantaged low achievers show similar levels of interest. For partner countries and economies, with some exceptions, resilient and disadvantaged low achievers are not very different in terms of their interest in science topics (Table A2.1a). The greatest level of interest expressed is in relation to human biology – over 70% of resilient students and almost 60% of disadvantaged low achievers in OECD countries – while the least interest is in learning about what is required for scientific explanations – 40% of resilient students and less than 30% of disadvantaged low achievers. In all countries except Latvia and the Russian Federation, a larger share of resilient students expresses interest in human biology than disadvantaged low achievers. Differences are particularly large (above 20 percentage points) in Australia, Iceland, Ireland, Japan, Norway, Portugal and Switzerland among OECD countries and in Azerbaijan and Hong Kong-China among partner countries and economies. Similarly, in all countries and economies except the United States and Latvia a larger share of resilient students than disadvantaged low achievers is interested in learning about what is required for scientific explanations. Among OECD countries, differences across resilient and disadvantaged low achievers on this item are particularly pronounced in Australia, Denmark, Iceland, Ireland, Japan, Korea, Norway, Sweden and Spain while among partner countries and economies differences are particularly strong in Hong Kong-China and Chinese Taipei (Table A2.1a).

As Figure 3.1 shows, the higher levels of interest shown by resilient students in most topics result in higher average indice of general interest in science among resilient students than disadvantaged low achievers in all OECD countries. Furthermore, resilient students in all OECD countries except the Netherlands have mean index values that are above the OECD students' average, while the mean index values for disadvantaged

A PROFILE OF STUDENT RESILIENCE

Figure 3.1
Internal and external motivation to learn science

■ Increased likelihood of being resilient associated with one unit on the PISA index
■ Same after accounting for school mean ESCS, ESCS, gender, immigrant status, language used at home, and grade
◆ Average index for resilient students (RES)   □ Average index for disadvantaged low achievers (DLA)

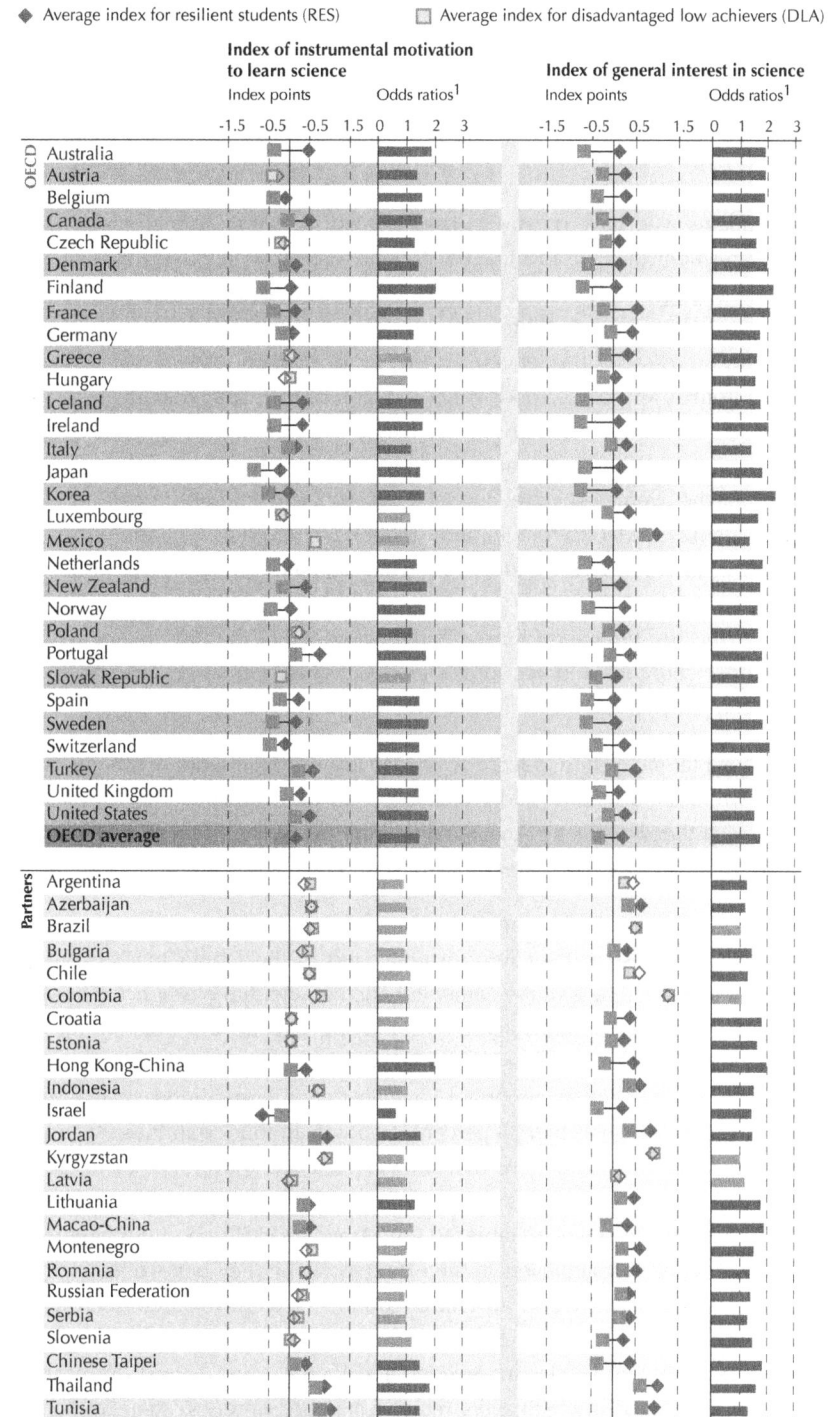

1. Odds ratios stand for the increase in the likelihood of being resilient associated with an increase of one standard deviation in the index. The results reported here refer to the logistic regressions explained in Annex A2.
2. Statistically significant differences are marked in a darker tone.
Note: Countries have been ordered alphabetically.
Source: *OECD PISA 2006 Database*, Table A2.1c and Table A2.2c.

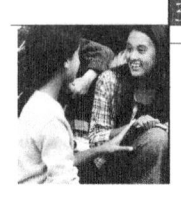

low achievers in all OECD countries (except Mexico) and some partner countries and economies are below the average of OECD students (Table A2.1b). Differences in means within all OECD countries and within 18 of the 25 partner countries and economies suggest that resilient students have greater general interest in science.[2] On average, across OECD countries, this difference is rather large, more than half of a standard deviation in the index and it is particularly marked in Australia, Denmark, Finland, France, Iceland, Ireland, Japan, Korea and Norway where it reaches more than three quarters of a standard deviation. This pattern is less marked among partner countries and economies with the exception of the partner economy Chinese Taipei where the difference in the index is close to three quarters of a standard deviation (Table A2.1b).

Disadvantaged students who have greater general interest in science (*i.e.* are internally motivated) are more likely to be resilient than disadvantaged students with low levels of internal motivation. This is quite a strong relationship. As Table A2.1c indicates, disadvantaged students in OECD countries who have a value on the index of general interest in science of 1 (that is a high value) are on average 1.66 times more likely to be resilient in science than the disadvantaged student who has an average interest in science. Apart from a few cases, odds ratios do not change dramatically across OECD countries when controlling for individual characteristics such as gender, immigration background, grade attended, language spoken and socio-economic background in the individual controls model (second column in Table A2.1c) and for the average socio-economic background of students attending the same school as the respondent in the full model (third column in Table A2.1c). The association between general interest in science and resilience is strongest in Korea where the estimated resilient odds ratio after accounting for school and student factors is 2.3. It is above two in Finland, France, Ireland and Switzerland. Except for Croatia, Lithuania, Macao-China and Chinese Taipei where the odds ratios are all above 1.75, estimated odds ratios in partner countries and economies are smaller and in some cases there appears to be no relationship between general interest in science and resilience (Table A2.1c).

The index of instrumental motivation to learn science measures the importance students attach to learning science for their own future academic and professional pursuits. This index combines students' responses on the extent to which they believe that making an effort in learning science will help them at work or in their future studies, will improve their career prospects and will help them find a job.

Both resilient students and disadvantaged low achievers appreciate the importance of scientific knowledge to achieve success in their future studies and in the labour market, but resilient students generally show a greater awareness of the career enhancing potential of science. For example, over 65% of resilient students in OECD countries agree that studying science will improve their career prospects while only less than 55% of disadvantaged low achievers do so. Resilient students in all OECD countries except Hungary perceive science as important for their future career, more so than disadvantaged low achievers. The difference is higher than 25 percentage points in four countries (Australia, Ireland, Korea and New Zealand). Most students believe that studying science is useful to them, but while over 70% of resilient students in OECD countries do so, only around 55% of disadvantaged low achievers agree on the usefulness of studying science (Table A2.2a). Among OECD countries, the difference between resilient and disadvantaged low achievers in the extent to which they believe learning science will help them in their future work is positive in all OECD countries except for the Czech Republic, Germany, Greece, Hungary, Luxembourg, Mexico, Poland and the Slovak Republic. This difference is particularly large in Australia, Finland, Iceland, Japan, Sweden and Portugal. In contrast, in most partner countries and economies disadvantaged low achievers report a higher awareness than resilient students on the extent to which learning science will help them in their future work. In 13 out of 25 partner countries and economies more disadvantaged low achievers than resilient students also report that studying science will improve their career prospects (Table A2.2a).

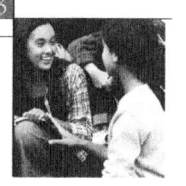

As summarised by differences in values on the index of instrumental motivation to learn science (see Table A2.2b), resilient students express a greater degree of instrumental motivation to learn science than disadvantaged low achievers in the majority of OECD countries and to a lesser extent in partner countries and economies. Figure 3.1 also indicates that differences in levels of instrumental motivation between resilient and disadvantaged low achievers are generally fewer and smaller than they are for the index of general interest in science (*i.e.* internal motivation). In eight out of 30 OECD countries and six out of 15 partner countries and economies the differences apparent in relation to general interest disappear when external motivation is considered (Table A2.2c).

Contrary to the findings for internal motivation, in several OECD countries disadvantaged students with greater instrumental motivation to learn science are not performing better than other less externally motivated disadvantaged students. Figure 3.1 highlights that the estimated odds ratios for instrumental motivation are smaller than for internal motivation and that the association with resilience disappears in practically all partner countries and economies (Table A2.2c). In the base model where factors such as gender and immigrant background are not taken into account, disadvantaged students who believe learning science will help them in their future work have a greater likelihood of being resilient in 22 out of 30 OECD countries and in eight partner countries and economies. This relationship is moderately strong. When individual and school-level information is taken into account, the relationship between instrumental motivation and academic resilience is positive in a further three OECD countries (Austria, the Czech Republic and Poland) but falls somewhat in two countries (Japan and Portugal). The base model (first column of Table A2.2c) shows that disadvantaged students who believe learning science will help them in their future work have a greater likelihood of being resilient in only eight partner countries and economies, with no major shift in the strength of the association occurring when individual and school-level variables are added to the model.

The evidence presented in this section suggests that student motivation to learn science, internal motivation more so than external is associated with resilience in most OECD countries and in some partner countries and economies. Fostering motivation to learn science among disadvantaged students could therefore lead to improvements in performance.

Student engagement with science activities outside of school

Increased awareness of the connections between science and everyday life is associated with higher academic achievement as students become more engaged with the academic material (OECD, 2003b; OECD, 2007a). Research indicates that resilient students have higher rates of engagement with science than low performing disadvantaged students (Borman and Overman, 2004; Catterall, 1998). This section presents analyses of the relationship between student engagement with science and student resilience using the index of engagement in science-related activities. Student engagement with science is measured by the frequency of their involvement in the following science-related activities: watching TV programmes about science, borrowing or buying books on science topics, visiting websites about science topics, listening to radio programmes about advances in science, reading science magazines or science articles in newspapers and attending a science club.

Across most science-related activities, resilient students are more engaged than disadvantaged low achievers. As evident in Table A2.3a, on average a larger share of resilient students than disadvantaged low achievers reports watching TV programmes about science, borrowing or buying books about science and reading science magazines or science articles, while more disadvantaged low achievers than resilient students listen to radio programmes about advances in science and attend a science club (possibly because such clubs offer remedial courses to low-performing students).

Overall, students in OECD countries report fairly low levels of engagement in science activities outside of school. The most popular activities, watching TV programmes about science and reading science magazines or science articles, were reported on average by only around 25% of resilient students and less than 18% of disadvantaged low achievers. Across OECD countries, even fewer students borrow or buy books on science topics (9% of resilient students and 7% of disadvantaged low achievers), visit web sites about science (12% of resilient students and 9% of disadvantaged low achievers), listen to radio programmes about advances in science (5% of resilient students and 8% of disadvantaged low achievers) and attend a science club (3% of resilient students and 5% of disadvantaged low achievers) (Table A2.3a).

Levels of engagement are generally higher in partner countries and economies. For example, while approximately 25% of resilient students and 18% of disadvantaged low achievers in OECD countries watch TV programmes about science, many more do so in partner countries and economies (Table A2.3a). Across OECD countries only in Poland and Portugal do over half of all resilient students watch TV programmes about science, while the majority of resilient students in five partner countries and economies do so (Azerbaijan, Chile, Colombia, Kyrgyzstan and Thailand). Participation rates are higher in partner countries and economies, especially among disadvantaged low achievers. For example, over 30% of disadvantaged low achievers borrow or buy books about science topics in Argentina, Azerbaijan, Brazil, Colombia, Kyrgyzstan and Tunisia and listen to radio programmes about advances in science in Azerbaijan, Colombia, Jordan, Kyrgyzstan, Montenegro and Tunisia (Table A2.3a).

Using the index of engagement in science-related activities, Figure 3.2 shows that resilient students generally participate in more science-related activities than disadvantaged low achievers. In all OECD countries except Poland and Mexico, the index of engagement in science-related activities is higher for the average resilient student than for the average disadvantaged low-achieving students (Table A2.3b). On average across OECD countries, this difference is about a third of a standard deviation, ranging from 0.15 of a standard deviation in the Czech Republic to more than 0.70 of a standard deviation in Iceland. The pattern is weaker across partner countries and economies but similar in that resilient students appear to be more engaged in seven partner countries and economies. However, the opposite is true in Brazil, Kyrgyzstan and Tunisia (Table A2.3b).

Figure 3.2 shows that disadvantaged students in OECD countries except Mexico and Poland who participate more in science-related activities have a greater likelihood of being resilient than disadvantaged students who do not participate in such activities. This relationship is moderately strong. In contrast, in most partner countries and economies participation in science-related activities is not associated with resilience except in Chile, Croatia, Hong Kong-China, Macao-China, Slovenia, Chinese Taipei and Thailand. Resilient odds ratios are relatively modest, even in OECD countries, ranging from 1.24 in the Czech Republic to 1.81 in Iceland. In fact, estimates of resilient odds ratios for most countries are under 1.5, suggesting that the odds of being resilient for a disadvantaged student who has an average value on the participation in science-related activities index that is one standard deviation above the OECD average is less than 1.5 times greater than those of a similarly disadvantaged student whose participation is the same as the average OECD student. In almost all OECD countries, adjusting for individual characteristics and the average socio-economic background at the school level strengthens the association between participation in science-related activities and the likelihood of being resilient (except Italy, Japan, Korea and Turkey as well as Poland) (Table A2.3c).

The evidence presented here suggests that student participation in science-related activities is associated with resilience in most OECD countries and in some partner countries and economies. Fostering student participation in science-related activities could therefore lead to improvements in performance in some countries.

A PROFILE OF STUDENT RESILIENCE

Figure 3.2
Engagement in science-related activities

■ Increased likelihood of being resilient associated with one unit on the PISA index
■ Same after accounting for school mean ESCS, ESCS, gender, immigrant status, language used at home, and grade

◆ Average index for resilient students (RES)   □ Average index for disadvantaged low achievers (DLA)

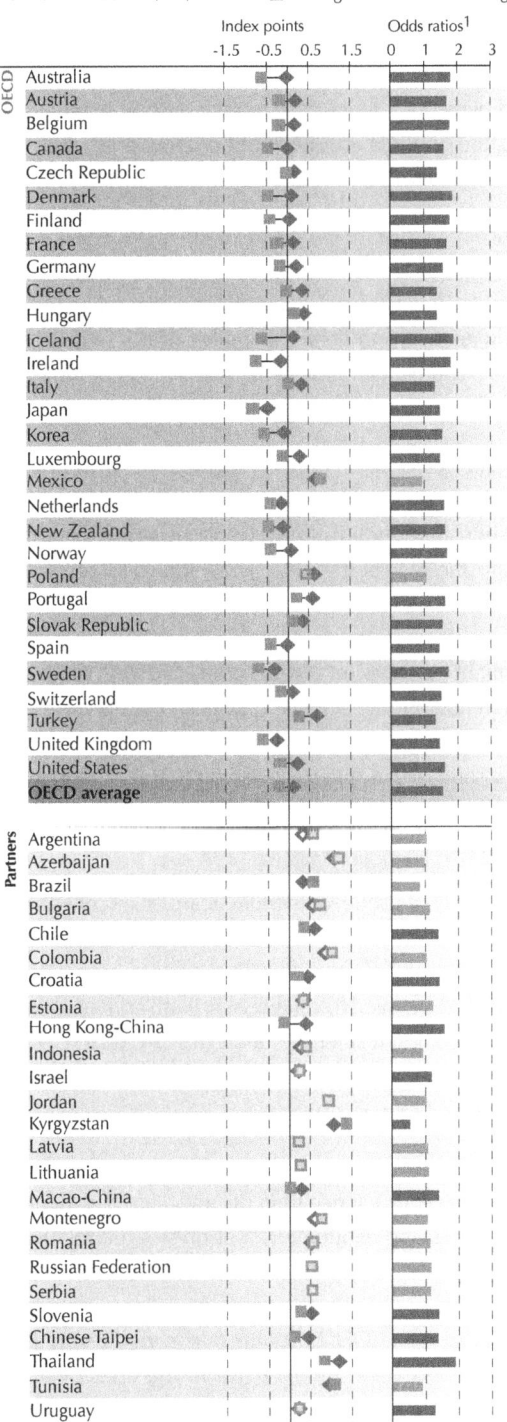

OECD
Australia, Austria, Belgium, Canada, Czech Republic, Denmark, Finland, France, Germany, Greece, Hungary, Iceland, Ireland, Italy, Japan, Korea, Luxembourg, Mexico, Netherlands, New Zealand, Norway, Poland, Portugal, Slovak Republic, Spain, Sweden, Switzerland, Turkey, United Kingdom, United States, OECD average

Partners
Argentina, Azerbaijan, Brazil, Bulgaria, Chile, Colombia, Croatia, Estonia, Hong Kong-China, Indonesia, Israel, Jordan, Kyrgyzstan, Latvia, Lithuania, Macao-China, Montenegro, Romania, Russian Federation, Serbia, Slovenia, Chinese Taipei, Thailand, Tunisia, Uruguay

1. Resilient odds ratios stand for the increase in the likelihood of being resilient associated with an increase of one standard deviation in the index. The results reported here refer to the logistic regressions explained in Annex A2.
2. Statistically significant differences are marked in a darker tone.
Note: Countries have been ordered alphabetically.
Source: *OECD PISA 2006 Database*, Table A2.3c.

Student confidence in their science ability

Student beliefs about their academic abilities can facilitate or hamper their academic performance (Bandura, 1994; Marsh, 1986; OECD, 2007a). Previous research has found resilient students to have greater confidence in their abilities than other disadvantaged students (Borman and Overman, 2004; Shumow et al., 1999). This analysis considers two measures: the index of student self-efficacy in science and the index of student self-concept in science. Higher values on both measures indicate greater confidence. The index of student self-efficacy in science assesses how much students believe in their own ability to handle tasks effectively and overcome difficulties and the ease with which students believe they can carry out specific tasks involving the application of scientific knowledge and skills. The index of student self-concept in science assesses students' beliefs in their own academic abilities.

The index of student self-efficacy in science measures whether students are able to do the following six tasks easily or with a bit of effort: recognise the science question that underlies a newspaper report on a health issue, explain why earthquakes occur more frequently in some areas than in others, describe the role of antibiotics in the treatment of disease, identify the science question associated with the disposal of garbage, predict how changes to an environment will affect the survival of certain species and interpret the scientific information provided on the labelling of food items.

Resilient students report greater ease in tackling all of these tasks in practically all OECD countries. For example, as depicted in Table A2.4a, in 18 out of 30 OECD countries 80% or more of resilient students recognise the science question that underlies a newspaper report on a health issue while in all OECD countries except Mexico and the Slovak Republic less than 70% of disadvantaged low achievers do so (Table A2.4a). Differences in the share of resilient and disadvantaged low achievers who can explain why earthquakes occur more frequently in some areas than in others exceeds 20% in all OECD countries (except Mexico). Over 70% of resilient students in partner countries and economies (expect Azerbaijan, Chile, Montenegro and Indonesia) recognise the science question that underlies a newspaper report on a health issue. The same can be said of disadvantaged low-achieving students in only Israel, Kyrgyzstan and Uruguay. Differences between resilient and disadvantaged low achievers in partner countries and economies range between around 2 percentage points in Azerbaijan and Kyrgyzstan to over 25 percentage points in Estonia and Chinese Taipei (Table A2.4a).

As Figure 3.3 shows, resilient students believe that they learn science with greater ease than disadvantaged low achievers and are more confident in their ability to apply their science knowledge. On the index of student self-efficacy, resilient students in most OECD countries report self-efficacy around one standard deviation greater than that of disadvantaged low achievers. In all countries except Azerbaijan and Kyrgyzstan, there is a sizable difference in favour of resilient students in self-efficacy. Across OECD countries on average the gap between the two groups of students is 0.8 of a standard deviation, almost reaching 1.2 of a standard deviation in the United Kingdom (Table A2.4b).

Disadvantaged students who believe in their own ability to handle tasks effectively and overcome difficulties are significantly more likely to excel in science than disadvantaged students with low levels of self-efficacy in all OECD and partner countries and economies. Not only is the relationship between self-efficacy and student resilience an essentially universal phenomenon, it is also quantitatively important. On average across OECD countries, self-efficacy has the strongest association with resilience of any of the variables considered in this chapter. In fact, in all OECD countries except Greece, Japan, Luxembourg, Mexico, the Netherlands, Turkey and the United States the increase in the odds of being resilient associated with an increase of one standard deviation in the self-efficacy index is above 2.0 and is as high as 3.1 in the United Kingdom. A similar pattern emerges for partner countries and economies. Odds ratios range between 1.1 in Azerbaijan and 2.8 in Estonia and are above 2.0 in eight partner countries and economies. When

A PROFILE OF STUDENT RESILIENCE

Figure 3.3
Student self-confidence in their science ability

- Increased likelihood of being resilient associated with one unit on the PISA index
- Same after accounting for school mean ESCS, ESCS, gender, immigrant status, language used at home, and grade
- ◆ Average index for resilient students (RES)
- ▫ Average index for disadvantaged low achievers (DLA)

Index of student self-concept in science | **Index of student self-efficacy in science**

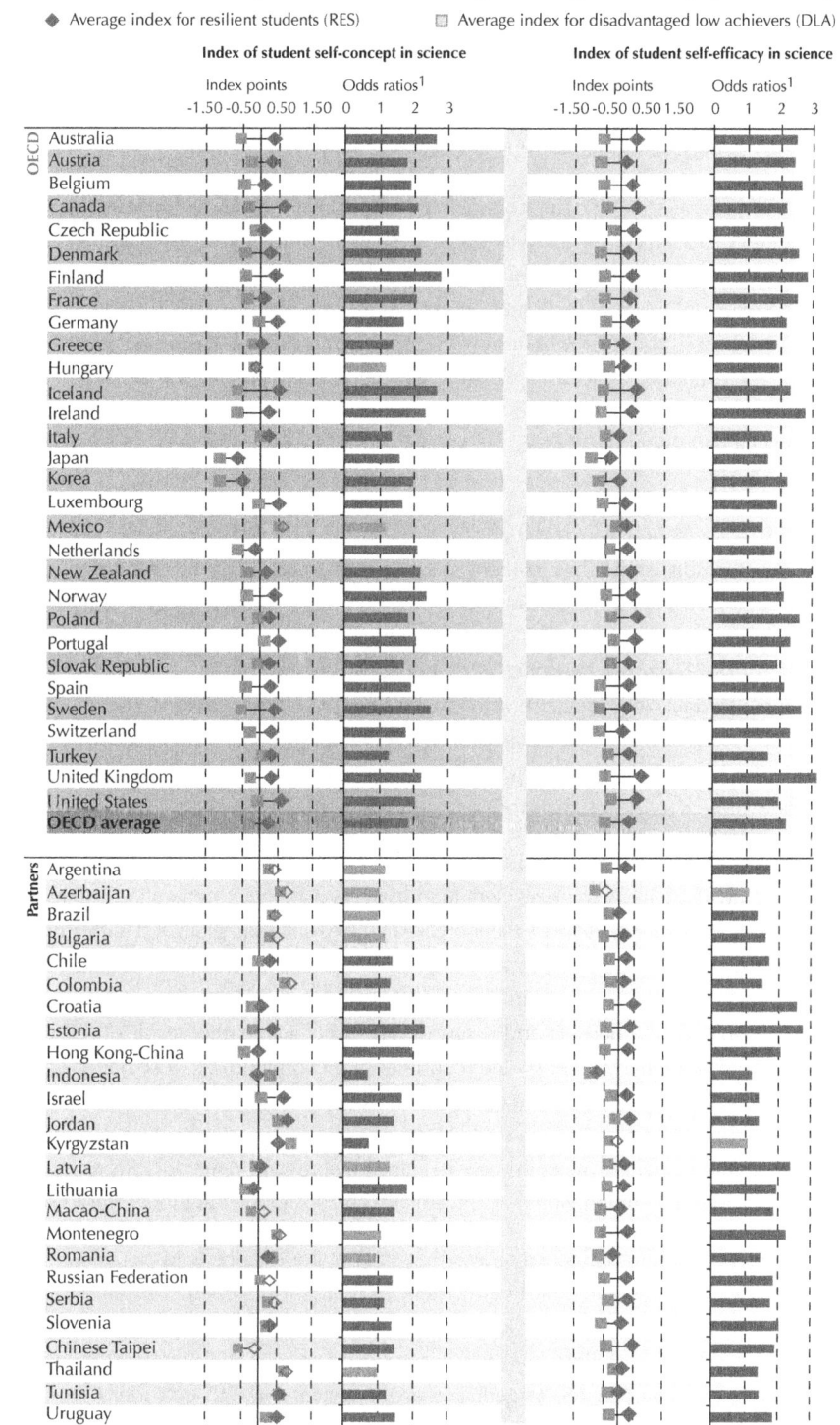

Index points (-1.50 -0.50 0.50 1.50) | Odds ratios[1] (0 1 2 3) | Index points (-1.50 -0.50 0.50 1.50) | Odds ratios[1] (0 1 2 3)

OECD:
Australia, Austria, Belgium, Canada, Czech Republic, Denmark, Finland, France, Germany, Greece, Hungary, Iceland, Ireland, Italy, Japan, Korea, Luxembourg, Mexico, Netherlands, New Zealand, Norway, Poland, Portugal, Slovak Republic, Spain, Sweden, Switzerland, Turkey, United Kingdom, United States, **OECD average**

Partners:
Argentina, Azerbaijan, Brazil, Bulgaria, Chile, Colombia, Croatia, Estonia, Hong Kong-China, Indonesia, Israel, Jordan, Kyrgyzstan, Latvia, Lithuania, Macao-China, Montenegro, Romania, Russian Federation, Serbia, Slovenia, Chinese Taipei, Thailand, Tunisia, Uruguay

1. Resilient odds ratios stand for the increase in the likelihood of being resilient associated with an increase of one standard deviation in the index. The results reported here refer to the logistic regressions explained in Annex A2.
2. Statistically significant differences are marked in a darker tone.
Note: Countries have been ordered alphabetically.
Source: *OECD PISA 2006 Database*, Tables A2.4c and A2.5c.

individual and school-level factors are included in the models, estimates of the change in the likelihood of being resilient remain significant and remarkably similar in strength in most countries, thus indicating little variation across demographic groups and schools in this relationship.

The index of self-concept combines students' responses regarding the extent that they agree with the following: learning advanced science topics would be easy for them, they can usually give good answers to test questions on science topics, they learn science topics quickly, they consider science topics easy, they believe that when they are being taught science, they can understand the concepts very well and they can easily understand new ideas in science.

Resilient students in general show greater confidence in their own academic abilities than disadvantaged low achievers. Across OECD countries over 50% of resilient students believe that learning advanced science topics would be easy for them compared to only about 40% of disadvantaged low achievers (Table A2.5a). Approximately 75% of resilient students believe they can give good answers to test questions on science topics while only about 50% of disadvantaged low achievers share this belief. There are however some exceptions. For example, disadvantaged low achievers report greater self-confidence in the Czech Republic, Hungary, Mexico, the Netherlands and Poland with respect to the ease with which they would learn advanced science topics and in Hungary with respect to the extent to which science topics are easy for them (Table A2.5a).

With respect to differences between resilient and disadvantaged low achievers in mean values on the index of self-concept, results show that resilient students have more confidence than disadvantaged low achievers (Table A2.5b). This is true in all but two OECD countries (Mexico and Hungary). The differences range from 0.22 standard deviations in the Czech Republic to 1.12 standard deviations in Iceland. There are differences in 14 of 25 partner countries and economies and all but two (Indonesia and Kyrgyzstan) indicate that resilient students learn science with greater ease than disadvantaged low achievers. The range of these significant differences is smaller than among OECD countries – from 0.13 standard deviations in the Russian Federation to 0.60 standard deviations in Israel. In Indonesia and Kyrgyzstan, disadvantaged low achievers show more confidence than resilient students (Table A2.5b).

While not as strong as for self-efficacy, disadvantaged students with more confidence in their own academic abilities are significantly more likely to be resilient than students with lower perceptions of their abilities. This is a strong relationship. As Figure 3.3 shows, the increase in the likelihood associated with a one unit increase in the self-concept index (corresponding to a change in 1 standard deviation at the mean) is statistically significant in all OECD countries except Hungary and Mexico, with odds ratios ranging between 1.32 in Greece and 2.84 in Finland. In Indonesia and Kyrgyzstan students with higher levels of self-concept are less likely to be resilient, while in many other partner countries and economies the association is significant and in the expected direction. In several OECD countries the association between students' confidence in their abilities and the likelihood that they will be resilient becomes stronger as individual and school factors are taken into account in the modelling, most notably in France where the estimated odds ratios are 1.56 in the base model, 1.9 after adjusting for individual characteristics and 2.1 in the full model (Table A2.5c).

The evidence presented on self-confidence shows that student confidence is associated with resilience in most countries. The evidence is particularly consistent in relation to self-efficacy where the relationship is significant in all OECD and partner countries and economies. Fostering students' self-confidence, particularly their self-efficacy, may therefore be a means of improving the performance of disadvantaged students. As discussed in next chapter, targeting is an important issue to consider when implementing policies to foster the motivation and engagement of students. It may prove harder to engage disadvantaged students and it is possible that policies to foster engagement across all socio-economic groups of students lead to a widening of the achievement gap between advantaged and disadvantaged students.

Student perspectives towards science-related careers

Indices developed to examine students' motivation to learn science, students' engagement with science and students' self-confidence in their science abilities describe the extent to which science material studied at school is perceived to be relevant by students and the extent to which science is an integral part of students' lives. For example, instrumental motivation to learn science measures students' perceptions on the role of science in their future academic and professional pursuits while the students' participation in science activities index explores whether science-related activities are part of students' leisure time.

The PISA student questionnaires allow the identification of a fourth dimension that characterises students' approaches to learning and that delves further into the theme of how relevant students perceive the science material they study at school. Students who feel stronger connections between this material and their career pursuits upon graduation may in fact perform better in school than students who view the studied material as less relevant to their future careers. This report considers the following two indices: the index of school preparation for science-related careers and the index of student information about science-related careers. The two are related: students who possess more information about science-related careers view these as a more likely occupational opportunity and thus view their current studies as more relevant for their future careers.

The index of school preparation for science-related careers measures how well students feel the curriculum provided by their schools prepares them for science-related careers. The school preparation for science-related careers index measures the extent to which students agree with the following four statements: the subjects available at my school provide students with the basic skills and knowledge for a science-related career, science subjects at my school provide students with the basic skills and knowledge for many different careers, the subjects I study provide me with the basic skills and knowledge for a science-related career, my teachers equip me with the basic skills and knowledge I need for a science-related career.

Across the OECD countries, disadvantaged students report their schools prepare them well for a science career. In most OECD countries there are small differences in favour of resilient students in specific areas of school preparation, but in only a small number of countries are these differences significant. For example, 80% of resilient students in France report that the subjects they study will provide them with the basic skills and knowledge for a science-related career, while only 58% of disadvantaged low achievers report this. Across partner countries and economies, the proportion of disadvantaged students who report being well prepared by their schools is even higher than in OECD countries and the differences between resilient and low achievers are smaller (Table A2.6a).

Using the index of school preparation for science-related careers, Table A2.6b shows that resilient students in OECD countries generally report feeling their schools prepare them for science-related careers to a greater extent than disadvantaged low achievers. There is a difference in 21 of the 30 OECD countries. In all countries except Hungary, Poland and the Slovak Republic, the results indicate that resilient students feel more prepared than disadvantaged low achievers. Differences are significant in ten out of 25 partner countries and economies; however no strong pattern emerges. In six of these partners resilient students feel more prepared than disadvantaged low achievers while in the others disadvantaged low achievers feel more prepared than resilient students (Table A2.6b).

Disadvantaged students who believe that they are receiving good preparation for science-related careers are more likely than other students to be resilient. This is a relatively weak relationship. As Figure 3.4 shows, in almost two thirds of OECD countries, the estimated resilient odds ratios are above 1.0. Only in Hungary and Poland is the likelihood that a disadvantaged student will be resilient reduced when the student reports greater school preparation for a science career. Estimated odds ratios are not affected by the inclusion of

A PROFILE OF STUDENT RESILIENCE

Figure 3.4
Students' perspectives towards science related careers

- ▇ Increased likelihood of being resilient associated with one unit on the PISA index
- ▒ Same after accounting for school mean ESCS, ESCS, gender, immigrant status, language used at home, and grade
- ◆ Average index for resilient students (RES)
- ☐ Average index for disadvantaged low achievers (DLA)

1. Resilient odds ratios stand for the increase in the likelihood of being resilient associated with an increase of one standard deviation in the index. The results reported here refer to the logistic regressions explained in Annex A2.
2. Statistically significant differences are marked in a darker tone.
Note: Countries have been ordered alphabetically.
Source: *OECD PISA 2006 Database*, Tables A2.6c and A2.7c.

© OECD 2011 Against the Odds: Disadvantaged Students Who Succeed in School

student characteristics and school factors in the models. Their size suggests that while the relationship between school preparation for science careers and student resilience is fairly widespread across OECD countries, it is not particularly strong. Odds ratios range between 1.26 in Spain and 1.73 in Australia in the full model. Contrary to findings for OECD countries, disadvantaged students in partner countries and economies who report that their school prepares them well for science-related careers are generally equally likely to be resilient as other disadvantaged students. Results presented in the full model indicate that the association between school preparation for science and resilience is statistically significant and positive only in Hong Kong-China and Thailand (odds ratios of 1.52 and 1.28 respectively), while it is significant and negative in four other countries: Brazil, Chile, Colombia and Montenegro (Table A2.6c).

The index of student information about science-related careers assesses how well informed students are about where science-related jobs are and what they need to do in order to work in such a job. The student information about science-related careers index combines students' responses on how well informed they are on the following four topics: science-related careers that are available in the job market, where to find information about science-related careers, the steps a student needs to take if they want a science-related career, and employers or companies that hire people to work in science-related careers.

Only a minority of resilient and disadvantaged low achievers in OECD countries is well informed about employers and companies that hire people to work in science-related careers. In all countries except Iceland, Korea and Turkey, a higher proportion of disadvantaged low achievers report being better informed on this aspect than resilient students (Table A2.7a). Students in partner countries and economies appear to be equally poorly informed about employers and companies that offer science-related job opportunities and results indicate that, as in OECD countries, resilient students are the ones that lack information the most. In addition, over half of resilient students in 15 out of 30 OECD countries reported that they are not sufficiently informed as to where they can find information about science-related careers. Over half of disadvantaged low achievers are not sufficiently informed on the steps they need to take if they want a science-related career in 21 out of 30 OECD countries (Table A2.7a).

Disadvantaged students who reported being better informed about science careers are not generally more resilient than students who feel less well informed. As Figure 3.4 depicts only in Australia, Denmark, Iceland, the Netherlands, Spain, Switzerland and Turkey is more information about science careers associated with an increase in the likelihood that a disadvantaged student will be resilient. While statistically significant, the association is quantitatively small. In the full model, odds ratios range from 1.18 in Spain to 1.46 in Iceland (Table A2.7c). The student information on science careers index is significantly associated with the likelihood that a disadvantaged student will be resilient in eight out of the 25 partner countries and economies. The association is, however, positive only in two countries and economies (Croatia and Chinese Taipei) and is quantitatively very small in both cases (odds ratios are at or below 1.3). In other partner countries and economies disadvantaged students who feel informed about science careers are generally less likely to be resilient than other disadvantaged students (Table A2.7c).

The evidence presented here suggests that students' perspectives on science-related careers are weakly related to student resilience, being somewhat stronger for school preparation than for student information about science-related careers. From this analysis there is little evidence that providing more career information is a strong contender as a policy option for raising the performance of disadvantaged students.

STUDENT ENGAGEMENT IN SCIENCE COURSES AT SCHOOL AND TIME SPENT LEARNING

In many schools, students can choose whether they want to enrol in science courses and if so, whether they prefer to attend general courses about science or discipline-specific modules such as physics, chemistry and biology. This section presents estimates of the association between participation in science courses and hours spent learning science at school and resilience. It uses two indicators to characterise students' participation in compulsory science courses and one indicator to characterise the time students spend learning science topics at school. The results for these indicators cannot be directly compared with the results for the PISA indices presented in earlier sections of this chapter because the scales are very different. In the indices presented earlier, student responses were converted to a standardised value to facilitate comparison to the average student in OECD countries. Thus, a one point difference in these indices equates to a one standard deviation difference. Here, the original response metrics are used.

The indicators for participation in science courses are derived from questions on the PISA student background questionnaire. These questions asked students whether they attended compulsory general science classes at school in the year in which the PISA assessment took place or in the previous year. They also asked students whether they attended compulsory classes in the year of the PISA assessment or the previous year in any of the following science topics: general science, biology, physics or chemistry. Annex A5 includes the questions addressed to students in this regard and a description of how the indicators were constructed.

In general, student resilience is associated with attending a compulsory general science course – across OECD countries on average this is the second strongest association found between resilience and the factors considered in this chapter. All students in nine OECD countries – Austria, France, Greece, Hungary, Japan, Luxembourg, Norway, Poland and the Slovak Republic – report having attended a compulsory general science course. In 15 of the other 21 OECD countries, a higher proportion of resilient students attended a compulsory general science course in the last two years than disadvantaged low achievers. Only in two countries, Italy and Spain, is the reverse true (Table A2.8a). The same pattern is apparent among partner countries and economies, where the differences are very similar and in the same direction (in this case with only one exception, Slovenia). After accounting for individual student and school characteristics, attending a compulsory general science course is associated with an increase in the likelihood of being resilient in 13 of the 21 OECD countries which have appropriate data for analysing this question. For both Italy and Spain, attending a compulsory science course is associated with a lower likelihood only when student and school background characteristics are not taken in account (Table A2.8b).

In relation to the number of science-related compulsory courses attended, the second indicator, the association with resilience is weaker, as Figure 3.5 depicts. In 19 of the 28 OECD countries for which data are available, the average resilient student engages in a larger number of courses than the average disadvantaged low achiever (Table A2.9a). The value of the indicator ranges between zero and eight, representing the total number of compulsory science courses students attended over a two-year period. The difference between the two student groups is more than three courses in Belgium and two courses in the United Kingdom, Sweden and Macao-China. The pattern is similar among partner countries and economies. After accounting for student and school background characteristics, the additional number of compulsory courses attended is associated with an increase in resilience in 20 of the 28 OECD countries.

The association is however weak in all cases (the highest odds ratio is slightly over 1.4 in France). Partner countries and economies have a similar pattern to OECD countries but in this case there is a relationship in every country and economy and (except in Argentina, Colombia and Thailand) all estimated odd ratios are above one (Table A2.9b).

A PROFILE OF STUDENT RESILIENCE

Figure 3.5
Student engagement in science courses at school

- ▬ Increased likelihood of being resilient associated with one unit on the PISA index
- ▬ Same after accounting for school mean ESCS, ESCS, gender, immigrant status, language used at home, and grade
- ◆ Average index for resilient students (RES)
- ☐ Average index for disadvantaged low achievers (DLA)

Number of attended compulsory courses in science | **Taking general science compulsory courses**

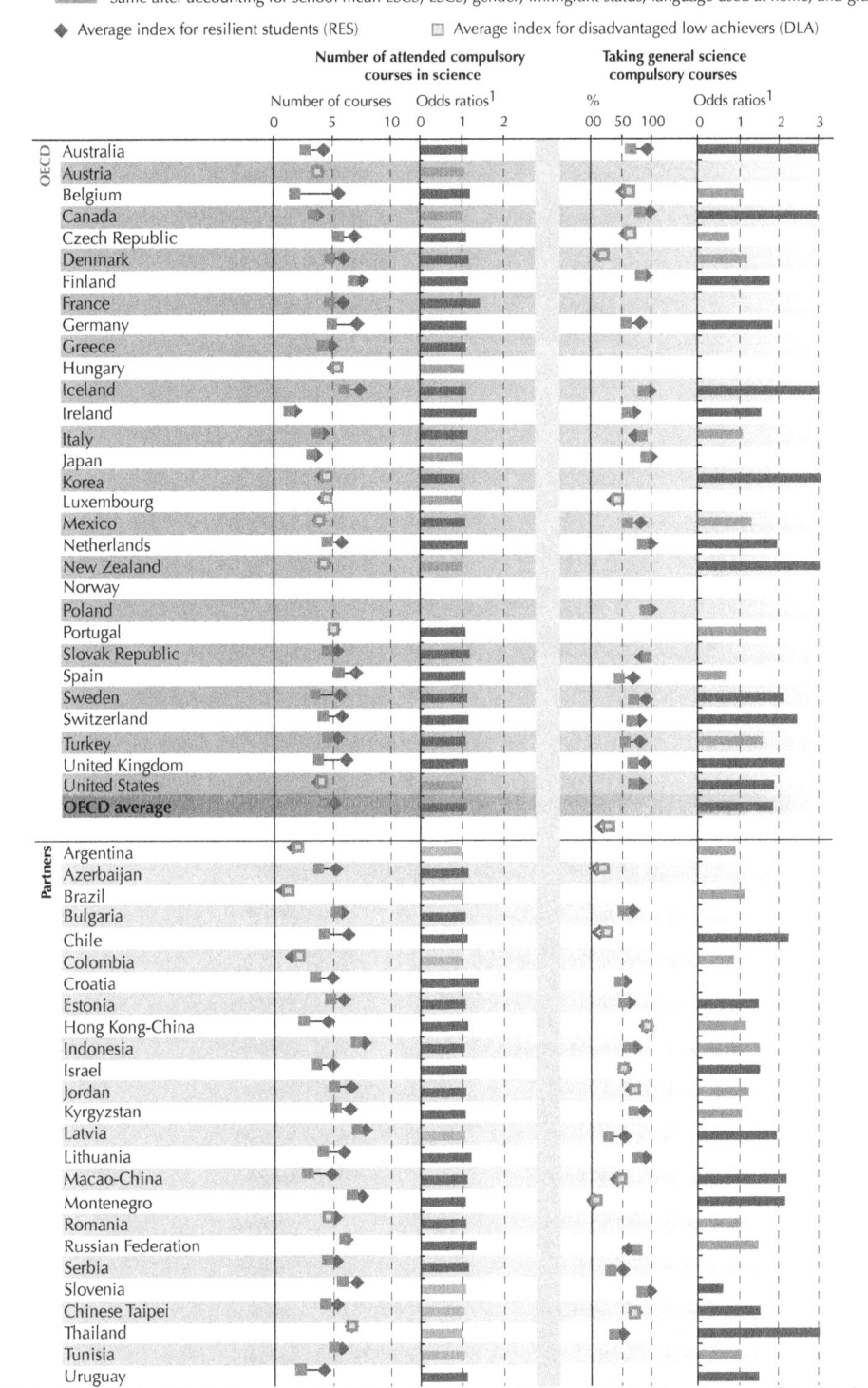

Number of courses (0, 5, 10) | Odds ratios[1] (0, 1, 2) | % (00, 50, 100) | Odds ratios[1] (0, 1, 2, 3)

OECD
- Australia
- Austria
- Belgium
- Canada
- Czech Republic
- Denmark
- Finland
- France
- Germany
- Greece
- Hungary
- Iceland
- Ireland
- Italy
- Japan
- Korea
- Luxembourg
- Mexico
- Netherlands
- New Zealand
- Norway
- Poland
- Portugal
- Slovak Republic
- Spain
- Sweden
- Switzerland
- Turkey
- United Kingdom
- United States
- **OECD average**

Partners
- Argentina
- Azerbaijan
- Brazil
- Bulgaria
- Chile
- Colombia
- Croatia
- Estonia
- Hong Kong-China
- Indonesia
- Israel
- Jordan
- Kyrgyzstan
- Latvia
- Lithuania
- Macao-China
- Montenegro
- Romania
- Russian Federation
- Serbia
- Slovenia
- Chinese Taipei
- Thailand
- Tunisia
- Uruguay

1. Resilient odds ratios stand for the increase in the likelihood of being resilient associated with an increase of one standard deviation in the index. The results reported here refer to the logistic regressions explained in Annex A2.
2. Statistically significant differences are marked in a darker tone.
Note: Countries have been ordered alphabetically.
Source: *OECD PISA 2006 Database*, Table A2.8c and Table A2.9c.

A PROFILE OF STUDENT RESILIENCE

Figure 3.6
Hours in science regular lessons at school

■ Increased likelihood of being resilient associated with one unit on the PISA index
■ Same after accounting for school mean ESCS, ESCS, gender, immigrant status, language used at home, and grade
◆ Average index for resilient students (RES)   □ Average index for disadvantaged low achievers (DLA)

	Hours	Odds ratios[1]
OECD	0.00 2.50 5.00	0 1 2
Australia		
Austria		
Belgium		
Canada		
Czech Republic		
Denmark		
Finland		
France		
Germany		
Greece		
Hungary		
Iceland		
Ireland		
Italy		
Japan		
Korea		
Luxembourg		
Mexico		
Netherlands		
New Zealand		
Norway		
Poland		
Portugal		
Slovak Republic		
Spain		
Sweden		
Switzerland		
Turkey		
United Kingdom		
United States		
OECD average		
Partners		
Argentina		
Azerbaijan		
Brazil		
Bulgaria		
Chile		
Colombia		
Croatia		
Estonia		
Hong Kong-China		
Indonesia		
Israel		
Jordan		
Kyrgyzstan		
Latvia		
Lithuania		
Macao-China		
Montenegro		
Romania		
Russian Federation		
Serbia		
Slovenia		
Chinese Taipei		
Thailand		
Tunisia		
Uruguay		

1. Resilient odds ratios stand for the increase in the likelihood of being resilient associated with an increase of one standard deviation in the index. The results reported here refer to the logistic regressions explained in Annex A2.
Note: Countries have been ordered alphabetically.
Source: *OECD PISA 2006 Database*, Table A2.10c.

The indicator for time spent learning science at school is the number of hours that students report spending in regular lessons at school learning science. This is also based on a question in the PISA student background questionnaire. The question asks students about the amount of time they spend each week studying science, mathematics, language and other subjects in regular school lessons, out-of-school time lessons and study or homework students do by themselves. Figure 3.6 highlights that in all OECD countries except Mexico and all partner countries and economies the average resilient student spends more time studying science at school than the average disadvantaged low achiever. On average the difference is between one and two hours (Table A2.10a). The association between more learning time at school in science and the likelihood of being resilient is strong; the relationship is consistent across almost all OECD countries but the estimated odd ratios are smaller than for compulsory courses. In all countries except for Mexico and Colombia, the more time a student spends the higher are his or her chances of being resilient. The estimated odd ratios in OECD countries range from less than 1.19 in Portugal to more than 1.5 the United Kingdom and the Czech Republic (Table A2.10b).

While increasing time spent at school will not alone raise overall performance, these results suggest that learning time at school is an important factor to take into account when designing interventions that raise the performance of disadvantaged students. Making science courses compulsory may be an option in some circumstances but the association between performance and an increase in the number of compulsory science courses is weak. One way to interpret these results is that it is not only the quantity of time spent in school matters but how that time is administered matters as well. Some disadvantaged students are vulnerable because they might end up in tracks or schools where there is very little choice and no possibility to take science courses, which does not help them in overcoming their disadvantaged socio-economic background.

LEARNING ENVIRONMENT AT SCHOOL

This section presents estimates of the association between the characteristics of the schools disadvantaged students attend and their resilience. Two broad areas of school factors are considered. First, school management, competition and admittance policies; then school resources its quality and use to promote science-related activities.

School management, competition and admittance policies are all areas the literature has identified as potential factors associated with student performance. This report presents results on whether schools are public or private (school management), whether they compete for students with other schools in their area (competition) and whether they use student academic records in admittance policies (academic selectivity). The PISA 2006 initial report (OECD, 2007a) presented results for all students. This section extends the analysis by comparing different groups of disadvantaged students. Given the definition of disadvantaged students used in this report, this focus implies analysing only a third of the sample of students that participated in PISA 2006. As a result, there are not enough data to offer reliable estimates for some of these variables. In particular, only in seven OECD countries do sizeable proportions of disadvantaged students attend a private school and only in 13 countries do sizeable proportions of disadvantaged students attend an academically selective school.[3] Annex A5 provides detailed information on how these variables were constructed. The PISA 2006 initial report and the Technical Report also provide details and summary statistics for these variables (OECD, 2007a and 2009b).

The PISA data show little association between school management and student resilience (Figure 3.7), *i.e.* in general, resilient students are as likely to be found in private schools as disadvantaged low achievers. Among the seven OECD countries with enough data, only in Spain is the proportion of resilient students in private schools higher than the proportion of disadvantaged low achievers and in Japan the opposite holds true (Table A2.11a). In terms of the likelihood of being resilient, only one OECD country, Japan, shows an association: in this country disadvantaged students attending private school are less likely to be resilient, although adjusting for individual and school characteristics lowers the estimated odds ratio (Table A2.11b). Among partner countries and economies, only in Argentina, Chile, Jordan and Macao-China is there a difference between the proportions observed: in this case resilient students are more likely to be found in private schools than are disadvantaged low achievers (the opposite is true in Chinese Taipei) (Table A2.11a). In terms of the likelihood of being resilient, there is a relationship in only a few partner countries and economies, all (except in Chinese Taipei) indicating that being at a private school increases the likelihood of resilience, but these associations disappear once student and school characteristics are taken into account (with two exceptions, each in a different direction: Jordan and Chinese Taipei) (Table A2.11b).

As Figure 3.7 shows, there is little evidence of an association between school competition and student resilience. Among OECD countries, it is only in Germany and Turkey that the proportion of resilient students in schools that compete with other schools for their students is higher than the proportion of disadvantaged low achievers. The opposite is true, however, in Korea. In the other OECD countries for which data are available, there is no difference between the two estimates. Among partner countries and economies the proportion resilient students in schools that compete with other schools for their students is higher than the proportion of disadvantaged lower achievers only in Argentina and Slovenia (Table A2.12a). After accounting for student and school factors, no country presents evidence of an association between school competition and the likelihood of being resilient (Table A2.12b).

In terms of school admittance policies, as Figure 3.8 displays, the proportion of resilient students in schools that use student academic records in admittance policies is higher than the proportion of disadvantaged low achievers in 8 countries out of the 13 OECD countries with sufficient data for this analysis and as well as in 13 countries out of the 21 partner countries and economies (Table A2.13a). However, the relationships with the likelihood of being resilient, which are also in favour of selective schools, disappear once student and school characteristics are taken into account in all countries except in Austria, Czech Republic, Hungary and Turkey as well as partner economy Chinese Taipei (Table A2.13b).

While the literature identifies these school characteristics as important factors associated with performance, there is no evidence in PISA 2006 supporting any widespread relationships between these factors and student resilience. Where an association was found, it turned out that students enrolled in schools that are privately managed (Japan) or that use academic selectivity (Austria) tend to have lower odds of being resilient, even after accounting for student and school characteristics. This evidence, however, is very limited and cannot be generalised as it could simply reflect country-specific circumstances.

The quality and use of school resources are also commonly thought to be associated with performance. For this second broad area of school characteristics, the report uses two measures, one on the overall quality of school resources and the other on a particular use schools can make of those resources, namely whether they organise school activities to promote science learning.

The quality of educational resources is measured in PISA by questions that ask school principals to rate how much their school's capacity to provide instruction is hindered by the lack of a series of resources such as laboratories or an internet connection. An index of the quality of educational resources is then constructed, with a mean of 0 and a standard deviation of 1 across the OECD, and where a higher value implies better quality. Therefore, a negative value simply means that the students in these schools enjoy a lower quality than the average OECD student.

Principals in schools with resilient and disadvantaged low achievers reported very similar levels of quality in terms of school resources (Figure 3.9). For example, in the Slovak Republic, about three quarters of both resilient and disadvantaged low achievers were in schools where the principals reported that the capacity of the school to provide instruction was hindered by the lack of or inadequacy of science laboratories. In

A PROFILE OF STUDENT RESILIENCE

Figure 3.7
Schools' competition, and management

■■■ Increased likelihood of being resilient associated with one unit on the PISA index
▬▬ Same after accounting for school mean ESCS, ESCS, gender, immigrant status, language used at home, and grade
◆ Average index for resilient students (RES)   ☐ Average index for disadvantaged low achievers (DLA)

1. Resilient odds ratios stand for the increase in the likelihood of being resilient associated with an increase of one standard deviation in the index. The results reported here refer to the logistic regressions explained in Annex A2.
2. Statistically significant differences are marked in a darker tone.
Note: Countries have been ordered alphabetically.
Source: *OECD PISA 2006 Database*, Tables A2.11c and A2.12c.

A PROFILE OF STUDENT RESILIENCE

Figure 3.8
Schools' academic selectivity

▬▬ Increased likelihood of being resilient associated with one unit on the PISA index
▬▬ Same after accounting for school mean ESCS, ESCS, gender, immigrant status, language used at home, and grade
◆ Average index for resilient students (RES)   ☐ Average index for disadvantaged low achievers (DLA)

OECD: Australia, Austria, Belgium, Canada, Czech Republic, Denmark, Finland, France, Germany, Greece, Hungary, Iceland, Ireland, Italy, Japan, Korea, Luxembourg, Mexico, Netherlands, New Zealand, Norway, Poland, Portugal, Slovak Republic, Spain, Sweden, Switzerland, Turkey, United Kingdom, United States, OECD average

Partners: Argentina, Azerbaijan, Brazil, Bulgaria, Chile, Colombia, Croatia, Estonia, Hong Kong-China, Indonesia, Israel, Jordan, Kyrgyzstan, Latvia, Lithuania, Macao-China, Montenegro, Romania, Russian Federation, Serbia, Slovenia, Chinese Taipei, Thailand, Tunisia, Uruguay

1. Resilient odds ratios stand for the increase in the likelihood of being resilient associated with an increase of one standard deviation in the index. The results reported here refer to the logistic regressions explained in Annex A2.
2. Statistically significant differences are marked in a darker tone.
Note: Countries have been ordered alphabetically.
Source: *OECD PISA 2006 Database,* Table A2.13c.

Japan, 24% of resilient students and 26% of disadvantaged low achievers were in schools whose principals reported a lack or the inadequacy of science laboratories hindered instruction (Table A2.14a). The same patterns are present for other school resources such as computers available for instruction, library materials and audio-visual resources. Differences between the two student groups appear only in exceptional cases.

On the index of quality of school educational resources, only six OECD countries (Denmark, Greece, Iceland, Italy, Mexico and Switzerland) have higher values for resilient students than for disadvantaged low achievers (a higher value on this index implies better quality resources). The size of the advantage for resilient students is modest, between 0.15 and 0.33 of a standard deviation across OECD countries (Table A2.14b). Where there is a difference, however, it is always in favour of resilient students; that is resilient students enjoy better resources than disadvantaged low achievers. The same pattern is observed among partner countries and economies. In this case, only Argentina, Brazil, Chile, Romania and Thailand have differences in favour of resilient students. But in these cases the gap tends to be larger, the differences in these countries range from a less than a third to close to two-thirds of a standard deviation.

Switzerland is the only OECD country where there is a statistically significant association between the quality of school resources index and the likelihood of being resilient. The estimated odds ratio is, however, very close to one after accounting for student and school characteristics. This result indicates that even in the case of Switzerland an increase of one standard deviation in the index is associated with only a marginal increase in the likelihood of being resilient. Among partner countries and economies, only in Macao-China is there evidence of an association and the estimated odds ratio is also very close to one (Table A2.14c).

A potential use for school resources is to offer school activities to promote the learning of science, such as organising science clubs, excursions and field trips or science competitions. PISA 2006 explored whether schools offered these kinds of activities by asking school principals to asses. An index of school activities to promote the learning of science was then constructed, with a mean of 0 and a standard deviation of 1 across the OECD, and where a higher value implies more involvement. Therefore, a negative value simply means that the students in these schools enjoy less a lower quality than the average OECD student.

Resilient and disadvantaged low achievers do not differ very much in the extent to which the schools they attend are involved in the promotion of activities aimed at enhancing science learning (with some exemptions). Excursions and field trips is the activity most commonly reported, across the OECD 89% of resilient students and 88% of disadvantaged low achievers attend schools that are involved in this activities. Only in a few cases there is a gap in this regard between these groups of disadvantaged students. For example, in Germany 57% of resilient students and 20% of disadvantaged low achievers attend schools that are involved in science competitions. In Austria, 39% of resilient students and 15% of disadvantaged low achievers attend schools involved in science fairs (Table A2.15a).

The index of school activities to promote the learning of science shows some differences between resilient and disadvantaged students. There is an advantage in favour of resilient students in 15 OECD countries. Only in Iceland the advantage is in favour of disadvantaged low achievers. Across OECD countries the difference ranges from one tenth (in Canada) to more than two thirds (in Austria) of a standard deviation (Table A2.15b). Among partner countries and economies, resilient students have a higher index of school activities to promote the learning of science in 11 countries while the reverse is true only in one. On average size of the difference is in general larger than for OECD countries but they still range from one tenth (in the Russian Federation) to more than two thirds of a standard deviation (in Indonesia and Chinese Taipei).

While the basic model shows an increased likelihood of resilience being associated with activities to promote the learning of science in quite a few countries (both OECD and partner countries and economies), after accounting for student and school factors, science promotion activity is generally not associated with

A PROFILE OF STUDENT RESILIENCE

Figure 3.9
School resources and science promotion activities

■ Increased likelihood of being resilient associated with one unit on the PISA index
■ Same after accounting for school mean ESCS, ESCS, gender, immigrant status, language used at home, and grade
◆ Average index for resilient students (RES)   ☐ Average index for disadvantaged low achievers (DLA)

1. Resilient odds ratios stand for the increase in the likelihood of being resilient associated with an increase of one standard deviation in the index. The results reported here refer to the logistic regressions explained in Annex A2.
2. Statistically significant differences are marked in a darker tone.
Note: Countries have been ordered alphabetically.
Source: *OECD PISA 2006 Database,* Tables A2.17c and A2.18c.

a higher likelihood of being resilient. An association is apparent in only seven OECD countries (Austria, Czech Republic, Germany, Iceland, Poland the Slovak Republic and Switzerland). In each of these the odds ratios are close to one indicating that a standard deviation in the index predicts that disadvantaged students at schools with science promotion activities are only marginally more likely to be resilient than students at schools that don't promote science activities (Table A2.15c). The same pattern is apparent for partner countries and economies, where there is evidence of an association in only four countries (Azerbaijan, Indonesia, Montenegro and Chinese Taipei. Only in Indonesia, with an estimate of nearly 1.4, is the odd ratio of a size worth some consideration.

These results provide little evidence that school resources, either their quality or use, are associated with student resilience across the board. The PISA 2006 data show that there is little difference among different groups of disadvantaged students in either the quality of school resources they experience or in the degree to which these resources are used to promote science learning activities at school. Similarly, the data show that neither resource quality nor resource use, as captured by PISA 2006, are consistently associated with an increased likelihood of resilience among disadvantaged students. These results ought to be interpreted with caution, however, as it is possible that not all the principals interpreted the questions in the same way, even within a country. One other possible reason for the lack of evidence of an association is that these measures are only a very rough approximation of the information they were intended to capture.

COMBINED EFFECTS OF STUDENT AND SCHOOL FACTORS ON STUDENT RESILIENCE

Having reviewed how student approaches to learning, engagement in courses and hours spent, and the learning environment at school are separately associated with resilience, the chapter now turns to a combined analysis of the relationships between these measures and resilience. For each of the areas, based on the previous analysis, the variable with the strongest relationship with the likelihood of resilience was included in the combined model. Annex A5 presents the details of this combined model. The main goal of this section is to analyse which relationships are robust to the inclusion of other important variables in the predictive model. As for the results presented above, the analysis is reported in terms of odds ratios for resilience.

A combined model allows for the estimation of the relative association with resilience for each factor accounting for all of the factors included. In the combined model the estimated coefficients are therefore relative; they assume all other factors remain constant. A comparison of the combined model with the previous models gives a sense of the degree to which other measures included in the model exert mediating effects on the measures of interest's association with performance. In general, given these mediating effects it is normal that the size of the estimates is smaller in the combined model.

Figure 3.10 highlights the strong association between resilience and the measures of student self-efficacy and number of hours, students report spending in regular lessons at school learning science. For the rest of the variables included in the model – internal motivation, participation in science-related activities, school preparation for science careers, school management, school competition, admission policies, the quality of resources and the promotion of science-related activities – the estimated associations (with some exceptions) are either close to one or there is no evidence of an association with the likelihood of resilience (Table A2.16).

Thus student confidence, represented in the model by the index of student self-efficacy, is the approach to learning that is most consistently associated with an increased likelihood that disadvantaged students will beat the odds, even when other factors are taken into account. This is the case in all OECD and almost all partner countries and economies (the exceptions being Azerbaijan, Indonesia and Thailand). Students who are more confident in their ability to carry out specific tasks involving the application of scientific

3 A PROFILE OF STUDENT RESILIENCE

Figure 3.10 [Part 1/2]
Combined model

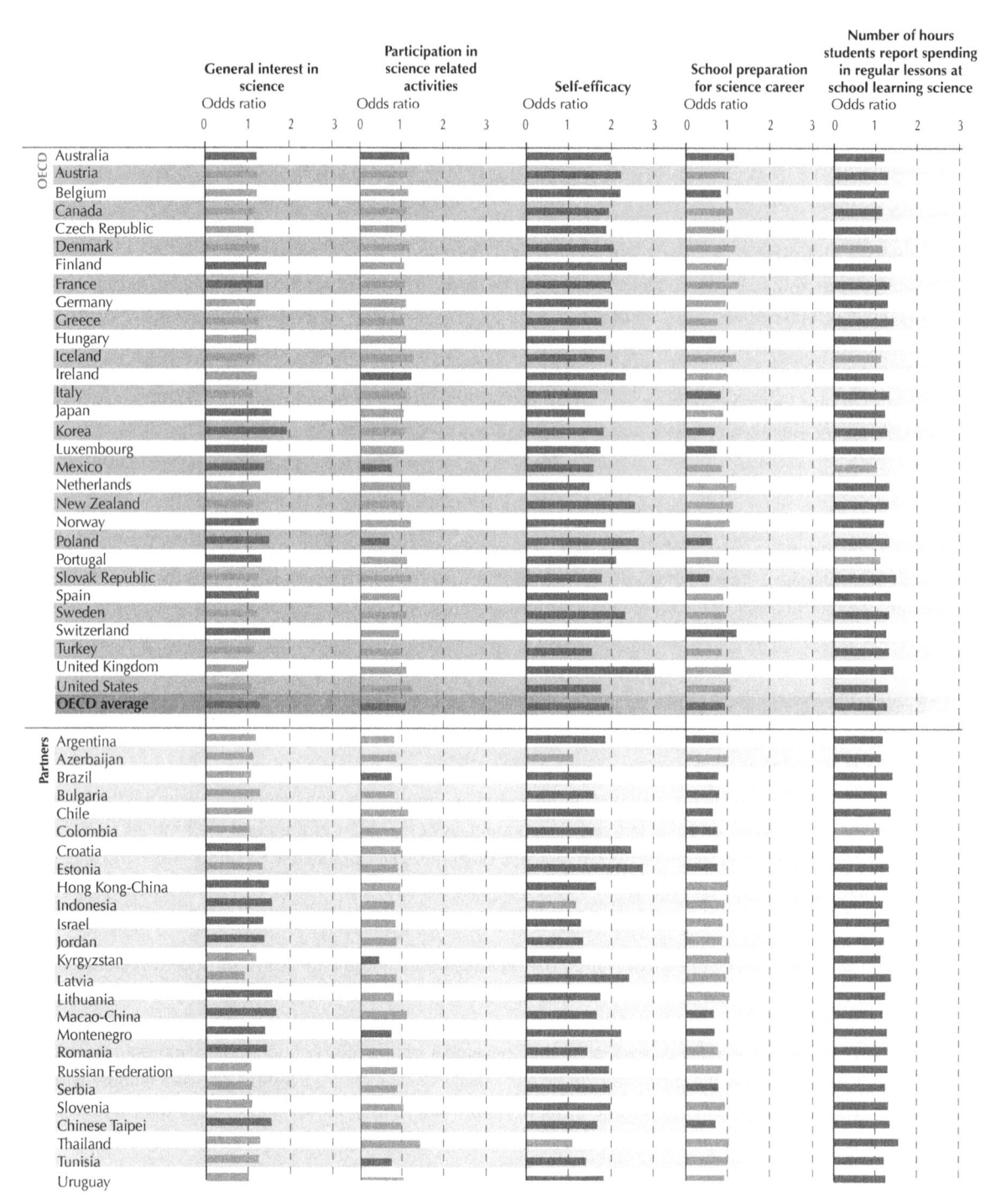

[Chart showing odds ratios for OECD countries and Partner countries across five variables: General interest in science, Participation in science related activities, Self-efficacy, School preparation for science career, and Number of hours students report spending in regular lessons at school learning science. Each variable has an odds ratio scale from 0 to 3.

OECD countries listed: Australia, Austria, Belgium, Canada, Czech Republic, Denmark, Finland, France, Germany, Greece, Hungary, Iceland, Ireland, Italy, Japan, Korea, Luxembourg, Mexico, Netherlands, New Zealand, Norway, Poland, Portugal, Slovak Republic, Spain, Sweden, Switzerland, Turkey, United Kingdom, United States, OECD average.

Partner countries listed: Argentina, Azerbaijan, Brazil, Bulgaria, Chile, Colombia, Croatia, Estonia, Hong Kong-China, Indonesia, Israel, Jordan, Kyrgyzstan, Latvia, Lithuania, Macao-China, Montenegro, Romania, Russian Federation, Serbia, Slovenia, Chinese Taipei, Thailand, Tunisia, Uruguay.]

1. Statistically significant differences are marked in a darker tone.
Source: *OECD PISA 2006 Database*, Table 3.16c.

A PROFILE OF STUDENT RESILIENCE

Figure 3.10 [Part 2/2]
Combined model

	Private Odds ratio	Students in schools which compete with other schools Odds ratio	Students in schools which select based on academic record Odds ratio	Index of school activities to promote the learning of science Odds ratio	Index of the quality of school educational resources Odds ratio

OECD
- Australia
- Austria
- Belgium
- Canada
- Czech Republic
- Denmark
- Finland
- France
- Germany
- Greece
- Hungary
- Iceland
- Ireland
- Italy
- Japan
- Korea
- Luxembourg
- Mexico
- Netherlands
- New Zealand
- Norway
- Poland
- Portugal
- Slovak Republic
- Spain
- Sweden
- Switzerland
- Turkey
- United Kingdom
- United States
- **OECD average**

Partners
- Argentina
- Azerbaijan
- Brazil
- Bulgaria
- Chile
- Colombia
- Croatia
- Estonia
- Hong Kong-China
- Indonesia
- Israel
- Jordan
- Kyrgyzstan
- Latvia
- Lithuania
- Macao-China
- Montenegro
- Romania
- Russian Federation
- Serbia
- Slovenia
- Chinese Taipei
- Thailand
- Tunisia
- Uruguay

1. Statistically significant differences are marked in a darker tone.
Source: *OECD PISA 2006 Database*, Table 3.16c.

knowledge have higher odds of being resilient than students who are less confident in their abilities. The association between student resilience and self-efficacy is strong in most countries. In a third of OECD countries, the odds ratios are above 2.0 and in many of the remaining countries they are over 1.9.

Motivation, particularly internal motivation as captured by the index of general interest in science, is also positively associated with the likelihood that disadvantaged students will be resilient, but less consistently so than self-efficacy. This association is seen in fewer than half of the OECD countries (12 out of 30) and in 10 out of 25 partner countries and economies (Table A2.16). In countries where the relationship between interest in science and academic resilience is significant, the odds ratios are smaller than for self-efficacy. They are below 1.5 except in Japan and Switzerland and in four partner countries and economies (Indonesia, Lithuania, Macao-China and Chinese Taipei).

The number of hours of regular science lessons at school is associated with greater odds of being resilient in all OECD countries except four (France, Iceland, Mexico and Portugal) and in all partner countries and economies except Colombia. As depicted in Figure 3.10, the association between learning time and resilience remains strong across the board when other factors are taken into account. Among OECD countries the estimated odds ratios range from about 1.2 in Canada to more than 1.4 in the Czech Republic, Greece, the Slovak Republic and the United Kingdom,. The range is even larger across partner countries and economies, from 1.12 in Azerbaijan to 1.58 in Thailand (Table A2.16). For OECD countries on average, the odds ratio for this measure (1.27) is about the same as the odds ratio for internal motivation (1.25), these two providing the strongest associations behind science efficacy (1.96).

The relationship between participation in science-related activities and student resilience is rather weak when other factors are taken into account (Figure 3.10). Across OECD countries, the relationship between participation in science-related activities and resilience is positive in only two countries (Australia and Ireland) and the relationships are very weak (Table A2.16). In most partner countries and economies students who participate in science-related activities are just as likely to be resilient as fellow students who do not participate in such activities. In four countries (Brazil, Kyrgyzstan, Montenegro and Tunisia) students who take part in science activities are less likely to be resilient than students who do not take part in such activities, although the association is quantitatively small.

Disadvantaged students who report being better prepared for science-related careers generally have no greater odds of being resilient than students who report being less prepared, when other factors are taken into account. Figure 3.10 shows that odds ratios for school preparation for science careers are below one in nine OECD countries and in 11 partner countries and economies (Table A2.16). Only in Switzerland and the United Kingdom are disadvantaged students who report better school preparation for a science career more likely to be resilient than other disadvantaged students.

The generally negative relationship between school preparation for science careers and resilience should be interpreted carefully. In OECD countries, students who perform satisfactorily at school on average tend to continue their education well beyond the age of 15. Conversely, students who are poor performers may be more likely to abandon school to enter the labour market immediately after completion of their compulsory education. Therefore, students who excel academically and plan on embarking on further studies are more likely to perceive the labour market in rather abstract terms. As a result, they may feel poorly prepared for science-related careers. On the other hand, poorly performing students may have already begun to evaluate different career opportunities and may have received additional support at school to help them in their early transition to the labour market.

The associations between school factors and resilience do not change when other variables are taken into account in the combined predictive model. Only in Japan, among OECD countries, and among the partner countries, Jordan and Chinese Taipei, there is an association between school management and the odds of being resilient: disadvantaged students who attend private schools in Japan and Jordan have lower odds of being resilient, whereas the opposite is true in Chinese Taipei. Further, as Figure 3.10 displays, there is evidence of an association between the quality of resources and/or the use schools make of them in only a small number of countries. Across both variables there are only five cases where there is an association; in four cases the estimated odds ratios are above one and in one case it is below one (Table A2.16).

The evidence from the combined model confirms the results of the previous analysis, highlighting the importance of students' confidence and learning time. With a small number of exceptions, there is very little evidence in PISA 2006 of associations between the other factors analysed in this report and student resilience. One possibility is that no relationships exist, but it is also possible that the data limitations in PISA 2006 are preventing associations from being found. Therefore, one should not conclude that there is no relationship, but rather that no relationship has been observed. What is clear, however, is that student confidence and learning time are closely associated with academic success among disadvantaged students across most OECD and partner countries and economies.

CONCLUSION

Having established a definition and measure of student resilience, Chapter 2 described the main individual features that characterise resilient students and disadvantaged low achievers. Chapter 3 extends this analysis to the approaches to learning, hours and courses, and the school's learning environment of these students. It shows that resilient students are engaged students who feel confident about their academic capabilities. Resilient students are more motivated, more engaged and more self-confident than their disadvantaged low-achieving peers.

Students' confidence in their academic abilities is one of the strongest predictors of resilience. Holding student demographics, school characteristics and other approaches to learning constant, the more confident students are, the greater are their odds of being resilient. Motivation, and in particular internal rather than instrumental motivation, is also associated with student resilience in many countries but the relationship is weaker.

Learning time is also one of the strongest predictors of resilience, even after accounting for student demographics, school characteristics and other factors that are considered to be closely related with performance.

PISA 2006 offers very little evidence of an association between school factors, such as the type of school management, admittance policies, school competition and school resources, and resilience. One should not interpret this as meaning that these factors are irrelevant, but rather that there is no empirical support in PISA 2006 for these hypotheses.

The results suggest that schools may have an important role to play in promoting resilience by developing activities, classroom practices and modes of instruction that foster disadvantaged students' motivation and confidence in their abilities and also by providing opportunities for disadvantaged students to spend more time learning science at school.

Notes

1. See Annex A5 for a technical description of the models used in analyses predicting the association between students' approaches to learning and the likelihood that disadvantaged students will be resilient.

2. Through the entire report, only statistically significant differences at 95% confidence levels are reported. If the estimates are not significant at this level they are not referred to in the main text of this report.

3. Because of sample size issues, no country-level estimates for a country are provided whenever a group considered in analyses is composed of less than 3% of the study population in the country.

Closing the Gap?
Enhancing the Performance of Socio-Economically Disadvantaged Students

INTRODUCTION

Chapters 2 and 3 analysed and compared different groups of socio-economically disadvantaged students defined by their performance on the PISA science scale. Chapter 2 classified them according to their performance and studied the main individual characteristics of two groups: resilient students (high achievers) and low achievers. Chapter 3 analysed whether differences in approaches to learning, hours spent and courses taken to learn science and in the types of schools disadvantaged students attend are associated with differences in performance and with an increased likelihood that disadvantaged students will be resilient.

This chapter compares socio-economically disadvantaged students with their more advantaged peers. In particular, it examines whether factors associated with better performance differ for socio-economically advantaged and disadvantaged students. The chapter analyses the same factors that were examined in Chapter 3. The central goal of this chapter is to assess whether these factors play a differential role in promoting performance improvements among disadvantaged students and by doing so to identify which policies may help disadvantaged students close their performance gap with students from more advantaged backgrounds.

The chapter presents results based on regression models estimating the change in the PISA science score that is associated with a one unit change in approaches to learning, hours and courses and school characteristics while controlling for gender, immigrant background, language spoken at home, socio-economic background, grade attended and the socio-economic background of the average student attending the same school as the respondent.[1]

MODELS OF STUDENT RESILIENCE

A crucial issue for school administrators and policy makers is to understand the role different sets of factors play in helping disadvantaged students overcome the adverse circumstances determined by their socio-economic background. Relevant educational factors highlighted by the literature include: student motivation and approaches to learning and the type of school students attend. The literature identifies two potential mechanisms through which educational resources may contribute to successful outcomes for students who are at a high risk of performing poorly at school (Luthar et al., 2000; Schoon, 2006).

The first mechanism is summarised by the "cumulative effects model" (Masten et al., 1990; Fergusson and Horwood, 2003) which predicts that the contribution of resources students can rely on to excel at school is independent of the circumstances of individual students. The cumulative effects model therefore suggests that students who are at a high risk of performing poorly at school and students who face no such risk will enjoy a similar benefit from possessing resources that promote academic performance.

The second mechanism is summarised by the "protective model" (Garmezy et al., 1984; Rutter, 1985; Rutter, 1987). This model predicts that the contribution of resources students can rely on to excel at school depends on the circumstances of individual students. It suggests that students who are at a high risk of performing poorly at school benefit more from resources that promote academic performance than students who face no such risk.

The analyses developed in this chapter are aimed at: *i)* assessing whether the following three sets of factors – approaches to learning, hours and courses and learning environment at school – contribute to improving students' performance in the PISA science assessment and if so, *ii)* whether the relationship follows the cumulative effects model or the protective model.

The rest of the chapter is structured as follows: for each of the three sets of factors considered, the chapter first identifies the overall association each of these has with performance and then explores whether such associations are stronger for disadvantaged students.

STUDENT APPROACHES TO LEARNING

Disadvantaged students tend to have less positive attitudes towards science and themselves, engage less in science activities, feel less prepared for science careers, attend fewer science courses and spend less time in science lessons at school (see Tables 4.1a and 4.2a). For example, disadvantaged students report being less interested in science and having lower levels of self-efficacy than their more advantaged peers in every OECD country and in most partner countries and economies. The differences in the extent to which disadvantaged students and their more advantaged peers report having low levels of instrumental motivation to learn science, participation in science-related activities, self-concept and information on science-related careers, as well as enrolment in fewer science courses and spending less time in science lessons at school are also significant in most OECD and partner countries and economies. Estimates presented in Table A3.1a on the other hand suggest that in almost a third of OECD countries and in all but six partner countries and economies there is no difference between disadvantaged students and their more advantaged peers in the extent to which they believe their schools prepare them for science careers.

Improved Performance

This section presents estimates of the associations between performance and the ten indices used in Chapter 3 to characterise students' approaches to learning and hours spent and courses taken.

Overall, students who have positive attitudes and approaches towards science learning on average perform better on the PISA science assessment than students who have less positive attitudes and approaches (Figure 4.1a and Table A3.1b).

The following student approaches to learning are associated with increased performance in the PISA science assessment in virtually all OECD countries: general interest (internal motivation) and instrumental (external) motivation to learn science, participation in science-related activities, self-efficacy and science self-concept, with self-efficacy having the strongest association. Across OECD countries, students who have values on the index of student self-efficacy that are one standard deviation above the OECD mean score 28 points higher on average than students with average levels of self-efficacy. The score point differences associated with one standard deviation rises in the index of general interest in science and in the index of student self-concept in science are also close to 20 points. The differences are lower in relation to both the index of student participation in science-related activities and the index of instrumental motivation to learn science (16 and 14 points respectively).

Figure 4.1A shows that the index of school preparation for science careers and the index of information on science-related careers are both positively associated with science performance in some countries but not in others. Across OECD countries, an increase of one standard deviation in the school preparation index is associated on average with a 9 point increase in the PISA science score, while a similar increase on the information index is associated with a 2 point increase in the PISA science score. The score point differences between students with an average value on the school preparation for science careers index and students that are one standard deviation above the OECD mean ranges from 5 points in Germany to 25 points or above in Australia, New Zealand and the United Kingdom.

The school preparation for science-related careers index is not associated with science performance in eight OECD countries while the information about science-related careers index is not associated with science performance in half of the OECD countries. In Poland, increases in the school preparation for science careers and information about science-related careers indices are even negatively associated with science performance.

4 CLOSING THE GAP? ENHANCING THE PERFORMANCE OF SOCIO-ECONOMICALLY DISADVANTAGED STUDENTS

Figure 4.1a
Association between student approaches to learning and performance in science

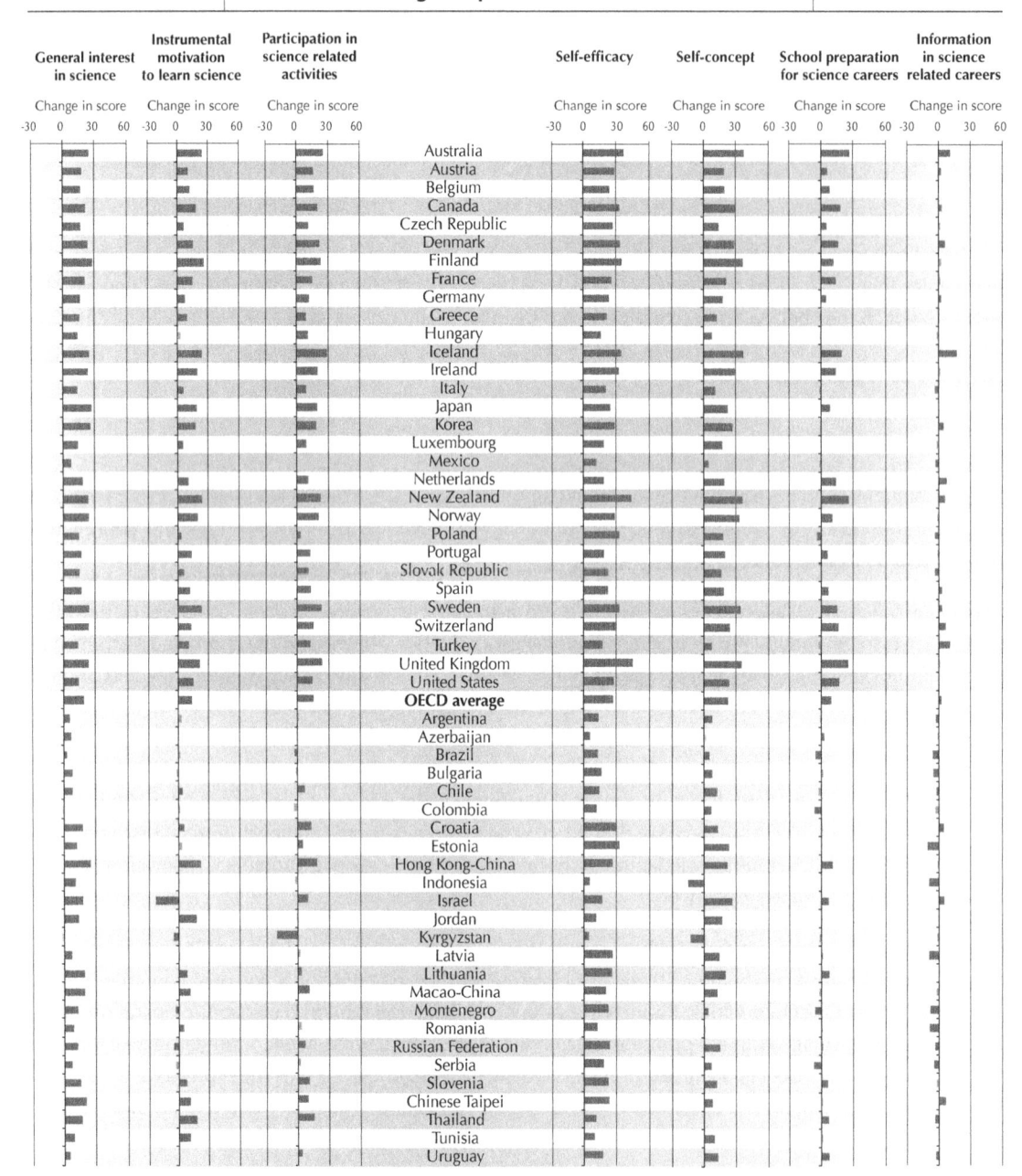

Note: Statistically significant differences are marked in a darker tone.
Source: *OECD PISA 2006 Database*, Table 4.1b.

Closing the gap

Results presented in Figure 4.1b and Table A3.1b indicate that both disadvantaged students and their more advantaged peers benefit from positive approaches to learning and high levels of motivation. With a few exceptions, disadvantaged students benefit on average as much as their more advantaged peers from having

Figure 4.1b
Differential effect for disadvantaged students of student approaches to learning

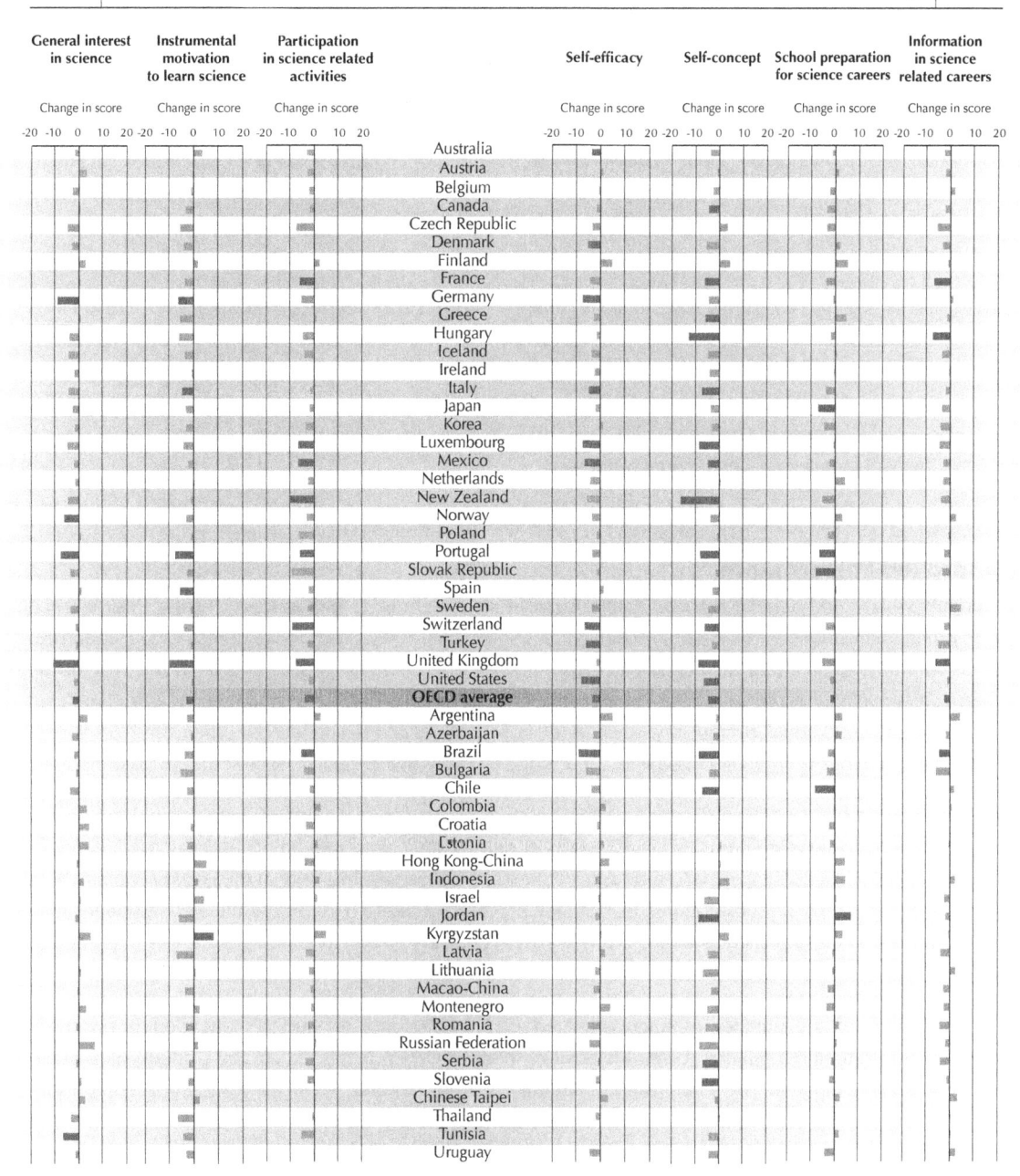

Note: Statistically significant differences are marked in a darker tone.
Source: OECD PISA 2006 Database, Table 4.1b

positive motivation, participation in science-related activities, confidence and perspectives future careers in science. These findings are in line with the "cumulative effects" hypothesis that both disadvantaged students and others benefit from having high levels of motivation and positive attitudes towards science learning.

There are, however, some important differences across areas. In a number of countries disadvantaged students appear to benefit less than their more advantaged peers. For example, self-efficacy and participation in science-related activities are associated with smaller gains for disadvantaged students in the PISA science score in nine and seven OECD countries respectively. In relation to self-efficacy, the difference in the PISA science assessment score between disadvantaged students and their peers is negative in 12 OECD countries. It is also negative in four OECD countries in the case of general interest, in three OECD countries in relation to each of the information on science careers and the school preparation for science careers indices, and in five OECD countries in the case of the instrumental motivation index. In almost all cases however the score point difference in the association between approaches to science learning and PISA science performance between disadvantaged and more advantaged students is below 10 points.

These results suggest that motivation to learn science and positive attitudes and approaches to science learning are associated with increases in the PISA score across all socio-economic groups, but the increases are smaller for disadvantaged students in some countries. Policies aimed at promoting greater motivation to learn science and positive attitudes and approaches to science learning may result in absolute improvements in science achievement but run the risk of contributing to wider performance gaps across social groups unless they are targeted at specific populations.

HOURS SPENT AND COURSES TAKEN TO LEARN SCIENCE

Improved Performance

Students who attend general science compulsory courses perform at higher levels in the PISA science assessment than students who do not. Results presented in Figure 4.2a show that, across OECD countries, students who report having attended at least one compulsory general science course in the year of the PISA assessment or the previous year score 26 points above students who did not attend any such course. Similarly, each additional compulsory science-related course students attended in either the PISA survey year or the previous year is associated with an average increase in the PISA science score of 7 score points.

The relationship between the indicator for having attended at least one general science compulsory course and the PISA science score is positive in 17 OECD countries, ranging from 6 points in Belgium to 66 points in Iceland (Table A3.2b). Figure 4.2a shows that the association is negative only in the case of Spain, where it may indicate a possible substitution effect: students who are interested in performing well in science may attend advanced courses such as biology, physics and chemistry while students who are less interested in performing well in science may attend general science courses.

The indicator for the number of science-related compulsory courses students attended is positively associated with the PISA science score. It is positive in all OECD countries except the United States where no association is apparent. The relationship is particularly strong in Korea where each additional compulsory course is associated with an increase of 32 score points in the PISA science score while in Canada and Portugal the change in the PISA science score associated with each additional compulsory course is below 2 score points (Table A3.2b).

Students who spend more time studying in regular science lessons at school perform better in the PISA science assessment than students who spend fewer hours. This association exists across all countries and is generally stronger than the association with the number of compulsory courses attended. Results presented in Figure 4.2a and Table A3.2b suggest that across OECD countries each additional hour is associated with a 12 score point increase in the PISA science score, but that estimate varies across countries. For example, the change in the PISA science score that is associated with an additional hour spent in a regular science lesson at school is as much as 22 score points in the United Kingdom and as little as 2 score points in Mexico.

Closing the gap

Results presented in Figure 4.2b and Table A3.2b indicate that in several countries the differential association between attending compulsory science courses and performance in the PISA science assessment is positive.

Figure 4.2a
Association between students' participation in science courses and student performance in science

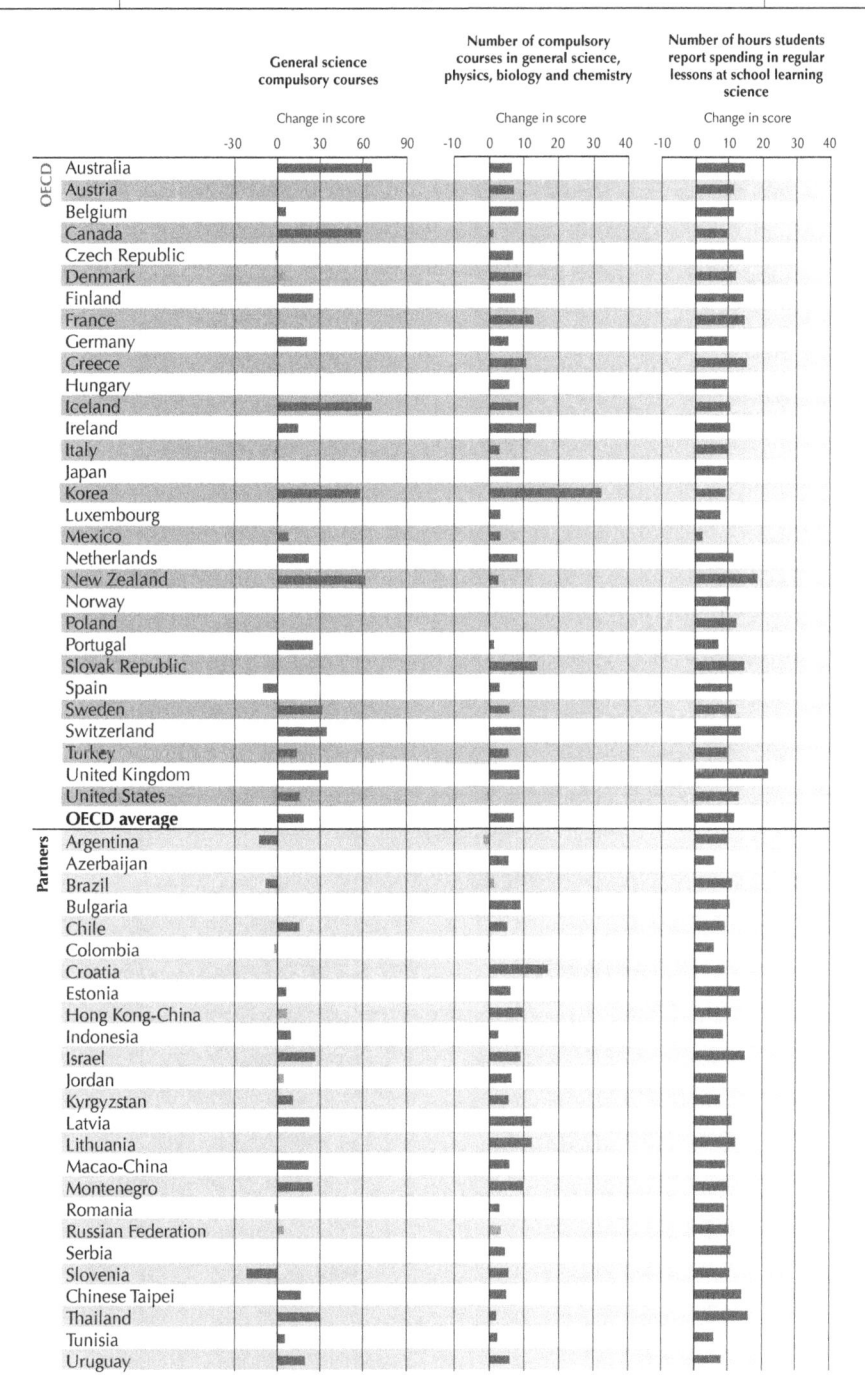

Note: Statistically significant differences are marked in a darker tone.
Source: *OECD PISA 2006 Database*, Table 4.2b

CLOSING THE GAP? ENHANCING THE PERFORMANCE OF SOCIO-ECONOMICALLY DISADVANTAGED STUDENTS

Figure 4.2b
Differential effect for disadvantaged students of students' participation in science courses

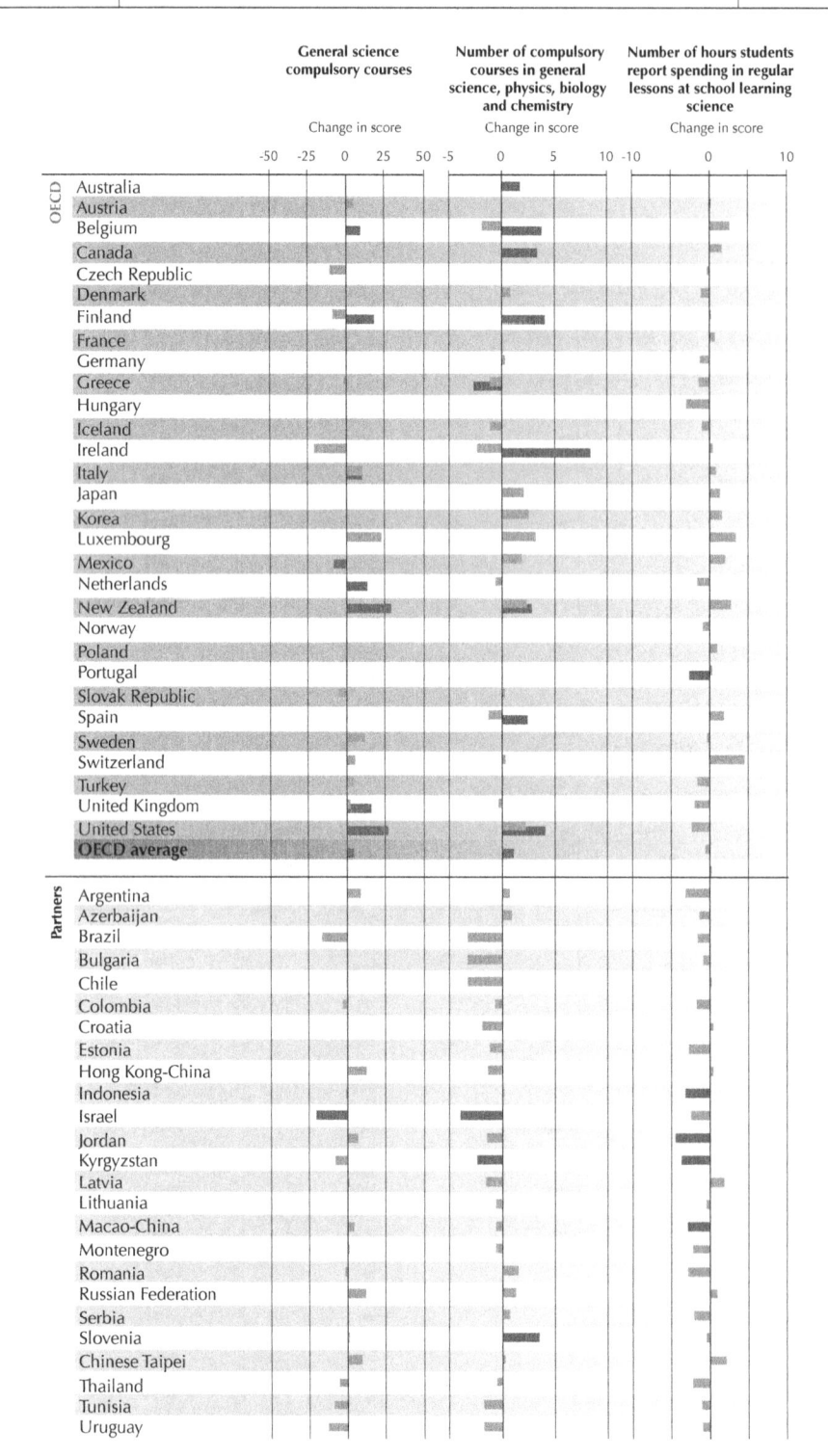

Note: Statistically significant differences are marked in a darker tone.
Source: *OECD PISA 2006 Database*, Table 4.2b

In seven OECD countries, disadvantaged students benefit more than more advantaged students from attending compulsory general science courses (Belgium, Finland, Italy, the Netherlands, New Zealand, the United Kingdom and the United States) while in eight OECD countries disadvantaged students benefit more from attending compulsory courses in physics, biology and chemistry (Australia, Belgium, Canada, Finland, Ireland, New Zealand, Spain and the United States). The findings also indicate the score point differences are substantial. For example, having attended a compulsory general science course is associated with a 29 point increase in the PISA science score in New Zealand while each additional compulsory course attended in Ireland is associated with an increase of 8 score points.

LEARNING ENVIRONMENT AT SCHOOL

Improved Performance

Disadvantaged students are somewhat less likely than their more advantaged peers to attend schools that are private, compete with other schools, select their students on the basis of academic record, organise activities that promote science learning and/or have good educational resources (see Table A3.3a). For example, the proportions of disadvantaged students that attend a private school are significantly lower than the proportions for more advantaged students in 18 OECD countries and 13 partner countries and economies. Similarly, the proportions of disadvantaged students attending schools that compete with other schools for students are significantly lower than the proportions for more advantaged students in 19 OECD countries and 12 partner countries and economies.

The performance of students in the PISA science assessment is associated with whether students attend a school that is private, competes with other schools for students, or organises activities to promote science learning in only a few countries. Attending a private school is associated with lower performance in seven OECD countries (and with higher performance in one) while academic selectivity is associated with higher performance in 11 out of 25 of OECD countries and science promotion activities are associated with higher performance in a third of OECD countries (see Figure 4.3a and Table A3.3b).

Closing the gap

Overall, school characteristics do not appear to play a major role in promoting performance in the PISA science assessment among disadvantaged students. Apart from a few exceptions, disadvantaged students and their more advantaged peers appear to perform equally well irrespective of the type of school they attend (Figure 4.3b).

CONCLUSION

This chapter examined the role played by approaches to learning, hours spent and courses taken to learn science and school characteristics in improving students' performance in the PISA science assessment and whether these factors play a differential role in promoting performance improvements for disadvantaged students. Some key findings emerge:

a) Students who believe in themselves, who are motivated and have positive attitudes towards science learning on average perform better in the PISA science assessment than other students. In particular, a one standard deviation difference in self-confidence or general interest in science is associated with a science assessment score difference of at least 20 points across OECD countries. However in a number of countries the benefit for disadvantaged students is lower than for other students.

b) Students who attend general science compulsory courses or compulsory courses in physics, biology and chemistry perform at higher levels in the PISA science assessment than students who do not. Both disadvantaged and non-disadvantaged students benefit from attending compulsory courses, but in several

4 CLOSING THE GAP? ENHANCING THE PERFORMANCE OF SOCIO-ECONOMICALLY DISADVANTAGED STUDENTS

Figure 4.3a
Association between school characteristics and student performance in science

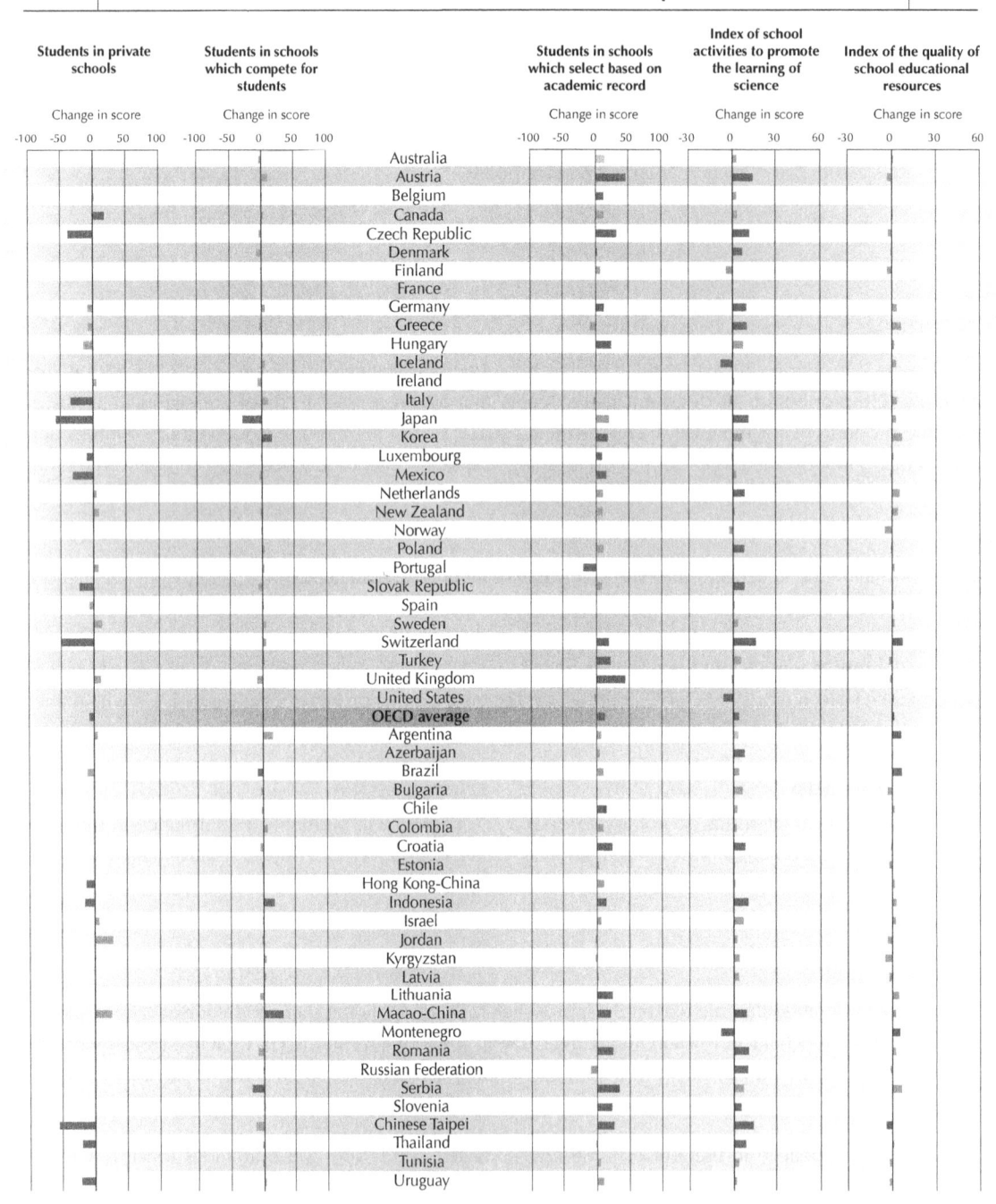

1. Statistically significant differences are marked in a darker tone.
Source: *OECD PISA 2006 Database*, Table 4.2b

countries disadvantaged students appear to benefit more than more advantaged students from attending compulsory courses. The actual number of compulsory courses taken does not show the same relationship: attending more courses does not seem to add more to close the performance gap of disadvantaged students with their more advantaged peers.

Figure 4.3b
Differential effect for disadvantaged students of school characteristics

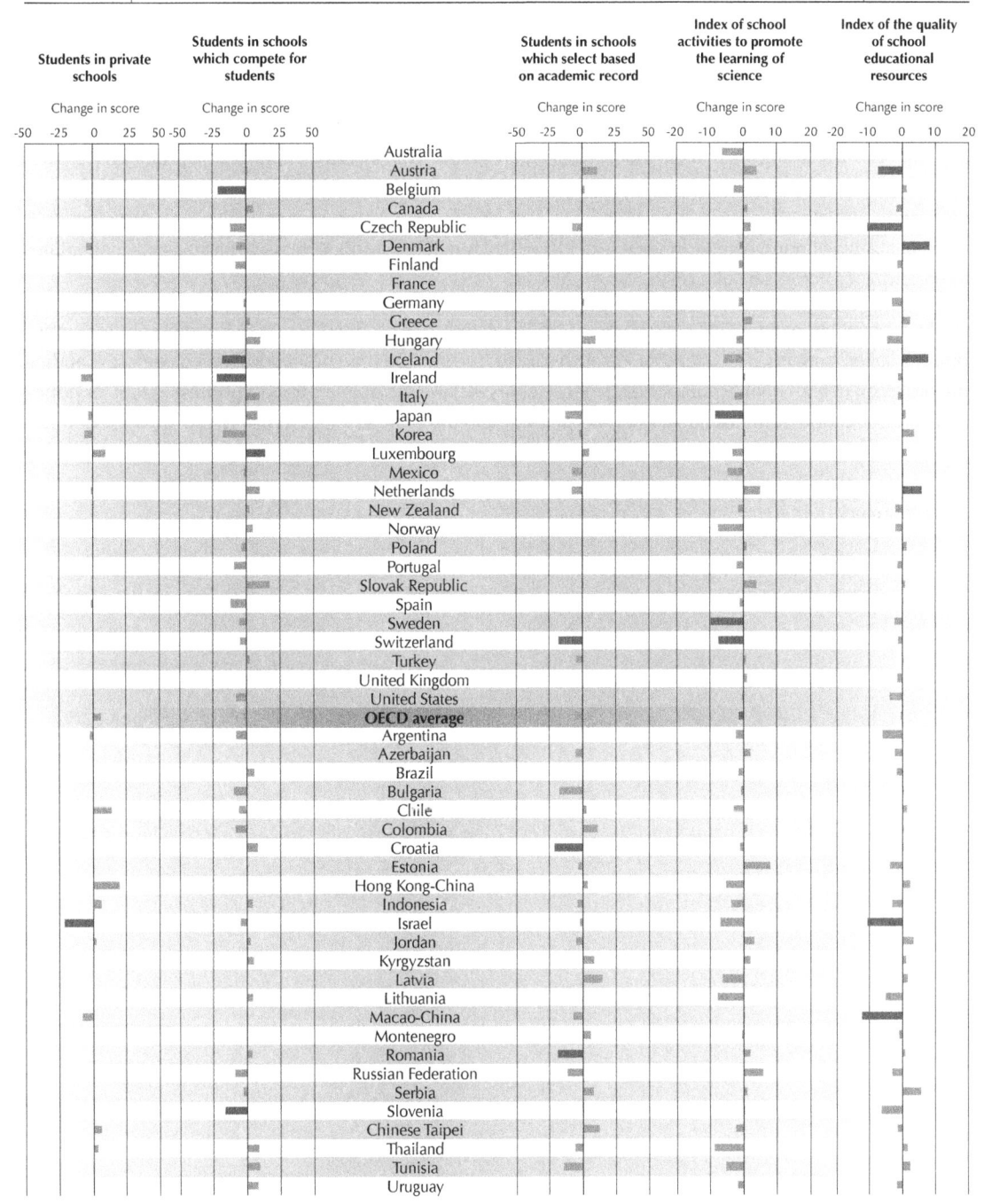

[Figure: Horizontal bar chart showing change in score across five indicators — Students in private schools, Students in schools which compete for students, Students in schools which select based on academic record, Index of school activities to promote the learning of science, Index of the quality of school educational resources — for OECD countries (Australia through United States), OECD average, and partner countries/economies (Argentina through Uruguay).]

1. Statistically significant differences are marked in a darker tone.
Source: *OECD PISA 2006 Database*, Table 4.3b

c) Students who spend more time in regular science lessons at school perform better than students who spend fewer hours and all students are equally likely to benefit from spending additional time in regular science lessons at school.

d) School characteristics such as whether the school is private, whether it competes with other schools for students, whether academic records play an important part in the school's admission criteria, whether the school provides activities that promote students' learning of science and whether the school has good educational resources do not play a significant role in promoting performance in the PISA science assessment for either disadvantaged or more advantaged students.

Overall, across most countries, disadvantaged students have lower levels of motivation and less positive approaches to learning than their more advantaged peers. Unless policies aimed at promoting greater motivation and positive attitudes to science learning are directed specifically at reducing disparities in motivation and attitudes towards science learning between social groups, this analysis suggests they will result in absolute improvements in science achievement but may contribute to widening existing inequalities in performance across social groups.

Students benefit from attending compulsory science-related courses in most countries and in some countries disadvantaged students who attend such courses benefit more than their more advantaged peers. Expanding the provision of high quality compulsory science courses therefore appears to be a promising tool for policy makers and schools administrators. Analyses presented in this chapter suggest that investing marginal funds in the provision of compulsory science-related courses should be considered as a possible policy priority as it may both help increase student achievement generally and mitigate socio-economic differences in performance.

Note

1. All models control for socio-economic background using both the PISA index of socio-economic background and an indicator of whether students are among the most disadvantaged in their country (bottom third of their country's socio-economic distribution). A detailed description of the models developed in the Chapter can be found in Annex A5.

Conclusions and Policy Implications

5
CONCLUSIONS AND POLICY IMPLICATIONS

INTRODUCTION

Education can improve the quality of life of individuals and societies. Ensuring that all children achieve their full potential academically is a major policy goal for countries worldwide both for equity and efficiency reasons. Education can in fact play a major role in promoting social mobility and ensuring that children's future is not determined by the socio-economic background of their parents. At the same time, ensuring that all students perform at high levels is an important component of policies aimed at promoting economic growth and success in a world that demands well-educated citizens and workers.

This report examines factors that are associated with the academic achievement of disadvantaged students. By doing so it helps educators and policy makers to promote the full realisation of the human potential of youth. Schools and countries seeking to promote the skills and knowledge of their most vulnerable and disadvantaged children have in fact so far relied mostly on country-specific evidence on how young people's socio-economic background is associated with poor achievement in school. However far less is known about the circumstances in which disadvantaged students can flourish and express their full potential. Consequently the report focuses on a group of students that "beat the odds" in the sense that they defy expectations and excel academically despite having a socio-economic background that in general is associated with poor outcomes at school. The goal is to infer what could be done to help more disadvantaged students "beat the odds".

The report defines students who "beat the odds" as resilient and uses data from the 2006 PISA science assessment to identify such students in different countries. In other words, a resilient student is a high-achieving socio-economically disadvantaged student. Resilient students are among the most disadvantaged third in their countries in terms of socio-economic background and among the third of students in their country with the highest scores in the PISA science assessment. The report examines three sets of factors – approaches to learning, participation in science courses and time spent learning science at school, and school characteristics – which may help explain the success in PISA science of this group of students.

The report maps resilience and the factors associated with students' ability to "beat the odds" in 55 countries using data from the 2006 PISA study. It represents the most extensive and rigorous treatment to date of academic resilience across countries. Because of the focus on science in the 2006 PISA study, the report uses performance in science as the measure of student achievement. By exploring which circumstances are associated with academic resilience, the report provides new insights into how educators, school administrators, policy makers and parents can better support disadvantaged students and help them to succeed in school.

This report provides a rich descriptive picture of resilience across a large number of countries. It shows that in all countries, disadvantaged students have the potential to overcome their economic and social disadvantage and to perform at levels similar to their more advantaged peers. The findings also confirm that disadvantaged students have the potential to become the leaders of the future and that socio-economic disadvantage can be overcome with the right set of circumstances and incentives. While the data do not allow causal inference, the results highlight key differences between students who beat the odds and those who do not. Most notably, resilient students generally have more positive learning approaches and spend more time in regular lessons at school than other disadvantaged students. These findings suggest that conditions that promote academic excellence among the most disadvantaged youngsters can be established.

This chapter reviews the report's main findings and discusses their implications for educational policy and practice. Two themes emerge from these findings and they are discussed in turn in the next section. Taken together these themes suggest several policy areas to which countries and schools may want to direct their efforts to increase school success and facilitate social mobility among their most disadvantaged citizens.

There are important areas of educational policy where this report is silent simply because they are not well covered in PISA. The report ends with a brief review of areas where PISA could look in the future to provide further policy insights for analysing resilience in student performance.

FINDINGS AND IMPLICATIONS FOR EDUCATIONAL POLICY AND PRACTICE

The majority of resilient students, especially in OECD countries, achieve scores in the PISA science assessment that place them in the top three PISA proficiency levels. In contrast, the great majority of disadvantaged low-achieving students perform below the baseline proficiency level. Disadvantaged low-achieving students are at a high risk of completing their studies without those skills and competencies that are essential to fully participate in society and succeed in the labour market.

The report identifies two factors that appear to be particularly strongly associated with successful academic performance among disadvantaged students: the extent to which disadvantaged students adopt positive approaches to learning and the amount of time they spend in regular science lessons.

First, disadvantaged students who exhibit more positive approaches to learning science are more likely to be resilient than other disadvantaged students. Resilient students are more motivated to learn to science, more engaged with science and have greater self-confidence in their ability to learn science. The level of self-confidence in their academic abilities is in fact one of the strongest correlates of resilience.

Policies aimed at fostering positive approaches to learning among disadvantaged students could help facilitate resilience. Programmes designed to increase disadvantaged students' confidence in their academic abilities may be a good place to start. Increased self-confidence may be achieved through instructional techniques that challenge false perceptions of inability. Programs that encourage students to engage and explore science topics may also help. Other research suggests that facilitating interactions between disadvantaged students and individuals who work in scientific industries may also help disadvantaged students believe they can do well in science. High quality mentoring programmes have been shown to be beneficial particularly to disadvantaged students (DuBois *et al.*, 2004).

Second, the amount of time spent learning science during regular school hours is significantly associated with resilience in almost all participating countries. Students who spend more hours in regular science lessons at school have significantly higher odds of being resilient than students who spend less time in science lessons. Furthermore, it appears that while all students benefit from attending compulsory science courses, in several countries disadvantaged students benefit more than more advantaged students from attending compulsory courses.

School science classrooms are the primary venue in which students can acquire science skills and knowledge. Yet this report's findings show that many disadvantaged students do not take any science courses. If science is important to success later in life and the betterment of society, then students need to be exposed to science in school. Increasing science course-taking requirements and expanding the science curricula could enable more disadvantaged students to achieve at the highest levels. Changes to school course-taking policies may therefore be effective policy tools to help foster academic resilience: time spent learning is strongly associated with skill development and conceptual understanding (Clark and Linn, 2003) and with the likelihood that students will be exposed to academic material they otherwise might not have been able to consult (Schiller and Muller, 2003; Teitlebaum, 2003). A note of caution is warranted, however, as increased course-taking requirements can also lead to higher failure rates (Gamoran and Hannigan, 2000) if teachers do not adequately adapt their classroom instructional techniques to reflect students' prior preparation and learning styles.

CONCLUSIONS AND POLICY IMPLICATIONS

The PISA study does not provide all the information that is relevant to student resilience. For example, it does not provide information about particular programmes or policies that may contribute to resilience or to the correlates of resilience (*i.e.* student confidence). The following paragraphs therefore explore other research studies to provide additional information about policies and programs that have shown promise in targeting those aspects of disadvantaged students' approaches to learning and educational experiences that may help facilitate and expand their resilience.

Teachers are an important, if not the most important, factor in improving student performance (Aaronson *et al.*, 2007; Hanushek, 1986). Policies and programmes designed to enhance and expand teachers' use of effective instructional techniques may prove useful to promoting resilience. A meta-analytic review of a decade's worth of teacher effectiveness literature offers some guidance to countries and schools. The review identifies the following strategies as having the strongest positive effects on "motivational-affective outcomes" (*i.e.* on those outcomes most similar to the student approaches to learning factors measured in PISA): subject domain-specific activities for processing information (*e.g.* mathematics problem solving, science inquiry), social experiences (*e.g.* cooperative learning, student discussion), time for learning, and regulation and monitoring (*e.g.* providing feedback and support, teaching students strategies of self-regulation and monitoring) (Seidel and Shavelson, 2007). Encouraging teachers to use these instructional strategies could help to improve students' motivation and confidence and, by extension, student resilience.

Finally, disadvantaged students may need better than average experiences to be able to perform at high levels and overcome their difficulties. If schools are going to be a catalyst for social mobility they may need to provide disadvantaged students with higher quality experiences and work hard to improve the students' motivation and confidence. The conversations and activities more advantaged students expose them to may make it clear why science matters, how science relates to their lives, and what they need to do to be successful in science-related career fields. Disadvantaged students' families may not be equipped to provide this information and exposure. Therefore, the schools these students attend could seek to provide these additional services to disadvantaged students to help them achieve at high levels.

The depth and pervasiveness of the current economic crisis has increased the number of youngsters that will face economic hardship in the coming years. The expectation of growing economic inequality and increases in poverty rates means that policy makers should renew their efforts to promote the academic achievement of all youngsters, with a special emphasis on the challenges disadvantaged students face. Failing to ensure that all youngsters have the opportunity to achieve their full potential at this critical stage could seriously challenge countries' chances of solid economic growth in the future and establish a cycle of underachievement and deprivation that will persist in the decades to come.

References

Aaronson, D., L. Barrow, and **W. Sander,** (2007), "Teachers and student achievement in the Chicago Public High Schools," *Journal of Labor Economics*, Vol. 25, No. 1, pp. 95-135.

Alexander, K. and **M. Cook** (1982), "Curricula and coursework: A surprise ending to a familiar story," *American Sociological Review*, Vol. 47, No. 5, pp. 626-640.

Baker, D., B. Goesling and **G. LeTendre** (2002), "Socioeconomic status, school quality and national economic development: A Cross-National Analysis of the 'Heyneman-Loxley effect' on Mathematics and Science Achievement," *Comparative Education Review*, Vol. 46, No. 3, pp. 291-312.

Bandura, A. (1984), "Recycling misconceptions of perceived self-efficacy," *Cognitive Therapy and Research*, Vol. 8, No. 3, pp. 231-255.

Borman, G.D. and **L.T. Overman** (2004), "Academic resilience in mathematics among poor and minority students," *Elementary School Journal*, Vol. 104, pp. 177-195.

Carbonaro, W. and **A. Gamoran** (2002), "The production of achievement inequality in high school English," *American Educational Research Journal*, Vol. 39, No. 4, pp. 801-27.

Catterall, J.S. (1998), "Risk and resilience in student transitions to high school," *American Journal of Education*, Vol. 106, No. 2, pp. 302-333.

Christensen, G. and **M. Segeritz** (2008), "An international perspective on student achievement," in *Immigrant Students Can Succeed*, Verlag Bertelsmann Stiftung, Gütersloh, pp. 11-33.

Clark, D. and **M.C. Linn** (2003), "Designing for knowledge integration: The impact of instructional time," *Journal of the Learning Sciences* Vol. 12, No. 4, pp. 451-493.

Connell, J.P., M.B. Spencer and **J.L. Aber** (1994), "Educational risk and resilience in African-American youth: context, self, action and outcomes in school," *Child Development*, Vol. 65, No. 2, pp. 493-506.

Coleman, J., E.Q. Campbell, C.J. Hobson, J. McPartland, A.M. Mood, F.D. Weinfield and **R.L York** (1966), *Equality of Educational Opportunity*, U.S. Government Printing Office, Washington, DC.

Connell, J.P., M.B. Spencer and **J.L. Aber** (1994), "Educational risk and resilience in African-American youth: context, self, action and outcomes in school," *Child Development*, Vol. 65, No. 2, pp. 493-506.

Crane, J. (1996), "Effects of home environment, SES and maternal test scores on mathematics achievement," *The Journal of Educational Research*, Vol. 89, No. 5, pp. 305-314.

Deci, E.L. and **R.M. Ryan** (1985), *Intrinsic Motivation and Self-Determination in Human Behavior*, Plenum Press, New York.

Deci, E., R.J. Vallerand, L.G. Pelletier and **R.M. Ryan** (1991), "Motivation and education: The self-determination perspective," *Educational Psychologist*, Vol. 26, No. 3 and 4, pp. 325-346.

DuBois, D. L., B.E. Holloway, J.C. Valentine and **H. Cooper** (2002). "Effectiveness of Mentoring Programs for Youth: A Meta-Analytic Review," *American Journal of Community Psychology*, Vol. 30, No. 2, pp. 157-197.

Eccles, J.S., A. Wigfiled and **U. Schiefele** (1998), "Motivation to succeed", in W. Damon and N. Eisenberg (eds.), *Handbook of Child Psychology*, Vol. 3, Wiley, New York, pp. 1017-1095.

Farkas, G., R. Grobe, D. Sheehan and **Y. Shuan** (1990), "Cultural resources and school success: gender, ethnicity and poverty groups within an urban school district," *American Sociological Review*, Vol. 67, pp. 148-55.

Farrington, D., B. Gallagher, L. Morley, R.J. Ledger and **D.J. West** (1986), "Unemployment, school leaving and crime," *British Journal of Criminology*, Vol. 26, No. 4, pp. 335-56.

Fergusson and **Horwood**, (2003), "Resilience to childhood adversity: results of a 21-year study," in Luthar, S.S. (Ed.) *Resilience and vulnerability: adaptation in the context of childhood adversities*, Cambridge University Press, Cambridge.

Finn, J.D. and **D.A. Rock** (1997), "Academic success among students at risk for school failure," *Journal of Applied Psychology*, Vol. 82, No. 2, pp. 221–234.

Flinn, C. (1986), "Dynamic models of criminal careers," in A. Blumstein, J. Cohen, J. Roth and C. Visher (eds.), *Criminal Careers*, Vol. 2, National Academy Press, Washington, D.C., pp. 356-379.

Fuller, B. and **P. Clarke** (1994), "Raising School Effects While Ignoring Culture? Local conditions and the Influence of Classroom Tools, Rules and Pedagogy," *Review of Educational Research*, Vol. 64, No. 1, pp. 119-157.

Gamoran, A. and **E.C. Hannigan** (2000), "Algebra for everyone? Benefits of college-preparatory mathematics for students with diverse abilities in early secondary school," *Educational Evaluation and Policy Analysis*, Vol. 22, No.3, pp. 241-254.

REFERENCES

Garmezy, N., A.S Masten and **A. Tellegen** (1984), "The study of stress and competence in children – a building block for developmental psychopathology," *Child Development* Vol. 55, pp. 97-111.

Goldhaber, D.D. and **D.J. Brewer** (1997), "Why Don't Schools and Teachers Seem to Matter? Assessing the Impact of Unobservables on Educational Productivity," *Journal of Human Resources*, Vol. 32, No. 3, summer, pp. 505-523.

Grossner, M. and **R. Kaestner** (1997), "Effects of education on health," in J.R. Behrman and N. Stacey (eds.), *Social Benefits of Education*, University of Michigan Press, Ann Arbor, pp. 69-124.

Hanushek, E.A. (1986), "The economics of schooling: production and efficiency in public schools," *Journal of Economic Literature*, Vol. 24, No. 3, pp. 1141-1178.

Hanushek, E.A., J.F. Kain and **S.G. Rivkin** (2002), "New evidence about Brown v. Board of Education: The complex effects of school racial composition on achievement," *Working Paper* no. W8741, National Bureau of Economic Research, Cambridge, MA.

Hanushek, E., D.T. Jamison, E.A. Jamison and **L. Woessmann** (2008), "Education and Economic Growth", *Education Next*, Vol. 8, No. 2, spring, pp. 62-70.

Hout, M. and **E. Beller** (2006), "Intergenerational social mobility in comparative perspective," *The Future of Children*, Vol. 16, No. 2, pp. 19-36.

Lee, V.E., L.F. Winfield and **T.C. Wilson** (1991), "Academic behaviors among high-achieving African-American students," *Education and Urban Society*, Vol. 24, No. 1, pp. 65-86.

Levy, F. and **R.J. Murnane** (2007), "How computerized work and globalization shape human skill demands," in M. Suárez-Orozco and C. Sattin (eds.), *Learning in the global era: International perspectives on globalization and education*, University of California Press, Berkeley, pp. 158–174.

Luthar, S.S., D. Cicchetti and **B. Becker** (2000), "The construct of resilience: A critical evaluation and guidelines for future work," *Child Development*, Vol. 71, No. 3, pp. 543-562.

Marsh, H.W. (1986), "Verbal and math self-concept: An internal/external frame of reference model," *American Educational Research Journal*, Vol. 23, No. 1, pp. 129-149.

Martin, A. and **H. Marsh** (2006), "Academic resilience and its psychological and educational correlates: A construct validity approach," *Psychology in the Schools*, Vol. 43, No. 3, pp. 267-281.

Martin, A. (2002), "Motivation and academic resilience: developing a model for student enhancement," *Australian Journal of Education*, Vol. 46, No. 1, pp. 34-49.

Masten, A.S., K.M. Best and **N. Garmzy**(1990), "Resilience and development: contributions from the study of children who overcome adversity," *Development and Psychopathology*, Vol. 2, pp. 425-444.

Masten, A.S. (1994), "Resilience in individual development: Successful adaptation despite risk and adversity," in M. Wang and E. Gordon (eds.), *Risk and Resilience in Inner-City America: Challenges and Prospects*, Erlbaum, Hillsdale, NJ, pp. 3-25.

OECD (2001), *Knowledge and Skills for Life: First Results from the OECD Program for International Student Assessment*, OECD, Paris.

OECD (2003a), *Learners for Life: Student Approaches to Learning: Results from PISA 2000*, OECD, Paris.

OECD (2003b), *Student Engagement in School: A Sense of Belonging and Participation. Results from PISA 2000*, OECD, Paris.

OECD (2004), *Learning for Tomorrow's World - First Results from PISA 2003*, OECD, Paris.

OECD (2006), *Where Immigrant Students Succeed – A Comparative Review of Performance and Engagement in PISA 2003*, OECD, Paris.

OECD (2007a), *PISA 2006 Science Competencies For Tomorrow's World Volume 1: Analysis*, OECD, Paris.

OECD (2007b), *PISA 2006 Science Competencies For Tomorrow's World Volume 2: Data*, OECD, Paris.

OECD (2009a), *Top of the Class - High Performers in Science in PISA 2006*, OECD, Paris.

OECD (2009b), *PISA 2006 Technical Report*, OECD, Paris.

Padrón, Y.N., H.C. Waxman, A.P. Brown and **R.A. Powers** (2000), *Improving the education of resilient and non-resilient English language learners (Technical Report 3.2)*, University of Houston and the Center for Research on Education, Diversity and Excellence, Houston, TX.

Power, C., O. Manor and **J. Fox.** (1991), *Health and Class: The Early Years*, Chapman and Hall, London.

Pulkkinen, L. and **R.E. Tremblay** (1992), "Adult life-styles and their precursors in the social behaviour of children and adolescents," *European Journal of Personality*, Vol. 4, No. 3, pp. 237-251.

Rigsby, L. (1994), "The Americanization of resilience: Deconstructing research practice." in M. Wang and E. Gordon (eds.), *Educational Resilience in Inner -city America: Challenges and Prospects*, Erlbaum, Hillsdale, NJ, pp. 85-92.

Rivkin, S.G., E.A. Hanushek and **J.F. Kain** (2005), "Teachers, schools and academic achievement," *Econometrica, Vol. 73, No. 2*, pp. 417-458.

Rodgers, B. (1990), "Behavior and personality in childhood as predictors of adult psychiatric disorder", *Journal of Child Psychology and Psychiatry*, Vol. 31, No. 3, pp. 393-414.

Rouse, K.A.G. (2001), "Resilient students' goals and motivation," *Journal of Adolescence, Vol. 24*, pp. 461-472.

REFERENCES

Rumberger, R.W. (1995), "Dropping out of middle school: A multi-level analysis of students and schools", *American Educational Research Journal*, Vol. 32, No. 3, pp. 583-625.

Rutter, M. (1985), "Resilience in the face of adversity – protective factors and resistance to psychiatric-disorder," *British Journal of Psychiatry*, Vol. 147, pp.598-611.

Rutter, M. (1987), "Psychosocial resilience and protective mechanisms," *American Journal of Orthopsychiatry*, Vol. 57, pp. 316-331.

Schiller, K.S. and **C. Muller** (2003), "Raising the bar and equity? Effects of state high school graduation requirements and accountability policies on students' mathematics course taking," *Education Evaluation and Policy Analysis*, Vol. 25, No. 3, pp. 229-318.

Schoon, I. (2006), *Risk and resilience. Adaptations in changing times*, Cambridge: Cambridge University Press.

Seidel, T. & **R. Shavelson** (2007), "Teaching Effectiveness Research in the Past Decade: The Role of Theory and Research Design in Disentangling Meta-Analysis Results," *Review of Educational Research*, Vol. 77, No. 4, pp. 454-499.

Shumow, L., D.L. Vandell and **J. Posner** (1999), "Risk and resilience in the urban neighborhood: Predictors of academic performance among low-income elementary school children," *Merrill-Palmer Quarterly*, Vol. 45, No. 2, pp. 309-331.

Sirin, S. (2005), "Socio-economic status and academic achievement: A meta-analytic review of research," *Review of Educational Research*, Vol. 75, No. 3, pp. 417-53.

Smith, B. (2002), "Quantity Matters: Annual Instructional Time in an Urban School System," *Educational Administration Quarterly*, 36(5), pp. 652–682.

Stacey, N. (1998), "Social benefits of education," *Annals of the American Academy of Political and Social Science*, Vol. 559, No. 1, pp. 54-63.

Teitlebaum, P. (2003), "The influence of high school graduation requirement policies in mathematics and science on student course-taking patterns and achievement" *Education Evaluation and Policy Analysis*, Vol. 25, No. 1, pp. 135-143.

Wanner, R. A. and **B.C. Hayes** (1996), "Intergenerational occupational mobility among men in Canada and Australia," *Canadian Journal of Sociology*, Vol. 21, No. 1, pp. 43-76.

Waxman, H. C. and **S.-Y.L. Huang** (1996), "Motivation and Learning Environment Differences in Inner-City Middle School Students," *The Journal of Educational Research, Vol. 90*, No. 2, pp. 93-102.

Wigfield, A., J.S. Eccles and **D. Rodriguez** (1998), "The development of children's motivation in school context," *Review of Research in Education*, Vol. 23, American Educational Research Association, pp. 73-118.

Wößmann, L. (2003), "School resources, educational institutions and student performance: The international evidence," *Oxford Bulletin of Economics and Statistics*, Vol. 65, No. 2, pp. 117-170.

Yoshikawa, H. (1994), "Prevention as cumulative protection: Effects of early family support and education on chronic delinquency and risks," *Psychological Bulletin*, Vol. 115, No. 1, pp. 28-54.

Annexes

Annex A1: Defining and characterising student resilience in PISA

Annex A2: A profile of student resilience

Annex A3: Closing the gap? Enhancing the performance of socio-economically disadvantaged students

Annex A4: Conclusions and policy implications

Annex A5: Technical notes

Table A1.1 Shares of resilient and disadvantaged low achievers among all students, by country and gender

| | | \multicolumn{6}{c|}{Resilient students} | | |
| | | All students | | Male | | Female | | Disadvantaged low achievers | |
		%	S.E.	%	S.E.	%	S.E.	%	S.E.
OECD	Australia	15.5	(0.4)	15.7	(0.6)	15.4	(0.6)	7.4	(0.4)
	Austria	12.7	(0.8)	13.5	(1.2)	11.9	(0.9)	9.9	(1.0)
	Belgium	12.4	(0.5)	11.9	(0.7)	12.9	(0.8)	9.8	(0.6)
	Canada	17.1	(0.6)	18.0	(0.8)	16.2	(0.6)	6.1	(0.4)
	Czech Republic	13.3	(0.8)	13.4	(1.1)	13.2	(1.0)	8.4	(0.7)
	Denmark	10.6	(0.5)	11.2	(0.8)	10.0	(0.8)	10.4	(0.8)
	Finland	22.2	(0.7)	21.5	(1.0)	22.9	(1.1)	2.6	(0.3)
	France	10.9	(0.7)	10.4	(0.9)	11.4	(0.8)	11.2	(0.9)
	Germany	12.6	(0.6)	11.8	(0.7)	13.4	(0.9)	8.8	(0.8)
	Greece	10.5	(0.7)	8.7	(0.8)	12.4	(0.9)	10.3	(0.9)
	Hungary	12.7	(0.7)	12.5	(0.9)	12.9	(1.0)	7.3	(0.6)
	Iceland	9.4	(0.5)	8.3	(0.7)	10.4	(0.8)	12.6	(0.6)
	Ireland	14.4	(0.7)	14.4	(1.0)	14.4	(0.9)	7.6	(0.8)
	Italy	11.0	(0.5)	10.9	(0.6)	11.0	(0.6)	10.4	(0.5)
	Japan	17.6	(0.8)	17.2	(0.9)	18.0	(1.0)	6.3	(0.7)
	Korea	17.7	(0.9)	17.8	(1.3)	17.7	(1.1)	5.3	(0.6)
	Luxembourg	9.7	(0.4)	10.0	(0.6)	9.5	(0.6)	11.2	(0.5)
	Mexico	7.7	(0.4)	8.3	(0.6)	7.2	(0.7)	10.5	(1.0)
	Netherlands	14.8	(0.7)	14.6	(1.0)	14.9	(1.0)	7.6	(0.7)
	New Zealand	15.2	(0.6)	15.5	(0.9)	14.9	(0.9)	7.6	(0.6)
	Norway	8.9	(0.5)	8.0	(0.7)	9.9	(0.9)	12.5	(0.8)
	Poland	14.1	(0.7)	12.9	(0.8)	15.2	(0.9)	7.1	(0.5)
	Portugal	15.4	(0.8)	15.8	(1.1)	15.0	(1.0)	5.4	(0.6)
	Slovak Republic	10.8	(0.6)	10.7	(0.8)	11.0	(0.9)	10.4	(0.7)
	Spain	14.7	(0.6)	14.8	(0.8)	14.6	(0.8)	6.5	(0.5)
	Sweden	12.1	(0.7)	12.4	(0.9)	11.7	(1.0)	9.1	(0.6)
	Switzerland	13.6	(0.5)	13.5	(0.6)	13.6	(0.7)	8.7	(0.5)
	Turkey	11.1	(0.8)	11.5	(1.1)	10.7	(0.9)	6.9	(0.8)
	United Kingdom	13.5	(0.6)	14.1	(0.7)	13.0	(0.8)	8.9	(0.5)
	United States	9.9	(0.7)	10.9	(0.9)	8.9	(0.8)	12.6	(1.4)
	OECD average	**13.0**	**(0.1)**	**13.0**	**(0.1)**	**13.1**	**(0.1)**	**8.6**	**(0.1)**
Partners	Argentina	4.2	(0.4)	4.1	(0.7)	4.3	(0.6)	18.9	(1.7)
	Azerbaijan	2.6	(0.7)	2.7	(0.8)	2.6	(0.7)	18.8	(1.0)
	Brazil	6.5	(0.5)	7.1	(0.7)	6.0	(0.6)	13.0	(0.8)
	Bulgaria	4.9	(0.4)	4.7	(0.6)	5.2	(0.6)	19.0	(1.6)
	Chile	8.2	(0.7)	8.7	(0.9)	7.7	(0.9)	11.6	(1.0)
	Colombia	6.3	(0.6)	7.3	(0.8)	5.5	(0.8)	13.1	(1.2)
	Croatia	12.3	(0.6)	12.3	(0.8)	12.3	(1.0)	7.3	(0.6)
	Estonia	18.4	(0.9)	16.3	(1.1)	20.6	(1.2)	4.2	(0.5)
	Hong Kong-China	24.8	(1.0)	27.2	(1.3)	22.5	(1.3)	2.1	(0.3)
	Indonesia	7.9	(0.8)	8.4	(1.0)	7.3	(0.9)	8.0	(0.8)
	Israel	6.4	(0.6)	6.9	(0.8)	6.0	(0.7)	17.3	(0.9)
	Jordan	7.3	(0.5)	5.2	(0.5)	9.4	(1.0)	12.6	(0.7)
	Kyrgyzstan	0.5	(0.1)	0.5	(0.2)	0.4	(0.2)	28.5	(1.0)
	Latvia	13.4	(0.8)	12.3	(1.2)	14.5	(0.9)	7.1	(0.7)
	Lithuania	11.3	(0.6)	10.2	(1.0)	12.5	(0.8)	9.9	(0.6)
	Macao-China	24.3	(0.8)	24.6	(1.1)	24.0	(1.1)	1.5	(0.3)
	Montenegro	3.7	(0.5)	3.2	(0.5)	4.2	(0.6)	19.4	(0.6)
	Romania	4.0	(0.6)	3.7	(0.6)	4.4	(1.0)	17.2	(1.5)
	Russian Federation	11.2	(0.9)	10.6	(1.0)	11.8	(1.1)	9.6	(0.8)
	Serbia	5.3	(0.5)	5.1	(0.6)	5.6	(0.6)	15.8	(1.1)
	Slovenia	13.6	(0.5)	12.4	(0.7)	14.7	(0.8)	8.2	(0.4)
	Chinese Taipei	19.2	(0.8)	19.8	(0.9)	18.5	(1.1)	4.5	(0.5)
	Thailand	11.7	(0.7)	10.4	(1.1)	12.7	(0.7)	5.5	(0.6)
	Tunisia	8.7	(0.8)	9.0	(1.0)	8.4	(0.9)	10.3	(0.7)
	Uruguay	7.6	(0.6)	7.3	(0.7)	7.8	(0.8)	13.1	(0.9)

Table A1.2 PISA index of economic, social and cultural status for system average, resilient and disadvantaged low achievers

		All students Mean index	S.E.	Disadvantaged low achievers Mean index	S.E.	Resilient Mean index	S.E.
OECD	Australia	0.21	(0.02)	-0.74	(0.01)	-0.57	(0.02)
	Austria	0.20	(0.02)	-0.80	(0.04)	-0.56	(0.02)
	Belgium	0.17	(0.02)	-0.94	(0.02)	-0.66	(0.02)
	Canada	0.37	(0.02)	-0.61	(0.02)	-0.43	(0.02)
	Czech Republic	0.03	(0.02)	-0.88	(0.02)	-0.70	(0.02)
	Denmark	0.31	(0.03)	-0.78	(0.03)	-0.54	(0.03)
	Finland	0.26	(0.02)	-0.67	(0.02)	-0.55	(0.02)
	France	-0.09	(0.03)	-1.10	(0.02)	-0.93	(0.04)
	Germany	0.29	(0.03)	-0.84	(0.03)	-0.51	(0.03)
	Greece	-0.15	(0.04)	-1.33	(0.02)	-1.09	(0.03)
	Hungary	-0.09	(0.03)	-1.19	(0.02)	-0.89	(0.03)
	Iceland	0.77	(0.01)	-0.30	(0.02)	-0.12	(0.03)
	Ireland	-0.02	(0.03)	-1.01	(0.02)	-0.85	(0.03)
	Italy	-0.07	(0.02)	-1.21	(0.01)	-1.02	(0.02)
	Japan	-0.01	(0.02)	-0.83	(0.02)	-0.71	(0.02)
	Korea	-0.01	(0.02)	-0.96	(0.03)	-0.83	(0.02)
	Luxembourg	0.09	(0.01)	-1.32	(0.02)	-0.92	(0.04)
	Mexico	-0.99	(0.04)	-2.50	(0.03)	-2.31	(0.03)
	Netherlands	0.25	(0.03)	-0.83	(0.04)	-0.59	(0.03)
	New Zealand	0.10	(0.02)	-0.89	(0.02)	-0.71	(0.02)
	Norway	0.42	(0.02)	-0.47	(0.02)	-0.31	(0.02)
	Poland	-0.30	(0.02)	-1.24	(0.02)	-1.11	(0.02)
	Portugal	-0.62	(0.04)	-2.06	(0.02)	-1.87	(0.02)
	Slovak Republic	-0.15	(0.03)	-1.17	(0.05)	-0.89	(0.02)
	Spain	-0.31	(0.03)	-1.56	(0.02)	-1.35	(0.02)
	Sweden	0.24	(0.02)	-0.72	(0.02)	-0.54	(0.03)
	Switzerland	0.09	(0.02)	-0.98	(0.02)	-0.75	(0.02)
	Turkey	-1.28	(0.05)	-2.48	(0.03)	-2.33	(0.03)
	United Kingdom	0.19	(0.02)	-0.79	(0.02)	-0.56	(0.02)
	United States	0.14	(0.04)	-0.96	(0.03)	-0.73	(0.02)
	OECD average	**0.00**	**(0.00)**	**-1.07**	**(0.00)**	**-0.86**	**(0.00)**
Partners	Argentina	-0.64	(0.07)	-2.02	(0.03)	-1.79	(0.04)
	Azerbaijan	-0.45	(0.03)	-1.62	(0.03)	-1.57	(0.05)
	Brazil	-1.12	(0.03)	-2.61	(0.02)	-2.41	(0.04)
	Bulgaria	-0.21	(0.05)	-1.42	(0.04)	-1.04	(0.03)
	Chile	-0.70	(0.06)	-2.03	(0.03)	-1.88	(0.06)
	Colombia	-1.00	(0.05)	-2.44	(0.04)	-2.28	(0.05)
	Croatia	-0.11	(0.02)	-1.09	(0.02)	-0.93	(0.03)
	Estonia	0.14	(0.02)	-0.79	(0.02)	-0.71	(0.03)
	Hong Kong-China	-0.67	(0.03)	-1.74	(0.02)	-1.60	(0.02)
	Indonesia	-1.52	(0.05)	-2.72	(0.02)	-2.65	(0.03)
	Israel	0.22	(0.02)	-0.81	(0.02)	-0.61	(0.04)
	Jordan	-0.57	(0.03)	-1.94	(0.05)	-1.66	(0.04)
	Kyrgyzstan	-0.66	(0.02)	-1.64	(0.03)	-1.57	(0.02)
	Latvia	-0.02	(0.02)	-1.10	(0.02)	-0.91	(0.02)
	Lithuania	0.04	(0.03)	-1.08	(0.02)	-0.87	(0.02)
	Macao-China	-0.91	(0.01)	-1.89	(0.02)	-1.77	(0.02)
	Montenegro	-0.02	(0.01)	-1.08	(0.02)	-0.93	(0.03)
	Romania	-0.37	(0.04)	-1.52	(0.04)	-1.14	(0.03)
	Russian Federation	-0.10	(0.03)	-1.01	(0.02)	-0.92	(0.02)
	Serbia	-0.14	(0.03)	-1.20	(0.02)	-1.04	(0.02)
	Slovenia	0.13	(0.01)	-0.88	(0.01)	-0.71	(0.03)
	Chinese Taipei	-0.31	(0.02)	-1.25	(0.02)	-1.10	(0.02)
	Thailand	-1.43	(0.03)	-2.57	(0.03)	-2.48	(0.02)
	Tunisia	-1.20	(0.07)	-2.75	(0.03)	-2.63	(0.03)
	Uruguay	-0.51	(0.03)	-1.95	(0.03)	-1.69	(0.04)

[Part 1/3]
Table A1.3 Differences in the components of the economic, social and cultural status index

		Wealth						Educational resources				
		Resilient students		Disadvantaged low achievers		Difference in the mean index between resilient students and disadvantaged low achievers		Resilient students		Disadvantaged low achievers		Difference in the mean index between resilient students and disadvantaged low achievers
		Mean	S.E.	Mean	S.E.	Dif	S.E.	Mean	S.E.	Mean	S.E.	Dif	S.E.

OECD

Country	Mean	S.E.	Mean	S.E.	Dif	S.E.	Mean	S.E.	Mean	S.E.	Dif	S.E.
Australia	-0.08	(0.03)	0.04	(0.02)	**-0.12**	(0.04)	-0.15	(0.04)	-0.47	(0.03)	**0.32**	(0.05)
Austria	-0.25	(0.04)	-0.34	(0.04)	0.10	(0.06)	0.24	(0.06)	-0.07	(0.05)	**0.31**	(0.08)
Belgium	-0.18	(0.04)	-0.31	(0.03)	**0.13**	(0.05)	0.00	(0.04)	-0.37	(0.04)	**0.37**	(0.05)
Canada	-0.23	(0.03)	-0.21	(0.02)	-0.02	(0.04)	-0.27	(0.04)	-0.49	(0.03)	**0.23**	(0.05)
Czech Republic	-0.97	(0.04)	-1.04	(0.03)	0.07	(0.05)	0.09	(0.06)	-0.56	(0.05)	**0.65**	(0.08)
Denmark	0.43	(0.07)	0.44	(0.04)	-0.01	(0.08)	-0.17	(0.06)	-0.20	(0.04)	0.03	(0.07)
Finland	-0.01	(0.05)	0.12	(0.03)	**-0.13**	(0.05)	-0.35	(0.08)	-0.45	(0.04)	0.10	(0.08)
France	-0.62	(0.04)	-0.69	(0.04)	0.07	(0.06)	0.18	(0.07)	-0.31	(0.05)	**0.49**	(0.09)
Germany	-0.22	(0.05)	-0.27	(0.03)	0.05	(0.06)	0.15	(0.08)	-0.15	(0.05)	**0.30**	(0.09)
Greece	-0.77	(0.05)	-0.75	(0.03)	-0.02	(0.05)	-0.80	(0.06)	-1.26	(0.03)	**0.46**	(0.07)
Hungary	-1.01	(0.05)	-0.98	(0.03)	-0.02	(0.05)	-0.26	(0.08)	-0.93	(0.05)	**0.67**	(0.10)
Iceland	0.56	(0.05)	0.68	(0.03)	**-0.12**	(0.06)	0.13	(0.05)	-0.14	(0.04)	**0.28**	(0.07)
Ireland	-0.34	(0.04)	-0.34	(0.03)	-0.00	(0.05)	-0.29	(0.06)	-0.72	(0.04)	**0.42**	(0.08)
Italy	-0.52	(0.02)	-0.60	(0.02)	**0.08**	(0.03)	0.14	(0.04)	-0.39	(0.04)	**0.52**	(0.06)
Japan	-0.56	(0.04)	-0.50	(0.03)	-0.06	(0.04)	-1.03	(0.05)	-1.19	(0.04)	**0.16**	(0.06)
Korea	-0.79	(0.04)	-0.87	(0.04)	0.08	(0.05)	-0.40	(0.05)	-0.74	(0.03)	**0.34**	(0.06)
Luxembourg	0.00	(0.06)	-0.20	(0.03)	**0.20**	(0.06)	0.02	(0.08)	-0.07	(0.04)	0.09	(0.09)
Mexico	-2.41	(0.05)	-2.56	(0.05)	**0.16**	(0.07)	-1.28	(0.05)	-1.59	(0.04)	**0.31**	(0.06)
Netherlands	0.19	(0.04)	0.22	(0.04)	-0.02	(0.06)	-0.07	(0.05)	-0.44	(0.05)	**0.36**	(0.07)
New Zealand	-0.15	(0.05)	-0.23	(0.03)	0.08	(0.05)	-0.40	(0.07)	-0.64	(0.04)	**0.24**	(0.07)
Norway	0.25	(0.05)	0.32	(0.04)	-0.06	(0.06)	-0.13	(0.05)	-0.43	(0.05)	**0.31**	(0.07)
Poland	-1.51	(0.04)	-1.46	(0.03)	-0.04	(0.05)	-0.23	(0.05)	-0.68	(0.04)	**0.45**	(0.07)
Portugal	-0.72	(0.04)	-0.91	(0.03)	**0.19**	(0.05)	0.06	(0.06)	-0.49	(0.04)	**0.55**	(0.08)
Slovak Republic	-1.42	(0.04)	-1.45	(0.04)	0.03	(0.05)	-0.29	(0.08)	-1.13	(0.07)	**0.84**	(0.12)
Spain	-0.59	(0.03)	-0.55	(0.03)	-0.05	(0.04)	0.15	(0.05)	-0.35	(0.03)	**0.51**	(0.06)
Sweden	0.25	(0.04)	0.31	(0.04)	-0.06	(0.05)	-0.49	(0.06)	-0.71	(0.04)	**0.22**	(0.08)
Switzerland	-0.35	(0.04)	-0.28	(0.02)	-0.07	(0.05)	0.06	(0.06)	-0.13	(0.04)	**0.18**	(0.07)
Turkey	-2.27	(0.06)	-2.48	(0.04)	**0.21**	(0.07)	-1.31	(0.08)	-1.95	(0.05)	**0.64**	(0.09)
United Kingdom	-0.21	(0.07)	-0.07	(0.03)	**-0.14**	(0.07)	-0.42	(0.06)	-0.64	(0.03)	**0.22**	(0.06)
United States	-0.39	(0.04)	-0.44	(0.03)	0.06	(0.05)	-0.73	(0.08)	-0.94	(0.05)	**0.21**	(0.09)
OECD average	-0.48	(0.01)	-0.52	(0.01)	**0.04**	(0.02)	-0.27	(0.01)	-0.61	(0.01)	**0.34**	(0.01)

Partners

Country	Mean	S.E.	Mean	S.E.	Dif	S.E.	Mean	S.E.	Mean	S.E.	Dif	S.E.
Argentina	-1.82	(0.06)	-2.05	(0.06)	**0.23**	(0.09)	-1.02	(0.09)	-1.49	(0.06)	**0.47**	(0.11)
Azerbaijan	-2.76	(0.06)	-2.59	(0.04)	**-0.17**	(0.07)	-1.90	(0.07)	-2.15	(0.07)	**0.25**	(0.09)
Brazil	-2.04	(0.05)	-2.34	(0.03)	**0.29**	(0.06)	-1.57	(0.07)	-1.87	(0.04)	**0.30**	(0.07)
Bulgaria	-1.25	(0.05)	-1.45	(0.04)	**0.20**	(0.06)	-1.10	(0.07)	-1.74	(0.05)	**0.63**	(0.08)
Chile	-1.78	(0.07)	-1.85	(0.04)	0.06	(0.07)	-1.22	(0.10)	-1.53	(0.04)	**0.30**	(0.11)
Colombia	-2.40	(0.10)	-2.57	(0.06)	0.17	(0.09)	-1.44	(0.12)	-1.86	(0.07)	**0.42**	(0.12)
Croatia	-0.98	(0.04)	-1.03	(0.03)	0.06	(0.06)	-0.21	(0.06)	-0.68	(0.04)	**0.47**	(0.07)
Estonia	-0.95	(0.04)	-0.93	(0.05)	-0.03	(0.07)	-0.46	(0.06)	-0.62	(0.04)	**0.16**	(0.07)
Hong Kong-China	-1.00	(0.04)	-1.01	(0.03)	0.01	(0.05)	-0.34	(0.05)	-0.59	(0.04)	**0.25**	(0.07)
Indonesia	-3.48	(0.08)	-3.58	(0.05)	0.10	(0.10)	-1.97	(0.06)	-2.18	(0.05)	**0.21**	(0.07)
Israel	-0.80	(0.06)	-0.80	(0.04)	0.00	(0.06)	-0.46	(0.06)	-0.68	(0.04)	**0.22**	(0.07)
Jordan	-2.15	(0.06)	-2.20	(0.04)	0.05	(0.06)	-1.59	(0.07)	-2.03	(0.05)	**0.44**	(0.08)
Kyrgyzstan	-3.02	(0.06)	-2.81	(0.04)	**-0.20**	(0.07)	-1.66	(0.06)	-1.87	(0.05)	**0.21**	(0.08)
Latvia	-1.25	(0.05)	-1.47	(0.04)	**0.22**	(0.06)	-0.23	(0.08)	-0.82	(0.05)	**0.59**	(0.09)
Lithuania	-1.04	(0.04)	-1.19	(0.03)	**0.16**	(0.04)	-0.17	(0.07)	-0.89	(0.04)	**0.72**	(0.08)
Macao-China	-1.13	(0.05)	-1.13	(0.04)	-0.01	(0.07)	-0.67	(0.05)	-0.99	(0.04)	**0.33**	(0.07)
Montenegro	-1.38	(0.04)	-1.12	(0.03)	**-0.26**	(0.04)	-0.78	(0.05)	-1.23	(0.05)	**0.45**	(0.08)
Romania	-1.91	(0.06)	-1.99	(0.05)	0.08	(0.07)	-1.20	(0.08)	-1.75	(0.07)	**0.55**	(0.10)
Russian Federation	-1.79	(0.04)	-1.72	(0.03)	-0.06	(0.05)	-0.72	(0.06)	-1.05	(0.05)	**0.33**	(0.08)
Serbia	-1.31	(0.04)	-1.28	(0.03)	-0.03	(0.05)	-0.60	(0.07)	-1.03	(0.05)	**0.43**	(0.09)
Slovenia	-0.36	(0.05)	-0.31	(0.03)	-0.05	(0.06)	0.19	(0.05)	-0.17	(0.03)	**0.36**	(0.06)
Chinese Taipei	-0.65	(0.03)	-0.56	(0.03)	**-0.09**	(0.04)	-0.71	(0.05)	-1.09	(0.04)	**0.38**	(0.06)
Thailand	-2.43	(0.05)	-2.44	(0.05)	0.01	(0.06)	-1.83	(0.05)	-2.15	(0.04)	**0.32**	(0.05)
Tunisia	-2.84	(0.05)	-2.90	(0.05)	0.07	(0.06)	-1.87	(0.05)	-2.31	(0.05)	**0.44**	(0.07)
Uruguay	-1.83	(0.07)	-1.91	(0.04)	0.08	(0.07)	-0.87	(0.07)	-1.28	(0.05)	**0.42**	(0.10)

Note: Values that are statistically different are indicated in bold.

[Part 2/3]
Table A1.3 Differences in the components of the economic, social and cultural status index

	Cultural possessions						Number of books					
	Resilient students		Disadvantaged low achievers		Difference in the mean index between resilient students and disadvantaged low achievers		Resilient students		Disadvantaged low achievers		Difference in the mean index between resilient students and disadvantaged low achievers	
	Mean	S.E.	Mean	S.E.	Dif	S.E.	Mean	S.E.	Mean	S.E.	Dif	S.E.

OECD
Country	Mean	S.E.	Mean	S.E.	Dif	S.E.	Mean	S.E.	Mean	S.E.	Dif	S.E.
Australia	-0.45	(0.04)	-0.73	(0.03)	**0.28**	(0.04)	3.53	(0.05)	2.74	(0.04)	**0.78**	(0.06)
Austria	-0.34	(0.05)	-0.51	(0.03)	**0.17**	(0.07)	3.24	(0.06)	2.14	(0.05)	**1.10**	(0.07)
Belgium	-0.62	(0.05)	-0.83	(0.03)	**0.21**	(0.05)	2.87	(0.06)	2.22	(0.04)	**0.66**	(0.07)
Canada	-0.48	(0.05)	-0.74	(0.04)	**0.25**	(0.06)	3.36	(0.05)	2.68	(0.04)	**0.67**	(0.06)
Czech Republic	-0.31	(0.06)	-0.52	(0.04)	**0.21**	(0.07)	3.45	(0.08)	2.67	(0.06)	**0.78**	(0.10)
Denmark	-0.64	(0.07)	-0.85	(0.04)	**0.21**	(0.07)	3.05	(0.10)	2.33	(0.07)	**0.73**	(0.13)
Finland	-0.08	(0.06)	-0.49	(0.03)	**0.42**	(0.07)	3.44	(0.07)	2.77	(0.04)	**0.68**	(0.08)
France	-0.37	(0.06)	-0.86	(0.03)	**0.49**	(0.07)	3.05	(0.08)	2.16	(0.05)	**0.90**	(0.09)
Germany	-0.24	(0.06)	-0.45	(0.03)	**0.21**	(0.07)	3.35	(0.09)	2.33	(0.06)	**1.02**	(0.11)
Greece	-0.38	(0.05)	-0.52	(0.04)	**0.14**	(0.07)	2.84	(0.09)	2.40	(0.05)	**0.44**	(0.10)
Hungary	0.08	(0.08)	-0.43	(0.05)	0.52	(0.10)	3.48	(0.09)	2.51	(0.06)	**0.97**	(0.11)
Iceland	0.52	(0.07)	0.18	(0.04)	**0.34**	(0.08)	3.87	(0.08)	3.09	(0.05)	**0.78**	(0.10)
Ireland	-0.52	(0.06)	-0.77	(0.04)	**0.24**	(0.06)	3.15	(0.08)	2.24	(0.06)	**0.91**	(0.10)
Italy	-0.03	(0.04)	-0.22	(0.03)	**0.19**	(0.05)	2.93	(0.06)	2.40	(0.04)	**0.53**	(0.07)
Japan	-0.76	(0.05)	-1.02	(0.02)	**0.26**	(0.05)	3.15	(0.07)	2.64	(0.06)	**0.51**	(0.09)
Korea	-0.22	(0.06)	-0.67	(0.04)	**0.45**	(0.07)	3.40	(0.06)	2.67	(0.04)	**0.73**	(0.08)
Luxembourg	-0.39	(0.08)	-0.70	(0.03)	**0.31**	(0.09)	3.41	(0.10)	2.39	(0.04)	**1.02**	(0.11)
Mexico	-0.80	(0.04)	-0.85	(0.03)	0.05	(0.05)	1.58	(0.04)	1.49	(0.03)	0.09	(0.05)
Netherlands	-0.76	(0.07)	-0.84	(0.04)	0.08	(0.09)	2.92	(0.10)	2.17	(0.06)	**0.75**	(0.11)
New Zealand	-0.58	(0.07)	-0.68	(0.04)	0.10	(0.09)	3.52	(0.09)	2.66	(0.05)	**0.86**	(0.10)
Norway	-0.09	(0.06)	-0.54	(0.05)	**0.46**	(0.08)	3.67	(0.09)	2.89	(0.06)	**0.77**	(0.10)
Poland	-0.29	(0.05)	-0.61	(0.04)	**0.32**	(0.06)	2.74	(0.06)	2.20	(0.04)	**0.54**	(0.07)
Portugal	-0.52	(0.06)	-0.75	(0.04)	**0.22**	(0.06)	2.35	(0.07)	1.98	(0.06)	**0.37**	(0.10)
Slovak Republic	0.11	(0.06)	-0.18	(0.04)	**0.29**	(0.07)	3.24	(0.07)	2.36	(0.06)	**0.88**	(0.09)
Spain	-0.09	(0.04)	-0.44	(0.02)	**0.35**	(0.05)	3.33	(0.05)	2.46	(0.04)	**0.86**	(0.06)
Sweden	-0.37	(0.07)	-0.69	(0.06)	**0.32**	(0.11)	3.62	(0.09)	2.77	(0.06)	**0.85**	(0.09)
Switzerland	-0.54	(0.06)	-0.63	(0.03)	0.08	(0.06)	3.29	(0.08)	2.19	(0.04)	**1.11**	(0.09)
Turkey	-0.37	(0.06)	-0.66	(0.03)	**0.29**	(0.07)	2.09	(0.08)	1.70	(0.04)	**0.39**	(0.09)
United Kingdom	-0.53	(0.07)	-0.71	(0.03)	**0.18**	(0.08)	3.22	(0.12)	2.22	(0.04)	**1.00**	(0.13)
United States	-0.35	(0.07)	-0.66	(0.05)	**0.31**	(0.08)	3.09	(0.12)	2.04	(0.08)	**1.05**	(0.13)
OECD average	-0.34	(0.01)	-0.61	(0.01)	**0.28**	(0.01)	3.16	(0.02)	2.38	(0.01)	**0.78**	(0.02)

Partners
Country	Mean	S.E.	Mean	S.E.	Dif	S.E.	Mean	S.E.	Mean	S.E.	Dif	S.E.
Argentina	-0.55	(0.07)	-0.67	(0.03)	0.12	(0.07)	1.93	(0.09)	1.58	(0.04)	**0.35**	(0.10)
Azerbaijan	0.14	(0.08)	0.11	(0.06)	0.03	(0.10)	1.77	(0.08)	1.65	(0.06)	0.13	(0.09)
Brazil	-0.48	(0.06)	-0.40	(0.04)	-0.08	(0.08)	1.59	(0.06)	1.53	(0.03)	0.06	(0.07)
Bulgaria	0.15	(0.07)	-0.38	(0.04)	**0.53**	(0.09)	2.79	(0.09)	1.73	(0.05)	**1.06**	(0.10)
Chile	-0.49	(0.06)	-0.56	(0.03)	0.07	(0.06)	2.07	(0.10)	1.70	(0.04)	**0.37**	(0.10)
Colombia	-0.43	(0.08)	-0.49	(0.05)	0.07	(0.09)	1.68	(0.08)	1.45	(0.06)	0.22	(0.09)
Croatia	-0.58	(0.05)	-0.85	(0.03)	**0.27**	(0.06)	2.06	(0.06)	1.63	(0.03)	**0.44**	(0.07)
Estonia	0.11	(0.06)	-0.07	(0.05)	**0.18**	(0.08)	3.79	(0.09)	2.98	(0.07)	**0.81**	(0.11)
Hong Kong-China	-0.66	(0.04)	-0.89	(0.03)	**0.24**	(0.05)	2.20	(0.06)	1.73	(0.04)	**0.47**	(0.07)
Indonesia	-1.05	(0.04)	-0.91	(0.04)	-0.14	(0.05)	1.94	(0.05)	1.93	(0.05)	0.01	(0.06)
Israel	-0.16	(0.07)	-0.45	(0.04)	**0.29**	(0.08)	3.26	(0.12)	2.73	(0.08)	**0.53**	(0.14)
Jordan	-0.59	(0.05)	-0.71	(0.04)	0.13	(0.06)	1.79	(0.06)	1.76	(0.04)	0.03	(0.06)
Kyrgyzstan	-0.19	(0.05)	-0.35	(0.04)	**0.16**	(0.07)	1.65	(0.06)	1.51	(0.04)	0.13	(0.07)
Latvia	0.24	(0.07)	-0.05	(0.05)	**0.30**	(0.09)	3.55	(0.09)	2.77	(0.08)	**0.79**	(0.11)
Lithuania	-0.04	(0.07)	-0.48	(0.04)	**0.44**	(0.07)	2.82	(0.09)	2.13	(0.04)	**0.69**	(0.09)
Macao-China	-0.72	(0.05)	-0.90	(0.03)	**0.17**	(0.05)	2.09	(0.07)	1.95	(0.06)	0.14	(0.09)
Montenegro	0.21	(0.06)	-0.20	(0.04)	**0.42**	(0.06)	2.32	(0.07)	1.87	(0.05)	**0.45**	(0.09)
Romania	0.43	(0.09)	-0.13	(0.06)	**0.56**	(0.10)	2.64	(0.08)	1.87	(0.05)	**0.77**	(0.09)
Russian Federation	0.31	(0.05)	0.14	(0.05)	**0.17**	(0.07)	3.10	(0.07)	2.56	(0.06)	**0.54**	(0.10)
Serbia	-0.05	(0.05)	-0.44	(0.04)	**0.38**	(0.07)	2.32	(0.07)	1.82	(0.05)	**0.49**	(0.09)
Slovenia	-0.05	(0.07)	-0.55	(0.04)	**0.50**	(0.08)	2.87	(0.09)	2.07	(0.04)	**0.79**	(0.10)
Chinese Taipei	-0.21	(0.05)	-0.60	(0.02)	**0.40**	(0.05)	2.72	(0.06)	2.04	(0.04)	**0.68**	(0.07)
Thailand	-0.45	(0.06)	-0.44	(0.04)	-0.01	(0.07)	1.94	(0.06)	1.77	(0.05)	**0.17**	(0.08)
Tunisia	-0.74	(0.05)	-0.91	(0.03)	**0.17**	(0.07)	1.52	(0.06)	1.47	(0.04)	0.05	(0.07)
Uruguay	-0.28	(0.07)	-0.64	(0.04)	**0.36**	(0.09)	2.17	(0.09)	1.74	(0.06)	**0.43**	(0.11)

Note: Values that are statistically different are indicated in bold.

[Part 3/3]
Table A1.3 Differences in the components of the economic, social and cultural status index

		\multicolumn{6}{c	}{Parental occupation}	\multicolumn{6}{c	}{Parental education}
		\multicolumn{2}{c	}{Resilient students}	\multicolumn{2}{c	}{Disadvantaged low achievers}	\multicolumn{2}{c	}{Difference in the mean index between resilient students and disadvantaged low achievers}	\multicolumn{2}{c	}{Resilient students}	\multicolumn{2}{c	}{Disadvantaged low achievers}	\multicolumn{2}{c	}{Difference in the mean index between resilient students and disadvantaged low achievers}
		Mean	S.E.	Mean	S.E.	Dif	S.E.	Mean	S.E.	Mean	S.E.	Dif	S.E.
OECD	Australia	38.40	(0.41)	35.67	(0.27)	**2.72**	(0.50)	11.78	(0.08)	11.40	(0.06)	**0.39**	(0.10)
	Austria	33.68	(0.80)	32.64	(0.35)	1.04	(0.89)	12.34	(0.10)	11.72	(0.23)	**0.62**	(0.25)
	Belgium	34.51	(0.53)	33.17	(0.42)	**1.34**	(0.67)	11.90	(0.10)	10.94	(0.15)	**0.95**	(0.17)
	Canada	40.51	(0.46)	37.58	(0.36)	**2.93**	(0.61)	12.77	(0.11)	12.41	(0.09)	**0.36**	(0.14)
	Czech Republic	36.56	(0.55)	34.85	(0.37)	**1.71**	(0.60)	11.91	(0.11)	11.81	(0.10)	0.10	(0.15)
	Denmark	34.53	(0.80)	33.01	(0.38)	1.52	(0.84)	12.30	(0.15)	11.39	(0.13)	**0.91**	(0.20)
	Finland	33.32	(0.59)	33.08	(0.43)	0.24	(0.76)	12.82	(0.16)	12.28	(0.12)	**0.54**	(0.20)
	France	33.46	(0.77)	32.76	(0.44)	0.70	(0.90)	10.31	(0.23)	10.18	(0.14)	0.14	(0.26)
	Germany	34.75	(0.73)	34.04	(0.33)	0.71	(0.81)	12.48	(0.15)	10.94	(0.18)	**1.54**	(0.25)
	Greece	33.33	(0.78)	32.11	(0.35)	1.22	(0.83)	10.72	(0.16)	9.73	(0.13)	**0.99**	(0.20)
	Hungary	35.30	(0.73)	33.84	(0.36)	1.45	(0.83)	11.04	(0.11)	10.26	(0.08)	**0.78**	(0.14)
	Iceland	37.48	(0.81)	37.97	(0.51)	-0.49	(0.96)	12.95	(0.18)	12.00	(0.14)	**0.94**	(0.24)
	Ireland	33.58	(0.70)	33.52	(0.39)	0.06	(0.81)	11.20	(0.14)	10.85	(0.11)	0.35	(0.18)
	Italy	33.82	(0.46)	32.21	(0.36)	**1.61**	(0.59)	9.24	(0.11)	8.91	(0.09)	**0.33**	(0.15)
	Japan	39.19	(0.48)	38.84	(0.34)	0.35	(0.62)	12.68	(0.09)	12.02	(0.06)	**0.66**	(0.10)
	Korea	37.56	(0.69)	39.17	(0.41)	-1.60	(0.75)	11.27	(0.12)	10.96	(0.10)	0.31	(0.15)
	Luxembourg	35.96	(1.09)	30.98	(0.32)	**4.98**	(1.16)	9.01	(0.32)	7.92	(0.16)	**1.09**	(0.36)
	Mexico	26.38	(0.39)	26.17	(0.48)	0.22	(0.60)	6.40	(0.15)	5.75	(0.12)	**0.65**	(0.20)
	Netherlands	39.02	(0.73)	35.31	(0.50)	**3.71**	(0.89)	11.37	(0.12)	10.89	(0.16)	**0.48**	(0.21)
	New Zealand	37.40	(0.84)	35.86	(0.44)	1.54	(1.01)	11.32	(0.15)	10.87	(0.11)	**0.45**	(0.20)
	Norway	39.33	(0.59)	38.61	(0.44)	0.72	(0.73)	12.61	(0.15)	12.31	(0.11)	0.30	(0.16)
	Poland	30.97	(0.52)	31.03	(0.37)	-0.07	(0.58)	11.18	(0.07)	10.72	(0.06)	**0.47**	(0.08)
	Portugal	30.17	(0.52)	28.56	(0.33)	**1.61**	(0.53)	4.56	(0.13)	4.45	(0.08)	0.11	(0.16)
	Slovak Republic	34.46	(0.50)	31.74	(0.49)	**2.72**	(0.66)	11.88	(0.06)	11.48	(0.14)	**0.40**	(0.16)
	Spain	31.52	(0.51)	30.99	(0.31)	0.52	(0.63)	7.26	(0.18)	6.51	(0.10)	**0.75**	(0.20)
	Sweden	37.68	(0.61)	35.04	(0.42)	**2.64**	(0.74)	12.12	(0.16)	11.84	(0.15)	0.28	(0.24)
	Switzerland	35.44	(0.63)	34.21	(0.32)	1.23	(0.65)	11.21	(0.15)	10.09	(0.11)	**1.12**	(0.17)
	Turkey	26.95	(0.82)	28.49	(0.63)	-1.54	(0.98)	5.52	(0.12)	5.61	(0.15)	-0.09	(0.20)
	United Kingdom	38.76	(0.87)	34.34	(0.36)	**4.41**	(0.81)	12.35	(0.09)	11.90	(0.12)	**0.45**	(0.16)
	United States	36.66	(0.79)	34.92	(0.42)	1.74	(0.93)	12.08	(0.13)	11.38	(0.20)	**0.70**	(0.22)
	OECD average	**35.15**	**(0.13)**	**33.65**	**(0.09)**	**1.51**	**(0.14)**	**10.95**	**(0.04)**	**10.29**	**(0.04)**	**0.66**	**(0.05)**
Partners	Argentina	33.21	(0.69)	31.85	(0.54)	1.35	(0.93)	7.51	(0.23)	7.11	(0.18)	0.40	(0.29)
	Azerbaijan	31.11	(0.79)	31.39	(0.60)	-0.28	(0.87)	11.26	(0.10)	11.00	(0.11)	0.25	(0.14)
	Brazil	26.12	(0.98)	24.49	(0.53)	1.63	(1.10)	5.31	(0.18)	4.94	(0.09)	0.37	(0.21)
	Bulgaria	33.44	(0.58)	32.06	(0.34)	**1.38**	(0.67)	11.62	(0.12)	10.87	(0.13)	**0.75**	(0.17)
	Chile	26.13	(0.67)	26.55	(0.52)	-0.42	(0.81)	8.45	(0.30)	7.80	(0.11)	**0.65**	(0.32)
	Colombia	28.73	(1.27)	28.12	(0.66)	0.62	(1.50)	5.98	(0.40)	5.80	(0.16)	0.17	(0.46)
	Croatia	34.85	(0.54)	33.43	(0.36)	**1.43**	(0.59)	11.48	(0.10)	11.23	(0.10)	0.25	(0.15)
	Estonia	34.84	(0.59)	33.52	(0.38)	**1.33**	(0.68)	12.15	(0.07)	12.28	(0.09)	-0.13	(0.12)
	Hong Kong-China	31.90	(0.53)	30.95	(0.38)	0.94	(0.60)	7.50	(0.12)	7.22	(0.11)	0.28	(0.15)
	Indonesia	25.28	(0.73)	25.48	(0.53)	-0.20	(0.84)	6.09	(0.16)	6.08	(0.10)	0.02	(0.19)
	Israel	37.70	(1.17)	36.95	(0.71)	0.76	(1.34)	12.50	(0.21)	11.65	(0.14)	**0.85**	(0.23)
	Jordan	33.86	(0.85)	33.68	(0.68)	0.18	(1.07)	9.97	(0.24)	8.90	(0.23)	**1.08**	(0.31)
	Kyrgyzstan	32.62	(0.55)	31.20	(0.48)	1.42	(0.75)	11.36	(0.14)	11.27	(0.12)	0.09	(0.17)
	Latvia	33.31	(0.72)	32.85	(0.47)	0.46	(0.69)	11.05	(0.09)	11.05	(0.11)	-0.00	(0.13)
	Lithuania	34.08	(0.66)	32.09	(0.34)	**1.99**	(0.81)	11.41	(0.09)	11.50	(0.07)	-0.09	(0.12)
	Macao-China	30.81	(0.48)	30.47	(0.42)	0.35	(0.61)	7.16	(0.14)	6.82	(0.11)	0.33	(0.17)
	Montenegro	36.99	(0.74)	34.21	(0.45)	**2.78**	(0.90)	11.51	(0.12)	11.16	(0.11)	**0.34**	(0.17)
	Romania	31.34	(0.77)	29.36	(0.93)	1.98	(1.17)	12.34	(0.12)	11.24	(0.21)	**1.10**	(0.25)
	Russian Federation	34.34	(0.62)	33.56	(0.38)	0.79	(0.83)	12.18	(0.07)	12.13	(0.05)	0.05	(0.09)
	Serbia	35.59	(0.78)	34.02	(0.51)	1.56	(0.89)	10.95	(0.09)	10.70	(0.08)	**0.25**	(0.10)
	Slovenia	34.92	(0.56)	34.95	(0.34)	-0.02	(0.66)	10.89	(0.12)	10.50	(0.10)	**0.38**	(0.17)
	Chinese Taipei	33.17	(0.36)	33.05	(0.39)	0.12	(0.55)	10.48	(0.10)	9.94	(0.10)	**0.54**	(0.15)
	Thailand	24.44	(0.34)	24.14	(0.25)	0.30	(0.42)	5.91	(0.12)	5.82	(0.09)	0.08	(0.15)
	Tunisia	23.29	(0.42)	23.42	(0.37)	-0.13	(0.50)	6.25	(0.19)	6.29	(0.13)	-0.05	(0.22)
	Uruguay	30.97	(0.73)	29.09	(0.53)	**1.88**	(0.86)	8.22	(0.23)	7.49	(0.15)	**0.72**	(0.26)

Note: Values that are statistically different are indicated in bold.

Table A1.4 **Performance in PISA science, system average, resilient and disadvantaged low achievers**

			Performance in PISA Science Scale			
			All students		Disadvantaged low achievers		Resilient students
		Mean score	S.E	Mean score	S.E	Mean score	S.E
OECD	Australia	528	(2.2)	414	(3.6)	615	(6.4)
	Austria	511	(3.9)	392	(5.8)	604	(5.5)
	Belgium	512	(2.5)	394	(4.1)	602	(5.0)
	Canada	536	(1.9)	430	(4.0)	619	(6.3)
	Czech Republic	513	(3.5)	402	(5.0)	595	(6.9)
	Denmark	497	(3.1)	391	(4.5)	579	(6.1)
	Finland	564	(2.0)	469	(4.2)	642	(6.1)
	France	497	(3.3)	379	(4.3)	582	(7.1)
	Germany	518	(3.7)	402	(4.7)	603	(6.5)
	Greece	474	(3.2)	368	(4.7)	551	(6.7)
	Hungary	504	(2.6)	402	(3.5)	577	(6.9)
	Iceland	492	(1.7)	386	(4.3)	579	(6.3)
	Ireland	509	(3.2)	402	(4.7)	594	(6.2)
	Italy	476	(2.0)	370	(3.7)	562	(5.0)
	Japan	533	(3.4)	418	(5.0)	619	(6.9)
	Korea	522	(3.4)	422	(5.5)	602	(6.3)
	Luxembourg	487	(1.0)	372	(3.1)	571	(6.1)
	Mexico	410	(2.7)	325	(4.9)	474	(6.9)
	Netherlands	526	(2.6)	413	(4.2)	611	(6.3)
	New Zealand	533	(2.6)	407	(4.2)	626	(6.6)
	Norway	489	(2.7)	387	(4.9)	575	(6.6)
	Poland	498	(2.3)	398	(4.0)	580	(6.1)
	Portugal	475	(3.0)	377	(4.0)	553	(5.7)
	Slovak Republic	489	(2.6)	380	(4.9)	570	(6.3)
	Spain	489	(2.6)	386	(4.0)	570	(5.4)
	Sweden	505	(2.4)	400	(4.1)	586	(6.6)
	Switzerland	512	(3.2)	395	(3.6)	599	(6.3)
	Turkey	424	(3.8)	339	(6.2)	487	(6.6)
	United Kingdom	518	(2.2)	399	(4.0)	612	(6.0)
	United States	490	(4.2)	370	(4.5)	583	(7.4)
	OECD average	**501**	**(0.5)**	**393**	**(0.8)**	**584**	**(1.2)**
Partners	Argentina	392	(6.0)	282	(7.0)	469	(9.0)
	Azerbaijan	383	(2.8)	332	(5.0)	436	(8.7)
	Brazil	391	(2.8)	299	(6.1)	458	(8.2)
	Bulgaria	435	(6.1)	316	(6.1)	529	(7.2)
	Chile	438	(4.4)	340	(5.0)	510	(7.9)
	Colombia	388	(3.4)	302	(6.3)	453	(8.6)
	Croatia	493	(2.4)	400	(4.2)	566	(5.6)
	Estonia	532	(2.5)	439	(4.2)	607	(6.3)
	Hong Kong-China	542	(2.4)	438	(4.6)	628	(5.5)
	Indonesia	393	(5.7)	328	(5.8)	450	(9.4)
	Israel	457	(3.7)	339	(6.1)	558	(7.8)
	Jordan	423	(2.8)	333	(5.3)	495	(7.3)
	Kyrgyzstan	322	(2.9)	243	(8.3)	380	(9.8)
	Latvia	490	(2.9)	397	(4.9)	564	(6.8)
	Lithuania	488	(2.8)	385	(3.5)	569	(6.1)
	Macao-China	511	(1.1)	428	(4.6)	585	(5.9)
	Montenegro	412	(1.1)	329	(4.4)	484	(6.2)
	Romania	418	(4.2)	332	(4.9)	489	(7.4)
	Russian Federation	480	(3.7)	384	(5.2)	557	(7.1)
	Serbia	436	(3.0)	343	(5.2)	511	(6.4)
	Slovenia	519	(1.1)	407	(3.6)	605	(6.8)
	Chinese Taipei	533	(3.6)	424	(3.7)	616	(6.3)
	Thailand	421	(2.1)	346	(6.1)	480	(6.8)
	Tunisia	386	(2.9)	307	(6.8)	452	(7.8)
	Uruguay	429	(2.7)	327	(5.0)	505	(7.1)

ANNEX A1

Table A1.5 Percentage of resilient students and disadvantaged low achievers above and below the basic level of proficiency

Proficiency in science

		Resilient students						Disadvantaged low achievers					
		Below Level 2		From Level 2 to Level 3		From Level 4 to Level 6		Below Level 2		From Level 2 to Level 3		From Level 4 to Level 6	
		%	S.E.	%	S.E.	%	S.E.	%	S.E.	%	S.E.	%	S.E.
OECD	Australia	0.0	(0.0)	22.5	(1.4)	77.5	(1.4)	34.3	(1.4)	64.7	(1.4)	1.0	(0.3)
	Austria	0.0	(0.0)	27.9	(2.4)	72.1	(2.4)	47.3	(3.5)	52.6	(3.5)	0.0	(0.0)
	Belgium	0.0	(0.0)	27.0	(2.3)	73.0	(2.3)	47.3	(2.3)	52.5	(2.2)	0.1	(0.1)
	Canada	0.0	(0.0)	17.3	(2.1)	82.7	(2.1)	25.8	(1.4)	72.3	(1.4)	1.9	(0.5)
	Czech Republic	0.0	(0.0)	35.2	(2.9)	64.8	(2.9)	41.4	(2.5)	58.5	(2.5)	0.0	(0.0)
	Denmark	0.0	(0.0)	51.2	(3.0)	48.7	(3.0)	48.7	(2.5)	51.3	(2.5)	0.0	(0.0)
	Finland	0.0	(0.0)	6.1	(1.3)	93.9	(1.3)	11.3	(1.4)	81.8	(2.1)	7.0	(1.3)
	France	0.0	(0.0)	47.3	(3.7)	52.7	(3.7)	55.3	(2.4)	44.7	(2.4)	0.0	(0.0)
	Germany	0.0	(0.0)	28.5	(2.8)	71.5	(2.8)	41.6	(3.0)	58.2	(2.9)	0.0	(0.0)
	Greece	0.0	(0.0)	72.6	(2.7)	27.3	(2.7)	61.4	(2.3)	38.5	(2.2)	0.0	(0.0)
	Hungary	0.7	(0.0)	48.8	(3.4)	51.2	(3.4)	42.2	(2.2)	57.6	(2.2)	0.0	(0.0)
	Iceland	0.0	(0.0)	50.8	(4.1)	49.1	(4.0)	49.3	(2.2)	50.6	(2.2)	0.0	(0.0)
	Ireland	0.0	(0.0)	38.1	(2.5)	61.9	(2.5)	40.1	(2.9)	59.6	(2.9)	0.3	(0.2)
	Italy	0.0	(0.0)	65.1	(1.7)	34.8	(1.7)	62.5	(1.7)	37.5	(1.7)	0.0	(0.0)
	Japan	0.0	(0.0)	18.3	(2.8)	81.7	(2.8)	32.3	(2.6)	66.2	(2.6)	1.5	(0.4)
	Korea	0.0	(0.0)	28.3	(1.9)	71.7	(1.9)	28.9	(3.1)	69.9	(3.0)	1.2	(0.4)
	Luxembourg	0.0	(0.0)	57.4	(3.4)	42.5	(3.4)	61.5	(1.8)	38.5	(1.8)	0.0	(0.0)
	Mexico	14.1	(1.7)	83.8	(1.6)	2.0	(0.6)	93.3	(0.9)	6.7	(0.9)	0.0	(0.0)
	Netherlands	0.0	(0.0)	21.3	(3.0)	78.7	(3.0)	36.8	(3.0)	62.9	(3.0)	0.3	(0.2)
	New Zealand	0.0	(0.0)	15.3	(2.6)	84.7	(2.6)	37.8	(2.2)	61.5	(2.3)	0.6	(0.4)
	Norway	0.0	(0.0)	56.8	(2.8)	43.2	(2.8)	49.2	(2.2)	50.7	(2.2)	0.0	(0.0)
	Poland	0.0	(0.0)	49.6	(2.7)	50.4	(2.7)	44.5	(2.2)	55.5	(2.2)	0.0	(0.0)
	Portugal	0.0	(0.0)	71.4	(2.7)	28.5	(2.7)	60.8	(2.0)	39.2	(2.0)	0.0	(0.0)
	Slovak Republic	0.0	(0.0)	56.8	(3.5)	43.2	(3.5)	54.9	(2.2)	45.0	(2.3)	0.0	(0.0)
	Spain	0.0	(0.0)	58.4	(2.1)	41.6	(2.1)	49.6	(1.8)	50.4	(1.8)	0.0	(0.0)
	Sweden	0.0	(0.0)	43.6	(3.0)	56.3	(3.0)	42.0	(2.0)	57.9	(2.0)	0.0	(0.0)
	Switzerland	0.0	(0.0)	32.7	(2.3)	67.3	(2.3)	45.7	(1.7)	54.3	(1.7)	0.1	(0.1)
	Turkey	8.1	(1.4)	87.3	(1.8)	4.6	(1.2)	87.6	(2.0)	12.4	(2.0)	0.0	(0.0)
	United Kingdom	0.0	(0.0)	24.2	(2.3)	75.8	(2.3)	42.6	(1.9)	57.2	(1.9)	0.3	(0.2)
	United States	0.0	(0.0)	50.3	(3.4)	49.6	(3.5)	62.7	(2.7)	37.3	(2.7)	0.0	(0.0)
	OECD average	0.7	(0.1)	43.1	(0.5)	56.1	(0.5)	48.0	(0.4)	51.5	(0.4)	0.5	(0.1)
Partners	Argentina	20.8	(3.0)	76.2	(3.2)	3.0	(1.2)	96.8	(0.6)	3.2	(0.6)	0.0	(0.0)
	Azerbaijan	51.0	(4.2)	48.3	(3.9)	0.7	(0.6)	97.5	(0.8)	2.5	(0.8)	0.0	(0.0)
	Brazil	27.5	(4.5)	70.4	(4.3)	2.0	(0.8)	97.2	(0.7)	2.8	(0.7)	0.0	(0.0)
	Bulgaria	2.8	(1.1)	79.0	(3.6)	18.2	(3.1)	91.2	(1.4)	8.8	(1.4)	0.0	(0.0)
	Chile	4.1	(1.5)	86.0	(3.0)	10.0	(2.6)	85.4	(1.8)	14.6	(1.8)	0.0	(0.0)
	Colombia	30.0	(3.9)	68.7	(3.9)	1.3	(0.9)	96.6	(0.9)	3.4	(0.9)	0.0	(0.0)
	Croatia	0.0	(0.0)	61.4	(2.3)	38.6	(2.4)	42.5	(2.0)	57.5	(2.0)	0.0	(0.0)
	Estonia	0.0	(0.0)	24.8	(3.7)	75.2	(3.7)	20.0	(2.0)	78.8	(2.0)	1.2	(0.6)
	Hong Kong-China	0.0	(0.0)	11.6	(2.3)	88.4	(2.3)	23.2	(2.3)	73.8	(2.6)	3.1	(0.9)
	Indonesia	30.7	(2.8)	68.1	(2.8)	1.2	(1.3)	96.3	(0.8)	3.7	(0.8)	0.0	(0.0)
	Israel	1.4	(0.8)	64.7	(3.6)	33.9	(3.5)	79.6	(2.4)	20.3	(2.5)	0.0	(0.0)
	Jordan	7.1	(1.5)	86.5	(2.2)	6.4	(1.6)	87.8	(1.3)	12.2	(1.3)	0.0	(0.0)
	Kyrgyzstan	85.2	(2.1)	14.7	(2.1)	0.2	(0.2)	99.8	(0.2)	0.2	(0.2)	0.0	(0.0)
	Latvia	0.0	(0.0)	64.0	(3.3)	35.9	(3.4)	43.4	(2.8)	56.4	(2.8)	0.0	(0.0)
	Lithuania	0.0	(0.0)	59.1	(3.2)	40.9	(3.2)	55.4	(2.2)	44.6	(2.1)	0.0	(0.0)
	Macao-China	0.0	(0.0)	44.6	(3.1)	55.4	(3.1)	24.3	(2.3)	75.3	(2.3)	0.0	(0.0)
	Montenegro	11.3	(1.6)	84.7	(2.2)	4.0	(1.3)	92.7	(1.1)	7.3	(1.1)	0.0	(0.0)
	Romania	8.6	(2.2)	87.4	(2.2)	4.0	(1.6)	90.3	(1.7)	9.7	(1.7)	0.0	(0.0)
	Russian Federation	0.0	(0.0)	68.7	(3.1)	31.2	(3.1)	52.3	(2.0)	47.6	(2.0)	0.0	(0.0)
	Serbia	2.7	(0.8)	87.1	(1.9)	10.3	(1.9)	82.9	(1.8)	17.1	(1.8)	0.0	(0.0)
	Slovenia	0.0	(0.0)	29.5	(2.9)	70.5	(2.9)	38.9	(2.1)	60.8	(2.0)	0.3	(0.3)
	Chinese Taipei	0.0	(0.0)	17.4	(1.9)	82.6	(1.9)	31.5	(2.3)	67.4	(2.2)	1.1	(0.5)
	Thailand	9.6	(1.6)	87.8	(1.7)	2.6	(0.9)	85.8	(1.5)	14.2	(1.5)	0.0	(0.0)
	Tunisia	31.6	(2.4)	67.3	(2.5)	1.1	(0.6)	96.7	(0.9)	3.3	(0.9)	0.0	(0.0)
	Uruguay	4.1	(1.5)	88.6	(2.1)	7.3	(1.6)	87.5	(1.8)	12.5	(1.8)	0.0	(0.0)

© OECD 2011 Against the Odds: Disadvantaged Students Who Succeed in School

[Part 1/2]
Table A1.6 Overlap of student resilience by subject

		\multicolumn{8}{c}{Students who are resilient in science}
		Resilient in science, mathematics and reading		Resilient in science and mathematics		Resilient in science and reading		Resilient only in science	
		%	S.E.	%	S.E.	%	S.E.	%	S.E.
OECD	Australia	54.4	(2.3)	16.4	(2.8)	14.9	(1.8)	14.2	(2.0)
	Austria	57.1	(3.9)	17.1	(3.4)	14.9	(3.1)	10.9	(2.2)
	Belgium	59.0	(3.5)	16.5	(2.3)	13.2	(2.5)	11.2	(2.2)
	Canada	49.4	(2.4)	20.7	(2.6)	14.5	(2.0)	15.4	(2.1)
	Czech Republic	52.4	(6.0)	18.1	(3.5)	16.4	(3.4)	13.1	(3.4)
	Denmark	56.0	(3.5)	17.7	(3.0)	15.3	(3.2)	11.0	(3.0)
	Finland	47.0	(3.2)	20.7	(3.0)	17.6	(2.3)	14.7	(2.8)
	France	46.5	(4.7)	22.8	(4.1)	16.2	(3.4)	14.5	(2.9)
	Germany	53.8	(3.5)	15.9	(3.3)	17.1	(3.1)	13.3	(3.2)
	Greece	45.8	(6.0)	16.4	(3.4)	21.7	(3.9)	16.2	(3.9)
	Hungary	47.7	(4.7)	20.3	(4.1)	16.4	(3.7)	15.6	(3.2)
	Iceland	56.8	(4.1)	14.1	(3.7)	13.0	(3.4)	16.1	(2.9)
	Ireland	53.0	(4.5)	15.4	(2.8)	16.4	(2.7)	15.2	(3.3)
	Italy	50.7	(2.7)	21.2	(1.9)	13.4	(2.3)	14.7	(2.0)
	Japan	48.0	(3.5)	15.9	(3.5)	18.7	(2.5)	17.5	(2.6)
	Korea	53.4	(4.1)	15.3	(2.7)	18.3	(3.7)	13.1	(2.1)
	Luxembourg	52.7	(5.2)	19.5	(4.6)	15.4	(3.7)	12.4	(2.9)
	Mexico	44.1	(3.4)	21.9	(3.2)	14.8	(2.4)	19.2	(3.5)
	Netherlands	59.3	(5.1)	16.8	(3.6)	13.4	(3.3)	10.5	(3.4)
	New Zealand	53.4	(3.7)	21.7	(3.7)	13.9	(2.6)	11.0	(2.4)
	Norway	53.2	(4.9)	20.0	(3.6)	13.6	(3.9)	13.2	(3.8)
	Poland	53.4	(3.0)	18.3	(2.8)	14.0	(2.8)	14.3	(2.5)
	Portugal	52.8	(3.4)	21.2	(2.8)	12.6	(2.6)	13.5	(2.8)
	Slovak Republic	53.4	(3.8)	16.6	(3.2)	16.9	(2.8)	13.1	(2.9)
	Spain	53.2	(3.0)	19.7	(3.0)	14.7	(1.9)	12.4	(2.1)
	Sweden	51.5	(4.7)	16.8	(3.0)	16.0	(2.7)	15.6	(2.9)
	Switzerland	56.4	(3.4)	16.7	(2.9)	15.1	(3.4)	11.8	(2.3)
	Turkey	44.5	(3.7)	21.0	(3.6)	16.6	(2.9)	18.0	(4.0)
	United Kingdom	54.4	(3.3)	17.3	(2.4)	14.0	(2.3)	14.3	(2.3)
	United States	m	m	m	m	m	m	m	m
	OECD average	52.2	(0.7)	18.3	(0.6)	15.5	(0.6)	14.0	(0.5)
Partners	Argentina	32.0	(4.2)	21.3	(5.5)	21.3	(4.0)	25.4	(5.2)
	Azerbaijan	39.5	(5.4)	28.0	(4.1)	13.6	(3.0)	18.9	(4.5)
	Brazil	39.4	(3.7)	19.6	(2.9)	14.9	(2.8)	26.1	(3.8)
	Bulgaria	46.9	(4.2)	17.4	(3.5)	15.3	(3.0)	20.5	(4.6)
	Chile	41.3	(4.6)	18.1	(3.0)	16.4	(2.9)	24.2	(4.4)
	Colombia	26.7	(4.9)	18.2	(4.3)	20.3	(3.5)	34.7	(4.6)
	Croatia	53.1	(4.2)	19.4	(2.9)	14.1	(2.9)	13.4	(2.7)
	Estonia	52.8	(3.7)	14.9	(2.5)	15.5	(2.9)	16.9	(3.3)
	Hong Kong-China	55.9	(3.9)	20.1	(2.3)	12.6	(2.2)	11.5	(2.8)
	Indonesia	47.2	(5.3)	16.3	(3.2)	12.2	(2.4)	24.3	(4.4)
	Israel	49.2	(4.9)	19.2	(3.5)	14.6	(3.5)	16.9	(3.7)
	Jordan	37.5	(3.8)	19.2	(2.6)	22.9	(3.3)	20.4	(2.7)
	Kyrgyzstan	29.5	(3.4)	20.2	(3.5)	17.9	(3.1)	32.3	(3.2)
	Latvia	47.0	(5.0)	19.1	(4.2)	18.2	(3.3)	15.7	(3.1)
	Lithuania	51.7	(3.5)	18.1	(3.2)	17.1	(3.0)	13.1	(3.3)
	Macao-China	48.4	(4.4)	22.8	(3.3)	14.7	(2.9)	14.2	(2.9)
	Montenegro	55.1	(3.2)	12.7	(2.7)	19.5	(3.0)	12.7	(2.7)
	Romania	53.0	(6.1)	18.3	(4.3)	13.0	(3.4)	15.7	(4.0)
	Russian Federation	41.4	(3.4)	20.5	(3.4)	17.8	(3.5)	20.3	(3.0)
	Serbia	48.4	(3.9)	20.3	(3.0)	15.4	(2.9)	15.9	(3.0)
	Slovenia	52.2	(4.8)	16.8	(3.5)	18.8	(4.2)	12.3	(2.6)
	Chinese Taipei	50.9	(3.3)	22.2	(3.0)	12.7	(1.8)	14.1	(1.8)
	Thailand	40.9	(3.8)	19.6	(3.1)	17.1	(2.6)	22.4	(3.0)
	Tunisia	35.0	(3.6)	15.2	(3.4)	22.3	(4.9)	27.5	(2.9)
	Uruguay	34.3	(4.1)	19.2	(4.7)	21.1	(3.5)	25.4	(3.5)

Table A1.6 Overlap of student resilience by subject [Part 2/2]

	Students who are resilient in mathematics								Students who are resilient in reading							
	Resilient in science, mathematics and reading		Resilient in reading and mathematics		Resilient in science and mathematics		Resilient only in mathematics		Resilient in science, mathematics and reading		Resilient in reading and mathematics		Resilient in science and reading		Resilient only in reading	
	%	S.E.	%	S.E.	%	S.E.	%	S.E.	%	S.E.	%	S.E.	%	S.E.	%	S.E.
OECD																
Australia	54.5	(2.3)	10.0	(1.7)	16.5	(2.8)	19.0	(2.1)	54.1	(2.4)	9.9	(1.6)	14.9	(1.7)	21.1	(2.1)
Austria	54.2	(4.6)	8.4	(2.0)	16.2	(3.1)	21.2	(4.3)	53.7	(4.2)	8.4	(1.9)	14.1	(3.1)	23.8	(3.9)
Belgium	58.6	(3.0)	8.1	(1.7)	16.6	(2.3)	16.8	(2.5)	54.3	(3.3)	7.5	(1.5)	12.0	(2.6)	26.2	(2.9)
Canada	46.9	(2.3)	10.5	(1.5)	19.7	(2.6)	23.0	(2.4)	49.4	(2.2)	11.0	(1.5)	14.7	(1.9)	24.9	(2.5)
Czech Republic	51.3	(4.8)	10.8	(3.5)	17.6	(3.4)	20.3	(3.3)	46.2	(4.9)	9.7	(3.1)	14.4	(3.0)	29.7	(3.2)
Denmark	54.9	(3.6)	9.2	(1.9)	17.4	(2.8)	18.5	(2.7)	50.7	(3.5)	8.5	(1.8)	13.7	(3.2)	27.1	(3.9)
Finland	50.8	(3.3)	8.3	(2.0)	22.6	(2.9)	18.3	(2.3)	47.4	(3.4)	7.7	(1.9)	17.7	(2.4)	27.2	(3.4)
France	45.4	(4.1)	8.8	(2.4)	22.2	(4.7)	23.5	(3.5)	41.1	(3.9)	8.0	(2.2)	14.4	(3.3)	36.5	(4.3)
Germany	54.8	(3.9)	12.8	(2.6)	16.3	(3.3)	16.1	(3.7)	45.8	(3.3)	10.7	(2.2)	14.7	(3.2)	28.8	(3.2)
Greece	44.9	(4.6)	12.1	(2.3)	16.1	(4.0)	26.9	(3.0)	39.4	(4.2)	10.6	(2.0)	19.1	(3.9)	30.9	(3.5)
Hungary	48.4	(5.7)	8.1	(3.1)	20.7	(3.9)	22.8	(5.9)	44.6	(5.1)	7.4	(2.9)	15.3	(3.9)	32.7	(6.8)
Iceland	58.3	(4.8)	10.7	(2.5)	14.6	(3.9)	16.5	(3.5)	52.7	(4.6)	9.7	(2.3)	12.2	(2.9)	25.4	(3.2)
Ireland	53.3	(4.0)	10.5	(3.2)	15.6	(2.8)	20.6	(3.0)	53.3	(4.1)	10.5	(3.0)	16.7	(2.9)	19.5	(3.3)
Italy	47.6	(2.5)	9.2	(1.5)	20.0	(1.9)	23.1	(2.2)	47.2	(3.0)	9.1	(1.5)	12.5	(2.5)	31.1	(3.1)
Japan	53.1	(4.3)	9.8	(2.3)	17.7	(3.9)	19.4	(2.9)	48.1	(3.0)	8.9	(2.3)	18.6	(2.5)	24.4	(3.6)
Korea	56.6	(3.8)	8.6	(2.3)	16.3	(2.9)	18.5	(2.7)	50.1	(4.0)	7.6	(1.9)	17.1	(3.5)	25.3	(2.9)
Luxembourg	49.2	(4.3)	10.5	(2.8)	18.2	(4.8)	22.1	(4.8)	52.1	(4.9)	11.1	(2.8)	15.1	(3.8)	21.7	(3.1)
Mexico	40.1	(3.9)	12.5	(1.8)	19.9	(2.8)	27.5	(3.1)	39.3	(3.1)	12.3	(2.1)	13.2	(2.3)	35.3	(4.1)
Netherlands	57.6	(4.2)	11.3	(2.1)	16.1	(3.6)	15.0	(2.3)	56.0	(4.3)	11.0	(1.9)	12.6	(3.4)	20.4	(3.0)
New Zealand	52.4	(4.3)	7.3	(1.9)	21.2	(3.7)	19.1	(2.9)	53.2	(3.6)	7.4	(2.0)	14.0	(2.5)	25.5	(2.9)
Norway	51.7	(4.2)	11.0	(2.1)	19.5	(3.7)	17.8	(3.2)	51.1	(4.7)	10.9	(2.3)	12.9	(3.8)	25.1	(5.2)
Poland	55.1	(3.4)	7.9	(1.9)	19.0	(2.8)	18.0	(2.7)	52.3	(3.0)	7.6	(2.0)	13.9	(2.8)	26.3	(3.3)
Portugal	50.8	(3.5)	7.1	(3.4)	20.3	(2.6)	21.8	(4.0)	55.6	(3.7)	7.7	(3.7)	13.1	(2.6)	23.6	(3.9)
Slovak Republic	52.5	(3.8)	11.0	(2.8)	16.5	(3.5)	20.0	(3.9)	48.2	(3.7)	10.1	(2.7)	15.2	(2.4)	26.4	(3.1)
Spain	50.0	(3.1)	11.8	(2.2)	18.5	(2.7)	19.8	(2.4)	47.2	(2.5)	11.1	(2.1)	13.1	(1.8)	28.7	(2.2)
Sweden	53.5	(4.9)	10.7	(2.5)	17.5	(3.3)	18.3	(3.4)	49.7	(4.8)	9.9	(2.4)	15.6	(2.7)	24.8	(4.1)
Switzerland	50.5	(3.5)	11.4	(2.2)	15.0	(2.5)	23.1	(3.0)	51.7	(3.0)	11.6	(2.3)	14.0	(3.2)	22.6	(3.1)
Turkey	44.2	(4.9)	9.5	(2.4)	21.0	(3.1)	25.3	(4.8)	41.1	(3.6)	8.9	(2.1)	15.3	(2.6)	34.7	(3.8)
United Kingdom	53.2	(3.0)	9.8	(1.9)	16.8	(2.5)	20.2	(3.6)	51.2	(3.3)	9.5	(1.7)	13.2	(2.1)	26.1	(2.9)
United States	m	m	m	m	m	m	m	m	m	m	m	m	m	m	m	m
OECD average	52.2	(0.7)	10.6	(0.4)	18.1	(0.6)	20.4	(0.6)	47.9	(0.7)	9.3	(0.4)	14.3	(0.5)	28.5	(0.6)
Partners																
Argentina	30.7	(3.8)	16.0	(3.4)	20.3	(5.0)	33.0	(4.5)	26.5	(3.6)	13.8	(2.8)	17.8	(3.4)	42.0	(5.5)
Azerbaijan	31.3	(4.8)	8.3	(2.4)	22.4	(3.5)	37.9	(4.9)	43.6	(6.0)	11.6	(3.0)	15.2	(3.1)	29.6	(5.3)
Brazil	40.9	(4.2)	13.2	(3.3)	20.3	(3.3)	25.6	(2.8)	36.1	(3.7)	11.7	(3.1)	13.6	(2.7)	38.7	(4.4)
Bulgaria	45.1	(3.9)	9.5	(2.4)	16.6	(3.4)	28.9	(4.2)	44.7	(4.8)	9.4	(2.2)	14.3	(2.5)	31.7	(4.2)
Chile	44.6	(4.1)	10.3	(2.8)	19.5	(3.3)	25.7	(4.2)	36.8	(3.5)	8.5	(2.5)	14.8	(3.0)	40.0	(4.2)
Colombia	27.7	(6.4)	16.2	(6.2)	19.2	(4.0)	36.9	(6.5)	25.7	(5.6)	14.9	(5.2)	20.0	(3.9)	39.4	(4.9)
Croatia	51.0	(4.1)	9.5	(1.9)	19.0	(3.0)	20.5	(3.0)	52.9	(3.8)	9.9	(2.0)	14.2	(2.6)	23.0	(2.7)
Estonia	58.2	(4.0)	8.4	(2.5)	16.5	(2.9)	16.8	(3.6)	50.8	(4.6)	7.4	(2.4)	15.0	(2.8)	26.8	(5.0)
Hong Kong-China	55.2	(3.1)	9.1	(2.0)	19.9	(2.3)	15.8	(3.0)	55.2	(3.5)	9.0	(1.9)	12.4	(2.3)	23.3	(2.9)
Indonesia	47.6	(5.7)	13.3	(3.1)	16.5	(3.1)	22.6	(4.0)	48.0	(5.3)	13.4	(3.1)	12.4	(2.5)	26.2	(4.0)
Israel	47.0	(4.4)	11.6	(3.0)	18.6	(3.2)	22.7	(3.3)	44.8	(3.9)	11.1	(3.0)	13.7	(3.5)	30.4	(4.4)
Jordan	39.0	(3.0)	11.4	(2.8)	20.3	(3.0)	29.3	(4.1)	34.8	(3.8)	10.1	(2.3)	21.4	(3.0)	33.7	(3.1)
Kyrgyzstan	32.3	(3.8)	14.7	(2.8)	22.3	(3.5)	30.6	(3.7)	31.4	(3.4)	14.3	(2.6)	19.1	(3.2)	35.1	(4.4)
Latvia	50.4	(5.7)	9.8	(2.4)	20.6	(4.3)	19.3	(3.8)	45.3	(4.3)	8.8	(2.2)	17.7	(3.3)	28.2	(3.7)
Lithuania	54.9	(3.9)	7.9	(2.9)	19.2	(3.4)	18.0	(3.7)	49.2	(3.4)	7.1	(2.4)	16.3	(3.3)	27.4	(3.5)
Macao-China	48.3	(3.5)	10.3	(2.6)	22.6	(3.4)	18.8	(3.1)	48.4	(4.0)	10.3	(2.2)	14.8	(3.1)	26.6	(3.5)
Montenegro	57.7	(3.7)	7.7	(2.5)	13.4	(2.8)	21.3	(3.8)	54.4	(3.5)	7.3	(2.4)	19.0	(3.1)	19.3	(4.9)
Romania	49.2	(5.4)	8.9	(3.3)	17.1	(4.7)	24.7	(4.6)	44.0	(5.2)	8.0	(2.8)	11.0	(3.3)	37.0	(4.8)
Russian Federation	40.8	(3.5)	10.8	(2.4)	20.6	(3.7)	27.7	(3.3)	40.4	(3.6)	10.7	(2.5)	17.5	(3.3)	31.4	(3.3)
Serbia	48.1	(4.3)	8.3	(2.5)	20.1	(3.0)	23.5	(3.4)	51.9	(4.2)	9.0	(2.8)	16.6	(3.1)	22.5	(3.5)
Slovenia	51.0	(5.8)	7.7	(2.9)	16.8	(3.0)	24.6	(3.7)	47.0	(4.7)	7.2	(3.0)	17.1	(3.6)	28.7	(3.5)
Chinese Taipei	50.8	(3.6)	9.1	(1.7)	22.2	(3.0)	17.9	(2.8)	52.8	(4.3)	9.4	(1.7)	13.2	(1.7)	24.6	(3.5)
Thailand	39.1	(3.9)	11.5	(2.4)	18.6	(3.3)	30.8	(4.2)	41.6	(3.5)	12.2	(2.4)	17.4	(2.6)	28.9	(3.0)
Tunisia	44.3	(4.0)	10.3	(2.2)	19.2	(4.0)	26.2	(6.2)	35.1	(4.2)	8.2	(1.8)	22.5	(4.5)	34.2	(3.9)
Uruguay	33.9	(5.6)	14.2	(3.7)	18.7	(3.8)	33.2	(4.6)	31.8	(4.5)	13.5	(4.4)	19.4	(2.7)	35.3	(4.3)

Table A1.7 — Percentage of male students among resilient, low achievers and all disadvantaged students

	Proportion of males among disadvantaged students		Science — Resilient students		Science — Disadvantaged low achievers		Reading — Resilient students		Reading — Disadvantaged low achievers		Mathematics — Resilient students		Mathematics — Disadvantaged low achievers	
	%	S.E	%	S.E	%	S.E	%	S.E	%	S.E	%	S.E	%	S.E
OECD														
Australia	51.5	(1.2)	53.2	(1.6)	50.5	(1.5)	40.8	(1.5)	57.5	(1.4)	56.8	(1.5)	48.8	(1.4)
Austria	50.1	(2.7)	52.9	(3.9)	47.8	(2.8)	40.0	(3.4)	55.3	(3.3)	57.7	(4.3)	45.6	(2.8)
Belgium	50.9	(2.2)	54.1	(2.4)	50.9	(2.7)	41.6	(2.3)	56.0	(2.7)	53.3	(2.6)	49.6	(2.6)
Canada	51.3	(0.8)	52.8	(1.5)	50.7	(1.1)	42.1	(1.6)	56.8	(1.0)	56.6	(1.5)	47.7	(1.2)
Czech Republic	53.6	(2.4)	56.5	(3.8)	51.5	(2.6)	41.4	(3.6)	60.1	(2.7)	58.9	(3.2)	51.5	(2.6)
Denmark	48.9	(1.4)	53.2	(3.0)	46.7	(1.6)	40.0	(2.5)	53.9	(1.6)	55.5	(2.5)	45.9	(1.5)
Finland	49.6	(1.4)	49.8	(2.4)	49.2	(1.7)	33.1	(2.3)	59.6	(1.6)	54.1	(2.4)	47.1	(1.8)
France	48.5	(1.7)	48.8	(2.8)	49.8	(1.8)	33.8	(2.4)	53.9	(1.9)	46.9	(2.8)	48.5	(1.7)
Germany	48.3	(1.5)	48.6	(3.2)	49.3	(1.9)	32.5	(2.9)	56.9	(1.9)	51.5	(3.3)	46.8	(1.7)
Greece	48.0	(1.7)	42.4	(2.5)	51.5	(2.4)	30.4	(2.2)	58.3	(2.3)	46.0	(2.2)	49.2	(2.3)
Hungary	52.3	(2.4)	55.6	(3.9)	52.8	(2.8)	36.9	(3.9)	59.0	(2.7)	57.8	(3.3)	50.7	(2.7)
Iceland	46.6	(1.2)	45.0	(2.4)	47.5	(1.8)	32.0	(1.9)	56.0	(1.6)	44.3	(2.3)	47.2	(1.7)
Ireland	50.0	(1.8)	49.7	(2.5)	50.4	(2.3)	42.4	(2.7)	54.1	(2.2)	55.4	(2.4)	47.1	(2.3)
Italy	45.7	(1.5)	48.6	(2.1)	44.0	(2.0)	35.4	(1.8)	51.6	(2.0)	52.9	(2.0)	42.2	(1.9)
Japan	48.4	(3.2)	49.4	(2.7)	48.0	(4.3)	41.4	(2.5)	52.3	(4.2)	57.0	(2.9)	44.6	(4.1)
Korea	49.9	(3.3)	52.9	(4.2)	48.7	(3.5)	41.2	(4.1)	56.3	(3.6)	56.0	(4.4)	48.0	(3.7)
Luxembourg	49.3	(1.2)	56.0	(2.6)	48.3	(1.4)	38.5	(2.3)	52.0	(1.4)	55.8	(2.7)	46.8	(1.5)
Mexico	48.1	(1.5)	50.5	(2.0)	46.2	(1.9)	36.3	(1.6)	52.7	(2.0)	52.7	(2.1)	46.4	(2.1)
Netherlands	47.4	(1.5)	48.3	(3.1)	45.7	(1.8)	43.2	(2.7)	49.4	(1.9)	52.0	(2.4)	45.6	(1.9)
New Zealand	48.9	(2.1)	49.9	(3.4)	48.3	(2.6)	38.6	(2.9)	54.1	(2.4)	53.5	(3.5)	46.8	(2.3)
Norway	48.7	(1.3)	47.2	(2.6)	49.8	(1.8)	35.8	(2.2)	57.0	(1.7)	50.3	(2.5)	47.9	(1.6)
Poland	46.0	(1.1)	48.9	(2.1)	45.5	(1.4)	35.1	(1.9)	51.8	(1.4)	49.9	(1.7)	44.5	(1.4)
Portugal	47.0	(1.5)	50.6	(2.7)	45.0	(2.0)	35.2	(2.7)	52.5	(1.9)	53.6	(2.5)	44.9	(1.9)
Slovak Republic	49.8	(2.4)	49.5	(3.4)	48.9	(2.9)	39.0	(3.7)	56.5	(2.8)	53.7	(3.0)	48.3	(2.8)
Spain	49.1	(1.1)	52.5	(1.9)	47.7	(1.4)	38.4	(1.7)	54.8	(1.4)	53.2	(1.8)	46.9	(1.4)
Sweden	49.8	(1.5)	52.8	(3.2)	49.0	(1.8)	39.1	(2.2)	56.5	(1.9)	53.4	(3.5)	47.8	(1.7)
Switzerland	50.8	(1.2)	51.8	(2.5)	49.2	(1.4)	38.8	(2.2)	56.7	(1.4)	54.3	(2.5)	48.5	(1.3)
Turkey	59.0	(2.4)	51.6	(3.2)	63.1	(3.0)	45.6	(2.8)	66.6	(2.8)	60.4	(2.8)	58.9	(2.8)
United Kingdom	47.5	(1.4)	52.9	(2.6)	44.8	(1.8)	41.0	(2.1)	51.1	(1.8)	54.4	(2.4)	44.3	(1.7)
United States	51.3	(1.1)	54.4	(2.6)	50.3	(1.6)	m	m	m	m	59.1	(2.4)	48.8	(1.6)
OECD average	49.5	(0.3)	51.0	(0.5)	49.0	(0.4)	38.3	(0.5)	55.5	(0.4)	53.9	(0.5)	47.6	(0.4)
Partners														
Argentina	45.9	(2.1)	43.5	(3.1)	47.1	(2.7)	31.4	(2.2)	52.5	(2.4)	52.3	(3.1)	43.7	(2.6)
Azerbaijan	53.7	(1.8)	50.7	(2.4)	55.9	(2.2)	49.1	(2.6)	57.3	(2.1)	54.9	(2.0)	51.9	(2.6)
Brazil	43.9	(1.4)	51.1	(2.4)	41.0	(1.5)	33.7	(2.2)	47.9	(1.7)	53.6	(2.6)	39.8	(1.5)
Bulgaria	52.3	(2.3)	47.6	(4.1)	53.6	(2.8)	33.5	(3.6)	59.8	(2.6)	54.0	(3.5)	52.6	(2.6)
Chile	50.5	(1.9)	61.7	(3.3)	46.2	(1.8)	40.3	(3.7)	53.9	(1.8)	63.4	(3.8)	45.7	(2.0)
Colombia	45.2	(2.3)	50.8	(4.1)	43.1	(3.0)	42.3	(2.8)	48.7	(2.4)	53.9	(3.0)	40.3	(2.5)
Croatia	49.6	(2.6)	50.5	(3.8)	49.2	(3.0)	34.4	(3.1)	57.6	(3.1)	55.6	(3.2)	45.3	(3.1)
Estonia	46.7	(1.5)	46.7	(2.5)	46.7	(2.1)	31.2	(2.5)	56.0	(1.8)	46.8	(2.4)	45.7	(2.0)
Hong Kong-China	53.4	(1.7)	60.1	(2.8)	50.0	(2.0)	45.7	(2.6)	59.5	(2.1)	59.4	(2.8)	50.2	(1.9)
Indonesia	50.1	(2.0)	54.1	(3.4)	47.9	(2.0)	42.6	(3.7)	55.6	(1.8)	56.8	(3.0)	47.2	(2.0)
Israel	45.4	(2.1)	50.1	(3.2)	45.4	(2.9)	34.5	(3.4)	52.0	(2.8)	51.3	(3.5)	43.6	(2.8)
Jordan	47.6	(2.4)	36.0	(3.1)	55.0	(2.7)	24.1	(2.5)	59.3	(2.4)	43.7	(3.8)	49.9	(2.9)
Kyrgyzstan	45.8	(1.3)	44.9	(2.0)	47.0	(1.9)	31.1	(1.9)	54.7	(1.7)	47.3	(2.2)	44.9	(1.7)
Latvia	44.2	(1.6)	43.9	(3.0)	45.5	(2.3)	30.4	(2.1)	52.6	(2.2)	47.4	(2.8)	43.0	(2.4)
Lithuania	48.3	(1.6)	45.2	(2.9)	50.4	(1.9)	29.8	(2.4)	57.0	(1.9)	47.3	(3.3)	48.9	(1.8)
Macao-China	50.6	(1.4)	51.1	(2.2)	51.2	(1.9)	43.7	(2.2)	57.4	(1.8)	54.4	(2.1)	47.7	(1.8)
Montenegro	47.7	(1.3)	49.5	(2.2)	46.7	(1.8)	37.2	(2.2)	54.5	(1.7)	52.5	(2.1)	45.0	(1.6)
Romania	46.0	(2.8)	46.1	(5.2)	46.5	(3.1)	33.8	(3.2)	52.7	(3.2)	47.4	(4.7)	44.2	(2.8)
Russian Federation	44.1	(1.5)	45.7	(2.2)	44.0	(1.9)	31.7	(1.5)	50.1	(1.9)	44.3	(1.9)	43.6	(2.0)
Serbia	49.9	(2.3)	48.3	(3.4)	50.9	(2.7)	34.6	(3.2)	57.1	(2.7)	50.4	(3.4)	48.9	(2.7)
Slovenia	48.4	(1.5)	44.7	(2.7)	50.3	(1.9)	26.7	(2.4)	58.3	(1.8)	49.3	(2.8)	48.4	(1.8)
Chinese Taipei	52.7	(2.2)	58.2	(2.5)	50.2	(2.6)	46.9	(2.2)	55.3	(2.5)	60.1	(2.6)	49.7	(2.6)
Thailand	44.0	(1.7)	37.8	(2.6)	47.6	(2.0)	23.4	(1.8)	55.5	(2.2)	42.7	(2.5)	44.7	(2.1)
Tunisia	46.5	(1.4)	48.4	(2.2)	45.3	(1.5)	37.9	(2.2)	51.0	(1.4)	53.9	(2.4)	41.7	(1.7)
Uruguay	46.7	(1.6)	44.6	(2.2)	47.6	(2.0)	36.0	(2.6)	51.8	(1.8)	53.6	(3.0)	44.3	(2.0)

Against the Odds: Disadvantaged Students Who Succeed in School © OECD 2011

Table A1.8 Percentage of native students among disadvantaged students and resilient students

		Proportion of native students among disadvantaged students		Science assesment - Proportion of native students among resilient students		Science assesment - Proportion of native students among low achievers		Reading assesment - Proportion of native students among resilient students		Reading assesment - Proportion of native students among low achievers		Mathematics assesment - Proportion of native students among resilient students		Mathematics assesment - Proportion of native students among low achievers	
		%	S.E	%	S.E	%	S.E	%	S.E	%	S.E	%	S.E	%	S.E
OECD	Australia	77.7	(1.7)	78.4	(2.2)	77.4	(1.8)	75.8	(2.2)	78.7	(1.7)	74.1	(2.5)	78.8	(1.7)
	Austria	77.2	(2.6)	93.3	(1.3)	67.8	(3.7)	87.3	(1.3)	70.9	(3.9)	90.2	(1.4)	69.5	(3.7)
	Belgium	78.2	(1.8)	92.9	(1.1)	71.7	(2.4)	91.4	(1.6)	72.4	(2.3)	91.6	(1.3)	71.7	(2.5)
	Canada	78.0	(1.7)	80.0	(1.9)	76.4	(2.3)	78.7	(1.9)	77.9	(2.0)	78.8	(1.8)	77.5	(2.2)
	Czech Republic	c	c	c	c	c	c	c	c	c	c	c	c	c	c
	Denmark	85.3	(1.6)	93.7	(1.3)	81.2	(2.1)	91.1	(1.5)	81.2	(2.2)	92.6	(1.6)	81.9	(1.9)
	Finland	c	c	c	c	c	c	c	c	c	c	c	c	c	c
	France	77.7	(2.1)	81.6	(2.7)	75.7	(2.7)	79.5	(2.5)	76.5	(2.7)	81.9	(2.9)	75.1	(2.7)
	Germany	75.6	(1.8)	86.9	(1.8)	69.0	(2.6)	85.2	(1.6)	70.9	(2.6)	86.0	(1.7)	70.8	(2.3)
	Greece	88.0	(1.5)	91.9	(1.9)	86.6	(2.3)	89.9	(1.7)	86.8	(2.0)	90.7	(1.5)	86.6	(1.8)
	Hungary	c	c	c	c	c	c	c	c	c	c	c	c	c	c
	Iceland	c	c	c	c	c	c	c	c	c	c	c	c	c	c
	Ireland	94.7	(0.9)	95.1	(1.2)	94.3	(1.2)	96.4	(0.9)	93.9	(1.3)	94.6	(1.1)	94.4	(1.2)
	Italy	94.4	(0.5)	96.1	(0.6)	93.3	(0.6)	96.2	(0.6)	93.5	(0.7)	96.1	(0.6)	93.6	(0.6)
	Japan	c	c	c	c	c	c	c	c	c	c	c	c	c	c
	Korea	c	c	c	c	c	c	c	c	c	c	c	c	c	c
	Luxembourg	37.3	(1.3)	63.0	(2.5)	27.3	(1.5)	57.1	(2.3)	30.2	(1.5)	53.0	(2.7)	31.9	(1.6)
	Mexico	c	c	c	c	c	c	c	c	c	c	c	c	c	c
	Netherlands	80.2	(1.8)	91.2	(1.7)	74.3	(2.4)	88.1	(2.0)	75.3	(2.4)	89.1	(2.1)	74.7	(2.4)
	New Zealand	78.6	(1.7)	80.6	(1.8)	76.0	(2.4)	80.2	(2.1)	77.3	(2.3)	80.9	(1.8)	77.1	(2.4)
	Norway	89.2	(1.3)	92.9	(1.4)	86.3	(1.8)	92.1	(1.6)	86.5	(1.6)	91.5	(1.7)	87.9	(1.6)
	Poland	c	c	c	c	c	c	c	c	c	c	c	c	c	c
	Portugal	95.1	(1.5)	99.3	(0.4)	93.0	(2.3)	98.4	(0.6)	93.0	(2.2)	98.3	(0.7)	93.2	(2.2)
	Slovak Republic	c	c	c	c	c	c	c	c	c	c	c	c	c	c
	Spain	91.9	(1.1)	96.7	(0.9)	88.9	(1.5)	95.3	(0.9)	89.6	(1.6)	96.3	(0.8)	89.4	(1.4)
	Sweden	84.3	(1.4)	93.7	(1.1)	79.0	(2.1)	92.2	(1.2)	81.0	(1.8)	91.1	(1.6)	80.2	(1.8)
	Switzerland	63.5	(1.4)	83.7	(1.6)	52.1	(1.8)	78.2	(1.7)	55.9	(1.9)	81.6	(1.7)	53.9	(1.8)
	Turkey	c	c	c	c	c	c	100.0	(0.0)	99.4	(0.2)	99.4	(0.3)	99.5	(0.2)
	United Kingdom	89.3	(1.7)	91.3	(1.5)	88.4	(2.1)	91.0	(1.5)	88.7	(2.1)	93.0	(1.2)	87.8	(2.1)
	United States	74.8	(2.4)	82.7	(2.9)	71.7	(2.8)	v	v	v	v	79.0	(3.0)	72.8	(2.7)
	OECD average	80.5	(0.4)	88.3	(0.4)	76.5	(0.5)	87.8	(0.4)	80.0	(0.5)	87.7	(0.4)	79.5	(0.5)
Partners	Argentina	c	c	c	c	c	c	c	c	c	c	c	c	c	c
	Azerbaijan	c	c	c	c	c	c	c	c	c	c	c	c	c	c
	Brazil	c	c	c	c	c	c	c	c	c	c	c	c	c	c
	Bulgaria	c	c	c	c	c	c	c	c	c	c	c	c	c	c
	Chile	c	c	c	c	c	c	c	c	c	c	c	c	c	c
	Colombia	c	c	c	c	c	c	c	c	c	c	c	c	c	c
	Croatia	82.9	(1.3)	85.8	(1.8)	81.8	(1.7)	84.6	(1.6)	82.3	(1.7)	84.2	(1.6)	81.9	(1.7)
	Estonia	87.8	(1.1)	94.3	(1.0)	83.2	(1.5)	94.3	(1.4)	83.2	(1.7)	91.7	(1.7)	85.3	(1.4)
	Hong Kong-China	36.9	(1.5)	37.2	(2.4)	36.4	(2.0)	37.3	(1.9)	36.6	(2.0)	36.5	(2.2)	36.1	(1.9)
	Indonesia	c	c	c	c	c	c	c	c	c	c	c	c	c	c
	Israel	71.5	(1.9)	69.5	(3.3)	72.0	(1.9)	70.9	(3.0)	71.3	(2.1)	69.1	(3.6)	72.5	(2.0)
	Jordan	87.7	(1.1)	81.8	(1.8)	90.5	(1.1)	81.7	(1.6)	90.9	(1.2)	82.2	(1.7)	89.8	(1.2)
	Kyrgyzstan	c	c	c	c	c	c	c	c	c	c	c	c	c	c
	Latvia	94.1	(0.8)	94.7	(1.0)	94.2	(0.9)	95.3	(1.1)	93.7	(1.0)	93.9	(1.1)	93.9	(0.9)
	Lithuania	c	c	c	c	c	c	c	c	c	c	c	c	c	c
	Macao-China	18.0	(1.0)	15.1	(1.3)	20.5	(1.5)	15.8	(1.5)	19.4	(1.4)	15.3	(1.2)	20.5	(1.4)
	Montenegro	93.9	(0.7)	90.5	(1.4)	95.4	(0.8)	90.5	(1.3)	95.4	(0.8)	90.8	(1.4)	95.1	(0.9)
	Romania	c	c	c	c	c	c	c	c	c	c	c	c	c	c
	Russian Federation	90.2	(1.1)	90.8	(1.5)	89.2	(1.4)	89.7	(1.8)	90.2	(1.2)	91.7	(1.1)	89.1	(1.4)
	Serbia	89.8	(0.9)	87.6	(1.5)	91.2	(1.0)	87.0	(1.5)	90.8	(1.1)	87.9	(1.5)	91.2	(1.1)
	Slovenia	81.1	(1.1)	87.0	(1.9)	78.0	(1.4)	82.5	(2.1)	80.8	(1.3)	83.1	(2.3)	79.9	(1.4)
	Chinese Taipei	c	c	c	c	c	c	c	c	c	c	c	c	c	c
	Thailand	c	c	c	c	c	c	c	c	c	c	c	c	c	c
	Tunisia	c	c	c	c	c	c	c	c	c	c	c	c	c	c
	Uruguay	c	c	c	c	c	c	c	c	c	c	c	c	c	c

Table A1.9 Percentage of students who speak the test language at home among disadvantaged students and resilient students

Percentage of students who speak at home the language of test among resilient, low achievers and all disadvantaged students

		Proportion of students who speak at home the test language among disadvantaged students		Science assessment				Reading assessment				Mathematics assessment			
				Proportion of students who speak at home the test language among resilient students		Proportion of students who speak at home the test language among low achievers		Proportion of students who speak at home the test language among resilient students		Proportion of students who speak at home the test language among low achievers		Proportion of students who speak at home the test language among resilient students		Proportion of students who speak at home the test language among low achievers	
		%	S.E	%	S.E	%	S.E	%	S.E	%	S.E	%	S.E	%	S.E
OECD	Australia	89.3	(1.1)	90.6	(1.6)	88.4	(1.1)	88.9	(1.6)	89.5	(1.1)	87.5	(1.9)	89.9	(1.0)
	Austria	81.6	(2.5)	95.2	(1.0)	73.6	(3.9)	89.2	(1.2)	76.5	(4.2)	92.4	(1.2)	75.0	(3.7)
	Belgium	73.6	(1.5)	71.5	(2.2)	74.0	(2.0)	70.6	(2.1)	74.5	(1.7)	69.9	(2.2)	75.0	(2.0)
	Canada	85.9	(1.2)	88.9	(1.3)	83.7	(1.6)	89.3	(1.3)	84.2	(1.4)	87.3	(1.4)	85.0	(1.5)
	Czech Republic	c	c	c	c	c	c	c	c	c	c	c	c	c	c
	Denmark	91.4	(1.2)	97.0	(1.0)	88.6	(1.5)	96.5	(1.0)	88.0	(1.7)	96.1	(1.1)	89.1	(1.5)
	Finland	c	c	c	c	c	c	c	c	c	c	c	c	c	c
	France	88.1	(1.3)	92.6	(1.5)	86.5	(1.7)	91.2	(1.5)	86.8	(1.8)	92.6	(1.6)	85.8	(1.7)
	Germany	84.8	(1.5)	95.2	(1.2)	78.7	(2.1)	94.0	(1.2)	80.3	(2.0)	94.0	(1.6)	80.4	(1.9)
	Greece	93.3	(1.3)	98.5	(0.8)	90.7	(1.9)	96.5	(1.0)	91.5	(1.8)	97.7	(0.8)	91.8	(1.6)
	Hungary	c	c	c	c	c	c	c	c	c	c	c	c	c	c
	Iceland	c	c	c	c	c	c	c	c	c	c	c	c	c	c
	Ireland	c	c	c	c	c	c	c	c	c	c	c	c	c	c
	Italy	c	c	c	c	c	c	c	c	c	c	c	c	c	c
	Japan	c	c	c	c	c	c	c	c	c	c	c	c	c	c
	Korea	c	c	c	c	c	c	c	c	c	c	c	c	c	c
	Luxembourg	5.2	(0.6)	2.6	(0.8)	5.5	(0.8)	4.1	(1.1)	5.9	(0.8)	5.8	(1.1)	5.3	(0.8)
	Mexico	c	c	c	c	c	c	c	c	c	c	c	c	c	c
	Netherlands	90.2	(1.4)	96.4	(0.9)	87.3	(2.1)	93.7	(1.4)	88.1	(2.2)	94.5	(1.4)	87.5	(2.1)
	New Zealand	89.5	(1.1)	91.4	(1.3)	87.7	(1.5)	91.1	(1.3)	88.0	(1.5)	90.7	(1.3)	88.9	(1.4)
	Norway	91.2	(0.9)	94.1	(1.2)	89.1	(1.2)	93.9	(1.2)	89.0	(1.1)	93.7	(1.2)	89.8	(1.1)
	Poland	c	c	c	c	c	c	c	c	c	c	c	c	c	c
	Portugal	c	c	c	c	c	c	c	c	c	c	c	c	c	c
	Slovak Republic	c	c	c	c	c	c	c	c	c	c	c	c	c	c
	Spain	c	c	c	c	c	c	c	c	c	c	c	c	c	c
	Sweden	88.0	(1.1)	95.3	(0.9)	83.6	(1.5)	93.7	(1.1)	85.3	(1.4)	93.2	(1.2)	84.8	(1.4)
	Switzerland	71.7	(1.4)	88.4	(1.5)	61.6	(1.9)	86.1	(1.6)	63.7	(1.7)	86.2	(1.5)	63.5	(1.8)
	Turkey	c	c	c	c	c	c	c	c	c	c	c	c	c	c
	United Kingdom	93.2	(1.3)	96.2	(1.0)	92.0	(1.6)	94.7	(1.4)	92.2	(1.6)	96.7	(0.8)	91.8	(1.7)
	United States	79.5	(2.1)	87.8	(2.1)	76.1	(2.7)	v	v	v	v	84.8	(2.4)	77.0	(2.6)
	OECD average	**81.0**	**(0.3)**	**86.4**	**(0.3)**	**78.0**	**(0.5)**	**84.9**	**(0.4)**	**78.9**	**(0.5)**	**85.2**	**(0.4)**	**78.8**	**(0.5)**
Partners	Argentina	c	c	c	c	c	c	c	c	c	c	c	c	c	c
	Azerbaijan	c	c	c	c	c	c	c	c	c	c	c	c	c	c
	Brazil	c	c	c	c	c	c	c	c	c	c	c	c	c	c
	Bulgaria	78.1	(2.3)	91.0	(1.8)	72.1	(2.9)	89.8	(2.2)	73.1	(2.7)	86.8	(2.2)	74.3	(2.6)
	Chile	c	c	c	c	c	c	c	c	c	c	c	c	c	c
	Colombia	c	c	c	c	c	c	c	c	c	c	c	c	c	c
	Croatia	c	c	c	c	c	c	c	c	c	c	c	c	c	c
	Estonia	c	c	c	c	c	c	c	c	c	c	c	c	c	c
	Hong Kong-China	c	c	c	c	c	c	c	c	c	c	c	c	c	c
	Indonesia	c	c	c	c	c	c	c	c	c	c	c	c	c	c
	Israel	83.6	(1.7)	81.2	(2.4)	84.1	(1.7)	84.7	(2.2)	82.9	(2.0)	81.1	(2.7)	84.3	(1.6)
	Jordan	c	c	c	c	c	c	c	c	c	c	c	c	c	c
	Kyrgyzstan	c	c	c	c	c	c	c	c	c	c	c	c	c	c
	Latvia	c	c	c	c	c	c	c	c	c	c	c	c	c	c
	Lithuania	c	c	c	c	c	c	c	c	c	c	c	c	c	c
	Macao-China	v	v	v	v	v	v	v	v	v	v	v	v	v	v
	Montenegro	48.5	(1.4)	53.5	(2.4)	45.4	(1.9)	53.9	(2.4)	44.7	(1.9)	56.5	(2.3)	45.0	(1.9)
	Romania	c	c	c	c	c	c	c	c	c	c	c	c	c	c
	Russian Federation	87.5	(2.2)	91.5	(2.0)	85.1	(2.7)	93.1	(1.9)	83.9	(2.8)	87.5	(2.2)	86.5	(2.6)
	Serbia	c	c	c	c	c	c	c	c	c	c	c	c	c	c
	Slovenia	88.5	(0.9)	93.9	(1.4)	85.7	(1.2)	91.0	(1.6)	87.3	(1.1)	91.3	(1.8)	86.7	(1.1)
	Chinese Taipei	c	c	c	c	c	c	c	c	c	c	c	c	c	c
	Thailand	c	c	c	c	c	c	c	c	c	c	c	c	c	c
	Tunisia	98.3	(0.3)	98.0	(0.7)	98.9	(0.3)	97.8	(0.6)	98.6	(0.4)	97.7	(0.8)	98.7	(0.4)
	Uruguay	c	c	c	c	c	c	c	c	c	c	c	c	c	c

ANNEX A2: A PROFILE OF STUDENT RESILIENCE

Table A2.1 Correlations among key indices

	ESCS	Performance on the science scale	General interest in science	Instrumental motivation to learn science	Science self-efficacy	Science self-concept	Participation in science related activities	School preparation for science-related careers	Students' information on science-related careers
ESCS	1								
Performance on the science scale	0.45	1							
General interest in science	-0.24	-0.02	1						
Instrumental motivation to learn science	-0.28	-0.12	0.49	1					
Science self-efficacy	0.12	0.24	0.35	0.22	1				
Science self-concept	-0.19	-0.06	0.48	0.52	0.37	1			
Participation in science related activities	-0.26	-0.13	0.53	0.44	0.31	0.46	1		
School preparation for science related careers	-0.12	-0.05	0.36	0.44	0.21	0.37	0.31	1	
Students' information on science-related careers	0.03	-0.05	0.27	0.30	0.27	0.33	0.31	0.33	1

Note: Correlations estimated on pooled sample of all disadvantaged students in all 55 countries included in the analysis.

[Part 1/2]
Table A2.1a Interest in science (underlying percentages), by student group

		Percentage of students having high or medium interest in following topics													
		Topics in physics				Topics in chemistry				The biology of plants				Human biology			
		Resilient students		Disadvantaged low achievers (DLA)		Resilient students		Disadvantaged low achievers (DLA)		Resilient students		Disadvantaged low achievers (DLA)		Resilient students		Disadvantaged low achievers (DLA)	
		%	S.E.	%	S.E.	%	S.E.	%	S.E.	%	S.E.	%	S.E.	%	S.E.	%	S.E.
OECD	Australia	57.3	(2.2)	29.5	(1.3)	60.8	(1.9)	33.0	(1.4)	46.8	(2.0)	27.1	(1.3)	67.5	(2.4)	45.8	(1.6)
	Austria	54.9	(3.7)	43.2	(2.3)	51.1	(4.2)	41.8	(2.4)	60.8	(3.3)	51.7	(2.4)	80.1	(2.3)	70.7	(2.1)
	Belgium	55.3	(3.0)	42.2	(1.7)	62.7	(2.7)	36.7	(1.6)	55.1	(2.9)	37.8	(1.7)	79.3	(2.1)	62.1	(1.6)
	Canada	64.0	(2.5)	44.4	(1.5)	73.7	(2.4)	48.3	(1.6)	53.7	(2.8)	42.2	(1.4)	73.6	(2.4)	57.4	(1.4)
	Czech Republic	47.6	(3.9)	42.0	(2.7)	44.2	(4.5)	38.2	(2.2)	43.2	(3.9)	39.0	(2.6)	71.7	(3.7)	65.0	(2.3)
	Denmark	64.9	(3.4)	39.9	(2.3)	68.4	(3.3)	39.4	(2.4)	41.4	(3.7)	28.8	(1.9)	60.7	(3.7)	47.8	(1.8)
	Finland	55.7	(3.4)	25.2	(1.7)	55.4	(3.4)	31.4	(2.0)	36.5	(2.6)	21.8	(1.9)	69.6	(2.6)	56.9	(2.2)
	France	73.8	(3.4)	56.3	(1.8)	75.3	(3.7)	42.5	(2.0)	60.2	(3.8)	38.7	(2.2)	83.2	(3.0)	65.2	(1.9)
	Germany	64.7	(3.3)	49.2	(2.5)	64.7	(3.2)	53.3	(2.1)	62.0	(3.8)	52.8	(2.0)	78.6	(3.5)	70.3	(1.8)
	Greece	56.6	(3.3)	40.8	(2.1)	62.0	(4.1)	41.3	(2.3)	64.4	(3.9)	51.7	(2.2)	84.9	(3.4)	69.7	(2.0)
	Hungary	44.4	(3.8)	35.4	(2.4)	43.2	(3.7)	35.7	(2.2)	47.2	(4.4)	41.7	(2.2)	72.6	(3.1)	67.3	(2.2)
	Iceland	62.1	(3.1)	27.2	(1.9)	57.8	(3.0)	28.9	(2.1)	44.4	(3.5)	24.7	(2.1)	71.5	(2.9)	47.0	(2.2)
	Ireland	44.9	(2.8)	28.1	(1.9)	50.7	(3.6)	30.1	(2.3)	59.4	(3.2)	37.8	(2.1)	84.1	(2.2)	61.4	(1.9)
	Italy	48.1	(2.5)	36.9	(1.4)	55.0	(2.3)	34.5	(1.5)	53.6	(2.1)	40.5	(1.5)	75.9	(2.0)	68.9	(1.7)
	Japan	49.1	(2.8)	25.6	(1.9)	61.4	(2.4)	28.8	(1.9)	66.2	(2.3)	45.5	(2.0)	74.5	(2.5)	51.6	(1.6)
	Korea	40.7	(2.7)	19.2	(1.8)	54.4	(2.6)	22.3	(1.6)	55.5	(3.1)	29.5	(1.9)	67.3	(2.4)	48.6	(2.4)
	Luxembourg	60.8	(4.2)	48.4	(2.0)	69.2	(3.7)	44.2	(1.8)	48.8	(4.8)	45.8	(1.7)	71.7	(3.4)	71.4	(1.6)
	Mexico	80.2	(2.4)	79.9	(1.7)	81.2	(2.6)	73.7	(2.0)	86.7	(1.7)	73.8	(2.0)	91.4	(1.4)	80.2	(2.1)
	Netherlands	47.6	(3.4)	30.5	(2.1)	45.3	(3.7)	25.7	(2.1)	46.4	(4.0)	34.1	(2.3)	68.0	(3.7)	57.8	(3.2)
	New Zealand	58.3	(3.2)	36.0	(1.8)	70.3	(3.4)	40.5	(2.2)	48.8	(4.2)	37.1	(2.4)	67.4	(3.7)	56.8	(2.6)
	Norway	65.6	(2.5)	38.5	(2.2)	70.5	(3.0)	41.1	(2.3)	45.5	(3.0)	25.8	(2.0)	59.2	(3.2)	31.7	(2.2)
	Poland	44.2	(3.1)	27.9	(1.8)	52.3	(3.4)	32.0	(2.2)	59.4	(2.6)	63.2	(2.1)	76.2	(2.6)	75.1	(1.9)
	Portugal	56.3	(3.3)	61.7	(2.4)	59.2	(3.5)	50.2	(2.1)	54.3	(3.6)	31.8	(1.9)	72.9	(2.9)	46.5	(2.0)
	Slovak Republic	50.9	(3.5)	42.1	(3.4)	43.9	(3.8)	40.3	(2.9)	51.3	(3.6)	41.7	(2.0)	74.1	(3.0)	59.7	(2.0)
	Spain	39.9	(3.0)	22.8	(1.4)	44.1	(2.7)	19.4	(1.3)	45.0	(2.6)	35.6	(1.9)	63.6	(2.7)	47.9	(1.8)
	Sweden	59.2	(3.8)	30.9	(2.0)	62.4	(4.1)	33.1	(2.0)	38.5	(4.0)	26.3	(1.9)	62.3	(3.5)	49.6	(2.1)
	Switzerland	60.0	(2.9)	44.6	(1.6)	68.2	(3.6)	47.5	(1.6)	54.8	(3.4)	26.8	(1.9)	59.4	(3.4)	30.9	(1.5)
	Turkey	58.0	(3.5)	38.0	(2.8)	59.4	(3.9)	42.3	(2.8)	71.5	(2.9)	59.5	(3.2)	86.8	(2.5)	66.9	(2.5)
	United Kingdom	56.2	(3.2)	41.0	(2.1)	62.1	(2.9)	45.6	(1.9)	47.8	(3.2)	38.6	(2.0)	78.5	(2.5)	63.7	(1.7)
	United States	56.9	(3.5)	46.9	(2.3)	69.5	(3.4)	47.5	(2.0)	47.8	(3.6)	48.5	(2.8)	71.2	(2.9)	66.3	(2.7)
	OECD average	55.9	(0.6)	39.1	(0.4)	60.0	(0.6)	39.0	(0.4)	53.2	(0.6)	40.0	(0.4)	73.3	(0.5)	58.7	(0.4)
Partners	Argentina	58.4	(4.3)	60.7	(2.6)	54.8	(5.1)	52.7	(2.8)	64.6	(3.8)	65.7	(2.2)	81.7	(3.3)	72.1	(2.3)
	Azerbaijan	76.0	(2.8)	65.5	(3.0)	72.4	(3.3)	62.6	(2.9)	79.0	(2.3)	64.3	(2.7)	75.5	(2.5)	53.9	(2.7)
	Brazil	53.2	(4.1)	61.4	(2.1)	57.7	(4.0)	60.8	(3.3)	72.2	(4.6)	71.6	(2.1)	77.7	(3.1)	74.9	(2.2)
	Bulgaria	55.1	(5.2)	58.5	(3.4)	53.1	(4.6)	58.7	(2.8)	53.3	(4.1)	41.0	(2.4)	79.0	(3.6)	61.4	(2.3)
	Chile	67.2	(3.9)	64.6	(2.3)	68.6	(4.9)	66.1	(2.1)	64.7	(3.9)	71.4	(2.0)	78.3	(3.5)	73.7	(2.0)
	Colombia	83.5	(3.4)	83.4	(2.6)	83.0	(3.4)	82.6	(2.4)	90.1	(2.3)	93.1	(1.3)	95.3	(1.6)	94.3	(0.9)
	Croatia	43.1	(4.1)	31.7	(1.9)	47.2	(3.4)	34.2	(2.1)	58.4	(3.0)	59.5	(2.2)	81.5	(2.5)	73.5	(1.8)
	Estonia	54.3	(4.6)	40.8	(2.9)	51.5	(3.9)	40.9	(3.3)	46.7	(5.2)	51.7	(2.5)	73.9	(2.9)	64.3	(2.0)
	Hong Kong-China	69.5	(2.5)	39.9	(2.2)	66.9	(2.7)	37.4	(2.2)	65.2	(3.3)	49.6	(2.4)	83.1	(2.2)	62.9	(2.3)
	Indonesia	61.2	(3.1)	58.0	(2.7)	57.6	(3.4)	45.5	(2.7)	85.9	(4.9)	90.2	(1.4)	86.8	(4.6)	86.7	(1.6)
	Israel	53.1	(3.7)	37.1	(2.6)	60.6	(4.6)	37.3	(2.7)	50.8	(4.0)	42.4	(2.8)	72.7	(3.8)	63.2	(2.7)
	Jordan	71.6	(3.5)	62.8	(2.4)	75.7	(3.4)	64.2	(2.3)	88.9	(2.0)	78.7	(1.9)	92.1	(1.8)	79.1	(1.9)
	Kyrgyzstan	73.7	(3.5)	83.9	(2.1)	75.6	(3.5)	81.4	(2.2)	91.4	(1.7)	92.5	(1.6)	95.0	(1.6)	93.1	(1.1)
	Latvia	56.9	(3.8)	52.8	(3.2)	44.2	(4.0)	46.1	(2.7)	40.1	(4.5)	48.0	(2.5)	69.1	(3.7)	73.4	(2.3)
	Lithuania	60.2	(3.6)	47.7	(2.4)	52.5	(3.5)	44.4	(1.9)	61.5	(4.1)	60.3	(2.1)	83.9	(3.5)	73.4	(1.9)
	Macao-China	62.2	(2.9)	39.0	(2.2)	60.6	(2.9)	35.4	(2.5)	61.4	(3.0)	54.3	(2.4)	77.4	(2.3)	65.7	(2.1)
	Montenegro	56.6	(3.5)	52.0	(2.6)	52.3	(3.6)	51.2	(2.4)	71.8	(2.9)	65.1	(2.2)	88.2	(2.2)	73.5	(2.0)
	Romania	63.3	(5.9)	50.0	(2.8)	52.3	(5.7)	47.8	(2.6)	69.6	(4.2)	63.5	(2.9)	89.1	(3.2)	73.0	(2.5)
	Russian Federation	53.2	(3.3)	49.8	(3.2)	50.0	(3.6)	44.6	(3.2)	57.5	(3.9)	66.9	(2.4)	77.3	(3.1)	78.9	(2.3)
	Serbia	40.1	(3.1)	47.0	(2.0)	48.3	(2.9)	44.1	(2.5)	68.8	(3.2)	70.5	(2.2)	85.2	(2.3)	78.9	(1.9)
	Slovenia	39.3	(3.8)	29.0	(1.7)	49.8	(3.7)	30.0	(1.7)	51.4	(3.9)	42.2	(2.2)	65.6	(3.5)	60.4	(1.7)
	Chinese Taipei	64.7	(2.5)	35.8	(2.2)	61.4	(2.8)	30.7	(1.8)	61.5	(2.2)	41.4	(2.0)	71.0	(2.2)	55.6	(1.7)
	Thailand	74.0	(2.4)	68.3	(2.6)	80.7	(2.4)	72.8	(2.3)	86.9	(2.6)	82.3	(2.0)	90.2	(2.0)	83.7	(2.0)
	Tunisia	81.5	(3.0)	78.8	(2.1)	72.4	(3.7)	56.7	(2.3)	78.1	(2.8)	73.8	(2.5)	89.6	(2.5)	85.8	(1.7)
	Uruguay	56.1	(4.0)	60.3	(2.5)	65.5	(3.5)	59.0	(2.2)	58.0	(5.0)	65.2	(2.6)	81.7	(2.8)	80.5	(2.2)

[Part 2/2]
Table A2.1a Interest in science (underlying percentages), by student group

Percentage of students having high or medium interest in following topics

		Topics in astronomy				Topics in geology				Ways scientists design experiments				What is required for scientific explanations			
		Resilient students		Disadvantaged low achievers (DLA)		Resilient students		Disadvantaged low achievers (DLA)		Resilient students		Disadvantaged low achievers (DLA)		Resilient students		Disadvantaged low achievers (DLA)	
		%	S.E.	%	S.E.	%	S.E.	%	S.E.	%	S.E.	%	S.E.	%	S.E.	%	S.E.
OECD	Australia	55.6	(2.2)	28.5	(1.3)	41.3	(1.8)	19.4	(1.1)	39.6	(1.9)	32.1	(1.4)	36.0	(1.8)	19.5	(1.0)
	Austria	58.8	(3.5)	32.6	(2.0)	52.7	(4.1)	28.6	(2.1)	54.6	(3.1)	40.9	(2.5)	39.3	(4.1)	26.2	(1.7)
	Belgium	63.7	(2.3)	40.6	(1.6)	47.8	(2.9)	28.8	(1.6)	57.2	(2.8)	38.6	(1.8)	42.8	(2.4)	29.1	(1.8)
	Canada	68.2	(2.2)	41.9	(1.3)	49.5	(2.3)	31.2	(1.3)	49.9	(2.6)	40.2	(1.3)	35.7	(2.1)	26.7	(1.2)
	Czech Republic	66.9	(3.5)	42.2	(2.4)	44.8	(3.9)	32.2	(2.5)	60.3	(3.4)	42.3	(2.5)	34.6	(3.6)	28.8	(2.0)
	Denmark	53.0	(3.7)	25.2	(2.0)	37.8	(3.0)	22.1	(1.8)	39.1	(3.1)	26.9	(1.9)	41.3	(3.6)	24.1	(1.8)
	Finland	60.1	(2.8)	35.2	(2.0)	41.3	(2.9)	16.3	(1.7)	29.2	(2.9)	16.8	(1.4)	31.1	(2.5)	16.8	(1.5)
	France	73.0	(3.4)	38.8	(1.7)	61.2	(3.7)	33.9	(1.7)	50.4	(3.4)	37.4	(1.8)	44.2	(3.7)	30.1	(1.9)
	Germany	62.6	(4.0)	41.8	(2.0)	59.7	(4.2)	38.6	(2.0)	58.3	(3.5)	42.3	(1.7)	42.7	(3.6)	32.8	(1.7)
	Greece	59.7	(4.3)	36.3	(2.0)	41.2	(3.6)	32.6	(2.0)	48.5	(3.2)	38.7	(1.9)	45.7	(3.5)	33.8	(2.2)
	Hungary	66.3	(4.3)	47.6	(1.8)	46.1	(3.9)	26.8	(2.0)	40.8	(3.2)	39.7	(2.2)	39.4	(3.5)	34.8	(2.0)
	Iceland	66.5	(3.2)	48.4	(2.4)	49.8	(3.6)	28.1	(2.1)	40.9	(3.5)	27.4	(2.3)	38.1	(3.1)	19.9	(1.8)
	Ireland	55.2	(3.1)	25.7	(1.9)	39.4	(2.9)	18.1	(1.9)	38.5	(3.5)	36.7	(2.0)	39.0	(3.3)	22.6	(1.4)
	Italy	73.1	(2.0)	50.0	(1.4)	53.1	(1.8)	37.9	(1.2)	61.2	(1.9)	56.3	(1.7)	40.6	(2.0)	35.6	(1.4)
	Japan	65.0	(2.7)	34.5	(2.2)	39.5	(3.0)	21.4	(1.9)	37.9	(2.9)	22.2	(1.5)	28.8	(2.1)	13.0	(1.1)
	Korea	65.6	(2.5)	31.2	(1.9)	51.9	(3.5)	26.9	(1.8)	27.9	(2.9)	13.5	(1.3)	37.7	(2.5)	12.1	(1.5)
	Luxembourg	58.8	(4.0)	41.7	(1.8)	52.1	(4.5)	37.5	(1.9)	69.0	(4.0)	47.9	(1.8)	43.6	(4.4)	34.8	(1.7)
	Mexico	80.9	(2.1)	63.3	(2.7)	76.3	(2.2)	62.0	(2.8)	80.0	(2.3)	72.9	(1.8)	76.4	(2.5)	65.3	(2.1)
	Netherlands	40.7	(3.0)	26.3	(2.5)	34.0	(3.0)	18.3	(1.8)	32.7	(3.2)	24.5	(2.3)	30.6	(3.3)	21.7	(2.2)
	New Zealand	58.3	(4.2)	38.1	(2.0)	45.3	(4.1)	24.9	(1.8)	38.4	(3.5)	40.6	(2.2)	36.2	(3.7)	24.5	(2.0)
	Norway	62.3	(3.3)	36.1	(2.7)	53.8	(2.9)	27.5	(2.1)	60.5	(2.9)	47.8	(2.2)	47.3	(3.2)	30.4	(1.9)
	Poland	67.2	(2.7)	38.6	(1.9)	51.1	(3.1)	35.2	(1.9)	51.4	(2.9)	42.2	(2.0)	34.3	(2.9)	32.5	(1.8)
	Portugal	60.4	(3.5)	39.0	(2.5)	58.0	(3.7)	35.9	(2.6)	67.1	(3.4)	48.8	(2.4)	53.2	(3.2)	42.2	(2.4)
	Slovak Republic	63.3	(4.3)	40.8	(2.0)	54.1	(3.5)	31.3	(2.2)	50.6	(3.3)	34.5	(2.5)	32.2	(3.2)	23.5	(2.0)
	Spain	52.1	(2.7)	26.4	(1.7)	38.1	(2.7)	23.9	(1.7)	50.5	(2.5)	29.7	(1.7)	34.4	(2.6)	17.5	(1.4)
	Sweden	56.7	(4.4)	35.0	(2.4)	39.5	(3.6)	19.5	(1.9)	46.6	(3.8)	33.0	(2.0)	38.6	(3.7)	22.8	(1.7)
	Switzerland	57.5	(3.4)	37.2	(1.7)	58.8	(2.8)	32.2	(1.5)	56.4	(3.2)	45.3	(1.9)	40.3	(2.6)	33.1	(2.0)
	Turkey	64.4	(3.2)	42.0	(3.3)	46.7	(4.0)	34.5	(2.2)	59.5	(3.6)	47.9	(2.5)	50.3	(3.6)	40.4	(2.7)
	United Kingdom	57.5	(2.7)	31.4	(1.7)	38.6	(2.9)	24.2	(1.6)	34.3	(2.6)	41.3	(1.7)	35.1	(2.7)	29.8	(1.9)
	United States	75.2	(2.5)	44.6	(2.1)	46.9	(3.1)	41.3	(3.3)	44.9	(3.9)	51.4	(2.3)	34.8	(3.4)	40.3	(3.4)
	OECD average	62.3	(0.6)	38.0	(0.4)	48.4	(0.6)	29.7	(0.4)	49.2	(0.6)	38.7	(0.4)	40.1	(0.6)	28.8	(0.3)
Partners	Argentina	55.7	(3.9)	41.2	(2.5)	45.7	(4.6)	41.3	(3.4)	56.3	(5.1)	57.7	(2.9)	50.1	(3.3)	47.9	(2.5)
	Azerbaijan	67.1	(3.2)	51.8	(2.8)	65.5	(3.6)	52.3	(3.0)	60.7	(3.9)	56.4	(3.3)	55.2	(3.6)	55.2	(3.7)
	Brazil	55.1	(3.0)	47.1	(2.6)	48.2	(3.9)	48.2	(2.3)	74.9	(3.4)	67.6	(1.8)	64.3	(3.6)	64.3	(2.0)
	Bulgaria	65.7	(4.4)	53.6	(2.6)	49.0	(4.3)	45.3	(2.3)	71.8	(4.8)	48.1	(2.6)	47.5	(4.0)	45.3	(2.6)
	Chile	68.6	(4.0)	56.7	(2.2)	59.4	(3.9)	49.2	(2.4)	57.0	(3.5)	51.1	(2.6)	46.4	(4.0)	45.2	(2.6)
	Colombia	85.2	(3.4)	73.2	(2.4)	80.3	(3.6)	73.5	(2.2)	79.1	(3.4)	79.9	(1.9)	75.7	(3.9)	73.3	(2.5)
	Croatia	74.9	(2.4)	44.0	(1.9)	62.3	(3.0)	34.0	(1.9)	67.8	(2.9)	55.0	(2.0)	56.8	(2.9)	45.6	(2.0)
	Estonia	73.2	(3.6)	48.4	(2.5)	46.2	(3.8)	35.3	(2.4)	60.4	(3.0)	56.3	(2.8)	39.8	(3.4)	37.6	(2.2)
	Hong Kong-China	68.1	(3.2)	50.3	(2.3)	44.3	(2.9)	34.1	(2.3)	57.0	(2.5)	45.2	(2.1)	51.1	(2.7)	33.7	(2.2)
	Indonesia	67.6	(3.0)	50.7	(2.2)	57.8	(4.1)	44.9	(2.2)	86.0	(2.7)	73.3	(2.0)	61.5	(3.9)	52.1	(2.4)
	Israel	60.7	(3.1)	40.9	(2.2)	40.1	(3.8)	31.4	(2.2)	52.7	(3.8)	44.4	(2.6)	41.3	(3.3)	36.5	(2.2)
	Jordan	63.3	(3.4)	51.7	(1.9)	63.8	(3.5)	49.0	(2.0)	72.4	(3.0)	58.4	(1.8)	60.6	(3.0)	52.0	(2.3)
	Kyrgyzstan	74.9	(3.3)	71.8	(2.5)	67.0	(3.1)	73.0	(2.5)	73.3	(3.2)	64.9	(2.8)	62.0	(3.1)	61.5	(3.0)
	Latvia	75.3	(3.4)	56.6	(2.5)	52.6	(3.3)	36.3	(3.2)	56.1	(4.8)	62.8	(3.1)	33.4	(4.4)	37.2	(2.7)
	Lithuania	76.1	(3.5)	42.4	(2.1)	59.8	(5.3)	45.1	(2.0)	74.9	(3.4)	66.3	(2.0)	47.6	(3.3)	46.3	(2.1)
	Macao-China	66.7	(3.2)	47.1	(3.0)	37.1	(2.8)	26.2	(2.2)	58.1	(3.3)	47.5	(2.9)	42.4	(3.0)	28.6	(3.1)
	Montenegro	72.7	(2.8)	47.4	(2.3)	63.3	(2.9)	43.4	(2.5)	65.0	(3.1)	49.1	(2.2)	62.3	(3.1)	51.5	(2.4)
	Romania	77.2	(5.2)	41.1	(2.4)	66.1	(5.4)	40.5	(3.3)	58.7	(6.0)	44.4	(2.9)	49.6	(4.4)	44.2	(2.7)
	Russian Federation	76.7	(3.1)	49.4	(2.5)	51.2	(3.4)	37.7	(2.7)	64.2	(3.4)	67.5	(1.8)	55.7	(3.4)	50.4	(2.9)
	Serbia	74.2	(2.6)	48.2	(2.4)	50.7	(3.3)	41.8	(2.3)	62.4	(3.0)	51.8	(2.3)	50.8	(2.6)	48.4	(2.4)
	Slovenia	67.4	(4.3)	47.5	(1.9)	65.1	(4.2)	46.0	(2.1)	54.9	(3.9)	43.7	(1.9)	41.9	(3.7)	37.4	(2.0)
	Chinese Taipei	74.6	(2.0)	50.9	(1.6)	54.7	(2.5)	35.9	(1.5)	58.4	(2.4)	37.0	(1.8)	49.8	(2.4)	30.3	(1.5)
	Thailand	87.0	(2.5)	69.6	(2.8)	82.9	(2.3)	67.8	(2.3)	82.9	(2.6)	79.2	(2.2)	77.1	(2.7)	72.3	(2.8)
	Tunisia	63.3	(2.8)	60.1	(2.7)	69.4	(3.0)	60.7	(2.1)	75.5	(3.5)	67.5	(2.2)	69.3	(2.9)	56.3	(2.2)
	Uruguay	60.3	(3.5)	56.1	(2.3)	53.4	(3.5)	49.1	(2.8)	58.4	(3.2)	55.9	(2.9)	51.3	(3.8)	48.5	(3.2)

Table A2.1b Interest in science (underlying percentages), by student group

		Resilient students		Disadvantaged low achievers (DLA)		Difference in the mean index between resilient students and disadvantaged low achievers	
		Mean	S.E.	Mean	S.E.	Dif	S.E.
OECD	Australia	0.11	(0.04)	-0.69	(0.04)	**0.79**	(0.06)
	Austria	0.24	(0.06)	-0.27	(0.04)	**0.51**	(0.07)
	Belgium	0.27	(0.05)	-0.37	(0.05)	**0.65**	(0.07)
	Canada	0.31	(0.05)	-0.27	(0.03)	**0.58**	(0.06)
	Czech Republic	0.11	(0.05)	-0.20	(0.05)	**0.31**	(0.07)
	Denmark	0.12	(0.06)	-0.58	(0.06)	**0.70**	(0.09)
	Finland	0.04	(0.05)	-0.70	(0.05)	**0.74**	(0.07)
	France	0.52	(0.06)	-0.24	(0.04)	**0.76**	(0.07)
	Germany	0.42	(0.05)	-0.06	(0.05)	**0.48**	(0.07)
	Greece	0.32	(0.06)	-0.20	(0.04)	**0.52**	(0.08)
	Hungary	0.05	(0.06)	-0.24	(0.04)	**0.28**	(0.07)
	Iceland	0.18	(0.06)	-0.70	(0.06)	**0.88**	(0.08)
	Ireland	0.11	(0.06)	-0.74	(0.05)	**0.85**	(0.08)
	Italy	0.29	(0.03)	-0.05	(0.03)	**0.35**	(0.04)
	Japan	0.15	(0.05)	-0.64	(0.05)	**0.79**	(0.06)
	Korea	0.06	(0.04)	-0.74	(0.04)	**0.79**	(0.06)
	Luxembourg	0.33	(0.09)	-0.14	(0.04)	**0.47**	(0.09)
	Mexico	0.99	(0.04)	0.73	(0.05)	**0.26**	(0.06)
	Netherlands	-0.13	(0.06)	-0.65	(0.06)	**0.52**	(0.09)
	New Zealand	0.15	(0.07)	-0.42	(0.06)	**0.57**	(0.09)
	Norway	0.24	(0.07)	-0.57	(0.07)	**0.80**	(0.09)
	Poland	0.21	(0.04)	-0.10	(0.03)	**0.32**	(0.05)
	Portugal	0.38	(0.05)	-0.07	(0.04)	**0.45**	(0.07)
	Slovak Republic	0.06	(0.05)	-0.40	(0.06)	**0.46**	(0.08)
	Spain	0.02	(0.05)	-0.59	(0.04)	**0.61**	(0.06)
	Sweden	0.04	(0.10)	-0.61	(0.06)	**0.65**	(0.10)
	Switzerland	0.24	(0.05)	-0.39	(0.04)	**0.63**	(0.06)
	Turkey	0.49	(0.06)	-0.04	(0.06)	**0.52**	(0.08)
	United Kingdom	0.11	(0.06)	-0.32	(0.04)	**0.43**	(0.07)
	United States	0.27	(0.05)	-0.11	(0.09)	**0.38**	(0.10)
	OECD average	**0.22**	**(0.01)**	**-0.35**	**(0.01)**	**0.57**	**(0.01)**
Partners	Argentina	0.34	(0.07)	0.24	(0.06)	0.10	(0.10)
	Azerbaijan	0.62	(0.07)	0.34	(0.07)	**0.28**	(0.09)
	Brazil	0.51	(0.07)	0.53	(0.06)	-0.02	(0.09)
	Bulgaria	0.30	(0.09)	0.02	(0.07)	**0.28**	(0.12)
	Chile	0.48	(0.09)	0.37	(0.05)	0.12	(0.09)
	Colombia	1.26	(0.09)	1.28	(0.06)	-0.02	(0.09)
	Croatia	0.37	(0.04)	-0.07	(0.04)	**0.44**	(0.06)
	Estonia	0.25	(0.07)	-0.03	(0.04)	**0.29**	(0.07)
	Hong Kong-China	0.46	(0.04)	-0.19	(0.06)	**0.65**	(0.07)
	Indonesia	0.61	(0.06)	0.38	(0.04)	**0.23**	(0.07)
	Israel	0.21	(0.10)	-0.36	(0.08)	**0.57**	(0.14)
	Jordan	0.85	(0.07)	0.38	(0.06)	**0.47**	(0.09)
	Kyrgyzstan	0.90	(0.06)	0.95	(0.05)	-0.05	(0.08)
	Latvia	0.15	(0.05)	0.07	(0.05)	0.08	(0.07)
	Lithuania	0.48	(0.05)	0.18	(0.03)	**0.30**	(0.06)
	Macao-China	0.32	(0.05)	-0.14	(0.05)	**0.46**	(0.07)
	Montenegro	0.61	(0.06)	0.21	(0.06)	**0.40**	(0.08)
	Romania	0.52	(0.08)	0.23	(0.06)	**0.30**	(0.10)
	Russian Federation	0.37	(0.05)	0.19	(0.05)	**0.17**	(0.06)
	Serbia	0.38	(0.05)	0.16	(0.05)	**0.23**	(0.06)
	Slovenia	0.22	(0.06)	-0.23	(0.04)	**0.45**	(0.07)
	Chinese Taipei	0.37	(0.04)	-0.36	(0.04)	**0.73**	(0.05)
	Thailand	1.02	(0.04)	0.63	(0.04)	**0.39**	(0.05)
	Tunisia	0.94	(0.07)	0.66	(0.04)	**0.29**	(0.08)
	Uruguay	0.39	(0.07)	0.24	(0.07)	0.15	(0.09)

Note: Values that are statistically different are indicated in bold.

Table A2.1c Interest in science (underlying percentages), by student group

		Ratio	S.E.	Ratio (After accounting for ESCS, gender, immigrant background, grade, using test language)	S.E.	Ratio (After accounting for Mean ESCS, ESCS, gender, immigrant background, grade, using test language)	S.E.
OECD	Australia	**1.83**	(0.06)	**1.89**	(0.06)	**1.92**	(0.06)
	Austria	**1.79**	(0.12)	**1.98**	(0.14)	**1.93**	(0.15)
	Belgium	**1.65**	(0.07)	**1.99**	(0.09)	**1.88**	(0.10)
	Canada	1.59	(0.07)	1.66	(0.08)	1.67	(0.08)
	Czech Republic	**1.43**	(0.10)	**1.51**	(0.11)	**1.56**	(0.12)
	Denmark	1.72	(0.08)	1.95	(0.08)	1.97	(0.09)
	Finland	**2.14**	(0.08)	**2.21**	(0.09)	**2.21**	(0.09)
	France	1.87	(0.07)	2.15	(0.11)	2.09	(0.12)
	Germany	**1.61**	(0.08)	**1.63**	(0.09)	**1.72**	(0.12)
	Greece	**1.60**	(0.10)	**1.63**	(0.10)	**1.61**	(0.11)
	Hungary	**1.41**	(0.10)	**1.56**	(0.12)	**1.54**	(0.14)
	Iceland	1.72	(0.07)	1.73	(0.08)	1.73	(0.08)
	Ireland	**1.87**	(0.09)	**1.98**	(0.10)	**2.03**	(0.11)
	Italy	1.55	(0.06)	1.52	(0.07)	1.40	(0.07)
	Japan	1.92	(0.08)	1.91	(0.08)	1.81	(0.09)
	Korea	2.47	(0.11)	2.45	(0.11)	2.31	(0.11)
	Luxembourg	**1.47**	(0.10)	**1.67**	(0.13)	**1.66**	(0.14)
	Mexico	1.33	(0.06)	1.33	(0.06)	1.35	(0.06)
	Netherlands	**1.54**	(0.09)	**1.88**	(0.10)	**1.83**	(0.12)
	New Zealand	1.59	(0.09)	1.72	(0.10)	1.75	(0.10)
	Norway	**1.63**	(0.06)	**1.65**	(0.07)	**1.64**	(0.07)
	Poland	1.66	(0.11)	1.67	(0.12)	1.67	(0.12)
	Portugal	1.67	(0.08)	1.74	(0.12)	1.81	(0.12)
	Slovak Republic	1.71	(0.10)	1.67	(0.11)	1.65	(0.11)
	Spain	**1.79**	(0.08)	**1.70**	(0.09)	**1.75**	(0.09)
	Sweden	**1.64**	(0.14)	**1.83**	(0.17)	**1.83**	(0.17)
	Switzerland	**1.88**	(0.10)	**2.22**	(0.11)	**2.10**	(0.12)
	Turkey	1.55	(0.07)	1.47	(0.08)	1.47	(0.08)
	United Kingdom	**1.40**	(0.08)	**1.41**	(0.08)	**1.42**	(0.08)
	United States	1.34	(0.07)	1.48	(0.07)	1.51	(0.07)
	OECD average	**1.66**	(0.07)	**1.75**	(0.02)	**1.74**	(0.07)
Partners	Argentina	1.10	(0.09)	1.24	(0.10)	1.26	(0.11)
	Azerbaijan	1.19	(0.07)	1.19	(0.07)	1.19	(0.07)
	Brazil	0.99	(0.07)	1.03	(0.07)	1.04	(0.07)
	Bulgaria	1.25	(0.10)	1.32	(0.11)	1.43	(0.12)
	Chile	1.14	(0.09)	1.21	(0.09)	1.27	(0.10)
	Colombia	0.99	(0.10)	1.06	(0.12)	1.06	(0.13)
	Croatia	**1.66**	(0.09)	**1.73**	(0.09)	**1.79**	(0.10)
	Estonia	**1.52**	(0.13)	**1.61**	(0.16)	**1.61**	(0.16)
	Hong Kong-China	**1.76**	(0.08)	**1.96**	(0.08)	**1.97**	(0.09)
	Indonesia	1.45	(0.14)	1.50	(0.14)	1.50	(0.14)
	Israel	**1.31**	(0.07)	**1.32**	(0.07)	**1.41**	(0.08)
	Jordan	**1.43**	(0.08)	**1.43**	(0.09)	**1.44**	(0.10)
	Kyrgyzstan	0.97	(0.10)	0.96	(0.11)	1.01	(0.11)
	Latvia	1.15	(0.14)	1.14	(0.17)	1.19	(0.18)
	Lithuania	**1.68**	(0.12)	**1.76**	(0.12)	**1.78**	(0.13)
	Macao-China	**1.85**	(0.10)	**1.88**	(0.12)	**1.89**	(0.11)
	Montenegro	**1.39**	(0.09)	**1.44**	(0.10)	**1.52**	(0.10)
	Romania	1.36	(0.10)	1.37	(0.11)	1.37	(0.12)
	Russian Federation	1.27	(0.10)	1.37	(0.11)	1.39	(0.12)
	Serbia	**1.25**	(0.07)	**1.25**	(0.07)	**1.28**	(0.08)
	Slovenia	**1.54**	(0.09)	**1.49**	(0.09)	**1.45**	(0.11)
	Chinese Taipei	**1.85**	(0.06)	**1.83**	(0.06)	**1.84**	(0.07)
	Thailand	**1.63**	(0.09)	**1.55**	(0.10)	**1.58**	(0.10)
	Tunisia	1.38	(0.10)	1.28	(0.11)	1.30	(0.11)
	Uruguay	1.16	(0.09)	1.22	(0.11)	1.23	(0.11)

Note: Values that are statistically different are indicated in bold.

[Part 1/2]
Table A2.2a Instrumental interest in science (underlying percentages), by student group

Percentage of students agreeing or strongly agreeing with the following statements

		Making an effort in my science is worth it because this will help me in the work I want to do later on				What I learn in my science is important for me because I need this for what I want to study later on				I study science because I know it is useful for me			
		Resilient students		Disadvantaged low achievers (DLA)		Resilient students		Disadvantaged low achievers (DLA)		Resilient students		Disadvantaged low achievers (DLA)	
		%	S.E.	%	S.E.	%	S.E.	%	S.E.	%	S.E.	%	S.E.
OECD	Australia	77.4	(1.9)	52.1	(1.6)	64.2	(2.4)	39.6	(1.7)	81.7	(2.0)	51.4	(1.6)
	Austria	49.9	(3.8)	47.6	(3.0)	39.7	(3.3)	34.6	(2.6)	58.2	(4.4)	50.8	(2.7)
	Belgium	58.9	(2.6)	52.9	(1.9)	52.8	(2.5)	46.1	(1.9)	60.2	(2.5)	48.5	(2.4)
	Canada	76.2	(2.3)	65.3	(1.6)	66.1	(2.2)	54.5	(2.0)	80.7	(2.1)	62.7	(1.7)
	Czech Republic	49.4	(4.1)	54.0	(2.5)	54.9	(4.0)	51.7	(2.7)	70.2	(3.9)	58.1	(2.8)
	Denmark	62.7	(3.4)	61.6	(2.5)	63.9	(3.2)	54.4	(2.3)	72.4	(3.1)	56.3	(2.5)
	Finland	58.9	(2.9)	39.2	(2.1)	50.9	(3.5)	28.2	(2.0)	73.9	(3.3)	44.3	(2.4)
	France	64.8	(4.1)	51.2	(2.2)	57.2	(3.8)	45.0	(2.5)	76.6	(3.2)	51.3	(2.2)
	Germany	60.2	(3.3)	60.4	(2.1)	49.2	(4.1)	46.8	(2.2)	74.3	(3.9)	59.0	(2.4)
	Greece	65.1	(3.1)	66.4	(2.2)	59.6	(3.4)	59.4	(2.2)	73.7	(4.0)	61.9	(2.1)
	Hungary	66.0	(3.3)	73.0	(2.0)	50.2	(3.8)	61.7	(2.4)	61.5	(3.5)	66.4	(2.1)
	Iceland	67.2	(3.4)	47.8	(2.3)	69.3	(3.2)	46.7	(2.3)	73.8	(3.0)	47.2	(2.2)
	Ireland	68.8	(3.3)	50.9	(2.6)	55.3	(3.5)	38.4	(2.7)	80.7	(2.5)	51.6	(2.2)
	Italy	65.1	(2.2)	60.7	(1.5)	61.0	(2.1)	61.9	(1.5)	80.2	(1.9)	67.9	(1.7)
	Japan	53.0	(3.1)	34.5	(2.1)	48.7	(2.8)	28.7	(2.0)	51.9	(2.7)	27.1	(1.8)
	Korea	66.4	(2.9)	49.3	(2.1)	50.2	(3.1)	39.3	(2.0)	66.6	(2.9)	45.2	(2.1)
	Luxembourg	52.8	(4.1)	57.9	(2.2)	47.5	(4.2)	49.1	(2.2)	60.6	(3.9)	55.1	(1.9)
	Mexico	86.7	(2.0)	91.2	(1.2)	83.7	(1.6)	88.1	(1.4)	89.7	(1.1)	86.5	(1.5)
	Netherlands	58.2	(3.2)	50.4	(2.7)	50.5	(4.0)	43.0	(2.4)	69.9	(3.5)	50.6	(2.6)
	New Zealand	77.1	(3.5)	63.3	(2.1)	61.9	(3.7)	49.3	(2.4)	81.6	(2.8)	57.1	(2.1)
	Norway	61.5	(4.0)	49.4	(2.5)	62.2	(3.2)	42.7	(2.5)	68.1	(2.7)	47.6	(2.3)
	Poland	69.5	(2.6)	74.8	(1.6)	74.9	(2.7)	74.3	(1.6)	76.7	(2.7)	72.5	(1.9)
	Portugal	82.2	(3.0)	64.2	(2.4)	83.0	(3.4)	67.9	(2.3)	89.3	(2.2)	75.0	(2.4)
	Slovak Republic	52.3	(3.5)	58.6	(2.6)	44.0	(3.7)	43.8	(2.8)	65.7	(3.3)	56.6	(2.2)
	Spain	69.9	(2.2)	59.6	(1.7)	59.2	(3.0)	45.3	(1.9)	72.6	(2.5)	53.8	(1.8)
	Sweden	67.8	(3.6)	49.6	(2.4)	56.9	(3.5)	44.8	(2.4)	69.1	(3.3)	48.0	(2.3)
	Switzerland	58.6	(2.8)	47.9	(2.0)	49.3	(2.7)	39.0	(1.7)	67.4	(3.0)	47.5	(1.7)
	Turkey	87.7	(2.4)	78.6	(2.2)	86.0	(2.5)	76.0	(2.3)	82.7	(2.7)	67.7	(2.5)
	United Kingdom	72.5	(3.1)	65.0	(1.7)	54.3	(3.5)	50.8	(1.9)	78.6	(2.6)	65.4	(1.8)
	United States	81.4	(2.2)	77.3	(2.2)	72.7	(3.5)	69.2	(2.3)	83.8	(2.5)	70.6	(1.4)
	OECD average	66.3	(0.6)	58.5	(0.4)	59.3	(0.6)	50.7	(0.4)	73.1	(0.5)	56.8	(0.4)
Partners	Argentina	77.9	(3.3)	84.3	(2.3)	71.4	(4.2)	83.9	(1.6)	81.2	(2.8)	80.1	(2.3)
	Azerbaijan	88.8	(2.3)	83.2	(2.1)	83.4	(2.4)	80.2	(2.7)	90.6	(2.2)	83.4	(2.2)
	Brazil	80.0	(2.7)	86.4	(1.9)	75.1	(2.6)	82.1	(2.2)	91.4	(2.4)	87.9	(1.7)
	Bulgaria	73.0	(3.5)	82.1	(2.1)	72.2	(3.9)	81.8	(2.0)	89.0	(2.5)	85.9	(1.9)
	Chile	83.2	(3.3)	85.2	(1.6)	69.8	(3.8)	76.8	(2.1)	81.3	(3.1)	77.4	(2.2)
	Colombia	86.6	(2.4)	91.0	(1.5)	83.3	(3.2)	88.4	(2.2)	91.6	(2.2)	90.9	(1.6)
	Croatia	62.3	(3.2)	64.7	(2.5)	71.7	(3.6)	71.2	(2.2)	72.6	(3.4)	69.1	(2.3)
	Estonia	68.0	(3.5)	72.3	(2.4)	60.4	(3.5)	64.8	(2.6)	82.4	(2.5)	71.3	(2.5)
	Hong Kong-China	78.4	(2.8)	70.7	(3.4)	72.1	(2.8)	63.1	(4.2)	82.4	(2.1)	68.9	(3.4)
	Indonesia	94.3	(2.0)	95.1	(1.1)	96.7	(1.1)	92.9	(1.3)	93.8	(2.0)	93.2	(1.1)
	Israel	32.0	(3.8)	56.3	(2.7)	30.2	(3.8)	49.5	(2.5)	30.2	(4.0)	45.1	(2.6)
	Jordan	96.0	(1.3)	90.0	(1.5)	92.3	(2.3)	81.6	(1.6)	93.0	(1.5)	82.2	(1.5)
	Kyrgyzstan	94.7	(1.5)	96.1	(0.9)	90.8	(2.1)	93.0	(1.4)	90.7	(2.0)	89.5	(1.6)
	Latvia	60.6	(4.8)	69.8	(2.4)	72.6	(3.3)	69.8	(2.7)	82.7	(3.0)	72.8	(2.5)
	Lithuania	83.9	(2.5)	82.8	(1.7)	82.4	(2.4)	79.9	(1.9)	91.0	(1.9)	81.9	(1.5)
	Macao-China	84.9	(3.6)	81.5	(1.9)	85.5	(3.3)	75.5	(2.3)	88.8	(2.8)	81.8	(2.1)
	Montenegro	80.3	(2.8)	85.9	(1.6)	72.1	(3.1)	78.2	(2.0)	88.5	(2.2)	84.5	(1.6)
	Romania	83.9	(2.9)	86.0	(1.8)	82.4	(3.1)	82.4	(2.2)	86.0	(3.3)	75.9	(3.0)
	Russian Federation	72.8	(2.9)	81.3	(1.6)	76.8	(3.1)	78.7	(1.7)	75.1	(3.2)	79.5	(1.6)
	Serbia	70.1	(2.6)	74.7	(2.2)	55.0	(3.4)	61.1	(2.6)	82.3	(2.2)	78.5	(1.9)
	Slovenia	71.8	(3.5)	70.0	(2.0)	62.2	(4.0)	62.5	(2.4)	80.0	(2.9)	69.5	(1.8)
	Chinese Taipei	77.2	(2.6)	75.4	(1.8)	68.1	(2.7)	64.4	(1.7)	89.2	(1.6)	76.1	(1.4)
	Thailand	94.9	(2.2)	95.4	(0.9)	97.0	(1.2)	91.5	(1.3)	98.8	(0.7)	93.7	(1.1)
	Tunisia	89.7	(2.2)	91.4	(1.6)	88.9	(2.3)	82.7	(2.1)	94.2	(2.1)	86.2	(2.3)
	Uruguay	71.0	(3.9)	80.4	(2.3)	57.1	(3.7)	72.1	(2.4)	73.1	(3.8)	75.4	(2.4)

ANNEX A2

Table A2.2a [Part 2/2] Instrumental interest in science (underlying percentages), by student group

Percentage of students agreeing or strongly agreeing with the following statements

		Studying science is worthwhile for me because what I learn will improve my career prospects				I will learn many things in science that will help me get a job			
		Resilient students		Disadvantaged low achievers (DLA)		Resilient students		Disadvantaged low achievers (DLA)	
		%	S.E.	%	S.E.	%	S.E.	%	S.E.
OECD	Australia	79.0	(2.2)	45.1	(1.7)	74.1	(2.3)	46.0	(1.6)
	Austria	50.1	(3.6)	45.4	(2.4)	37.3	(3.4)	40.3	(3.0)
	Belgium	56.8	(2.7)	48.3	(2.6)	49.7	(2.6)	43.7	(2.1)
	Canada	78.3	(1.9)	58.4	(1.9)	74.2	(2.1)	59.1	(1.8)
	Czech Republic	51.2	(3.8)	47.7	(2.5)	48.6	(3.6)	48.5	(2.5)
	Denmark	63.9	(3.4)	53.8	(2.3)	52.5	(3.5)	52.5	(2.3)
	Finland	57.0	(3.5)	33.6	(2.3)	57.5	(3.5)	31.6	(2.1)
	France	66.7	(3.9)	50.4	(2.4)	51.9	(3.4)	41.6	(2.0)
	Germany	65.0	(3.2)	52.1	(1.9)	54.8	(4.2)	49.9	(2.2)
	Greece	64.1	(3.4)	61.0	(2.1)	59.4	(3.6)	59.9	(2.2)
	Hungary	46.6	(4.2)	59.4	(2.2)	47.4	(3.8)	60.0	(2.3)
	Iceland	62.7	(3.3)	44.8	(2.2)	59.9	(3.3)	42.0	(2.5)
	Ireland	75.1	(2.8)	48.0	(2.5)	70.2	(3.2)	51.8	(2.4)
	Italy	73.2	(2.0)	64.6	(1.7)	62.0	(2.1)	59.8	(1.5)
	Japan	48.5	(2.8)	24.7	(1.7)	46.4	(2.8)	26.0	(1.8)
	Korea	65.0	(3.4)	39.6	(2.1)	53.1	(2.6)	38.1	(2.0)
	Luxembourg	53.2	(4.4)	52.9	(2.1)	47.0	(4.7)	50.5	(2.0)
	Mexico	88.9	(1.4)	85.4	(1.7)	81.3	(2.0)	84.5	(1.4)
	Netherlands	60.3	(4.1)	50.5	(2.4)	44.1	(3.6)	41.7	(2.3)
	New Zealand	79.0	(3.5)	54.0	(2.1)	74.6	(3.4)	56.2	(2.0)
	Norway	65.6	(3.2)	47.0	(2.5)	52.6	(3.0)	39.3	(2.0)
	Poland	75.6	(2.3)	75.0	(1.7)	66.7	(3.0)	71.9	(2.1)
	Portugal	86.9	(3.3)	72.5	(2.1)	80.7	(3.5)	68.4	(1.9)
	Slovak Republic	55.1	(3.9)	51.9	(2.4)	50.0	(3.5)	52.4	(2.6)
	Spain	66.9	(2.6)	51.3	(1.5)	64.5	(2.8)	57.3	(1.7)
	Sweden	69.7	(3.6)	47.7	(2.3)	58.0	(3.7)	39.8	(2.7)
	Switzerland	52.3	(2.9)	41.2	(1.5)	41.0	(3.2)	38.2	(1.7)
	Turkey	79.3	(2.8)	71.9	(2.5)	73.3	(2.9)	69.5	(2.5)
	United Kingdom	71.7	(2.8)	61.3	(2.0)	66.4	(3.0)	57.1	(1.9)
	United States	74.7	(3.2)	65.9	(1.7)	74.6	(3.3)	68.0	(2.3)
	OECD average	66.1	(0.6)	53.5	(0.4)	59.1	(0.6)	51.5	(0.4)
Partners	Argentina	81.0	(3.2)	79.3	(2.3)	74.3	(3.0)	80.5	(2.2)
	Azerbaijan	85.8	(2.3)	81.0	(2.6)	81.7	(2.1)	80.6	(2.3)
	Brazil	83.2	(2.6)	83.9	(1.9)	79.3	(2.7)	82.5	(2.3)
	Bulgaria	76.9	(3.3)	79.5	(2.0)	69.5	(4.1)	81.1	(2.0)
	Chile	75.3	(3.6)	78.8	(2.1)	66.1	(3.7)	78.5	(2.0)
	Colombia	83.7	(2.9)	89.9	(1.7)	80.2	(4.0)	86.7	(2.8)
	Croatia	61.6	(3.8)	59.1	(2.6)	64.5	(3.5)	64.1	(2.4)
	Estonia	64.4	(3.1)	66.4	(2.3)	48.3	(3.2)	54.2	(2.4)
	Hong Kong-China	81.1	(2.2)	68.3	(3.2)	73.5	(2.6)	64.4	(3.7)
	Indonesia	86.7	(1.9)	89.7	(1.4)	84.8	(2.5)	88.0	(1.3)
	Israel	29.6	(3.4)	45.2	(2.5)	35.6	(3.7)	48.2	(2.2)
	Jordan	91.1	(2.6)	79.8	(1.8)	88.1	(2.3)	80.4	(1.8)
	Kyrgyzstan	84.9	(2.6)	89.5	(1.8)	86.7	(2.5)	91.1	(2.0)
	Latvia	46.9	(5.2)	53.5	(2.5)	53.6	(4.6)	62.0	(2.4)
	Lithuania	71.8	(3.1)	71.4	(1.9)	67.6	(2.9)	73.2	(1.7)
	Macao-China	84.6	(3.9)	76.4	(2.3)	78.7	(4.0)	76.0	(2.2)
	Montenegro	72.1	(3.1)	77.7	(2.0)	70.8	(3.0)	78.4	(2.0)
	Romania	84.5	(3.6)	77.5	(3.0)	79.9	(3.4)	81.4	(2.4)
	Russian Federation	64.1	(2.9)	71.8	(1.7)	63.7	(2.9)	72.9	(1.9)
	Serbia	66.9	(2.6)	71.1	(2.2)	63.3	(3.2)	70.2	(2.1)
	Slovenia	65.9	(3.5)	60.6	(1.8)	61.3	(4.0)	62.9	(1.8)
	Chinese Taipei	78.0	(2.4)	71.7	(1.9)	74.5	(2.0)	72.7	(1.8)
	Thailand	94.9	(1.6)	93.0	(1.2)	92.6	(2.5)	90.8	(1.5)
	Tunisia	90.0	(1.7)	82.2	(1.9)	89.0	(2.2)	79.8	(2.0)
	Uruguay	57.0	(4.1)	66.6	(2.5)	59.8	(3.7)	70.7	(2.5)

Table A2.2b Instrumental motivation by student group

		\multicolumn{6}{c}{Instrumental motivation to learn science}

		Resilient students		Disadvantaged low achievers (DLA)		Difference in the mean index between resilient students and disadvantaged low achievers	
		Mean	S.E.	Mean	S.E.	Dif	S.E.
OECD	Australia	0.46	(0.05)	-0.36	(0.03)	**0.82**	(0.05)
	Austria	-0.30	(0.08)	-0.43	(0.07)	0.14	(0.11)
	Belgium	-0.12	(0.05)	-0.38	(0.04)	**0.26**	(0.07)
	Canada	0.48	(0.05)	-0.04	(0.03)	**0.52**	(0.06)
	Czech Republic	-0.14	(0.07)	-0.24	(0.04)	0.10	(0.08)
	Denmark	0.15	(0.07)	-0.13	(0.04)	**0.28**	(0.09)
	Finland	0.01	(0.06)	-0.60	(0.04)	**0.62**	(0.08)
	France	0.12	(0.08)	-0.38	(0.06)	**0.50**	(0.09)
	Germany	0.07	(0.08)	-0.17	(0.05)	**0.24**	(0.09)
	Greece	0.08	(0.07)	-0.01	(0.04)	0.09	(0.08)
	Hungary	-0.12	(0.06)	0.02	(0.04)	-0.13	(0.07)
	Iceland	0.30	(0.08)	-0.38	(0.04)	**0.69**	(0.09)
	Ireland	0.31	(0.08)	-0.35	(0.05)	**0.66**	(0.09)
	Italy	0.15	(0.03)	-0.02	(0.03)	**0.17**	(0.04)
	Japan	-0.25	(0.05)	-0.83	(0.05)	**0.58**	(0.06)
	Korea	-0.03	(0.06)	-0.49	(0.04)	**0.46**	(0.07)
	Luxembourg	-0.14	(0.10)	-0.21	(0.04)	0.07	(0.11)
	Mexico	0.61	(0.03)	0.64	(0.04)	-0.03	(0.05)
	Netherlands	-0.06	(0.08)	-0.36	(0.05)	**0.30**	(0.10)
	New Zealand	0.39	(0.07)	-0.15	(0.05)	**0.54**	(0.09)
	Norway	0.02	(0.07)	-0.42	(0.04)	**0.43**	(0.08)
	Poland	0.25	(0.05)	0.18	(0.04)	0.07	(0.06)
	Portugal	0.75	(0.08)	0.11	(0.05)	**0.64**	(0.10)
	Slovak Republic	-0.16	(0.06)	-0.21	(0.05)	0.05	(0.08)
	Spain	0.22	(0.06)	-0.21	(0.03)	**0.42**	(0.07)
	Sweden	0.14	(0.07)	-0.40	(0.05)	**0.54**	(0.09)
	Switzerland	-0.12	(0.05)	-0.45	(0.03)	**0.33**	(0.06)
	Turkey	0.59	(0.07)	0.20	(0.06)	**0.39**	(0.10)
	United Kingdom	0.27	(0.06)	-0.05	(0.04)	**0.33**	(0.07)
	United States	0.51	(0.07)	0.14	(0.04)	**0.37**	(0.09)
	OECD average	**0.15**	**(0.01)**	**-0.20**	**(0.01)**	**0.35**	**(0.01)**
Partners	Argentina	0.37	(0.07)	0.52	(0.06)	-0.15	(0.09)
	Azerbaijan	0.56	(0.05)	0.54	(0.06)	0.02	(0.07)
	Brazil	0.51	(0.04)	0.58	(0.04)	-0.07	(0.05)
	Bulgaria	0.32	(0.08)	0.45	(0.04)	-0.13	(0.09)
	Chile	0.49	(0.09)	0.50	(0.05)	-0.01	(0.09)
	Colombia	0.65	(0.06)	0.79	(0.06)	-0.14	(0.08)
	Croatia	0.06	(0.07)	0.04	(0.06)	0.02	(0.09)
	Estonia	0.04	(0.05)	0.04	(0.03)	0.00	(0.07)
	Hong Kong-China	0.39	(0.05)	0.02	(0.05)	**0.37**	(0.08)
	Indonesia	0.71	(0.07)	0.73	(0.03)	-0.02	(0.08)
	Israel	-0.68	(0.07)	-0.18	(0.06)	**-0.49**	(0.09)
	Jordan	0.94	(0.06)	0.59	(0.04)	**0.35**	(0.07)
	Kyrgyzstan	0.86	(0.06)	0.92	(0.04)	-0.06	(0.07)
	Latvia	-0.03	(0.07)	0.06	(0.04)	-0.08	(0.08)
	Lithuania	0.47	(0.05)	0.34	(0.03)	**0.13**	(0.05)
	Macao-China	0.51	(0.07)	0.25	(0.04)	**0.26**	(0.08)
	Montenegro	0.42	(0.06)	0.57	(0.04)	-0.14	(0.08)
	Romania	0.44	(0.07)	0.39	(0.05)	0.05	(0.09)
	Russian Federation	0.22	(0.06)	0.31	(0.03)	-0.09	(0.06)
	Serbia	0.12	(0.05)	0.22	(0.05)	-0.10	(0.07)
	Slovenia	0.12	(0.06)	0.01	(0.04)	0.11	(0.08)
	Chinese Taipei	0.39	(0.05)	0.10	(0.03)	**0.29**	(0.06)
	Thailand	0.87	(0.04)	0.62	(0.02)	**0.24**	(0.05)
	Tunisia	1.03	(0.07)	0.71	(0.05)	**0.32**	(0.07)
	Uruguay	0.10	(0.07)	0.28	(0.05)	**-0.18**	(0.08)

Note: Values that are statistically different are indicated in bold.

Table A2.2c — Relationship between being resilient and PISA index of instrumental motivation in science learning

Increased likelihood of being resilient associated with one unit on the PISA index of instrumental motivation in science learning

		Ratio	S.E.	Ratio (After accounting for ESCS, gender, immigrant background, grade, using test language)	S.E.	Ratio (After accounting for Mean ESCS, ESCS, gender, immigrant background, grade, using test language)	S.E.
OECD	Australia	**1.90**	(0.06)	**1.86**	(0.06)	**1.87**	(0.06)
	Austria	1.15	(0.08)	**1.37**	(0.09)	**1.38**	(0.10)
	Belgium	**1.30**	(0.07)	**1.48**	(0.08)	**1.55**	(0.09)
	Canada	**1.55**	(0.06)	**1.55**	(0.07)	**1.55**	(0.07)
	Czech Republic	1.21	(0.12)	1.29	(0.12)	**1.28**	(0.12)
	Denmark	**1.33**	(0.09)	**1.42**	(0.09)	**1.42**	(0.09)
	Finland	**1.99**	(0.10)	**2.02**	(0.10)	**2.02**	(0.10)
	France	**1.60**	(0.09)	**1.60**	(0.10)	**1.60**	(0.10)
	Germany	**1.25**	(0.08)	1.18	(0.09)	**1.24**	(0.10)
	Greece	1.13	(0.10)	1.19	(0.11)	1.19	(0.11)
	Hungary	0.90	(0.10)	1.04	(0.11)	1.04	(0.12)
	Iceland	**1.64**	(0.08)	**1.61**	(0.08)	**1.61**	(0.08)
	Ireland	**1.57**	(0.08)	**1.60**	(0.08)	**1.58**	(0.08)
	Italy	**1.31**	(0.06)	**1.32**	(0.07)	**1.17**	(0.06)
	Japan	**1.60**	(0.06)	**1.60**	(0.06)	**1.48**	(0.06)
	Korea	**1.68**	(0.09)	**1.68**	(0.09)	**1.64**	(0.10)
	Luxembourg	1.07	(0.10)	1.13	(0.11)	1.15	(0.11)
	Mexico	1.00	(0.08)	1.08	(0.08)	1.10	(0.08)
	Netherlands	**1.36**	(0.10)	**1.42**	(0.10)	**1.38**	(0.11)
	New Zealand	**1.65**	(0.10)	**1.71**	(0.10)	**1.72**	(0.10)
	Norway	**1.59**	(0.09)	**1.64**	(0.09)	**1.64**	(0.09)
	Poland	1.15	(0.09)	**1.21**	(0.09)	**1.21**	(0.09)
	Portugal	**2.22**	(0.14)	**1.63**	(0.15)	**1.68**	(0.15)
	Slovak Republic	1.09	(0.10)	1.20	(0.10)	1.19	(0.11)
	Spain	**1.54**	(0.08)	**1.46**	(0.08)	**1.47**	(0.08)
	Sweden	**1.63**	(0.08)	**1.78**	(0.09)	**1.77**	(0.09)
	Switzerland	**1.41**	(0.07)	**1.51**	(0.07)	**1.46**	(0.07)
	Turkey	**1.49**	(0.11)	**1.42**	(0.12)	**1.42**	(0.12)
	United Kingdom	**1.39**	(0.08)	**1.40**	(0.09)	**1.41**	(0.09)
	United States	**1.66**	(0.11)	**1.73**	(0.12)	**1.76**	(0.12)
	OECD average	**1.41**	(0.02)	**1.45**	(0.02)	**1.45**	(0.02)
Partners	Argentina	0.83	(0.11)	0.89	(0.12)	0.91	(0.12)
	Azerbaijan	1.01	(0.10)	1.00	(0.10)	1.00	(0.10)
	Brazil	0.93	(0.09)	1.01	(0.10)	1.02	(0.10)
	Bulgaria	0.86	(0.13)	0.89	(0.13)	0.95	(0.13)
	Chile	1.03	(0.11)	1.11	(0.10)	1.15	(0.10)
	Colombia	0.86	(0.12)	1.07	(0.13)	1.08	(0.11)
	Croatia	1.01	(0.09)	1.04	(0.09)	1.09	(0.10)
	Estonia	1.05	(0.12)	1.11	(0.13)	1.12	(0.13)
	Hong Kong-China	**1.57**	(0.09)	**1.84**	(0.11)	**1.97**	(0.12)
	Indonesia	0.96	(0.16)	1.07	(0.15)	1.05	(0.14)
	Israel	**0.70**	(0.09)	**0.67**	(0.09)	**0.65**	(0.09)
	Jordan	**1.64**	(0.14)	**1.50**	(0.15)	**1.51**	(0.15)
	Kyrgyzstan	0.87	(0.14)	0.86	(0.15)	0.92	(0.15)
	Latvia	0.93	(0.16)	0.92	(0.17)	0.97	(0.17)
	Lithuania	**1.23**	(0.09)	**1.26**	(0.09)	**1.31**	(0.09)
	Macao-China	**1.41**	(0.14)	1.25	(0.15)	1.25	(0.16)
	Montenegro	0.90	(0.08)	0.94	(0.09)	1.01	(0.09)
	Romania	1.10	(0.17)	1.07	(0.17)	1.08	(0.18)
	Russian Federation	0.91	(0.12)	0.95	(0.12)	0.95	(0.12)
	Serbia	0.95	(0.08)	0.96	(0.08)	1.00	(0.09)
	Slovenia	1.16	(0.10)	**1.22**	(0.10)	**1.20**	(0.10)
	Chinese Taipei	**1.53**	(0.10)	**1.49**	(0.10)	**1.47**	(0.11)
	Thailand	**1.92**	(0.13)	**1.84**	(0.13)	**1.84**	(0.13)
	Tunisia	**1.59**	(0.16)	**1.45**	(0.17)	**1.49**	(0.17)
	Uruguay	0.91	(0.09)	1.02	(0.09)	1.03	(0.09)

Note: Values that are statistically different are indicated in bold.

Table A2.3a [Part 1/2] Engagement in science-related activities outside school (underlying percentages), by student group

	Watch TV programmes about science				Borrow or buy books on science topics				Visit web sites about science topics			
	Resilient students		Disadvantaged low achievers (DLA)		Resilient students		Disadvantaged low achievers (DLA)		Resilient students		Disadvantaged low achievers (DLA)	
	%	S.E.	%	S.E.	%	S.E.	%	S.E.	%	S.E.	%	S.E.
OECD												
Australia	19.9	(1.6)	12.7	(0.9)	7.6	(1.1)	2.9	(0.5)	14.5	(1.3)	5.7	(0.6)
Austria	23.3	(2.5)	13.1	(1.8)	8.0	(1.2)	6.1	(1.2)	11.5	(2.4)	9.7	(1.6)
Belgium	27.9	(2.1)	21.2	(1.5)	9.1	(1.8)	6.6	(0.9)	16.7	(1.8)	11.1	(1.0)
Canada	24.2	(2.0)	12.5	(1.0)	6.0	(0.8)	3.7	(0.7)	15.5	(1.4)	6.9	(0.8)
Czech Republic	13.0	(2.2)	13.8	(1.8)	6.1	(1.6)	5.3	(1.3)	5.5	(1.6)	5.8	(0.8)
Denmark	28.2	(3.0)	15.1	(1.5)	6.1	(1.6)	4.6	(0.9)	10.8	(2.2)	6.1	(1.2)
Finland	19.0	(2.3)	12.4	(1.3)	4.3	(1.2)	2.2	(0.6)	5.6	(1.3)	1.9	(0.5)
France	22.3	(3.4)	22.6	(1.6)	10.1	(2.3)	7.4	(1.0)	12.2	(3.0)	9.2	(1.0)
Germany	25.3	(3.8)	13.0	(1.4)	7.3	(2.0)	4.5	(0.8)	12.3	(2.6)	7.8	(1.2)
Greece	24.8	(2.8)	18.8	(1.5)	14.4	(2.1)	11.3	(1.4)	11.5	(1.9)	9.4	(1.3)
Hungary	37.2	(3.6)	28.7	(1.8)	9.1	(2.1)	12.3	(1.8)	11.5	(2.2)	10.4	(1.4)
Iceland	25.7	(3.0)	7.2	(1.3)	10.6	(2.0)	3.9	(0.9)	17.4	(2.8)	5.3	(1.0)
Ireland	21.3	(2.7)	12.0	(1.3)	6.4	(1.7)	2.5	(0.9)	9.9	(2.1)	5.8	(1.1)
Italy	28.7	(2.0)	21.7	(1.0)	9.6	(1.3)	7.2	(0.6)	15.5	(1.7)	8.8	(0.8)
Japan	8.3	(1.5)	5.8	(0.7)	2.5	(0.9)	3.5	(0.8)	4.2	(1.1)	2.7	(0.6)
Korea	8.1	(1.7)	6.7	(1.0)	7.0	(1.5)	3.0	(0.6)	6.2	(1.3)	2.7	(0.6)
Luxembourg	30.4	(4.9)	17.9	(1.4)	12.0	(2.4)	8.2	(1.0)	15.5	(3.4)	10.4	(1.1)
Mexico	39.2	(3.0)	44.2	(2.3)	23.0	(2.9)	35.3	(2.2)	26.5	(2.6)	27.8	(2.3)
Netherlands	28.9	(3.1)	20.0	(2.0)	6.6	(1.8)	6.3	(1.4)	11.6	(2.1)	7.8	(1.1)
New Zealand	16.7	(2.5)	13.9	(1.3)	7.7	(1.8)	6.9	(1.2)	9.6	(1.7)	7.3	(1.2)
Norway	24.5	(2.8)	17.5	(1.7)	2.3	(1.0)	4.9	(1.2)	15.1	(2.5)	10.8	(1.5)
Poland	53.3	(2.9)	43.5	(1.9)	16.1	(2.2)	12.7	(1.2)	12.7	(2.1)	13.7	(1.4)
Portugal	51.3	(3.5)	33.9	(2.0)	14.2	(2.7)	15.6	(1.8)	20.7	(3.2)	15.1	(1.4)
Slovak Republic	24.5	(3.1)	17.6	(1.7)	10.4	(2.3)	5.7	(1.0)	6.2	(1.7)	6.5	(1.2)
Spain	12.5	(1.8)	10.5	(1.1)	4.7	(1.1)	3.8	(0.7)	8.6	(1.3)	5.4	(0.7)
Sweden	10.0	(2.1)	6.8	(1.0)	0.9	(0.7)	1.4	(0.5)	4.9	(1.6)	3.2	(0.7)
Switzerland	18.2	(2.2)	14.0	(1.2)	6.1	(1.3)	4.8	(0.6)	8.4	(1.7)	8.6	(1.0)
Turkey	31.0	(3.5)	21.1	(2.2)	26.3	(3.1)	15.9	(2.0)	17.4	(3.4)	12.1	(1.7)
United Kingdom	16.8	(2.4)	9.4	(1.1)	5.9	(1.5)	3.5	(0.7)	12.1	(1.8)	6.8	(1.0)
United States	27.2	(3.3)	19.8	(1.6)	8.4	(2.5)	6.6	(1.0)	18.5	(3.4)	9.3	(1.3)
OECD average	24.7	(0.5)	17.6	(0.3)	9.0	(0.3)	7.3	(0.2)	12.3	(0.4)	8.5	(0.2)
Partners												
Argentina	36.1	(4.6)	34.3	(3.3)	25.6	(4.0)	30.9	(3.1)	19.7	(3.4)	21.5	(2.0)
Azerbaijan	60.0	(2.7)	61.2	(2.9)	42.8	(3.9)	39.5	(3.3)	14.4	(3.2)	20.0	(2.5)
Brazil	30.2	(3.8)	42.4	(3.0)	19.8	(2.8)	30.0	(2.2)	11.6	(2.2)	15.7	(1.5)
Bulgaria	45.6	(4.3)	40.4	(2.4)	6.9	(2.1)	15.6	(2.1)	19.9	(2.9)	23.6	(1.8)
Chile	53.4	(4.3)	32.2	(2.1)	22.2	(3.3)	22.1	(2.1)	27.5	(3.4)	25.3	(2.1)
Colombia	58.0	(3.9)	50.2	(3.2)	34.0	(3.6)	39.9	(3.0)	29.7	(4.4)	31.8	(3.6)
Croatia	36.7	(3.0)	25.6	(2.0)	11.9	(1.9)	5.9	(0.8)	10.3	(1.9)	5.4	(1.0)
Estonia	26.3	(3.2)	22.0	(1.9)	4.7	(2.0)	6.0	(1.1)	15.6	(3.0)	14.8	(1.7)
Hong Kong-China	17.4	(2.1)	9.1	(1.3)	15.3	(1.9)	3.7	(1.0)	11.6	(2.1)	5.3	(1.2)
Indonesia	11.9	(2.1)	13.2	(1.8)	4.1	(1.1)	5.8	(1.0)	1.9	(1.0)	4.4	(0.8)
Israel	27.3	(3.3)	31.3	(2.8)	15.5	(3.4)	19.7	(2.2)	22.4	(3.5)	21.9	(1.8)
Jordan	43.1	(3.4)	47.0	(1.8)	21.4	(2.9)	27.5	(1.8)	16.0	(2.5)	27.1	(1.7)
Kyrgyzstan	62.4	(2.9)	72.0	(3.2)	33.1	(3.2)	48.0	(2.9)	18.0	(2.4)	34.0	(3.4)
Latvia	22.8	(3.2)	13.8	(1.6)	4.2	(1.4)	5.9	(1.1)	5.2	(1.5)	7.9	(1.1)
Lithuania	28.7	(3.5)	28.6	(2.3)	4.2	(1.4)	8.3	(1.3)	12.0	(2.6)	10.9	(1.5)
Macao-China	20.1	(2.6)	14.4	(1.7)	9.2	(1.8)	5.6	(0.9)	8.3	(1.5)	6.7	(1.3)
Montenegro	38.0	(3.2)	38.4	(2.5)	13.5	(2.0)	13.3	(1.6)	10.2	(2.1)	13.6	(1.3)
Romania	27.2	(5.4)	27.9	(2.9)	12.9	(3.8)	16.9	(1.8)	11.2	(5.3)	12.9	(1.9)
Russian Federation	39.0	(3.6)	31.7	(2.9)	20.1	(3.0)	19.9	(3.8)	6.7	(2.2)	14.4	(3.4)
Serbia	37.2	(3.3)	36.5	(2.2)	12.3	(2.8)	11.9	(1.5)	9.5	(2.0)	8.1	(1.0)
Slovenia	37.8	(3.9)	26.9	(2.0)	10.9	(2.0)	8.9	(1.0)	16.3	(3.0)	13.1	(1.4)
Chinese Taipei	20.1	(1.8)	11.8	(1.1)	11.1	(1.7)	6.1	(0.8)	14.5	(2.0)	8.9	(1.0)
Thailand	62.9	(3.4)	32.5	(2.3)	35.3	(3.3)	17.1	(1.7)	24.0	(3.0)	12.9	(1.4)
Tunisia	40.5	(3.8)	47.3	(2.5)	28.5	(3.1)	37.2	(2.8)	8.5	(2.0)	24.3	(2.1)
Uruguay	33.1	(2.9)	25.1	(2.2)	19.3	(2.8)	22.7	(1.9)	13.4	(2.6)	15.9	(1.4)

Table A2.3a [Part 2/2] **Engagement in science-related activities outside school (underlying percentages), by student group**

Percentage of students doing the following activities very often or regularly

		Listen to radio programmes about advances in science				Read science magazines or science articles in newspapers				Attend a science club			
		Resilient students		Disadvantaged low achievers (DLA)		Resilient students		Disadvantaged low achievers (DLA)		Resilient students		Disadvantaged low achievers (DLA)	
		%	S.E.	%	S.E.	%	S.E.	%	S.E.	%	S.E.	%	S.E.
OECD	Australia	4.8	(0.9)	2.6	(0.4)	12.9	(1.4)	4.0	(0.5)	1.1	(0.4)	1.3	(0.4)
	Austria	6.2	(1.5)	10.4	(1.5)	28.7	(2.7)	17.8	(2.2)	0.7	(0.6)	4.0	(0.8)
	Belgium	5.5	(1.4)	8.8	(1.0)	23.9	(2.3)	11.9	(1.0)	0.1	(0.2)	3.3	(0.7)
	Canada	3.9	(0.8)	5.0	(0.9)	15.5	(1.4)	7.7	(1.0)	0.7	(0.4)	1.6	(0.4)
	Czech Republic	1.3	(0.6)	6.5	(1.3)	19.8	(2.7)	12.0	(1.8)	5.6	(1.6)	4.4	(1.1)
	Denmark	5.6	(1.8)	4.5	(0.9)	25.4	(3.0)	9.0	(1.1)	1.5	(0.7)	2.6	(0.6)
	Finland	2.1	(0.9)	2.7	(0.7)	23.2	(2.7)	7.0	(1.0)	0.5	(0.4)	0.6	(0.3)
	France	3.8	(1.5)	8.0	(0.9)	25.2	(3.4)	15.3	(1.5)	1.4	(1.3)	2.8	(0.7)
	Germany	4.2	(1.7)	7.5	(1.0)	24.3	(3.2)	12.0	(1.5)	3.5	(1.6)	2.8	(0.8)
	Greece	4.5	(1.4)	10.8	(1.4)	40.5	(3.5)	20.5	(1.8)	17.4	(3.4)	15.1	(1.7)
	Hungary	7.5	(2.3)	7.6	(1.2)	28.4	(3.5)	17.5	(1.9)	8.4	(2.3)	11.1	(1.7)
	Iceland	3.6	(1.5)	2.2	(0.7)	42.6	(3.6)	12.3	(1.6)	0.5	(0.5)	1.5	(0.6)
	Ireland	4.9	(1.4)	3.1	(0.7)	13.5	(2.1)	6.5	(1.0)	0.5	(0.5)	1.0	(0.4)
	Italy	5.7	(1.4)	7.8	(0.8)	38.7	(1.9)	19.3	(1.1)	2.1	(0.7)	6.9	(0.9)
	Japan	0.7	(0.2)	1.4	(0.4)	5.9	(1.2)	5.0	(0.7)	1.2	(0.7)	2.1	(0.6)
	Korea	c	c	1.2	(0.4)	14.9	(1.7)	4.6	(1.0)	3.7	(1.1)	1.5	(0.6)
	Luxembourg	6.6	(1.9)	8.4	(1.0)	23.5	(2.8)	13.8	(1.3)	2.3	(1.1)	5.8	(0.8)
	Mexico	19.7	(2.4)	35.5	(2.5)	41.4	(2.9)	41.4	(2.5)	4.0	(1.5)	16.4	(1.7)
	Netherlands	2.8	(1.0)	9.1	(1.7)	15.4	(2.5)	11.9	(1.8)	2.2	(1.1)	5.8	(1.2)
	New Zealand	1.8	(0.9)	4.1	(0.7)	8.9	(1.9)	7.8	(1.4)	0.5	(0.5)	1.9	(0.6)
	Norway	3.0	(1.2)	3.6	(0.8)	18.7	(2.6)	8.9	(1.3)	3.0	(1.1)	5.8	(1.1)
	Poland	12.5	(1.8)	19.1	(1.5)	37.0	(2.4)	24.8	(1.6)	13.3	(2.4)	8.3	(1.3)
	Portugal	8.8	(1.9)	11.3	(1.3)	37.4	(3.8)	18.2	(1.8)	1.8	(0.8)	8.1	(1.2)
	Slovak Republic	6.7	(1.8)	8.9	(1.7)	29.0	(3.1)	14.7	(2.3)	4.0	(1.8)	4.8	(1.2)
	Spain	4.0	(1.2)	3.4	(0.7)	21.0	(2.1)	7.6	(0.9)	3.6	(1.0)	4.0	(0.9)
	Sweden	1.9	(1.1)	2.6	(0.6)	13.3	(2.7)	4.1	(0.9)	0.4	(0.6)	1.3	(0.4)
	Switzerland	5.9	(1.9)	6.9	(0.7)	21.9	(2.0)	12.1	(1.1)	2.7	(0.7)	6.1	(0.7)
	Turkey	16.9	(2.9)	17.0	(2.4)	37.4	(3.8)	25.7	(2.3)	7.2	(2.3)	10.4	(1.8)
	United Kingdom	1.6	(0.7)	2.0	(0.5)	8.2	(1.4)	3.7	(0.7)	1.0	(0.5)	3.2	(0.9)
	United States	2.5	(1.0)	7.6	(1.4)	22.2	(3.0)	12.0	(1.1)	4.7	(1.4)	5.0	(1.4)
	OECD average	**5.5**	**(0.3)**	**7.6**	**(0.2)**	**24.0**	**(0.5)**	**13.0**	**(0.3)**	**3.3**	**(0.2)**	**5.0**	**(0.2)**
Partners	Argentina	8.5	(2.3)	25.0	(2.5)	37.4	(3.7)	33.8	(2.5)	4.1	(1.5)	18.0	(2.7)
	Azerbaijan	42.6	(2.9)	40.8	(2.7)	40.1	(3.2)	38.2	(3.2)	34.7	(3.2)	30.5	(2.8)
	Brazil	13.4	(2.5)	27.5	(1.9)	36.6	(3.5)	38.1	(2.0)	5.6	(1.7)	22.3	(1.8)
	Bulgaria	12.2	(2.7)	19.2	(2.2)	33.3	(3.4)	24.2	(2.1)	4.6	(1.6)	13.0	(1.8)
	Chile	15.2	(2.5)	18.4	(1.4)	42.2	(3.7)	23.4	(1.7)	5.9	(2.4)	15.0	(1.8)
	Colombia	32.8	(4.0)	40.2	(3.4)	57.8	(4.2)	51.4	(2.7)	7.7	(2.3)	18.9	(2.2)
	Croatia	6.2	(1.4)	11.3	(1.2)	39.9	(3.1)	23.1	(1.4)	1.9	(0.9)	5.1	(0.9)
	Estonia	9.2	(2.2)	10.1	(1.7)	28.0	(4.0)	18.3	(2.2)	6.5	(2.4)	5.8	(1.2)
	Hong Kong-China	6.8	(1.5)	5.5	(1.1)	18.6	(2.0)	8.2	(1.4)	10.9	(1.7)	5.6	(1.1)
	Indonesia	6.0	(1.6)	14.0	(1.8)	7.2	(1.6)	12.3	(1.2)	3.5	(1.1)	7.1	(1.1)
	Israel	12.5	(3.2)	23.9	(2.2)	36.4	(4.6)	26.2	(2.0)	9.7	(2.4)	17.5	(2.0)
	Jordan	38.8	(3.4)	42.1	(2.3)	46.1	(4.2)	43.2	(2.5)	15.3	(2.9)	27.1	(1.7)
	Kyrgyzstan	51.5	(3.5)	66.0	(2.3)	59.5	(3.4)	64.0	(2.3)	25.1	(3.1)	41.0	(2.7)
	Latvia	5.7	(1.7)	12.1	(1.6)	21.0	(3.2)	15.9	(2.0)	1.7	(1.2)	2.6	(0.8)
	Lithuania	7.3	(1.6)	10.9	(1.2)	21.8	(2.8)	18.0	(1.6)	4.3	(1.5)	3.6	(0.8)
	Macao-China	6.6	(1.3)	7.1	(1.2)	22.1	(2.5)	10.4	(1.7)	2.4	(0.8)	2.7	(0.6)
	Montenegro	25.3	(3.2)	30.4	(1.8)	44.9	(3.7)	36.1	(2.4)	1.3	(0.7)	10.6	(1.2)
	Romania	9.2	(2.5)	18.4	(2.9)	30.9	(5.0)	26.1	(2.1)	4.8	(3.2)	12.6	(1.9)
	Russian Federation	19.8	(2.8)	23.5	(3.1)	35.8	(2.9)	28.7	(2.9)	8.9	(3.0)	12.9	(3.1)
	Serbia	17.5	(2.6)	25.2	(1.8)	34.0	(3.7)	22.4	(1.9)	5.0	(1.6)	6.7	(1.0)
	Slovenia	10.1	(2.1)	11.1	(1.3)	29.1	(3.1)	16.0	(1.2)	6.4	(1.7)	7.6	(1.3)
	Chinese Taipei	4.4	(1.0)	7.0	(0.9)	24.4	(2.6)	11.7	(1.3)	5.5	(1.4)	7.4	(0.9)
	Thailand	24.9	(3.0)	24.7	(2.4)	43.6	(2.6)	29.3	(2.3)	37.6	(3.1)	30.3	(2.2)
	Tunisia	38.5	(3.3)	44.4	(2.2)	46.3	(3.1)	50.3	(2.8)	14.5	(2.7)	31.2	(2.3)
	Uruguay	7.5	(2.0)	12.1	(1.6)	25.9	(3.4)	20.3	(2.1)	5.4	(1.7)	10.2	(1.3)

Table A2.3b Engagement in science-related activities outside school, by student group

		Participation in science-related activities				
		Resilient students		Disadvantaged low achievers (DLA)		Difference in the mean index between resilient students and disadvantaged low achievers	
		Mean	S.E.	Mean	S.E.	Dif	S.E.
OECD	Australia	-0.04	(0.03)	-0.65	(0.03)	**0.59**	(0.04)
	Austria	0.17	(0.05)	-0.21	(0.05)	**0.37**	(0.08)
	Belgium	0.16	(0.04)	-0.21	(0.03)	**0.37**	(0.06)
	Canada	-0.01	(0.03)	-0.49	(0.04)	**0.45**	(0.06)
	Czech Republic	0.15	(0.05)	-0.01	(0.05)	**0.15**	(0.07)
	Denmark	0.08	(0.06)	-0.49	(0.04)	**0.54**	(0.07)
	Finland	0.04	(0.04)	-0.45	(0.03)	**0.47**	(0.05)
	France	0.13	(0.07)	-0.27	(0.04)	**0.39**	(0.08)
	Germany	0.20	(0.06)	-0.19	(0.04)	**0.42**	(0.07)
	Greece	0.35	(0.05)	-0.03	(0.05)	**0.37**	(0.07)
	Hungary	0.39	(0.06)	0.18	(0.04)	**0.19**	(0.08)
	Iceland	0.12	(0.06)	-0.64	(0.04)	**0.73**	(0.09)
	Ireland	-0.19	(0.07)	-0.82	(0.04)	**0.61**	(0.08)
	Italy	0.33	(0.03)	0.02	(0.02)	**0.31**	(0.04)
	Japan	-0.50	(0.04)	-0.89	(0.03)	**0.39**	(0.06)
	Korea	-0.10	(0.04)	-0.59	(0.05)	**0.48**	(0.07)
	Luxembourg	0.27	(0.06)	-0.12	(0.04)	**0.38**	(0.08)
	Mexico	0.65	(0.04)	0.87	(0.05)	**-0.20**	(0.08)
	Netherlands	-0.18	(0.06)	-0.46	(0.06)	**0.26**	(0.08)
	New Zealand	-0.13	(0.05)	-0.50	(0.05)	**0.35**	(0.07)
	Norway	0.07	(0.05)	-0.43	(0.04)	**0.49**	(0.07)
	Poland	0.62	(0.04)	0.58	(0.03)	0.03	(0.05)
	Portugal	0.58	(0.05)	0.24	(0.05)	**0.32**	(0.06)
	Slovak Republic	0.34	(0.05)	0.14	(0.07)	**0.22**	(0.09)
	Spain	-0.04	(0.04)	-0.45	(0.03)	**0.37**	(0.06)
	Sweden	-0.34	(0.07)	-0.77	(0.04)	**0.40**	(0.08)
	Switzerland	0.08	(0.05)	-0.19	(0.03)	**0.27**	(0.06)
	Turkey	0.67	(0.05)	0.31	(0.07)	**0.32**	(0.09)
	United Kingdom	-0.29	(0.06)	-0.68	(0.04)	**0.37**	(0.08)
	United States	0.20	(0.05)	-0.21	(0.06)	**0.38**	(0.10)
	OECD average	**0.13**	**(0.01)**	**-0.25**	**(0.01)**	**0.36**	**(0.01)**
Partners	Argentina	0.40	(0.07)	0.55	(0.06)	-0.17	(0.10)
	Azerbaijan	1.16	(0.06)	1.18	(0.06)	-0.03	(0.08)
	Brazil	0.33	(0.05)	0.64	(0.04)	**-0.33**	(0.07)
	Bulgaria	0.64	(0.04)	0.71	(0.05)	-0.06	(0.08)
	Chile	0.60	(0.07)	0.38	(0.05)	**0.23**	(0.07)
	Colombia	0.94	(0.05)	1.01	(0.05)	-0.08	(0.07)
	Croatia	0.44	(0.04)	0.22	(0.03)	**0.23**	(0.06)
	Estonia	0.40	(0.05)	0.29	(0.04)	0.11	(0.07)
	Hong Kong-China	0.39	(0.05)	-0.12	(0.05)	**0.46**	(0.07)
	Indonesia	0.34	(0.04)	0.36	(0.06)	-0.03	(0.07)
	Israel	0.28	(0.07)	0.19	(0.07)	0.09	(0.13)
	Jordan	0.93	(0.06)	0.92	(0.04)	-0.02	(0.07)
	Kyrgyzstan	1.06	(0.04)	1.49	(0.04)	**-0.35**	(0.07)
	Latvia	0.24	(0.05)	0.16	(0.04)	0.07	(0.08)
	Lithuania	0.27	(0.05)	0.21	(0.04)	0.06	(0.07)
	Macao-China	0.28	(0.05)	0.01	(0.04)	**0.25**	(0.07)
	Montenegro	0.68	(0.05)	0.74	(0.04)	-0.08	(0.06)
	Romania	0.59	(0.05)	0.53	(0.06)	0.03	(0.09)
	Russian Federation	0.56	(0.05)	0.49	(0.08)	0.05	(0.07)
	Serbia	0.55	(0.06)	0.50	(0.04)	0.04	(0.08)
	Slovenia	0.52	(0.05)	0.29	(0.04)	**0.24**	(0.07)
	Chinese Taipei	0.43	(0.04)	0.11	(0.03)	**0.31**	(0.06)
	Thailand	1.19	(0.04)	0.90	(0.02)	**0.26**	(0.04)
	Tunisia	0.94	(0.04)	1.16	(0.03)	**-0.20**	(0.06)
	Uruguay	0.28	(0.06)	0.17	(0.05)	0.08	(0.08)

Note: Values that are statistically different are indicated in bold.

Table A2.3c Relationship between being resilient and PISA index of science activities outside the school

			Increased likelihood of being resilient associated with one unit on the PISA index of science activities			
			After accounting for ESCS, gender, immigrant background, grade, using test language		After accounting for Mean ESCS, ESCS, gender, immigrant background, grade, using test language	
		Ratio	S.E.	Ratio	S.E.	Ratio	S.E.

OECD

	Ratio	S.E.	Ratio	S.E.	Ratio	S.E.
Australia	**1.76**	(0.04)	**1.77**	(0.04)	**1.79**	(0.05)
Austria	**1.47**	(0.08)	**1.68**	(0.09)	**1.68**	(0.09)
Belgium	**1.43**	(0.06)	**1.74**	(0.08)	**1.78**	(0.09)
Canada	**1.46**	(0.06)	**1.58**	(0.06)	**1.59**	(0.06)
Czech Republic	**1.24**	(0.09)	**1.34**	(0.10)	**1.38**	(0.10)
Denmark	**1.66**	(0.08)	**1.83**	(0.08)	**1.85**	(0.08)
Finland	**1.74**	(0.07)	**1.76**	(0.08)	**1.76**	(0.08)
France	**1.51**	(0.08)	**1.71**	(0.11)	**1.69**	(0.12)
Germany	**1.52**	(0.09)	**1.50**	(0.11)	**1.58**	(0.14)
Greece	**1.36**	(0.06)	**1.39**	(0.07)	**1.39**	(0.07)
Hungary	**1.26**	(0.10)	**1.37**	(0.11)	**1.39**	(0.13)
Iceland	**1.81**	(0.09)	**1.88**	(0.10)	**1.88**	(0.10)
Ireland	**1.73**	(0.07)	**1.79**	(0.08)	**1.81**	(0.08)
Italy	**1.42**	(0.05)	**1.38**	(0.06)	**1.32**	(0.06)
Japan	**1.48**	(0.07)	**1.46**	(0.07)	**1.48**	(0.08)
Korea	**1.57**	(0.07)	**1.58**	(0.07)	**1.53**	(0.07)
Luxembourg	**1.42**	(0.09)	**1.50**	(0.11)	**1.47**	(0.11)
Mexico	0.88	(0.09)	0.94	(0.09)	0.95	(0.09)
Netherlands	**1.30**	(0.07)	**1.52**	(0.07)	**1.60**	(0.10)
New Zealand	**1.47**	(0.08)	**1.60**	(0.09)	**1.64**	(0.09)
Norway	**1.56**	(0.08)	**1.68**	(0.08)	**1.68**	(0.09)
Poland	1.10	(0.09)	1.08	(0.09)	1.08	(0.09)
Portugal	**1.38**	(0.07)	**1.59**	(0.09)	**1.63**	(0.10)
Slovak Republic	**1.43**	(0.13)	**1.51**	(0.13)	**1.54**	(0.13)
Spain	**1.39**	(0.06)	**1.42**	(0.07)	**1.44**	(0.07)
Sweden	**1.50**	(0.10)	**1.70**	(0.12)	**1.71**	(0.11)
Switzerland	**1.31**	(0.07)	**1.52**	(0.09)	**1.51**	(0.09)
Turkey	**1.36**	(0.09)	**1.33**	(0.09)	**1.33**	(0.09)
United Kingdom	**1.39**	(0.08)	**1.44**	(0.08)	**1.46**	(0.08)
United States	**1.46**	(0.11)	**1.56**	(0.14)	**1.58**	(0.14)
OECD average	**1.43**	(0.01)	**1.52**	(0.02)	**1.54**	(0.02)

Partners

	Ratio	S.E.	Ratio	S.E.	Ratio	S.E.
Argentina	0.92	(0.09)	1.02	(0.10)	1.06	(0.11)
Azerbaijan	0.99	(0.10)	1.00	(0.10)	1.00	(0.10)
Brazil	**0.79**	(0.07)	0.84	(0.09)	0.86	(0.09)
Bulgaria	1.00	(0.10)	1.05	(0.11)	1.15	(0.11)
Chile	**1.26**	(0.07)	**1.32**	(0.08)	**1.39**	(0.09)
Colombia	0.95	(0.11)	1.05	(0.13)	1.05	(0.13)
Croatia	**1.34**	(0.08)	**1.36**	(0.09)	**1.41**	(0.09)
Estonia	1.18	(0.12)	1.23	(0.14)	1.24	(0.14)
Hong Kong-China	**1.52**	(0.07)	**1.57**	(0.08)	**1.56**	(0.08)
Indonesia	0.95	(0.11)	0.97	(0.12)	0.94	(0.12)
Israel	1.04	(0.08)	1.07	(0.08)	**1.18**	(0.09)
Jordan	1.01	(0.08)	1.04	(0.09)	1.04	(0.10)
Kyrgyzstan	**0.53**	(0.12)	**0.50**	(0.12)	**0.54**	(0.12)
Latvia	1.14	(0.14)	1.04	(0.14)	1.08	(0.14)
Lithuania	1.11	(0.11)	1.08	(0.11)	1.10	(0.12)
Macao-China	**1.38**	(0.08)	**1.41**	(0.09)	**1.41**	(0.10)
Montenegro	0.96	(0.09)	0.99	(0.10)	1.07	(0.10)
Romania	1.08	(0.13)	1.06	(0.14)	1.15	(0.16)
Russian Federation	1.08	(0.09)	1.16	(0.08)	1.17	(0.08)
Serbia	1.11	(0.11)	1.11	(0.11)	1.16	(0.12)
Slovenia	**1.32**	(0.10)	**1.28**	(0.09)	**1.39**	(0.11)
Chinese Taipei	**1.37**	(0.08)	**1.33**	(0.08)	**1.37**	(0.09)
Thailand	**2.02**	(0.14)	**1.85**	(0.15)	**1.88**	(0.16)
Tunisia	**0.77**	(0.11)	0.90	(0.13)	0.92	(0.14)
Uruguay	1.14	(0.08)	**1.27**	(0.09)	**1.28**	(0.10)

Note: Values that are statistically different are indicated in bold.

[Part 1/2]
Table A2.4a Science self-efficacy (underlying percentages), by student group

Percentage of students being able to do easily or with a bit of effort in following tasks

		Recognise the science question that underlies a newspaper report on a health issue			Explain why earthquakes occur more frequently in some areas than in others			Describe the role of antibiotics in the treatment of disease			Identify the science question associated with the disposal of garbage		
		Resilient students		Disadvantaged low achievers (DLA)		Resilient students		Disadvantaged low achievers (DLA)		Resilient students		Disadvantaged low achievers (DLA)		Resilient students		Disadvantaged low achievers (DLA)	
		%	S.E.	%	S.E.	%	S.E.	%	S.E.	%	S.E.	%	S.E.	%	S.E.	%	S.E.
OECD	Australia	89.3	(1.7)	57.3	(1.4)	91.2	(1.1)	59.0	(1.4)	73.6	(2.0)	35.3	(1.5)	66.2	(2.1)	45.6	(1.3)
	Austria	83.7	(2.7)	52.8	(2.2)	91.9	(1.7)	53.6	(2.1)	62.3	(3.2)	38.1	(2.2)	70.3	(3.0)	50.2	(2.2)
	Belgium	83.8	(1.7)	59.1	(1.8)	80.5	(2.1)	53.1	(2.0)	71.1	(2.7)	44.0	(1.9)	58.4	(2.9)	40.8	(1.6)
	Canada	86.9	(2.0)	59.0	(1.7)	84.5	(2.0)	58.2	(1.5)	69.0	(2.1)	38.3	(1.7)	71.1	(2.4)	46.2	(1.8)
	Czech Republic	86.3	(2.3)	63.3	(2.2)	88.2	(2.4)	66.7	(2.3)	75.1	(3.3)	63.3	(2.0)	66.3	(3.3)	53.0	(2.3)
	Denmark	85.5	(2.8)	60.6	(2.3)	84.8	(2.8)	60.5	(1.8)	51.0	(3.7)	32.9	(2.0)	60.7	(3.2)	40.0	(2.2)
	Finland	85.4	(2.4)	61.5	(2.0)	94.2	(1.3)	67.4	(1.8)	63.4	(2.4)	32.6	(2.1)	75.2	(3.7)	44.9	(2.0)
	France	73.5	(3.5)	52.6	(2.0)	89.5	(3.4)	61.9	(1.9)	77.3	(3.4)	54.8	(1.8)	59.5	(4.0)	41.2	(1.9)
	Germany	87.5	(2.4)	60.9	(2.8)	91.9	(2.5)	69.3	(2.3)	75.7	(4.2)	46.6	(2.2)	68.3	(4.0)	49.9	(2.2)
	Greece	67.4	(3.3)	54.7	(1.7)	78.6	(2.8)	48.3	(2.1)	67.3	(3.9)	41.3	(2.0)	62.7	(3.1)	55.2	(2.0)
	Hungary	79.7	(3.3)	61.7	(2.1)	82.2	(3.0)	49.4	(1.8)	69.9	(4.7)	47.7	(2.1)	72.7	(4.3)	66.3	(2.3)
	Iceland	83.2	(2.7)	51.5	(2.3)	90.9	(2.4)	58.0	(2.2)	70.6	(2.9)	46.8	(2.3)	66.7	(3.1)	42.1	(2.2)
	Ireland	79.6	(2.6)	48.7	(1.8)	89.9	(2.6)	60.1	(2.6)	73.5	(3.1)	33.6	(2.2)	78.1	(2.7)	54.0	(2.1)
	Italy	73.0	(2.4)	54.5	(1.8)	85.8	(1.4)	65.1	(1.4)	51.9	(1.7)	34.8	(1.4)	60.4	(2.1)	48.2	(1.7)
	Japan	70.0	(2.5)	51.6	(2.1)	74.0	(2.7)	40.7	(1.9)	35.1	(3.0)	24.2	(1.6)	63.5	(2.8)	53.1	(2.1)
	Korea	77.1	(2.6)	44.8	(2.4)	86.8	(2.0)	45.3	(2.5)	64.3	(3.1)	39.5	(2.1)	68.3	(3.2)	53.3	(2.5)
	Luxembourg	76.5	(3.3)	59.2	(1.8)	89.1	(2.6)	58.7	(1.7)	63.0	(4.0)	40.7	(1.8)	65.7	(4.2)	39.9	(1.8)
	Mexico	84.0	(1.7)	70.1	(2.0)	78.4	(2.5)	64.2	(1.9)	56.5	(2.9)	54.8	(2.2)	79.5	(2.3)	75.1	(1.6)
	Netherlands	83.6	(2.3)	68.8	(2.7)	90.5	(2.1)	67.1	(2.4)	73.4	(2.8)	53.7	(2.1)	58.2	(2.8)	54.2	(2.1)
	New Zealand	85.1	(2.8)	53.9	(2.1)	91.3	(2.0)	56.8	(1.6)	75.9	(3.6)	32.1	(2.1)	71.6	(3.5)	43.6	(2.3)
	Norway	71.6	(3.1)	47.7	(2.0)	90.1	(2.0)	58.1	(2.2)	85.6	(2.1)	61.8	(2.0)	76.6	(2.8)	50.3	(2.1)
	Poland	83.4	(2.2)	60.4	(1.8)	87.7	(2.1)	55.8	(1.9)	81.8	(2.4)	55.6	(2.1)	72.3	(3.0)	46.4	(2.2)
	Portugal	82.6	(2.4)	61.8	(2.1)	87.5	(2.7)	59.5	(2.4)	69.2	(3.1)	49.1	(2.1)	78.5	(3.3)	70.6	(2.0)
	Slovak Republic	88.6	(2.6)	71.5	(2.6)	86.5	(3.0)	57.4	(2.7)	66.1	(3.3)	54.0	(3.3)	64.8	(3.3)	52.0	(2.5)
	Spain	69.5	(2.5)	43.2	(2.0)	85.1	(1.9)	52.8	(1.7)	65.7	(2.7)	38.3	(1.7)	61.7	(2.4)	42.9	(1.7)
	Sweden	75.7	(4.0)	47.4	(2.3)	90.8	(2.5)	60.0	(2.2)	63.4	(3.8)	39.4	(2.1)	70.2	(3.3)	37.0	(2.2)
	Switzerland	79.5	(2.7)	50.2	(1.7)	87.2	(2.0)	58.4	(1.5)	61.0	(2.8)	35.1	(1.5)	63.0	(2.7)	38.8	(1.7)
	Turkey	84.5	(2.6)	64.2	(2.7)	85.2	(3.0)	56.4	(2.5)	72.8	(3.3)	44.6	(2.8)	75.3	(3.0)	52.8	(2.9)
	United Kingdom	89.7	(2.2)	60.2	(2.0)	87.9	(2.3)	53.1	(1.9)	73.1	(3.2)	37.0	(1.7)	79.1	(2.5)	51.4	(1.6)
	United States	87.2	(2.3)	65.9	(2.5)	87.2	(2.9)	60.2	(1.9)	74.6	(4.3)	45.6	(2.8)	69.2	(3.5)	55.0	(3.0)
	OECD average	81.1	(0.5)	57.3	(0.4)	87.0	(0.4)	57.8	(0.4)	67.8	(0.6)	43.2	(0.4)	68.5	(0.6)	49.8	(0.4)
Partners	Argentina	84.3	(2.7)	59.5	(2.9)	71.5	(4.2)	52.8	(2.9)	53.4	(3.9)	40.1	(2.9)	69.9	(3.7)	59.2	(3.1)
	Azerbaijan	57.3	(4.0)	55.4	(3.5)	50.8	(3.6)	37.9	(3.2)	44.7	(3.2)	36.0	(3.7)	52.5	(4.8)	48.9	(2.7)
	Brazil	81.0	(2.7)	63.8	(2.4)	67.4	(3.9)	49.2	(2.1)	55.2	(3.6)	45.6	(2.0)	78.3	(3.2)	71.1	(2.1)
	Bulgaria	75.3	(3.7)	58.4	(2.4)	76.5	(3.6)	45.9	(2.2)	62.9	(3.9)	42.8	(2.7)	75.5	(3.7)	61.2	(2.8)
	Chile	64.8	(3.6)	53.6	(2.1)	80.9	(3.1)	57.2	(2.1)	58.1	(3.7)	46.2	(2.4)	62.8	(4.0)	52.8	(2.0)
	Colombia	70.5	(4.1)	60.5	(2.8)	74.6	(3.6)	53.7	(2.5)	59.4	(5.6)	50.7	(3.1)	79.7	(4.2)	67.0	(2.7)
	Croatia	85.9	(2.0)	64.5	(1.9)	84.2	(2.3)	55.4	(2.0)	82.6	(2.4)	59.2	(1.5)	79.7	(2.7)	63.0	(1.8)
	Estonia	88.4	(2.1)	61.8	(3.2)	82.4	(3.2)	52.1	(2.2)	65.0	(3.1)	46.5	(2.1)	75.7	(3.0)	59.1	(2.5)
	Hong Kong-China	85.6	(2.2)	63.6	(1.7)	80.0	(2.2)	47.6	(1.9)	58.2	(2.8)	40.7	(2.4)	82.8	(2.5)	59.9	(2.3)
	Indonesia	55.1	(3.2)	52.9	(2.4)	40.2	(3.3)	34.1	(2.3)	42.7	(3.8)	36.5	(2.3)	60.6	(2.9)	55.7	(2.0)
	Israel	84.0	(3.2)	70.7	(2.4)	74.2	(3.5)	57.0	(2.6)	65.7	(4.0)	48.8	(1.9)	72.1	(3.5)	58.0	(2.1)
	Jordan	75.6	(3.7)	62.5	(2.5)	80.3	(2.3)	58.0	(1.8)	75.7	(3.1)	55.1	(2.0)	77.9	(2.6)	70.5	(1.9)
	Kyrgyzstan	81.9	(3.1)	79.8	(2.0)	63.0	(3.5)	51.5	(3.3)	53.5	(3.9)	45.6	(2.9)	65.8	(3.9)	57.9	(3.0)
	Latvia	80.2	(2.3)	66.6	(2.1)	85.7	(2.2)	61.8	(2.8)	59.2	(4.1)	38.0	(3.2)	66.0	(3.6)	56.9	(3.1)
	Lithuania	84.6	(2.6)	69.2	(2.2)	92.0	(2.3)	60.2	(2.0)	73.9	(3.4)	47.6	(2.2)	68.8	(4.0)	60.9	(2.0)
	Macao-China	73.3	(3.0)	57.2	(2.5)	82.5	(2.4)	46.3	(2.4)	55.9	(3.5)	36.7	(2.4)	69.5	(3.0)	59.3	(2.5)
	Montenegro	67.8	(2.8)	48.3	(2.3)	79.7	(2.9)	44.4	(2.0)	76.8	(2.6)	44.8	(2.2)	73.7	(3.1)	53.0	(2.5)
	Romania	70.2	(5.0)	61.9	(2.9)	61.8	(4.4)	41.1	(2.2)	45.4	(6.2)	33.6	(2.4)	46.8	(6.1)	42.1	(2.9)
	Russian Federation	74.1	(2.9)	56.1	(2.3)	75.4	(2.2)	50.9	(2.9)	62.8	(3.0)	46.5	(2.7)	77.0	(2.5)	59.1	(2.5)
	Serbia	80.2	(2.5)	64.1	(2.0)	73.2	(3.5)	46.8	(2.4)	67.9	(3.6)	44.2	(2.0)	77.8	(3.3)	66.4	(1.7)
	Slovenia	79.8	(3.4)	59.8	(1.7)	85.8	(2.6)	52.8	(2.1)	54.3	(4.4)	34.6	(1.7)	72.1	(3.7)	45.8	(2.5)
	Chinese Taipei	82.0	(2.5)	55.1	(1.8)	88.2	(1.5)	53.3	(1.6)	66.1	(2.3)	39.4	(1.6)	78.0	(2.3)	63.1	(1.9)
	Thailand	87.3	(2.2)	83.0	(1.9)	81.4	(2.4)	58.8	(2.3)	62.8	(2.9)	56.3	(3.4)	88.6	(2.4)	81.0	(1.6)
	Tunisia	77.5	(3.0)	60.7	(2.4)	63.0	(3.4)	39.7	(2.3)	47.1	(3.1)	38.6	(2.4)	70.0	(2.8)	64.2	(2.6)
	Uruguay	86.7	(3.0)	70.2	(1.8)	82.3	(2.8)	56.5	(2.5)	59.3	(3.7)	50.2	(2.3)	68.6	(4.2)	59.9	(2.5)

Table A2.4a [Part 2/2] Science self-efficacy (underlying percentages), by student group

Percentage of students being able to do easily or with a bit of effort in following tasks

	Predict how changes to an environment will affect the survival of certain species				Interpret the scientific information provided on the labelling of food items				Discuss how new evidence can lead you to change your understanding about the possibility of life on mars				Identify the better of two explanations for the formation of acid rain			
	Resilient students		Disadvantaged low achievers (DLA)		Resilient students		Disadvantaged low achievers (DLA)		Resilient students		Disadvantaged low achievers (DLA)		Resilient students		Disadvantaged low achievers (DLA)	
	%	S.E.	%	S.E.	%	S.E.	%	S.E.	%	S.E.	%	S.E.	%	S.E.	%	S.E.

OECD

Australia	84.2	(1.7)	54.7	(1.4)	73.3	(1.9)	50.8	(1.3)	65.6	(2.1)	37.4	(1.4)	68.2	(2.0)	33.5	(1.3)
Austria	69.6	(2.6)	41.2	(1.8)	57.8	(2.9)	38.8	(1.9)	40.0	(2.9)	28.5	(2.1)	74.1	(2.9)	37.9	(2.4)
Belgium	72.2	(2.3)	46.4	(1.7)	73.1	(2.6)	53.3	(1.7)	64.0	(2.6)	39.4	(1.5)	75.8	(2.3)	39.7	(1.5)
Canada	85.4	(1.7)	60.9	(1.4)	79.9	(2.0)	56.2	(1.4)	67.4	(2.0)	40.2	(1.6)	74.3	(1.7)	41.1	(1.5)
Czech Republic	74.9	(3.0)	52.9	(2.1)	63.8	(3.8)	59.7	(2.0)	66.2	(3.7)	46.4	(2.3)	65.5	(3.6)	49.2	(1.9)
Denmark	71.7	(3.2)	39.4	(2.3)	80.6	(2.8)	51.7	(2.3)	71.1	(3.0)	46.1	(2.2)	60.5	(3.2)	33.8	(2.3)
Finland	67.1	(3.4)	40.4	(2.3)	74.2	(3.0)	56.6	(1.9)	76.0	(2.3)	44.1	(2.1)	61.0	(2.7)	28.2	(1.9)
France	70.7	(3.6)	42.8	(2.0)	71.2	(3.4)	58.6	(1.9)	61.5	(3.6)	36.7	(1.7)	55.0	(3.4)	32.3	(1.7)
Germany	77.1	(3.6)	54.4	(1.9)	65.5	(3.8)	45.7	(2.0)	53.9	(4.5)	30.8	(1.7)	81.7	(3.4)	42.9	(2.0)
Greece	61.7	(3.4)	44.9	(2.1)	53.3	(3.5)	47.0	(2.1)	43.5	(3.3)	33.6	(2.0)	71.8	(3.6)	40.3	(2.0)
Hungary	51.3	(3.5)	40.4	(2.3)	63.3	(3.9)	62.0	(2.1)	35.1	(3.5)	31.7	(2.6)	73.7	(3.3)	47.5	(2.6)
Iceland	83.2	(2.9)	48.8	(2.1)	79.9	(2.8)	55.6	(2.0)	65.6	(3.3)	39.9	(2.3)	63.6	(3.2)	35.8	(2.2)
Ireland	67.8	(3.3)	49.8	(2.0)	72.3	(3.2)	47.5	(2.2)	46.9	(3.4)	28.8	(1.9)	75.3	(2.6)	43.4	(2.0)
Italy	73.4	(1.9)	49.2	(1.7)	64.5	(2.3)	52.2	(1.7)	51.2	(2.2)	36.9	(1.5)	66.1	(2.1)	44.5	(1.8)
Japan	62.0	(2.4)	41.4	(2.0)	46.3	(2.9)	34.4	(1.9)	30.4	(2.6)	17.4	(1.4)	52.1	(3.1)	31.2	(1.8)
Korea	55.0	(2.7)	36.8	(2.0)	50.4	(2.9)	29.9	(1.6)	41.1	(2.6)	25.9	(1.8)	67.5	(3.8)	39.5	(1.8)
Luxembourg	67.8	(3.8)	47.2	(1.8)	61.2	(4.7)	46.0	(1.8)	42.4	(4.4)	42.8	(1.8)	59.8	(4.3)	38.6	(1.8)
Mexico	67.5	(2.6)	63.8	(2.4)	66.9	(2.8)	57.7	(2.5)	55.3	(3.0)	42.8	(2.2)	64.9	(2.7)	56.0	(2.6)
Netherlands	64.2	(3.7)	50.4	(2.2)	63.2	(3.4)	48.0	(2.2)	58.9	(3.7)	41.9	(2.2)	75.7	(3.0)	49.7	(2.0)
New Zealand	80.4	(3.0)	45.0	(1.8)	69.5	(3.2)	51.6	(2.3)	62.4	(3.9)	37.3	(2.2)	64.4	(3.4)	31.0	(2.0)
Norway	71.4	(3.1)	53.0	(2.1)	72.9	(2.6)	48.9	(2.4)	66.5	(2.7)	43.8	(2.2)	87.8	(2.0)	58.9	(2.1)
Poland	79.3	(2.8)	55.7	(1.9)	84.2	(2.3)	71.9	(1.8)	68.4	(2.7)	41.4	(1.7)	82.6	(2.4)	56.1	(1.8)
Portugal	81.4	(2.7)	61.1	(2.3)	80.7	(2.5)	62.1	(2.2)	65.9	(2.7)	44.5	(2.3)	77.5	(3.3)	50.1	(2.1)
Slovak Republic	51.2	(3.5)	45.9	(2.9)	77.9	(3.1)	71.2	(1.8)	67.5	(3.5)	44.0	(2.5)	79.3	(3.2)	54.0	(2.2)
Spain	65.6	(2.4)	41.6	(1.9)	67.9	(2.9)	50.3	(2.0)	65.4	(2.4)	37.9	(1.8)	77.3	(3.0)	39.6	(1.8)
Sweden	75.3	(3.1)	46.9	(2.3)	70.6	(3.2)	43.7	(2.1)	63.2	(3.8)	36.9	(2.3)	65.7	(3.6)	42.4	(2.5)
Switzerland	70.6	(3.7)	42.5	(1.7)	65.0	(3.0)	38.4	(1.5)	44.0	(2.9)	31.3	(1.3)	59.5	(3.8)	32.4	(1.5)
Turkey	73.6	(3.8)	56.0	(2.7)	76.5	(3.0)	63.3	(2.7)	56.6	(4.0)	43.7	(2.4)	65.2	(3.1)	42.1	(2.9)
United Kingdom	87.9	(2.1)	54.3	(1.7)	78.0	(2.5)	53.7	(1.7)	65.2	(3.0)	35.0	(1.7)	77.5	(2.4)	40.0	(1.7)
United States	89.1	(2.1)	61.3	(2.7)	76.8	(3.1)	60.1	(2.9)	67.3	(3.2)	47.2	(2.6)	67.1	(3.3)	45.9	(3.1)
OECD average	71.7	(0.5)	49.0	(0.4)	69.4	(0.6)	52.2	(0.4)	57.6	(0.6)	37.8	(0.4)	69.7	(0.6)	41.9	(0.4)

Partners

Argentina	73.6	(4.1)	52.9	(3.4)	73.6	(3.4)	60.8	(2.7)	55.3	(3.7)	38.6	(3.1)	64.6	(3.9)	47.6	(2.9)
Azerbaijan	47.8	(5.0)	42.4	(4.0)	52.7	(3.8)	49.2	(3.6)	30.4	(3.9)	32.7	(2.9)	36.2	(3.3)	33.9	(3.2)
Brazil	68.1	(3.7)	58.8	(2.4)	67.1	(3.4)	60.2	(2.2)	38.0	(3.5)	37.4	(2.3)	51.8	(3.9)	39.8	(2.3)
Bulgaria	68.9	(4.1)	49.0	(2.2)	76.2	(3.0)	58.3	(2.5)	49.4	(4.1)	34.5	(2.6)	52.5	(3.8)	36.3	(2.3)
Chile	73.5	(3.1)	54.7	(2.4)	71.8	(3.6)	63.0	(1.8)	52.4	(3.1)	43.3	(2.5)	72.8	(4.1)	51.0	(2.1)
Colombia	76.0	(4.0)	62.6	(3.3)	67.6	(5.7)	63.4	(2.9)	48.1	(5.0)	39.5	(2.9)	63.6	(4.3)	48.3	(3.2)
Croatia	70.6	(2.7)	54.3	(2.0)	59.0	(2.7)	51.9	(2.1)	60.7	(2.7)	37.4	(1.9)	83.0	(2.2)	56.9	(2.1)
Estonia	65.4	(3.2)	44.5	(3.0)	73.6	(3.2)	64.2	(2.7)	55.1	(3.4)	29.1	(2.4)	71.8	(3.4)	33.0	(2.2)
Hong Kong-China	73.2	(2.7)	53.1	(2.2)	67.3	(2.5)	54.9	(2.4)	47.2	(3.1)	31.7	(2.0)	87.1	(1.9)	56.7	(2.4)
Indonesia	38.3	(3.0)	34.1	(2.2)	38.1	(3.1)	38.2	(2.4)	21.8	(3.2)	21.4	(1.9)	26.1	(3.2)	23.2	(2.0)
Israel	69.0	(3.7)	57.6	(2.2)	70.8	(3.9)	61.7	(2.2)	54.5	(4.6)	50.6	(2.3)	50.6	(4.5)	47.9	(2.7)
Jordan	64.6	(3.5)	57.3	(2.1)	77.9	(3.0)	73.8	(2.0)	50.1	(3.6)	45.8	(2.2)	73.4	(3.3)	48.8	(2.2)
Kyrgyzstan	61.6	(3.8)	61.7	(2.6)	68.8	(3.4)	61.5	(2.5)	42.7	(3.7)	45.2	(2.8)	41.2	(2.9)	44.0	(2.7)
Latvia	69.8	(3.5)	54.5	(3.2)	71.1	(3.3)	65.0	(2.4)	57.4	(4.1)	34.5	(2.2)	61.5	(3.7)	45.6	(2.3)
Lithuania	64.6	(3.5)	49.0	(2.0)	71.7	(3.0)	61.2	(2.6)	53.9	(3.8)	41.1	(2.0)	62.3	(3.4)	43.3	(2.2)
Macao-China	61.6	(2.8)	45.3	(2.5)	56.6	(2.9)	51.8	(2.4)	36.6	(2.6)	27.4	(2.1)	73.9	(2.8)	41.4	(2.3)
Montenegro	63.8	(3.3)	43.2	(2.5)	72.6	(2.8)	58.7	(2.2)	50.3	(3.2)	31.2	(2.3)	70.8	(3.9)	41.3	(2.3)
Romania	60.3	(5.1)	48.0	(3.4)	69.2	(4.8)	58.8	(3.6)	33.0	(3.7)	32.4	(2.1)	56.2	(4.1)	42.5	(3.0)
Russian Federation	51.2	(3.7)	45.0	(2.4)	77.0	(2.5)	66.9	(2.4)	30.5	(2.8)	31.1	(3.1)	62.0	(3.6)	37.6	(3.3)
Serbia	70.0	(4.3)	51.4	(2.3)	69.4	(2.9)	60.1	(1.6)	57.6	(3.9)	37.9	(2.1)	72.2	(3.0)	44.2	(2.4)
Slovenia	55.1	(3.7)	39.9	(2.4)	60.7	(3.5)	52.4	(2.3)	51.2	(4.2)	31.1	(1.8)	76.4	(3.5)	39.8	(2.0)
Chinese Taipei	71.2	(2.4)	51.9	(2.1)	80.5	(2.6)	59.1	(1.8)	56.0	(3.1)	37.1	(1.7)	75.7	(2.0)	48.6	(1.7)
Thailand	76.5	(2.9)	70.3	(1.8)	73.2	(3.1)	70.0	(2.1)	53.3	(3.1)	52.3	(2.4)	60.4	(3.4)	57.5	(2.1)
Tunisia	64.5	(3.1)	53.5	(2.9)	79.1	(2.4)	70.1	(2.1)	42.2	(3.3)	31.6	(2.2)	39.4	(2.9)	36.0	(1.8)
Uruguay	73.4	(3.2)	57.8	(2.6)	72.7	(3.1)	64.4	(2.4)	60.8	(4.0)	43.1	(2.6)	79.4	(2.9)	53.9	(2.5)

Table A2.4b Science self-efficacy by student group

<table>
<tr><th rowspan="3"></th><th colspan="6">Science self-efficacy</th></tr>
<tr><th colspan="2">Resilient students</th><th colspan="2">Disadvantaged low achievers (DLA)</th><th colspan="2">Difference in the mean index between resilient students and disadvantaged low achievers</th></tr>
<tr><th>Mean</th><th>S.E.</th><th>Mean</th><th>S.E.</th><th>Dif</th><th>S.E.</th></tr>
<tr><td colspan="7">OECD</td></tr>
<tr><td>Australia</td><td>0.50</td><td>(0.03)</td><td>-0.59</td><td>(0.03)</td><td>1.06</td><td>(0.04)</td></tr>
<tr><td>Austria</td><td>0.18</td><td>(0.05)</td><td>-0.69</td><td>(0.05)</td><td>0.88</td><td>(0.07)</td></tr>
<tr><td>Belgium</td><td>0.36</td><td>(0.04)</td><td>-0.58</td><td>(0.04)</td><td>0.91</td><td>(0.06)</td></tr>
<tr><td>Canada</td><td>0.54</td><td>(0.04)</td><td>-0.48</td><td>(0.04)</td><td>1.00</td><td>(0.06)</td></tr>
<tr><td>Czech Republic</td><td>0.39</td><td>(0.04)</td><td>-0.25</td><td>(0.04)</td><td>0.60</td><td>(0.07)</td></tr>
<tr><td>Denmark</td><td>0.25</td><td>(0.05)</td><td>-0.68</td><td>(0.04)</td><td>0.92</td><td>(0.07)</td></tr>
<tr><td>Finland</td><td>0.36</td><td>(0.04)</td><td>-0.55</td><td>(0.04)</td><td>0.90</td><td>(0.07)</td></tr>
<tr><td>France</td><td>0.31</td><td>(0.05)</td><td>-0.55</td><td>(0.04)</td><td>0.81</td><td>(0.08)</td></tr>
<tr><td>Germany</td><td>0.37</td><td>(0.05)</td><td>-0.51</td><td>(0.04)</td><td>0.86</td><td>(0.07)</td></tr>
<tr><td>Greece</td><td>0.07</td><td>(0.05)</td><td>-0.56</td><td>(0.03)</td><td>0.62</td><td>(0.06)</td></tr>
<tr><td>Hungary</td><td>0.10</td><td>(0.05)</td><td>-0.42</td><td>(0.03)</td><td>0.50</td><td>(0.08)</td></tr>
<tr><td>Iceland</td><td>0.53</td><td>(0.05)</td><td>-0.60</td><td>(0.04)</td><td>1.08</td><td>(0.08)</td></tr>
<tr><td>Ireland</td><td>0.38</td><td>(0.05)</td><td>-0.67</td><td>(0.04)</td><td>1.02</td><td>(0.07)</td></tr>
<tr><td>Italy</td><td>-0.05</td><td>(0.03)</td><td>-0.53</td><td>(0.03)</td><td>0.47</td><td>(0.03)</td></tr>
<tr><td>Japan</td><td>-0.34</td><td>(0.04)</td><td>-0.98</td><td>(0.04)</td><td>0.64</td><td>(0.07)</td></tr>
<tr><td>Korea</td><td>-0.04</td><td>(0.04)</td><td>-0.76</td><td>(0.04)</td><td>0.71</td><td>(0.07)</td></tr>
<tr><td>Luxembourg</td><td>0.16</td><td>(0.07)</td><td>-0.61</td><td>(0.04)</td><td>0.71</td><td>(0.09)</td></tr>
<tr><td>Mexico</td><td>0.20</td><td>(0.04)</td><td>-0.14</td><td>(0.05)</td><td>0.33</td><td>(0.07)</td></tr>
<tr><td>Netherlands</td><td>0.23</td><td>(0.04)</td><td>-0.37</td><td>(0.04)</td><td>0.58</td><td>(0.07)</td></tr>
<tr><td>New Zealand</td><td>0.38</td><td>(0.06)</td><td>-0.63</td><td>(0.04)</td><td>1.00</td><td>(0.07)</td></tr>
<tr><td>Norway</td><td>0.41</td><td>(0.05)</td><td>-0.48</td><td>(0.04)</td><td>0.86</td><td>(0.07)</td></tr>
<tr><td>Poland</td><td>0.59</td><td>(0.04)</td><td>-0.31</td><td>(0.03)</td><td>0.85</td><td>(0.07)</td></tr>
<tr><td>Portugal</td><td>0.52</td><td>(0.05)</td><td>-0.21</td><td>(0.04)</td><td>0.71</td><td>(0.08)</td></tr>
<tr><td>Slovak Republic</td><td>0.29</td><td>(0.05)</td><td>-0.30</td><td>(0.06)</td><td>0.59</td><td>(0.09)</td></tr>
<tr><td>Spain</td><td>0.31</td><td>(0.05)</td><td>-0.69</td><td>(0.04)</td><td>0.96</td><td>(0.07)</td></tr>
<tr><td>Sweden</td><td>0.24</td><td>(0.05)</td><td>-0.70</td><td>(0.05)</td><td>0.91</td><td>(0.07)</td></tr>
<tr><td>Switzerland</td><td>0.09</td><td>(0.04)</td><td>-0.73</td><td>(0.03)</td><td>0.79</td><td>(0.05)</td></tr>
<tr><td>Turkey</td><td>0.30</td><td>(0.04)</td><td>-0.41</td><td>(0.07)</td><td>0.66</td><td>(0.10)</td></tr>
<tr><td>United Kingdom</td><td>0.73</td><td>(0.05)</td><td>-0.51</td><td>(0.03)</td><td>1.18</td><td>(0.06)</td></tr>
<tr><td>United States</td><td>0.58</td><td>(0.06)</td><td>-0.31</td><td>(0.09)</td><td>0.84</td><td>(0.11)</td></tr>
<tr><td>OECD average</td><td>0.30</td><td>(0.01)</td><td>-0.53</td><td>(0.01)</td><td>0.80</td><td>(0.01)</td></tr>
<tr><td colspan="7">Partners</td></tr>
<tr><td>Argentina</td><td>0.21</td><td>(0.06)</td><td>-0.45</td><td>(0.05)</td><td>0.61</td><td>(0.09)</td></tr>
<tr><td>Azerbaijan</td><td>-0.61</td><td>(0.09)</td><td>-0.85</td><td>(0.11)</td><td>0.25</td><td>(0.14)</td></tr>
<tr><td>Brazil</td><td>0.01</td><td>(0.06)</td><td>-0.37</td><td>(0.05)</td><td>0.33</td><td>(0.08)</td></tr>
<tr><td>Bulgaria</td><td>0.18</td><td>(0.05)</td><td>-0.53</td><td>(0.06)</td><td>0.67</td><td>(0.09)</td></tr>
<tr><td>Chile</td><td>0.22</td><td>(0.06)</td><td>-0.35</td><td>(0.04)</td><td>0.55</td><td>(0.09)</td></tr>
<tr><td>Colombia</td><td>0.18</td><td>(0.06)</td><td>-0.28</td><td>(0.04)</td><td>0.41</td><td>(0.09)</td></tr>
<tr><td>Croatia</td><td>0.48</td><td>(0.04)</td><td>-0.37</td><td>(0.03)</td><td>0.80</td><td>(0.06)</td></tr>
<tr><td>Estonia</td><td>0.37</td><td>(0.05)</td><td>-0.45</td><td>(0.03)</td><td>0.79</td><td>(0.06)</td></tr>
<tr><td>Hong Kong-China</td><td>0.31</td><td>(0.05)</td><td>-0.49</td><td>(0.04)</td><td>0.77</td><td>(0.07)</td></tr>
<tr><td>Indonesia</td><td>-0.75</td><td>(0.05)</td><td>-0.97</td><td>(0.05)</td><td>0.20</td><td>(0.07)</td></tr>
<tr><td>Israel</td><td>0.27</td><td>(0.08)</td><td>-0.25</td><td>(0.06)</td><td>0.49</td><td>(0.12)</td></tr>
<tr><td>Jordan</td><td>0.38</td><td>(0.05)</td><td>-0.12</td><td>(0.04)</td><td>0.46</td><td>(0.08)</td></tr>
<tr><td>Kyrgyzstan</td><td>-0.22</td><td>(0.06)</td><td>-0.35</td><td>(0.06)</td><td>0.12</td><td>(0.11)</td></tr>
<tr><td>Latvia</td><td>0.21</td><td>(0.05)</td><td>-0.37</td><td>(0.04)</td><td>0.57</td><td>(0.06)</td></tr>
<tr><td>Lithuania</td><td>0.16</td><td>(0.05)</td><td>-0.40</td><td>(0.04)</td><td>0.57</td><td>(0.07)</td></tr>
<tr><td>Macao-China</td><td>0.07</td><td>(0.05)</td><td>-0.61</td><td>(0.05)</td><td>0.65</td><td>(0.07)</td></tr>
<tr><td>Montenegro</td><td>0.29</td><td>(0.05)</td><td>-0.63</td><td>(0.05)</td><td>0.87</td><td>(0.07)</td></tr>
<tr><td>Romania</td><td>-0.19</td><td>(0.07)</td><td>-0.69</td><td>(0.06)</td><td>0.43</td><td>(0.12)</td></tr>
<tr><td>Russian Federation</td><td>0.27</td><td>(0.05)</td><td>-0.49</td><td>(0.08)</td><td>0.68</td><td>(0.09)</td></tr>
<tr><td>Serbia</td><td>0.32</td><td>(0.06)</td><td>-0.35</td><td>(0.04)</td><td>0.63</td><td>(0.09)</td></tr>
<tr><td>Slovenia</td><td>0.09</td><td>(0.05)</td><td>-0.59</td><td>(0.04)</td><td>0.68</td><td>(0.07)</td></tr>
<tr><td>Chinese Taipei</td><td>0.46</td><td>(0.04)</td><td>-0.41</td><td>(0.04)</td><td>0.84</td><td>(0.06)</td></tr>
<tr><td>Thailand</td><td>0.13</td><td>(0.04)</td><td>-0.15</td><td>(0.04)</td><td>0.25</td><td>(0.06)</td></tr>
<tr><td>Tunisia</td><td>0.02</td><td>(0.04)</td><td>-0.35</td><td>(0.04)</td><td>0.36</td><td>(0.06)</td></tr>
<tr><td>Uruguay</td><td>0.36</td><td>(0.05)</td><td>-0.31</td><td>(0.05)</td><td>0.68</td><td>(0.07)</td></tr>
</table>

Note: Values that are statistically different are indicated in bold.

Table A2.4c Relationship between being resilient and PISA index of science efficacy

		Increased likelihood of being resilient associate with one unit on the PISA index of science efficacy				
				After accounting for ESCS, gender, immigrant, grade, using test language		After accounting for Mean ESCS, ESCS, gender, immigrant, grade, using test language
		Ratio	S.E.	Ratio	S.E.	Ratio	S.E.

OECD

Country	Ratio	S.E.	Ratio	S.E.	Ratio	S.E.
Australia	2.50	(0.06)	2.46	(0.06)	2.48	(0.06)
Austria	2.60	(0.09)	2.63	(0.11)	2.42	(0.10)
Belgium	2.57	(0.08)	2.84	(0.09)	2.63	(0.09)
Canada	2.20	(0.08)	2.18	(0.08)	2.19	(0.08)
Czech Republic	2.04	(0.11)	2.15	(0.13)	2.09	(0.14)
Denmark	2.43	(0.10)	2.55	(0.11)	2.56	(0.11)
Finland	2.87	(0.12)	2.81	(0.12)	2.82	(0.12)
France	2.49	(0.11)	2.64	(0.14)	2.51	(0.15)
Germany	2.55	(0.12)	2.25	(0.13)	2.18	(0.15)
Greece	1.91	(0.09)	1.94	(0.10)	1.89	(0.10)
Hungary	2.00	(0.15)	1.99	(0.17)	1.98	(0.19)
Iceland	2.28	(0.10)	2.31	(0.10)	2.31	(0.10)
Ireland	2.62	(0.11)	2.73	(0.12)	2.75	(0.12)
Italy	2.05	(0.06)	1.89	(0.06)	1.77	(0.06)
Japan	1.74	(0.08)	1.71	(0.08)	1.64	(0.09)
Korea	2.25	(0.13)	2.22	(0.12)	2.23	(0.13)
Luxembourg	1.89	(0.12)	1.91	(0.13)	1.90	(0.13)
Mexico	1.50	(0.08)	1.51	(0.08)	1.49	(0.08)
Netherlands	1.65	(0.07)	1.76	(0.08)	1.86	(0.10)
New Zealand	2.87	(0.12)	2.85	(0.12)	2.98	(0.13)
Norway	2.06	(0.11)	2.13	(0.11)	2.14	(0.11)
Poland	2.61	(0.11)	2.60	(0.11)	2.60	(0.11)
Portugal	2.15	(0.09)	2.28	(0.14)	2.33	(0.14)
Slovak Republic	2.00	(0.12)	2.00	(0.13)	1.93	(0.13)
Spain	2.29	(0.09)	2.16	(0.09)	2.16	(0.09)
Sweden	2.48	(0.09)	2.68	(0.11)	2.67	(0.11)
Switzerland	2.36	(0.09)	2.38	(0.11)	2.35	(0.11)
Turkey	1.76	(0.09)	1.69	(0.10)	1.67	(0.10)
United Kingdom	3.10	(0.09)	3.10	(0.09)	3.16	(0.10)
United States	1.86	(0.08)	1.91	(0.08)	1.96	(0.08)
OECD average	**2.22**	**(0.02)**	**2.24**	**(0.02)**	**2.22**	**(0.02)**

Partners

Country	Ratio	S.E.	Ratio	S.E.	Ratio	S.E.
Argentina	1.97	(0.11)	1.80	(0.12)	1.76	(0.13)
Azerbaijan	1.11	(0.08)	1.11	(0.08)	1.11	(0.08)
Brazil	1.39	(0.09)	1.34	(0.09)	1.35	(0.09)
Bulgaria	1.64	(0.07)	1.60	(0.08)	1.61	(0.08)
Chile	1.84	(0.11)	1.70	(0.12)	1.75	(0.12)
Colombia	1.55	(0.13)	1.52	(0.14)	1.52	(0.14)
Croatia	2.68	(0.10)	2.64	(0.10)	2.59	(0.11)
Estonia	2.83	(0.11)	2.75	(0.11)	2.78	(0.11)
Hong Kong-China	2.21	(0.10)	2.13	(0.10)	2.09	(0.10)
Indonesia	1.27	(0.10)	1.24	(0.10)	1.21	(0.10)
Israel	1.39	(0.09)	1.37	(0.09)	1.42	(0.09)
Jordan	1.39	(0.07)	1.42	(0.08)	1.42	(0.08)
Kyrgyzstan	1.09	(0.10)	1.08	(0.10)	1.09	(0.10)
Latvia	2.37	(0.11)	2.35	(0.13)	2.39	(0.13)
Lithuania	2.06	(0.13)	1.93	(0.13)	1.98	(0.13)
Macao-China	1.91	(0.10)	1.89	(0.12)	1.87	(0.12)
Montenegro	2.36	(0.11)	2.31	(0.11)	2.27	(0.11)
Romania	1.46	(0.12)	1.44	(0.13)	1.48	(0.14)
Russian Federation	1.84	(0.09)	1.86	(0.09)	1.87	(0.09)
Serbia	1.81	(0.09)	1.83	(0.10)	1.78	(0.10)
Slovenia	2.07	(0.11)	2.16	(0.10)	2.07	(0.11)
Chinese Taipei	2.10	(0.08)	2.07	(0.08)	1.94	(0.08)
Thailand	1.46	(0.10)	1.40	(0.10)	1.43	(0.10)
Tunisia	1.62	(0.09)	1.46	(0.11)	1.46	(0.11)
Uruguay	1.96	(0.09)	1.85	(0.09)	1.89	(0.10)

Note: Values that are statistically different are indicated in bold.

[Part 1/2]
Table A2.5a Science self-concept (underlying percentages), by student group

<table>
<tr><th colspan="13">Percentage of students agreeing or strongly agreeing with following statements</th></tr>
<tr><th></th><th colspan="4">Learning advance science topics would be easy for me</th><th colspan="4">I can usually give good answers to test questions on science topics</th><th colspan="4">I learn science topics quickly</th></tr>
<tr><th></th><th colspan="2">Resilient students</th><th colspan="2">Disadvantaged low achievers (DLA)</th><th colspan="2">Resilient students</th><th colspan="2">Disadvantaged low achievers (DLA)</th><th colspan="2">Resilient students</th><th colspan="2">Disadvantaged low achievers (DLA)</th></tr>
<tr><th></th><th>%</th><th>S.E.</th><th>%</th><th>S.E.</th><th>%</th><th>S.E.</th><th>%</th><th>S.E.</th><th>%</th><th>S.E.</th><th>%</th><th>S.E.</th></tr>
<tr><td>Australia</td><td>54.0</td><td>(2.3)</td><td>25.2</td><td>(1.3)</td><td>81.9</td><td>(1.7)</td><td>42.1</td><td>(1.7)</td><td>71.4</td><td>(2.2)</td><td>34.8</td><td>(1.5)</td></tr>
<tr><td>Austria</td><td>49.7</td><td>(3.9)</td><td>44.9</td><td>(3.0)</td><td>79.6</td><td>(2.8)</td><td>53.8</td><td>(2.1)</td><td>72.2</td><td>(3.0)</td><td>45.9</td><td>(2.4)</td></tr>
<tr><td>Belgium</td><td>42.2</td><td>(2.4)</td><td>38.2</td><td>(2.0)</td><td>77.2</td><td>(2.6)</td><td>46.9</td><td>(2.5)</td><td>60.6</td><td>(2.7)</td><td>41.1</td><td>(2.0)</td></tr>
<tr><td>Canada</td><td>68.9</td><td>(2.2)</td><td>37.0</td><td>(1.9)</td><td>86.7</td><td>(1.9)</td><td>51.9</td><td>(2.0)</td><td>80.7</td><td>(2.2)</td><td>45.1</td><td>(2.0)</td></tr>
<tr><td>Czech Republic</td><td>30.2</td><td>(3.5)</td><td>40.4</td><td>(2.6)</td><td>74.7</td><td>(3.5)</td><td>54.3</td><td>(2.2)</td><td>62.0</td><td>(3.6)</td><td>48.1</td><td>(2.6)</td></tr>
<tr><td>Denmark</td><td>45.2</td><td>(3.6)</td><td>24.0</td><td>(2.0)</td><td>77.6</td><td>(2.9)</td><td>46.7</td><td>(2.3)</td><td>69.5</td><td>(4.0)</td><td>40.4</td><td>(2.3)</td></tr>
<tr><td>Finland</td><td>63.0</td><td>(3.2)</td><td>34.1</td><td>(2.2)</td><td>84.6</td><td>(2.8)</td><td>46.4</td><td>(2.2)</td><td>76.1</td><td>(2.7)</td><td>39.1</td><td>(2.3)</td></tr>
<tr><td>France</td><td>49.8</td><td>(3.8)</td><td>37.3</td><td>(2.0)</td><td>69.9</td><td>(3.3)</td><td>50.7</td><td>(2.0)</td><td>64.4</td><td>(3.9)</td><td>38.9</td><td>(1.8)</td></tr>
<tr><td>Germany</td><td>71.6</td><td>(2.9)</td><td>63.7</td><td>(2.4)</td><td>76.6</td><td>(2.9)</td><td>51.8</td><td>(2.2)</td><td>75.2</td><td>(2.9)</td><td>49.5</td><td>(2.7)</td></tr>
<tr><td>Greece</td><td>51.4</td><td>(3.2)</td><td>48.8</td><td>(2.2)</td><td>66.4</td><td>(2.7)</td><td>48.5</td><td>(2.0)</td><td>56.5</td><td>(3.3)</td><td>42.6</td><td>(2.5)</td></tr>
<tr><td>Hungary</td><td>23.9</td><td>(3.2)</td><td>43.1</td><td>(3.4)</td><td>52.9</td><td>(3.3)</td><td>53.0</td><td>(2.6)</td><td>48.9</td><td>(3.6)</td><td>41.9</td><td>(2.0)</td></tr>
<tr><td>Iceland</td><td>63.1</td><td>(3.2)</td><td>24.4</td><td>(2.2)</td><td>85.4</td><td>(2.3)</td><td>37.9</td><td>(2.6)</td><td>78.2</td><td>(2.5)</td><td>31.5</td><td>(2.3)</td></tr>
<tr><td>Ireland</td><td>43.6</td><td>(3.5)</td><td>29.3</td><td>(2.6)</td><td>73.4</td><td>(3.3)</td><td>39.3</td><td>(2.3)</td><td>64.4</td><td>(3.2)</td><td>27.7</td><td>(2.5)</td></tr>
<tr><td>Italy</td><td>54.3</td><td>(2.2)</td><td>52.7</td><td>(1.5)</td><td>86.9</td><td>(1.4)</td><td>70.4</td><td>(1.3)</td><td>64.9</td><td>(2.2)</td><td>48.5</td><td>(1.6)</td></tr>
<tr><td>Japan</td><td>12.8</td><td>(2.0)</td><td>9.6</td><td>(1.3)</td><td>36.2</td><td>(3.4)</td><td>22.2</td><td>(1.8)</td><td>32.1</td><td>(3.2)</td><td>17.0</td><td>(1.3)</td></tr>
<tr><td>Korea</td><td>20.6</td><td>(2.2)</td><td>6.7</td><td>(1.2)</td><td>47.1</td><td>(2.8)</td><td>15.5</td><td>(1.5)</td><td>37.5</td><td>(2.8)</td><td>14.3</td><td>(1.5)</td></tr>
<tr><td>Luxembourg</td><td>72.5</td><td>(3.8)</td><td>56.5</td><td>(1.8)</td><td>78.8</td><td>(3.4)</td><td>55.3</td><td>(1.9)</td><td>67.5</td><td>(3.9)</td><td>50.9</td><td>(2.1)</td></tr>
<tr><td>Mexico</td><td>83.6</td><td>(2.0)</td><td>86.7</td><td>(1.5)</td><td>79.9</td><td>(3.2)</td><td>74.6</td><td>(1.6)</td><td>80.5</td><td>(2.4)</td><td>71.1</td><td>(2.3)</td></tr>
<tr><td>Netherlands</td><td>25.7</td><td>(2.8)</td><td>26.9</td><td>(2.5)</td><td>63.9</td><td>(3.9)</td><td>34.2</td><td>(2.4)</td><td>52.0</td><td>(3.7)</td><td>29.7</td><td>(2.6)</td></tr>
<tr><td>New Zealand</td><td>45.0</td><td>(3.2)</td><td>35.1</td><td>(2.0)</td><td>82.2</td><td>(2.8)</td><td>51.1</td><td>(2.1)</td><td>65.9</td><td>(3.0)</td><td>39.0</td><td>(2.4)</td></tr>
<tr><td>Norway</td><td>49.4</td><td>(3.8)</td><td>35.7</td><td>(2.2)</td><td>89.5</td><td>(2.3)</td><td>53.7</td><td>(2.3)</td><td>74.5</td><td>(3.7)</td><td>39.3</td><td>(2.2)</td></tr>
<tr><td>Poland</td><td>58.9</td><td>(3.2)</td><td>61.9</td><td>(2.0)</td><td>82.3</td><td>(2.3)</td><td>58.5</td><td>(2.1)</td><td>63.1</td><td>(2.9)</td><td>47.7</td><td>(2.1)</td></tr>
<tr><td>Portugal</td><td>53.5</td><td>(3.3)</td><td>48.5</td><td>(2.4)</td><td>92.5</td><td>(2.1)</td><td>72.4</td><td>(2.3)</td><td>84.8</td><td>(2.8)</td><td>62.3</td><td>(2.2)</td></tr>
<tr><td>Slovak Republic</td><td>53.7</td><td>(3.7)</td><td>46.1</td><td>(3.0)</td><td>74.5</td><td>(3.7)</td><td>50.6</td><td>(2.7)</td><td>64.2</td><td>(3.0)</td><td>50.5</td><td>(2.1)</td></tr>
<tr><td>Spain</td><td>61.0</td><td>(2.8)</td><td>49.1</td><td>(1.7)</td><td>74.2</td><td>(2.2)</td><td>42.5</td><td>(1.9)</td><td>62.6</td><td>(2.3)</td><td>34.6</td><td>(1.5)</td></tr>
<tr><td>Sweden</td><td>54.6</td><td>(4.0)</td><td>28.5</td><td>(2.4)</td><td>87.5</td><td>(3.3)</td><td>48.8</td><td>(2.0)</td><td>71.3</td><td>(3.2)</td><td>35.9</td><td>(2.5)</td></tr>
<tr><td>Switzerland</td><td>61.0</td><td>(2.7)</td><td>48.0</td><td>(1.8)</td><td>76.3</td><td>(2.5)</td><td>48.3</td><td>(1.5)</td><td>65.1</td><td>(3.0)</td><td>45.2</td><td>(1.7)</td></tr>
<tr><td>Turkey</td><td>70.0</td><td>(3.7)</td><td>67.8</td><td>(3.1)</td><td>65.5</td><td>(3.3)</td><td>58.1</td><td>(3.3)</td><td>71.5</td><td>(2.9)</td><td>57.7</td><td>(2.7)</td></tr>
<tr><td>United Kingdom</td><td>50.7</td><td>(2.9)</td><td>41.4</td><td>(2.1)</td><td>84.9</td><td>(2.3)</td><td>57.2</td><td>(1.7)</td><td>66.3</td><td>(2.7)</td><td>38.1</td><td>(1.8)</td></tr>
<tr><td>United States</td><td>73.7</td><td>(3.6)</td><td>43.6</td><td>(2.3)</td><td>77.1</td><td>(2.9)</td><td>53.3</td><td>(2.7)</td><td>73.5</td><td>(3.1)</td><td>52.6</td><td>(1.9)</td></tr>
<tr><td>OECD average</td><td>51.9</td><td>(0.6)</td><td>41.2</td><td>(0.4)</td><td>75.5</td><td>(0.5)</td><td>49.7</td><td>(0.4)</td><td>65.9</td><td>(0.6)</td><td>42.0</td><td>(0.4)</td></tr>
<tr><td>Argentina</td><td>64.6</td><td>(4.2)</td><td>70.3</td><td>(3.1)</td><td>74.6</td><td>(3.5)</td><td>65.3</td><td>(3.8)</td><td>67.6</td><td>(4.0)</td><td>65.8</td><td>(3.0)</td></tr>
<tr><td>Azerbaijan</td><td>85.3</td><td>(2.3)</td><td>82.4</td><td>(2.4)</td><td>78.1</td><td>(3.2)</td><td>71.5</td><td>(3.5)</td><td>78.4</td><td>(3.5)</td><td>74.5</td><td>(3.5)</td></tr>
<tr><td>Brazil</td><td>57.6</td><td>(3.7)</td><td>77.1</td><td>(1.9)</td><td>84.2</td><td>(3.0)</td><td>76.3</td><td>(1.8)</td><td>63.6</td><td>(4.1)</td><td>60.1</td><td>(2.3)</td></tr>
<tr><td>Bulgaria</td><td>63.4</td><td>(3.7)</td><td>65.8</td><td>(2.7)</td><td>88.5</td><td>(3.0)</td><td>72.5</td><td>(2.8)</td><td>78.3</td><td>(3.8)</td><td>64.7</td><td>(2.3)</td></tr>
<tr><td>Chile</td><td>64.7</td><td>(4.1)</td><td>57.1</td><td>(2.3)</td><td>65.0</td><td>(3.5)</td><td>50.5</td><td>(2.4)</td><td>68.7</td><td>(4.2)</td><td>49.7</td><td>(2.4)</td></tr>
<tr><td>Colombia</td><td>88.9</td><td>(2.2)</td><td>84.0</td><td>(2.2)</td><td>86.8</td><td>(3.2)</td><td>79.6</td><td>(3.0)</td><td>89.1</td><td>(2.0)</td><td>78.9</td><td>(2.6)</td></tr>
<tr><td>Croatia</td><td>53.9</td><td>(3.1)</td><td>50.1</td><td>(2.6)</td><td>71.1</td><td>(3.2)</td><td>52.5</td><td>(2.5)</td><td>62.1</td><td>(2.9)</td><td>45.2</td><td>(2.2)</td></tr>
<tr><td>Estonia</td><td>48.4</td><td>(3.3)</td><td>29.0</td><td>(2.5)</td><td>74.7</td><td>(3.0)</td><td>48.5</td><td>(2.6)</td><td>76.8</td><td>(2.9)</td><td>59.8</td><td>(2.4)</td></tr>
<tr><td>Hong Kong-China</td><td>34.2</td><td>(3.2)</td><td>34.1</td><td>(2.7)</td><td>47.3</td><td>(3.4)</td><td>34.0</td><td>(2.7)</td><td>58.0</td><td>(3.4)</td><td>36.7</td><td>(3.0)</td></tr>
<tr><td>Indonesia</td><td>54.4</td><td>(4.5)</td><td>74.1</td><td>(2.2)</td><td>60.1</td><td>(4.3)</td><td>73.1</td><td>(2.4)</td><td>41.3</td><td>(4.3)</td><td>54.9</td><td>(2.8)</td></tr>
<tr><td>Israel</td><td>73.1</td><td>(3.5)</td><td>57.8</td><td>(2.6)</td><td>84.6</td><td>(2.9)</td><td>62.6</td><td>(2.3)</td><td>73.6</td><td>(3.5)</td><td>51.2</td><td>(2.3)</td></tr>
<tr><td>Jordan</td><td>88.8</td><td>(1.9)</td><td>84.8</td><td>(1.7)</td><td>90.0</td><td>(2.0)</td><td>79.5</td><td>(1.4)</td><td>81.3</td><td>(2.9)</td><td>71.5</td><td>(1.9)</td></tr>
<tr><td>Kyrgyzstan</td><td>82.9</td><td>(2.5)</td><td>92.6</td><td>(1.4)</td><td>79.5</td><td>(2.7)</td><td>86.9</td><td>(2.1)</td><td>74.7</td><td>(3.3)</td><td>81.8</td><td>(2.3)</td></tr>
<tr><td>Latvia</td><td>54.1</td><td>(3.4)</td><td>55.1</td><td>(3.3)</td><td>77.6</td><td>(3.3)</td><td>53.6</td><td>(3.1)</td><td>62.9</td><td>(3.6)</td><td>46.7</td><td>(3.4)</td></tr>
<tr><td>Lithuania</td><td>34.8</td><td>(3.1)</td><td>31.8</td><td>(2.0)</td><td>62.3</td><td>(3.5)</td><td>37.7</td><td>(2.1)</td><td>57.4</td><td>(3.5)</td><td>35.2</td><td>(2.1)</td></tr>
<tr><td>Macao-China</td><td>48.4</td><td>(4.1)</td><td>42.0</td><td>(2.5)</td><td>71.4</td><td>(3.9)</td><td>54.4</td><td>(2.9)</td><td>56.2</td><td>(4.1)</td><td>44.1</td><td>(3.2)</td></tr>
<tr><td>Montenegro</td><td>72.7</td><td>(2.9)</td><td>83.4</td><td>(1.9)</td><td>79.6</td><td>(2.8)</td><td>73.7</td><td>(2.3)</td><td>81.6</td><td>(3.2)</td><td>72.9</td><td>(2.2)</td></tr>
<tr><td>Romania</td><td>67.0</td><td>(5.7)</td><td>80.9</td><td>(2.3)</td><td>80.5</td><td>(4.5)</td><td>80.7</td><td>(1.9)</td><td>68.7</td><td>(4.1)</td><td>64.0</td><td>(2.9)</td></tr>
<tr><td>Russian Federation</td><td>42.0</td><td>(3.4)</td><td>51.5</td><td>(2.4)</td><td>72.8</td><td>(3.0)</td><td>58.1</td><td>(2.3)</td><td>72.1</td><td>(3.4)</td><td>53.1</td><td>(2.7)</td></tr>
<tr><td>Serbia</td><td>62.7</td><td>(2.9)</td><td>69.4</td><td>(1.8)</td><td>69.3</td><td>(2.6)</td><td>67.0</td><td>(2.2)</td><td>64.5</td><td>(3.2)</td><td>60.4</td><td>(2.3)</td></tr>
<tr><td>Slovenia</td><td>71.6</td><td>(3.2)</td><td>72.5</td><td>(2.0)</td><td>78.7</td><td>(3.4)</td><td>74.5</td><td>(1.8)</td><td>66.2</td><td>(3.9)</td><td>65.0</td><td>(2.0)</td></tr>
<tr><td>Chinese Taipei</td><td>28.1</td><td>(2.4)</td><td>25.4</td><td>(1.9)</td><td>41.3</td><td>(2.5)</td><td>29.5</td><td>(2.0)</td><td>43.9</td><td>(2.4)</td><td>28.6</td><td>(1.6)</td></tr>
<tr><td>Thailand</td><td>90.7</td><td>(2.3)</td><td>92.1</td><td>(1.2)</td><td>83.7</td><td>(2.7)</td><td>81.2</td><td>(1.6)</td><td>82.8</td><td>(3.0)</td><td>79.3</td><td>(1.8)</td></tr>
<tr><td>Tunisia</td><td>80.3</td><td>(2.5)</td><td>82.9</td><td>(2.1)</td><td>64.2</td><td>(3.4)</td><td>70.1</td><td>(2.2)</td><td>76.6</td><td>(2.5)</td><td>70.8</td><td>(2.5)</td></tr>
<tr><td>Uruguay</td><td>72.4</td><td>(3.6)</td><td>70.9</td><td>(2.3)</td><td>85.8</td><td>(2.5)</td><td>69.3</td><td>(2.0)</td><td>76.4</td><td>(3.5)</td><td>58.4</td><td>(2.8)</td></tr>
</table>

[Part 2/2]
Table A2.5a Science self-concept (underlying percentages), by student group

Percentage of students agreeing or strongly agreeing with following statements

		Science topics are easy for me				When I am being taught science, I can understand the concepts very well				I can easily understand new ideas in science			
		Resilient students		Disadvantaged low achievers (DLA)		Resilient students		Disadvantaged low achievers (DLA)		Resilient students		Disadvantaged low achievers (DLA)	
		%	S.E.	%	S.E.	%	S.E.	%	S.E.	%	S.E.	%	S.E.
OECD	Australia	64.4	(2.0)	26.9	(1.5)	73.7	(2.0)	38.7	(1.6)	73.9	(2.0)	38.9	(1.8)
	Austria	48.5	(3.3)	38.9	(2.6)	76.4	(2.8)	43.6	(2.4)	57.4	(3.6)	40.5	(3.0)
	Belgium	41.6	(2.8)	32.6	(1.8)	68.3	(3.2)	42.9	(2.1)	60.1	(2.5)	38.7	(1.9)
	Canada	75.2	(2.3)	39.6	(1.8)	80.9	(2.2)	48.5	(1.8)	80.2	(2.0)	47.1	(1.8)
	Czech Republic	48.4	(4.0)	41.9	(2.6)	67.3	(3.3)	48.6	(2.6)	64.8	(2.9)	49.4	(2.5)
	Denmark	56.7	(3.9)	26.9	(2.1)	75.1	(3.5)	41.5	(2.3)	68.3	(3.6)	37.1	(2.5)
	Finland	68.9	(2.9)	29.1	(2.1)	67.2	(2.8)	33.0	(2.4)	75.7	(2.9)	38.7	(2.1)
	France	47.5	(4.1)	30.1	(2.1)	65.1	(3.9)	44.0	(1.7)	58.8	(4.3)	39.9	(2.0)
	Germany	56.1	(3.7)	42.9	(2.2)	68.1	(3.0)	49.7	(3.1)	72.3	(2.7)	49.1	(2.1)
	Greece	44.0	(3.6)	36.1	(2.4)	54.2	(3.2)	47.1	(2.3)	50.9	(3.1)	45.2	(2.0)
	Hungary	33.8	(3.8)	40.1	(2.8)	50.7	(3.7)	44.7	(2.2)	47.4	(4.0)	44.0	(2.5)
	Iceland	79.3	(2.6)	29.1	(2.2)	72.7	(2.9)	32.3	(2.0)	75.3	(3.1)	31.6	(2.3)
	Ireland	57.1	(3.5)	19.9	(2.2)	69.8	(3.7)	33.7	(2.5)	63.8	(3.6)	32.6	(2.7)
	Italy	54.1	(2.2)	45.7	(1.6)	68.3	(2.0)	57.0	(1.3)	59.5	(2.4)	50.5	(1.6)
	Japan	16.1	(2.3)	10.0	(1.4)	47.7	(2.9)	26.0	(1.8)	21.4	(2.4)	14.0	(1.4)
	Korea	27.9	(2.7)	9.1	(1.3)	35.8	(2.7)	12.0	(1.4)	34.3	(2.8)	14.8	(1.5)
	Luxembourg	63.9	(3.9)	47.1	(2.0)	70.6	(3.5)	51.3	(1.9)	68.2	(3.6)	49.7	(1.9)
	Mexico	74.5	(2.8)	69.8	(1.9)	75.3	(2.9)	71.6	(1.8)	73.4	(3.1)	72.2	(1.8)
	Netherlands	40.0	(3.5)	27.4	(2.6)	72.1	(3.4)	34.8	(2.9)	52.2	(3.6)	33.0	(2.9)
	New Zealand	55.2	(3.5)	29.2	(1.9)	71.3	(3.0)	43.8	(2.0)	66.8	(3.1)	45.5	(1.9)
	Norway	61.9	(3.9)	31.4	(2.2)	69.8	(4.0)	38.9	(2.4)	70.7	(3.6)	38.9	(2.5)
	Poland	50.8	(2.8)	35.0	(2.2)	71.1	(2.5)	53.5	(2.0)	60.1	(3.0)	42.3	(2.2)
	Portugal	75.7	(3.3)	59.5	(2.4)	80.9	(3.4)	62.7	(2.5)	77.0	(3.2)	61.5	(2.6)
	Slovak Republic	52.2	(3.4)	48.0	(2.5)	83.9	(2.5)	64.4	(2.1)	71.9	(3.3)	56.1	(2.2)
	Spain	67.0	(2.7)	32.8	(1.9)	66.7	(2.7)	37.5	(1.8)	63.5	(2.5)	33.8	(1.6)
	Sweden	65.1	(3.6)	28.7	(2.3)	68.6	(3.5)	37.2	(1.9)	63.0	(4.8)	31.4	(2.3)
	Switzerland	58.2	(2.8)	37.9	(1.7)	66.5	(2.8)	41.3	(1.7)	61.6	(2.8)	44.1	(1.8)
	Turkey	58.3	(4.3)	52.9	(2.9)	67.7	(3.6)	57.6	(2.4)	72.4	(3.4)	56.8	(3.1)
	United Kingdom	56.7	(2.8)	30.9	(1.8)	77.2	(2.3)	48.1	(1.8)	76.6	(2.7)	50.0	(1.7)
	United States	64.1	(3.6)	48.1	(3.3)	85.9	(2.9)	57.2	(2.0)	75.0	(3.6)	46.2	(2.5)
	OECD average	55.4	(0.6)	35.9	(0.4)	69.0	(0.6)	44.8	(0.4)	63.9	(0.6)	42.5	(0.4)
Partners	Argentina	59.1	(4.4)	55.7	(3.0)	67.0	(4.2)	65.9	(2.9)	62.0	(3.8)	58.9	(2.9)
	Azerbaijan	73.8	(3.7)	68.6	(3.7)	82.0	(2.9)	75.0	(3.1)	76.5	(3.0)	72.5	(3.1)
	Brazil	58.3	(4.2)	62.2	(2.9)	65.5	(3.4)	67.4	(2.2)	52.6	(3.3)	63.4	(2.2)
	Bulgaria	63.8	(4.1)	62.8	(3.0)	68.9	(3.9)	65.1	(2.7)	70.8	(4.4)	65.7	(2.9)
	Chile	56.0	(4.1)	38.2	(2.3)	69.9	(3.2)	57.7	(2.3)	69.7	(3.5)	57.8	(2.2)
	Colombia	79.9	(4.1)	75.7	(2.5)	83.9	(3.1)	84.5	(2.2)	89.3	(2.2)	82.5	(2.4)
	Croatia	35.0	(2.7)	31.5	(2.0)	65.2	(2.8)	48.1	(2.5)	61.8	(3.0)	47.3	(2.4)
	Estonia	67.2	(3.1)	43.5	(2.6)	72.4	(3.2)	49.7	(2.4)	76.9	(3.0)	46.9	(2.2)
	Hong Kong-China	42.9	(2.9)	29.2	(2.5)	65.9	(2.7)	46.1	(3.8)	61.1	(2.7)	42.3	(3.5)
	Indonesia	33.8	(4.4)	51.9	(2.9)	64.5	(2.9)	76.8	(2.1)	49.7	(4.5)	68.2	(2.5)
	Israel	70.2	(3.5)	47.6	(2.4)	82.9	(3.1)	60.8	(2.5)	76.7	(3.4)	56.2	(2.5)
	Jordan	73.9	(2.9)	66.2	(2.0)	87.4	(2.2)	76.1	(1.7)	82.9	(2.8)	72.6	(1.7)
	Kyrgyzstan	77.6	(2.8)	83.6	(2.4)	76.8	(2.7)	86.1	(1.9)	69.8	(3.5)	83.7	(1.9)
	Latvia	41.9	(4.0)	39.0	(3.0)	52.1	(5.0)	50.0	(2.8)	63.0	(4.4)	45.3	(2.9)
	Lithuania	32.1	(3.4)	26.5	(2.0)	46.7	(3.6)	32.4	(1.9)	47.4	(3.7)	35.3	(2.1)
	Macao-China	46.4	(4.4)	36.0	(2.6)	58.8	(4.2)	52.6	(3.2)	52.7	(4.0)	45.1	(3.0)
	Montenegro	54.7	(3.2)	62.4	(2.6)	79.2	(2.8)	71.7	(2.2)	68.7	(3.3)	72.5	(2.4)
	Romania	58.4	(5.2)	65.0	(2.5)	64.1	(3.6)	68.5	(2.3)	65.3	(4.0)	67.7	(2.7)
	Russian Federation	60.1	(3.1)	47.9	(3.0)	66.0	(3.2)	59.6	(2.2)	60.1	(3.3)	50.3	(2.1)
	Serbia	57.1	(3.5)	63.4	(2.2)	81.2	(2.5)	66.3	(1.8)	62.0	(3.1)	63.7	(2.0)
	Slovenia	49.3	(3.9)	53.7	(2.2)	70.7	(3.8)	63.5	(2.1)	59.1	(3.9)	53.4	(2.4)
	Chinese Taipei	32.9	(3.0)	23.2	(1.6)	55.0	(2.4)	38.9	(1.9)	53.9	(2.7)	35.3	(2.0)
	Thailand	76.1	(3.1)	78.0	(2.1)	84.9	(2.4)	83.0	(1.8)	84.7	(3.2)	84.0	(1.5)
	Tunisia	69.5	(2.9)	69.0	(2.6)	81.7	(2.5)	77.0	(2.4)	72.6	(2.6)	74.3	(2.4)
	Uruguay	69.7	(3.5)	58.8	(2.9)	77.0	(3.7)	63.9	(2.9)	66.4	(4.4)	55.1	(2.6)

© OECD 2011 Against the Odds: Disadvantaged Students Who Succeed in School

Table A2.5b Science self-concept by student group

		Resilient students		Disadvantaged low achievers (DLA)		Difference in the mean index between resilient students and disadvantaged low achievers	
		Mean	S.E.	Mean	S.E.	Dif	S.E.
OECD	Australia	0.37	(0.03)	-0.56	(0.03)	**0.90**	(0.05)
	Austria	0.33	(0.06)	-0.26	(0.06)	**0.55**	(0.09)
	Belgium	0.10	(0.05)	-0.46	(0.04)	**0.52**	(0.08)
	Canada	0.67	(0.04)	-0.33	(0.03)	**0.97**	(0.06)
	Czech Republic	0.09	(0.04)	-0.15	(0.04)	**0.22**	(0.07)
	Denmark	0.26	(0.06)	-0.44	(0.04)	**0.68**	(0.08)
	Finland	0.41	(0.04)	-0.42	(0.03)	**0.79**	(0.06)
	France	0.09	(0.07)	-0.37	(0.04)	**0.47**	(0.09)
	Germany	0.47	(0.06)	-0.06	(0.04)	**0.53**	(0.08)
	Greece	0.04	(0.05)	-0.20	(0.04)	**0.25**	(0.07)
	Hungary	-0.26	(0.05)	-0.19	(0.05)	-0.06	(0.08)
	Iceland	0.52	(0.05)	-0.65	(0.05)	**1.12**	(0.07)
	Ireland	0.23	(0.06)	-0.66	(0.05)	**0.86**	(0.09)
	Italy	0.24	(0.04)	0.00	(0.02)	**0.24**	(0.05)
	Japan	-0.62	(0.05)	-1.13	(0.04)	**0.51**	(0.07)
	Korea	-0.48	(0.05)	-1.13	(0.04)	**0.63**	(0.06)
	Luxembourg	0.52	(0.07)	-0.07	(0.04)	**0.56**	(0.08)
	Mexico	0.50	(0.03)	0.52	(0.03)	0.01	(0.05)
	Netherlands	-0.14	(0.05)	-0.63	(0.06)	**0.48**	(0.08)
	New Zealand	0.19	(0.05)	-0.38	(0.04)	**0.55**	(0.06)
	Norway	0.41	(0.05)	-0.37	(0.04)	**0.74**	(0.08)
	Poland	0.27	(0.04)	-0.08	(0.03)	**0.35**	(0.06)
	Portugal	0.51	(0.05)	0.10	(0.05)	**0.39**	(0.08)
	Slovak Republic	0.27	(0.05)	-0.08	(0.04)	**0.34**	(0.07)
	Spain	0.30	(0.04)	-0.41	(0.03)	**0.68**	(0.06)
	Sweden	0.40	(0.06)	-0.53	(0.04)	**0.90**	(0.08)
	Switzerland	0.31	(0.05)	-0.30	(0.03)	**0.58**	(0.06)
	Turkey	0.33	(0.06)	0.05	(0.06)	**0.26**	(0.09)
	United Kingdom	0.32	(0.05)	-0.28	(0.03)	**0.56**	(0.06)
	United States	0.60	(0.05)	-0.10	(0.08)	**0.66**	(0.09)
	OECD average	**0.24**	**(0.01)**	**-0.32**	**(0.01)**	**0.54**	**(0.01)**
Partners	Argentina	0.29	(0.07)	0.24	(0.06)	0.02	(0.09)
	Azerbaijan	0.63	(0.07)	0.58	(0.07)	0.05	(0.09)
	Brazil	0.30	(0.06)	0.37	(0.03)	-0.08	(0.07)
	Bulgaria	0.36	(0.05)	0.28	(0.05)	0.08	(0.08)
	Chile	0.29	(0.05)	-0.03	(0.04)	**0.29**	(0.07)
	Colombia	0.76	(0.04)	0.72	(0.06)	0.02	(0.08)
	Croatia	0.06	(0.04)	-0.21	(0.05)	**0.25**	(0.06)
	Estonia	0.37	(0.06)	-0.19	(0.03)	**0.53**	(0.07)
	Hong Kong-China	-0.02	(0.05)	-0.44	(0.07)	**0.39**	(0.08)
	Indonesia	-0.06	(0.08)	0.31	(0.05)	**-0.37**	(0.10)
	Israel	0.69	(0.09)	0.06	(0.05)	**0.60**	(0.12)
	Jordan	0.82	(0.05)	0.52	(0.04)	**0.29**	(0.06)
	Kyrgyzstan	0.54	(0.05)	0.90	(0.04)	**-0.30**	(0.08)
	Latvia	0.07	(0.06)	-0.09	(0.04)	0.14	(0.07)
	Lithuania	-0.13	(0.05)	-0.38	(0.03)	**0.26**	(0.06)
	Macao-China	0.02	(0.07)	-0.21	(0.04)	0.21	(0.10)
	Montenegro	0.46	(0.06)	0.50	(0.04)	-0.05	(0.08)
	Romania	0.26	(0.05)	0.36	(0.04)	-0.10	(0.08)
	Russian Federation	0.18	(0.04)	0.04	(0.04)	**0.13**	(0.05)
	Serbia	0.32	(0.05)	0.25	(0.04)	0.07	(0.07)
	Slovenia	0.31	(0.06)	0.21	(0.04)	0.09	(0.08)
	Chinese Taipei	-0.23	(0.04)	-0.58	(0.03)	**0.33**	(0.06)
	Thailand	0.66	(0.05)	0.71	(0.03)	-0.03	(0.06)
	Tunisia	0.59	(0.06)	0.58	(0.05)	0.02	(0.06)
	Uruguay	0.51	(0.06)	0.23	(0.05)	**0.25**	(0.08)

Note: Values that are statistically different are indicated in bold.

Table A2.5c Relationship between being resilient and PISA index of science self-concept

			After accounting for ESCS, gender, immigrant background, grade, using test language		After accounting for Mean ESCS, ESCS, gender, immigrant background, grade, using test language	
	Ratio	S.E.	Ratio	S.E.	Ratio	S.E.
OECD						
Australia	**2.49**	(0.07)	**2.56**	(0.08)	**2.63**	(0.08)
Austria	**1.57**	(0.08)	**1.79**	(0.08)	**1.79**	(0.09)
Belgium	**1.60**	(0.08)	**1.85**	(0.11)	**1.92**	(0.12)
Canada	**2.10**	(0.06)	**2.09**	(0.06)	**2.11**	(0.06)
Czech Republic	**1.37**	(0.12)	**1.47**	(0.14)	**1.56**	(0.15)
Denmark	**1.99**	(0.10)	**2.17**	(0.11)	**2.20**	(0.11)
Finland	**2.84**	(0.11)	**2.80**	(0.11)	**2.80**	(0.11)
France	**1.59**	(0.09)	**1.91**	(0.11)	**2.08**	(0.14)
Germany	**1.63**	(0.08)	**1.61**	(0.10)	**1.70**	(0.12)
Greece	**1.32**	(0.08)	**1.37**	(0.09)	**1.38**	(0.09)
Hungary	1.01	(0.09)	**1.03**	(0.10)	1.17	(0.11)
Iceland	**2.54**	(0.09)	**2.66**	(0.09)	**2.68**	(0.09)
Ireland	**2.20**	(0.11)	**2.31**	(0.12)	**2.34**	(0.13)
Italy	**1.39**	(0.06)	**1.35**	(0.07)	**1.35**	(0.07)
Japan	**1.56**	(0.08)	**1.58**	(0.07)	**1.59**	(0.08)
Korea	**2.08**	(0.08)	**2.07**	(0.09)	**2.01**	(0.09)
Luxembourg	**1.65**	(0.09)	**1.68**	(0.10)	**1.68**	(0.11)
Mexico	1.11	(0.10)	1.18	(0.11)	1.18	(0.11)
Netherlands	**1.72**	(0.10)	**2.00**	(0.11)	**2.12**	(0.13)
New Zealand	**1.94**	(0.09)	**2.02**	(0.09)	**2.22**	(0.09)
Norway	**2.15**	(0.11)	**2.35**	(0.13)	**2.37**	(0.13)
Poland	**1.79**	(0.10)	**1.85**	(0.10)	**1.85**	(0.10)
Portugal	**1.70**	(0.11)	**2.06**	(0.16)	**2.08**	(0.16)
Slovak Republic	**1.62**	(0.11)	**1.66**	(0.11)	**1.73**	(0.12)
Spain	**1.96**	(0.07)	**1.91**	(0.07)	**1.93**	(0.07)
Sweden	**2.37**	(0.11)	**2.50**	(0.13)	**2.51**	(0.13)
Switzerland	**1.71**	(0.07)	**1.80**	(0.08)	**1.80**	(0.08)
Turkey	**1.28**	(0.08)	**1.23**	(0.09)	**1.29**	(0.09)
United Kingdom	**2.16**	(0.09)	**2.16**	(0.10)	**2.23**	(0.10)
United States	**1.94**	(0.09)	**2.02**	(0.09)	**2.05**	(0.09)
OECD average	**1.76**	(0.02)	**1.76**	(0.02)	**1.90**	(0.02)
Partners						
Argentina	1.08	(0.11)	1.17	(0.12)	1.19	(0.13)
Azerbaijan	1.02	(0.12)	1.01	(0.12)	1.02	(0.12)
Brazil	0.93	(0.09)	0.99	(0.10)	1.00	(0.10)
Bulgaria	1.07	(0.11)	1.04	(0.13)	1.20	(0.12)
Chile	**1.41**	(0.08)	**1.39**	(0.09)	**1.40**	(0.09)
Colombia	1.12	(0.13)	**1.35**	(0.13)	**1.35**	(0.13)
Croatia	**1.30**	(0.08)	**1.31**	(0.09)	**1.36**	(0.10)
Estonia	**2.22**	(0.12)	**2.31**	(0.13)	**2.35**	(0.13)
Hong Kong-China	**1.59**	(0.09)	**1.85**	(0.09)	**1.99**	(0.10)
Indonesia	**0.59**	(0.16)	**0.66**	(0.15)	**0.69**	(0.14)
Israel	**1.55**	(0.10)	**1.57**	(0.10)	**1.70**	(0.10)
Jordan	**1.43**	(0.09)	**1.46**	(0.10)	**1.48**	(0.10)
Kyrgyzstan	**0.68**	(0.13)	**0.67**	(0.13)	**0.72**	(0.13)
Latvia	1.28	(0.14)	1.29	(0.15)	1.34	(0.16)
Lithuania	**1.67**	(0.10)	**1.81**	(0.11)	**1.86**	(0.11)
Macao-China	**1.35**	(0.12)	**1.48**	(0.15)	**1.49**	(0.15)
Montenegro	1.03	(0.09)	1.05	(0.09)	1.11	(0.08)
Romania	0.93	(0.14)	0.86	(0.15)	0.96	(0.15)
Russian Federation	**1.33**	(0.09)	**1.42**	(0.10)	**1.44**	(0.11)
Serbia	1.12	(0.08)	1.13	(0.08)	1.21	(0.09)
Slovenia	1.19	(0.11)	**1.24**	(0.11)	**1.42**	(0.12)
Chinese Taipei	**1.48**	(0.07)	**1.46**	(0.07)	**1.51**	(0.08)
Thailand	0.99	(0.11)	0.99	(0.12)	1.01	(0.12)
Tunisia	1.02	(0.08)	**1.25**	(0.09)	**1.27**	(0.10)
Uruguay	**1.38**	(0.10)	**1.53**	(0.11)	**1.54**	(0.11)

Note: Values that are statistically different are indicated in bold.

Table A2.6a Science-related careers (underlying percentages), by student group

Percentage of students agreeing or strongly agreeing with the following statements

		The subjects available at my school provide students with the basic skills and knowledge for a science-related career				The school science subjects at my school provide students with the basic skills and knowledge for many different careers				The subjects I study provide me with the basic skills and knowledge for a science-related career				My teachers equip me with the basic skills and knowledge I need for a science-related career			
		Resilient students		Disadvantaged low achievers (DLA)		Resilient students		Disadvantaged low achievers (DLA)		Resilient students		Disadvantaged low achievers (DLA)		Resilient students		Disadvantaged low achievers (DLA)	
		%	S.E.	%	S.E.	%	S.E.	%	S.E.	%	S.E.	%	S.E.	%	S.E.	%	S.E.
OECD	Australia	96.8	(1.0)	84.4	(1.2)	92.7	(1.2)	80.5	(1.1)	76.7	(1.8)	58.4	(1.3)	86.0	(1.5)	68.0	(1.4)
	Austria	74.2	(3.5)	69.0	(2.1)	66.4	(3.2)	61.6	(2.3)	69.7	(3.7)	57.9	(2.4)	69.6	(3.4)	55.2	(2.1)
	Belgium	85.4	(1.9)	74.0	(1.5)	79.0	(1.9)	69.4	(1.5)	68.4	(2.6)	56.5	(1.6)	69.5	(2.6)	60.1	(1.5)
	Canada	93.9	(1.0)	86.5	(1.0)	92.1	(1.1)	84.8	(1.0)	86.0	(1.8)	71.7	(1.3)	89.7	(1.2)	77.3	(1.4)
	Czech Republic	82.6	(3.1)	83.8	(1.7)	76.1	(3.1)	73.6	(1.9)	69.6	(3.6)	67.2	(2.4)	74.2	(3.3)	67.9	(2.2)
	Denmark	84.0	(2.5)	74.1	(2.1)	90.7	(1.7)	80.6	(1.9)	82.8	(2.8)	66.1	(2.0)	79.1	(3.0)	66.1	(2.1)
	Finland	93.2	(1.5)	87.1	(1.5)	87.5	(2.0)	81.5	(1.6)	92.2	(1.5)	78.9	(1.8)	85.5	(2.0)	78.5	(1.6)
	France	88.4	(3.5)	74.3	(1.5)	91.9	(2.0)	74.8	(1.5)	80.4	(3.4)	58.2	(2.1)	83.7	(3.1)	63.5	(1.7)
	Germany	83.7	(2.9)	75.0	(1.6)	83.2	(2.8)	76.2	(1.9)	78.1	(3.3)	65.2	(2.4)	76.5	(3.5)	65.4	(2.3)
	Greece	76.1	(3.5)	83.7	(1.5)	70.5	(3.2)	76.8	(1.7)	70.0	(3.1)	65.7	(1.8)	66.2	(3.4)	66.8	(1.7)
	Hungary	77.9	(3.0)	85.2	(1.6)	82.8	(2.7)	84.6	(1.6)	67.6	(3.6)	75.8	(1.7)	71.2	(4.5)	74.7	(1.9)
	Iceland	89.7	(2.4)	78.0	(2.1)	87.5	(2.4)	75.1	(2.0)	84.9	(3.0)	62.6	(2.3)	80.2	(2.7)	63.0	(2.4)
	Ireland	95.9	(1.6)	85.4	(1.8)	88.6	(2.2)	80.3	(2.0)	83.6	(2.3)	62.0	(2.0)	75.6	(3.2)	65.3	(1.8)
	Italy	74.8	(2.2)	76.7	(1.2)	78.3	(1.9)	77.4	(1.4)	66.0	(1.8)	64.6	(1.8)	69.4	(2.0)	70.5	(1.6)
	Japan	72.0	(2.9)	54.7	(2.0)	47.8	(3.6)	49.5	(2.0)	52.4	(2.9)	52.8	(2.2)	49.6	(3.3)	52.6	(2.2)
	Korea	78.1	(2.8)	79.8	(1.5)	63.9	(2.8)	68.7	(1.6)	70.5	(2.6)	67.5	(1.8)	67.6	(3.0)	71.1	(1.7)
	Luxembourg	78.4	(3.5)	76.4	(1.7)	76.1	(3.3)	78.0	(1.6)	61.6	(3.5)	67.2	(1.7)	60.6	(3.8)	66.3	(1.8)
	Mexico	91.9	(1.4)	92.9	(1.2)	86.2	(1.5)	87.3	(1.6)	85.9	(2.1)	88.0	(1.6)	86.5	(1.7)	89.5	(1.3)
	Netherlands	92.7	(1.4)	71.3	(1.8)	93.3	(1.6)	70.2	(2.1)	62.7	(3.4)	51.8	(1.9)	69.1	(3.5)	55.8	(2.7)
	New Zealand	97.0	(1.3)	86.7	(1.3)	92.8	(1.6)	83.1	(1.4)	82.7	(2.7)	63.8	(2.0)	88.0	(2.5)	74.8	(1.7)
	Norway	61.8	(3.4)	64.3	(2.5)	79.7	(2.4)	71.6	(2.3)	70.5	(2.7)	55.1	(2.5)	73.4	(3.5)	57.1	(3.0)
	Poland	86.0	(2.2)	90.7	(1.2)	75.5	(2.9)	84.7	(1.3)	79.6	(2.6)	83.7	(1.4)	78.5	(2.3)	80.6	(1.8)
	Portugal	91.5	(2.2)	91.4	(1.2)	91.7	(2.8)	88.3	(1.4)	78.4	(3.7)	81.3	(1.6)	79.0	(3.4)	80.3	(1.5)
	Slovak Republic	69.3	(3.2)	82.6	(1.8)	78.0	(3.5)	81.1	(2.0)	64.6	(2.9)	72.1	(2.1)	64.5	(3.0)	67.4	(2.5)
	Spain	89.5	(1.6)	82.3	(1.2)	84.0	(2.1)	79.5	(1.4)	76.5	(2.1)	69.3	(1.7)	76.3	(1.8)	71.6	(1.5)
	Sweden	80.9	(3.1)	74.5	(2.1)	76.9	(4.7)	74.4	(2.1)	77.6	(3.6)	63.0	(2.4)	77.5	(2.8)	67.1	(2.2)
	Switzerland	86.7	(2.5)	75.6	(1.4)	85.8	(2.5)	71.2	(1.4)	77.2	(2.8)	60.3	(1.7)	78.6	(3.0)	63.3	(1.5)
	Turkey	77.5	(3.4)	79.8	(2.6)	74.3	(3.3)	78.8	(1.9)	68.7	(3.8)	66.4	(3.3)	66.7	(3.6)	68.4	(2.2)
	United Kingdom	92.7	(1.6)	84.6	(1.3)	89.6	(1.7)	79.2	(1.5)	80.7	(2.3)	68.2	(1.5)	84.3	(2.0)	76.0	(1.5)
	United States	92.5	(1.7)	85.4	(1.3)	88.6	(2.2)	78.9	(1.7)	82.2	(2.6)	73.9	(1.7)	88.0	(2.3)	76.4	(1.5)
	OECD average	84.5	(0.5)	79.7	(0.3)	81.7	(0.5)	76.7	(0.3)	74.9	(0.5)	66.5	(0.4)	75.5	(0.5)	68.7	(0.3)
Partners	Argentina	82.9	(2.7)	87.7	(2.2)	84.0	(2.9)	82.9	(2.2)	75.0	(3.8)	79.5	(2.2)	77.2	(3.5)	77.4	(3.0)
	Azerbaijan	95.7	(1.1)	93.2	(1.1)	90.8	(1.6)	86.1	(1.9)	92.2	(1.7)	86.8	(1.8)	93.9	(1.5)	89.3	(2.0)
	Brazil	79.3	(2.6)	86.3	(1.7)	75.2	(2.9)	84.3	(1.8)	70.5	(3.2)	83.5	(1.7)	74.7	(3.1)	82.7	(1.8)
	Bulgaria	89.6	(2.1)	92.7	(1.2)	89.9	(2.8)	86.6	(2.0)	82.1	(2.6)	85.0	(1.9)	84.3	(3.9)	84.5	(2.3)
	Chile	64.8	(3.9)	81.6	(2.0)	75.7	(4.0)	85.6	(1.6)	64.9	(4.5)	79.4	(1.7)	66.2	(4.2)	79.0	(1.9)
	Colombia	84.4	(2.2)	94.3	(1.0)	90.9	(2.4)	94.6	(1.0)	78.6	(3.5)	87.9	(2.4)	77.0	(3.4)	87.6	(2.1)
	Croatia	86.6	(2.3)	89.3	(1.2)	85.2	(2.4)	85.0	(1.5)	78.6	(2.9)	81.3	(1.5)	79.1	(2.4)	82.8	(1.4)
	Estonia	86.5	(2.4)	88.6	(1.6)	88.8	(2.3)	88.0	(1.6)	90.6	(1.8)	83.9	(1.7)	79.5	(3.5)	79.8	(2.1)
	Hong Kong-China	87.3	(2.1)	80.6	(1.8)	79.5	(2.6)	74.5	(2.3)	71.4	(2.7)	65.3	(2.1)	80.2	(2.5)	76.5	(2.0)
	Indonesia	93.0	(1.9)	92.6	(1.1)	87.2	(2.3)	80.5	(1.8)	85.6	(2.4)	85.7	(2.2)	88.2	(2.5)	91.1	(1.3)
	Israel	79.2	(3.7)	79.8	(1.7)	76.9	(3.5)	74.2	(2.1)	71.5	(4.0)	65.2	(2.1)	66.4	(4.7)	62.7	(2.0)
	Jordan	87.7	(2.0)	89.4	(1.4)	87.1	(2.2)	84.6	(1.6)	94.0	(2.0)	81.6	(1.7)	86.0	(2.5)	80.2	(2.0)
	Kyrgyzstan	92.5	(1.6)	94.3	(1.2)	88.2	(2.0)	89.1	(1.6)	88.6	(1.4)	88.1	(1.9)	90.5	(1.7)	91.2	(1.4)
	Latvia	92.6	(1.6)	90.7	(1.4)	86.9	(2.8)	88.3	(1.4)	84.9	(2.7)	82.6	(2.0)	86.1	(2.5)	84.2	(1.8)
	Lithuania	96.7	(1.4)	93.8	(0.9)	92.3	(2.3)	86.0	(1.5)	92.9	(1.9)	84.7	(1.1)	90.9	(1.9)	85.5	(1.4)
	Macao-China	74.7	(2.5)	83.5	(2.0)	72.1	(2.6)	81.3	(1.7)	62.8	(3.0)	71.6	(2.6)	65.9	(2.9)	78.2	(1.9)
	Montenegro	81.8	(2.7)	91.3	(1.4)	80.9	(2.6)	88.1	(1.5)	79.6	(3.2)	87.5	(1.8)	83.2	(2.8)	90.5	(1.2)
	Romania	93.2	(2.2)	92.2	(1.8)	90.3	(3.0)	86.7	(1.5)	81.4	(5.0)	83.0	(2.1)	78.0	(5.1)	83.9	(2.0)
	Russian Federation	88.6	(2.1)	89.0	(1.3)	85.8	(2.6)	90.0	(1.2)	85.2	(3.2)	83.9	(1.6)	85.2	(2.2)	84.7	(1.5)
	Serbia	80.5	(2.6)	88.9	(1.4)	80.2	(2.6)	85.1	(1.5)	76.5	(3.0)	84.0	(1.6)	76.2	(3.3)	85.8	(1.5)
	Slovenia	85.7	(3.2)	86.5	(1.3)	86.9	(2.9)	83.0	(1.4)	81.3	(3.1)	75.1	(1.5)	83.1	(3.4)	80.1	(1.4)
	Chinese Taipei	85.4	(2.1)	88.9	(1.0)	81.2	(2.0)	85.1	(1.2)	87.1	(1.5)	86.3	(1.1)	87.2	(1.8)	87.6	(0.9)
	Thailand	97.9	(1.0)	96.7	(0.7)	96.0	(1.5)	93.6	(1.2)	96.5	(1.4)	93.6	(1.0)	95.7	(1.3)	94.4	(1.3)
	Tunisia	93.3	(1.7)	92.3	(1.6)	88.5	(2.2)	83.6	(1.5)	86.8	(2.1)	82.1	(2.6)	87.0	(2.1)	80.4	(2.1)
	Uruguay	83.9	(3.2)	83.5	(2.4)	90.1	(2.7)	84.4	(2.0)	73.2	(4.0)	76.5	(1.8)	75.3	(4.0)	79.7	(2.0)

Table A2.6b Science-related careers by country and student group

		\multicolumn{4}{c	}{School preparation for science-related careers}		
		\multicolumn{2}{c	}{Resilient students}	\multicolumn{2}{c	}{Disadvantaged low achievers (DLA)}	\multicolumn{2}{c	}{Difference in the mean index between resilient students and disadvantaged low achievers}
		Mean	S.E.	Mean	S.E.	Dif	S.E.
OECD	Australia	0.36	(0.03)	-0.26	(0.02)	**0.60**	(0.04)
	Austria	0.00	(0.08)	-0.32	(0.06)	**0.28**	(0.10)
	Belgium	-0.03	(0.04)	-0.32	(0.03)	**0.29**	(0.06)
	Canada	0.45	(0.04)	0.00	(0.03)	**0.43**	(0.05)
	Czech Republic	-0.06	(0.07)	-0.14	(0.04)	0.04	(0.10)
	Denmark	0.18	(0.05)	-0.23	(0.04)	**0.38**	(0.08)
	Finland	0.27	(0.04)	-0.02	(0.04)	**0.27**	(0.06)
	France	0.36	(0.07)	-0.25	(0.04)	**0.60**	(0.09)
	Germany	0.25	(0.08)	-0.05	(0.05)	**0.31**	(0.10)
	Greece	-0.16	(0.06)	-0.07	(0.03)	-0.12	(0.08)
	Hungary	-0.09	(0.06)	0.10	(0.04)	**-0.17**	(0.07)
	Iceland	0.27	(0.06)	-0.30	(0.04)	**0.53**	(0.09)
	Ireland	0.35	(0.05)	-0.15	(0.04)	**0.47**	(0.07)
	Italy	-0.09	(0.04)	-0.11	(0.03)	0.01	(0.05)
	Japan	-0.56	(0.07)	-0.66	(0.04)	0.14	(0.09)
	Korea	-0.32	(0.05)	-0.24	(0.03)	-0.06	(0.07)
	Luxembourg	-0.11	(0.07)	-0.06	(0.04)	-0.09	(0.09)
	Mexico	0.45	(0.05)	0.57	(0.03)	-0.11	(0.07)
	Netherlands	-0.07	(0.05)	-0.46	(0.04)	**0.41**	(0.07)
	New Zealand	0.34	(0.05)	-0.10	(0.04)	**0.40**	(0.07)
	Norway	-0.23	(0.05)	-0.51	(0.06)	**0.29**	(0.08)
	Poland	0.00	(0.05)	0.18	(0.04)	**-0.20**	(0.06)
	Portugal	0.22	(0.05)	0.14	(0.03)	0.09	(0.08)
	Slovak Republic	-0.27	(0.06)	-0.07	(0.06)	**-0.19**	(0.09)
	Spain	0.15	(0.04)	-0.06	(0.03)	**0.19**	(0.05)
	Sweden	0.02	(0.06)	-0.31	(0.04)	**0.32**	(0.09)
	Switzerland	0.22	(0.06)	-0.19	(0.03)	**0.41**	(0.07)
	Turkey	-0.06	(0.08)	-0.01	(0.05)	-0.01	(0.09)
	United Kingdom	0.31	(0.05)	-0.12	(0.03)	**0.40**	(0.05)
	United States	0.37	(0.06)	-0.03	(0.03)	**0.42**	(0.07)
	OECD average	0.08	(0.01)	-0.14	(0.01)	**0.21**	(0.01)
Partners	Argentina	0.09	(0.07)	0.24	(0.04)	-0.19	(0.10)
	Azerbaijan	0.67	(0.04)	0.53	(0.05)	0.14	(0.07)
	Brazil	-0.10	(0.07)	0.29	(0.03)	**-0.37**	(0.08)
	Bulgaria	0.39	(0.07)	0.42	(0.05)	-0.04	(0.09)
	Chile	-0.15	(0.08)	0.27	(0.04)	**-0.39**	(0.10)
	Colombia	0.32	(0.09)	0.73	(0.04)	**-0.40**	(0.09)
	Croatia	0.17	(0.06)	0.23	(0.04)	-0.05	(0.08)
	Estonia	0.19	(0.05)	0.25	(0.04)	-0.05	(0.07)
	Hong Kong-China	0.06	(0.06)	-0.23	(0.05)	**0.26**	(0.08)
	Indonesia	0.30	(0.06)	0.27	(0.03)	0.02	(0.06)
	Israel	0.04	(0.09)	-0.08	(0.05)	0.08	(0.11)
	Jordan	0.54	(0.06)	0.39	(0.04)	0.16	(0.09)
	Kyrgyzstan	0.59	(0.06)	0.67	(0.04)	-0.06	(0.09)
	Latvia	0.28	(0.05)	0.26	(0.04)	0.01	(0.06)
	Lithuania	0.52	(0.06)	0.33	(0.03)	**0.18**	(0.07)
	Macao-China	-0.34	(0.05)	-0.09	(0.03)	**-0.24**	(0.07)
	Montenegro	0.14	(0.06)	0.55	(0.04)	**-0.38**	(0.10)
	Romania	0.27	(0.10)	0.32	(0.04)	-0.03	(0.12)
	Russian Federation	0.29	(0.05)	0.26	(0.03)	0.00	(0.06)
	Serbia	0.09	(0.06)	0.34	(0.04)	**-0.25**	(0.08)
	Slovenia	0.20	(0.07)	0.03	(0.03)	0.10	(0.08)
	Chinese Taipei	0.18	(0.04)	0.20	(0.03)	-0.03	(0.06)
	Thailand	0.72	(0.05)	0.52	(0.03)	**0.19**	(0.06)
	Tunisia	0.61	(0.06)	0.53	(0.05)	0.10	(0.08)
	Uruguay	0.06	(0.06)	0.08	(0.05)	0.02	(0.10)

Note: Values that are statistically different are indicated in bold.

Table A2.6c **Relationship between being resilient and PISA index of school preparation for science career**

| | | Increased likelihood of being resilient associated with one unit on the PISA index of school preparation for science career ||||||
		Ratio	S.E.	After accounting for ESCS, gender, immigrant, grade, using test language ‖ Ratio	S.E.	After accounting for Mean ESCS, ESCS, gender, immigrant, grade, using test language ‖ Ratio	S.E.
OECD	Australia	**1.74**	(0.04)	**1.76**	(0.05)	**1.73**	(0.05)
	Austria	**1.28**	(0.07)	**1.42**	(0.08)	**1.38**	(0.08)
	Belgium	**1.29**	(0.06)	**1.40**	(0.07)	**1.30**	(0.08)
	Canada	**1.49**	(0.06)	**1.45**	(0.06)	**1.45**	(0.06)
	Czech Republic	1.14	(0.12)	1.24	(0.13)	1.27	(0.13)
	Denmark	**1.57**	(0.08)	**1.71**	(0.09)	**1.69**	(0.09)
	Finland	**1.31**	(0.07)	**1.32**	(0.07)	**1.32**	(0.07)
	France	**1.72**	(0.09)	**1.79**	(0.11)	**1.71**	(0.12)
	Germany	**1.25**	(0.08)	1.18	(0.08)	1.17	(0.10)
	Greece	0.89	(0.09)	0.93	(0.10)	0.96	(0.10)
	Hungary	**0.85**	(0.09)	0.89	(0.09)	0.89	(0.11)
	Iceland	**1.56**	(0.09)	**1.54**	(0.09)	**1.54**	(0.09)
	Ireland	**1.45**	(0.07)	**1.46**	(0.08)	**1.43**	(0.08)
	Italy	1.07	(0.06)	1.08	(0.06)	1.00	(0.06)
	Japan	1.14	(0.08)	1.13	(0.09)	1.10	(0.09)
	Korea	0.97	(0.08)	0.96	(0.08)	0.93	(0.09)
	Luxembourg	0.94	(0.08)	0.98	(0.09)	0.99	(0.10)
	Mexico	0.93	(0.07)	0.94	(0.08)	0.94	(0.07)
	Netherlands	**1.63**	(0.11)	**1.82**	(0.12)	**1.63**	(0.14)
	New Zealand	**1.53**	(0.09)	**1.60**	(0.09)	**1.60**	(0.09)
	Norway	**1.30**	(0.08)	**1.30**	(0.08)	**1.30**	(0.08)
	Poland	**0.79**	(0.08)	**0.81**	(0.08)	**0.80**	(0.08)
	Portugal	1.17	(0.11)	1.14	(0.13)	1.14	(0.13)
	Slovak Republic	0.85	(0.10)	0.91	(0.10)	0.88	(0.10)
	Spain	**1.22**	(0.06)	**1.25**	(0.08)	**1.26**	(0.08)
	Sweden	**1.28**	(0.09)	**1.32**	(0.10)	**1.32**	(0.10)
	Switzerland	**1.42**	(0.07)	**1.60**	(0.07)	**1.60**	(0.07)
	Turkey	1.05	(0.07)	1.02	(0.08)	1.01	(0.08)
	United Kingdom	**1.49**	(0.06)	**1.49**	(0.07)	**1.48**	(0.07)
	United States	**1.50**	(0.08)	**1.46**	(0.09)	**1.47**	(0.09)
	OECD average	**1.23**	(0.01)	**1.26**	(0.02)	**1.25**	(0.02)
Partners	Argentina	0.86	(0.10)	0.89	(0.11)	0.91	(0.12)
	Azerbaijan	1.15	(0.09)	1.13	(0.09)	1.13	(0.09)
	Brazil	**0.73**	(0.08)	**0.82**	(0.09)	**0.82**	(0.09)
	Bulgaria	0.95	(0.10)	0.92	(0.10)	0.97	(0.10)
	Chile	**0.73**	(0.10)	**0.76**	(0.10)	**0.74**	(0.10)
	Colombia	**0.70**	(0.10)	**0.78**	(0.10)	**0.78**	(0.10)
	Croatia	0.96	(0.09)	0.97	(0.09)	1.00	(0.10)
	Estonia	0.94	(0.10)	0.92	(0.11)	0.92	(0.11)
	Hong Kong-China	**1.38**	(0.09)	**1.54**	(0.10)	**1.52**	(0.11)
	Indonesia	1.01	(0.10)	1.08	(0.10)	1.07	(0.10)
	Israel	1.04	(0.09)	1.05	(0.09)	1.10	(0.09)
	Jordan	1.10	(0.09)	1.04	(0.10)	1.05	(0.10)
	Kyrgyzstan	0.91	(0.10)	0.91	(0.10)	0.95	(0.10)
	Latvia	1.07	(0.10)	1.06	(0.11)	1.11	(0.11)
	Lithuania	**1.22**	(0.10)	1.20	(0.10)	1.20	(0.10)
	Macao-China	**0.79**	(0.09)	0.84	(0.10)	0.85	(0.10)
	Montenegro	**0.73**	(0.09)	**0.76**	(0.10)	**0.79**	(0.10)
	Romania	0.93	(0.16)	0.93	(0.17)	0.93	(0.17)
	Russian Federation	1.01	(0.08)	1.02	(0.08)	1.02	(0.08)
	Serbia	**0.85**	(0.09)	0.84	(0.09)	0.86	(0.10)
	Slovenia	1.15	(0.11)	1.19	(0.11)	1.14	(0.12)
	Chinese Taipei	0.94	(0.07)	0.92	(0.07)	0.93	(0.07)
	Thailand	**1.31**	(0.09)	**1.26**	(0.09)	**1.28**	(0.09)
	Tunisia	1.06	(0.08)	1.04	(0.09)	1.05	(0.09)
	Uruguay	1.04	(0.12)	1.14	(0.13)	1.14	(0.13)

Note: Values that are statistically different are indicated in bold.

Table A2.7a Students' information on science-related careers (underlying percentages), by student group

Percentage of students answered informed or very well informed about the following topics

	Science-related careers that are available in the job market				Where to find information about science-related careers				The steps a student needs to take if they want a science-related career				Employers or companies that hire people to work in science-related careers			
	Resilient students		Disadvantaged low achievers (DLA)		Resilient students		Disadvantaged low achievers (DLA)		Resilient students		Disadvantaged low achievers (DLA)		Resilient students		Disadvantaged low achievers (DLA)	
	%	S.E.	%	S.E.	%	S.E.	%	S.E.	%	S.E.	%	S.E.	%	S.E.	%	S.E.
---	---	---	---	---	---	---	---	---	---	---	---	---	---	---	---	---
OECD																
Australia	61.2	(2.1)	45.8	(1.3)	60.9	(1.9)	49.3	(1.5)	58.2	(1.9)	49.0	(1.4)	34.9	(2.1)	41.9	(1.4)
Austria	41.2	(3.4)	40.9	(2.2)	48.6	(3.3)	41.9	(2.2)	37.0	(3.8)	43.6	(2.4)	25.5	(3.3)	40.2	(2.4)
Belgium	44.7	(2.4)	39.1	(1.7)	38.3	(2.6)	43.0	(1.5)	38.5	(2.1)	46.3	(1.7)	20.5	(2.2)	36.1	(1.7)
Canada	64.4	(2.4)	55.2	(1.3)	62.6	(2.4)	55.9	(1.6)	60.7	(2.1)	55.5	(1.6)	33.3	(2.3)	44.4	(1.6)
Czech Republic	30.3	(3.6)	41.5	(2.4)	59.5	(4.2)	52.7	(2.2)	44.6	(4.9)	46.6	(2.5)	31.5	(3.7)	37.5	(2.3)
Denmark	40.3	(3.6)	32.1	(1.6)	49.6	(3.6)	40.8	(2.2)	42.6	(3.6)	43.1	(2.2)	26.2	(3.2)	37.1	(1.9)
Finland	45.0	(3.0)	45.9	(2.4)	67.7	(3.2)	59.9	(2.2)	58.4	(2.8)	53.1	(2.2)	37.2	(3.0)	42.0	(2.1)
France	47.4	(4.3)	43.0	(2.1)	53.6	(4.6)	43.7	(1.9)	64.4	(3.2)	48.8	(1.9)	20.1	(2.6)	38.9	(1.8)
Germany	41.6	(4.0)	37.2	(2.0)	61.9	(3.8)	46.3	(2.7)	42.0	(3.4)	41.5	(1.7)	34.0	(4.2)	34.5	(1.9)
Greece	59.2	(3.5)	60.2	(2.1)	62.7	(3.3)	54.6	(2.2)	63.7	(4.1)	58.7	(1.9)	36.5	(2.9)	48.9	(2.1)
Hungary	19.1	(3.2)	36.0	(2.8)	44.2	(4.1)	50.0	(2.2)	43.9	(4.2)	51.7	(2.4)	27.4	(3.6)	40.4	(2.2)
Iceland	45.3	(3.0)	25.0	(2.0)	42.9	(3.5)	36.2	(2.3)	59.9	(3.8)	36.4	(2.3)	37.7	(3.5)	27.9	(2.3)
Ireland	55.0	(3.7)	44.7	(2.1)	50.7	(3.3)	47.2	(2.2)	46.7	(3.8)	46.1	(2.1)	31.6	(3.0)	34.7	(1.9)
Italy	54.5	(2.0)	44.7	(1.4)	47.2	(2.0)	40.8	(1.6)	50.6	(2.2)	54.9	(1.6)	27.1	(1.7)	40.2	(1.5)
Japan	23.3	(2.2)	28.5	(1.5)	27.1	(2.1)	27.8	(1.7)	29.1	(2.5)	29.3	(1.8)	20.1	(2.0)	28.7	(2.0)
Korea	28.4	(2.7)	26.8	(1.9)	40.4	(2.5)	32.3	(1.9)	24.7	(2.6)	22.5	(1.7)	20.0	(2.6)	16.7	(1.5)
Luxembourg	39.7	(3.6)	38.6	(2.1)	35.2	(5.2)	40.8	(2.0)	41.6	(4.4)	44.9	(1.8)	22.9	(3.5)	40.6	(1.7)
Mexico	12.9	(1.4)	29.5	(2.6)	30.1	(2.4)	36.3	(2.1)	20.7	(2.2)	38.0	(2.7)	19.3	(1.8)	33.4	(2.4)
Netherlands	36.1	(3.1)	32.8	(2.8)	44.5	(3.2)	39.6	(2.6)	31.6	(3.1)	28.8	(2.3)	26.1	(3.1)	29.6	(2.2)
New Zealand	55.7	(4.1)	49.5	(2.0)	63.7	(3.6)	54.7	(2.6)	54.2	(3.7)	53.8	(1.9)	33.1	(4.5)	43.8	(2.2)
Norway	37.1	(2.9)	40.2	(2.3)	41.5	(3.1)	43.3	(2.1)	40.5	(3.9)	41.2	(2.2)	32.6	(3.8)	36.3	(2.2)
Poland	59.5	(3.6)	60.1	(1.8)	55.2	(2.8)	61.0	(2.0)	50.5	(3.3)	59.3	(1.9)	38.2	(2.8)	49.9	(2.1)
Portugal	73.2	(3.5)	61.5	(1.9)	67.2	(3.3)	54.8	(1.9)	64.4	(3.5)	59.3	(1.8)	38.9	(4.1)	52.8	(2.2)
Slovak Republic	39.9	(3.6)	50.0	(2.6)	56.1	(3.8)	53.0	(2.2)	36.4	(3.0)	44.2	(2.6)	33.9	(3.6)	41.5	(2.4)
Spain	45.7	(2.9)	33.8	(1.9)	47.5	(3.0)	40.2	(2.0)	65.6	(2.7)	44.1	(1.8)	24.0	(2.6)	31.1	(1.7)
Sweden	42.6	(4.2)	38.5	(2.2)	40.7	(3.3)	41.1	(2.2)	50.7	(4.3)	46.4	(2.2)	24.4	(3.2)	34.1	(2.3)
Switzerland	44.8	(3.5)	42.1	(1.9)	65.8	(2.9)	48.9	(1.6)	47.9	(3.0)	44.7	(1.6)	31.9	(2.3)	40.7	(1.7)
Turkey	71.5	(3.1)	48.9	(2.6)	71.7	(3.1)	51.2	(3.4)	63.8	(3.4)	45.7	(3.1)	46.5	(4.0)	45.2	(2.9)
United Kingdom	46.3	(3.4)	45.1	(1.8)	46.0	(3.1)	49.6	(2.1)	39.7	(3.1)	47.5	(2.2)	26.7	(2.5)	40.7	(1.9)
United States	63.0	(3.4)	58.9	(1.9)	63.5	(3.4)	63.5	(1.9)	55.5	(3.1)	59.2	(1.9)	40.8	(3.6)	57.5	(2.3)
OECD average	45.6	(0.6)	42.5	(0.4)	51.6	(0.6)	46.7	(0.4)	47.6	(0.6)	46.1	(0.4)	30.1	(0.6)	38.9	(0.4)
Partners																
Argentina	20.2	(3.3)	27.3	(2.5)	28.1	(3.5)	31.6	(2.9)	24.9	(3.7)	36.0	(2.8)	17.9	(2.8)	32.2	(2.5)
Azerbaijan	56.4	(4.1)	57.7	(2.5)	51.1	(3.7)	50.5	(3.6)	61.1	(4.0)	55.2	(2.9)	42.5	(4.1)	49.5	(2.6)
Brazil	51.6	(3.6)	63.5	(2.4)	47.4	(3.8)	59.0	(2.3)	48.2	(3.8)	61.3	(2.0)	38.2	(3.2)	53.3	(2.5)
Bulgaria	36.6	(3.4)	53.2	(2.5)	48.9	(4.2)	51.9	(2.7)	55.4	(4.5)	58.2	(2.5)	52.4	(4.9)	53.5	(2.4)
Chile	46.5	(4.4)	45.5	(2.2)	56.8	(3.9)	53.4	(2.1)	43.2	(4.6)	53.0	(2.4)	42.3	(3.9)	47.9	(2.2)
Colombia	24.2	(4.3)	25.5	(2.0)	42.0	(4.7)	35.2	(3.0)	37.2	(6.4)	48.0	(3.9)	27.4	(3.7)	40.7	(3.7)
Croatia	40.7	(3.2)	31.7	(1.7)	55.3	(2.9)	44.2	(1.8)	46.0	(3.1)	43.8	(1.9)	35.3	(3.4)	36.8	(1.8)
Estonia	28.5	(3.5)	40.3	(2.5)	42.8	(3.5)	56.9	(2.1)	48.1	(4.6)	53.6	(2.7)	26.1	(3.0)	44.2	(2.8)
Hong Kong-China	67.3	(2.7)	59.3	(2.0)	68.1	(3.0)	60.8	(2.4)	44.7	(2.5)	50.8	(1.9)	32.5	(2.2)	44.3	(2.1)
Indonesia	39.8	(3.5)	48.8	(2.2)	43.6	(4.0)	53.7	(2.4)	50.8	(3.6)	60.8	(2.2)	42.9	(3.2)	56.5	(2.7)
Israel	60.6	(3.3)	63.8	(2.1)	61.4	(3.7)	56.6	(2.4)	64.2	(3.6)	59.0	(2.7)	44.7	(3.5)	52.9	(2.3)
Jordan	59.9	(3.4)	63.6	(2.3)	63.7	(3.1)	62.7	(1.9)	66.5	(2.9)	62.3	(2.1)	48.8	(3.3)	55.0	(2.5)
Kyrgyzstan	45.9	(3.2)	56.2	(2.9)	46.6	(4.3)	45.7	(3.2)	69.6	(3.1)	63.1	(3.2)	50.6	(3.3)	46.8	(3.4)
Latvia	33.8	(3.9)	46.7	(2.7)	43.4	(4.5)	53.4	(2.5)	52.8	(3.7)	53.6	(2.9)	30.0	(4.0)	46.0	(2.6)
Lithuania	50.3	(3.7)	42.4	(2.2)	65.2	(3.3)	57.6	(1.8)	59.3	(3.2)	56.3	(2.1)	30.4	(3.1)	40.6	(1.9)
Macao-China	50.0	(3.6)	49.0	(2.5)	50.1	(3.9)	48.6	(2.5)	30.7	(2.8)	36.2	(2.4)	20.6	(2.4)	28.9	(2.8)
Montenegro	27.0	(2.7)	41.6	(2.3)	28.9	(4.0)	44.7	(2.4)	40.2	(3.2)	52.0	(2.2)	30.4	(3.1)	44.0	(2.5)
Romania	28.5	(3.3)	47.4	(2.8)	39.6	(4.4)	39.1	(3.0)	29.7	(5.2)	52.0	(4.1)	27.3	(3.1)	48.0	(3.1)
Russian Federation	46.5	(3.9)	55.1	(2.6)	56.2	(2.8)	64.0	(1.9)	61.0	(2.4)	66.2	(1.7)	58.4	(2.9)	61.1	(2.5)
Serbia	37.6	(3.3)	46.2	(2.4)	39.6	(3.3)	42.7	(1.7)	47.1	(2.6)	54.2	(1.7)	34.8	(4.3)	49.6	(2.1)
Slovenia	37.7	(4.6)	41.9	(2.0)	51.7	(3.9)	53.6	(2.1)	42.7	(3.8)	48.4	(2.1)	31.8	(3.7)	43.2	(2.4)
Chinese Taipei	62.9	(2.6)	45.7	(1.7)	72.0	(2.4)	53.6	(1.7)	32.8	(2.4)	36.4	(1.8)	30.1	(2.5)	28.1	(1.6)
Thailand	58.7	(4.9)	60.7	(1.9)	68.5	(3.2)	61.6	(2.2)	56.4	(3.4)	59.6	(2.2)	40.7	(3.8)	49.5	(2.7)
Tunisia	54.5	(3.2)	64.8	(2.4)	52.1	(3.8)	58.7	(2.2)	61.6	(3.0)	60.0	(2.2)	45.3	(3.5)	56.3	(2.7)
Uruguay	19.7	(3.5)	33.9	(2.7)	43.0	(4.3)	42.9	(2.6)	46.9	(3.3)	45.8	(2.7)	23.9	(2.8)	35.8	(2.5)

Table A2.7b Students' information on science-related careers by student group

		\multicolumn{4}{c}{Students' information on science-related careers}	\multicolumn{2}{c}{Difference in the mean index between resilient students and disadvantaged low achievers}
		\multicolumn{2}{c}{Resilient students}	\multicolumn{2}{c}{Disadvantaged low achievers (DLA)}		
		Mean	S.E.	Mean	S.E.	Dif	S.E.
OECD	Australia	0.21	(0.04)	-0.11	(0.03)	**0.31**	(0.04)
	Austria	-0.17	(0.05)	-0.13	(0.05)	-0.06	(0.08)
	Belgium	-0.30	(0.04)	-0.23	(0.04)	-0.05	(0.06)
	Canada	0.22	(0.04)	0.09	(0.04)	**0.13**	(0.06)
	Czech Republic	-0.22	(0.06)	-0.10	(0.05)	-0.09	(0.10)
	Denmark	-0.08	(0.06)	-0.18	(0.04)	0.08	(0.08)
	Finland	0.12	(0.04)	0.04	(0.03)	0.07	(0.07)
	France	-0.01	(0.06)	-0.15	(0.04)	0.15	(0.08)
	Germany	-0.02	(0.06)	-0.19	(0.04)	**0.17**	(0.08)
	Greece	0.15	(0.07)	0.13	(0.05)	0.04	(0.09)
	Hungary	-0.28	(0.06)	-0.03	(0.04)	**-0.25**	(0.09)
	Iceland	0.04	(0.05)	-0.37	(0.04)	**0.40**	(0.08)
	Ireland	-0.08	(0.07)	-0.21	(0.05)	**0.16**	(0.08)
	Italy	-0.03	(0.03)	-0.01	(0.03)	-0.01	(0.04)
	Japan	-0.43	(0.04)	-0.44	(0.04)	0.02	(0.06)
	Korea	-0.43	(0.04)	-0.52	(0.03)	0.09	(0.06)
	Luxembourg	-0.24	(0.07)	-0.14	(0.04)	-0.09	(0.11)
	Mexico	-0.68	(0.06)	-0.37	(0.07)	**-0.30**	(0.09)
	Netherlands	-0.35	(0.05)	-0.45	(0.07)	0.12	(0.08)
	New Zealand	0.12	(0.07)	0.07	(0.05)	0.04	(0.10)
	Norway	-0.17	(0.06)	-0.18	(0.05)	-0.01	(0.09)
	Poland	0.10	(0.05)	0.25	(0.03)	**-0.13**	(0.07)
	Portugal	0.32	(0.06)	0.23	(0.04)	0.08	(0.07)
	Slovak Republic	-0.16	(0.06)	-0.03	(0.05)	-0.13	(0.09)
	Spain	0.03	(0.05)	-0.25	(0.04)	**0.24**	(0.06)
	Sweden	-0.18	(0.07)	-0.37	(0.05)	**0.17**	(0.08)
	Switzerland	0.07	(0.04)	-0.07	(0.03)	**0.15**	(0.05)
	Turkey	0.44	(0.06)	-0.14	(0.08)	**0.55**	(0.10)
	United Kingdom	-0.17	(0.05)	-0.08	(0.04)	-0.11	(0.07)
	United States	0.23	(0.05)	0.27	(0.06)	-0.03	(0.09)
	OECD average	**-0.07**	**(0.01)**	**-0.12**	**(0.01)**	**0.06**	**(0.01)**
Partners	Argentina	-0.77	(0.08)	-0.58	(0.08)	-0.18	(0.11)
	Azerbaijan	0.18	(0.07)	0.30	(0.06)	-0.07	(0.10)
	Brazil	-0.12	(0.08)	0.38	(0.04)	**-0.47**	(0.09)
	Bulgaria	0.01	(0.07)	0.26	(0.06)	**-0.22**	(0.10)
	Chile	0.05	(0.07)	0.13	(0.05)	-0.08	(0.09)
	Colombia	-0.19	(0.07)	-0.03	(0.06)	-0.18	(0.11)
	Croatia	0.01	(0.05)	-0.17	(0.03)	**0.16**	(0.06)
	Estonia	-0.27	(0.05)	0.04	(0.04)	**-0.31**	(0.07)
	Hong Kong-China	0.14	(0.03)	0.13	(0.03)	-0.01	(0.06)
	Indonesia	-0.10	(0.07)	0.21	(0.04)	**-0.31**	(0.09)
	Israel	0.23	(0.08)	0.20	(0.05)	0.01	(0.09)
	Jordan	0.30	(0.06)	0.33	(0.04)	-0.05	(0.08)
	Kyrgyzstan	0.16	(0.07)	0.21	(0.06)	-0.01	(0.11)
	Latvia	-0.15	(0.05)	0.13	(0.05)	**-0.26**	(0.09)
	Lithuania	0.11	(0.06)	0.06	(0.03)	0.07	(0.07)
	Macao-China	-0.32	(0.04)	-0.25	(0.04)	-0.08	(0.08)
	Montenegro	-0.36	(0.06)	0.04	(0.05)	**-0.36**	(0.09)
	Romania	-0.32	(0.04)	0.12	(0.06)	**-0.44**	(0.08)
	Russian Federation	0.26	(0.04)	0.37	(0.04)	**-0.13**	(0.06)
	Serbia	-0.12	(0.05)	0.13	(0.04)	**-0.24**	(0.07)
	Slovenia	-0.08	(0.05)	0.06	(0.03)	**-0.13**	(0.07)
	Chinese Taipei	0.06	(0.04)	-0.18	(0.03)	**0.23**	(0.05)
	Thailand	0.15	(0.05)	0.19	(0.03)	-0.05	(0.07)
	Tunisia	0.21	(0.08)	0.41	(0.04)	-0.14	(0.09)
	Uruguay	-0.45	(0.07)	-0.30	(0.07)	-0.17	(0.12)

Note: Values that are statistically different are indicated in bold.

Table A2.7c Relationship between being resilient and PISA index of student information on science careers

| | | Increased likelihood of being resilient associated with one unit on the PISA index of student information on science careers ||||||
| | | | | After accounting for ESCS, gender, immigrant, grade, using test language || After accounting for Mean ESCS, ESCS, gender, immigrant, grade, using test language ||
		Ratio	S.E.	Ratio	S.E.	Ratio	S.E.
OECD	Australia	**1.27**	(0.04)	**1.26**	(0.04)	**1.26**	(0.04)
	Austria	0.98	(0.08)	1.07	(0.09)	1.15	(0.10)
	Belgium	0.96	(0.05)	1.07	(0.06)	1.11	(0.07)
	Canada	1.11	(0.06)	1.06	(0.06)	1.07	(0.06)
	Czech Republic	0.93	(0.12)	0.93	(0.13)	0.92	(0.13)
	Denmark	1.15	(0.09)	**1.24**	(0.09)	**1.24**	(0.09)
	Finland	1.09	(0.09)	1.07	(0.09)	1.07	(0.09)
	France	1.15	(0.06)	1.09	(0.08)	1.02	(0.09)
	Germany	1.15	(0.09)	1.02	(0.10)	1.04	(0.12)
	Greece	1.03	(0.09)	1.00	(0.09)	0.98	(0.09)
	Hungary	**0.74**	(0.11)	**0.75**	(0.13)	0.80	(0.15)
	Iceland	**1.44**	(0.08)	**1.46**	(0.10)	**1.46**	(0.10)
	Ireland	1.11	(0.07)	1.06	(0.07)	1.06	(0.08)
	Italy	0.98	(0.05)	0.93	(0.05)	0.90	(0.06)
	Japan	1.05	(0.06)	1.04	(0.07)	1.02	(0.07)
	Korea	1.15	(0.08)	1.15	(0.08)	1.12	(0.09)
	Luxembourg	0.93	(0.10)	0.92	(0.13)	0.91	(0.13)
	Mexico	**0.90**	(0.05)	0.96	(0.05)	0.96	(0.05)
	Netherlands	1.14	(0.07)	**1.24**	(0.06)	**1.19**	(0.08)
	New Zealand	1.08	(0.10)	1.09	(0.11)	1.11	(0.11)
	Norway	1.02	(0.08)	1.02	(0.08)	1.03	(0.08)
	Poland	0.87	(0.08)	0.88	(0.08)	0.88	(0.09)
	Portugal	1.10	(0.08)	0.96	(0.12)	0.97	(0.11)
	Slovak Republic	0.93	(0.09)	0.95	(0.09)	0.94	(0.10)
	Spain	**1.27**	(0.06)	**1.17**	(0.07)	**1.18**	(0.07)
	Sweden	1.11	(0.07)	1.16	(0.08)	1.15	(0.08)
	Switzerland	**1.19**	(0.06)	**1.28**	(0.08)	**1.33**	(0.09)
	Turkey	**1.55**	(0.09)	**1.47**	(0.09)	**1.39**	(0.10)
	United Kingdom	0.93	(0.07)	0.92	(0.07)	0.92	(0.07)
	United States	1.00	(0.07)	1.00	(0.08)	1.01	(0.08)
	OECD average	**1.07**	(0.01)	**1.00**	(0.00)	**1.06**	(0.02)
Partners	Argentina	0.92	(0.07)	0.93	(0.08)	0.93	(0.08)
	Azerbaijan	0.96	(0.09)	0.94	(0.09)	0.94	(0.09)
	Brazil	**0.73**	(0.08)	**0.73**	(0.09)	**0.73**	(0.09)
	Bulgaria	0.88	(0.08)	0.85	(0.09)	0.87	(0.09)
	Chile	0.98	(0.09)	1.04	(0.09)	1.04	(0.09)
	Colombia	0.89	(0.12)	0.95	(0.13)	0.95	(0.13)
	Croatia	**1.20**	(0.07)	**1.17**	(0.07)	**1.21**	(0.08)
	Estonia	**0.74**	(0.08)	**0.73**	(0.09)	**0.73**	(0.09)
	Hong Kong-China	1.00	(0.09)	1.00	(0.10)	1.00	(0.11)
	Indonesia	**0.75**	(0.09)	0.76	(0.08)	0.75	(0.09)
	Israel	1.02	(0.06)	1.03	(0.06)	1.06	(0.06)
	Jordan	0.95	(0.08)	0.95	(0.09)	0.96	(0.09)
	Kyrgyzstan	1.02	(0.09)	1.00	(0.09)	1.01	(0.09)
	Latvia	**0.75**	(0.13)	**0.69**	(0.15)	**0.72**	(0.15)
	Lithuania	1.09	(0.10)	1.01	(0.10)	1.03	(0.10)
	Macao-China	0.96	(0.08)	0.89	(0.09)	0.87	(0.09)
	Montenegro	**0.80**	(0.07)	**0.78**	(0.07)	**0.81**	(0.08)
	Romania	0.67	(0.10)	0.66	(0.11)	0.71	(0.11)
	Russian Federation	0.92	(0.08)	0.95	(0.08)	0.95	(0.08)
	Serbia	**0.85**	(0.08)	**0.83**	(0.08)	0.86	(0.09)
	Slovenia	0.91	(0.07)	0.95	(0.08)	1.00	(0.10)
	Chinese Taipei	**1.28**	(0.07)	**1.24**	(0.07)	**1.30**	(0.08)
	Thailand	1.00	(0.11)	0.95	(0.12)	0.97	(0.13)
	Tunisia	0.90	(0.08)	0.94	(0.08)	0.96	(0.08)
	Uruguay	0.92	(0.07)	0.97	(0.09)	0.97	(0.10)

Note: Values that are statistically different are indicated in bold.

Table A2.8a — Share of students who took general science compulsory courses this or last year, by student group

	Resilient students %	S.E.	Disadvantaged low achievers (DLA) %	S.E.	Dif	S.E.
OECD						
Australia	93.0	(0.9)	65.0	(1.5)	**28.0**	(1.7)
Austria	a	a	a	a	a	a
Belgium	54.7	(3.4)	58.7	(2.7)	-4.0	(4.1)
Canada	96.7	(0.8)	79.6	(1.2)	**17.1**	(1.3)
Czech Republic	59.8	(4.1)	60.1	(2.5)	-0.3	(5.2)
Denmark	15.4	(2.8)	15.6	(1.4)	-0.2	(3.3)
Finland	91.3	(1.7)	81.3	(1.8)	**10.0**	(2.4)
France	a	a	a	a	a	a
Germany	80.9	(3.4)	56.7	(2.0)	**24.1**	(3.8)
Greece	a	a	a	a	a	a
Hungary	a	a	a	a	a	a
Iceland	97.1	(1.2)	86.6	(1.4)	**10.5**	(1.8)
Ireland	70.9	(4.2)	58.3	(3.4)	**12.6**	(4.2)
Italy	72.4	(2.6)	83.8	(1.3)	**-11.4**	(3.0)
Japan	a	a	a	a	a	a
Korea	99.2	(0.6)	90.8	(1.4)	**8.4**	(1.5)
Luxembourg	a	a	a	a	a	a
Mexico	38.9	(3.1)	38.8	(2.4)	0.1	(4.4)
Netherlands	82.0	(2.8)	58.7	(2.9)	**23.3**	(3.6)
New Zealand	98.3	(0.9)	84.4	(1.5)	**13.9**	(1.6)
Norway	a	a	a	a	a	a
Poland	a	a	a	a	a	a
Portugal	98.5	(1.0)	89.6	(1.8)	**8.8**	(2.1)
Slovak Republic	a	a	a	a	a	a
Spain	83.6	(1.9)	91.8	(1.1)	**-8.3**	(2.2)
Sweden	69.0	(4.0)	44.8	(2.1)	**24.2**	(4.3)
Switzerland	91.2	(1.6)	69.6	(1.9)	**21.5**	(2.3)
Turkey	80.3	(3.2)	66.5	(2.9)	**13.8**	(4.3)
United Kingdom	80.4	(3.6)	55.1	(2.0)	**25.3**	(4.1)
United States	87.9	(2.3)	67.5	(2.9)	**20.4**	(3.3)
OECD average	**80.1**	**(0.5)**	**69.7**	**(0.4)**	**10.3**	**(0.7)**
Partners						
Argentina	18.5	(3.4)	23.1	(2.1)	-4.5	(3.8)
Azerbaijan	a	a	a	a	a	a
Brazil	9.4	(2.0)	14.0	(2.4)	-4.6	(3.1)
Bulgaria	a	a	a	a	a	a
Chile	67.9	(3.1)	50.7	(2.1)	**17.2**	(3.6)
Colombia	13.5	(3.6)	20.8	(3.0)	-7.3	(5.3)
Croatia	a	a	a	a	a	a
Estonia	55.6	(3.7)	44.4	(2.8)	**11.2**	(5.2)
Hong Kong-China	61.3	(3.8)	52.1	(2.5)	**9.2**	(4.1)
Indonesia	91.4	(1.9)	87.9	(1.8)	3.5	(2.7)
Israel	72.2	(3.1)	59.5	(2.7)	**12.7**	(3.6)
Jordan	55.6	(4.5)	48.7	(2.6)	6.9	(4.7)
Kyrgyzstan	66.2	(3.2)	67.2	(2.6)	-1.0	(4.4)
Latvia	86.8	(3.2)	68.9	(2.3)	**18.0**	(4.3)
Lithuania	a	a	a	a	a	a
Macao-China	53.7	(2.9)	25.8	(2.0)	**27.8**	(3.5)
Montenegro	88.5	(2.1)	74.8	(2.2)	**13.8**	(3.2)
Romania	42.6	(5.0)	44.1	(2.8)	-1.6	(5.2)
Russian Federation	3.4	(1.3)	2.4	(1.0)	1.0	(1.3)
Serbia	a	a	a	a	a	a
Slovenia	61.0	(3.7)	74.9	(2.2)	**-13.9**	(3.9)
Chinese Taipei	51.0	(3.1)	30.2	(2.3)	**20.8**	(3.7)
Thailand	96.8	(1.1)	82.8	(2.3)	**14.0**	(2.6)
Tunisia	72.8	(2.6)	66.9	(2.3)	5.8	(3.6)
Uruguay	50.8	(4.2)	35.3	(2.0)	**15.5**	(4.9)

Note: Values that are statistically different are indicated in bold.

Table A2.8b Relationship between being resilient and taking general science compulsory courses

		Increased likelihood of being resilient associated with taking general science compulsory courses				
				After accounting for ESCS, gender, immigrant, grade, using test language		After accounting for Mean ESCS, ESCS, gender, immigrant, grade, using test language
		Ratio	S.E.	Ratio	S.E.	Ratio	S.E.

OECD

Country	Ratio	S.E.	Ratio	S.E.	Ratio	S.E.
Australia	**4.58**	(0.15)	**4.44**	(0.15)	**4.15**	(0.15)
Austria	a	a	a	a	a	a
Belgium	0.88	(0.15)	1.23	(0.14)	1.12	(0.16)
Canada	**5.38**	(0.25)	**4.26**	(0.26)	**4.12**	(0.26)
Czech Republic	0.86	(0.19)	0.78	(0.20)	0.78	(0.21)
Denmark	1.10	(0.26)	1.14	(0.27)	1.21	(0.28)
Finland	**1.86**	(0.24)	**1.80**	(0.24)	**1.80**	(0.24)
France	a	a	a	a	a	a
Germany	**2.59**	(0.23)	**2.25**	(0.22)	**1.86**	(0.23)
Greece	a	a	a	a	a	a
Hungary	a	a	a	a	a	a
Iceland	**3.88**	(0.44)	**3.50**	(0.45)	**3.45**	(0.45)
Ireland	**1.55**	(0.19)	**1.56**	(0.19)	**1.58**	(0.19)
Italy	**0.57**	(0.15)	**0.65**	(0.14)	1.11	(0.15)
Japan	a	a	a	a	a	a
Korea	**8.71**	(0.77)	**8.33**	(0.78)	**8.35**	(0.77)
Luxembourg	a	a	a	a	a	a
Mexico	1.11	(0.16)	1.29	(0.18)	1.33	(0.18)
Netherlands	**2.50**	(0.19)	**2.88**	(0.21)	**1.98**	(0.22)
New Zealand	**7.22**	(0.57)	**6.67**	(0.56)	**6.11**	(0.56)
Norway	a	a	a	a	a	a
Poland	a	a	a	a	a	a
Portugal	**5.53**	(0.86)	1.71	(0.98)	1.71	(0.99)
Slovak Republic	a	a	a	a	a	a
Spain	**0.51**	(0.17)	0.72	(0.19)	0.71	(0.18)
Sweden	**2.25**	(0.20)	**2.19**	(0.20)	**2.15**	(0.20)
Switzerland	**3.22**	(0.20)	**2.57**	(0.23)	**2.48**	(0.23)
Turkey	**1.75**	(0.23)	1.63	(0.25)	1.61	(0.26)
United Kingdom	**2.32**	(0.24)	**2.20**	(0.24)	**2.17**	(0.24)
United States	**2.55**	(0.23)	**1.94**	(0.22)	**1.90**	(0.22)
OECD average	**2.04**	(0.07)	**1.91**	(0.07)	**1.88**	(0.07)

Partners

Country	Ratio	S.E.	Ratio	S.E.	Ratio	S.E.
Argentina	0.87	(0.26)	0.89	(0.28)	0.93	(0.27)
Azerbaijan	a	a	a	a	a	a
Brazil	0.95	(0.28)	1.14	(0.30)	1.15	(0.31)
Bulgaria	a	a	a	a	a	a
Chile	**2.04**	(0.15)	**2.30**	(0.17)	**2.27**	(0.18)
Colombia	0.70	(0.34)	0.88	(0.36)	0.88	(0.36)
Croatia	a	a	a	a	a	a
Estonia	**1.54**	(0.18)	**1.52**	(0.18)	**1.51**	(0.18)
Hong Kong-China	1.22	(0.18)	1.16	(0.19)	1.20	(0.19)
Indonesia	1.47	(0.28)	1.64	(0.27)	1.55	(0.27)
Israel	**1.75**	(0.16)	**1.68**	(0.17)	**1.55**	(0.18)
Jordan	1.26	(0.17)	1.26	(0.17)	1.27	(0.17)
Kyrgyzstan	1.02	(0.18)	1.03	(0.18)	1.09	(0.18)
Latvia	**2.40**	(0.30)	**1.97**	(0.32)	**1.97**	(0.33)
Lithuania	a	a	a	a	a	a
Macao-China	**2.72**	(0.14)	**2.23**	(0.15)	**2.22**	(0.15)
Montenegro	**2.24**	(0.24)	**2.20**	(0.24)	**2.18**	(0.25)
Romania	0.99	(0.25)	0.98	(0.28)	1.06	(0.29)
Russian Federation	1.42	(0.34)	1.56	(0.36)	1.51	(0.37)
Serbia	a	a	a	a	a	a
Slovenia	**0.59**	(0.17)	**0.55**	(0.17)	**0.62**	(0.20)
Chinese Taipei	**2.03**	(0.14)	**2.12**	(0.16)	**1.56**	(0.16)
Thailand	**4.89**	(0.39)	**3.89**	(0.40)	**3.77**	(0.41)
Tunisia	1.30	(0.15)	1.05	(0.18)	1.08	(0.18)
Uruguay	**1.70**	(0.19)	**1.55**	(0.21)	**1.53**	(0.21)

Note: Values that are statistically different are indicated in bold.

Table A2.9a Number of attended compulsory courses in general science, physics, biology and chemistry, by student group

		\multicolumn{4}{c	}{Number of attended compulsory courses in general science, physics, biology and chemistry}	Difference in the mean index between resilient students and disadvantaged low achievers	
		Resilient students		Disadvantaged low achievers (DLA)			
		Mean	S.E.	Mean	S.E.	Dif	S.E.
OECD	Australia	4.20	(0.12)	2.66	(0.08)	**1.54**	(0.14)
	Austria	3.68	(0.15)	3.51	(0.14)	0.17	(0.20)
	Belgium	5.50	(0.19)	1.74	(0.08)	**3.76**	(0.21)
	Canada	3.72	(0.11)	3.36	(0.09)	0.35	(0.14)
	Czech Republic	6.88	(0.14)	5.50	(0.20)	**1.38**	(0.24)
	Denmark	5.97	(0.12)	4.78	(0.13)	**1.19**	(0.18)
	Finland	7.50	(0.11)	6.76	(0.11)	**0.74**	(0.13)
	France	5.90	(0.09)	4.72	(0.08)	**1.18**	(0.11)
	Germany	7.11	(0.15)	4.94	(0.15)	**2.17**	(0.22)
	Greece	4.88	(0.10)	4.13	(0.12)	**0.75**	(0.16)
	Hungary	5.10	(0.12)	5.18	(0.10)	-0.08	(0.15)
	Iceland	7.38	(0.18)	6.03	(0.16)	**1.34**	(0.23)
	Ireland	1.78	(0.07)	1.20	(0.05)	**0.57**	(0.09)
	Italy	4.14	(0.13)	3.68	(0.09)	0.46	(0.17)
	Japan	3.56	(0.10)	3.18	(0.09)	**0.38**	(0.12)
	Korea	4.03	(0.16)	4.24	(0.16)	-0.21	(0.21)
	Luxembourg	4.26	(0.15)	4.25	(0.10)	0.00	(0.17)
	Mexico	3.86	(0.18)	3.64	(0.15)	0.22	(0.23)
	Netherlands	5.75	(0.19)	4.53	(0.24)	**1.22**	(0.28)
	New Zealand	4.33	(0.26)	3.98	(0.14)	0.35	(0.27)
	Norway	a	a	a	a	a	a
	Poland	a	a	a	a	a	a
	Portugal	5.04	(0.21)	4.82	(0.18)	0.21	(0.25)
	Slovak Republic	5.36	(0.11)	4.54	(0.14)	**0.83**	(0.18)
	Spain	7.00	(0.16)	5.51	(0.12)	**1.49**	(0.19)
	Sweden	5.59	(0.27)	3.47	(0.15)	**2.12**	(0.30)
	Switzerland	5.74	(0.13)	4.14	(0.09)	**1.60**	(0.15)
	Turkey	5.37	(0.23)	4.49	(0.25)	**0.88**	(0.32)
	United Kingdom	6.11	(0.25)	3.72	(0.13)	**2.40**	(0.27)
	United States	3.65	(0.11)	3.76	(0.10)	-0.12	(0.15)
	OECD average	**5.12**	**(0.03)**	**4.16**	**(0.03)**	**0.96**	**(0.04)**
Partners	Argentina	1.55	(0.28)	1.75	(0.15)	-0.20	(0.31)
	Azerbaijan	5.20	(0.25)	3.71	(0.20)	**1.49**	(0.33)
	Brazil	0.70	(0.13)	0.87	(0.10)	-0.17	(0.16)
	Bulgaria	5.73	(0.12)	5.25	(0.18)	**0.48**	(0.22)
	Chile	6.27	(0.21)	4.19	(0.15)	**2.08**	(0.26)
	Colombia	1.41	(0.24)	1.84	(0.19)	-0.43	(0.31)
	Croatia	4.90	(0.13)	3.46	(0.09)	**1.44**	(0.15)
	Estonia	5.94	(0.24)	4.74	(0.19)	**1.19**	(0.35)
	Hong Kong-China	4.51	(0.17)	2.43	(0.15)	**2.08**	(0.21)
	Indonesia	7.69	(0.24)	6.94	(0.16)	**0.75**	(0.28)
	Israel	4.88	(0.27)	3.56	(0.16)	**1.32**	(0.30)
	Jordan	6.52	(0.21)	5.03	(0.17)	**1.49**	(0.26)
	Kyrgyzstan	6.47	(0.27)	5.22	(0.26)	**1.25**	(0.39)
	Latvia	7.78	(0.19)	7.01	(0.14)	**0.77**	(0.23)
	Lithuania	5.88	(0.11)	4.05	(0.13)	**1.83**	(0.18)
	Macao-China	4.81	(0.20)	2.74	(0.17)	**2.06**	(0.28)
	Montenegro	7.47	(0.13)	6.59	(0.17)	**0.88**	(0.22)
	Romania	5.17	(0.48)	4.30	(0.19)	0.86	(0.45)
	Russian Federation	6.06	(0.03)	5.96	(0.03)	**0.11**	(0.04)
	Serbia	5.19	(0.11)	4.46	(0.09)	**0.73**	(0.13)
	Slovenia	6.95	(0.15)	5.71	(0.08)	**1.24**	(0.17)
	Chinese Taipei	5.29	(0.17)	4.26	(0.11)	**1.03**	(0.19)
	Thailand	6.49	(0.22)	6.34	(0.20)	0.15	(0.32)
	Tunisia	5.71	(0.20)	5.01	(0.19)	**0.70**	(0.27)
	Uruguay	4.12	(0.26)	2.12	(0.13)	**2.00**	(0.29)

Note: Values that are statistically different are indicated in bold.

Table A2.9b Relationship between being resilient and number of attended compulsory courses in general science, physics, biology and chemistry

		\multicolumn{6}{c}{Increased likelihood of being resilient associate with one additional compulsory courses in general science, physics, biology and chemistry}
				After accounting for ESCS, gender, immigrant, grade, using test language		After accounting for Mean ESCS, ESCS, gender, immigrant, grade, using test language	
		Ratio	S.E.	Ratio	S.E.	Ratio	S.E.
OECD	Australia	**1.14**	(0.01)	**1.15**	(0.01)	**1.14**	(0.01)
	Austria	1.05	(0.04)	**1.12**	(0.04)	1.04	(0.05)
	Belgium	**1.34**	(0.02)	**1.25**	(0.02)	**1.18**	(0.02)
	Canada	**1.04**	(0.02)	1.02	(0.02)	1.02	(0.02)
	Czech Republic	**1.14**	(0.02)	**1.15**	(0.03)	**1.09**	(0.03)
	Denmark	**1.15**	(0.03)	**1.15**	(0.03)	**1.16**	(0.03)
	Finland	**1.15**	(0.03)	**1.14**	(0.03)	**1.14**	(0.03)
	France	**1.35**	(0.05)	**1.56**	(0.09)	**1.44**	(0.09)
	Germany	**1.22**	(0.03)	**1.15**	(0.03)	**1.11**	(0.04)
	Greece	**1.11**	(0.03)	**1.09**	(0.03)	**1.08**	(0.03)
	Hungary	0.99	(0.04)	1.01	(0.05)	1.06	(0.07)
	Iceland	**1.10**	(0.02)	**1.09**	(0.03)	**1.09**	(0.03)
	Ireland	**1.42**	(0.06)	**1.35**	(0.06)	**1.35**	(0.07)
	Italy	**1.07**	(0.03)	1.04	(0.03)	**1.13**	(0.03)
	Japan	**1.09**	(0.04)	**1.08**	(0.04)	1.02	(0.05)
	Korea	0.95	(0.03)	0.95	(0.03)	**0.92**	(0.04)
	Luxembourg	0.99	(0.02)	0.96	(0.03)	1.00	(0.04)
	Mexico	1.03	(0.02)	**1.06**	(0.02)	**1.06**	(0.02)
	Netherlands	**1.09**	(0.03)	**1.16**	(0.03)	**1.14**	(0.04)
	New Zealand	1.02	(0.03)	1.02	(0.03)	1.02	(0.03)
	Norway	a	a	a	a	a	a
	Poland	a	a	a	a	a	a
	Portugal	1.04	(0.03)	**1.07**	(0.03)	**1.08**	(0.03)
	Slovak Republic	**1.19**	(0.04)	**1.21**	(0.05)	**1.17**	(0.05)
	Spain	**1.13**	(0.02)	**1.07**	(0.02)	**1.07**	(0.02)
	Sweden	**1.12**	(0.02)	**1.12**	(0.02)	**1.11**	(0.02)
	Switzerland	**1.16**	(0.02)	**1.16**	(0.02)	**1.15**	(0.02)
	Turkey	**1.07**	(0.03)	**1.06**	(0.03)	**1.08**	(0.03)
	United Kingdom	**1.13**	(0.02)	**1.13**	(0.02)	**1.13**	(0.02)
	United States	1.00	(0.02)	0.98	(0.03)	0.98	(0.03)
	OECD average	**1.10**	(0.01)	**1.10**	(0.01)	**1.09**	(0.01)
Partners	Argentina	0.97	(0.04)	0.95	(0.05)	0.97	(0.05)
	Azerbaijan	**1.14**	(0.03)	**1.13**	(0.03)	**1.13**	(0.03)
	Brazil	1.00	(0.04)	1.01	(0.04)	1.02	(0.04)
	Bulgaria	1.05	(0.02)	1.04	(0.03)	**1.07**	(0.03)
	Chile	**1.15**	(0.02)	**1.13**	(0.02)	**1.12**	(0.02)
	Colombia	0.96	(0.04)	0.98	(0.04)	0.98	(0.05)
	Croatia	**1.41**	(0.05)	**1.50**	(0.05)	**1.39**	(0.05)
	Estonia	**1.10**	(0.03)	**1.07**	(0.03)	**1.07**	(0.03)
	Hong Kong-China	**1.19**	(0.03)	**1.13**	(0.03)	**1.13**	(0.03)
	Indonesia	**1.06**	(0.02)	**1.06**	(0.02)	**1.05**	(0.02)
	Israel	**1.10**	(0.02)	**1.10**	(0.02)	**1.09**	(0.03)
	Jordan	**1.10**	(0.02)	**1.08**	(0.02)	**1.08**	(0.02)
	Kyrgyzstan	**1.06**	(0.02)	**1.05**	(0.02)	**1.06**	(0.02)
	Latvia	**1.09**	(0.04)	1.04	(0.04)	1.05	(0.04)
	Lithuania	**1.22**	(0.03)	**1.20**	(0.03)	**1.21**	(0.03)
	Macao-China	**1.15**	(0.02)	**1.11**	(0.02)	**1.11**	(0.02)
	Montenegro	**1.06**	(0.02)	**1.06**	(0.02)	**1.06**	(0.02)
	Romania	1.06	(0.04)	1.07	(0.04)	1.08	(0.04)
	Russian Federation	**1.34**	(0.09)	**1.35**	(0.10)	**1.33**	(0.10)
	Serbia	**1.21**	(0.06)	**1.19**	(0.06)	**1.15**	(0.06)
	Slovenia	**1.25**	(0.05)	**1.27**	(0.05)	1.07	(0.06)
	Chinese Taipei	**1.09**	(0.02)	**1.07**	(0.02)	1.03	(0.02)
	Thailand	1.01	(0.02)	0.99	(0.03)	0.99	(0.03)
	Tunisia	**1.06**	(0.02)	1.03	(0.02)	1.04	(0.02)
	Uruguay	**1.17**	(0.03)	**1.13**	(0.03)	**1.12**	(1.03)

Note: Values that are statistically different are indicated in bold.

Table A2.10a — Number of hours students report spending in regular lessons at school learning science

		Resilient students Mean	S.E.	Disadvantaged low achievers (DLA) Mean	S.E.	Difference Dif	S.E.
OECD	Australia	3.60	(0.07)	2.33	(0.06)	**1.27**	(0.09)
	Austria	3.13	(0.15)	1.52	(0.06)	**1.62**	(0.16)
	Belgium	3.02	(0.11)	1.47	(0.08)	**1.55**	(0.13)
	Canada	4.13	(0.11)	2.81	(0.07)	**1.31**	(0.13)
	Czech Republic	3.50	(0.16)	1.89	(0.07)	**1.61**	(0.17)
	Denmark	3.44	(0.10)	2.72	(0.08)	**0.72**	(0.13)
	Finland	3.52	(0.09)	2.44	(0.08)	**1.08**	(0.10)
	France	3.45	(0.12)	1.55	(0.06)	**1.90**	(0.13)
	Germany	3.68	(0.14)	1.93	(0.08)	**1.75**	(0.17)
	Greece	3.59	(0.12)	2.02	(0.08)	**1.57**	(0.15)
	Hungary	2.93	(0.14)	1.87	(0.06)	**1.06**	(0.15)
	Iceland	3.11	(0.08)	2.49	(0.06)	**0.62**	(0.11)
	Ireland	2.84	(0.11)	1.95	(0.10)	**0.89**	(0.16)
	Italy	3.52	(0.10)	2.16	(0.07)	**1.35**	(0.13)
	Japan	2.85	(0.09)	2.22	(0.06)	**0.63**	(0.11)
	Korea	3.78	(0.09)	2.95	(0.09)	**0.83**	(0.12)
	Luxembourg	2.66	(0.14)	1.69	(0.06)	**0.97**	(0.14)
	Mexico	3.00	(0.11)	2.91	(0.11)	0.09	(0.16)
	Netherlands	3.01	(0.11)	1.23	(0.08)	**1.79**	(0.12)
	New Zealand	4.51	(0.09)	2.91	(0.11)	**1.60**	(0.15)
	Norway	2.75	(0.07)	2.32	(0.07)	**0.43**	(0.10)
	Poland	3.17	(0.11)	2.16	(0.07)	**1.01**	(0.11)
	Portugal	3.62	(0.18)	2.10	(0.07)	**1.52**	(0.20)
	Slovak Republic	2.95	(0.14)	1.35	(0.07)	**1.60**	(0.15)
	Spain	3.53	(0.08)	2.27	(0.06)	**1.26**	(0.10)
	Sweden	3.06	(0.06)	2.46	(0.06)	**0.59**	(0.08)
	Switzerland	2.84	(0.13)	1.54	(0.05)	**1.30**	(0.14)
	Turkey	3.54	(0.18)	1.86	(0.12)	**1.68**	(0.21)
	United Kingdom	4.54	(0.09)	3.27	(0.07)	**1.26**	(0.11)
	United States	3.91	(0.13)	2.21	(0.11)	**1.70**	(0.17)
	OECD average	**3.37**	**(0.02)**	**2.15**	**(0.01)**	**1.22**	**(0.03)**
Partners	Argentina	2.43	(0.18)	1.64	(0.09)	**0.79**	(0.21)
	Azerbaijan	2.92	(0.14)	2.27	(0.08)	**0.65**	(0.17)
	Brazil	2.44	(0.12)	1.64	(0.08)	**0.81**	(0.15)
	Bulgaria	2.88	(0.21)	1.69	(0.10)	**1.18**	(0.22)
	Chile	2.58	(0.16)	1.44	(0.06)	**1.13**	(0.19)
	Colombia	3.63	(0.19)	3.04	(0.15)	**0.59**	(0.21)
	Croatia	2.18	(0.10)	1.29	(0.07)	**0.88**	(0.12)
	Estonia	3.74	(0.12)	2.54	(0.09)	**1.19**	(0.13)
	Hong Kong-China	3.92	(0.14)	1.80	(0.11)	**2.12**	(0.18)
	Indonesia	3.30	(0.15)	2.52	(0.08)	**0.78**	(0.14)
	Israel	2.86	(0.14)	1.57	(0.08)	**1.28**	(0.17)
	Jordan	3.53	(0.18)	2.24	(0.10)	**1.29**	(0.22)
	Kyrgyzstan	2.08	(0.14)	1.64	(0.19)	**0.44**	(0.20)
	Latvia	3.31	(0.16)	2.04	(0.10)	**1.27**	(0.18)
	Lithuania	3.02	(0.12)	2.00	(0.09)	**1.02**	(0.14)
	Macao-China	4.11	(0.13)	2.74	(0.10)	**1.38**	(0.14)
	Montenegro	3.13	(0.14)	1.95	(0.09)	**1.18**	(0.16)
	Romania	2.67	(0.21)	1.50	(0.10)	**1.17**	(0.22)
	Russian Federation	4.14	(0.17)	2.63	(0.12)	**1.51**	(0.20)
	Serbia	3.15	(0.12)	1.93	(0.09)	**1.22**	(0.15)
	Slovenia	3.41	(0.15)	1.68	(0.06)	**1.72**	(0.15)
	Chinese Taipei	3.31	(0.12)	1.80	(0.08)	**1.52**	(0.14)
	Thailand	4.16	(0.11)	3.27	(0.05)	**0.89**	(0.11)
	Tunisia	3.01	(0.10)	1.87	(0.09)	**1.14**	(0.13)
	Uruguay	2.53	(0.16)	1.74	(0.08)	**0.79**	(0.17)

Note: Values that are statistically different are indicated in bold.

Table A2.10b **Relationship between being resilient and hours spent in regular lessons at school learning science**

| | | Increased likelihood of being resilient associate with one additional hour regular lessons at school learning science ||||||
| | | Ratio | S.E. | After accounting for ESCS, gender, immigrant background, grade, using test language || After accounting for Mean ESCS, ESCS, gender, immigrant background, grade, using test language ||
				Ratio	S.E.	Ratio	S.E.
OECD	Australia	**1.33**	(0.03)	**1.37**	(0.03)	**1.36**	(0.03)
	Austria	**1.54**	(0.05)	**1.55**	(0.05)	**1.40**	(0.05)
	Belgium	**1.44**	(0.03)	**1.49**	(0.04)	**1.41**	(0.04)
	Canada	**1.26**	(0.03)	**1.21**	(0.03)	**1.20**	(0.03)
	Czech Republic	**1.49**	(0.05)	**1.55**	(0.05)	**1.50**	(0.06)
	Denmark	**1.30**	(0.06)	**1.29**	(0.06)	**1.29**	(0.07)
	Finland	**1.44**	(0.04)	**1.44**	(0.04)	**1.44**	(0.04)
	France	**1.8**	(0.05)	**1.55**	(0.06)	**1.44**	(0.07)
	Germany	**1.53**	(0.05)	**1.45**	(0.06)	**1.33**	(0.06)
	Greece	**1.5**	(0.05)	**1.48**	(0.05)	**1.45**	(0.05)
	Hungary	**1.4**	(0.06)	**1.42**	(0.06)	**1.37**	(0.07)
	Iceland	**1.27**	(0.05)	**1.25**	(0.06)	**1.25**	(0.06)
	Ireland	**1.28**	(0.05)	**1.32**	(0.05)	**1.30**	(0.05)
	Italy	**1.38**	(0.04)	**1.33**	(0.04)	**1.32**	(0.04)
	Japan	**1.4**	(0.06)	**1.37**	(0.07)	**1.25**	(0.07)
	Korea	**1.44**	(0.06)	**1.43**	(0.06)	**1.31**	(0.06)
	Luxembourg	**1.3**	(0.05)	**1.19**	(0.05)	**1.23**	(0.06)
	Mexico	1.01	(0.03)	1.02	(0.03)	1.02	(0.03)
	Netherlands	**1.59**	(0.04)	**1.63**	(0.04)	**1.48**	(0.06)
	New Zealand	**1.48**	(0.05)	**1.46**	(0.05)	**1.44**	(0.06)
	Norway	**1.3**	(0.07)	**1.26**	(0.07)	**1.26**	(0.07)
	Poland	**1.4**	(0.05)	**1.41**	(0.05)	**1.41**	(0.05)
	Portugal	**1.40**	(0.06)	**1.18**	(0.06)	**1.19**	(0.06)
	Slovak Republic	**1.5**	(0.04)	**1.55**	(0.05)	**1.46**	(0.05)
	Spain	**1.47**	(0.03)	**1.42**	(0.04)	**1.42**	(0.04)
	Sweden	**1.38**	(0.05)	**1.40**	(0.06)	**1.39**	(0.06)
	Switzerland	**1.47**	(0.05)	**1.44**	(0.05)	**1.37**	(0.05)
	Turkey	**1.40**	(0.05)	**1.39**	(0.05)	**1.33**	(0.05)
	United Kingdom	**1.50**	(0.06)	**1.51**	(0.06)	**1.50**	(0.06)
	United States	**1.37**	(0.04)	**1.34**	(0.05)	**1.34**	(0.05)
	OECD average	**1.41**	(0.01)	**1.38**	(0.01)	**1.34**	(0.01)
Partners	Argentina	**1.24**	(0.07)	**1.22**	(0.07)	**1.18**	(0.07)
	Azerbaijan	1.2	(0.05)	1.17	(0.05)	1.17	(0.05)
	Brazil	**1.36**	(0.06)	**1.41**	(0.06)	**1.41**	(0.06)
	Bulgaria	**1.29**	(0.06)	**1.31**	(0.07)	**1.28**	(0.07)
	Chile	**1.37**	(0.06)	**1.40**	(0.06)	**1.37**	(0.06)
	Colombia	1.15	(0.07)	1.10	(0.08)	1.10	(0.08)
	Croatia	**1.3**	(0.04)	**1.27**	(0.04)	**1.22**	(0.04)
	Estonia	**1.37**	(0.04)	**1.35**	(0.05)	**1.36**	(0.05)
	Hong Kong-China	**1.38**	(0.03)	**1.35**	(0.03)	**1.34**	(0.03)
	Indonesia	**1.26**	(0.06)	**1.24**	(0.05)	**1.21**	(0.05)
	Israel	**1.30**	(0.04)	**1.33**	(0.04)	**1.34**	(0.04)
	Jordan	**1.26**	(0.05)	**1.21**	(0.05)	**1.22**	(0.05)
	Kyrgyzstan	**1.11**	(0.05)	**1.12**	(0.04)	**1.14**	(0.04)
	Latvia	**1.44**	(0.07)	**1.40**	(0.07)	**1.40**	(0.08)
	Lithuania	**1.3**	(0.05)	**1.27**	(0.05)	**1.27**	(0.05)
	Macao-China	**1.28**	(0.04)	**1.21**	(0.04)	**1.21**	(0.04)
	Montenegro	**1.30**	(0.04)	**1.31**	(0.05)	**1.31**	(0.05)
	Romania	**1.32**	(0.07)	**1.31**	(0.08)	**1.29**	(0.08)
	Russian Federation	**1.30**	(0.05)	**1.29**	(0.06)	**1.29**	(0.06)
	Serbia	**1.3**	(0.04)	**1.32**	(0.04)	**1.27**	(0.04)
	Slovenia	**1.52**	(0.05)	**1.55**	(0.05)	**1.35**	(0.06)
	Chinese Taipei	**1.39**	(0.04)	**1.53**	(0.05)	**1.42**	(0.05)
	Thailand	**1.72**	(0.08)	**1.64**	(0.08)	**1.62**	(0.08)
	Tunisia	**1.33**	(0.04)	**1.21**	(0.05)	**1.21**	(0.05)
	Uruguay	**1.23**	(0.05)	**1.28**	(0.06)	**1.27**	(0.06)

Note: Values that are statistically different are indicated in bold.

Table A2.11a Share of students in private schools

		Share of students in private schools				Difference in the mean index between resilient students and disadvantaged low achievers	
		Resilient students		Disadvantaged low achievers (DLA)			
		%	S.E.	%	S.E.	Dif	S.E.
OECD	Australia	w	w	w	w	w	w
	Austria	c	c	c	c	c	c
	Belgium	w	w	w	w	w	w
	Canada	c	c	c	c	c	c
	Czech Republic	c	c	c	c	c	c
	Denmark	23.7	(4.7)	18.5	(3.6)	5.3	(4.2)
	Finland	c	c	c	c	c	c
	France	w	w	w	w	w	w
	Germany	c	c	c	c	c	c
	Greece	c	c	c	c	c	c
	Hungary	c	c	c	c	c	c
	Iceland	c	c	c	c	c	c
	Ireland	54.1	(4.3)	44.1	(3.3)	9.9	(5.7)
	Italy	c	c	c	c	c	c
	Japan	18.2	(2.6)	28.9	(4.1)	**-10.7**	(4.4)
	Korea	48.4	(6.0)	51.0	(6.0)	-2.6	(6.6)
	Luxembourg	11.5	(2.2)	16.4	(1.2)	**-4.9**	(2.5)
	Mexico	c	c	c	c	c	c
	Netherlands	73.7	(5.2)	66.2	(7.2)	7.5	(7.2)
	New Zealand	c	c	c	c	c	c
	Norway	c	c	c	c	c	c
	Poland	c	c	c	c	c	c
	Portugal	c	c	c	c	c	c
	Slovak Republic	c	c	c	c	c	c
	Spain	24.0	(2.6)	18.0	(2.0)	**6.0**	(2.9)
	Sweden	c	c	c	c	c	c
	Switzerland	c	c	c	c	c	c
	Turkey	c	c	c	c	c	c
	United Kingdom	c	c	c	c	c	c
	United States	c	c	c	c	c	c
	OECD average	**14.8**	**(0.5)**	**12.7**	**(0.5)**	**2.1**	**(0.6)**
Partners	Argentina	26.9	(4.6)	11.0	(3.6)	15.9	(5.7)
	Azerbaijan	c	c	c	c	c	c
	Brazil	c	c	c	c	c	c
	Bulgaria	m	m	m	m	m	m
	Chile	50.3	(5.7)	32.1	(4.6)	**18.2**	(6.4)
	Colombia	c	c	c	c	c	c
	Croatia	c	c	c	c	c	c
	Estonia	c	c	c	c	c	c
	Hong Kong-China	93.3	(2.6)	94.4	(1.2)	-1.1	(2.6)
	Indonesia	37.5	(7.0)	48.5	(5.2)	-11.0	(7.9)
	Israel	31.2	(5.8)	26.2	(3.9)	5.0	(4.9)
	Jordan	18.8	(2.5)	7.2	(0.9)	**11.5**	(2.5)
	Kyrgyzstan	c	c	c	c	c	c
	Latvia	c	c	c	c	c	c
	Lithuania	c	c	c	c	c	c
	Macao-China	95.6	(1.0)	89.2	(0.9)	**6.4**	(1.4)
	Montenegro	c	c	c	c	c	c
	Romania	c	c	c	c	c	c
	Russian Federation	c	c	c	c	c	c
	Serbia	c	c	c	c	c	c
	Slovenia	c	c	c	c	c	c
	Chinese Taipei	15.5	(2.5)	47.3	(6.2)	**-31.8**	(6.0)
	Thailand	9.4	(3.3)	10.2	(2.1)	-0.8	(3.1)
	Tunisia	c	c	c	c	c	c
	Uruguay	c	c	c	c	c	c

Note: Values that are statistically different are indicated in bold.

Table A2.11b Relationship between being resilient and being in private schools

		\multicolumn{6}{c}{Increased likelihood of being resilient associate with being in private schools}
				After accounting for ESCS, gender, immigrant, grade, using test language		After accounting for Mean ESCS, ESCS, gender, immigrant, grade, using test language	
		Ratio	S.E.	Ratio	S.E.	Ratio	S.E.
OECD	Australia	w	w	w	w	w	w
	Austria	c	c	c	c	c	c
	Belgium	w	w	w	w	w	w
	Canada	c	c	c	c	c	c
	Czech Republic	c	c	c	c	c	c
	Denmark	1.27	(0.22)	1.08	(0.22)	0.95	(0.23)
	Finland	c	c	c	c	c	c
	France	w	w	w	w	w	w
	Germany	c	c	c	c	c	c
	Greece	c	c	c	c	c	c
	Hungary	c	c	c	c	c	c
	Iceland	c	c	c	c	c	c
	Ireland	1.30	(0.21)	1.18	(0.22)	0.86	(0.20)
	Italy	c	c	c	c	c	c
	Japan	**0.64**	(0.21)	**0.63**	(0.20)	**0.35**	(0.22)
	Korea	0.91	(0.21)	0.89	(0.21)	0.98	(0.20)
	Luxembourg	0.67	(0.24)	0.68	(0.28)	0.78	(0.29)
	Mexico	c	c	c	c	c	c
	Netherlands	1.33	(0.30)	1.20	(0.30)	1.24	(0.27)
	New Zealand	c	c	c	c	c	c
	Norway	c	c	c	c	c	c
	Poland	c	c	c	c	c	c
	Portugal	c	c	c	c	c	c
	Slovak Republic	c	c	c	c	c	c
	Spain	1.38	(0.16)	0.97	(0.19)	0.78	(0.19)
	Sweden	c	c	c	c	c	c
	Switzerland	c	c	c	c	c	c
	Turkey	c	c	c	c	c	c
	United Kingdom	c	c	c	c	c	c
	United States	c	c	c	c	c	c
	OECD average	0.87	(0.10)	1.00	(0.00)	**0.58**	(0.10)
Partners	Argentina	**2.52**	(0.32)	**1.98**	(0.27)	1.10	(0.31)
	Azerbaijan	c	c	c	c	c	c
	Brazil	c	c	c	c	c	c
	Bulgaria	m	m	m	m	m	m
	Chile	**1.76**	(0.23)	1.46	(0.24)	1.12	(0.24)
	Colombia	c	c	c	c	c	c
	Croatia	c	c	c	c	c	c
	Estonia	c	c	c	c	c	c
	Hong Kong-China	0.83	(0.38)	0.73	(0.38)	0.91	(0.42)
	Indonesia	0.67	(0.29)	**0.52**	(0.30)	0.70	(0.26)
	Israel	1.28	(0.24)	1.14	(0.25)	1.01	(0.24)
	Jordan	**2.19**	(0.20)	**1.99**	(0.23)	**1.96**	(0.23)
	Kyrgyzstan	c	c	c	c	c	c
	Latvia	c	c	c	c	c	c
	Lithuania	c	c	c	c	c	c
	Macao-China	**1.95**	(0.29)	1.84	(0.33)	1.59	(0.37)
	Montenegro	c	c	c	c	c	c
	Romania	c	c	c	c	c	c
	Russian Federation	c	c	c	c	c	c
	Serbia	c	c	c	c	c	c
	Slovenia	c	c	c	c	c	c
	Chinese Taipei	**0.27**	(0.23)	**0.19**	(0.27)	**0.22**	(0.23)
	Thailand	0.82	(0.38)	0.59	(0.40)	0.54	(0.41)
	Tunisia	c	c	c	c	c	c
	Uruguay	c	c	c	c	c	c

Note: Values that are statistically different are indicated in bold.

Table A2.12a Share of students in schools which compete with other schools

		Share of students in schools which compete with other schools				
	Resilient students		Disadvantaged low achievers (DLA)		Difference in the mean index between resilient students and disadvantaged low achievers	
	%	S.E.	%	S.E.	Dif	S.E.
OECD						
Australia	c	c	c	c	c	c
Austria	55.1	(5.7)	52.8	(6.2)	2.3	(7.8)
Belgium	90.1	(2.9)	92.0	(2.8)	-1.9	(3.7)
Canada	76.5	(3.0)	72.0	(2.7)	4.5	(2.6)
Czech Republic	85.4	(3.7)	82.3	(3.7)	3.1	(4.2)
Denmark	74.5	(4.8)	82.0	(3.4)	-7.5	(4.3)
Finland	46.5	(4.3)	50.8	(4.0)	-4.3	(4.1)
France	w	w	w	w	w	w
Germany	86.2	(4.2)	71.9	(5.0)	**14.3**	(6.2)
Greece	57.9	(5.1)	51.7	(4.9)	6.3	(5.7)
Hungary	77.7	(5.8)	69.2	(5.6)	8.5	(7.4)
Iceland	24.8	(2.8)	29.2	(2.0)	-4.4	(3.4)
Ireland	78.1	(4.0)	84.2	(3.4)	-6.2	(3.8)
Italy	83.2	(3.0)	77.0	(3.5)	6.1	(3.7)
Japan	88.5	(4.1)	88.2	(3.5)	0.3	(4.3)
Korea	86.1	(3.7)	92.5	(2.1)	**-6.4**	(2.7)
Luxembourg	62.1	(3.6)	64.2	(1.3)	-2.1	(3.9)
Mexico	80.7	(3.8)	74.2	(5.5)	6.5	(5.8)
Netherlands	87.5	(5.2)	85.0	(4.5)	2.5	(6.9)
New Zealand	89.0	(3.5)	90.7	(2.5)	-1.6	(2.4)
Norway	28.7	(4.4)	27.5	(4.0)	1.3	(3.7)
Poland	50.7	(5.6)	51.5	(4.8)	-0.8	(4.1)
Portugal	68.4	(6.2)	63.9	(5.4)	4.5	(6.2)
Slovak Republic	90.0	(3.4)	81.7	(5.8)	8.4	(5.7)
Spain	72.9	(3.8)	76.5	(3.3)	-3.7	(3.4)
Sweden	55.8	(5.5)	56.8	(4.5)	-0.9	(4.6)
Switzerland	38.1	(4.0)	36.1	(3.6)	2.0	(4.6)
Turkey	68.6	(5.3)	51.6	(6.0)	**17.0**	(6.2)
United Kingdom	c	c	c	c	c	c
United States	67.8	(5.2)	74.6	(4.6)	-6.8	(5.3)
OECD average	**70.8**	**(0.8)**	**69.5**	**(0.8)**	**1.3**	**(0.9)**
Partners						
Argentina	79.1	(4.6)	63.0	(6.9)	**16.1**	(7.2)
Azerbaijan	m	m	m	m	m	m
Brazil	54.4	(4.5)	53.3	(4.1)	1.1	(5.6)
Bulgaria	84.2	(5.2)	73.8	(6.3)	10.4	(6.9)
Chile	67.5	(8.2)	71.0	(5.8)	-3.4	(7.0)
Colombia	72.4	(7.5)	69.6	(6.8)	2.8	(5.6)
Croatia	75.4	(5.2)	74.5	(4.6)	0.9	(5.1)
Estonia	77.1	(4.9)	75.0	(3.9)	2.2	(5.5)
Hong Kong-China	c	c	c	c	c	c
Indonesia	c	c	c	c	c	c
Israel	82.3	(4.1)	85.0	(4.0)	-2.6	(4.3)
Jordan	50.9	(5.8)	49.9	(4.9)	0.9	(5.5)
Kyrgyzstan	64.4	(5.2)	60.7	(4.7)	3.7	(6.8)
Latvia	c	c	c	c	c	c
Lithuania	66.5	(4.8)	64.0	(4.5)	2.4	(4.7)
Macao-China	c	c	c	c	c	c
Montenegro	c	c	c	c	c	c
Romania	53.2	(10.4)	45.5	(5.9)	7.7	(10.4)
Russian Federation	65.7	(6.3)	71.2	(4.5)	-5.5	(4.5)
Serbia	64.6	(5.5)	75.5	(5.0)	-10.9	(6.0)
Slovenia	56.7	(3.8)	39.4	(2.0)	**17.3**	(4.0)
Chinese Taipei	c	c	c	c	c	c
Thailand	87.3	(3.9)	86.1	(4.4)	1.2	(4.2)
Tunisia	46.0	(7.4)	47.2	(6.4)	-1.2	(7.3)
Uruguay	38.2	(5.0)	31.9	(4.9)	6.3	(6.2)

Note: Values that are statistically different are indicated in bold.

Table A2.12b **Relationship between being resilient and being in schools which compete with other schools**

		Increased likelihood of being resilient associate with being in schools which compete with other schools					
				After accounting for ESCS, gender, immigrant background, grade, using test language		After accounting for Mean ESCS, ESCS, gender, immigrant background, grade, using test language	
		Ratio	S.E.	Ratio	S.E.	Ratio	S.E.
OECD	Australia	c	c	c	c	c	c
	Austria	1.02	(0.25)	1.61	(0.25)	1.08	(0.25)
	Belgium	0.93	(0.38)	0.96	(0.32)	0.92	(0.30)
	Canada	1.19	(0.12)	1.14	(0.13)	1.09	(0.13)
	Czech Republic	1.26	(0.29)	1.08	(0.31)	0.84	(0.31)
	Denmark	0.71	(0.26)	0.71	(0.28)	0.74	(0.28)
	Finland	0.85	(0.15)	0.89	(0.15)	0.87	(0.17)
	France	w	w	w	w	w	w
	Germany	1.91	(0.39)	1.42	(0.37)	1.06	(0.30)
	Greece	1.22	(0.19)	1.07	(0.18)	0.89	(0.19)
	Hungary	1.34	(0.34)	1.19	(0.34)	0.86	(0.29)
	Iceland	0.88	(0.17)	0.90	(0.17)	0.90	(0.17)
	Ireland	0.79	(0.24)	0.76	(0.24)	0.72	(0.25)
	Italy	1.30	(0.20)	1.23	(0.20)	1.28	(0.20)
	Japan	1.03	(0.35)	1.04	(0.34)	0.79	(0.35)
	Korea	**0.64**	(0.21)	0.66	(0.22)	1.11	(0.28)
	Luxembourg	0.90	(0.17)	0.99	(0.17)	0.96	(0.18)
	Mexico	1.33	(0.29)	0.80	(0.29)	0.72	(0.30)
	Netherlands	1.06	(0.50)	1.02	(0.48)	0.62	(0.53)
	New Zealand	0.87	(0.25)	0.91	(0.25)	0.91	(0.26)
	Norway	1.03	(0.16)	1.08	(0.16)	0.99	(0.16)
	Poland	0.96	(0.15)	0.94	(0.15)	0.97	(0.15)
	Portugal	1.22	(0.24)	1.00	(0.22)	0.93	(0.22)
	Slovak Republic	1.61	(0.39)	0.92	(0.33)	0.59	(0.33)
	Spain	0.88	(0.17)	0.86	(0.20)	0.77	(0.20)
	Sweden	1.04	(0.18)	1.23	(0.19)	1.16	(0.20)
	Switzerland	1.10	(0.17)	1.18	(0.18)	1.00	(0.15)
	Turkey	**1.79**	(0.24)	1.55	(0.24)	1.09	(0.24)
	United Kingdom	c	c	c	c	c	c
	United States	0.81	(0.21)	0.97	(0.18)	0.95	(0.18)
	OECD average	1.04	(0.05)	1.01	(0.05)	**0.91**	(0.05)
Partners	Argentina	**1.94**	(0.29)	**1.86**	(0.29)	1.25	(0.30)
	Azerbaijan	m	m	m	m	m	m
	Brazil	0.97	(0.20)	0.87	(0.21)	0.81	(0.20)
	Bulgaria	1.65	(0.39)	1.00	(0.41)	0.73	(0.37)
	Chile	0.83	(0.30)	0.89	(0.30)	0.59	(0.33)
	Colombia	1.19	(0.26)	1.10	(0.29)	1.07	(0.29)
	Croatia	1.04	(0.24)	0.96	(0.24)	0.91	(0.25)
	Estonia	1.17	(0.27)	1.16	(0.27)	1.13	(0.28)
	Hong Kong-China	c	c	c	c	c	c
	Indonesia	c	c	c	c	c	c
	Israel	0.85	(0.28)	0.85	(0.28)	0.89	(0.25)
	Jordan	1.02	(0.20)	0.93	(0.20)	0.92	(0.20)
	Kyrgyzstan	1.06	(0.24)	1.05	(0.24)	1.01	(0.25)
	Latvia	c	c	c	c	c	c
	Lithuania	1.05	(0.20)	0.96	(0.20)	0.77	(0.19)
	Macao-China	c	c	c	c	c	c
	Montenegro	c	c	c	c	c	c
	Romania	1.25	(0.37)	1.06	(0.38)	0.81	(0.39)
	Russian Federation	0.86	(0.18)	0.85	(0.18)	0.85	(0.19)
	Serbia	0.67	(0.25)	0.63	(0.25)	0.61	(0.27)
	Slovenia	**1.97**	(0.16)	**2.01**	(0.17)	1.09	(0.19)
	Chinese Taipei	c	c	c	c	c	c
	Thailand	1.00	(0.29)	0.90	(0.27)	0.96	(0.27)
	Tunisia	1.01	(0.25)	1.21	(0.19)	1.09	(0.19)
	Uruguay	1.21	(0.23)	1.25	(0.22)	1.13	(0.24)

Note: Values that are statistically different are indicated in bold.

Table A2.13a Share of students in schools which select students based on academic record

		Share of students in schools which select students based on academic record				
	Resilient students		**Disadvantaged low achievers (DLA)**		**Difference in the mean index between resilient students and disadvantaged low achievers**	
	%	S.E.	%	S.E.	Dif	S.E.
OECD						
Australia	c	c	c	c	c	c
Austria	80.6	(3.5)	34.8	(4.4)	**45.8**	(5.7)
Belgium	30.3	(4.7)	24.5	(3.7)	5.8	(5.3)
Canada	c	c	c	c	c	c
Czech Republic	52.3	(4.5)	25.5	(4.5)	**26.8**	(5.9)
Denmark	c	c	c	c	c	c
Finland	c	c	c	c	c	c
France	w	w	w	w	w	w
Germany	54.0	(6.0)	21.2	(4.2)	**32.9**	(6.5)
Greece	1.2	(1.1)	0.2	(0.2)	1.0	(0.9)
Hungary	78.7	(5.3)	32.1	(5.6)	**46.6**	(7.0)
Iceland	c	c	c	c	c	c
Ireland	c	c	c	c	c	c
Italy	c	c	c	c	c	c
Japan	91.1	(3.1)	84.1	(4.1)	7.0	(4.6)
Korea	64.9	(5.2)	63.6	(6.0)	1.3	(6.1)
Luxembourg	46.7	(4.6)	46.2	(1.7)	0.5	(4.9)
Mexico	40.3	(3.6)	21.1	(5.1)	**19.3**	(5.1)
Netherlands	68.2	(6.0)	59.9	(6.0)	8.3	(7.0)
New Zealand	c	c	c	c	c	c
Norway	c	c	c	c	c	c
Poland	c	c	c	c	c	c
Portugal	c	c	c	c	c	c
Slovak Republic	55.1	(4.5)	34.3	(5.6)	**20.8**	(6.4)
Spain	c	c	c	c	c	c
Sweden	c	c	c	c	c	c
Switzerland	58.8	(5.0)	46.6	(3.5)	**12.3**	(5.3)
Turkey	34.0	(5.3)	14.3	(2.9)	**19.8**	(5.2)
United Kingdom	c	c	c	c	c	c
United States	c	c	c	c	c	c
OECD average	**54.0**	**(1.2)**	**36.3**	**(1.2)**	**17.7**	**(1.5)**
Partners						
Argentina	c	c	c	c	c	c
Azerbaijan	14.8	(5.1)	15.8	(4.4)	-1.0	(5.8)
Brazil	c	c	c	c	c	c
Bulgaria	86.9	(4.4)	65.5	(5.3)	**21.4**	(6.3)
Chile	35.0	(7.2)	15.4	(4.4)	**19.5**	(6.7)
Colombia	17.4	(4.4)	8.6	(2.3)	**8.7**	(3.7)
Croatia	92.7	(2.6)	81.0	(3.8)	**11.8**	(3.3)
Estonia	35.6	(5.7)	30.2	(4.1)	5.4	(5.7)
Hong Kong-China	85.2	(3.7)	73.8	(4.8)	**11.3**	(4.7)
Indonesia	66.5	(7.1)	43.3	(5.0)	**23.2**	(6.4)
Israel	33.7	(5.6)	28.4	(5.6)	5.3	(5.6)
Jordan	20.3	(4.9)	24.0	(4.6)	-3.8	(4.8)
Kyrgyzstan	22.8	(5.6)	22.5	(4.3)	0.3	(5.7)
Latvia	15.6	(3.3)	6.2	(1.6)	**9.4**	(3.1)
Lithuania	c	c	c	c	c	c
Macao-China	72.0	(3.3)	62.4	(1.9)	**9.6**	(3.8)
Montenegro	67.9	(2.7)	57.6	(2.3)	**10.3**	(3.7)
Romania	68.8	(8.2)	48.0	(6.5)	**20.8**	(8.6)
Russian Federation	8.9	(2.6)	10.1	(2.5)	-1.3	(3.4)
Serbia	94.9	(2.3)	81.0	(4.9)	**13.9**	(4.8)
Slovenia	45.1	(3.8)	18.3	(1.3)	**26.9**	(4.0)
Chinese Taipei	64.9	(3.6)	28.3	(5.9)	**36.6**	(6.1)
Thailand	38.5	(6.3)	35.0	(5.6)	3.4	(5.2)
Tunisia	21.8	(5.8)	27.3	(5.8)	-5.5	(6.5)
Uruguay	c	c	c	c	c	c

Note: Values that are statistically different are indicated in bold.

Table A2.13b Relationship between being resilient and being in schools which select based on academic record

			Increased likelihood of being resilient associate with being in schools which select based on academic record
				After accounting for ESCS, gender, immigrant background, grade, using test language		After accounting for Mean ESCS, ESCS, gender, immigrant background, grade, using test language	
		Ratio	S.E.	Ratio	S.E.	Ratio	S.E.

OECD

Country	Ratio	S.E.	Ratio	S.E.	Ratio	S.E.
Australia	c	c	c	c	c	c
Austria	**5.06**	(0.24)	**6.69**	(0.27)	**3.80**	(0.33)
Belgium	1.30	(0.23)	1.27	(0.21)	1.21	(0.19)
Canada	c	c	c	c	c	c
Czech Republic	**2.32**	(0.22)	**2.86**	(0.32)	**2.24**	(0.31)
Denmark	c	c	c	c	c	c
Finland	c	c	c	c	c	c
France	w	w	w	w	w	w
Germany	**3.30**	(0.25)	**2.96**	(0.26)	1.62	(0.25)
Greece	c	c	c	c	c	c
Hungary	**4.62**	(0.32)	**2.99**	(0.34)	**2.05**	(0.34)
Iceland	c	c	c	c	c	c
Ireland	c	c	c	c	c	c
Italy	c	c	c	c	c	c
Japan	1.69	(0.41)	1.69	(0.41)	1.77	(0.40)
Korea	1.04	(0.22)	1.02	(0.21)	1.33	(0.18)
Luxembourg	1.00	(0.20)	1.03	(0.22)	1.18	(0.24)
Mexico	**1.97**	(0.23)	1.33	(0.19)	1.17	(0.18)
Netherlands	1.32	(0.27)	1.45	(0.28)	0.97	(0.30)
New Zealand	c	c	c	c	c	c
Norway	c	c	c	c	c	c
Poland	c	c	c	c	c	c
Portugal	c	c	c	c	c	c
Slovak Republic	**1.97**	(0.21)	1.70	(0.29)	1.58	(0.28)
Spain	c	c	c	c	c	c
Sweden	c	c	c	c	c	c
Switzerland	**1.65**	(0.20)	**1.63**	(0.20)	1.45	(0.20)
Turkey	**2.71**	(0.24)	**3.96**	(0.32)	**1.80**	(0.24)
United Kingdom	c	c	c	c	c	c
United States	c	c	c	c	c	c
OECD average	**2.02**	(0.07)	**1.93**	(0.08)	**1.60**	(0.08)

Partners

Country	Ratio	S.E.	Ratio	S.E.	Ratio	S.E.
Argentina	c	c	c	c	c	c
Azerbaijan	0.88	(0.41)	0.91	(0.41)	0.91	(0.42)
Brazil	c	c	c	c	c	c
Bulgaria	**2.99**	(0.41)	1.66	(0.37)	0.96	(0.34)
Chile	**2.18**	(0.31)	1.67	(0.32)	1.34	(0.29)
Colombia	**1.79**	(0.24)	**1.83**	(0.28)	1.77	(0.29)
Croatia	**2.47**	(0.33)	**2.19**	(0.34)	1.43	(0.33)
Estonia	1.14	(0.24)	1.07	(0.24)	0.99	(0.22)
Hong Kong-China	1.53	(0.27)	1.48	(0.29)	1.20	(0.29)
Indonesia	**2.14**	(0.26)	**1.76**	(0.26)	1.43	(0.25)
Israel	1.16	(0.21)	1.12	(0.21)	1.00	(0.20)
Jordan	0.87	(0.27)	0.94	(0.26)	0.93	(0.26)
Kyrgyzstan	1.05	(0.28)	1.03	(0.28)	1.11	(0.29)
Latvia	**1.88**	(0.24)	1.62	(0.24)	1.25	(0.25)
Lithuania	c	c	c	c	c	c
Macao-China	1.34	(0.21)	1.41	(0.25)	1.41	(0.25)
Montenegro	**1.46**	(0.15)	**1.43**	(0.16)	1.22	(0.16)
Romania	2.06	(0.33)	1.99	(0.32)	1.85	(0.34)
Russian Federation	0.94	(0.34)	0.78	(0.37)	0.77	(0.37)
Serbia	**3.16**	(0.46)	**2.86**	(0.49)	2.40	(0.46)
Slovenia	**2.67**	(0.16)	**2.45**	(0.17)	1.47	(0.20)
Chinese Taipei	**3.16**	(0.22)	**3.13**	(0.25)	1.89	(0.20)
Thailand	1.07	(0.23)	0.89	(0.22)	0.82	(0.22)
Tunisia	0.76	(0.30)	0.73	(0.23)	0.77	(0.24)
Uruguay	c	c	c	c	c	c

Note: Values that are statistically different are indicated in bold.

[Part 1/2]
Table A2.14a Quality of educational resources (underlying percentages), by student group

Percentage of principal reported school capacity to provide instruction hindered by any of the following

		Shortage or inadequacy of science laboratory equipment				Shortage or inadequacy of instructional materials (e.g. textbooks)				Shortage or inadequacy of computers for instruction				Lack or inadequacy of internet connectivity			
		Resilient students		Disadvantaged low achievers (DLA)		Resilient students		Disadvantaged low achievers (DLA)		Resilient students		Disadvantaged low achievers (DLA)		Resilient students		Disadvantaged low achievers (DLA)	
		%	S.E.	%	S.E.	%	S.E.	%	S.E.	%	S.E.	%	S.E.	%	S.E.	%	S.E.
OECD	Australia	27.1	(4.0)	30.1	(3.8)	14.7	(3.0)	19.5	(2.6)	37.0	(3.6)	35.5	(3.3)	20.4	(3.1)	17.3	(2.7)
	Austria	40.8	(5.9)	47.4	(6.0)	25.5	(5.3)	21.2	(4.5)	21.7	(4.9)	27.4	(5.2)	7.6	(3.1)	14.6	(4.2)
	Belgium	41.7	(5.4)	36.8	(4.1)	17.0	(3.8)	28.6	(4.0)	47.0	(5.1)	35.3	(4.4)	21.7	(4.3)	26.8	(4.3)
	Canada	39.2	(3.6)	37.2	(3.0)	25.7	(3.2)	24.0	(2.5)	37.2	(3.6)	35.2	(2.5)	18.9	(3.0)	20.3	(2.8)
	Czech Republic	44.6	(5.8)	39.7	(4.8)	31.2	(5.7)	34.1	(4.9)	37.3	(6.1)	44.1	(5.5)	11.2	(2.9)	19.9	(4.4)
	Denmark	27.4	(5.1)	37.3	(4.4)	34.0	(5.6)	35.4	(4.7)	33.0	(4.5)	42.0	(4.5)	16.7	(4.2)	18.3	(3.7)
	Finland	40.0	(4.8)	38.4	(4.1)	24.0	(4.1)	22.4	(3.9)	34.9	(4.4)	33.1	(4.0)	18.6	(3.5)	16.5	(2.5)
	France	w	w	w	w	w	w	w	w	w	w	w	w	w	w	w	w
	Germany	33.0	(5.3)	42.3	(5.3)	18.1	(4.7)	24.3	(5.2)	26.3	(5.1)	27.3	(5.1)	17.9	(5.0)	20.1	(4.1)
	Greece	32.4	(5.0)	53.1	(4.6)	9.5	(3.3)	8.7	(2.4)	22.4	(5.0)	27.6	(4.8)	8.4	(3.3)	17.9	(4.4)
	Hungary	45.9	(5.3)	61.7	(4.8)	35.9	(6.3)	35.7	(5.7)	11.5	(3.9)	18.7	(4.7)	8.7	(3.3)	12.3	(4.0)
	Iceland	55.6	(3.7)	65.1	(2.2)	33.7	(3.2)	38.5	(2.3)	21.6	(2.4)	28.7	(2.1)	7.0	(1.7)	7.0	(1.1)
	Ireland	47.1	(5.0)	48.3	(4.8)	15.6	(4.3)	16.3	(4.5)	52.7	(4.9)	52.5	(5.8)	30.2	(5.0)	33.2	(5.4)
	Italy	37.3	(3.9)	54.9	(3.6)	11.0	(2.3)	28.5	(3.4)	18.4	(2.9)	25.6	(3.2)	11.0	(2.6)	18.9	(2.3)
	Japan	24.0	(4.8)	26.1	(5.0)	4.8	(2.7)	7.9	(3.2)	18.0	(3.4)	22.1	(4.8)	17.5	(3.7)	19.4	(3.9)
	Korea	45.8	(5.7)	56.4	(6.8)	15.3	(4.0)	15.2	(3.7)	25.6	(4.3)	33.1	(5.3)	12.4	(3.1)	16.9	(5.0)
	Luxembourg	18.3	(2.8)	12.5	(1.0)	14.7	(2.6)	13.0	(1.1)	46.6	(3.7)	37.4	(1.5)	15.7	(2.8)	7.7	(0.9)
	Mexico	69.8	(3.9)	83.3	(3.5)	56.1	(4.2)	45.8	(5.8)	63.4	(4.2)	72.8	(4.7)	65.2	(3.5)	81.4	(2.9)
	Netherlands	27.5	(4.7)	35.7	(5.8)	8.8	(2.8)	20.2	(4.7)	28.6	(4.9)	39.7	(6.8)	19.5	(4.5)	23.6	(6.1)
	New Zealand	19.2	(4.5)	20.0	(4.6)	20.3	(4.7)	22.5	(4.4)	43.9	(4.9)	44.2	(5.1)	20.2	(3.5)	20.3	(3.4)
	Norway	54.3	(5.3)	54.4	(4.6)	38.0	(5.2)	39.2	(5.2)	47.3	(4.7)	43.9	(4.8)	26.0	(4.7)	21.7	(3.6)
	Poland	59.2	(5.4)	62.0	(4.6)	31.6	(4.8)	33.3	(4.2)	35.5	(5.3)	32.1	(4.5)	14.5	(4.4)	7.5	(2.5)
	Portugal	48.7	(5.4)	49.7	(6.2)	30.3	(5.7)	28.1	(5.3)	54.1	(5.7)	57.5	(6.1)	27.1	(5.1)	29.3	(4.9)
	Slovak Republic	75.9	(4.1)	70.6	(4.7)	68.8	(4.3)	57.6	(5.2)	38.8	(5.5)	36.8	(6.8)	25.3	(5.0)	22.1	(5.2)
	Spain	40.8	(4.1)	42.6	(4.4)	15.0	(2.3)	16.7	(2.5)	45.2	(4.1)	46.3	(4.0)	24.3	(3.5)	25.7	(3.1)
	Sweden	27.2	(4.5)	33.9	(4.3)	27.0	(5.3)	29.0	(4.6)	52.2	(5.5)	51.2	(4.1)	16.1	(3.7)	16.6	(3.2)
	Switzerland	25.1	(3.8)	35.1	(3.7)	10.6	(2.4)	17.3	(2.8)	9.6	(2.8)	16.1	(3.0)	5.4	(2.2)	11.8	(2.8)
	Turkey	77.7	(4.9)	68.4	(7.3)	67.5	(5.8)	59.4	(4.8)	64.6	(5.9)	69.3	(4.2)	35.6	(5.9)	42.5	(5.2)
	United Kingdom	31.0	(4.6)	29.2	(4.2)	24.0	(4.7)	26.6	(4.0)	40.1	(4.5)	42.8	(4.0)	19.9	(4.4)	23.0	(3.5)
	United States	33.7	(5.7)	41.4	(7.1)	15.0	(3.7)	24.8	(7.7)	32.2	(6.0)	37.5	(7.4)	14.4	(5.4)	21.5	(8.1)
	OECD average	**41.0**	**(0.9)**	**45.3**	**(0.9)**	**25.6**	**(0.8)**	**27.4**	**(0.8)**	**36.1**	**(0.9)**	**38.5**	**(0.9)**	**19.2**	**(0.7)**	**21.9**	**(0.8)**
Partners	Argentina	49.1	(5.7)	72.1	(3.9)	33.5	(5.6)	42.6	(5.8)	47.9	(6.1)	66.2	(5.4)	55.4	(6.9)	75.4	(4.5)
	Azerbaijan	87.9	(3.8)	81.9	(4.6)	54.1	(7.6)	63.5	(6.3)	85.9	(4.8)	83.0	(3.7)	80.9	(6.7)	92.5	(3.6)
	Brazil	83.7	(4.1)	90.6	(2.2)	54.9	(5.1)	57.3	(4.3)	85.6	(3.1)	89.1	(2.2)	63.6	(4.1)	80.3	(3.2)
	Bulgaria	68.8	(6.8)	79.2	(4.9)	40.5	(6.1)	54.6	(6.8)	50.7	(6.4)	41.7	(6.4)	28.5	(5.6)	36.9	(6.0)
	Chile	74.5	(6.2)	82.4	(4.4)	45.2	(8.2)	56.6	(6.3)	45.6	(6.6)	57.6	(6.1)	22.2	(7.6)	37.2	(6.4)
	Colombia	71.3	(6.3)	81.9	(4.2)	79.0	(5.1)	81.1	(4.7)	73.6	(6.8)	80.3	(4.6)	69.3	(8.0)	66.6	(6.1)
	Croatia	73.0	(5.2)	78.7	(4.5)	50.8	(5.7)	56.1	(4.0)	43.3	(5.0)	50.2	(5.1)	26.3	(4.7)	27.6	(5.5)
	Estonia	65.5	(5.0)	70.0	(4.9)	31.2	(5.2)	33.9	(5.4)	40.8	(6.1)	45.2	(5.0)	7.5	(2.6)	11.1	(3.4)
	Hong Kong-China	11.7	(3.4)	16.4	(5.7)	11.9	(3.2)	24.6	(4.9)	23.5	(5.3)	24.7	(5.6)	6.6	(2.6)	12.0	(4.3)
	Indonesia	69.6	(7.1)	80.6	(4.1)	57.9	(7.1)	71.0	(5.2)	56.3	(7.6)	77.3	(3.9)	85.6	(4.2)	87.3	(3.3)
	Israel	45.8	(6.2)	44.0	(5.9)	24.5	(4.6)	26.6	(5.7)	36.0	(5.2)	36.1	(5.0)	15.9	(4.3)	17.0	(4.1)
	Jordan	58.3	(5.5)	58.0	(5.4)	45.8	(5.7)	47.4	(5.5)	77.4	(4.5)	74.5	(5.9)	73.6	(5.2)	72.7	(5.7)
	Kyrgyzstan	95.8	(1.8)	95.6	(2.4)	95.5	(2.2)	97.2	(1.4)	94.0	(1.9)	90.0	(3.9)	96.7	(1.8)	99.2	(0.4)
	Latvia	80.6	(4.0)	79.2	(4.8)	44.8	(6.3)	44.3	(6.4)	45.2	(5.4)	47.2	(5.4)	17.2	(4.0)	21.7	(5.8)
	Lithuania	66.1	(5.7)	66.6	(4.5)	27.4	(5.0)	28.8	(4.0)	51.5	(5.4)	52.3	(5.4)	18.7	(4.4)	19.9	(3.3)
	Macao-China	16.3	(1.7)	17.8	(1.3)	23.0	(2.0)	14.8	(1.2)	18.1	(2.3)	20.6	(1.4)	14.2	(1.9)	14.2	(1.2)
	Montenegro	81.2	(2.4)	89.3	(1.1)	60.4	(2.8)	73.8	(1.8)	77.7	(3.4)	77.8	(1.5)	65.4	(3.4)	62.3	(2.0)
	Romania	73.7	(7.9)	78.4	(6.6)	66.8	(7.4)	68.2	(6.1)	55.2	(8.8)	65.1	(6.7)	27.1	(6.7)	61.2	(5.4)
	Russian Federation	88.7	(3.1)	88.2	(3.1)	64.6	(3.9)	65.9	(3.4)	78.8	(4.6)	79.4	(3.0)	69.8	(4.9)	70.3	(4.0)
	Serbia	62.8	(6.1)	65.6	(5.4)	51.3	(5.8)	48.5	(5.2)	56.4	(5.2)	63.5	(5.8)	44.6	(5.5)	46.7	(5.5)
	Slovenia	25.1	(3.5)	30.0	(2.5)	19.5	(2.6)	27.7	(1.6)	20.2	(3.2)	22.2	(1.5)	8.7	(1.9)	7.9	(0.8)
	Chinese Taipei	25.5	(4.6)	39.9	(6.9)	12.5	(4.1)	21.3	(6.9)	17.6	(4.7)	27.0	(7.2)	13.3	(4.2)	23.6	(7.3)
	Thailand	69.1	(5.8)	73.2	(5.0)	51.5	(5.8)	55.8	(5.0)	52.0	(6.0)	64.6	(4.2)	44.2	(6.9)	58.4	(4.3)
	Tunisia	40.4	(6.8)	36.4	(5.6)	31.3	(5.9)	29.9	(5.6)	79.7	(5.6)	82.6	(4.1)	48.5	(6.0)	58.3	(6.1)
	Uruguay	50.0	(4.7)	53.4	(5.3)	57.2	(4.6)	63.5	(4.9)	67.5	(4.6)	73.1	(5.8)	65.1	(4.2)	71.0	(5.4)

[Part 2/2]
Table A2.14a Quality of educational resources (underlying percentages), by student group

Percentage of principal reported school capacity to provide instruction hindered by any of the following

		Shortage or inadequacy of computer software for instruction				Shortage or inadequacy of library materials				Shortage or inadequacy of audio-visual resources			
		Resilient students		Disadvantaged low achievers (DLA)		Resilient students		Disadvantaged low achievers (DLA)		Resilient students		Disadvantaged low achievers (DLA)	
		%	S.E.	%	S.E.	%	S.E.	%	S.E.	%	S.E.	%	S.E.
OECD	Australia	27.3	(3.6)	28.7	(3.2)	15.7	(3.0)	19.0	(3.2)	19.6	(3.3)	19.8	(3.1)
	Austria	17.9	(4.1)	23.1	(5.5)	19.7	(4.7)	22.9	(4.5)	25.6	(5.4)	27.0	(5.8)
	Belgium	31.7	(4.5)	33.4	(4.5)	38.9	(5.0)	37.3	(5.1)	39.0	(5.1)	34.6	(4.4)
	Canada	32.1	(3.4)	33.1	(2.6)	29.4	(3.5)	31.7	(2.9)	30.2	(3.3)	33.4	(2.8)
	Czech Republic	29.4	(5.9)	36.5	(5.7)	38.7	(5.2)	31.6	(4.6)	44.9	(6.5)	39.2	(5.9)
	Denmark	33.0	(5.1)	35.0	(5.2)	16.5	(4.3)	18.2	(3.7)	36.2	(5.0)	42.3	(5.3)
	Finland	40.8	(5.1)	36.7	(4.2)	38.4	(4.9)	36.5	(4.0)	42.1	(5.4)	44.6	(4.8)
	France	w	w	w	w	w	w	w	w	w	w	w	w
	Germany	33.6	(5.4)	26.8	(4.2)	28.8	(4.8)	36.4	(5.5)	28.6	(5.4)	28.2	(5.0)
	Greece	53.8	(6.3)	63.0	(4.4)	51.6	(6.1)	60.4	(5.4)	46.7	(5.8)	57.7	(5.6)
	Hungary	17.5	(4.3)	32.3	(5.2)	19.0	(4.5)	30.7	(5.5)	18.0	(5.0)	26.3	(5.7)
	Iceland	18.7	(2.8)	32.4	(2.1)	20.2	(3.2)	27.1	(1.9)	16.5	(2.4)	27.6	(1.7)
	Ireland	54.4	(5.5)	54.6	(5.7)	52.7	(5.2)	61.1	(5.2)	50.8	(4.9)	56.7	(5.0)
	Italy	30.6	(4.1)	40.2	(3.7)	21.2	(2.9)	34.9	(3.3)	28.3	(3.8)	38.2	(3.6)
	Japan	27.3	(4.5)	29.8	(4.6)	21.8	(4.1)	31.5	(4.7)	29.9	(4.8)	37.9	(5.4)
	Korea	28.3	(5.0)	37.1	(5.6)	47.8	(5.5)	56.0	(6.6)	49.7	(6.3)	59.8	(6.1)
	Luxembourg	18.2	(2.9)	14.5	(1.0)	39.0	(3.4)	47.5	(1.5)	27.4	(3.4)	38.9	(1.3)
	Mexico	70.2	(3.6)	79.9	(4.0)	62.3	(4.1)	59.1	(5.8)	69.4	(3.9)	79.4	(3.5)
	Netherlands	27.0	(5.1)	32.4	(6.1)	8.6	(2.3)	17.0	(4.9)	17.6	(4.1)	23.2	(6.6)
	New Zealand	30.8	(4.8)	26.7	(4.3)	15.0	(4.0)	14.8	(4.0)	28.4	(4.5)	26.8	(4.5)
	Norway	70.3	(1.0)	63.2	(4.9)	48.3	(5.0)	48.5	(4.4)	45.2	(5.1)	38.7	(4.7)
	Poland	52.2	(5.6)	49.7	(4.5)	41.5	(5.2)	37.7	(4.5)	41.6	(5.9)	39.4	(5.0)
	Portugal	67.8	(5.6)	71.3	(4.9)	35.6	(5.9)	48.0	(6.1)	55.2	(5.8)	47.1	(5.8)
	Slovak Republic	58.2	(5.9)	44.6	(6.5)	66.1	(5.5)	62.9	(5.2)	62.4	(4.8)	58.7	(6.2)
	Spain	49.7	(4.2)	54.8	(4.1)	36.6	(4.0)	41.4	(4.2)	40.6	(4.0)	45.4	(4.0)
	Sweden	49.5	(5.4)	43.5	(4.1)	32.2	(5.1)	30.4	(4.3)	35.5	(5.0)	41.3	(4.3)
	Switzerland	10.8	(2.5)	17.7	(3.2)	13.3	(3.0)	22.2	(3.9)	16.3	(3.6)	15.3	(2.8)
	Turkey	63.2	(5.7)	61.5	(5.0)	66.8	(6.1)	67.5	(5.2)	75.3	(4.8)	74.5	(3.9)
	United Kingdom	31.7	(5.1)	30.3	(4.3)	29.3	(4.8)	26.9	(4.5)	27.0	(4.4)	23.7	(4.2)
	United States	25.3	(5.1)	30.3	(7.3)	20.6	(5.0)	20.5	(4.7)	25.5	(5.2)	22.1	(5.0)
	OECD average	**38.0**	**(0.9)**	**40.1**	**(0.9)**	**33.6**	**(0.9)**	**37.2**	**(0.9)**	**37.0**	**(0.9)**	**39.6**	**(0.9)**
Partners	Argentina	59.3	(6.4)	69.6	(6.2)	27.2	(4.8)	46.0	(6.1)	52.9	(5.9)	64.8	(4.5)
	Azerbaijan	87.2	(4.5)	91.0	(3.9)	72.3	(6.2)	68.8	(4.5)	89.8	(3.9)	84.9	(5.9)
	Brazil	83.1	(3.1)	84.8	(2.9)	66.3	(5.5)	71.3	(3.6)	65.1	(5.0)	68.0	(3.6)
	Bulgaria	51.8	(6.5)	51.4	(6.7)	59.1	(6.2)	64.6	(6.1)	67.5	(5.8)	71.4	(5.6)
	Chile	62.2	(7.6)	58.7	(5.9)	55.1	(8.2)	62.1	(6.0)	42.4	(6.4)	60.0	(6.2)
	Colombia	80.6	(6.7)	82.8	(4.3)	74.3	(6.3)	79.1	(5.3)	69.5	(7.1)	80.0	(5.0)
	Croatia	67.0	(5.0)	64.7	(4.8)	46.4	(5.7)	42.7	(5.2)	60.7	(4.9)	65.6	(4.6)
	Estonia	45.8	(5.6)	51.4	(5.1)	47.7	(5.7)	40.8	(5.4)	55.0	(5.9)	62.6	(5.3)
	Hong Kong-China	30.2	(4.6)	34.8	(4.8)	19.4	(4.3)	27.8	(5.8)	24.9	(4.8)	26.1	(5.0)
	Indonesia	67.4	(6.5)	82.4	(4.0)	82.2	(4.0)	77.2	(4.7)	80.6	(4.8)	83.7	(3.3)
	Israel	26.1	(5.0)	32.4	(5.4)	37.2	(5.6)	35.6	(4.6)	45.2	(6.1)	44.8	(6.4)
	Jordan	73.9	(5.0)	73.8	(4.8)	55.3	(6.0)	55.0	(6.0)	65.3	(4.8)	66.7	(5.4)
	Kyrgyzstan	97.1	(1.4)	96.0	(2.1)	93.0	(2.5)	94.7	(2.6)	95.0	(1.9)	97.5	(1.4)
	Latvia	36.5	(5.4)	39.3	(6.4)	39.4	(6.7)	44.8	(6.0)	56.1	(5.8)	50.8	(6.7)
	Lithuania	47.1	(5.4)	56.0	(4.4)	35.1	(5.2)	38.2	(3.8)	53.3	(5.7)	53.5	(5.1)
	Macao-China	30.5	(2.2)	25.1	(1.4)	33.0	(2.5)	33.6	(1.8)	29.5	(2.4)	29.3	(1.6)
	Montenegro	73.0	(3.9)	70.3	(1.7)	66.3	(2.9)	63.4	(1.7)	72.3	(2.8)	75.2	(1.6)
	Romania	63.6	(8.7)	71.4	(6.3)	47.6	(9.9)	46.7	(6.3)	50.0	(9.8)	82.8	(3.5)
	Russian Federation	85.0	(3.2)	86.5	(2.8)	80.3	(3.5)	81.5	(2.8)	87.6	(2.8)	87.6	(2.8)
	Serbia	60.7	(5.8)	55.2	(5.1)	50.5	(6.3)	54.9	(5.4)	53.5	(5.4)	68.4	(4.8)
	Slovenia	22.7	(2.7)	26.9	(1.9)	9.1	(2.4)	15.0	(1.6)	22.3	(3.6)	25.7	(2.5)
	Chinese Taipei	25.1	(4.8)	32.2	(7.1)	24.8	(4.5)	34.2	(7.0)	24.2	(4.3)	34.2	(7.2)
	Thailand	64.3	(5.8)	71.7	(4.7)	63.0	(6.0)	73.5	(4.9)	66.2	(6.1)	76.7	(4.8)
	Tunisia	66.9	(6.3)	67.6	(5.3)	74.6	(6.2)	75.5	(4.6)	65.7	(6.1)	62.3	(4.6)
	Uruguay	65.9	(4.2)	69.9	(5.5)	58.5	(4.5)	53.5	(5.8)	64.6	(4.1)	61.1	(5.0)

Table A2.14b Quality of school educational resources, by student group

| | | Quality of school educational resources | | | | |
| | | Resilient students | | Disadvantaged low achievers (DLA) | | Difference in the mean index between resilient students and disadvantaged low achievers | |
		Mean	S.E.	Mean	S.E.	Dif	S.E.
OECD	Australia	0.26	(0.08)	0.15	(0.06)	0.11	(0.06)
	Austria	0.35	(0.10)	0.30	(0.13)	0.05	(0.15)
	Belgium	-0.08	(0.08)	-0.01	(0.08)	-0.07	(0.10)
	Canada	0.06	(0.08)	0.04	(0.05)	0.02	(0.06)
	Czech Republic	-0.11	(0.08)	-0.12	(0.08)	0.01	(0.09)
	Denmark	-0.03	(0.10)	-0.18	(0.07)	0.15	(0.07)
	Finland	-0.25	(0.07)	-0.19	(0.06)	-0.06	(0.06)
	France	w	w	w	w	w	w
	Germany	0.19	(0.11)	0.02	(0.11)	0.17	(0.12)
	Greece	-0.04	(0.09)	-0.26	(0.08)	**0.22**	(0.10)
	Hungary	0.24	(0.08)	0.13	(0.11)	0.11	(0.12)
	Iceland	0.22	(0.07)	0.04	(0.04)	**0.18**	(0.08)
	Ireland	-0.34	(0.08)	-0.33	(0.11)	-0.01	(0.09)
	Italy	0.31	(0.08)	-0.03	(0.07)	**0.33**	(0.10)
	Japan	0.46	(0.09)	0.28	(0.09)	0.17	(0.10)
	Korea	-0.12	(0.08)	-0.23	(0.12)	0.11	(0.12)
	Luxembourg	0.28	(0.08)	0.29	(0.03)	-0.01	(0.08)
	Mexico	-1.13	(0.08)	-1.33	(0.08)	**0.21**	(0.10)
	Netherlands	0.43	(0.10)	0.16	(0.11)	0.27	(0.15)
	New Zealand	0.26	(0.10)	0.18	(0.10)	0.07	(0.10)
	Norway	-0.48	(0.06)	-0.41	(0.06)	-0.06	(0.06)
	Poland	-0.15	(0.09)	-0.14	(0.06)	-0.00	(0.07)
	Portugal	-0.37	(0.08)	-0.42	(0.08)	0.05	(0.09)
	Slovak Republic	-0.60	(0.09)	-0.47	(0.09)	-0.13	(0.11)
	Spain	-0.06	(0.08)	-0.17	(0.07)	0.11	(0.08)
	Sweden	-0.05	(0.08)	-0.06	(0.08)	0.01	(0.08)
	Switzerland	0.82	(0.09)	0.53	(0.07)	**0.30**	(0.09)
	Turkey	-0.95	(0.10)	-0.96	(0.09)	0.01	(0.11)
	United Kingdom	0.08	(0.11)	0.11	(0.09)	-0.03	(0.10)
	United States	0.27	(0.10)	0.14	(0.14)	0.13	(0.14)
	OECD average	**-0.02**	**(0.02)**	**-0.10**	**(0.02)**	**0.08**	**(0.02)**
Partners	Argentina	-0.47	(0.12)	-1.06	(0.11)	**0.60**	(0.15)
	Azerbaijan	-1.51	(0.15)	-1.50	(0.09)	-0.01	(0.17)
	Brazil	-1.32	(0.08)	-1.63	(0.07)	**0.31**	(0.10)
	Bulgaria	-0.57	(0.10)	-0.67	(0.08)	0.10	(0.11)
	Chile	-0.66	(0.14)	-1.03	(0.15)	**0.36**	(0.15)
	Colombia	-1.36	(0.15)	-1.50	(0.09)	0.14	(0.14)
	Croatia	-0.54	(0.09)	-0.61	(0.08)	0.07	(0.09)
	Estonia	-0.33	(0.06)	-0.29	(0.07)	-0.04	(0.07)
	Hong Kong-China	0.33	(0.10)	0.22	(0.11)	0.11	(0.12)
	Indonesia	-1.70	(0.19)	-2.05	(0.14)	0.35	(0.22)
	Israel	-0.05	(0.11)	-0.04	(0.13)	-0.02	(0.12)
	Jordan	-0.95	(0.11)	-0.96	(0.09)	0.01	(0.10)
	Kyrgyzstan	-2.47	(0.07)	-2.52	(0.10)	0.05	(0.11)
	Latvia	-0.53	(0.07)	-0.55	(0.07)	0.02	(0.08)
	Lithuania	-0.45	(0.07)	-0.44	(0.06)	-0.01	(0.07)
	Macao-China	0.07	(0.04)	0.07	(0.02)	0.01	(0.04)
	Montenegro	-1.18	(0.07)	-1.26	(0.04)	0.08	(0.08)
	Romania	-0.65	(0.10)	-1.10	(0.12)	**0.45**	(0.14)
	Russian Federation	-1.22	(0.06)	-1.31	(0.05)	0.09	(0.06)
	Serbia	-0.62	(0.07)	-0.74	(0.06)	0.12	(0.08)
	Slovenia	0.26	(0.06)	0.20	(0.05)	0.06	(0.07)
	Chinese Taipei	0.54	(0.15)	0.19	(0.30)	0.35	(0.28)
	Thailand	-0.91	(0.11)	-1.21	(0.09)	**0.30**	(0.11)
	Tunisia	-0.69	(0.10)	-0.72	(0.09)	0.03	(0.10)
	Uruguay	-1.06	(0.12)	-1.20	(0.12)	0.14	(0.15)

Note: Values that are statistically different are indicated in bold.

Table A2.14c Relationship between being resilient and index of the quality of school educational resources

Increased likelihood of being resilient associate with one unit increase of index of the quality of school educational resources

		Ratio	S.E.	Ratio (After accounting for ESCS, gender, immigrant background, grade, using test language)	S.E.	Ratio (After accounting for Mean ESCS, ESCS, gender, immigrant background, grade, using test language)	S.E.
OECD	Australia	1.08	(0.06)	1.00	(0.07)	1.07	(0.07)
	Austria	1.03	(0.11)	1.00	-(0.10)	1.14	(0.12)
	Belgium	0.92	(0.11)	1.00	-(0.11)	1.13	(0.12)
	Canada	1.03	(0.07)	1.00	(0.00)	1.08	(0.07)
	Czech Republic	1.07	(0.14)	1.00	(0.08)	1.16	(0.14)
	Denmark	**1.22**	(0.10)	**2.72**	(0.20)	1.11	(0.11)
	Finland	0.94	(0.10)	1.00	-(0.03)	1.11	(0.11)
	France	w	w	w	w	w	w
	Germany	1.15	(0.11)	1.00	(0.12)	1.13	(0.12)
	Greece	1.22	(0.13)	1.00	(0.13)	1.14	(0.11)
	Hungary	1.14	(0.12)	1.00	(0.07)	1.11	(0.13)
	Iceland	1.19	(0.11)	1.00	(0.17)	1.11	(0.12)
	Ireland	0.98	(0.10)	1.00	-(0.02)	1.09	(0.10)
	Italy	**1.29**	(0.08)	**2.72**	(0.21)	1.10	(0.09)
	Japan	1.18	(0.09)	1.00	(0.17)	1.16	(0.09)
	Korea	1.13	(0.15)	1.00	(0.17)	1.10	(0.13)
	Luxembourg	1.00	(0.09)	1.00	(0.04)	1.09	(0.10)
	Mexico	1.16	(0.09)	1.00	-(0.01)	1.16	(0.09)
	Netherlands	1.30	(0.15)	1.00	(0.24)	1.10	(0.14)
	New Zealand	1.10	(0.10)	1.00	(0.12)	1.16	(0.09)
	Norway	0.94	(0.15)	1.00	-(0.04)	1.10	(0.14)
	Poland	0.96	(0.09)	1.00	-(0.06)	1.13	(0.09)
	Portugal	1.05	(0.14)	1.00	-(0.00)	1.14	(0.12)
	Slovak Republic	0.83	(0.14)	1.00	-(0.15)	1.09	(0.14)
	Spain	1.08	(0.07)	1.00	(0.02)	1.10	(0.08)
	Sweden	0.99	(0.09)	1.00	-(0.00)	1.09	(0.09)
	Switzerland	**1.27**	(0.07)	**2.72**	(0.17)	**1.14**	(0.08)
	Turkey	0.94	(0.12)	1.00	-(0.16)	1.09	(0.11)
	United Kingdom	0.95	(0.09)	1.00	-(0.05)	1.09	(0.08)
	United States	1.06	(0.10)	1.00	-(0.05)	1.08	(0.09)
	OECD average	**1.07**	(0.02)	**2.72**	(0.04)	**1.26**	(0.02)
Partners	Argentina	**1.38**	(0.08)	**1.00**	(0.20)	1.13	(0.08)
	Azerbaijan	0.93	(0.23)	1.00	-(0.07)	1.16	(0.23)
	Brazil	**1.28**	(0.11)	**2.72**	(0.09)	1.14	(0.13)
	Bulgaria	1.19	(0.18)	1.00	(0.12)	1.14	(0.18)
	Chile	**1.34**	(0.11)	**2.72**	(0.28)	1.12	(0.13)
	Colombia	1.16	(0.16)	1.00	(0.12)	1.11	(0.14)
	Croatia	1.10	(0.13)	1.00	(0.08)	1.08	(0.14)
	Estonia	0.95	(0.13)	1.00	-(0.00)	1.12	(0.14)
	Hong Kong-China	1.04	(0.10)	1.00	(0.03)	1.11	(0.10)
	Indonesia	1.22	(0.12)	1.00	(0.13)	1.18	(0.11)
	Israel	0.98	(0.07)	1.00	-(0.04)	1.15	(0.07)
	Jordan	1.01	(0.12)	1.00	-(0.01)	1.13	(0.11)
	Kyrgyzstan	1.03	(0.11)	1.00	(0.04)	1.09	(0.11)
	Latvia	1.04	(0.17)	1.00	-(0.00)	1.18	(0.16)
	Lithuania	0.92	(0.14)	1.00	-(0.10)	1.10	(0.13)
	Macao-China	0.95	(0.10)	**1.00**	-(0.25)	**1.19**	(0.12)
	Montenegro	1.06	(0.08)	1.00	(0.06)	1.11	(0.10)
	Romania	**1.57**	(0.16)	2.72	(0.31)	1.09	(0.17)
	Russian Federation	1.13	(0.09)	1.00	(0.03)	1.11	(0.10)
	Serbia	1.15	(0.17)	1.00	(0.15)	1.14	(0.17)
	Slovenia	1.10	(0.10)	1.00	(0.11)	1.09	(0.16)
	Chinese Taipei	1.10	(0.08)	1.00	(0.05)	1.00	(0.08)
	Thailand	**1.26**	(0.11)	**2.72**	(0.14)	1.00	(0.11)
	Tunisia	1.08	(0.14)	1.00	(0.08)	1.00	(0.14)
	Uruguay	1.06	(0.09)	1.00	-(0.04)	1.00	(0.09)

Note: Values that are statistically different are indicated in bold.

[Part 1/2] **Table A2.15a** School activities to promote the learning of science (underlying percentages), by student group

	Science clubs - Resilient students %	S.E.	Science clubs - DLA %	S.E.	Science fairs - Resilient students %	S.E.	Science fairs - DLA %	S.E.	Science competitions - Resilient students %	S.E.	Science competitions - DLA %	S.E.
OECD												
Australia	28.8	(3.9)	24.1	(3.5)	27.6	(3.8)	29.8	(3.4)	96.9	(1.4)	96.8	(1.3)
Austria	26.5	(5.1)	12.8	(3.5)	38.9	(6.3)	15.1	(4.7)	35.8	(5.6)	14.1	(3.9)
Belgium	6.6	(3.4)	3.4	(1.3)	34.8	(4.5)	37.5	(5.1)	62.6	(4.3)	34.3	(4.5)
Canada	48.0	(3.3)	41.3	(3.0)	58.8	(3.4)	53.0	(3.2)	64.9	(3.1)	61.7	(2.7)
Czech Republic	51.7	(6.4)	40.9	(3.9)	67.3	(5.8)	51.2	(5.0)	80.4	(4.8)	71.9	(4.7)
Denmark	3.4	(3.0)	2.8	(1.7)	28.4	(4.9)	25.2	(4.5)	10.7	(3.9)	9.4	(3.1)
Finland	7.1	(2.5)	9.2	(2.9)	6.7	(2.4)	9.2	(2.5)	29.2	(5.1)	34.4	(4.8)
France	w	w	w	w	w	w	w	w	w	w	w	w
Germany	55.7	(5.0)	30.4	(4.3)	38.2	(5.8)	15.0	(3.4)	56.8	(5.4)	20.1	(3.7)
Greece	9.9	(3.5)	7.6	(3.1)	5.3	(2.8)	5.8	(2.7)	71.1	(5.1)	39.4	(4.1)
Hungary	66.1	(6.5)	63.7	(6.2)	72.2	(5.5)	60.7	(5.3)	86.7	(4.3)	76.1	(4.8)
Iceland	4.0	(1.3)	4.6	(0.9)	6.2	(1.9)	8.7	(1.1)	19.3	(2.8)	23.0	(2.0)
Ireland	21.1	(4.4)	14.4	(3.2)	57.6	(5.6)	60.3	(5.4)	55.0	(5.2)	39.5	(4.5)
Italy	36.1	(3.6)	32.8	(3.8)	13.6	(3.1)	11.1	(2.4)	33.0	(3.4)	22.2	(2.9)
Japan	54.3	(5.1)	29.3	(4.7)	14.7	(4.2)	3.9	(1.6)	9.2	(3.2)	2.0	(1.1)
Korea	87.4	(3.7)	75.6	(5.6)	45.1	(6.2)	43.2	(6.9)	86.2	(5.7)	73.7	(5.6)
Luxembourg	35.5	(3.6)	20.8	(1.1)	62.3	(4.5)	66.9	(1.4)	40.4	(3.6)	36.6	(1.3)
Mexico	18.9	(2.7)	9.6	(3.0)	35.3	(3.2)	18.0	(3.7)	75.1	(4.3)	54.1	(5.6)
Netherlands	10.3	(3.2)	4.9	(2.4)	29.0	(5.7)	8.9	(2.9)	51.9	(6.7)	13.3	(4.5)
New Zealand	32.3	(4.2)	24.3	(3.7)	75.8	(4.5)	71.8	(4.3)	90.2	(3.7)	87.8	(3.7)
Norway	1.1	(1.0)	0.8	(0.7)	34.9	(5.1)	40.3	(4.9)	13.1	(3.1)	16.5	(3.4)
Poland	79.0	(4.5)	74.4	(4.3)	21.9	(4.6)	18.0	(3.3)	100.0	(0.0)	100.0	(0.0)
Portugal	71.3	(5.4)	72.2	(4.6)	61.6	(6.4)	55.7	(5.9)	65.3	(6.1)	60.7	(5.5)
Slovak Republic	78.2	(4.7)	75.1	(4.4)	70.2	(5.5)	59.2	(5.6)	84.2	(3.8)	75.4	(5.9)
Spain	67.4	(4.3)	70.9	(3.9)	54.8	(3.9)	54.8	(4.0)	33.9	(3.8)	32.5	(4.0)
Sweden	7.3	(3.2)	5.3	(1.6)	19.2	(4.0)	27.7	(3.4)	55.5	(5.5)	54.7	(3.8)
Switzerland	38.1	(3.9)	35.2	(4.0)	49.5	(4.1)	36.0	(3.5)	24.2	(3.3)	10.5	(1.6)
Turkey	39.6	(5.8)	27.4	(5.5)	25.6	(5.0)	14.3	(3.9)	53.7	(6.7)	39.8	(7.1)
United Kingdom	71.1	(3.8)	75.0	(3.0)	34.6	(4.2)	34.1	(4.2)	69.6	(4.2)	65.6	(4.1)
United States	69.2	(5.2)	71.0	(5.6)	40.0	(5.6)	57.8	(5.3)	54.5	(5.9)	51.2	(6.0)
OECD average	**38.8**	**(0.8)**	**33.1**	**(0.7)**	**39.0**	**(0.9)**	**34.3**	**(0.8)**	**55.5**	**(0.8)**	**45.4**	**(0.8)**
Partners												
Argentina	19.3	(5.3)	10.6	(3.6)	73.1	(5.1)	70.0	(5.9)	54.6	(5.7)	40.1	(7.5)
Azerbaijan	75.7	(6.1)	64.7	(6.3)	33.7	(6.7)	29.3	(5.8)	83.2	(6.3)	65.6	(7.5)
Brazil	4.6	(1.9)	3.3	(1.2)	84.3	(3.7)	76.2	(4.5)	28.4	(4.8)	38.4	(4.8)
Bulgaria					16.1	(4.3)	10.0	(3.2)	84.1	(5.0)	61.5	(7.2)
Chile	38.9	(7.0)	32.9	(5.7)	40.8	(6.8)	32.2	(6.4)	35.7	(6.7)	26.5	(6.4)
Colombia	95.1	(2.2)	92.5	(2.6)	73.0	(8.4)	63.3	(7.5)	58.3	(7.5)	53.7	(6.6)
Croatia	19.9	(4.4)	17.7	(4.2)	44.7	(5.2)	41.7	(5.7)	78.3	(4.5)	63.5	(4.8)
Estonia	49.2	(5.6)	44.3	(5.1)	87.0	(3.0)	84.6	(3.2)	76.9	(5.6)	86.9	(3.3)
Hong Kong-China	93.5	(2.5)	85.9	(5.3)	56.9	(5.9)	53.3	(6.0)	90.5	(3.3)	87.8	(4.2)
Indonesia	61.8	(6.6)	47.7	(5.8)	34.7	(7.9)	7.1	(2.4)	68.9	(6.2)	47.5	(5.2)
Israel	55.9	(6.1)	62.0	(5.0)	25.5	(4.8)	37.0	(6.7)	58.2	(5.5)	58.4	(5.2)
Jordan	70.6	(4.6)	57.8	(5.8)	82.4	(3.8)	77.1	(3.0)	75.7	(4.9)	72.1	(4.5)
Kyrgyzstan	81.4	(5.6)	77.6	(5.3)	71.6	(6.2)	71.2	(4.8)	98.6	(1.1)	97.2	(2.0)
Latvia	14.2	(3.7)	10.6	(2.9)	5.1	(2.5)	8.6	(4.2)	92.2	(4.1)	93.1	(2.7)
Lithuania	76.3	(4.9)	73.3	(4.4)	98.0	(1.3)	96.1	(1.8)	88.9	(3.7)	89.5	(2.5)
Macao-China	56.7	(2.8)	43.8	(2.2)	33.5	(2.9)	32.8	(2.3)	92.6	(1.3)	91.1	(1.2)
Montenegro	68.0	(3.4)	65.3	(2.1)	22.7	(2.9)	39.3	(1.8)	76.3	(2.6)	77.3	(1.5)
Romania	80.7	(5.4)	51.4	(6.2)	69.3	(7.0)	43.3	(5.9)	92.6	(3.7)	86.5	(4.7)
Russian Federation	84.9	(3.8)	81.2	(4.2)	82.7	(3.3)	82.0	(3.2)	98.5	(0.9)	96.8	(1.9)
Serbia	79.9	(5.1)	78.4	(5.0)	41.6	(4.7)	28.5	(4.1)	85.3	(4.6)	77.1	(5.0)
Slovenia	94.8	(1.1)	88.0	(1.3)	90.3	(1.8)	75.3	(1.7)	89.9	(2.4)	70.4	(1.3)
Chinese Taipei	84.8	(3.5)	60.4	(5.8)	80.8	(4.0)	53.6	(6.3)	78.4	(4.3)	52.9	(6.4)
Thailand	82.8	(5.6)	76.5	(5.1)	97.5	(1.4)	98.6	(0.9)	97.1	(1.3)	95.6	(1.2)
Tunisia	85.5	(4.1)	84.6	(4.9)	60.6	(7.3)	52.6	(7.2)	60.4	(6.9)	38.2	(6.9)
Uruguay	27.5	(3.8)	37.5	(5.4)	55.5	(5.1)	60.1	(5.4)	32.9	(4.5)	26.4	(5.0)

Note: Values that are statistically different are indicated in bold.

Table A2.15a [Part 2/2] **School activities to promote the learning of science (underlying percentages), by student group**

		Extracurricular science projects (including research)				Excursions and field trips			
		Resilient students		Disadvantaged low achievers (DLA)		Resilient students		Disadvantaged low achievers (DLA)	
		%	S.E.	%	S.E.	%	S.E.	%	S.E.
OECD	Australia	67.4	(3.9)	65.6	(3.7)	96.6	(1.7)	96.5	(1.3)
	Austria	41.0	(5.9)	12.0	(2.7)	94.1	(2.0)	84.2	(3.5)
	Belgium	56.4	(5.2)	40.3	(4.7)	88.7	(3.3)	88.5	(3.1)
	Canada	65.1	(3.2)	63.4	(3.4)	93.6	(1.5)	92.8	(1.3)
	Czech Republic	53.1	(6.0)	35.1	(4.2)	97.6	(2.8)	98.3	(1.0)
	Denmark	19.1	(4.3)	13.2	(3.1)	90.3	(2.7)	85.1	(3.6)
	Finland	24.1	(4.7)	24.5	(4.4)	93.3	(2.7)	92.5	(2.8)
	France	w	w	w	w	w	w	w	w
	Germany	45.7	(5.7)	22.4	(4.2)	96.3	(2.2)	92.4	(3.0)
	Greece	20.1	(4.8)	18.4	(4.5)	86.8	(4.3)	81.8	(4.6)
	Hungary	37.3	(7.1)	28.7	(4.9)	98.0	(1.8)	96.6	(1.8)
	Iceland	13.6	(2.6)	24.0	(2.2)	94.5	(1.3)	92.6	(1.2)
	Ireland	52.0	(5.2)	49.1	(5.5)	93.8	(2.3)	93.2	(2.6)
	Italy	77.4	(3.3)	66.2	(3.8)	98.0	(0.6)	93.6	(1.7)
	Japan	22.5	(4.9)	15.0	(4.5)	30.0	(4.6)	30.7	(6.4)
	Korea	44.5	(6.0)	27.2	(5.5)	81.0	(4.2)	78.8	(5.3)
	Luxembourg	52.9	(4.1)	35.4	(1.4)	92.4	(2.6)	88.2	(0.8)
	Mexico	50.2	(4.1)	37.7	(5.2)	78.1	(3.4)	69.9	(4.8)
	Netherlands	44.0	(5.6)	26.0	(5.0)	85.3	(4.4)	85.2	(5.1)
	New Zealand	60.6	(4.8)	56.3	(5.0)	92.2	(3.5)	95.4	(1.8)
	Norway	36.9	(5.2)	42.6	(5.0)	94.1	(2.1)	92.9	(3.1)
	Poland	48.8	(5.2)	42.5	(4.5)	99.3	(0.8)	97.9	(1.8)
	Portugal	88.6	(4.0)	79.1	(5.3)	95.3	(2.2)	89.7	(4.1)
	Slovak Republic	46.3	(6.1)	37.4	(6.1)	99.6	(0.6)	99.5	(0.6)
	Spain	33.8	(4.1)	31.6	(4.5)	95.9	(1.1)	95.3	(1.7)
	Sweden	26.3	(4.9)	31.3	(4.8)	78.7	(5.7)	80.6	(4.0)
	Switzerland	28.0	(3.8)	21.2	(2.6)	95.9	(1.4)	94.9	(1.3)
	Turkey	51.1	(6.1)	39.5	(6.7)	76.7	(4.5)	73.1	(4.8)
	United Kingdom	56.9	(5.2)	61.2	(4.7)	84.1	(4.2)	83.9	(3.6)
	United States	60.5	(5.7)	70.9	(4.5)	88.8	(5.0)	92.5	(3.5)
	OECD average	**45.7**	**(0.9)**	**38.5**	**(0.8)**	**89.3**	**(0.6)**	**87.5**	**(0.6)**
Partners	Argentina	67.5	(6.7)	68.6	(6.0)	85.0	(4.3)	67.6	(6.8)
	Azerbaijan	19.6	(6.6)	22.9	(5.7)	95.8	(1.5)	89.7	(3.3)
	Brazil	87.0	(3.4)	77.8	(4.2)	83.9	(3.7)	76.6	(4.2)
	Bulgaria	54.7	(6.9)	28.2	(5.4)	87.3	(3.6)	86.6	(5.3)
	Chile	43.3	(7.7)	31.4	(6.5)	70.3	(7.9)	67.4	(7.4)
	Colombia	70.0	(7.7)	66.8	(7.4)	85.6	(4.0)	82.9	(4.6)
	Croatia	59.7	(5.6)	48.1	(4.7)	93.3	(2.8)	85.5	(4.6)
	Estonia	92.5	(3.4)	82.7	(4.6)	97.7	(1.6)	91.7	(3.7)
	Hong Kong-China	77.2	(4.4)	81.0	(4.3)	86.6	(4.3)	92.2	(3.2)
	Indonesia	49.8	(6.7)	31.2	(5.4)	78.5	(5.7)	62.9	(5.9)
	Israel	61.2	(6.3)	59.2	(5.2)	88.5	(4.1)	89.1	(2.9)
	Jordan	87.3	(4.7)	79.8	(4.0)	90.4	(3.5)	90.9	(2.9)
	Kyrgyzstan	37.5	(6.1)	24.6	(4.4)	92.7	(3.0)	95.7	(1.7)
	Latvia	87.8	(4.5)	84.3	(4.5)	98.6	(1.1)	98.6	(0.8)
	Lithuania	67.0	(5.3)	69.5	(4.6)	98.7	(1.3)	99.0	(0.8)
	Macao-China	94.7	(1.0)	95.2	(0.7)	62.7	(2.6)	70.9	(1.8)
	Montenegro	56.3	(3.3)	62.4	(1.9)	75.1	(3.1)	86.8	(1.5)
	Romania	67.0	(7.5)	35.9	(5.0)	100.0	(0.0)	100.0	(0.0)
	Russian Federation	81.0	(3.3)	72.2	(3.9)	99.3	(0.6)	97.9	(1.5)
	Serbia	51.8	(5.9)	27.5	(4.9)	68.3	(5.8)	61.2	(5.6)
	Slovenia	79.3	(3.2)	72.9	(1.7)	93.5	(2.3)	96.8	(0.3)
	Chinese Taipei	78.5	(3.8)	57.5	(5.8)	87.1	(3.2)	90.5	(3.4)
	Thailand	90.8	(2.8)	85.2	(4.2)	95.9	(2.9)	95.4	(2.7)
	Tunisia	57.6	(6.6)	47.8	(6.4)	79.5	(5.7)	67.2	(5.5)
	Uruguay	60.0	(5.0)	52.3	(4.8)	83.3	(3.7)	83.1	(4.1)

Table A2.15b School activities to promote the learning of science, by student group

		\multicolumn{4}{c	}{School activities to promote the learning of science}	\multicolumn{2}{c}{Difference in the mean index between resilient students and disadvantaged low achievers}

		Resilient students		Disadvantaged low achievers (DLA)		Difference in the mean index between resilient students and disadvantaged low achievers	
		Mean	S.E.	Mean	S.E.	Dif	S.E.
OECD	Australia	0.35	(0.05)	0.32	(0.04)	0.03	(0.04)
	Austria	-0.19	(0.11)	-0.88	(0.09)	**0.69**	(0.13)
	Belgium	-0.09	(0.08)	-0.42	(0.09)	**0.33**	(0.10)
	Canada	0.45	(0.07)	0.32	(0.05)	0.13	(0.06)
	Czech Republic	0.56	(0.10)	0.21	(0.07)	**0.35**	(0.11)
	Denmark	-0.76	(0.08)	-0.90	(0.08)	0.14	(0.08)
	Finland	-0.68	(0.07)	-0.62	(0.08)	-0.06	(0.06)
	France	w	w	w	w	w	w
	Germany	0.17	(0.10)	-0.57	(0.08)	**0.74**	(0.12)
	Greece	-0.41	(0.09)	-0.74	(0.08)	**0.33**	(0.11)
	Hungary	0.62	(0.11)	0.38	(0.09)	0.24	(0.13)
	Iceland	-0.83	(0.04)	-0.71	(0.03)	**-0.12**	(0.05)
	Ireland	0.11	(0.09)	-0.05	(0.09)	0.15	(0.08)
	Italy	-0.00	(0.05)	-0.23	(0.07)	**0.22**	(0.07)
	Japan	-1.04	(0.13)	-1.43	(0.10)	**0.38**	(0.15)
	Korea	0.53	(0.09)	0.21	(0.12)	**0.33**	(0.11)
	Luxembourg	0.10	(0.10)	-0.15	(0.03)	**0.24**	(0.11)
	Mexico	-0.04	(0.06)	-0.49	(0.08)	**0.45**	(0.09)
	Netherlands	-0.35	(0.14)	-0.87	(0.11)	**0.52**	(0.15)
	New Zealand	0.52	(0.11)	0.43	(0.08)	0.10	(0.11)
	Norway	-0.55	(0.07)	-0.48	(0.07)	-0.07	(0.08)
	Poland	0.53	(0.05)	0.44	(0.05)	0.09	(0.05)
	Portugal	0.75	(0.09)	0.60	(0.11)	0.15	(0.11)
	Slovak Republic	0.73	(0.07)	0.52	(0.08)	**0.20**	(0.09)
	Spain	0.15	(0.07)	0.13	(0.08)	0.02	(0.07)
	Sweden	-0.58	(0.12)	-0.49	(0.09)	-0.09	(0.09)
	Switzerland	-0.20	(0.06)	-0.44	(0.04)	**0.23**	(0.06)
	Turkey	-0.16	(0.12)	-0.54	(0.14)	**0.38**	(0.16)
	United Kingdom	0.35	(0.10)	0.38	(0.08)	-0.02	(0.09)
	United States	0.29	(0.13)	0.50	(0.12)	-0.21	(0.13)
	OECD average	0.01	(0.02)	-0.19	(0.02)	**0.20**	(0.02)
Partners	Argentina	0.20	(0.13)	-0.01	(0.11)	0.21	(0.15)
	Azerbaijan	0.30	(0.11)	0.03	(0.11)	**0.27**	(0.13)
	Brazil	0.22	(0.06)	0.07	(0.07)	0.15	(0.09)
	Bulgaria	0.08	(0.08)	-0.37	(0.12)	**0.44**	(0.14)
	Chile	-0.36	(0.22)	-0.62	(0.20)	0.26	(0.21)
	Colombia	0.78	(0.12)	0.66	(0.11)	0.12	(0.08)
	Croatia	0.19	(0.10)	-0.09	(0.12)	**0.28**	(0.12)
	Estonia	0.88	(0.06)	0.80	(0.07)	0.07	(0.07)
	Hong Kong-China	0.91	(0.08)	0.88	(0.09)	0.03	(0.09)
	Indonesia	0.13	(0.19)	-0.51	(0.12)	**0.64**	(0.21)
	Israel	0.15	(0.11)	0.26	(0.11)	-0.12	(0.11)
	Jordan	0.95	(0.09)	0.75	(0.08)	**0.20**	(0.10)
	Kyrgyzstan	0.76	(0.10)	0.64	(0.07)	0.12	(0.10)
	Latvia	0.21	(0.06)	0.18	(0.05)	0.03	(0.06)
	Lithuania	1.08	(0.07)	1.06	(0.05)	0.02	(0.07)
	Macao-China	0.48	(0.03)	0.41	(0.03)	0.07	(0.05)
	Montenegro	0.15	(0.09)	0.42	(0.04)	**-0.27**	(0.10)
	Romania	0.97	(0.14)	0.37	(0.10)	**0.60**	(0.16)
	Russian Federation	1.22	(0.06)	1.09	(0.06)	0.14	(0.06)
	Serbia	0.37	(0.13)	0.02	(0.10)	**0.36**	(0.13)
	Slovenia	1.26	(0.04)	0.92	(0.02)	**0.33**	(0.05)
	Chinese Taipei	0.96	(0.09)	0.33	(0.13)	**0.64**	(0.17)
	Thailand	1.36	(0.07)	1.26	(0.07)	0.10	(0.06)
	Tunisia	0.51	(0.13)	0.16	(0.15)	**0.34**	(0.15)
	Uruguay	-0.06	(0.09)	-0.06	(0.09)	0.00	(0.11)

Note: Values that are statistically different are indicated in bold.

Table A2.15c Relationship between being resilient and index of school activities to promote the learning of science

		Increased likelihood of being resilient associate with one unit increase of index of school activities to promote the learning of science					
				After accounting for ESCS, gender, immigrant background, grade, using test language		After accounting for Mean ESCS, ESCS, gender, immigrant background, grade, using test language	
		Ratio	S.E.	Ratio	S.E.	Ratio	S.E.
OECD	Australia	1.05	(0.10)	1.00	(0.01)	1.10	(0.10)
	Austria	**2.00**	(0.12)	**2.72**	(0.78)	**1.13**	(0.13)
	Belgium	**1.49**	(0.13)	**2.72**	(0.33)	1.13	(0.14)
	Canada	**1.14**	(0.06)	**2.72**	(0.14)	1.07	(0.07)
	Czech Republic	**1.42**	(0.11)	**2.72**	(0.57)	**1.13**	(0.13)
	Denmark	1.27	(0.12)	2.72	(0.27)	1.14	(0.13)
	Finland	0.91	(0.11)	1.00	-(0.08)	1.11	(0.11)
	France	w	w	w	w	w	w
	Germany	**2.01**	(0.14)	**2.72**	(0.55)	**1.15**	(0.14)
	Greece	**1.38**	(0.14)	2.72	(0.23)	1.22	(0.14)
	Hungary	1.40	(0.20)	1.00	(0.36)	1.14	(0.19)
	Iceland	**0.74**	(0.13)	2.72	-(0.30)	**1.09**	(0.13)
	Ireland	1.10	(0.09)	1.00	(0.07)	1.10	(0.09)
	Italy	**1.29**	(0.10)	2.72	(0.21)	1.12	(0.09)
	Japan	**1.40**	(0.11)	2.72	(0.31)	1.13	(0.11)
	Korea	**1.33**	(0.12)	2.72	(0.28)	1.12	(0.12)
	Luxembourg	1.20	(0.10)	1.00	(0.20)	1.09	(0.12)
	Mexico	**1.53**	(0.09)	**2.72**	(0.03)	1.21	(0.08)
	Netherlands	**1.71**	(0.19)	2.72	(0.57)	1.17	(0.19)
	New Zealand	1.14	(0.16)	1.00	(0.15)	1.13	(0.15)
	Norway	0.95	(0.13)	1.00	-(0.05)	1.14	(0.12)
	Poland	**1.36**	(0.13)	2.72	(0.34)	1.17	(0.14)
	Portugal	1.13	(0.14)	1.00	-(0.20)	1.14	(0.16)
	Slovak Republic	**1.33**	(0.12)	2.72	(0.46)	**1.10**	(0.12)
	Spain	1.03	(0.09)	1.00	(0.06)	1.09	(0.09)
	Sweden	0.91	(0.09)	1.00	-(0.07)	1.11	(0.09)
	Switzerland	**1.49**	(0.11)	2.72	(0.45)	**1.12**	(0.10)
	Turkey	**1.31**	(0.11)	2.72	(0.29)	1.10	(0.11)
	United Kingdom	0.98	(0.09)	1.00	(0.01)	1.11	(0.10)
	United States	0.84	(0.12)	1.00	-(0.14)	1.16	(0.10)
	OECD average	**1.24**	(0.02)	**2.72**	(0.20)	**1.20**	(0.02)
Partners	Argentina	1.18	(0.15)	1.00	(0.13)	1.13	(0.13)
	Azerbaijan	1.42	(0.18)	1.00	(0.32)	**1.14**	(0.18)
	Brazil	1.18	(0.12)	1.00	(0.06)	1.09	(0.14)
	Bulgaria	**1.83**	(0.17)	**2.72**	(0.52)	1.18	(0.17)
	Chile	1.17	(0.12)	1.00	(0.15)	1.19	(0.11)
	Colombia	1.19	(0.11)	1.00	(0.15)	1.13	(0.14)
	Croatia	**1.20**	(0.09)	**2.72**	(0.20)	1.10	(0.09)
	Estonia	1.10	(0.15)	1.00	(0.04)	1.13	(0.17)
	Hong Kong-China	1.05	(0.17)	1.00	(0.06)	1.19	(0.17)
	Indonesia	**1.50**	(0.14)	**2.72**	(0.31)	**1.38**	(0.13)
	Israel	0.90	(0.09)	1.00	-(0.10)	1.15	(0.10)
	Jordan	**1.29**	(0.13)	**2.72**	(0.19)	1.10	(0.12)
	Kyrgyzstan	1.18	(0.18)	1.00	(0.17)	1.10	(0.18)
	Latvia	1.21	(0.32)	1.00	(0.11)	1.26	(0.31)
	Lithuania	0.98	(0.15)	1.00	-(0.10)	1.18	(0.14)
	Macao-China	1.05	(0.09)	1.00	(0.09)	1.16	(0.10)
	Montenegro	0.84	(0.09)	1.00	-(0.20)	**1.14**	(0.10)
	Romania	**1.95**	(0.24)	**2.72**	(0.57)	1.17	(0.23)
	Russian Federation	1.32	(0.16)	1.00	(0.33)	1.18	(0.17)
	Serbia	**1.37**	(0.15)	**2.72**	(0.32)	1.10	(0.14)
	Slovenia	**1.73**	(0.13)	**2.72**	(0.52)	1.10	(0.14)
	Chinese Taipei	**1.62**	(0.15)	**2.72**	(0.56)	1.00	(0.15)
	Thailand	1.27	(0.19)	1.00	(0.17)	1.00	(0.16)
	Tunisia	**1.29**	(0.11)	**2.72**	(0.08)	1.00	(0.10)
	Uruguay	0.98	(0.09)	1.00	-(0.02)	1.00	(0.10)

Note: Values that are statistically different are indicated in bold.

[Part 1/2]
Table A2.16 Combined model

		Interest in science		Science activities		Science efficacy		School preparation for science career		Number of hours students report spending in regular lessons at school learning science	
		Ratio	S.E.	Ratio	S.E.	Ratio	S.E.	Ratio	S.E.	Ratio	S.E.
OECD	Australia	**1.20**	0.08	**1.18**	0.06	**1.99**	0.06	**1.15**	0.05	**1.20**	0.03
	Austria	**1.22**	0.23	1.13	0.14	**2.23**	0.14	0.95	0.10	**1.28**	0.06
	Belgium	**1.22**	0.12	1.15	0.10	**2.22**	0.11	**0.83**	0.09	**1.31**	0.04
	Canada	1.16	0.10	1.12	0.07	**1.94**	0.09	1.12	0.06	**1.15**	0.04
	Czech Republic	1.15	0.17	1.10	0.12	**1.88**	0.16	0.93	0.16	**1.46**	0.06
	Denmark	1.28	0.13	1.19	0.10	**2.06**	0.14	1.17	0.11	1.16	0.08
	Finland	**1.43**	0.13	1.06	0.11	**2.37**	0.15	0.97	0.09	**1.36**	0.05
	France	**1.35**	0.14	1.06	0.15	**1.98**	0.18	1.25	0.14	**1.32**	0.07
	Germany	1.17	0.14	1.11	0.16	**1.93**	0.17	0.94	0.10	**1.28**	0.07
	Greece	1.26	0.18	1.06	0.11	**1.76**	0.13	0.76	0.14	**1.42**	0.05
	Hungary	**1.20**	0.14	1.09	0.16	**1.88**	0.23	**0.72**	0.12	**1.36**	0.08
	Iceland	1.15	0.10	1.27	0.14	**1.84**	0.13	1.19	0.11	1.13	0.06
	Ireland	**1.22**	(0.12)	**1.22**	(0.10)	**2.34**	(0.13)	0.96	(0.10)	**1.19**	(0.06)
	Italy	1.12	(0.09)	1.11	(0.07)	**1.67**	(0.07)	**0.83**	(0.08)	**1.31**	(0.04)
	Japan	**1.55**	(0.11)	1.05	(0.10)	**1.37**	(0.11)	0.90	(0.11)	**1.22**	(0.08)
	Korea	**1.92**	(0.13)	1.05	(0.09)	**1.81**	(0.16)	**0.68**	(0.11)	**1.27**	(0.07)
	Luxembourg	**1.44**	(0.14)	1.05	(0.12)	**1.74**	(0.16)	**0.74**	(0.11)	**1.20**	(0.07)
	Mexico	**1.37**	(0.07)	**0.75**	(0.11)	**1.58**	(0.09)	0.86	(0.08)	1.02	(0.03)
	Netherlands	**1.28**	(0.17)	1.19	(0.14)	**1.48**	(0.14)	1.20	(0.17)	**1.32**	(0.07)
	New Zealand	1.12	(0.12)	1.05	(0.11)	**2.56**	(0.15)	1.12	(0.11)	**1.31**	(0.07)
	Norway	**1.23**	(0.08)	1.20	(0.10)	**1.86**	(0.11)	1.04	(0.10)	**1.19**	(0.08)
	Poland	**1.49**	(0.15)	**0.70**	(0.12)	**2.64**	(0.14)	**0.62**	(0.10)	**1.32**	(0.06)
	Portugal	**1.31**	(0.13)	1.12	(0.14)	**2.11**	(0.15)	0.80	(0.15)	1.12	(0.06)
	Slovak Republic	1.24	(0.15)	1.23	(0.18)	**1.76**	(0.15)	**0.55**	(0.12)	**1.48**	(0.06)
	Spain	**1.24**	(0.10)	0.95	(0.09)	**1.92**	(0.10)	0.90	(0.09)	**1.36**	(0.04)
	Sweden	1.21	(0.20)	1.10	(0.12)	**2.33**	(0.12)	0.96	(0.12)	**1.32**	(0.07)
	Switzerland	**1.51**	(0.15)	0.94	(0.13)	**1.98**	(0.10)	**1.20**	(0.08)	**1.26**	(0.06)
	Turkey	1.12	(0.12)	0.94	(0.14)	**1.55**	(0.13)	0.85	(0.11)	**1.32**	(0.05)
	United Kingdom	0.96	(0.10)	1.10	(0.10)	**3.02**	(0.09)	1.09	(0.08)	**1.43**	(0.06)
	United States	1.07	(0.09)	1.25	(0.17)	**1.75**	(0.09)	1.07	(0.11)	**1.29**	(0.05)
	OECD average	**1.26**	(0.02)	1.08	(0.02)	**1.95**	(0.02)	0.93	(0.02)	**1.27**	(0.01)
Partners	Argentina	1.17	(0.14)	0.82	(0.12)	**1.86**	(0.14)	0.77	(0.12)	**1.17**	(0.07)
	Azerbaijan	1.13	(0.08)	0.86	(0.13)	1.11	(0.09)	1.01	(0.10)	**1.13**	(0.05)
	Brazil	1.05	(0.08)	**0.74**	(0.12)	**1.54**	(0.13)	**0.76**	(0.10)	**1.41**	(0.06)
	Bulgaria	1.26	(0.13)	0.82	(0.14)	**1.59**	(0.10)	**0.79**	(0.10)	**1.27**	(0.08)
	Chile	1.10	(0.14)	1.14	(0.12)	**1.61**	(0.14)	**0.64**	(0.12)	**1.36**	(0.07)
	Colombia	1.03	(0.13)	1.00	(0.16)	**1.59**	(0.15)	**0.74**	(0.11)	1.10	(0.08)
	Croatia	**1.39**	(0.14)	0.96	(0.13)	**2.47**	(0.12)	0.75	(0.13)	**1.18**	(0.04)
	Estonia	1.34	(0.16)	0.90	(0.15)	**2.75**	(0.12)	0.74	(0.12)	**1.31**	(0.06)
	Hong Kong-China	**1.47**	(0.11)	0.95	(0.10)	**1.64**	(0.11)	0.99	(0.12)	**1.29**	(0.04)
	Indonesia	**1.54**	(0.16)	0.82	(0.14)	1.18	(0.11)	0.92	(0.11)	**1.18**	(0.05)
	Israel	**1.34**	(0.11)	0.83	(0.13)	**1.29**	(0.11)	0.87	(0.10)	**1.32**	(0.05)
	Jordan	**1.36**	(0.10)	0.85	(0.10)	**1.35**	(0.09)	0.85	(0.10)	**1.20**	(0.05)
	Kyrgyzstan	1.18	(0.10)	**0.43**	(0.14)	**1.30**	(0.12)	1.03	(0.10)	**1.12**	(0.04)
	Latvia	0.91	(0.18)	0.86	(0.15)	**2.42**	(0.14)	0.94	(0.13)	**1.37**	(0.08)
	Lithuania	**1.55**	(0.14)	0.79	(0.14)	**1.75**	(0.13)	1.04	(0.12)	**1.23**	(0.05)
	Macao-China	**1.64**	(0.14)	1.10	(0.13)	**1.66**	(0.14)	**0.65**	(0.12)	**1.17**	(0.05)
	Montenegro	**1.38**	(0.14)	**0.73**	(0.14)	**2.23**	(0.11)	**0.67**	(0.15)	**1.27**	(0.05)
	Romania	**1.42**	(0.11)	0.77	(0.17)	**1.45**	(0.15)	0.76	(0.18)	**1.29**	(0.08)
	Russian Federation	1.05	(0.15)	0.87	(0.10)	**1.95**	(0.10)	**0.85**	(0.08)	**1.30**	(0.06)
	Serbia	1.07	(0.11)	0.87	(0.15)	**1.97**	(0.11)	**0.76**	(0.12)	**1.23**	(0.05)
	Slovenia	1.09	(0.14)	1.02	(0.14)	**1.98**	(0.12)	0.93	(0.14)	**1.31**	(0.06)
	Chinese Taipei	**1.53**	(0.09)	0.97	(0.13)	**1.68**	(0.10)	**0.70**	(0.10)	**1.35**	(0.06)
	Thailand	1.26	(0.12)	**1.41**	(0.20)	1.10	(0.12)	1.02	(0.10)	**1.56**	(0.08)
	Tunisia	1.23	(0.13)	**0.74**	(0.15)	**1.41**	(0.12)	0.99	(0.10)	**1.20**	(0.05)
	Uruguay	1.01	(0.16)	1.03	(0.12)	**1.83**	(0.12)	0.91	(0.15)	**1.25**	(0.06)

Note: Values that are statistically different are indicated in bold.

Table A2.16 Combined model [Part 2/2]

		Students in private schools		Students in schools which compete with other schools		Students in schools which select based on academic record		Index of school activities to promote the learning of science		Index of the quality of school educational resources	
		Ratio	S.E.	Ratio	S.E.	Ratio	S.E.	Ratio	S.E.	Ratio	S.E.
OECD	Australia	w	w	0.96	0.21	c	c	0.94	0.10	1.04	0.08
	Austria	c	c	0.79	0.27	**2.67**	0.36	1.15	0.13	0.96	0.14
	Belgium	w	w	0.88	0.41	1.23	0.22	1.09	0.14	0.93	0.12
	Canada	c	c	1.05	0.15	c	c	**1.19**	0.08	0.95	0.08
	Czech Republic	c	c	0.90	0.36	1.70	0.42	1.25	0.16	0.97	0.14
	Denmark	0.88	0.27	0.81	0.32	c	c	1.21	0.14	1.12	0.13
	Finland	c	c	0.85	0.18	c	c	0.97	0.14	0.96	0.12
	France	w	w	w	w	w	w	w	w	w	w
	Germany	c	c	0.83	0.34	1.45	0.26	1.24	0.14	0.98	0.13
	Greece	c	c	0.89	0.22	0.71	0.59	1.06	0.16	1.05	0.10
	Hungary	c	c	0.91	0.32	1.85	0.36	1.18	0.18	1.22	0.15
	Iceland	c	c	0.80	0.22	c	c	**0.69**	0.15	1.17	0.14
	Ireland	0.92	(0.22)	0.80	(0.29)	c	c	0.94	(0.11)	0.97	(0.11)
	Italy	c	c	1.28	(0.20)	c	c	0.88	(0.10)	1.09	(0.09)
	Japan	**0.35**	(0.22)	0.88	(0.40)	1.45	(0.35)	1.13	(0.12)	1.12	(0.08)
	Korea	1.02	(0.19)	1.05	(0.31)	1.30	(0.21)	0.96	(0.13)	1.17	(0.13)
	Luxembourg	0.65	(0.37)	1.14	(0.23)	1.24	(0.36)	1.04	(0.14)	1.09	(0.15)
	Mexico	c	c	0.70	(0.28)	1.25	(0.17)	0.93	(0.08)	1.00	(0.09)
	Netherlands	1.20	(0.29)	0.62	(0.52)	0.97	(0.29)	1.16	(0.18)	1.29	(0.14)
	New Zealand	c	c	0.64	(0.32)	c	c	1.12	(0.15)	1.05	(0.10)
	Norway	c	c	0.90	(0.18)	c	c	0.96	(0.13)	0.98	(0.16)
	Poland	c	c	0.90	(0.17)	c	c	**1.45**	(0.16)	1.00	(0.10)
	Portugal	c	c	0.95	(0.26)	c	c	0.80	(0.19)	0.94	(0.13)
	Slovak Republic	c	c	0.47	(0.46)	1.58	(0.31)	1.15	(0.15)	0.85	(0.13)
	Spain	0.78	(0.20)	0.92	(0.23)	c	c	1.04	(0.09)	1.04	(0.09)
	Sweden	c	c	1.06	(0.19)	c	c	0.89	(0.10)	0.94	(0.11)
	Switzerland	c	c	0.77	(0.19)	1.32	(0.27)	1.13	(0.11)	1.24	(0.09)
	Turkey	c	c	1.08	(0.25)	1.71	(0.29)	1.04	(0.11)	0.86	(0.11)
	United Kingdom	c	c	c	c	c	c	1.05	(0.12)	0.90	(0.08)
	United States	c	c	0.89	(0.19)	c	c	0.86	(0.11)	0.97	(0.11)
	OECD average	**0.62**	(0.10)	**0.87**	(0.05)	1.64	(0.32)	1.04	(0.02)	1.02	(0.02)
Partners	Argentina	1.04	(0.28)	1.31	(0.29)	c	c	1.01	(0.12)	1.10	(0.09)
	Azerbaijan	c	c	m	m	0.83	(0.39)	**1.49**	(0.19)	0.84	(0.28)
	Brazil	c	c	0.82	(0.20)	c	c	1.13	(0.15)	1.06	(0.13)
	Bulgaria	m	m	0.77	(0.34)	0.77	(0.37)	1.19	(0.16)	0.94	(0.17)
	Chile	1.17	(0.28)	0.64	(0.35)	1.20	(0.29)	1.01	(0.11)	1.16	(0.15)
	Colombia	c	c	0.97	(0.30)	1.71	(0.32)	1.18	(0.14)	1.00	(0.13)
	Croatia	c	c	0.99	(0.26)	1.19	(0.34)	1.05	(0.09)	1.07	(0.14)
	Estonia	c	c	1.07	(0.32)	0.99	(0.26)	1.05	(0.19)	0.97	(0.15)
	Hong Kong-China	0.89	(0.52)	c	c	1.18	(0.34)	1.01	(0.18)	0.99	(0.11)
	Indonesia	0.84	(0.28)	c	c	1.33	(0.23)	1.27	(0.13)	1.01	(0.10)
	Israel	1.00	(0.31)	0.92	(0.27)	1.12	(0.23)	0.83	(0.12)	0.96	(0.07)
	Jordan	**2.13**	(0.26)	0.83	(0.22)	1.07	(0.26)	1.19	(0.12)	1.00	(0.12)
	Kyrgyzstan	c	c	0.98	(0.25)	1.14	(0.32)	1.04	(0.17)	0.92	(0.11)
	Latvia	c	c	c	c	1.16	(0.25)	1.11	(0.30)	0.99	(0.17)
	Lithuania	c	c	0.76	(0.21)	c	c	0.77	(0.14)	0.84	(0.13)
	Macao-China	1.01	(0.52)	1.59	(0.43)	c	c	0.99	(0.10)	0.75	(0.17)
	Montenegro	c	c	2.08	(0.89)	1.25	(0.20)	0.85	(0.12)	1.02	(0.12)
	Romania	c	c	0.90	(0.36)	1.64	(0.26)	1.41	(0.23)	0.94	(0.16)
	Russian Federation	c	c	0.85	(0.19)	0.71	(0.36)	1.23	(0.17)	1.07	(0.10)
	Serbia	c	c	0.64	(0.27)	2.33	(0.47)	1.14	(0.13)	1.19	(0.17)
	Slovenia	c	c	1.06	(0.22)	1.16	(0.25)	0.98	(0.15)	1.00	(0.17)
	Chinese Taipei	0.31	(0.26)	c	c	1.26	(0.22)	1.19	(0.12)	0.91	(0.08)
	Thailand	0.64	(0.51)	1.14	(0.28)	0.86	(0.22)	0.88	(0.21)	1.10	(0.12)
	Tunisia	c	c	1.08	(0.19)	0.82	(0.25)	1.16	(0.10)	1.08	(0.14)
	Uruguay	c	c	1.06	(0.24)	c	c	0.97	(0.10)	0.90	(0.11)

Note: Values that are statistically different are indicated in bold.

ANNEX A3: CLOSING THE GAP? ENHANCING THE PERFORMANCE OF SOCIO-ECONOMICALLY DISADVANTAGED STUDENTS

[Part 1/3]

Table A3.1a Approaches to learning among disadvantaged and non-disadvantaged students

		\multicolumn{6}{c	}{General interest in science}	\multicolumn{6}{c	}{Instrumental motivation to learn science}	\multicolumn{6}{c	}{Participation in science related activities}
		\multicolumn{2}{c	}{Non-disadvantaged students}	\multicolumn{2}{c	}{Disadvantaged students}	\multicolumn{2}{c	}{Difference}	\multicolumn{2}{c	}{Non-disadvantaged students}	\multicolumn{2}{c	}{Disadvantaged students}	\multicolumn{2}{c	}{Difference}	\multicolumn{2}{c	}{Non-disadvantaged students}	\multicolumn{2}{c	}{Disadvantaged students}	\multicolumn{2}{c	}{Difference}
		Mean	S.E.	Mean	S.E.	Dif.	S.E.	Mean	S.E.	Mean	S.E.	Dif.	S.E.	Mean	S.E.	Mean	S.E.	Dif.	S.E.
OECD	Australia	-0.12	(0.01)	-0.40	(0.02)	**0.28**	(0.03)	0.19	(0.02)	-0.06	(0.02)	**0.25**	(0.03)	-0.20	(0.02)	-0.46	(0.02)	**0.26**	(0.02)
	Austria	0.12	(0.02)	-0.09	(0.03)	**0.21**	(0.03)	-0.39	(0.03)	-0.43	(0.05)	**0.04**	(0.05)	0.08	(0.02)	-0.12	(0.03)	**0.19**	(0.04)
	Belgium	0.13	(0.02)	-0.18	(0.03)	**0.31**	(0.04)	-0.17	(0.02)	-0.32	(0.03)	**0.15**	(0.03)	0.08	(0.02)	-0.12	(0.03)	**0.20**	(0.03)
	Canada	0.18	(0.01)	-0.04	(0.02)	**0.22**	(0.02)	0.41	(0.02)	0.14	(0.03)	**0.27**	(0.03)	-0.07	(0.02)	-0.31	(0.02)	**0.24**	(0.03)
	Czech Republic	-0.00	(0.02)	-0.09	(0.03)	**0.09**	(0.03)	-0.24	(0.02)	-0.24	(0.03)	**0.00**	(0.03)	0.08	(0.02)	0.01	(0.03)	**0.07**	(0.03)
	Denmark	-0.07	(0.02)	-0.37	(0.04)	**0.29**	(0.04)	0.09	(0.02)	-0.06	(0.02)	**0.15**	(0.03)	-0.05	(0.02)	-0.34	(0.03)	**0.29**	(0.03)
	Finland	-0.16	(0.02)	-0.42	(0.03)	**0.26**	(0.03)	-0.13	(0.02)	-0.38	(0.03)	**0.25**	(0.03)	-0.10	(0.02)	-0.27	(0.03)	**0.17**	(0.03)
	France	0.31	(0.02)	-0.01	(0.03)	**0.32**	(0.04)	0.03	(0.03)	-0.28	(0.03)	**0.31**	(0.04)	0.09	(0.02)	-0.20	(0.03)	**0.29**	(0.03)
	Germany	0.24	(0.02)	0.09	(0.03)	**0.16**	(0.03)	-0.04	(0.02)	-0.13	(0.03)	**0.08**	(0.04)	0.21	(0.02)	-0.07	(0.03)	**0.28**	(0.03)
	Greece	0.30	(0.02)	-0.02	(0.03)	**0.31**	(0.03)	0.12	(0.03)	0.00	(0.03)	**0.12**	(0.03)	0.36	(0.02)	0.10	(0.03)	**0.26**	(0.03)
	Hungary	-0.02	(0.02)	-0.17	(0.02)	**0.15**	(0.03)	-0.08	(0.03)	-0.06	(0.03)	**-0.02**	(0.03)	0.38	(0.02)	0.22	(0.03)	**0.16**	(0.03)
	Iceland	-0.04	(0.02)	-0.35	(0.04)	**0.31**	(0.04)	0.20	(0.03)	-0.13	(0.03)	**0.33**	(0.04)	-0.12	(0.02)	-0.39	(0.03)	**0.26**	(0.04)
	Ireland	-0.01	(0.02)	-0.42	(0.03)	**0.41**	(0.03)	0.26	(0.02)	-0.09	(0.03)	**0.35**	(0.04)	-0.33	(0.02)	-0.64	(0.03)	**0.31**	(0.03)
	Italy	0.24	(0.01)	0.07	(0.02)	**0.17**	(0.02)	0.17	(0.02)	0.01	(0.02)	**0.16**	(0.02)	0.33	(0.01)	0.12	(0.02)	**0.22**	(0.02)
	Japan	-0.03	(0.02)	-0.32	(0.03)	**0.29**	(0.04)	-0.33	(0.02)	-0.63	(0.03)	**0.29**	(0.03)	-0.56	(0.02)	-0.75	(0.02)	**0.20**	(0.03)
	Korea	-0.15	(0.02)	-0.43	(0.03)	**0.27**	(0.03)	-0.22	(0.03)	-0.34	(0.02)	**0.12**	(0.04)	-0.07	(0.03)	-0.41	(0.03)	**0.34**	(0.04)
	Luxembourg	0.22	(0.02)	-0.01	(0.03)	**0.23**	(0.03)	-0.11	(0.02)	-0.20	(0.03)	**0.09**	(0.04)	0.19	(0.02)	-0.05	(0.03)	**0.24**	(0.03)
	Mexico	0.74	(0.01)	0.81	(0.03)	**-0.07**	(0.03)	0.51	(0.01)	0.60	(0.02)	**-0.10**	(0.02)	0.73	(0.01)	0.73	(0.03)	**-0.00**	(0.03)
	Netherlands	-0.27	(0.02)	-0.50	(0.04)	**0.23**	(0.04)	-0.19	(0.02)	-0.28	(0.03)	**0.09**	(0.04)	-0.18	(0.02)	-0.44	(0.03)	**0.26**	(0.03)
	New Zealand	-0.02	(0.02)	-0.24	(0.04)	**0.23**	(0.04)	0.26	(0.02)	0.02	(0.03)	**0.25**	(0.04)	-0.17	(0.02)	-0.42	(0.03)	**0.25**	(0.03)
	Norway	0.08	(0.03)	-0.26	(0.04)	**0.34**	(0.04)	-0.09	(0.02)	-0.30	(0.03)	**0.21**	(0.03)	-0.02	(0.02)	-0.29	(0.03)	**0.28**	(0.04)
	Poland	0.09	(0.02)	-0.01	(0.02)	**0.10**	(0.02)	0.15	(0.02)	0.18	(0.02)	**-0.03**	(0.02)	0.68	(0.01)	0.57	(0.03)	**0.11**	(0.02)
	Portugal	0.22	(0.02)	0.05	(0.03)	**0.17**	(0.03)	0.57	(0.02)	0.25	(0.03)	**0.32**	(0.04)	0.51	(0.02)	0.33	(0.03)	**0.18**	(0.03)
	Slovak Republic	-0.04	(0.02)	-0.26	(0.03)	**0.22**	(0.04)	-0.18	(0.02)	-0.20	(0.03)	**0.03**	(0.03)	0.27	(0.02)	0.16	(0.04)	**0.10**	(0.03)
	Spain	-0.09	(0.01)	-0.36	(0.03)	**0.27**	(0.03)	0.14	(0.02)	-0.11	(0.02)	**0.26**	(0.03)	-0.06	(0.02)	-0.31	(0.03)	**0.25**	(0.03)
	Sweden	-0.02	(0.03)	-0.35	(0.04)	**0.33**	(0.04)	0.03	(0.02)	-0.22	(0.03)	**0.25**	(0.04)	-0.31	(0.02)	-0.62	(0.03)	**0.32**	(0.03)
	Switzerland	0.10	(0.02)	-0.19	(0.02)	**0.29**	(0.02)	-0.19	(0.02)	-0.38	(0.02)	**0.18**	(0.02)	0.10	(0.02)	-0.12	(0.02)	**0.23**	(0.02)
	Turkey	0.26	(0.03)	0.16	(0.03)	**0.09**	(0.04)	0.34	(0.03)	0.34	(0.03)	**0.00**	(0.04)	0.63	(0.03)	0.45	(0.04)	**0.18**	(0.05)
	United Kingdom	0.06	(0.02)	-0.16	(0.03)	**0.22**	(0.03)	0.24	(0.02)	0.04	(0.03)	**0.20**	(0.03)	-0.25	(0.02)	-0.56	(0.03)	**0.32**	(0.03)
	United States	0.07	(0.02)	-0.04	(0.04)	**0.10**	(0.04)	0.33	(0.02)	0.19	(0.02)	**0.14**	(0.03)	-0.05	(0.02)	-0.15	(0.03)	**0.10**	(0.03)
	OECD average	**0.08**	**(0.00)**	**-0.15**	**(0.01)**	**0.23**	**(0.01)**	**0.06**	**(0.00)**	**-0.10**	**(0.01)**	**0.16**	**(0.01)**	**0.7**	**(0.00)**	**-0.15**	**(0.01)**	**0.22**	**(0.01)**
Partners	Argentina	0.20	(0.03)	0.26	(0.04)	**-0.06**	(0.05)	0.42	(0.02)	0.49	(0.03)	**-0.07**	(0.04)	0.42	(0.04)	0.45	(0.04)	**-0.03**	(0.05)
	Azerbaijan	0.67	(0.03)	0.47	(0.04)	**0.20**	(0.04)	0.55	(0.03)	0.55	(0.03)	**-0.01**	(0.03)	1.25	(0.02)	1.16	(0.03)	**0.09**	(0.03)
	Brazil	0.51	(0.02)	0.52	(0.04)	**-0.01**	(0.04)	0.45	(0.02)	0.55	(0.02)	**-0.10**	(0.03)	0.55	(0.02)	0.50	(0.03)	**0.05**	(0.03)
	Bulgaria	0.24	(0.02)	0.07	(0.04)	**0.17**	(0.05)	0.34	(0.02)	0.39	(0.03)	**-0.06**	(0.03)	0.84	(0.02)	0.64	(0.03)	**0.20**	(0.03)
	Chile	0.35	(0.02)	0.37	(0.03)	**-0.02**	(0.04)	0.54	(0.04)	0.47	(0.04)	**0.07**	(0.04)	0.51	(0.02)	0.44	(0.03)	**0.07**	(0.04)
	Colombia	1.09	(0.03)	1.27	(0.03)	**-0.18**	(0.04)	0.61	(0.02)	0.72	(0.04)	**-0.11**	(0.04)	1.01	(0.02)	0.96	(0.03)	**0.06**	(0.03)
	Croatia	0.21	(0.02)	0.10	(0.03)	**0.11**	(0.03)	0.04	(0.03)	0.06	(0.04)	**-0.02**	(0.04)	0.40	(0.02)	0.28	(0.02)	**0.13**	(0.03)
	Estonia	0.25	(0.01)	0.07	(0.03)	**0.18**	(0.03)	0.08	(0.02)	0.02	(0.02)	**0.06**	(0.02)	0.43	(0.02)	0.33	(0.03)	**0.10**	(0.03)
	Hong Kong-China	0.25	(0.02)	0.07	(0.03)	**0.18**	(0.04)	0.16	(0.02)	0.16	(0.03)	**0.00**	(0.04)	0.36	(0.02)	0.06	(0.03)	**0.29**	(0.03)
	Indonesia	0.60	(0.03)	0.47	(0.03)	**0.13**	(0.03)	0.78	(0.03)	0.73	(0.03)	**0.05**	(0.03)	0.68	(0.02)	0.35	(0.03)	**0.32**	(0.03)
	Israel	-0.22	(0.03)	-0.17	(0.05)	**-0.05**	(0.06)	-0.37	(0.03)	-0.36	(0.04)	**-0.02**	(0.05)	0.08	(0.03)	0.22	(0.04)	**-0.13**	(0.05)
	Jordan	0.74	(0.02)	0.55	(0.03)	**0.18**	(0.04)	0.85	(0.02)	0.72	(0.02)	**0.13**	(0.02)	1.00	(0.02)	0.90	(0.02)	**0.10**	(0.04)
	Kyrgyzstan	0.90	(0.02)	0.92	(0.03)	**-0.02**	(0.03)	0.81	(0.02)	0.92	(0.03)	**-0.11**	(0.03)	1.31	(0.02)	1.36	(0.03)	**-0.05**	(0.03)
	Latvia	0.20	(0.02)	0.10	(0.03)	**0.10**	(0.03)	0.01	(0.02)	0.00	(0.03)	**0.01**	(0.03)	0.29	(0.02)	0.18	(0.03)	**0.11**	(0.03)
	Lithuania	0.39	(0.01)	0.27	(0.02)	**0.12**	(0.02)	0.37	(0.02)	0.37	(0.02)	**-0.01**	(0.02)	0.28	(0.02)	0.22	(0.03)	**0.06**	(0.03)
	Macao-China	0.13	(0.02)	0.04	(0.02)	**0.09**	(0.03)	0.40	(0.02)	0.35	(0.03)	**0.05**	(0.04)	0.36	(0.02)	0.09	(0.02)	**0.27**	(0.03)
	Montenegro	0.44	(0.02)	0.36	(0.03)	**0.08**	(0.04)	0.42	(0.02)	0.50	(0.03)	**-0.07**	(0.03)	0.79	(0.02)	0.67	(0.02)	**0.12**	(0.03)
	Romania	0.43	(0.02)	0.29	(0.03)	**0.14**	(0.03)	0.40	(0.03)	0.40	(0.03)	**-0.00**	(0.03)	0.70	(0.02)	0.51	(0.03)	**0.19**	(0.04)
	Russian Federation	0.29	(0.02)	0.26	(0.04)	**0.02**	(0.03)	0.19	(0.02)	0.26	(0.02)	**-0.07**	(0.02)	0.59	(0.02)	0.51	(0.05)	**0.08**	(0.04)
	Serbia	0.27	(0.02)	0.23	(0.03)	**0.04**	(0.03)	0.08	(0.02)	0.16	(0.03)	**-0.08**	(0.04)	0.57	(0.02)	0.48	(0.02)	**0.09**	(0.02)
	Slovenia	0.07	(0.02)	-0.05	(0.02)	**0.12**	(0.03)	0.08	(0.02)	0.03	(0.03)	**0.05**	(0.03)	0.47	(0.02)	0.35	(0.02)	**0.12**	(0.02)
	Chinese Taipei	0.17	(0.02)	-0.08	(0.02)	**0.25**	(0.02)	0.32	(0.01)	0.18	(0.02)	**0.14**	(0.02)	0.50	(0.01)	0.21	(0.02)	**0.29**	(0.02)
	Thailand	0.80	(0.02)	0.77	(0.03)	**0.04**	(0.04)	0.73	(0.01)	0.68	(0.02)	**0.05**	(0.02)	1.16	(0.01)	0.99	(0.02)	**0.16**	(0.02)
	Tunisia	0.79	(0.02)	0.75	(0.03)	**0.04**	(0.03)	0.84	(0.02)	0.82	(0.03)	**0.02**	(0.04)	1.14	(0.02)	1.05	(0.02)	**0.09**	(0.02)
	Uruguay	0.24	(0.02)	0.26	(0.04)	**-0.02**	(0.05)	0.20	(0.02)	0.17	(0.03)	**0.03**	(0.04)	0.15	(0.02)	0.15	(0.03)	**-0.01**	(0.04)

[Part 2/3]
Table A3.1a Approaches to learning among disadvantaged and non-disadvantaged students

		Self-efficacy						Self-concept				
		Non-disadvantaged students		Disadvantaged students		Difference		Non-disadvantaged students		Disadvantaged students		Difference	
		Mean	S.E.	Mean	S.E.	Dif.	S.E.	Mean	S.E.	Mean	S.E.	Dif.	S.E.
OECD	Australia	0.28	(0.02)	-0.21	(0.02)	**0.49**	(0.02)	0.07	(0.02)	-0.25	(0.02)	**0.31**	(0.02)
	Austria	0.03	(0.02)	-0.40	(0.03)	**0.43**	(0.03)	0.17	(0.02)	-0.10	(0.04)	**0.27**	(0.04)
	Belgium	0.04	(0.02)	-0.30	(0.03)	**0.34**	(0.03)	-0.07	(0.02)	-0.29	(0.03)	**0.22**	(0.03)
	Canada	0.36	(0.02)	-0.08	(0.02)	**0.44**	(0.03)	0.37	(0.02)	0.05	(0.02)	**0.32**	(0.03)
	Czech Republic	0.22	(0.02)	-0.03	(0.03)	**0.25**	(0.03)	-0.01	(0.02)	-0.09	(0.02)	**0.08**	(0.03)
	Denmark	0.08	(0.03)	-0.39	(0.04)	**0.47**	(0.04)	0.01	(0.02)	-0.26	(0.03)	**0.27**	(0.03)
	Finland	0.14	(0.02)	-0.20	(0.03)	**0.34**	(0.03)	0.15	(0.02)	-0.11	(0.02)	**0.26**	(0.03)
	France	0.09	(0.02)	-0.35	(0.02)	**0.43**	(0.03)	-0.03	(0.02)	-0.27	(0.03)	**0.23**	(0.04)
	Germany	0.20	(0.02)	-0.22	(0.03)	**0.42**	(0.03)	0.33	(0.02)	0.10	(0.03)	**0.23**	(0.03)
	Greece	-0.01	(0.02)	-0.36	(0.03)	**0.35**	(0.04)	0.13	(0.02)	-0.16	(0.02)	**0.29**	(0.03)
	Hungary	0.06	(0.02)	-0.28	(0.02)	**0.34**	(0.03)	-0.19	(0.02)	-0.27	(0.03)	**0.08**	(0.04)
	Iceland	0.30	(0.02)	-0.18	(0.03)	**0.48**	(0.04)	0.27	(0.02)	-0.23	(0.03)	**0.50**	(0.04)
	Ireland	0.16	(0.02)	-0.31	(0.03)	**0.47**	(0.04)	-0.01	(0.02)	-0.37	(0.03)	**0.36**	(0.04)
	Italy	-0.12	(0.01)	-0.36	(0.02)	**0.24**	(0.02)	0.21	(0.02)	0.06	(0.02)	**0.16**	(0.02)
	Japan	-0.44	(0.02)	-0.72	(0.03)	**0.29**	(0.03)	-0.83	(0.02)	-0.96	(0.03)	**0.13**	(0.03)
	Korea	-0.10	(0.02)	-0.45	(0.04)	**0.35**	(0.05)	-0.61	(0.03)	-0.91	(0.03)	**0.30**	(0.04)
	Luxembourg	0.02	(0.02)	-0.43	(0.03)	**0.45**	(0.03)	0.33	(0.02)	0.06	(0.03)	**0.26**	(0.03)
	Mexico	0.18	(0.01)	-0.08	(0.03)	**0.26**	(0.03)	0.56	(0.01)	0.46	(0.02)	**0.10**	(0.02)
	Netherlands	0.12	(0.02)	-0.17	(0.03)	**0.29**	(0.03)	-0.26	(0.02)	-0.48	(0.04)	**0.22**	(0.04)
	New Zealand	0.14	(0.02)	-0.32	(0.03)	**0.46**	(0.03)	0.03	(0.02)	-0.23	(0.02)	**0.26**	(0.03)
	Norway	0.27	(0.02)	-0.17	(0.03)	**0.44**	(0.04)	0.14	(0.02)	-0.13	(0.03)	**0.28**	(0.04)
	Poland	0.39	(0.02)	0.00	(0.02)	**0.39**	(0.03)	0.13	(0.02)	-0.02	(0.02)	**0.15**	(0.02)
	Portugal	0.31	(0.02)	-0.01	(0.03)	**0.33**	(0.03)	0.37	(0.02)	0.18	(0.03)	**0.19**	(0.03)
	Slovak Republic	0.21	(0.02)	-0.11	(0.04)	**0.32**	(0.04)	0.21	(0.02)	0.03	(0.03)	**0.17**	(0.03)
	Spain	0.07	(0.02)	-0.34	(0.03)	**0.41**	(0.03)	0.09	(0.02)	-0.21	(0.02)	**0.30**	(0.03)
	Sweden	0.09	(0.03)	-0.38	(0.03)	**0.46**	(0.04)	0.13	(0.02)	-0.23	(0.03)	**0.36**	(0.03)
	Switzerland	-0.05	(0.02)	-0.48	(0.02)	**0.43**	(0.02)	0.19	(0.02)	-0.09	(0.02)	**0.28**	(0.03)
	Turkey	0.11	(0.03)	-0.17	(0.04)	**0.28**	(0.05)	0.18	(0.04)	0.11	(0.04)	**0.07**	(0.05)
	United Kingdom	0.35	(0.02)	-0.12	(0.02)	**0.48**	(0.03)	0.09	(0.02)	-0.13	(0.02)	**0.22**	(0.03)
	United States	0.38	(0.02)	-0.08	(0.04)	**0.46**	(0.05)	0.30	(0.02)	0.02	(0.04)	**0.28**	(0.04)
	OECD average	**0.13**	**(0.00)**	**-0.26**	**(0.01)**	**0.39**	**(0.01)**	**0.08**	**(0.00)**	**-0.16**	**(0.01)**	**0.24**	**(0.01)**
Partners	Argentina	0.06	(0.02)	-0.27	(0.03)	**0.32**	(0.04)	0.29	(0.03)	0.20	(0.04)	**0.09**	(0.05)
	Azerbaijan	-0.34	(0.03)	-0.69	(0.06)	**0.36**	(0.06)	0.66	(0.03)	0.61	(0.05)	**0.05**	(0.05)
	Brazil	0.06	(0.02)	-0.28	(0.03)	**0.34**	(0.04)	0.38	(0.02)	0.33	(0.03)	**0.05**	(0.03)
	Bulgaria	0.10	(0.03)	-0.34	(0.04)	**0.44**	(0.05)	0.39	(0.02)	0.32	(0.03)	**0.07**	(0.04)
	Chile	0.20	(0.02)	-0.22	(0.03)	**0.42**	(0.04)	0.24	(0.02)	0.05	(0.03)	**0.19**	(0.03)
	Colombia	0.19	(0.02)	-0.11	(0.03)	**0.29**	(0.03)	0.78	(0.02)	0.69	(0.04)	**0.09**	(0.03)
	Croatia	0.26	(0.02)	-0.09	(0.02)	**0.35**	(0.03)	0.01	(0.02)	-0.10	(0.03)	**0.11**	(0.03)
	Estonia	0.12	(0.02)	-0.15	(0.02)	**0.27**	(0.03)	0.18	(0.02)	-0.04	(0.02)	**0.22**	(0.03)
	Hong Kong-China	0.18	(0.02)	-0.17	(0.03)	**0.35**	(0.04)	-0.22	(0.02)	-0.32	(0.03)	**0.10**	(0.03)
	Indonesia	-0.61	(0.02)	-0.88	(0.03)	**0.27**	(0.03)	0.16	(0.04)	0.16	(0.03)	**-0.00**	(0.04)
	Israel	0.09	(0.03)	-0.12	(0.04)	**0.21**	(0.05)	0.30	(0.03)	0.21	(0.04)	**0.09**	(0.04)
	Jordan	0.30	(0.03)	0.04	(0.03)	**0.26**	(0.03)	0.82	(0.02)	0.60	(0.03)	**0.22**	(0.03)
	Kyrgyzstan	-0.08	(0.02)	-0.29	(0.03)	**0.21**	(0.03)	0.67	(0.02)	0.74	(0.03)	**-0.08**	(0.03)
	Latvia	0.07	(0.02)	-0.19	(0.03)	**0.26**	(0.03)	0.06	(0.02)	-0.03	(0.03)	**0.09**	(0.03)
	Lithuania	0.11	(0.02)	-0.18	(0.03)	**0.29**	(0.03)	-0.19	(0.02)	-0.34	(0.02)	**0.15**	(0.03)
	Macao-China	-0.00	(0.02)	-0.32	(0.03)	**0.32**	(0.03)	-0.08	(0.02)	-0.18	(0.03)	**0.11**	(0.04)
	Montenegro	0.12	(0.02)	-0.31	(0.03)	**0.44**	(0.03)	0.52	(0.02)	0.43	(0.03)	**0.10**	(0.03)
	Romania	-0.24	(0.03)	-0.56	(0.04)	**0.32**	(0.04)	0.37	(0.02)	0.30	(0.03)	**0.06**	(0.03)
	Russian Federation	0.10	(0.02)	-0.23	(0.04)	**0.33**	(0.04)	0.21	(0.02)	0.06	(0.03)	**0.15**	(0.03)
	Serbia	0.16	(0.02)	-0.17	(0.03)	**0.33**	(0.03)	0.25	(0.02)	0.23	(0.03)	**0.02**	(0.03)
	Slovenia	0.03	(0.01)	-0.37	(0.02)	**0.40**	(0.02)	0.23	(0.02)	0.21	(0.02)	**0.03**	(0.03)
	Chinese Taipei	0.32	(0.02)	-0.10	(0.03)	**0.42**	(0.03)	-0.34	(0.02)	-0.53	(0.02)	**0.19**	(0.02)
	Thailand	0.12	(0.02)	-0.05	(0.02)	**0.17**	(0.03)	0.70	(0.02)	0.67	(0.02)	**0.03**	(0.03)
	Tunisia	-0.05	(0.02)	-0.23	(0.02)	**0.18**	(0.03)	0.67	(0.02)	0.58	(0.03)	**0.08**	(0.03)
	Uruguay	0.23	(0.02)	-0.09	(0.03)	**0.32**	(0.04)	0.39	(0.02)	0.26	(0.03)	**0.13**	(0.03)

[Part 3/3]
Table A3.1a Approaches to learning among disadvantaged and non-disadvantaged students

		School preparation for science careers						Information in science related careers					
		Non-disadvantaged students		Disadvantaged students		Difference		Non-disadvantaged students		Disadvantaged students		Difference	
		Mean	S.E.	Mean	S.E.	Dif.	S.E.	Mean	S.E.	Mean	S.E.	Dif.	S.E.
OECD	Australia	0.30	(0.02)	-0.04	(0.02)	**0.34**	(0.02)	0.26	(0.01)	-0.01	(0.02)	**0.27**	(0.02)
	Austria	-0.21	(0.04)	-0.30	(0.04)	**0.10**	(0.05)	-0.07	(0.02)	-0.16	(0.03)	**0.10**	(0.04)
	Belgium	-0.07	(0.02)	-0.24	(0.03)	**0.17**	(0.03)	-0.22	(0.02)	-0.26	(0.02)	**0.04**	(0.03)
	Canada	0.41	(0.02)	0.17	(0.02)	**0.24**	(0.02)	0.36	(0.02)	0.13	(0.02)	**0.23**	(0.03)
	Czech Republic	-0.17	(0.03)	-0.18	(0.03)	**0.01**	(0.03)	-0.07	(0.02)	-0.15	(0.03)	**0.07**	(0.04)
	Denmark	0.00	(0.02)	-0.14	(0.03)	**0.14**	(0.03)	-0.06	(0.02)	-0.20	(0.03)	**0.15**	(0.03)
	Finland	0.20	(0.02)	0.09	(0.02)	**0.11**	(0.03)	0.17	(0.02)	0.06	(0.02)	**0.11**	(0.03)
	France	0.17	(0.03)	-0.12	(0.03)	**0.29**	(0.04)	0.07	(0.02)	-0.14	(0.03)	**0.21**	(0.04)
	Germany	0.14	(0.03)	0.04	(0.03)	**0.09**	(0.04)	0.08	(0.02)	-0.10	(0.03)	**0.19**	(0.04)
	Greece	-0.14	(0.02)	-0.09	(0.03)	**-0.05**	(0.03)	0.42	(0.02)	0.16	(0.03)	**0.27**	(0.03)
	Hungary	0.04	(0.03)	0.04	(0.03)	**0.00**	(0.03)	0.01	(0.02)	-0.11	(0.03)	**0.11**	(0.03)
	Iceland	0.13	(0.02)	-0.09	(0.03)	**0.22**	(0.04)	0.02	(0.02)	-0.23	(0.03)	**0.25**	(0.03)
	Ireland	0.26	(0.03)	0.03	(0.03)	**0.23**	(0.03)	0.08	(0.02)	-0.17	(0.04)	**0.26**	(0.04)
	Italy	-0.06	(0.02)	-0.16	(0.02)	**0.10**	(0.03)	0.11	(0.01)	-0.01	(0.02)	**0.13**	(0.02)
	Japan	-0.46	(0.03)	-0.64	(0.03)	**0.18**	(0.03)	-0.35	(0.02)	-0.46	(0.02)	**0.10**	(0.02)
	Korea	-0.27	(0.03)	-0.28	(0.02)	**0.01**	(0.04)	-0.25	(0.02)	-0.50	(0.02)	**0.24**	(0.03)
	Luxembourg	-0.11	(0.02)	-0.11	(0.03)	**0.00**	(0.04)	-0.07	(0.02)	-0.17	(0.03)	**0.10**	(0.03)
	Mexico	0.47	(0.02)	0.50	(0.02)	**-0.03**	(0.02)	-0.38	(0.02)	-0.58	(0.05)	**0.20**	(0.04)
	Netherlands	-0.19	(0.01)	-0.34	(0.02)	**0.14**	(0.03)	-0.30	(0.02)	-0.44	(0.04)	**0.14**	(0.04)
	New Zealand	0.30	(0.02)	0.03	(0.02)	**0.27**	(0.03)	0.19	(0.02)	0.05	(0.03)	**0.14**	(0.04)
	Norway	-0.25	(0.03)	-0.43	(0.04)	**0.17**	(0.04)	-0.06	(0.02)	-0.22	(0.03)	**0.16**	(0.04)
	Poland	-0.02	(0.02)	0.13	(0.03)	**-0.15**	(0.03)	0.36	(0.02)	0.19	(0.02)	**0.17**	(0.03)
	Portugal	0.26	(0.02)	0.13	(0.02)	**0.14**	(0.03)	0.48	(0.02)	0.24	(0.03)	**0.24**	(0.03)
	Slovak Republic	-0.13	(0.03)	-0.16	(0.04)	**0.03**	(0.04)	-0.02	(0.02)	-0.11	(0.03)	**0.09**	(0.03)
	Spain	0.11	(0.02)	-0.02	(0.02)	**0.14**	(0.03)	0.10	(0.02)	-0.17	(0.02)	**0.27**	(0.03)
	Sweden	-0.03	(0.02)	-0.17	(0.03)	**0.14**	(0.03)	-0.05	(0.02)	-0.28	(0.03)	**0.23**	(0.03)
	Switzerland	0.08	(0.02)	-0.09	(0.03)	**0.17**	(0.03)	0.09	(0.02)	-0.05	(0.02)	**0.14**	(0.02)
	Turkey	-0.16	(0.03)	-0.09	(0.03)	**-0.07**	(0.04)	0.40	(0.04)	0.03	(0.05)	**0.37**	(0.05)
	United Kingdom	0.31	(0.02)	0.02	(0.02)	**0.29**	(0.03)	0.05	(0.02)	-0.12	(0.03)	**0.17**	(0.03)
	United States	0.32	(0.02)	0.10	(0.02)	**0.22**	(0.03)	0.39	(0.02)	0.26	(0.04)	**0.14**	(0.04)
	OECD average	**0.04**	**(0.00)**	**-0.08**	**(0.01)**	**0.12**	**(0.01)**	**0.06**	**(0.00)**	**-0.12**	**(0.01)**	**0.18**	**(0.01)**
Partners	Argentina	0.10	(0.03)	0.17	(0.03)	**-0.08**	(0.05)	-0.40	(0.04)	-0.67	(0.04)	**0.27**	(0.05)
	Azerbaijan	0.69	(0.02)	0.59	(0.03)	**0.10**	(0.03)	0.43	(0.02)	0.23	(0.04)	**0.19**	(0.04)
	Brazil	0.18	(0.02)	0.14	(0.03)	**0.04**	(0.03)	0.40	(0.02)	0.19	(0.03)	**0.21**	(0.03)
	Bulgaria	0.39	(0.02)	0.41	(0.03)	**-0.02**	(0.04)	0.29	(0.02)	0.16	(0.04)	**0.13**	(0.04)
	Chile	0.27	(0.04)	0.13	(0.04)	**0.14**	(0.04)	0.35	(0.03)	0.06	(0.04)	**0.30**	(0.04)
	Colombia	0.48	(0.03)	0.57	(0.04)	**-0.09**	(0.05)	0.02	(0.02)	-0.12	(0.04)	**0.14**	(0.04)
	Croatia	0.17	(0.02)	0.20	(0.03)	**-0.03**	(0.03)	0.09	(0.02)	-0.11	(0.02)	**0.21**	(0.03)
	Estonia	0.29	(0.02)	0.25	(0.02)	**0.05**	(0.03)	0.02	(0.02)	-0.08	(0.02)	**0.09**	(0.03)
	Hong Kong-China	-0.12	(0.02)	-0.15	(0.03)	**0.03**	(0.03)	0.28	(0.02)	0.12	(0.03)	**0.15**	(0.04)
	Indonesia	0.35	(0.04)	0.29	(0.02)	**0.06**	(0.05)	0.44	(0.03)	0.14	(0.03)	**0.30**	(0.03)
	Israel	-0.10	(0.03)	-0.04	(0.04)	**-0.05**	(0.05)	0.21	(0.03)	0.17	(0.04)	**0.04**	(0.05)
	Jordan	0.51	(0.02)	0.48	(0.03)	**0.02**	(0.03)	0.49	(0.02)	0.34	(0.03)	**0.15**	(0.03)
	Kyrgyzstan	0.63	(0.02)	0.65	(0.03)	**-0.02**	(0.03)	0.37	(0.02)	0.16	(0.04)	**0.20**	(0.04)
	Latvia	0.22	(0.02)	0.22	(0.03)	**-0.00**	(0.03)	0.08	(0.02)	-0.00	(0.03)	**0.08**	(0.03)
	Lithuania	0.45	(0.02)	0.39	(0.03)	**0.05**	(0.03)	0.31	(0.02)	0.07	(0.02)	**0.24**	(0.02)
	Macao-China	-0.15	(0.02)	-0.20	(0.02)	**0.04**	(0.02)	-0.03	(0.02)	-0.29	(0.02)	**0.26**	(0.03)
	Montenegro	0.31	(0.02)	0.39	(0.03)	**-0.08**	(0.04)	0.04	(0.02)	-0.17	(0.03)	**0.20**	(0.03)
	Romania	0.43	(0.04)	0.35	(0.03)	**0.08**	(0.05)	0.13	(0.02)	-0.08	(0.05)	**0.20**	(0.05)
	Russian Federation	0.31	(0.02)	0.28	(0.02)	**0.03**	(0.03)	0.43	(0.02)	0.31	(0.03)	**0.12**	(0.03)
	Serbia	0.12	(0.02)	0.22	(0.03)	**-0.10**	(0.04)	0.18	(0.02)	0.02	(0.02)	**0.16**	(0.03)
	Slovenia	0.08	(0.02)	0.06	(0.02)	**0.02**	(0.03)	0.05	(0.02)	-0.03	(0.02)	**0.08**	(0.03)
	Chinese Taipei	0.27	(0.02)	0.22	(0.01)	**0.05**	(0.02)	0.14	(0.01)	-0.12	(0.02)	**0.26**	(0.02)
	Thailand	0.66	(0.02)	0.59	(0.02)	**0.06**	(0.02)	0.32	(0.02)	0.13	(0.03)	**0.19**	(0.03)
	Tunisia	0.53	(0.02)	0.59	(0.03)	**-0.06**	(0.03)	0.45	(0.02)	0.33	(0.04)	**0.12**	(0.04)
	Uruguay	0.10	(0.02)	0.06	(0.03)	**0.05**	(0.03)	-0.16	(0.02)	-0.38	(0.03)	**0.22**	(0.04)

Note: Values that are statistically different are indicated in bold.

[Part 1/2] **Table A3.1b** **Approaches to learning, overall performance effect and differential effect for disadvantaged students**

		General interest in science		Instrumental motivation to learn science		Participation in science related activities		Self-efficacy			
		Average association with performance for all students		Differential effect for disadvantaged students		Average association with performance for all students		Differential effect for disadvantaged students		Average association with performance for all students		Differential effect for disadvantaged students		Average association with performance for all students		Differential effect for disadvantaged students	
		Coef.	S.E.	Coef.	S.E.	Coef.	S.E.	Coef.	S.E.	Coef.	S.E.	Coef.	S.E.	Coef.	S.E.	Coef.	S.E.
OECD	Australia	25.3	(0.8)	-1.6	(1.7)	24.9	(0.8)	3.5	(2.0)	25.1	(1.0)	-3.1	(2.1)	37.6	(0.8)	-3.7	(1.8)
	Austria	18.3	(1.4)	3.1	(2.7)	10.6	(1.5)	0.2	(2.8)	15.9	(1.6)	-2.7	(3.2)	29.1	(1.4)	1.0	(2.7)
	Belgium	17.1	(1.2)	-2.6	(1.8)	12.5	(1.3)	-0.8	(2.1)	16.8	(1.0)	-2.1	(1.9)	24.6	(1.0)	-0.6	(1.7)
	Canada	21.6	(1.0)	0.4	(1.7)	18.8	(1.1)	-3.0	(2.0)	20.1	(1.0)	-1.7	(2.4)	33.4	(1.0)	-1.6	(1.9)
	Czech Republic	17.1	(1.7)	-4.7	(3.3)	6.8	(2.2)	-5.5	(3.4)	11.5	(2.3)	-7.4	(3.9)	27.2	(1.6)	-3.3	(2.7)
	Denmark	24.0	(1.3)	-2.8	(2.8)	15.4	(1.5)	-3.9	(3.2)	21.8	(1.4)	-0.2	(2.6)	34.4	(1.4)	-5.2	(2.6)
	Finland	28.5	(1.5)	2.6	(2.9)	26.3	(1.5)	1.7	(3.5)	22.9	(1.5)	2.1	(3.0)	35.9	(1.6)	4.9	(3.1)
	France	21.3	(1.4)	0.4	(2.6)	15.1	(1.1)	-3.5	(2.8)	14.8	(1.5)	-6.0	(2.9)	26.1	(1.3)	-4.4	(3.3)
	Germany	16.8	(1.8)	-8.9	(2.5)	7.9	(1.2)	-6.1	(2.6)	12.3	(1.4)	-5.4	(2.9)	23.9	(1.6)	-7.4	(2.8)
	Greece	16.2	(1.5)	0.8	(2.6)	9.4	(1.5)	-5.4	(2.8)	9.4	(1.4)	0.8	(2.3)	21.7	(1.5)	-2.7	(2.9)
	Hungary	14.3	(1.7)	-3.9	(3.3)	3.2	(1.7)	-5.8	(3.4)	10.8	(1.4)	-4.7	(3.2)	16.6	(1.7)	-1.4	(3.2)
	Iceland	24.9	(1.3)	-4.2	(2.7)	24.2	(1.6)	-3.5	(3.2)	28.8	(1.7)	-4.1	(3.7)	35.4	(1.6)	-3.7	(2.9)
	Ireland	24.3	(1.2)	-1.8	(2.2)	19.9	(1.5)	-0.7	(2.6)	20.1	(1.4)	-0.2	(2.8)	33.1	(1.2)	-2.4	(2.8)
	Italy	13.8	(1.2)	-4.2	(1.7)	6.2	(1.4)	-4.6	(1.9)	9.1	(1.1)	-1.6	(1.8)	21.2	(1.4)	-4.8	(2.2)
	Japan	27.4	(1.5)	-2.6	(2.5)	19.3	(1.5)	-3.0	(2.5)	19.8	(1.6)	-1.9	(3.0)	25.0	(1.3)	-2.0	(2.4)
	Korea	26.2	(1.5)	-1.6	(2.4)	18.3	(1.8)	-2.8	(2.9)	18.4	(1.4)	-3.4	(2.7)	28.9	(1.6)	1.1	(2.9)
	Luxembourg	14.4	(1.4)	-4.7	(2.4)	5.6	(1.1)	-4.1	(2.3)	9.2	(1.3)	-6.7	(3.0)	18.7	(1.4)	-7.5	(2.5)
	Mexico	7.2	(1.1)	-1.9	(2.0)	2.0	(1.2)	-2.2	(2.9)	-0.5	(1.2)	-6.7	(2.3)	12.3	(1.2)	-6.6	(2.3)
	Netherlands	18.8	(1.1)	-1.5	(2.5)	10.7	(1.2)	0.3	(2.8)	11.0	(1.2)	-2.6	(2.1)	18.6	(1.3)	-4.2	(2.5)
	New Zealand	24.2	(1.4)	-4.5	(3.1)	24.4	(1.4)	-0.9	(3.2)	22.4	(1.6)	-10.0	(3.6)	44.5	(1.5)	-5.5	(3.3)
	Norway	24.4	(1.3)	-6.1	(2.3)	20.1	(1.4)	-2.9	(3.3)	20.7	(1.5)	-3.1	(3.3)	29.1	(1.7)	3.5	(3.3)
	Poland	14.9	(1.5)	0.9	(3.2)	3.7	(1.3)	-0.9	(3.1)	3.6	(1.5)	-6.3	(3.3)	33.2	(1.4)	-1.5	(2.8)
	Portugal	17.1	(1.3)	-7.6	(2.6)	14.0	(1.2)	-7.5	(2.7)	12.5	(1.2)	-6.1	(2.4)	18.7	(1.4)	-3.4	(2.6)
	Slovak Republic	15.4	(1.8)	-3.5	(3.8)	6.4	(1.7)	-2.5	(3.7)	10.6	(2.6)	-9.3	(4.8)	22.9	(1.3)	-1.2	(3.1)
	Spain	17.1	(1.0)	1.2	(1.9)	11.9	(0.9)	-5.5	(2.1)	13.2	(1.0)	-2.4	(2.1)	22.7	(0.9)	1.4	(2.0)
	Sweden	24.6	(1.3)	-3.4	(3.2)	23.8	(1.6)	-1.0	(3.1)	23.2	(1.5)	-2.7	(3.7)	33.3	(1.6)	-3.5	(2.6)
	Switzerland	24.3	(1.1)	-1.3	(2.6)	13.0	(1.1)	-3.9	(2.1)	15.4	(1.2)	-9.2	(2.5)	30.7	(1.2)	-6.4	(2.8)
	Turkey	13.8	(1.3)	-1.0	(2.7)	11.0	(1.3)	-1.1	(3.0)	12.8	(1.5)	-2.7	(3.3)	17.5	(1.4)	-5.9	(2.3)
	United Kingdom	24.3	(1.3)	-10.5	(2.6)	22.0	(1.4)	-9.8	(2.7)	23.5	(1.5)	-7.7	(2.5)	45.6	(1.1)	-1.5	(2.3)
	United States	14.2	(1.4)	-2.0	(2.1)	15.1	(1.7)	-0.7	(3.1)	14.6	(1.7)	-2.3	(3.1)	28.0	(1.2)	-7.9	(2.8)
	OECD average	**19.7**	**(0.2)**	**-2.6**	**(0.5)**	**14.1**	**(0.3)**	**-2.9**	**(0.5)**	**15.7**	**(0.3)**	**-4.0**	**(0.5)**	**27.7**	**(0.3)**	**-3.1**	**(0.5)**
Partners	Argentina	5.9	(1.5)	3.5	(3.9)	3.4	(2.2)	-2.6	(4.1)	1.2	(1.8)	2.6	(4.0)	13.9	(2.0)	4.9	(4.9)
	Azerbaijan	7.1	(1.2)	-2.8	(2.1)	0.4	(1.4)	-1.0	(2.6)	-0.4	(1.6)	-0.0	(2.8)	5.7	(1.1)	-2.9	(2.0)
	Brazil	2.9	(1.0)	-2.0	(2.4)	1.8	(1.3)	-3.7	(2.6)	-3.1	(1.2)	-5.4	(2.3)	13.2	(1.2)	-8.9	(2.2)
	Bulgaria	7.9	(1.7)	-1.1	(3.6)	-1.6	(2.0)	-5.4	(4.0)	-1.3	(1.9)	-4.4	(4.1)	16.6	(1.5)	-5.8	(3.4)
	Chile	8.0	(1.4)	-3.8	(2.9)	4.3	(1.3)	-2.8	(3.1)	6.9	(1.3)	-2.0	(3.1)	14.5	(1.7)	-3.7	(3.1)
	Colombia	-1.1	(1.6)	3.1	(3.2)	1.3	(2.2)	-0.3	(4.0)	-3.7	(2.1)	2.4	(4.0)	11.9	(1.6)	2.1	(3.8)
	Croatia	17.6	(1.6)	4.1	(3.0)	5.6	(1.5)	-1.2	(2.7)	13.2	(1.2)	-3.5	(3.1)	30.7	(1.3)	-1.2	(2.5)
	Estonia	12.2	(2.3)	4.1	(3.5)	3.5	(2.1)	-2.7	(3.2)	4.9	(2.1)	1.2	(3.8)	33.2	(1.6)	1.2	(3.1)
	Hong Kong-China	25.4	(1.4)	-0.8	(2.9)	22.2	(1.5)	5.1	(3.2)	18.4	(1.2)	-4.1	(3.1)	27.0	(1.4)	3.6	(2.9)
	Indonesia	11.1	(2.2)	1.9	(3.1)	0.5	(2.9)	1.7	(2.3)	-2.4	(2.1)	1.9	(3.1)	5.2	(1.6)	-1.9	(2.3)
	Israel	17.5	(1.8)	0.6	(2.7)	-22.9	(1.7)	4.0	(3.4)	10.0	(1.9)	1.0	(3.3)	17.2	(2.2)	-0.7	(3.7)
	Jordan	13.5	(1.5)	-1.6	(2.4)	18.1	(1.8)	-6.2	(3.8)	-0.9	(1.6)	-0.2	(2.4)	11.6	(1.2)	-1.9	(2.4)
	Kyrgyzstan	-1.9	(1.7)	4.8	(3.0)	-5.0	(1.8)	8.0	(3.4)	-20.0	(2.2)	4.7	(3.5)	4.9	(1.5)	0.1	(2.4)
	Latvia	6.7	(2.6)	0.1	(5.1)	0.9	(1.9)	-7.1	(4.1)	2.2	(2.1)	-3.6	(3.9)	26.9	(1.7)	1.9	(3.2)
	Lithuania	19.4	(1.7)	0.7	(3.4)	8.6	(1.6)	0.6	(3.3)	3.6	(1.6)	-2.2	(3.2)	26.1	(1.7)	-2.1	(3.6)
	Macao-China	19.5	(1.4)	-0.5	(3.0)	11.6	(2.0)	-3.6	(3.7)	10.9	(1.3)	-1.7	(2.5)	20.8	(1.1)	-2.7	(2.9)
	Montenegro	12.6	(1.2)	2.9	(2.8)	-2.9	(1.2)	2.3	(3.0)	-1.8	(1.6)	-1.3	(3.4)	22.8	(1.1)	4.0	(2.6)
	Romania	8.4	(1.7)	-0.9	(3.3)	4.8	(2.2)	-3.2	(4.7)	3.6	(2.1)	-2.5	(5.3)	12.8	(1.7)	-4.9	(3.1)
	Russian Federation	12.4	(2.2)	6.5	(3.6)	-4.6	(1.8)	1.5	(3.5)	6.8	(2.1)	0.6	(3.2)	24.2	(1.5)	-4.3	(3.3)
	Serbia	7.1	(1.3)	-1.1	(2.8)	-3.0	(1.6)	-1.9	(3.0)	2.3	(1.8)	-3.7	(3.1)	18.2	(1.5)	-0.9	(3.1)
	Slovenia	15.7	(1.6)	1.0	(2.9)	7.7	(1.4)	-2.1	(2.7)	10.6	(1.3)	-2.8	(2.7)	22.6	(1.7)	-1.7	(3.5)
	Chinese Taipei	20.8	(0.9)	2.6	(1.9)	11.7	(1.1)	2.3	(2.4)	9.6	(1.2)	0.3	(2.6)	23.6	(1.1)	3.0	(1.9)
	Thailand	16.4	(1.3)	-3.3	(2.9)	18.3	(1.7)	-6.6	(3.9)	15.6	(1.6)	-0.9	(4.5)	11.4	(1.6)	-1.8	(3.3)
	Tunisia	9.4	(1.4)	-6.6	(2.7)	11.6	(1.4)	-4.3	(3.0)	0.7	(1.6)	-5.4	(3.5)	9.6	(1.4)	0.3	(3.0)
	Uruguay	5.2	(1.3)	-1.3	(2.7)	0.9	(1.5)	-3.0	(2.5)	3.8	(1.4)	-0.1	(2.9)	17.9	(1.7)	-4.3	(2.8)

Note: Values that are statistically different are indicated in bold.

Table A3.1b [Part 2/2] **Approaches to learning, overall performance effect and differential effect for disadvantaged students**

		\multicolumn{4}{c	}{Self-concept}	\multicolumn{4}{c	}{School preparation for science careers}	\multicolumn{4}{c}{Information in science related careers}
		\multicolumn{2}{c	}{Average association with performance for all students}	\multicolumn{2}{c	}{Differential effect for disadvantaged students}	\multicolumn{2}{c	}{Average association with performance for all students}	\multicolumn{2}{c	}{Differential effect for disadvantaged students}	\multicolumn{2}{c	}{Average association with performance for all students}	\multicolumn{2}{c}{Differential effect for disadvantaged students}
		Coef.	S.E.	Coef.	S.E.	Coef.	S.E.	Coef.	S.E.	Coef.	S.E.	Coef.	S.E.
OECD	Australia	**38.4**	(1.0)	-3.7	(2.1)	**26.8**	(1.0)	-1.2	(2.0)	**11.2**	(0.9)	-2.5	(1.9)
	Austria	**19.2**	(1.3)	-0.9	(2.2)	**6.3**	(1.4)	1.3	(2.4)	**2.5**	(1.3)	-1.9	(2.6)
	Belgium	**20.0**	(1.3)	-2.5	(2.3)	**8.7**	(1.2)	-2.2	(1.8)	0.3	(1.0)	1.8	(2.3)
	Canada	**30.2**	(1.0)	**-4.5**	(2.0)	**18.6**	(1.3)	-3.5	(2.0)	**3.1**	(1.0)	-2.1	(2.1)
	Czech Republic	**14.1**	(2.1)	3.3	(3.7)	**5.3**	(2.0)	-3.5	(3.2)	1.4	(1.5)	-5.6	(3.1)
	Denmark	**29.4**	(1.3)	**-5.4**	(3.2)	**16.2**	(1.8)	1.8	(3.3)	**5.7**	(1.6)	-3.1	(3.3)
	Finland	**37.1**	(1.5)	4.3	(3.0)	**11.7**	(1.7)	5.0	(2.9)	2.2	(1.6)	-1.0	(3.6)
	France	**21.7**	(1.4)	**-6.1**	(2.7)	**14.3**	(1.2)	-3.8	(2.3)	1.6	(1.2)	**-6.8**	(2.5)
	Germany	**18.3**	(1.2)	**-4.4**	(2.5)	**4.9**	(1.3)	-0.9	(2.3)	2.4	(1.2)	1.0	(2.7)
	Greece	**12.4**	(1.4)	**-5.9**	(2.5)	-1.0	(1.6)	4.4	(2.8)	0.3	(1.2)	-1.4	(2.5)
	Hungary	**7.9**	(1.7)	**-12.9**	(3.3)	-0.6	(1.4)	-1.8	(3.0)	-1.8	(1.5)	**-7.4**	(3.2)
	Iceland	**37.8**	(1.7)	-4.8	(2.9)	**19.9**	(1.8)	0.5	(3.3)	**17.2**	(1.7)	-3.4	(3.9)
	Ireland	**30.2**	(1.4)	**-4.0**	(3.1)	**14.2**	(1.2)	-0.3	(2.8)	1.4	(1.5)	-0.5	(2.5)
	Italy	**10.8**	(1.2)	**-7.3**	(2.3)	-1.4	(1.1)	-3.8	(2.0)	**-3.6**	(1.2)	-1.9	(2.2)
	Japan	**23.1**	(1.5)	-3.6	(2.9)	**8.6**	(1.8)	-7.1	(3.0)	-0.2	(1.5)	-3.4	(2.7)
	Korea	**27.3**	(1.4)	-3.2	(3.2)	0.4	(1.7)	-4.5	(3.0)	**4.8**	(1.6)	-3.9	(3.4)
	Luxembourg	**18.0**	(1.0)	**-8.5**	(2.2)	0.5	(1.0)	-0.6	(2.3)	**-1.9**	(1.2)	**-4.4**	(2.6)
	Mexico	**4.5**	(1.3)	**-4.7**	(2.3)	-1.6	(1.0)	-2.2	(2.3)	**-2.9**	(0.8)	-2.7	(1.6)
	Netherlands	**19.6**	(1.6)	-0.0	(2.9)	**14.1**	(1.5)	4.0	(2.5)	**7.4**	(1.3)	-2.9	(2.3)
	New Zealand	**36.8**	(1.5)	**-16.3**	(4.0)	**25.9**	(1.5)	-5.3	(3.4)	**5.8**	(1.4)	-3.9	(3.5)
	Norway	**33.5**	(1.6)	-3.8	(3.2)	**10.4**	(1.7)	2.9	(3.4)	-1.5	(1.5)	2.4	(2.8)
	Poland	**18.2**	(1.5)	-0.9	(3.0)	-3.5	(1.5)	-3.1	(3.1)	**-3.3**	(1.2)	-0.7	(2.6)
	Portugal	**20.1**	(1.4)	**-8.0**	(3.0)	**5.9**	(1.4)	**-6.5**	(2.5)	-1.2	(1.3)	-2.5	(2.4)
	Slovak Republic	**16.5**	(1.4)	-1.3	(3.5)	0.7	(1.9)	**-8.0**	(3.7)	**-3.7**	(1.4)	-3.3	(3.1)
	Spain	**19.1**	(0.9)	-2.8	(2.0)	**7.0**	(1.0)	0.4	(2.1)	**2.8**	(0.9)	-0.3	(1.7)
	Sweden	**34.7**	(1.4)	-4.5	(2.6)	**15.0**	(1.5)	0.4	(2.7)	**3.1**	(1.4)	4.4	(3.1)
	Switzerland	**24.7**	(1.3)	**-6.0**	(2.2)	**16.5**	(1.2)	-3.6	(2.3)	**6.2**	(1.4)	-2.4	(2.3)
	Turkey	**7.3**	(1.2)	-2.9	(3.0)	-2.2	(1.3)	-0.1	(2.3)	**10.5**	(1.4)	-4.8	(2.5)
	United Kingdom	**35.9**	(1.6)	**-8.7**	(2.7)	**25.2**	(1.3)	-5.2	(2.9)	1.1	(1.3)	**-6.0**	(2.8)
	United States	**23.9**	(1.5)	**-6.3**	(2.7)	**16.6**	(1.7)	-1.8	(3.3)	-0.4	(1.7)	-1.0	(2.8)
	OECD average	**23.0**	**(0.3)**	**-4.5**	**(0.5)**	**9.4**	**(0.3)**	**-1.6**	**(0.5)**	**2.4**	**(0.2)**	**-2.3**	**(0.5)**
Partners	Argentina	**7.9**	(2.1)	-1.2	(4.8)	-1.4	(1.7)	3.0	(3.5)	**-2.9**	(1.2)	4.2	(4.5)
	Azerbaijan	2.4	(1.5)	-2.5	(2.5)	**2.6**	(1.2)	2.8	(2.1)	-1.0	(1.2)	-1.6	(2.5)
	Brazil	**5.1**	(1.5)	**-8.5**	(2.5)	**-5.1**	(1.4)	-2.9	(2.5)	**-5.7**	(1.2)	**-4.5**	(2.2)
	Bulgaria	**8.0**	(1.8)	-4.1	(3.6)	1.6	(1.6)	-3.1	(3.2)	**-5.5**	(1.5)	-5.7	(3.5)
	Chile	**12.6**	(1.3)	**-7.0**	(2.9)	-2.5	(1.4)	**-8.2**	(2.7)	**-2.6**	(1.1)	1.7	(2.4)
	Colombia	6.8	(2.3)	0.3	(4.4)	**-6.2**	(1.7)	-0.3	(3.4)	**-3.3**	(1.9)	0.6	(3.2)
	Croatia	**13.0**	(1.8)	-0.2	(3.7)	1.0	(1.4)	-2.3	(2.7)	**4.4**	(1.3)	0.3	(3.2)
	Estonia	**23.7**	(1.7)	0.9	(3.0)	0.7	(1.6)	-1.9	(3.1)	**-10.9**	(1.5)	-0.5	(2.7)
	Hong Kong-China	**22.6**	(1.5)	0.6	(3.8)	**10.8**	(1.4)	4.2	(4.7)	-1.1	(1.7)	0.2	(3.9)
	Indonesia	**-14.5**	(2.8)	4.4	(2.3)	0.0	(1.8)	4.3	(2.7)	**-9.2**	(1.9)	2.0	(2.0)
	Israel	**26.7**	(1.9)	**-6.2**	(3.6)	**6.5**	(1.6)	0.6	(3.2)	**5.2**	(1.5)	-2.3	(2.8)
	Jordan	**16.9**	(1.8)	**-8.6**	(3.0)	0.1	(1.5)	**6.8**	(2.7)	-0.5	(1.5)	-1.8	(2.8)
	Kyrgyzstan	**-12.4**	(1.7)	4.1	(4.0)	-1.5	(1.7)	3.3	(3.1)	-1.6	(1.4)	-0.5	(2.8)
	Latvia	**14.4**	(2.1)	-4.6	(4.6)	1.4	(1.5)	-0.9	(3.9)	**-9.3**	(1.6)	-3.9	(3.5)
	Lithuania	**20.3**	(1.6)	**-6.6**	(3.8)	**7.6**	(1.5)	-1.0	(3.1)	0.6	(1.6)	2.2	(3.8)
	Macao-China	**12.5**	(1.6)	-3.2	(3.5)	-1.8	(1.2)	-2.7	(3.1)	-2.1	(1.4)	-2.7	(2.7)
	Montenegro	**4.3**	(1.6)	-4.8	(3.0)	**-5.7**	(1.4)	-3.3	(3.1)	**-8.2**	(1.2)	-2.4	(2.7)
	Romania	1.6	(2.4)	-5.5	(3.8)	0.9	(1.4)	1.8	(4.5)	**-8.7**	(1.8)	-4.2	(3.4)
	Russian Federation	**15.2**	(2.0)	**-8.3**	(4.3)	1.3	(1.6)	0.9	(3.3)	**-3.6**	(1.3)	-1.8	(3.4)
	Serbia	**7.1**	(1.3)	**-6.8**	(2.8)	**-7.0**	(1.4)	-1.3	(2.5)	**-4.6**	(1.3)	-3.9	(2.6)
	Slovenia	**12.3**	(1.3)	**-7.0**	(2.8)	**6.0**	(1.4)	-2.1	(3.1)	-2.3	(1.5)	-1.2	(2.4)
	Chinese Taipei	**8.1**	(1.4)	-1.5	(2.7)	1.1	(1.1)	2.2	(2.5)	**6.5**	(1.2)	3.3	(2.4)
	Thailand	-0.3	(1.6)	-0.1	(2.8)	**6.8**	(1.1)	0.3	(2.9)	**-3.8**	(1.4)	-0.1	(2.8)
	Tunisia	**9.9**	(1.4)	-4.2	(2.5)	1.0	(1.2)	1.8	(2.4)	-0.4	(1.3)	0.3	(2.2)
	Uruguay	**13.1**	(1.7)	-4.4	(2.9)	**7.4**	(1.6)	-4.1	(3.5)	**-3.0**	(1.5)	2.3	(2.5)

Note: Values that are statistically different are indicated in bold.

Table A3.2a — Number of science courses and learning hours among disadvantaged and non-disadvantaged students

	Share of students who attended general science compulsory courses						The number of compulsory courses in general science, physics, biology and chemistry*						The number of science regular hours					
	Non-disadvantaged students		Disadvantaged students		Difference		Non-disadvantaged students		Disadvantaged students		Difference		Non-disadvantaged students		Disadvantaged students		Difference	
	%	S.E.	%	S.E.	Dif.	S.E.	Mean	S.E.	Mean	S.E.	Dif.	S.E.	Mean	S.E.	Mean	S.E.	Dif.	S.E.
OECD																		
Australia	88.1	(0.7)	78.0	(0.9)	10.1	(0.9)	3.40	(0.08)	2.59	(0.06)	0.81	(0.07)	3.36	(0.03)	2.82	(0.04)	0.54	(0.04)
Austria	a	a	a	a	a	a	3.43	(0.06)	3.22	(0.07)	0.21	(0.07)	2.58	(0.07)	2.03	(0.06)	0.55	(0.08)
Belgium	63.5	(1.1)	57.0	(2.0)	6.5	(1.9)	3.88	(0.07)	2.77	(0.08)	1.11	(0.09)	2.83	(0.04)	1.97	(0.06)	0.86	(0.06)
Canada	93.2	(0.4)	87.0	(0.7)	6.2	(0.8)	3.43	(0.04)	3.02	(0.05)	0.41	(0.06)	3.99	(0.04)	3.36	(0.04)	0.63	(0.05)
Czech Republic	62.4	(1.0)	61.8	(1.6)	0.7	(1.7)	6.04	(0.09)	5.87	(0.09)	0.17	(0.08)	2.98	(0.07)	2.38	(0.06)	0.60	(0.07)
Denmark	17.7	(0.9)	13.7	(0.9)	4.0	(1.2)	5.31	(0.04)	4.96	(0.07)	0.35	(0.07)	3.28	(0.04)	3.00	(0.05)	0.28	(0.05)
Finland	88.8	(0.9)	86.4	(1.2)	2.4	(1.3)	7.10	(0.05)	6.85	(0.07)	0.25	(0.06)	3.20	(0.04)	2.87	(0.06)	0.33	(0.06)
France	a	a	a	a	a	a	5.47	(0.04)	5.02	(0.06)	0.46	(0.07)	3.10	(0.06)	2.10	(0.05)	1.00	(0.07)
Germany	75.5	(1.1)	64.0	(1.5)	11.5	(1.6)	6.02	(0.05)	5.48	(0.08)	0.53	(0.07)	3.19	(0.04)	2.49	(0.07)	0.70	(0.07)
Greece	a	a	a	a	a	a	4.19	(0.04)	3.62	(0.06)	0.56	(0.07)	3.36	(0.05)	2.58	(0.06)	0.78	(0.07)
Hungary	a	a	a	a	a	a	4.66	(0.06)	4.81	(0.06)	-0.15	(0.07)	2.62	(0.05)	2.16	(0.05)	0.46	(0.07)
Iceland	92.1	(0.5)	91.2	(0.8)	0.9	(0.9)	6.02	(0.04)	5.84	(0.08)	0.17	(0.08)	3.05	(0.03)	2.74	(0.04)	0.32	(0.05)
Ireland	66.3	(2.6)	61.6	(2.7)	4.7	(2.4)	0.86	(0.04)	0.77	(0.03)	0.09	(0.04)	2.64	(0.04)	2.28	(0.07)	0.36	(0.06)
Italy	70.4	(1.5)	79.9	(0.9)	-9.5	(1.5)	3.63	(0.08)	3.96	(0.08)	-0.33	(0.08)	2.88	(0.06)	2.65	(0.06)	0.23	(0.06)
Japan	100.0	v	100.0	v	v	v	3.44	(0.05)	3.11	(0.06)	0.33	(0.06)	2.80	(0.06)	2.45	(0.05)	0.35	(0.05)
Korea	96.8	(0.4)	94.8	(0.7)	2.0	(0.7)	1.84	(0.01)	1.79	(0.02)	0.04	(0.02)	3.67	(0.06)	3.28	(0.07)	0.39	(0.07)
Luxembourg	a	a	a	a	a	a	3.77	(0.03)	3.75	(0.05)	0.02	(0.06)	2.44	(0.03)	1.99	(0.05)	0.44	(0.06)
Mexico	39.9	(0.8)	36.3	(1.5)	3.6	(1.7)	2.68	(0.05)	2.40	(0.07)	0.28	(0.09)	2.97	(0.04)	2.95	(0.07)	0.03	(0.09)
Netherlands	75.5	(1.1)	66.8	(1.8)	8.7	(2.1)	4.71	(0.07)	4.35	(0.10)	0.37	(0.11)	2.27	(0.04)	1.82	(0.06)	0.44	(0.06)
New Zealand	94.6	(0.6)	90.6	(0.9)	4.0	(1.1)	3.62	(0.08)	3.21	(0.09)	0.41	(0.09)	4.18	(0.04)	3.55	(0.07)	0.63	(0.08)
Norway	100.0	v	100.0	v	v	v	2.00	v	2.00	v	v	v	2.69	(0.03)	2.51	(0.05)	0.18	(0.05)
Poland	a	a	a	a	a	a	6.00	v	6.00	v	v	v	2.77	(0.04)	2.51	(0.05)	0.26	(0.05)
Portugal	96.4	(0.4)	93.6	(1.0)	2.9	(0.9)	3.98	(0.05)	3.83	(0.08)	0.15	(0.09)	3.25	(0.05)	2.56	(0.06)	0.69	(0.07)
Slovak Republic	a	a	a	a	a	a	5.03	(0.05)	4.58	(0.06)	0.45	(0.06)	2.60	(0.08)	1.85	(0.06)	0.75	(0.07)
Spain	87.8	(0.7)	89.1	(0.8)	-1.3	(1.0)	5.25	(0.05)	4.92	(0.06)	0.34	(0.06)	3.17	(0.04)	2.65	(0.04)	0.52	(0.05)
Sweden	61.7	(1.5)	53.2	(1.7)	8.5	(2.0)	4.90	(0.09)	4.13	(0.12)	0.77	(0.13)	2.85	(0.03)	2.69	(0.03)	0.15	(0.04)
Switzerland	85.4	(0.7)	78.5	(1.4)	6.8	(1.3)	4.92	(0.06)	4.14	(0.07)	0.78	(0.08)	2.51	(0.05)	1.92	(0.04)	0.60	(0.05)
Turkey	77.6	(1.1)	71.1	(1.6)	6.5	(1.9)	4.20	(0.06)	3.85	(0.09)	0.35	(0.10)	2.85	(0.10)	2.33	(0.09)	0.52	(0.12)
United Kingdom	74.4	(0.9)	64.9	(1.3)	9.5	(1.5)	3.32	(0.05)	2.87	(0.06)	0.45	(0.06)	4.31	(0.03)	3.80	(0.05)	0.51	(0.04)
United States	83.4	(0.8)	76.0	(2.0)	7.4	(2.2)	3.07	(0.05)	2.79	(0.04)	0.28	(0.07)	3.66	(0.04)	2.81	(0.10)	0.85	(0.10)
OECD average	77.9	(0.2)	73.7	(0.3)	4.6	(0.3)	4.21	(0.01)	3.88	(0.01)	0.34	(0.01)	3.07	0.01	2.57	(0.01)	0.50	(0.01)
Partners																		
Argentina	21.8	(1.3)	20.3	(1.2)	1.5	(1.6)	1.29	(0.08)	1.25	(0.07)	0.04	(0.08)	2.35	(0.07)	1.92	(0.06)	0.43	(0.09)
Azerbaijan	a	a	a	a	a	a	3.69	(0.07)	3.35	(0.11)	0.34	(0.12)	2.81	(0.06)	2.56	(0.06)	0.24	(0.07)
Brazil	12.4	(0.8)	9.8	(1.2)	2.6	(1.3)	0.82	(0.05)	0.45	(0.04)	0.37	(0.05)	2.32	(0.03)	1.90	(0.04)	0.42	(0.05)
Bulgaria	a	a	a	a	a	a	4.70	(0.06)	4.72	(0.06)	-0.02	(0.07)	2.74	(0.08)	2.05	(0.08)	0.69	(0.09)
Chile	62.1	(1.0)	53.3	(1.5)	8.8	(1.5)	5.08	(0.09)	3.87	(0.11)	1.21	(0.10)	2.50	(0.05)	1.78	(0.05)	0.72	(0.05)
Colombia	17.4	(1.1)	17.3	(1.6)	0.0	(1.6)	1.07	(0.06)	0.84	(0.07)	0.24	(0.08)	3.46	(0.10)	3.29	(0.12)	0.17	(0.09)
Croatia	a	a	a	a	a	a	4.62	(0.06)	3.81	(0.08)	0.81	(0.06)	2.16	(0.05)	1.66	(0.05)	0.50	(0.05)
Estonia	52.5	(1.0)	46.1	(1.5)	6.4	(1.7)	5.42	(0.08)	4.69	(0.09)	0.73	(0.11)	3.23	(0.04)	2.99	(0.06)	0.24	(0.07)
Hong Kong-China	59.9	(1.9)	57.5	(1.8)	2.5	(2.1)	3.89	(0.07)	3.09	(0.09)	0.80	(0.09)	3.03	(0.06)	2.58	(0.08)	0.45	(0.09)
Indonesia	91.4	(0.8)	88.3	(0.8)	3.1	(1.2)	5.55	(0.08)	5.04	(0.08)	0.51	(0.11)	3.24	(0.08)	2.84	(0.07)	0.40	(0.08)
Israel	74.0	(1.1)	61.5	(1.7)	12.5	(2.0)	3.96	(0.08)	3.08	(0.08)	0.88	(0.10)	2.51	(0.06)	2.02	(0.06)	0.48	(0.07)
Jordan	59.1	(2.0)	50.1	(2.1)	9.0	(2.1)	5.18	(0.08)	4.16	(0.12)	1.03	(0.11)	3.27	(0.06)	2.72	(0.08)	0.55	(0.09)
Kyrgyzstan	70.3	(1.2)	64.3	(1.4)	6.0	(1.7)	4.71	(0.07)	4.26	(0.10)	0.45	(0.10)	2.09	(0.05)	1.81	(0.11)	0.28	(0.11)
Latvia	79.7	(0.8)	75.9	(1.4)	3.8	(1.5)	6.75	(0.05)	6.28	(0.09)	0.47	(0.09)	2.91	(0.06)	2.54	(0.08)	0.37	(0.08)
Lithuania	a	a	a	a	a	a	4.90	(0.05)	4.32	(0.07)	0.59	(0.08)	2.75	(0.04)	2.43	(0.05)	0.32	(0.05)
Macao-China	46.8	(1.1)	35.9	(1.2)	11.0	(1.8)	3.46	(0.06)	2.78	(0.08)	0.68	(0.11)	3.58	(0.03)	3.38	(0.06)	0.19	(0.07)
Montenegro	84.3	(0.7)	78.9	(1.1)	5.4	(1.4)	6.24	(0.04)	5.73	(0.07)	0.51	(0.08)	2.89	(0.05)	2.35	(0.06)	0.53	(0.08)
Romania	38.2	(1.3)	42.5	(1.9)	-4.3	(2.3)	3.04	(0.10)	3.19	(0.19)	-0.15	(0.18)	2.34	(0.07)	1.86	(0.08)	0.48	(0.08)
Russian Federation	3.7	(1.1)	2.6	(0.8)	1.1	(0.7)	5.99	(0.02)	5.91	(0.03)	0.08	(0.03)	3.60	(0.06)	3.26	(0.09)	0.34	(0.07)
Serbia	a	a	a	a	a	a	4.85	(0.04)	4.81	(0.06)	0.03	(0.07)	2.92	(0.06)	2.38	(0.06)	0.54	(0.07)
Slovenia	64.9	(0.8)	70.1	(1.6)	-5.3	(1.6)	6.40	(0.02)	5.90	(0.05)	0.50	(0.06)	2.95	(0.03)	2.21	(0.05)	0.73	(0.06)
Chinese Taipei	46.5	(1.2)	37.2	(1.5)	9.3	(1.9)	4.48	(0.07)	3.82	(0.08)	0.67	(0.06)	3.00	(0.05)	2.43	(0.07)	0.58	(0.07)
Thailand	93.0	(0.5)	88.1	(1.3)	4.9	(1.4)	4.55	(0.08)	4.15	(0.10)	0.40	(0.12)	3.73	(0.04)	3.52	(0.04)	0.21	(0.05)
Tunisia	74.6	(1.2)	68.3	(1.4)	6.3	(2.0)	3.83	(0.06)	3.40	(0.09)	0.43	(0.10)	2.63	(0.05)	2.30	(0.06)	0.33	(0.07)
Uruguay	49.4	(1.2)	39.3	(1.4)	10.2	(1.9)	4.03	(0.08)	2.65	(0.09)	1.38	(0.10)	2.49	(0.05)	1.98	(0.06)	0.51	(0.07)

Note: * the number of additional courses was calculated treating missing values as zeroes.
a - The category does not apply in the country concerned. Data are therefore missing.
v - There is no variation in this indicator in this country.

Table A3.2b — Courses and hours, overall performance effect and differential effect for disadvantaged students

		\multicolumn{4}{c	}{Students who attended general science compulsory courses this or last year}	\multicolumn{4}{c	}{Number of attended compulsory courses in general science, physics, biology and chemistry*}	\multicolumn{4}{c}{Number of hours students report spending in regular lessons at school learning science}
		\multicolumn{2}{c	}{Average association with performance for all students}	\multicolumn{2}{c	}{Differential effect for disadvantaged students}	\multicolumn{2}{c	}{Average association with performance for all students}	\multicolumn{2}{c	}{Differential effect for disadvantaged students}	\multicolumn{2}{c	}{Average association with performance for all students}	\multicolumn{2}{c}{Differential effect for disadvantaged students}
		Coef.	S.E.	Coef.	S.E.	Coef.	S.E.	Coef.	S.E.	Coef.	S.E.	Coef.	S.E.
OECD	Australia	65.6	(2.9)	4.8	(5.6)	6.5	(0.4)	1.7	(0.9)	14.4	(0.5)	0.1	(1.0)
	Austria	a	a	a	a	7.0	(1.2)	-1.8	(2.0)	11.4	(0.9)	2.6	(1.4)
	Belgium	5.7	(2.9)	9.2	(4.7)	8.3	(0.6)	3.8	(0.8)	11.3	(0.6)	1.6	(1.1)
	Canada	58.4	(3.4)	-10.8	(6.8)	1.1	(0.4)	3.3	(0.9)	9.3	(0.5)	-0.3	(0.8)
	Czech Republic	-1.2	(3.4)	-0.5	(6.4)	6.7	(1.2)	0.8	(1.6)	14.3	(0.8)	-1.1	(1.7)
	Denmark	5.1	(4.2)	-8.7	(7.4)	9.4	(1.0)	-0.0	(1.5)	11.8	(1.2)	0.0	(2.2)
	Finland	24.7	(4.7)	18.1	(8.3)	7.4	(0.9)	4.0	(1.7)	14.1	(0.8)	0.8	(1.6)
	France	a	a	a	a	12.9	(1.1)	0.4	(1.8)	14.4	(0.9)	-1.3	(1.7)
	Germany	20.5	(2.8)	-1.9	(4.7)	5.4	(0.6)	-1.1	(1.0)	9.4	(0.6)	-1.4	(1.4)
	Greece	a	a	a	a	10.4	(0.8)	-2.7	(1.3)	15.1	(0.9)	-3.0	(1.6)
	Hungary	a	a	a	a	5.8	(1.3)	-1.1	(2.0)	9.4	(1.0)	-1.0	(1.7)
	Iceland	65.7	(6.7)	-20.4	(13.3)	8.2	(0.7)	-2.3	(1.4)	10.3	(1.2)	0.5	(2.3)
	Ireland	14.3	(3.4)	10.6	(6.2)	13.5	(2.2)	8.4	(4.3)	10.5	(1.0)	0.8	(1.9)
	Italy	-1.6	(3.0)	10.0	(4.6)	3.0	(0.8)	2.0	(1.1)	9.6	(0.7)	1.3	(1.1)
	Japan	v	v	v	v	8.8	(1.9)	2.5	(2.7)	9.6	(1.5)	1.5	(2.7)
	Korea	57.8	(8.6)	22.6	(17.4)	32.2	(4.0)	3.2	(7.3)	9.1	(1.3)	3.4	(2.0)
	Luxembourg	a	a	a	a	3.1	(0.5)	1.8	(1.1)	7.5	(0.7)	2.0	(1.7)
	Mexico	7.6	(1.9)	-8.0	(3.9)	3.2	(0.4)	-0.6	(0.9)	2.2	(0.4)	-1.5	(0.9)
	Netherlands	21.6	(2.8)	13.2	(5.7)	8.1	(0.8)	2.3	(1.3)	11.4	(0.7)	2.7	(1.5)
	New Zealand	61.5	(7.4)	28.9	(11.0)	2.6	(0.6)	2.8	(1.1)	18.4	(0.9)	-0.8	(1.7)
	Norway	v	v	v	v	v	v	v	v	10.4	(1.3)	0.9	(3.3)
	Poland	a	a	a	a	v	v	v	v	12.4	(0.8)	0.3	(1.6)
	Portugal	24.4	(5.9)	-5.4	(9.5)	1.5	(0.5)	0.2	(1.1)	6.8	(0.5)	-2.6	(1.2)
	Slovak Republic	a	a	a	a	13.7	(1.1)	-1.3	(1.8)	14.5	(0.9)	1.9	(1.4)
	Spain	-10.3	(3.2)	11.6	(6.8)	2.9	(0.5)	2.4	(0.9)	11.0	(0.6)	-0.3	(1.2)
	Sweden	31.0	(3.3)	5.2	(5.8)	5.7	(0.5)	0.4	(0.8)	12.0	(1.4)	4.6	(2.7)
	Switzerland	34.1	(3.0)	5.0	(4.8)	8.8	(0.5)	0.1	(0.9)	13.4	(0.7)	-1.6	(1.3)
	Turkey	13.5	(3.5)	2.3	(6.1)	5.6	(0.6)	-0.4	(1.3)	9.3	(0.6)	-1.9	(1.1)
	United Kingdom	35.2	(3.4)	15.9	(7.2)	8.5	(0.7)	2.3	(1.5)	21.6	(1.0)	-2.3	(1.6)
	United States	15.4	(5.4)	26.6	(8.1)	-0.5	(1.1)	4.1	(1.8)	12.9	(0.9)	-0.6	(1.7)
	OECD average	**26.2**	**(1.0)**	**6.1**	**(1.7)**	**7.5**	**(0.2)**	**1.2**	**(0.4)**	**11.6**	**(0.2)**	**0.2**	**(0.3)**
Partners	Argentina	-13.1	(4.5)	8.8	(10.5)	-1.6	(0.9)	0.7	(1.8)	9.9	(1.0)	-3.2	(2.3)
	Azerbaijan	a	a	a	a	5.3	(0.6)	0.9	(1.3)	5.6	(0.7)	-1.3	(1.1)
	Brazil	-8.5	(4.2)	-16.5	(10.4)	1.4	(0.8)	-3.3	(1.9)	11.1	(0.9)	-1.6	(1.6)
	Bulgaria	a	a	a	a	8.9	(1.0)	1.1	(1.9)	10.5	(0.9)	-0.8	(1.9)
	Chile	15.2	(2.5)	-0.3	(5.4)	5.3	(0.4)	-0.6	(0.6)	8.9	(0.7)	0.2	(1.5)
	Colombia	-2.3	(4.3)	-3.1	(8.8)	-0.2	(1.1)	-0.8	(1.6)	5.7	(0.9)	-1.7	(1.9)
	Croatia	a	a	a	a	16.7	(0.9)	-2.0	(1.5)	8.9	(0.9)	0.4	(1.2)
	Estonia	6.1	(2.8)	-0.3	(6.5)	6.0	(0.7)	-1.2	(1.2)	13.3	(0.8)	-2.8	(1.7)
	Hong Kong-China	6.4	(3.9)	12.5	(6.4)	9.5	(0.8)	-1.4	(1.3)	10.6	(0.6)	0.4	(1.1)
	Indonesia	9.3	(2.6)	-1.2	(6.2)	2.6	(0.4)	-0.0	(0.8)	8.5	(1.0)	-3.2	(1.3)
	Israel	26.4	(4.0)	-20.2	(7.7)	8.9	(0.8)	-4.0	(1.6)	14.8	(1.0)	-2.5	(1.9)
	Jordan	4.4	(3.4)	7.0	(5.2)	6.3	(0.5)	-1.5	(0.9)	9.6	(0.6)	-4.5	(1.5)
	Kyrgyzstan	10.6	(3.0)	-8.1	(4.6)	5.6	(0.6)	-2.4	(1.0)	7.6	(0.7)	-3.7	(1.2)
	Latvia	22.2	(3.7)	1.2	(7.5)	12.3	(0.8)	-1.6	(1.6)	11.0	(0.6)	1.9	(1.9)
	Lithuania	a	a	a	a	12.0	(0.5)	-0.7	(1.0)	12.0	(0.7)	-0.5	(1.5)
	Macao-China	21.4	(2.9)	3.9	(4.8)	5.7	(0.4)	-0.6	(0.8)	9.2	(0.5)	-2.9	(1.2)
	Montenegro	24.2	(3.0)	0.2	(5.9)	9.9	(0.5)	-0.6	(1.0)	9.6	(0.6)	-2.3	(1.3)
	Romania	-1.6	(3.2)	-1.9	(4.7)	3.0	(0.6)	1.4	(1.0)	8.9	(0.8)	-2.8	(2.1)
	Russian Federation	4.4	(6.9)	12.0	(14.8)	3.4	(2.2)	1.3	(3.4)	10.1	(0.8)	0.9	(1.2)
	Serbia	a	a	a	a	4.5	(0.7)	0.7	(1.4)	10.6	(0.8)	-2.1	(1.6)
	Slovenia	-21.6	(2.9)	0.3	(7.1)	5.6	(0.7)	3.5	(1.6)	10.4	(0.7)	-0.4	(1.3)
	Chinese Taipei	16.4	(3.1)	9.2	(5.5)	4.7	(0.6)	0.2	(0.9)	13.8	(0.7)	2.0	(1.4)
	Thailand	29.3	(3.2)	-5.1	(6.0)	1.9	(0.5)	-0.5	(1.0)	15.7	(1.0)	-2.2	(1.7)
	Tunisia	5.3	(2.6)	-8.6	(5.1)	2.3	(0.5)	-1.8	(1.0)	5.6	(0.7)	-1.1	(1.3)
	Uruguay	19.1	(2.5)	-12.1	(6.6)	5.7	(0.4)	-1.8	(1.0)	7.9	(0.7)	-1.0	(1.5)

Note: * the number of additional courses was calculated treating missing values as zeroes.
a - The category does not apply in the country concerned. Data are therefore missing.
v - There is no variation in this indicator in this country.

[Part 1/2] **Learning environment at school among disadvantaged and non-disadvantaged students**
Table A3.3a

		Share of students in private schools			Share of students in schools which compete for students			Share of students in schools which select students based on academic record		
		Non-disadvantaged students	Disadvantaged students	Difference	Non-disadvantaged students	Disadvantaged students	Difference	Non-disadvantaged students	Disadvantaged students	Difference
		% S.E.	% S.E.	Dif. S.E.	% S.E.	% S.E.	Dif. S.E.	% S.E.	% S.E.	Dif. S.E.
OECD	Australia	w w	w w	w w	94.7 (1.0)	91.5 (1.7)	3.3 (1.2)	9.6 (1.9)	9.0 (2.0)	0.6 (1.8)
	Austria	10.0 (2.1)	8.1 (3.0)	1.9 (2.2)	69.0 (3.5)	54.8 (4.3)	14.2 (3.3)	71.9 (2.4)	52.1 (2.5)	19.8 (2.8)
	Belgium	w w	w w	w w	90.6 (2.1)	90.7 (2.4)	-0.1 (2.0)	25.6 (2.7)	25.9 (3.1)	-0.2 (2.5)
	Canada	9.5 (0.8)	3.2 (0.5)	6.3 (0.8)	78.2 (2.4)	74.0 (2.5)	4.2 (1.6)	12.7 (1.4)	6.4 (1.0)	6.4 (1.1)
	Czech Republic	7.2 (2.9)	5.4 (2.6)	1.8 (1.8)	87.4 (2.4)	82.9 (3.1)	4.5 (2.0)	45.6 (3.4)	35.4 (3.8)	10.2 (3.0)
	Denmark	26.0 (3.3)	20.5 (3.2)	5.5 (2.4)	76.6 (3.5)	79.2 (3.3)	-2.6 (2.1)	4.2 (1.7)	3.5 (1.5)	0.7 (1.1)
	Finland	3.5 (1.4)	1.9 (1.0)	1.6 (1.0)	59.3 (4.0)	49.5 (3.4)	9.8 (2.0)	5.0 (2.3)	2.8 (1.3)	2.3 (1.6)
	France	w w	w w	w w	w w	w w	w w	w w	w w	w w
	Germany	7.0 (2.2)	3.5 (1.2)	3.5 (1.5)	85.1 (2.5)	78.1 (3.5)	7.0 (2.5)	42.7 (4.0)	30.7 (4.0)	12.0 (2.9)
	Greece	7.6 (1.8)	0.3 (0.2)	7.4 (1.7)	62.6 (3.7)	54.0 (3.9)	8.7 (3.4)	6.4 (2.5)	0.7 (0.5)	5.7 (2.3)
	Hungary	19.9 (4.2)	8.8 (2.5)	11.1 (3.8)	77.0 (3.9)	73.1 (4.2)	3.9 (3.6)	71.9 (4.0)	49.8 (4.7)	22.2 (4.2)
	Iceland	1.4 (0.1)	0.5 (0.2)	1.0 (0.3)	28.3 (0.7)	26.6 (0.9)	1.7 (1.4)	0.8 (0.1)	1.8 (0.3)	-1.1 (0.4)
	Ireland	66.9 (1.4)	48.6 (2.2)	18.3 (2.5)	84.7 (2.7)	81.1 (3.0)	3.6 (1.8)	2.5 (1.2)	2.7 (1.4)	-0.2 (0.8)
	Italy	4.2 (0.8)	3.2 (0.9)	1.0 (0.8)	81.3 (2.5)	79.8 (2.7)	1.5 (1.5)	6.6 (1.5)	7.9 (2.6)	-1.3 (2.0)
	Japan	34.5 (1.1)	24.2 (2.7)	10.4 (2.5)	90.2 (2.3)	88.3 (3.1)	1.9 (2.7)	86.1 (2.7)	86.9 (3.0)	-0.7 (2.6)
	Korea	44.4 (3.8)	50.2 (5.1)	-5.7 (3.8)	81.7 (3.4)	89.7 (2.5)	-8.0 (2.3)	56.4 (4.2)	64.3 (4.8)	-7.8 (3.9)
	Luxembourg	13.9 (0.4)	15.6 (0.8)	-1.7 (1.2)	68.1 (0.5)	64.2 (0.9)	3.9 (1.3)	39.0 (0.6)	46.9 (1.1)	-7.9 (1.7)
	Mexico	20.9 (2.7)	3.1 (1.3)	17.8 (2.4)	88.0 (1.4)	76.8 (4.0)	11.2 (3.6)	43.1 (2.6)	28.0 (4.2)	15.1 (3.4)
	Netherlands	67.2 (4.1)	68.9 (5.5)	-1.7 (3.5)	90.9 (2.0)	87.0 (2.8)	3.9 (1.9)	66.5 (3.8)	63.0 (4.8)	3.6 (2.9)
	New Zealand	8.0 (0.5)	1.5 (0.4)	6.5 (0.6)	88.8 (2.2)	90.1 (2.4)	-1.4 (2.0)	10.4 (2.1)	7.3 (2.3)	3.2 (1.4)
	Norway	2.4 (1.2)	1.1 (0.5)	1.4 (0.9)	37.2 (3.8)	28.3 (3.8)	8.9 (2.7)	0.0 (0.0)	0.0 (0.0)	0.0 (0.0)
	Poland	2.2 (0.2)	0.3 (0.1)	1.9 (0.2)	71.5 (3.3)	51.4 (4.6)	20.1 (3.3)	15.8 (3.0)	8.7 (1.8)	7.1 (2.3)
	Portugal	11.2 (1.4)	8.0 (1.3)	3.2 (0.9)	76.8 (3.8)	64.8 (4.8)	12.0 (3.3)	6.8 (2.2)	6.6 (2.6)	0.2 (2.3)
	Slovak Republic	9.0 (2.1)	5.1 (1.8)	4.0 (1.6)	94.2 (1.6)	86.0 (3.7)	8.2 (2.9)	49.0 (2.4)	41.4 (3.8)	7.6 (3.0)
	Spain	43.4 (1.2)	19.6 (1.5)	23.8 (2.0)	82.3 (2.2)	74.8 (3.0)	7.5 (2.4)	4.0 (1.4)	1.0 (0.6)	3.0 (1.7)
	Sweden	10.3 (0.8)	4.7 (1.1)	5.6 (0.9)	66.9 (3.6)	55.0 (4.1)	11.9 (1.7)	2.5 (1.0)	0.6 (0.3)	1.9 (1.0)
	Switzerland	6.3 (0.7)	2.6 (0.7)	3.7 (0.7)	44.2 (2.9)	36.3 (3.0)	7.9 (2.6)	52.6 (2.7)	48.4 (2.9)	4.2 (2.3)
	Turkey	3.2 (2.0)	0.6 (0.6)	2.5 (1.8)	73.7 (3.8)	57.7 (4.9)	16.0 (3.4)	33.8 (4.0)	19.6 (3.0)	14.2 (3.0)
	United Kingdom	10.5 (0.8)	2.0 (0.9)	8.4 (0.8)	91.6 (1.6)	93.6 (1.3)	-2.0 (0.9)	13.5 (1.8)	2.6 (0.5)	10.9 (1.6)
	United States	10.4 (1.3)	2.7 (0.9)	7.7 (1.2)	75.4 (3.2)	71.4 (3.9)	3.9 (3.4)	9.1 (2.1)	5.7 (1.9)	3.4 (1.9)
	OECD average	17.1 (0.4)	11.6 (0.4)	5.4 (0.4)	75.7 (0.5)	70.0 (0.6)	5.7 (0.5)	27.4 (0.5)	22.7 (0.5)	4.6 (0.4)
Partners	Argentina	44.1 (4.5)	14.8 (2.6)	29.3 (4.2)	86.7 (2.6)	68.3 (5.1)	18.4 (3.4)	9.0 (2.7)	3.4 (1.7)	5.6 (2.6)
	Azerbaijan	1.4 (0.6)	0.0 (0.0)	1.4 (0.6)	m m	m m	m m	17.9 (3.3)	15.9 (3.8)	2.0 (3.5)
	Brazil	20.0 (1.6)	0.7 (0.2)	19.2 (1.5)	73.3 (2.5)	55.2 (3.2)	18.2 (3.0)	8.8 (1.8)	6.5 (2.4)	2.3 (2.6)
	Bulgaria	m m	m m	m m	88.5 (3.0)	77.8 (4.7)	10.7 (3.9)	89.9 (2.3)	72.0 (4.0)	18.0 (3.0)
	Chile	65.4 (2.0)	38.5 (4.4)	27.0 (4.3)	85.9 (2.7)	70.9 (5.8)	15.0 (4.8)	38.0 (3.9)	21.9 (4.8)	16.1 (4.5)
	Colombia	25.2 (3.2)	7.1 (2.3)	18.1 (2.8)	79.0 (4.3)	69.5 (7.2)	9.5 (4.9)	23.7 (3.9)	11.8 (2.7)	11.9 (3.0)
	Croatia	2.0 (1.4)	0.2 (0.1)	1.8 (1.3)	78.1 (3.5)	74.8 (4.0)	3.4 (2.5)	93.1 (1.7)	85.5 (2.9)	7.6 (2.3)
	Estonia	2.5 (1.2)	0.9 (0.5)	1.6 (0.9)	80.5 (2.5)	74.9 (3.3)	5.6 (2.2)	49.9 (3.5)	33.1 (3.6)	16.8 (2.4)
	Hong Kong-China	91.7 (0.6)	94.2 (1.1)	-2.5 (1.6)	98.4 (1.1)	99.4 (0.6)	-1.0 (0.9)	84.1 (3.4)	80.4 (3.5)	3.6 (2.6)
	Indonesia	37.2 (3.7)	45.3 (3.9)	-8.1 (3.2)	95.9 (1.5)	92.6 (2.0)	3.3 (1.8)	68.3 (4.6)	52.0 (4.8)	16.3 (3.9)
	Israel	32.5 (4.0)	26.8 (4.5)	5.7 (3.1)	80.3 (3.5)	84.3 (3.6)	-2.3 (3.3)	38.0 (4.9)	31.0 (4.8)	7.0 (3.9)
	Jordan	24.5 (2.2)	11.1 (1.0)	13.5 (2.3)	58.4 (4.1)	50.6 (4.3)	7.8 (2.7)	29.5 (3.8)	22.0 (3.7)	7.6 (3.5)
	Kyrgyzstan	2.2 (1.1)	0.1 (0.1)	2.1 (1.0)	65.7 (2.9)	63.3 (3.5)	2.4 (2.5)	22.9 (3.3)	22.3 (3.8)	0.7 (2.7)
	Latvia	0.0 (0.0)	0.0 (0.0)	0.0 (0.0)	96.3 (1.6)	95.1 (2.0)	1.2 (1.7)	21.2 (2.8)	10.3 (1.9)	10.9 (1.7)
	Lithuania	1.1 (1.1)	0.0 (0.0)	1.1 (1.1)	76.1 (3.1)	65.7 (3.7)	10.4 (3.3)	14.5 (3.0)	4.3 (1.2)	10.1 (2.4)
	Macao-China	97.9 (0.2)	92.9 (0.3)	5.0 (0.5)	88.4 (0.3)	91.3 (0.5)	-3.0 (0.8)	66.0 (0.5)	67.2 (1.0)	-1.3 (1.5)
	Montenegro	0.3 (0.0)	0.0 (0.0)	0.3 (0.0)	99.1 (0.1)	97.2 (0.4)	1.9 (0.5)	69.7 (0.6)	61.1 (1.1)	8.5 (1.7)
	Romania	0.0 (0.0)	0.0 (0.0)	0.0 (0.0)	57.9 (6.0)	48.5 (5.4)	9.4 (4.4)	64.9 (4.1)	55.0 (5.5)	9.9 (4.1)
	Russian Federation	0.0 (0.0)	0.0 (0.0)	0.0 (0.0)	67.8 (4.4)	68.4 (4.7)	-0.5 (3.0)	11.7 (2.6)	9.2 (1.7)	2.5 (2.2)
	Serbia	0.6 (0.6)	0.7 (0.7)	-0.1 (0.1)	73.4 (3.7)	71.8 (4.3)	1.7 (3.2)	93.4 (1.8)	87.2 (3.2)	6.1 (2.2)
	Slovenia	3.2 (0.1)	0.6 (0.2)	2.6 (0.3)	57.3 (0.5)	42.5 (1.3)	14.9 (1.4)	43.8 (0.6)	26.8 (1.2)	17.0 (1.7)
	Chinese Taipei	35.0 (1.9)	35.5 (4.4)	-0.5 (3.7)	94.2 (2.0)	92.7 (2.7)	1.5 (1.9)	57.9 (2.9)	42.4 (4.4)	15.5 (3.5)
	Thailand	19.4 (0.9)	10.7 (2.0)	8.7 (2.5)	88.8 (2.9)	87.3 (3.4)	1.5 (2.4)	46.7 (4.3)	37.1 (5.0)	9.6 (4.6)
	Tunisia	2.9 (1.2)	1.1 (0.5)	1.8 (0.9)	53.8 (5.4)	45.9 (5.7)	7.9 (4.5)	22.6 (3.8)	25.6 (4.8)	-3.1 (4.2)
	Uruguay	21.9 (1.1)	1.3 (0.3)	20.6 (1.1)	54.9 (2.6)	34.3 (3.9)	20.5 (2.7)	9.4 (1.9)	8.3 (2.1)	1.1 (2.3)

Note:
m - Data are not available. These data were collected but subsequently removed from the publication for technical reasons.
w - Data have been withdrawn at the request of the country concerned.

Table A3.3a [Part 2/2] **Learning environment at school among disadvantaged and non-disadvantaged students**

		Index of school activities to promote the learning of science						Index of the quality of school educational resources					
		Non-disadvantaged students		Disadvantaged students		Difference		Non-disadvantaged students		Disadvantaged students		Difference	
		Mean	S.E.	Mean	S.E.	Dif.	S.E.	Mean	S.E.	Mean	S.E.	Dif.	S.E.
OECD	Australia	0.44	(0.04)	0.34	(0.04)	**0.10**	(0.03)	0.51	(0.05)	0.20	(0.06)	**0.32**	(0.05)
	Austria	-0.25	(0.08)	-0.65	(0.07)	**0.41**	(0.06)	0.38	(0.09)	0.33	(0.10)	0.05	(0.08)
	Belgium	-0.17	(0.05)	-0.33	(0.07)	**0.15**	(0.04)	-0.04	(0.06)	-0.02	(0.07)	-0.02	(0.05)
	Canada	0.44	(0.04)	0.36	(0.04)	**0.09**	(0.03)	0.11	(0.06)	0.03	(0.05)	0.08	(0.04)
	Czech Republic	0.53	(0.07)	0.31	(0.07)	**0.21**	(0.05)	-0.04	(0.07)	-0.14	(0.07)	**0.10**	(0.05)
	Denmark	-0.81	(0.07)	-0.86	(0.07)	0.05	(0.04)	-0.06	(0.06)	-0.14	(0.07)	0.08	(0.05)
	Finland	-0.58	(0.05)	-0.64	(0.07)	0.06	(0.04)	-0.23	(0.07)	-0.23	(0.05)	0.00	(0.05)
	France	w	w	w	w	w	w	w	w	w	w	w	w
	Germany	0.02	(0.05)	-0.34	(0.06)	**0.36**	(0.05)	0.12	(0.08)	0.07	(0.08)	0.05	(0.06)
	Greece	-0.34	(0.07)	-0.58	(0.07)	**0.24**	(0.06)	0.04	(0.09)	-0.15	(0.07)	**0.18**	(0.07)
	Hungary	0.70	(0.06)	0.46	(0.07)	**0.24**	(0.06)	0.22	(0.07)	0.15	(0.08)	0.08	(0.07)
	Iceland	-0.69	(0.01)	-0.74	(0.02)	**0.05**	(0.02)	0.24	(0.01)	0.12	(0.02)	**0.12**	(0.03)
	Ireland	0.16	(0.08)	0.04	(0.08)	**0.12**	(0.06)	-0.32	(0.08)	-0.32	(0.08)	-0.00	(0.06)
	Italy	0.08	(0.04)	-0.14	(0.05)	**0.23**	(0.04)	0.23	(0.05)	0.09	(0.06)	**0.14**	(0.04)
	Japan	-1.07	(0.08)	-1.31	(0.08)	**0.24**	(0.06)	0.50	(0.07)	0.34	(0.08)	**0.17**	(0.06)
	Korea	0.63	(0.07)	0.37	(0.09)	**0.27**	(0.06)	-0.19	(0.07)	-0.19	(0.09)	-0.00	(0.07)
	Luxembourg	0.27	(0.01)	-0.08	(0.02)	**0.35**	(0.03)	0.25	(0.01)	0.28	(0.02)	-0.03	(0.03)
	Mexico	0.12	(0.04)	-0.32	(0.06)	**0.45**	(0.06)	-0.66	(0.06)	-1.25	(0.06)	**0.58**	(0.06)
	Netherlands	-0.41	(0.08)	-0.70	(0.09)	**0.29**	(0.05)	0.27	(0.07)	0.24	(0.08)	0.02	(0.06)
	New Zealand	0.54	(0.06)	0.44	(0.07)	0.10	(0.06)	0.37	(0.06)	0.19	(0.08)	**0.17**	(0.06)
	Norway	-0.48	(0.05)	-0.53	(0.06)	0.06	(0.05)	-0.42	(0.05)	-0.46	(0.05)	0.03	(0.03)
	Poland	0.64	(0.05)	0.46	(0.05)	**0.18**	(0.04)	-0.07	(0.07)	-0.13	(0.07)	0.06	(0.05)
	Portugal	0.65	(0.06)	0.68	(0.09)	-0.03	(0.07)	-0.38	(0.06)	-0.39	(0.07)	0.01	(0.05)
	Slovak Republic	0.76	(0.06)	0.58	(0.06)	**0.18**	(0.05)	-0.57	(0.05)	-0.50	(0.07)	-0.07	(0.06)
	Spain	0.23	(0.07)	0.13	(0.07)	0.10	(0.05)	0.04	(0.06)	-0.13	(0.07)	**0.16**	(0.05)
	Sweden	-0.47	(0.07)	-0.52	(0.09)	0.05	(0.05)	0.09	(0.07)	-0.04	(0.07)	**0.13**	(0.05)
	Switzerland	-0.19	(0.04)	-0.37	(0.04)	**0.17**	(0.03)	0.70	(0.07)	0.62	(0.07)	0.08	(0.05)
	Turkey	-0.03	(0.09)	-0.41	(0.10)	**0.38**	(0.09)	-0.80	(0.10)	-0.91	(0.07)	0.11	(0.06)
	United Kingdom	0.44	(0.06)	0.36	(0.07)	0.07	(0.05)	0.34	(0.09)	0.12	(0.08)	**0.22**	(0.07)
	United States	0.49	(0.08)	0.44	(0.11)	0.05	(0.09)	0.32	(0.08)	0.22	(0.11)	0.10	(0.09)
	OECD average	0.06	(0.01)	-0.12	(0.01)	**0.18**	(0.01)	0.03	(0.01)	-0.07	(0.01)	**0.10**	(0.01)
Partners	Argentina	0.13	(0.08)	0.07	(0.08)	0.06	(0.09)	-0.38	(0.10)	-0.87	(0.09)	**0.49**	(0.10)
	Azerbaijan	0.34	(0.08)	0.13	(0.08)	**0.21**	(0.07)	-1.32	(0.05)	-1.47	(0.07)	**0.16**	(0.06)
	Brazil	0.29	(0.04)	0.15	(0.05)	**0.14**	(0.05)	-0.71	(0.07)	-1.49	(0.06)	**0.78**	(0.07)
	Bulgaria	0.15	(0.07)	-0.24	(0.08)	**0.39**	(0.08)	-0.55	(0.06)	-0.64	(0.07)	0.09	(0.06)
	Chile	-0.12	(0.11)	-0.57	(0.18)	**0.45**	(0.15)	-0.47	(0.08)	-0.95	(0.14)	**0.48**	(0.12)
	Colombia	0.89	(0.06)	0.69	(0.11)	**0.20**	(0.08)	-1.03	(0.08)	-1.46	(0.09)	**0.43**	(0.07)
	Croatia	0.21	(0.08)	0.03	(0.10)	**0.19**	(0.07)	-0.54	(0.06)	-0.59	(0.07)	0.05	(0.06)
	Estonia	0.92	(0.04)	0.85	(0.05)	**0.07**	(0.03)	-0.27	(0.05)	-0.31	(0.05)	0.04	(0.04)
	Hong Kong-China	0.93	(0.06)	0.89	(0.07)	0.04	(0.05)	0.37	(0.08)	0.30	(0.09)	0.07	(0.06)
	Indonesia	0.08	(0.10)	-0.28	(0.11)	**0.36**	(0.10)	-1.46	(0.10)	-1.95	(0.11)	**0.49**	(0.12)
	Israel	0.19	(0.10)	0.24	(0.09)	-0.05	(0.08)	0.11	(0.09)	-0.02	(0.11)	0.13	(0.07)
	Jordan	0.91	(0.08)	0.81	(0.07)	0.10	(0.05)	-0.63	(0.08)	-0.95	(0.09)	**0.33**	(0.07)
	Kyrgyzstan	0.79	(0.05)	0.69	(0.07)	**0.09**	(0.04)	-2.23	(0.07)	-2.48	(0.07)	**0.25**	(0.06)
	Latvia	0.20	(0.03)	0.18	(0.04)	0.02	(0.04)	-0.53	(0.05)	-0.54	(0.06)	0.00	(0.04)
	Lithuania	1.24	(0.04)	1.09	(0.05)	**0.15**	(0.03)	-0.37	(0.05)	-0.42	(0.05)	0.05	(0.04)
	Macao-China	0.44	(0.01)	0.47	(0.01)	-0.03	(0.02)	0.05	(0.01)	0.09	(0.01)	**-0.04**	(0.02)
	Montenegro	0.36	(0.01)	0.31	(0.02)	0.05	(0.04)	-1.28	(0.01)	-1.22	(0.02)	-0.06	(0.03)
	Romania	0.86	(0.09)	0.60	(0.09)	**0.25**	(0.06)	-0.67	(0.07)	-0.90	(0.09)	**0.24**	(0.08)
	Russian Federation	1.22	(0.05)	1.14	(0.05)	**0.08**	(0.04)	-1.13	(0.05)	-1.28	(0.05)	**0.15**	(0.06)
	Serbia	0.40	(0.08)	0.13	(0.09)	**0.27**	(0.07)	-0.70	(0.06)	-0.67	(0.05)	-0.03	(0.05)
	Slovenia	1.21	(0.01)	1.03	(0.02)	**0.17**	(0.02)	0.22	(0.01)	0.21	(0.03)	0.02	(0.03)
	Chinese Taipei	0.87	(0.05)	0.56	(0.09)	**0.30**	(0.07)	0.71	(0.10)	0.36	(0.20)	**0.35**	(0.16)
	Thailand	1.36	(0.06)	1.30	(0.06)	0.06	(0.06)	-0.46	(0.07)	-1.09	(0.08)	**0.63**	(0.08)
	Tunisia	0.40	(0.08)	0.29	(0.12)	0.11	(0.11)	-0.67	(0.06)	-0.73	(0.07)	0.06	(0.06)
	Uruguay	0.00	(0.05)	-0.04	(0.07)	0.04	(0.06)	-0.51	(0.07)	-1.13	(0.09)	**0.62**	(0.08)

Note:
m - Data are not available. These data were collected but subsequently removed from the publication for technical reasons.
w - Data have been withdrawn at the request of the country concerned.

Table A3.3b [Part 1/2] Learning environment at school, overall performance effect and differential effect for disadvantaged students

		Students in private schools				Students in schools which compete for students				Students in schools wchich select based on academic record			
		Average association with performance for all students		Differential effect for disadvantaged students		Average association with performance for all students		Differential effect for disadvantaged students		Average association with performance for all students		Differential effect for disadvantaged students	
		Coef.	S.E.	Coef.	S.E.	Coef.	S.E.	Coef.	S.E.	Coef.	S.E.	Coef.	S.E.
OECD	Australia	w	w	w	w	-3.8	(6.3)	-2.4	(7.2)	13.1	(9.6)	c	c
	Austria	-0.0	(10.5)	c	c	10.3	(6.9)	0.9	(6.4)	**46.3**	(7.2)	11.3	(7.0)
	Belgium	1.8	(4.3)	w	w	1.1	(7.1)	-21.0	(8.5)	**11.6**	(4.5)	1.9	(5.1)
	Canada	17.7	(4.8)	c	c	2.2	(3.6)	5.5	(5.5)	11.5	(8.9)	c	c
	Czech Republic	**-38.5**	(9.4)	c	c	-3.8	(8.4)	-11.8	(8.2)	**31.7**	(9.7)	-6.9	(6.7)
	Denmark	-0.9	(6.8)	-4.5	(7.8)	-8.1	(4.2)	-7.4	(8.0)	0.5	(8.2)	c	c
	Finland	c	c	c	c	-1.4	(3.5)	-7.7	(5.1)	6.6	(13.3)	c	c
	France	w	w	w	w	w	w	w	w	w	w	w	w
	Germany	-8.2	(15.7)	c	c	4.7	(5.5)	-1.3	(8.1)	**12.0**	(5.9)	1.6	(6.6)
	Greece	-7.8	(13.7)	c	c	-4.8	(6.1)	3.0	(6.7)	-8.7	(10.9)	c	c
	Hungary	-14.8	(9.8)	c	c	0.6	(6.3)	10.4	(7.7)	**23.0**	(7.1)	9.8	(6.9)
	Iceland	c	c	c	c	4.2	(3.7)	**-17.6**	(7.4)	c	c	c	c
	Ireland	4.9	(4.7)	-8.4	(6.8)	-6.7	(5.3)	**-21.8**	(6.2)	c	c	c	c
	Italy	**-34.2**	(13.2)	c	c	9.7	(7.2)	9.9	(7.3)	-3.6	(14.0)	c	c
	Japan	**-57.3**	(6.6)	-3.4	(8.0)	**-30.1**	(9.8)	8.5	(15.5)	19.5	(11.5)	-12.3	(10.6)
	Korea	-1.5	(6.1)	-5.6	(8.2)	**15.7**	(5.7)	-17.2	(10.1)	**17.2**	(5.4)	-1.9	(7.3)
	Luxembourg	**-10.0**	(3.4)	9.9	(5.9)	-2.3	(2.5)	**14.0**	(4.7)	**8.6**	(2.5)	5.1	(5.2)
	Mexico	**-31.5**	(5.5)	c	c	-4.1	(4.0)	-1.6	(7.1)	**15.2**	(3.3)	-7.4	(6.0)
	Netherlands	4.6	(5.7)	-1.2	(6.4)	-2.3	(12.7)	9.8	(7.4)	9.9	(7.1)	-7.5	(5.6)
	New Zealand	8.6	(6.0)	c	c	-2.3	(5.6)	2.4	(10.4)	8.9	(6.1)	c	c
	Norway	c	c	c	c	-1.6	(4.8)	4.9	(7.7)	0.0	0.0	c	c
	Poland	c	c	c	c	3.2	(4.4)	-3.3	(5.4)	10.7	(6.1)	c	c
	Portugal	7.1	(6.2)	c	c	1.6	(4.2)	-9.1	(5.6)	**-19.7**	(7.4)	c	c
	Slovak Republic	**-22.1**	(9.2)	c	c	-6.9	(11.2)	17.6	(16.6)	7.8	(7.5)	0.6	(10.0)
	Spain	-6.8	(3.5)	-1.2	(5.1)	-0.5	(3.3)	**-11.7**	(6.3)	c	c	c	c
	Sweden	12.4	(7.2)	c	c	4.6	(4.5)	-5.1	(9.2)	c	c	c	c
	Switzerland	**-50.3**	(16.7)	c	c	4.6	(4.9)	-4.9	(5.6)	**18.5**	(4.7)	**-17.8**	(5.2)
	Turkey	c	c	c	c	2.4	(6.0)	2.3	(6.5)	**20.8**	(6.8)	-4.5	(5.8)
	United Kingdom	10.3	(12.5)	c	c	**-10.0**	(6.5)	c	c	**43.4**	(12.0)	c	c
	United States	1.5	(8.7)	c	c	0.2	(5.9)	-7.6	(8.1)	-3.5	(9.5)	c	c
	OECD average	**-9.3**	**(1.9)**	**-2.1**	**(2.6)**	**-0.8**	**(1.2)**	**-2.3**	**(1.5)**	**12.0**	**(1.7)**	**-2.1**	**(1.9)**
Partners	Argentina	5.2	(7.5)	-2.2	(10.1)	14.9	(9.6)	-7.6	(11.1)	6.7	(8.1)	c	c
	Azerbaijan	c	c	c	c	m	m	m	m	3.9	(6.3)	-5.0	(7.3)
	Brazil	-10.8	(8.3)	c	c	**-8.4**	(4.0)	5.1	(5.7)	9.8	(9.3)	c	c
	Bulgaria	m	m	m	m	-4.2	(9.8)	-9.4	(11.6)	-0.6	(8.3)	-17.3	(9.6)
	Chile	-1.4	(5.5)	14.3	(7.4)	-2.9	(5.8)	-5.8	(7.7)	**14.7**	(5.4)	2.7	(8.8)
	Colombia	0.3	(12.8)	c	c	5.8	(7.4)	-8.3	(8.1)	9.5	(6.6)	10.9	(8.2)
	Croatia	c	c	c	c	-5.2	(7.0)	7.8	(7.0)	**23.5**	(9.5)	**-21.0**	(9.1)
	Estonia	c	c	c	c	-2.5	(5.8)	-0.5	(8.6)	2.8	(4.0)	-3.2	(7.8)
	Hong Kong-China	**-13.0**	(6.3)	19.8	(13.4)	c	c	c	c	10.2	(9.6)	3.5	(9.3)
	Indonesia	**-15.0**	(7.1)	5.6	(6.8)	**17.2**	(6.1)	c	c	**13.8**	(5.0)	-3.8	(5.4)
	Israel	6.5	(8.8)	-21.8	(8.2)	-2.3	(12.3)	-4.7	(13.2)	6.0	(9.4)	-1.9	(10.1)
	Jordan	27.7	(7.2)	2.3	(7.6)	-3.4	(5.1)	2.2	(7.1)	-2.3	(5.5)	-4.9	(7.6)
	Kyrgyzstan	c	c	c	c	2.8	(5.6)	5.1	(6.3)	-2.4	(6.8)	8.1	(7.9)
	Latvia	c	c	c	c	1.7	(13.5)	c	c	-0.1	(6.4)	14.3	(8.0)
	Lithuania	c	c	c	c	-6.7	(5.2)	4.0	(5.8)	**23.5**	(7.7)	c	c
	Macao-China	25.7	(5.1)	-8.2	(11.6)	**30.6**	(3.3)	c	c	**20.3**	(2.2)	-7.0	(5.1)
	Montenegro	c	c	c	c	c	c	c	c	-1.1	(2.3)	5.7	(5.3)
	Romania	c	c	c	c	-9.2	(7.5)	3.3	(7.7)	**24.1**	(7.5)	**-18.5**	(7.8)
	Russian Federation	c	c	c	c	-1.1	(4.8)	-8.9	(6.3)	-10.2	(9.2)	-11.2	(9.5)
	Serbia	c	c	c	c	**-18.2**	(6.7)	-2.7	(8.3)	**33.9**	(10.9)	7.8	(10.5)
	Slovenia	c	c	c	c	0.0	(2.2)	**-16.5**	(5.0)	**22.4**	(2.8)	-0.2	(5.2)
	Chinese Taipei	**-55.8**	(4.6)	6.0	(6.3)	-12.9	(11.5)	c	c	**25.8**	(7.5)	12.2	(6.5)
	Thailand	**-19.7**	(6.1)	3.1	(10.4)	-3.5	(5.8)	8.5	(8.9)	-2.1	(4.2)	-5.7	(5.7)
	Tunisia	c	c	c	c	-2.9	(4.7)	9.4	(6.0)	4.4	(6.1)	-14.0	(8.5)
	Uruguay	**-21.2**	(7.8)	c	c	1.7	(5.5)	7.7	(6.4)	9.6	(5.4)	c	c

Note:
m - Data are not available. These data were collected but subsequently removed from the publication for technical reasons.
w - Data have been withdrawn at the request of the country concerned.
c - There are too few observations to provide reliable estimates (i.e. there are fewer than 30 students or less than 3% of students for this cell or too few schools for valid inferences).

Table A3.3b [Part 2/2] **Learning environment at school, overall performance effect and differential effect for disadvantaged students**

	\multicolumn{4}{c	}{Index of school activities to promote the learning of science}	\multicolumn{4}{c	}{Index of the quality of school educational resources}
	\multicolumn{2}{c	}{Average association with performance for all students}	\multicolumn{2}{c	}{Differential effect for disadvantaged students}	\multicolumn{2}{c	}{Average association with performance for all students}	\multicolumn{2}{c	}{Differential effect for disadvantaged students}
	Coef.	S.E.	Coef.	S.E.	Coef.	S.E.	Coef.	S.E.
OECD								
Australia	2.9	(2.8)	-6.4	(3.7)	1.3	(1.8)	-0.1	(2.3)
Austria	**14.4**	(3.4)	4.1	(3.5)	-2.9	(2.8)	**-7.3**	(2.7)
Belgium	2.8	(2.6)	-2.7	(3.0)	-0.3	(2.8)	1.3	(3.1)
Canada	3.2	(1.8)	1.3	(3.0)	-0.3	(1.5)	-1.8	(2.2)
Czech Republic	**11.9**	(4.1)	2.5	(3.3)	-2.1	(4.3)	**-10.6**	(4.1)
Denmark	**6.8**	(2.7)	-1.0	(3.8)	-0.9	(2.6)	**8.1**	(4.1)
Finland	-4.4	(2.6)	-1.2	(4.2)	-2.9	(2.4)	-1.4	(3.4)
France	w	w	w	w	w	w	w	w
Germany	**9.8**	(2.5)	-1.3	(2.8)	3.3	(1.8)	-2.9	(3.2)
Greece	**10.0**	(3.4)	2.9	(3.9)	6.3	(3.5)	2.3	(4.8)
Hungary	7.4	(3.8)	-1.9	(4.7)	1.9	(3.0)	-4.6	(4.2)
Iceland	**-8.0**	(2.4)	-5.8	(4.7)	3.0	(1.6)	**7.8**	(3.6)
Ireland	1.2	(2.1)	0.6	(3.4)	0.5	(2.8)	-1.3	(3.1)
Italy	-1.6	(2.6)	-2.5	(3.0)	3.4	(2.9)	-1.3	(2.2)
Japan	**11.2**	(3.7)	**-8.4**	(4.1)	2.6	(3.1)	1.1	(4.0)
Korea	6.2	(3.4)	0.5	(3.4)	6.8	(3.5)	3.7	(5.0)
Luxembourg	-0.4	(1.1)	-3.2	(2.8)	1.0	(1.2)	1.3	(2.6)
Mexico	2.4	(1.8)	-4.7	(2.6)	-0.7	(1.5)	0.2	(2.7)
Netherlands	**8.1**	(4.1)	5.2	(3.2)	5.2	(3.0)	**5.8**	(2.7)
New Zealand	1.3	(3.5)	-1.4	(4.8)	3.7	(2.7)	-1.9	(4.0)
Norway	-2.5	(3.1)	-7.5	(4.0)	-4.7	(3.3)	-2.0	(5.9)
Poland	**7.7**	(3.9)	1.2	(5.1)	-0.8	(2.0)	1.4	(3.1)
Portugal	0.7	(1.8)	-1.9	(2.6)	1.7	(1.8)	-1.5	(2.5)
Slovak Republic	**7.8**	(3.3)	4.2	(4.4)	-0.4	(3.7)	0.8	(3.6)
Spain	1.1	(2.4)	-1.0	(2.6)	1.2	(1.9)	-0.0	(2.7)
Sweden	3.2	(2.4)	**-9.8**	(4.2)	1.6	(1.9)	-2.1	(3.7)
Switzerland	**16.0**	(2.9)	**-7.5**	(3.1)	**6.8**	(2.2)	-1.2	(2.4)
Turkey	5.4	(2.9)	0.9	(3.6)	-1.9	(3.1)	0.4	(3.2)
United Kingdom	-0.8	(2.4)	0.9	(3.7)	-1.1	(2.4)	-1.4	(3.4)
United States	**-6.6**	(2.5)	-0.4	(3.2)	1.3	(2.2)	-3.8	(3.5)
OECD average	**4.0**	(0.5)	**-1.5**	(0.7)	**1.1**	(0.5)	**-0.4**	(0.6)
Partners								
Argentina	3.5	(3.0)	-2.2	(2.8)	**5.9**	(2.2)	-6.0	(3.2)
Azerbaijan	**7.9**	(2.7)	2.0	(3.4)	0.6	(3.9)	-2.1	(5.1)
Brazil	4.0	(2.6)	-1.5	(3.6)	**6.2**	(1.9)	-1.7	(3.0)
Bulgaria	6.4	(4.5)	-0.8	(4.6)	-2.9	(4.6)	0.3	(6.3)
Chile	2.8	(2.2)	-3.1	(3.1)	1.8	(2.5)	1.4	(3.9)
Colombia	2.1	(3.6)	1.2	(4.6)	-0.4	(3.0)	0.4	(3.5)
Croatia	**8.0**	(2.2)	-1.1	(2.8)	-0.4	(5.6)	0.2	(6.0)
Estonia	1.1	(4.3)	8.0	(6.1)	-1.6	(4.0)	-3.9	(4.5)
Hong Kong-China	1.4	(6.0)	-5.3	(4.9)	1.7	(3.5)	2.3	(3.0)
Indonesia	**10.4**	(3.7)	-3.7	(2.8)	2.9	(2.4)	-3.1	(2.2)
Israel	6.7	(3.6)	-7.0	(4.2)	2.1	(2.9)	**-10.7**	(3.3)
Jordan	2.3	(3.3)	3.4	(3.2)	-3.0	(2.8)	3.3	(3.6)
Kyrgyzstan	4.2	(3.7)	2.1	(4.9)	-4.7	(2.9)	1.1	(4.1)
Latvia	3.6	(4.9)	-6.2	(8.7)	-1.7	(3.5)	1.5	(4.9)
Lithuania	0.1	(4.0)	-7.8	(4.6)	4.8	(3.2)	-5.0	(4.2)
Macao-China	**8.8**	(1.5)	0.2	(3.3)	2.2	(1.3)	**-12.3**	(3.4)
Montenegro	**-8.7**	(1.2)	-0.6	(2.5)	**4.9**	(0.9)	-0.9	(2.5)
Romania	**10.3**	(5.0)	2.1	(5.3)	2.2	(3.5)	0.8	(4.4)
Russian Federation	**9.8**	(4.2)	5.9	(4.5)	-1.2	(2.5)	-3.0	(4.0)
Serbia	6.7	(3.5)	0.9	(4.1)	6.3	(4.3)	5.7	(5.6)
Slovenia	**5.1**	(1.5)	0.2	(3.1)	-0.3	(1.5)	-6.3	(3.3)
Chinese Taipei	**13.5**	(5.1)	-2.2	(3.5)	**-4.1**	(2.1)	-1.4	(2.2)
Thailand	**8.2**	(3.4)	-8.9	(4.8)	0.9	(1.7)	1.5	(2.9)
Tunisia	3.3	(2.0)	-5.3	(2.8)	-1.9	(2.7)	2.3	(4.1)
Uruguay	1.9	(1.6)	-1.8	(2.6)	-1.8	(2.1)	-1.7	(2.5)

Note:
m - Data are not available. These data were collected but subsequently removed from the publication for technical reasons.
w - Data have been withdrawn at the request of the country concerned.
c - There are too few observations to provide reliable estimates (i.e. there are fewer than 30 students or less than 3% of students for this cell or too few schools for valid inferences).

ANNEX A4: CONCLUSIONS AND POLICY IMPLICATIONS

Table A4.1 **Missing data analysis and agreement analysis for parental occupation by country and ESCS tertile**

| | | Highest Parental Occupation Status (HISEI versus PQHISEI) ||||||||||||
| | | Percent of students with no useable data |||| Percent of students that accurately indicate their parents' highest occupation status |||| Average disagreement between student and parent report[1] ||||
		Low ESCS	Mid ESCS	High ESCS	Overall	Low ESCS	Mid ESCS	High ESCS	Overall	Low ESCS	Mid ESCS	High ESCS	Overall
OECD	Denmark	52.3	38.0	32.3	40.9	46.5	45.8	54.7	49.4	7.8	7.3	5.5	6.7
	Germany	31.6	21.6	16.3	23.2	48.2	42.9	45.9	45.6	6.0	6.5	6.7	6.4
	Iceland	38.3	38.7	35.3	37.4	42.5	42.0	52.5	45.8	7.1	8.0	5.7	6.9
	Italy	19.5	16.4	15.9	17.3	49.2	42.1	47.4	46.2	4.7	5.7	5.7	5.4
	Korea	5.6	3.8	2.7	4.0	33.5	29.8	35.8	33.1	8.0	9.0	7.9	8.3
	Luxembourg	34.2	27.4	26.2	29.3	48.6	38.8	38.4	41.7	5.5	6.4	6.9	6.3
	New Zealand	45.5	31.8	23.5	33.6	45.1	44.5	60.7	50.9	7.5	7.2	5.4	6.6
	Poland	6.4	4.3	3.1	4.6	56.6	47.4	44.6	49.5	4.3	5.5	6.0	5.3
	Portugal	16.9	16.3	16.2	16.5	55.1	48.7	50.5	51.4	3.5	5.7	6.5	5.2
	Turkey	15.6	14.1	10.9	13.5	76.6	77.7	77.4	77.3	3.1	3.3	3.1	3.2
Partners	Bulgaria	11.4	8.6	10.7	10.3	99.0	99.4	99.7	99.4	0.1	0.1	0.0	0.1
	Colombia	17.5	15.5	10.7	14.6	60.4	54.6	50.7	55.1	4.9	6.2	6.7	6.0
	Croatia	12.6	8.8	8.2	9.9	68.2	68.5	69.3	68.7	3.3	3.6	3.9	3.6
	Hong Kong-China	13.6	8.2	6.4	9.4	62.7	55.4	50.7	56.1	3.6	4.6	5.2	4.5
	Macao-China	8.64	6.28	4.58	6.51	46.18	44.32	42.99	44.48	5.11	5.68	6.88	5.90

1 Occupation status values range from 16 to 90.

Table A4.2 **Missing data analysis and agreement analysis for parental education by country and ESCS tertile**

| | | Highest Parental Education (HISCED versus PQISCED) ||||||||||||
| | | Percent of students with no useable data |||| Percent of students that accurately indicate their parents' highest education |||| Average disagreement between student and parent report[1] ||||
		Low ESCS	Mid ESCS	High ESCS	Overall	Low ESCS	Mid ESCS	High ESCS	Overall	Low ESCS	Mid ESCS	High ESCS	Overall
OECD	Denmark	51.90	37.49	30.44	39.95	45.56	52.89	66.44	56.17	0.69	0.60	0.39	0.54
	Germany	29.90	21.56	15.18	22.22	45.81	42.05	67.64	52.49	0.74	0.84	0.49	0.68
	Iceland	38.25	37.85	34.58	36.89	59.72	47.56	71.86	59.94	0.49	0.67	0.35	0.50
	Italy	26.05	17.15	15.27	19.49	63.52	69.65	75.16	69.71	0.38	0.35	0.35	0.36
	Korea	4.10	2.19	1.72	2.67	68.40	70.12	85.06	74.59	0.37	0.38	0.18	0.31
	Luxembourg	39.19	32.38	26.98	32.85	62.80	49.61	52.70	54.71	0.45	0.64	0.61	0.57
	New Zealand	48.41	34.39	24.42	35.74	55.67	53.95	68.30	60.04	0.59	0.61	0.39	0.52
	Poland	1.89	1.83	1.52	1.75	84.92	81.34	86.85	84.39	0.16	0.22	0.24	0.21
	Portugal	19.01	16.17	14.27	16.49	83.06	57.48	72.13	70.79	0.20	0.48	0.39	0.36
	Turkey	13.80	10.63	3.40	9.28	92.60	83.23	81.54	85.60	0.09	0.19	0.22	0.17
Partners	Bulgaria	7.20	5.57	10.12	7.65	74.59	72.22	85.21	77.27	0.28	0.39	0.24	0.30
	Colombia	18.31	12.37	6.93	12.54	81.68	58.00	65.35	67.98	0.25	0.55	0.47	0.43
	Croatia	9.17	6.13	5.48	6.93	61.01	62.48	67.70	63.77	0.47	0.43	0.41	0.43
	Hong Kong-China	5.26	3.68	4.18	4.38	97.69	84.90	62.24	81.54	0.03	0.17	0.47	0.22
	Macao-China	5.61	3.37	2.79	3.93	87.95	71.37	58.65	72.57	0.13	0.32	0.52	0.32

1 Parental education is measured by ISCED level.

[Part 1/2]
Table A4.3 **Difference in means test results on matched sample for selected variables**

		General interest in science						Science self-concept						Percentage of students who spend no time in school in regular lessons in science					
		Resilient students		Disadvantaged low achievers (DLA)		Difference		Resilient students		Disadvantaged low achievers (DLA)		Difference		Resilient students		Disadvantaged low achievers (DLA)		Difference	
		Mean	S.E.	Mean	S.E.	Diff.	S.E.	Mean	S.E.	Mean	S.E.	Diff.	S.E.	Percent	S.E.	Percent	S.E.	Diff.	S.E.
OECD	Australia	0.11	(0.04)	-0.70	(0.05)	0.80	(0.06)	0.34	(0.03)	-0.57	(0.04)	0.91	(0.06)	9.68	(1.34)	23.12	(1.92)	-13.44	(2.20)
	Austria	0.24	(0.06)	-0.25	(0.07)	0.49	(0.08)	0.30	(0.07)	-0.20	(0.08)	0.50	(0.11)	7.63	(1.66)	26.32	(2.50)	-18.70	(2.83)
	Belgium	0.27	(0.05)	-0.47	(0.06)	0.74	(0.08)	0.07	(0.06)	-0.47	(0.06)	0.54	(0.08)	5.28	(1.15)	40.99	(2.84)	-35.71	(2.94)
	Canada	0.31	(0.05)	-0.34	(0.05)	0.64	(0.07)	0.67	(0.05)	-0.29	(0.05)	0.96	(0.07)	6.46	(1.39)	19.95	(2.08)	-13.49	(2.23)
	Czech Republic	0.11	(0.05)	-0.20	(0.08)	0.31	(0.09)	0.06	(0.06)	-0.18	(0.07)	0.23	(0.09)	7.92	(2.13)	18.01	(2.98)	-10.09	(3.83)
	Denmark	0.12	(0.06)	-0.68	(0.08)	0.80	(0.11)	0.23	(0.07)	-0.46	(0.07)	0.69	(0.10)	1.11	(0.87)	10.54	(2.47)	-9.43	(2.53)
	Finland	0.04	(0.05)	-0.68	(0.07)	0.72	(0.09)	0.38	(0.05)	-0.41	(0.05)	0.79	(0.07)	0.99	(0.68)	8.87	(1.84)	-7.88	(2.00)
	France	0.52	(0.06)	-0.17	(0.07)	0.69	(0.08)	0.11	(0.07)	-0.40	(0.08)	0.51	(0.11)	1.40	(1.19)	19.37	(3.19)	-17.97	(3.55)
	Germany	0.42	(0.05)	0.01	(0.07)	0.41	(0.08)	0.48	(0.06)	-0.03	(0.07)	0.51	(0.09)	5.34	(2.16)	23.01	(3.50)	-17.68	(4.05)
	Greece	0.32	(0.06)	-0.16	(0.07)	0.48	(0.10)	0.04	(0.06)	-0.18	(0.05)	0.22	(0.08)	1.25	(1.11)	20.14	(2.65)	-18.88	(2.90)
	Hungary	0.05	(0.06)	-0.20	(0.07)	0.25	(0.09)	-0.26	(0.06)	-0.05	(0.09)	-0.21	(0.10)	6.94	(2.43)	9.76	(2.40)	-2.82	(3.10)
	Iceland	0.18	(0.06)	-0.77	(0.09)	0.95	(0.11)	0.48	(0.06)	-0.75	(0.07)	1.22	(0.09)	0.51	(0.49)	4.39	(1.25)	-3.89	(1.31)
	Ireland	0.11	(0.06)	-0.69	(0.09)	0.80	(0.11)	0.20	(0.07)	-0.61	(0.08)	0.82	(0.11)	8.35	(1.90)	31.50	(4.34)	-23.15	(4.36)
	Italy	0.29	(0.03)	-0.01	(0.04)	0.30	(0.05)	0.24	(0.03)	0.05	(0.04)	0.19	(0.05)	5.84	(1.68)	13.67	(1.35)	-7.83	(2.08)
	Japan	0.15	(0.05)	-0.62	(0.06)	0.77	(0.08)	-0.63	(0.06)	-1.12	(0.06)	0.50	(0.08)	2.47	(1.19)	6.15	(1.97)	-3.68	(2.21)
	Korea	0.06	(0.04)	-0.78	(0.06)	0.84	(0.08)	-0.49	(0.05)	-1.13	(0.05)	0.64	(0.07)	1.43	(0.82)	8.48	(2.55)	-7.06	(2.14)
	Luxembourg	0.33	(0.09)	-0.12	(0.09)	0.45	(0.12)	0.49	(0.08)	-0.08	(0.07)	0.57	(0.10)	4.45	(1.60)	19.90	(2.69)	-15.45	(3.18)
	Mexico	0.99	(0.04)	0.65	(0.07)	0.34	(0.08)	0.51	(0.04)	0.46	(0.04)	0.05	(0.06)	19.21	(1.93)	9.29	(1.80)	9.92	(2.60)
	Netherlands	-0.13	(0.06)	-0.64	(0.08)	0.51	(0.10)	-0.14	(0.05)	-0.58	(0.06)	0.44	(0.08)	8.07	(1.84)	41.00	(3.67)	-32.93	(3.81)
	New Zealand	0.15	(0.07)	-0.37	(0.08)	0.52	(0.10)	0.18	(0.05)	-0.31	(0.06)	0.49	(0.08)	4.08	(1.33)	17.43	(2.77)	-13.35	(3.03)
	Norway	0.24	(0.07)	-0.46	(0.06)	0.70	(0.12)	0.37	(0.07)	-0.34	(0.06)	0.71	(0.09)	0.92	(0.77)	4.97	(1.38)	-4.05	(1.56)
	Poland	0.21	(0.04)	-0.15	(0.05)	0.36	(0.06)	0.26	(0.05)	-0.07	(0.05)	0.34	(0.07)	0.80	(0.54)	5.68	(1.32)	-4.88	(1.45)
	Portugal	0.38	(0.05)	-0.02	(0.06)	0.40	(0.08)	0.48	(0.06)	0.06	(0.06)	0.42	(0.08)	13.09	(3.10)	7.94	(1.87)	5.14	(3.67)
	Slovak Republic	0.06	(0.05)	-0.30	(0.06)	0.36	(0.07)	0.27	(0.06)	-0.04	(0.05)	0.31	(0.07)	5.51	(1.69)	21.07	(2.79)	-15.56	(3.35)
	Spain	0.02	(0.05)	-0.65	(0.05)	0.67	(0.07)	0.27	(0.05)	-0.42	(0.04)	0.69	(0.06)	7.24	(1.35)	13.77	(1.50)	-6.53	(1.87)
	Sweden	0.04	(0.10)	-0.66	(0.09)	0.70	(0.11)	0.38	(0.07)	-0.55	(0.07)	0.93	(0.09)	1.12	(0.96)	9.35	(1.98)	-8.24	(2.16)
	Switzerland	0.24	(0.05)	-0.46	(0.05)	0.70	(0.07)	0.29	(0.05)	-0.37	(0.05)	0.67	(0.07)	7.49	(2.14)	28.50	(2.32)	-21.01	(2.99)
	Turkey	0.49	(0.06)	0.05	(0.08)	0.43	(0.09)	0.29	(0.06)	0.03	(0.09)	0.26	(0.11)	18.48	(2.65)	28.09	(3.41)	-9.61	(4.31)
	United Kingdom	0.11	(0.06)	-0.28	(0.06)	0.39	(0.08)	0.28	(0.05)	-0.27	(0.04)	0.55	(0.06)	1.07	(0.61)	7.97	(1.36)	-6.90	(1.48)
	United States	0.27	(0.05)	-0.10	(0.13)	0.36	(0.15)	0.58	(0.07)	-0.04	(0.12)	0.62	(0.14)	5.37	(1.41)	17.10	(3.47)	-11.73	(3.56)
	OECD average	**0.22**	**(0.02)**	**-0.33**	**(0.01)**	**0.55**	**(0.02)**	**0.22**	**(0.01)**	**-0.30**	**(0.01)**	**0.52**	**(0.02)**	**5.49**	**(0.30)**	**(17.12)**	**(0.68)**	**-11.62**	**(0.76)**
Partners	Argentina	0.34	(0.07)	0.19	(0.07)	0.15	(0.10)	0.25	(0.08)	0.13	(0.07)	0.12	(0.10)	11.93	(3.28)	25.30	(3.92)	-13.37	(4.89)
	Azerbaijan	0.62	(0.07)	0.37	(0.07)	0.24	(0.10)	0.62	(0.08)	0.56	(0.08)	0.06	(0.11)	6.21	(2.34)	12.94	(2.45)	-6.73	(3.69)
	Brazil	0.51	(0.07)	0.59	(0.08)	-0.08	(0.10)	0.29	(0.06)	0.32	(0.06)	-0.03	(0.08)	3.18	(1.63)	15.46	(2.66)	-12.28	(3.25)
	Bulgaria	0.30	(0.09)	-0.13	(0.09)	0.43	(0.13)	0.36	(0.07)	0.31	(0.08)	0.06	(0.10)	8.54	(2.88)	24.96	(3.70)	-16.42	(4.81)
	Chile	0.48	(0.09)	0.27	(0.07)	0.21	(0.11)	0.27	(0.06)	-0.03	(0.08)	0.30	(0.09)	11.75	(2.04)	28.19	(3.20)	-16.45	(3.63)
	Colombia	1.26	(0.09)	1.24	(0.08)	0.02	(0.11)	0.74	(0.06)	0.73	(0.07)	0.00	(0.10)	3.17	(1.94)	5.90	(1.73)	-2.72	(2.84)
	Croatia	0.37	(0.04)	-0.16	(0.05)	0.54	(0.07)	0.05	(0.05)	-0.22	(0.07)	0.27	(0.08)	14.99	(2.32)	45.65	(3.38)	-30.66	(4.00)
	Estonia	0.25	(0.07)	-0.02	(0.05)	0.28	(0.08)	0.35	(0.06)	-0.18	(0.05)	0.54	(0.07)	1.02	(0.65)	6.12	(1.33)	-5.09	(1.37)
	Hong Kong-China	0.46	(0.04)	-0.21	(0.07)	0.67	(0.08)	-0.05	(0.05)	-0.52	(0.10)	0.47	(0.11)	21.91	(2.40)	36.53	(3.34)	-14.62	(4.27)
	Indonesia	0.61	(0.06)	0.37	(0.05)	0.23	(0.08)	-0.06	(0.08)	0.31	(0.06)	-0.37	(0.10)	4.86	(1.65)	5.44	(1.50)	-0.58	(2.11)
	Israel	0.21	(0.10)	-0.37	(0.11)	0.57	(0.15)	0.65	(0.10)	-0.09	(0.11)	0.73	(0.16)	17.42	(3.17)	39.08	(4.82)	-21.67	(5.60)
	Jordan	0.85	(0.07)	0.38	(0.07)	0.47	(0.09)	0.80	(0.05)	0.56	(0.05)	0.24	(0.07)	6.94	(1.75)	21.18	(2.72)	-14.24	(3.01)
	Kyrgyzstan	0.90	(0.06)	0.99	(0.07)	-0.09	(0.10)	0.58	(0.06)	0.92	(0.06)	-0.35	(0.08)	18.63	(2.61)	24.92	(3.76)	-6.29	(4.37)
	Latvia	0.15	(0.05)	0.15	(0.06)	0.01	(0.08)	0.06	(0.06)	-0.06	(0.05)	0.12	(0.08)	1.87	(1.36)	15.15	(3.02)	-13.28	(3.48)
	Lithuania	0.48	(0.05)	0.20	(0.05)	0.28	(0.08)	-0.12	(0.05)	-0.40	(0.05)	0.27	(0.07)	2.26	(1.12)	10.25	(2.80)	-7.99	(2.98)
	Macao-China	0.32	(0.05)	-0.12	(0.06)	0.43	(0.08)	0.00	(0.08)	-0.26	(0.06)	0.26	(0.10)	10.83	(1.58)	11.87	(2.26)	-1.05	(2.89)
	Montenegro	0.61	(0.06)	0.18	(0.08)	0.43	(0.10)	0.44	(0.06)	0.47	(0.07)	-0.03	(0.10)	5.84	(1.79)	21.56	(2.81)	-15.72	(3.30)
	Romania	0.52	(0.08)	0.19	(0.10)	0.33	(0.13)	0.27	(0.07)	0.34	(0.05)	-0.07	(0.09)	10.29	(4.08)	36.13	(3.30)	-25.84	(5.41)
	Russian Federation	0.37	(0.05)	0.19	(0.08)	0.18	(0.09)	0.18	(0.05)	0.05	(0.05)	0.13	(0.06)	3.13	(1.32)	14.18	(2.96)	-11.05	(3.36)
	Serbia	0.38	(0.05)	0.11	(0.09)	0.27	(0.09)	0.31	(0.06)	0.20	(0.06)	0.11	(0.09)	6.00	(1.62)	26.90	(3.03)	-20.90	(3.52)
	Slovenia	0.22	(0.06)	-0.22	(0.07)	0.44	(0.10)	0.31	(0.06)	0.29	(0.07)	0.02	(0.11)	4.10	(1.69)	20.10	(3.59)	-15.99	(4.11)
	Chinese Taipei	0.37	(0.04)	-0.42	(0.06)	0.80	(0.07)	-0.26	(0.05)	-0.55	(0.04)	0.29	(0.06)	5.22	(1.85)	24.70	(2.50)	-19.48	(3.21)
	Thailand	1.02	(0.04)	0.62	(0.05)	0.40	(0.06)	0.66	(0.05)	0.69	(0.06)	-0.02	(0.07)	0.00	(0.00)	0.00	(0.00)	0.00	(0.00)
	Tunisia	0.94	(0.07)	0.63	(0.05)	0.31	(0.08)	0.59	(0.05)	0.59	(0.06)	0.00	(0.07)	3.35	(1.24)	18.27	(2.95)	-14.92	(2.96)
	Uruguay	0.39	(0.07)	0.04	(0.10)	0.35	(0.12)	0.47	(0.07)	0.19	(0.09)	0.28	(0.12)	11.41	(3.40)	26.75	(3.28)	-15.34	(4.45)

[Part 2/2]
Table A4.3 Difference in means test results on matched sample for selected variables

| | | Percentage of students who spend less than 2 hours or 2 to up to 4 hours in school learning science in regular lessons |||||| Percentage of students who spend 4 up to 6 hours or 6 hours or more in school learning science in regular lessons ||||||
| | | Resilient || Disadvantaged low achievers (DLA) || Difference || Resilient || Disadvantaged low achievers (DLA) || Difference ||
		Percent	S.E.	Percent	S.E.	Diff.	S.E.	Percent	S.E.	Percent	S.E.	Diff.	S.E.
OECD	Australia	44.63	(2.11)	53.58	(2.15)	-8.94	(2.83)	45.20	(2.03)	18.92	(1.87)	26.28	(2.58)
	Austria	55.22	(3.53)	62.17	(3.11)	-6.95	(4.52)	33.10	(3.45)	5.38	(1.36)	27.72	(3.86)
	Belgium	63.89	(2.58)	43.63	(2.49)	20.27	(3.35)	30.25	(2.54)	4.61	(1.06)	25.64	(2.70)
	Canada	29.37	(2.15)	41.95	(2.57)	-12.58	(3.23)	60.63	(2.47)	32.87	(2.32)	27.76	(2.96)
	Czech Republic	46.55	(3.79)	66.59	(3.58)	-20.04	(5.17)	44.20	(3.86)	6.17	(1.71)	38.03	(4.07)
	Denmark	66.93	(3.81)	68.04	(4.24)	-1.11	(5.23)	30.71	(3.68)	17.74	(3.00)	12.97	(4.10)
	Finland	63.39	(3.30)	73.29	(2.87)	-9.91	(3.87)	35.35	(3.08)	14.76	(2.37)	20.59	(3.31)
	France	61.34	(3.93)	68.87	(3.19)	-7.53	(5.28)	36.36	(3.74)	4.27	(1.37)	32.09	(4.08)
	Germany	45.15	(3.94)	56.64	(3.54)	-11.50	(5.58)	48.03	(3.59)	10.91	(2.12)	37.12	(4.28)
	Greece	57.95	(3.74)	62.24	(3.68)	-4.29	(5.27)	40.27	(3.47)	13.47	(2.87)	26.80	(4.35)
	Hungary	62.52	(3.61)	78.49	(3.30)	-15.97	(4.96)	27.65	(3.52)	7.05	(1.68)	20.60	(3.76)
	Iceland	79.01	(2.70)	78.44	(2.56)	0.57	(3.70)	20.41	(2.68)	16.09	(2.16)	4.31	(3.45)
	Ireland	72.77	(3.11)	50.89	(3.83)	21.88	(5.08)	18.36	(2.66)	14.77	(2.51)	3.59	(3.73)
	Italy	55.11	(2.51)	68.30	(2.27)	-13.19	(3.18)	37.77	(2.54)	12.97	(1.82)	24.80	(3.13)
	Japan	82.48	(2.56)	87.51	(2.39)	-5.02	(3.46)	14.86	(2.26)	4.73	(0.96)	10.13	(2.44)
	Korea	57.38	(4.00)	66.84	(3.13)	-9.46	(4.76)	40.67	(3.93)	20.21	(2.17)	20.47	(4.32)
	Luxembourg	67.11	(3.90)	66.53	(3.06)	0.58	(5.00)	24.67	(3.47)	9.14	(1.63)	15.54	(3.77)
	Mexico	39.98	(2.40)	49.49	(3.07)	-9.51	(3.69)	39.05	(2.54)	33.78	(3.40)	5.27	(4.35)
	Netherlands	59.18	(3.41)	48.56	(3.81)	10.61	(5.03)	26.77	(2.74)	3.50	(1.23)	23.27	(2.93)
	New Zealand	16.83	(2.67)	37.59	(2.95)	-20.76	(4.07)	78.94	(2.78)	41.45	(3.21)	37.49	(4.46)
	Norway	93.22	(2.00)	87.07	(2.06)	6.15	(2.76)	5.86	(1.72)	3.97	(1.40)	1.89	(2.01)
	Poland	65.83	(3.03)	82.70	(2.25)	-16.87	(3.67)	31.95	(3.14)	10.46	(1.90)	21.49	(3.62)
	Portugal	36.76	(3.35)	76.55	(3.00)	-39.79	(4.62)	48.62	(3.63)	11.98	(2.02)	36.64	(4.24)
	Slovak Republic	59.92	(3.52)	68.71	(3.11)	-8.78	(4.90)	34.09	(3.37)	6.14	(1.50)	27.94	(3.57)
	Spain	54.89	(2.23)	66.02	(2.25)	-11.13	(3.04)	36.72	(2.23)	12.15	(1.68)	24.57	(2.69)
	Sweden	85.28	(2.28)	79.16	(3.58)	6.11	(4.55)	12.43	(2.19)	8.14	(1.96)	4.29	(3.00)
	Switzerland	62.68	(3.33)	63.63	(2.47)	-0.96	(3.75)	28.34	(3.12)	4.66	(0.95)	23.68	(3.36)
	Turkey	34.53	(3.32)	54.14	(3.66)	-19.61	(5.41)	46.74	(3.87)	15.00	(3.02)	31.74	(4.77)
	United Kingdom	25.95	(3.53)	50.81	(2.91)	-24.86	(4.48)	72.12	(3.69)	38.32	(3.05)	33.80	(4.65)
	United States	33.10	(2.99)	55.80	(3.50)	-22.70	(4.57)	60.16	(3.22)	20.83	(2.79)	39.33	(4.02)
	OECD average	**56.13**	**(0.67)**	**(63.64)**	**(0.70)**	**-7.51**	**(1.07)**	**37.00**	**(0.65)**	**(14.05)**	**(0.52)**	**22.95**	**(0.80)**
Partners	Argentina	66.26	(4.32)	53.80	(4.34)	12.46	(6.11)	19.41	(3.73)	5.16	(1.46)	14.25	(4.23)
	Azerbaijan	61.03	(3.04)	56.29	(3.80)	4.75	(5.31)	24.80	(2.98)	14.38	(2.87)	10.42	(4.14)
	Brazil	82.00	(2.99)	70.50	(3.57)	11.50	(4.71)	11.94	(2.69)	3.09	(1.29)	8.85	(3.04)
	Bulgaria	61.59	(4.65)	58.54	(4.21)	3.05	(5.80)	28.05	(4.62)	9.18	(2.63)	18.87	(5.01)
	Chile	63.23	(4.06)	59.57	(3.95)	3.66	(5.65)	23.37	(3.90)	5.84	(1.87)	17.52	(4.55)
	Colombia	49.93	(5.17)	56.70	(5.79)	-6.77	(8.09)	46.12	(5.24)	29.13	(6.53)	16.99	(8.71)
	Croatia	71.65	(2.68)	46.19	(3.17)	25.46	(4.36)	10.27	(1.74)	4.53	(1.00)	5.75	(1.91)
	Estonia	53.66	(3.36)	72.31	(2.79)	-18.65	(4.51)	44.61	(3.35)	18.55	(2.95)	26.06	(4.28)
	Hong Kong-China	17.36	(2.14)	43.75	(3.04)	-26.40	(4.11)	60.26	(2.72)	17.03	(2.24)	43.24	(3.57)
	Indonesia	63.92	(3.30)	80.09	(3.17)	-16.17	(4.76)	30.28	(3.50)	12.13	(2.40)	18.15	(4.14)
	Israel	49.15	(3.89)	38.02	(4.22)	11.13	(6.06)	29.41	(3.66)	8.07	(1.75)	21.34	(4.07)
	Jordan	44.66	(4.15)	53.60	(3.14)	-8.93	(5.21)	45.67	(4.24)	18.55	(2.70)	27.12	(5.02)
	Kyrgyzstan	60.08	(3.70)	46.75	(4.19)	13.32	(4.89)	15.78	(2.78)	11.53	(4.74)	4.25	(4.87)
	Latvia	64.89	(4.77)	71.32	(3.21)	-6.43	(5.76)	32.31	(4.42)	11.47	(2.87)	20.83	(4.89)
	Lithuania	67.44	(2.80)	73.43	(3.46)	-5.99	(3.84)	29.65	(2.74)	12.21	(2.57)	17.44	(3.30)
	Macao-China	28.15	(2.58)	64.45	(3.08)	-36.30	(3.71)	60.70	(3.08)	22.59	(2.97)	38.11	(3.90)
	Montenegro	58.71	(3.34)	54.79	(3.53)	3.92	(5.06)	33.90	(3.30)	15.19	(2.24)	18.71	(4.22)
	Romania	63.73	(5.97)	52.42	(4.15)	11.31	(7.18)	25.76	(5.02)	9.61	(2.66)	16.14	(5.32)
	Russian Federation	37.25	(3.14)	58.42	(3.84)	-21.17	(4.83)	58.21	(3.86)	24.83	(2.94)	33.38	(4.80)
	Serbia	60.57	(3.42)	55.55	(3.47)	5.03	(4.96)	31.88	(3.44)	11.23	(1.78)	20.65	(3.96)
	Slovenia	54.16	(4.16)	66.96	(3.70)	-12.80	(5.80)	38.83	(3.64)	7.69	(1.90)	31.14	(4.01)
	Chinese Taipei	62.28	(3.53)	58.17	(2.25)	4.11	(4.31)	32.45	(3.31)	10.48	(1.73)	21.97	(3.78)
	Thailand	50.77	(3.24)	82.10	(2.74)	-31.33	(4.43)	49.06	(3.21)	17.48	(2.81)	31.58	(4.44)
	Tunisia	66.63	(2.86)	65.26	(3.36)	1.37	(4.25)	28.22	(2.60)	7.93	(1.53)	20.29	(2.93)
	Uruguay	65.56	(3.92)	50.61	(3.37)	14.95	(5.14)	21.07	(2.97)	9.02	(1.81)	12.05	(3.45)

[Part 1/3]
Table A4.4 Difference in means test results on alternative definition for selected variables

		General interest in science						Science self-concept					
		Resilient students		Disadvantaged low achievers (DLA)		Difference		Resilient		Disadvantaged low achievers (DLA)		Difference	
		Mean	S.E.	Mean	S.E.	Diff.	S.E.	Mean	S.E.	Mean	S.E.	Diff.	S.E.
OECD	Australia	-0.04	(0.03)	-0.69	(0.04)	0.65	(0.05)	0.16	(0.03)	-0.55	(0.03)	0.72	(0.04)
	Austria	0.17	(0.04)	-0.27	(0.04)	0.44	(0.06)	0.16	(0.06)	-0.26	(0.06)	0.42	(0.08)
	Belgium	0.15	(0.04)	-0.38	(0.05)	0.52	(0.06)	-0.06	(0.04)	-0.45	(0.05)	0.39	(0.06)
	Canada	0.22	(0.03)	-0.27	(0.03)	0.49	(0.04)	0.48	(0.04)	-0.30	(0.03)	0.79	(0.06)
	Czech Republic	0.06	(0.04)	-0.20	(0.05)	0.26	(0.07)	0.02	(0.04)	-0.16	(0.05)	0.18	(0.07)
	Denmark	-0.03	(0.06)	-0.58	(0.06)	0.54	(0.08)	0.04	(0.06)	-0.45	(0.05)	0.49	(0.07)
	Finland	-0.09	(0.04)	-0.70	(0.05)	0.61	(0.07)	0.25	(0.04)	-0.41	(0.04)	0.65	(0.05)
	France	0.42	(0.06)	-0.23	(0.04)	0.66	(0.08)	-0.05	(0.05)	-0.36	(0.04)	0.31	(0.06)
	Germany	0.34	(0.05)	-0.06	(0.05)	0.40	(0.07)	0.38	(0.04)	-0.05	(0.04)	0.43	(0.06)
	Greece	0.24	(0.04)	-0.20	(0.04)	0.44	(0.06)	-0.05	(0.04)	-0.20	(0.04)	0.15	(0.06)
	Hungary	-0.05	(0.05)	-0.23	(0.04)	0.19	(0.07)	-0.31	(0.05)	-0.20	(0.05)	-0.12	(0.07)
	Iceland	0.05	(0.05)	-0.71	(0.06)	0.75	(0.08)	0.24	(0.05)	-0.64	(0.05)	0.89	(0.07)
	Ireland	-0.03	(0.05)	-0.74	(0.05)	0.71	(0.07)	-0.01	(0.06)	-0.65	(0.05)	0.64	(0.08)
	Italy	0.24	(0.03)	-0.05	(0.03)	0.29	(0.04)	0.16	(0.03)	0.00	(0.03)	0.16	(0.04)
	Japan	0.05	(0.04)	-0.64	(0.05)	0.69	(0.06)	-0.72	(0.04)	-1.14	(0.04)	0.42	(0.06)
	Korea	-0.06	(0.04)	-0.73	(0.04)	0.67	(0.05)	-0.61	(0.05)	-1.12	(0.04)	0.52	(0.05)
	Luxembourg	0.24	(0.06)	-0.14	(0.04)	0.38	(0.07)	0.35	(0.06)	-0.07	(0.04)	0.42	(0.07)
	Mexico	0.92	(0.03)	0.73	(0.05)	0.19	(0.06)	0.44	(0.03)	0.49	(0.03)	-0.05	(0.05)
	Netherlands	-0.26	(0.05)	-0.65	(0.06)	0.39	(0.08)	-0.25	(0.05)	-0.62	(0.06)	0.38	(0.08)
	New Zealand	0.04	(0.05)	-0.42	(0.06)	0.46	(0.07)	0.04	(0.04)	-0.37	(0.04)	0.40	(0.06)
	Norway	0.14	(0.05)	-0.57	(0.07)	0.70	(0.06)	0.21	(0.04)	-0.37	(0.04)	0.58	(0.06)
	Poland	0.13	(0.03)	-0.10	(0.03)	0.23	(0.04)	0.12	(0.03)	-0.09	(0.04)	0.21	(0.05)
	Portugal	0.28	(0.04)	-0.07	(0.04)	0.36	(0.06)	0.38	(0.04)	0.09	(0.05)	0.29	(0.07)
	Slovak Republic	-0.01	(0.04)	-0.40	(0.06)	0.39	(0.07)	0.20	(0.04)	-0.07	(0.04)	0.27	(0.05)
	Spain	-0.08	(0.03)	-0.59	(0.04)	0.51	(0.05)	0.10	(0.04)	-0.41	(0.03)	0.51	(0.05)
	Sweden	-0.02	(0.06)	-0.61	(0.06)	0.59	(0.08)	0.21	(0.05)	-0.52	(0.04)	0.73	(0.06)
	Switzerland	0.11	(0.03)	-0.39	(0.04)	0.50	(0.05)	0.19	(0.04)	-0.29	(0.03)	0.47	(0.05)
	Turkey	0.39	(0.05)	-0.04	(0.06)	0.43	(0.08)	0.20	(0.06)	0.04	(0.06)	0.17	(0.08)
	United Kingdom	0.04	(0.05)	-0.33	(0.04)	0.37	(0.06)	0.12	(0.04)	-0.28	(0.03)	0.40	(0.05)
	United States	0.16	(0.05)	-0.11	(0.09)	0.27	(0.10)	0.31	(0.06)	-0.09	(0.07)	0.40	(0.09)
	OECD average	**0.12**	**(0.01)**	**-0.34**	**(0.01)**	**0.46**	**(0.01)**	**0.08**	**(0.01)**	**-0.31**	**(0.01)**	**0.39**	**(0.01)**
Partners	Argentina	0.31	(0.05)	0.24	(0.06)	0.06	(0.08)	0.18	(0.05)	0.23	(0.07)	-0.05	(0.07)
	Azerbaijan	0.57	(0.05)	0.34	(0.07)	0.23	(0.08)	0.63	(0.06)	0.57	(0.06)	0.06	(0.07)
	Brazil	0.50	(0.05)	0.53	(0.06)	-0.03	(0.08)	0.28	(0.04)	0.37	(0.04)	-0.09	(0.06)
	Bulgaria	0.21	(0.06)	0.01	(0.07)	0.20	(0.09)	0.34	(0.05)	0.29	(0.05)	0.06	(0.07)
	Chile	0.44	(0.06)	0.37	(0.05)	0.07	(0.07)	0.18	(0.05)	-0.02	(0.04)	0.20	(0.06)
	Colombia	1.25	(0.05)	1.27	(0.06)	-0.02	(0.09)	0.68	(0.06)	0.71	(0.06)	-0.03	(0.07)
	Croatia	0.31	(0.03)	-0.07	(0.04)	0.38	(0.06)	0.02	(0.04)	-0.20	(0.05)	0.22	(0.07)
	Estonia	0.19	(0.05)	-0.03	(0.04)	0.23	(0.05)	0.20	(0.05)	-0.18	(0.03)	0.38	(0.06)
	Hong Kong-China	0.37	(0.03)	-0.19	(0.06)	0.56	(0.06)	-0.18	(0.05)	-0.44	(0.07)	0.26	(0.09)
	Indonesia	0.57	(0.04)	0.37	(0.03)	0.19	(0.05)	-0.00	(0.05)	0.30	(0.05)	-0.30	(0.07)
	Israel	0.10	(0.08)	-0.36	(0.08)	0.46	(0.11)	0.47	(0.07)	0.04	(0.06)	0.43	(0.10)
	Jordan	0.78	(0.05)	0.38	(0.06)	0.40	(0.07)	0.72	(0.04)	0.52	(0.04)	0.20	(0.06)
	Kyrgyzstan	0.89	(0.04)	0.95	(0.05)	-0.05	(0.06)	0.63	(0.04)	0.87	(0.04)	-0.24	(0.06)
	Latvia	0.13	(0.04)	0.07	(0.05)	0.06	(0.06)	0.04	(0.05)	-0.08	(0.05)	0.12	(0.06)
	Lithuania	0.40	(0.04)	0.18	(0.03)	0.22	(0.06)	-0.25	(0.04)	-0.39	(0.03)	0.14	(0.04)
	Macao-China	0.23	(0.03)	-0.15	(0.05)	0.38	(0.06)	-0.08	(0.07)	-0.21	(0.04)	0.13	(0.08)
	Montenegro	0.53	(0.05)	0.21	(0.06)	0.32	(0.08)	0.38	(0.05)	0.49	(0.05)	-0.11	(0.07)
	Romania	0.42	(0.05)	0.22	(0.06)	0.19	(0.08)	0.24	(0.06)	0.37	(0.04)	-0.13	(0.08)
	Russian Federation	0.33	(0.04)	0.19	(0.05)	0.14	(0.06)	0.12	(0.04)	0.05	(0.04)	0.07	(0.04)
	Serbia	0.34	(0.04)	0.15	(0.05)	0.19	(0.06)	0.25	(0.04)	0.24	(0.04)	0.01	(0.05)
	Slovenia	0.17	(0.04)	-0.23	(0.04)	0.40	(0.06)	0.23	(0.04)	0.22	(0.04)	0.02	(0.06)
	Chinese Taipei	0.28	(0.03)	-0.36	(0.04)	0.64	(0.04)	-0.39	(0.03)	-0.59	(0.04)	0.20	(0.05)
	Thailand	0.93	(0.04)	0.63	(0.04)	0.31	(0.05)	0.63	(0.04)	0.70	(0.03)	-0.06	(0.05)
	Tunisia	0.86	(0.05)	0.66	(0.05)	0.21	(0.06)	0.59	(0.04)	0.58	(0.04)	0.01	(0.06)
	Uruguay	0.32	(0.05)	0.24	(0.07)	0.08	(0.08)	0.38	(0.05)	0.22	(0.05)	0.16	(0.07)

[Part 2/3]
Table A4.4 **Difference in means test results on alternative definition for selected variables**

		Percentage of students who spend no time in school in regular lessons in science						Percentage of students who spend less than 2 hours or 2 to up to 4 hours in school learning science in regular lessons					
		Resilient		Disadvantaged low achievers (DLA)		Difference		Resilient		Disadvantaged low achievers (DLA)		Difference	
		Percent	S.E.	Percent	S.E.	Diff.	S.E.	Percent	S.E.	Percent	S.E.	Diff.	S.E.
OECD	Australia	12.15	(1.22)	24.08	(1.39)	-11.93	(1.67)	46.08	(1.85)	51.99	(1.29)	-5.91	(2.06)
	Austria	12.35	(1.67)	28.06	(1.94)	-15.72	(2.47)	57.18	(2.49)	59.80	(2.33)	-2.62	(3.09)
	Belgium	7.81	(1.41)	37.45	(2.34)	-29.64	(2.71)	65.12	(2.24)	43.51	(2.24)	21.62	(3.38)
	Canada	7.76	(0.91)	18.51	(1.21)	-10.75	(1.27)	30.01	(1.57)	42.27	(1.39)	-12.26	(1.85)
	Czech Republic	9.47	(2.00)	15.85	(2.05)	-6.38	(2.72)	54.71	(3.28)	63.85	(2.83)	-9.14	(4.30)
	Denmark	1.81	(0.74)	7.93	(1.52)	-6.12	(1.56)	67.79	(2.74)	69.13	(2.18)	-1.35	(3.27)
	Finland	1.51	(0.66)	7.80	(1.25)	-6.29	(1.46)	66.56	(2.72)	74.74	(2.14)	-8.17	(2.92)
	France	2.91	(1.04)	18.94	(1.82)	-16.03	(1.78)	67.48	(2.78)	69.90	(1.99)	-2.42	(3.28)
	Germany	6.29	(1.41)	20.18	(2.32)	-13.89	(2.58)	51.22	(2.61)	56.95	(2.13)	-5.72	(3.62)
	Greece	3.95	(1.10)	20.96	(1.50)	-17.01	(1.87)	59.98	(2.59)	62.33	(2.05)	-2.35	(3.27)
	Hungary	7.25	(1.84)	10.07	(1.36)	-2.82	(2.21)	67.92	(2.87)	80.07	(1.99)	-12.15	(3.24)
	Iceland	1.20	(0.58)	7.09	(1.03)	-5.89	(1.17)	79.80	(2.07)	76.15	(1.70)	3.65	(2.76)
	Ireland	11.26	(1.63)	29.63	(2.74)	-18.38	(2.95)	71.79	(2.09)	54.47	(2.36)	17.33	(3.27)
	Italy	6.56	(1.18)	15.16	(1.10)	-8.60	(1.50)	58.73	(2.11)	68.52	(1.76)	-9.79	(2.59)
	Japan	3.08	(1.24)	5.88	(1.68)	-2.81	(1.66)	84.09	(2.06)	88.24	(2.04)	-4.15	(2.50)
	Korea	1.78	(0.87)	7.26	(2.18)	-5.48	(1.56)	61.51	(3.19)	69.62	(2.52)	-8.11	(3.75)
	Luxembourg	7.17	(1.27)	18.61	(1.49)	-11.45	(1.95)	66.54	(2.85)	67.86	(1.67)	-1.33	(3.47)
	Mexico	17.55	(1.40)	9.57	(1.31)	7.98	(1.99)	42.56	(2.12)	50.46	(2.18)	-7.90	(2.90)
	Netherlands	11.38	(1.57)	38.45	(2.41)	-27.07	(2.72)	59.31	(2.64)	49.39	(2.84)	9.92	(3.86)
	New Zealand	4.69	(1.17)	18.10	(2.51)	-13.41	(2.69)	18.74	(1.72)	39.68	(2.08)	-20.94	(2.56)
	Norway	1.36	(0.54)	5.25	(1.06)	-3.89	(1.14)	92.58	(1.28)	83.09	(1.88)	9.49	(2.25)
	Poland	1.11	(0.47)	4.62	(0.81)	-3.51	(0.98)	69.54	(2.35)	83.42	(1.47)	-13.87	(2.63)
	Portugal	13.34	(2.10)	9.18	(1.22)	4.16	(2.58)	44.34	(3.05)	74.55	(2.05)	-30.21	(4.03)
	Slovak Republic	7.78	(1.39)	22.63	(1.96)	-14.85	(2.32)	63.70	(3.07)	63.68	(2.17)	0.02	(3.55)
	Spain	8.69	(1.34)	12.73	(1.19)	-4.04	(1.90)	60.29	(1.71)	68.36	(1.88)	-8.07	(2.54)
	Sweden	1.03	(0.45)	8.02	(1.33)	-7.00	(1.42)	87.30	(1.85)	79.02	(2.00)	8.28	(2.98)
	Switzerland	10.04	(1.24)	25.69	(1.22)	-15.65	(1.60)	66.25	(2.06)	65.08	(1.38)	1.17	(2.54)
	Turkey	22.98	(2.53)	30.38	(2.49)	-7.39	(3.82)	40.54	(2.98)	53.93	(2.61)	-13.38	(4.36)
	United Kingdom	1.09	(0.45)	7.45	(1.00)	-6.36	(1.03)	29.90	(2.62)	51.79	(1.98)	-21.89	(2.86)
	United States	7.43	(1.25)	14.46	(1.60)	-7.04	(1.99)	36.80	(2.40)	57.15	(2.27)	-20.35	(3.44)
	OECD average	**7.01**	**(0.25)**	**16.62**	**(0.36)**	**-9.61**	**(0.43)**	**59.14**	**(0.45)**	**63.82**	**(0.47)**	**-4.68**	**(0.69)**
Partners	Argentina	13.21	(2.14)	21.76	(2.40)	-8.55	(3.13)	68.90	(3.10)	59.07	(2.76)	9.83	(4.14)
	Azerbaijan	6.96	(1.68)	13.82	(2.10)	-6.86	(2.81)	61.68	(2.52)	56.58	(3.04)	5.10	(3.56)
	Brazil	6.15	(1.12)	15.88	(1.81)	-9.73	(2.30)	81.42	(1.98)	70.43	(2.11)	11.00	(2.98)
	Bulgaria	11.11	(1.87)	25.82	(2.29)	-14.71	(2.86)	60.10	(2.70)	53.36	(2.91)	6.74	(3.66)
	Chile	12.75	(1.60)	25.36	(1.92)	-12.61	(2.38)	66.62	(2.14)	63.27	(2.15)	3.35	(2.92)
	Colombia	3.86	(1.38)	5.35	(1.00)	-1.49	(1.56)	50.51	(3.99)	56.93	(3.47)	-6.42	(4.89)
	Croatia	18.14	(2.07)	45.00	(2.29)	-26.86	(2.98)	68.63	(2.05)	47.42	(2.08)	21.21	(3.02)
	Estonia	1.51	(0.54)	5.69	(1.20)	-4.17	(1.29)	59.33	(2.81)	74.31	(1.68)	-14.97	(3.24)
	Hong Kong-China	26.41	(2.28)	38.64	(2.53)	-12.23	(3.11)	21.53	(2.05)	42.75	(2.18)	-21.22	(2.81)
	Indonesia	5.04	(1.59)	4.53	(0.95)	0.50	(1.41)	67.26	(2.63)	80.40	(2.08)	-13.14	(3.39)
	Israel	19.15	(2.25)	34.64	(2.80)	-15.49	(3.39)	50.98	(3.05)	43.72	(2.51)	7.26	(3.61)
	Jordan	7.86	(1.40)	19.16	(1.86)	-11.30	(2.17)	48.21	(2.87)	51.79	(2.22)	-3.58	(3.43)
	Kyrgyzstan	21.57	(2.02)	27.16	(2.53)	-5.59	(3.15)	56.89	(2.78)	45.57	(2.60)	11.32	(3.02)
	Latvia	3.68	(1.18)	13.42	(2.17)	-9.74	(2.43)	67.26	(3.95)	75.36	(2.59)	-8.10	(5.00)
	Lithuania	2.48	(0.93)	9.44	(1.54)	-6.96	(1.75)	69.71	(2.12)	76.76	(1.52)	-7.05	(2.33)
	Macao-China	10.45	(1.42)	12.21	(1.64)	-1.76	(2.50)	33.12	(2.10)	61.08	(2.16)	-27.95	(2.83)
	Montenegro	7.84	(1.54)	19.97	(1.79)	-12.13	(2.66)	60.96	(2.46)	57.26	(2.45)	3.70	(3.77)
	Romania	13.46	(3.16)	30.68	(2.49)	-17.22	(4.34)	63.68	(4.81)	57.50	(2.54)	6.18	(5.81)
	Russian Federation	4.47	(1.04)	12.93	(1.74)	-8.46	(1.90)	39.06	(2.58)	56.56	(2.64)	-17.50	(3.62)
	Serbia	7.52	(1.29)	23.61	(1.84)	-16.09	(2.36)	62.60	(2.36)	59.09	(1.94)	3.51	(3.10)
	Slovenia	6.65	(1.64)	17.08	(1.47)	-10.42	(2.18)	59.32	(2.94)	68.51	(1.82)	-9.18	(3.37)
	Chinese Taipei	6.45	(1.57)	24.70	(1.77)	-18.24	(2.34)	62.34	(2.17)	57.63	(1.64)	4.71	(2.48)
	Thailand	0.00	(0.00)	0.00	(0.00)	0.00	(0.00)	59.32	(2.43)	82.94	(2.10)	-23.63	(3.05)
	Tunisia	5.18	(1.33)	17.73	(2.15)	-12.55	(2.67)	69.48	(2.17)	65.08	(2.44)	4.41	(3.23)
	Uruguay	13.27	(2.74)	25.77	(2.46)	-12.49	(3.12)	65.76	(2.95)	51.06	(2.43)	14.71	(3.62)

[Part 3/3]
Table A4.4 Difference in means test results on alternative definition for selected variables

Percentage of students who spend 4 up to 6 hours or 6 hours or more in school learning science in regular lessons

		Resilient Percent	Resilient S.E.	DLA Percent	DLA S.E.	Diff.	Diff. S.E.
OECD	Australia	41.18	(1.75)	19.77	(1.12)	21.41	(1.87)
	Austria	26.76	(2.45)	5.25	(0.92)	21.51	(2.50)
	Belgium	25.62	(2.07)	7.32	(1.02)	18.30	(2.11)
	Canada	58.34	(1.68)	33.75	(1.51)	24.58	(2.17)
	Czech Republic	33.36	(2.67)	6.53	(1.03)	26.83	(2.81)
	Denmark	28.94	(2.61)	18.47	(1.64)	10.47	(2.85)
	Finland	31.29	(2.54)	14.85	(1.75)	16.44	(2.62)
	France	28.60	(2.69)	4.49	(0.75)	24.11	(2.68)
	Germany	40.00	(2.63)	10.66	(1.27)	29.34	(3.18)
	Greece	35.48	(2.51)	12.11	(1.74)	23.37	(3.22)
	Hungary	22.52	(2.65)	6.03	(1.09)	16.49	(2.72)
	Iceland	18.71	(1.90)	14.87	(1.38)	3.83	(2.45)
	Ireland	15.85	(1.81)	12.96	(1.59)	2.89	(2.53)
	Italy	33.27	(2.11)	12.14	(1.48)	21.13	(2.48)
	Japan	12.46	(1.67)	4.54	(0.78)	7.92	(1.79)
	Korea	36.22	(3.10)	19.20	(1.70)	17.03	(3.41)
	Luxembourg	22.72	(2.68)	8.19	(0.98)	14.53	(2.75)
	Mexico	37.69	(2.37)	31.74	(2.16)	5.95	(3.23)
	Netherlands	22.85	(1.89)	4.11	(0.89)	18.74	(2.02)
	New Zealand	76.16	(1.94)	38.76	(2.34)	37.39	(3.03)
	Norway	5.93	(1.25)	4.94	(1.02)	0.99	(1.49)
	Poland	28.01	(2.39)	10.21	(1.18)	17.80	(2.59)
	Portugal	40.53	(2.57)	12.11	(1.37)	28.42	(3.02)
	Slovak Republic	27.41	(2.44)	6.62	(1.18)	20.80	(2.54)
	Spain	29.63	(1.63)	11.33	(1.10)	18.30	(1.94)
	Sweden	10.65	(1.79)	9.30	(1.12)	1.35	(2.28)
	Switzerland	22.09	(1.88)	5.99	(0.80)	16.10	(2.00)
	Turkey	35.74	(2.55)	12.43	(1.80)	23.32	(3.11)
	United Kingdom	68.12	(2.70)	37.73	(1.94)	30.39	(2.96)
	United States	53.16	(2.76)	22.23	(2.11)	30.93	(3.45)
	OECD average	**32.21**	**(0.46)**	**13.81**	**(0.32)**	**18.39**	**(0.53)**
Partners	Argentina	14.84	(2.07)	5.97	(1.37)	8.87	(2.33)
	Azerbaijan	21.74	(2.42)	14.32	(1.81)	7.41	(2.97)
	Brazil	9.38	(1.72)	3.90	(1.08)	5.49	(2.10)
	Bulgaria	25.43	(2.92)	10.40	(1.75)	15.03	(3.04)
	Chile	18.48	(1.95)	6.00	(1.02)	12.48	(2.26)
	Colombia	44.22	(3.70)	29.94	(3.64)	14.28	(4.14)
	Croatia	10.02	(1.26)	4.57	(0.87)	5.45	(1.39)
	Estonia	38.06	(2.75)	17.74	(1.71)	20.33	(3.00)
	Hong Kong-China	51.68	(2.45)	16.22	(1.78)	35.46	(2.97)
	Indonesia	26.71	(2.63)	12.93	(1.66)	13.78	(3.21)
	Israel	24.43	(2.31)	8.78	(1.08)	15.65	(2.51)
	Jordan	40.89	(2.94)	20.27	(2.04)	20.62	(3.37)
	Kyrgyzstan	15.22	(2.19)	10.45	(2.95)	4.77	(2.91)
	Latvia	28.50	(3.40)	9.58	(1.89)	18.92	(3.95)
	Lithuania	27.23	(1.94)	11.31	(1.27)	15.92	(2.31)
	Macao-China	56.10	(2.30)	25.61	(2.14)	30.49	(2.89)
	Montenegro	29.28	(2.60)	15.38	(1.59)	13.89	(3.32)
	Romania	22.26	(2.54)	9.68	(1.28)	12.58	(2.72)
	Russian Federation	54.72	(2.79)	27.20	(2.49)	27.52	(3.51)
	Serbia	28.28	(2.46)	12.04	(1.38)	16.24	(2.81)
	Slovenia	31.80	(2.63)	7.43	(1.21)	24.36	(2.50)
	Chinese Taipei	30.94	(1.89)	11.23	(1.43)	19.71	(2.12)
	Thailand	40.48	(2.42)	16.73	(2.11)	23.75	(3.06)
	Tunisia	23.23	(1.75)	9.21	(1.40)	14.03	(2.21)
	Uruguay	17.66	(2.11)	10.39	(1.38)	7.27	(2.49)

[Part 1/2]
Table A4.5 Country means of student approaches to learning

	General interest in science		Instrumental motivation to learn science		Participation in science related activities		Self-concept		Self-efficacy	
	Mean	S.E.	Mean	S.E.	Mean	S.E.	Mean	S.E.	Mean	S.E.
OECD										
Australia	-0.22	(0.01)	0.11	(0.02)	-0.29	(0.01)	-0.03	(0.01)	0.12	(0.01)
Austria	0.05	(0.02)	-0.40	(0.03)	0.01	(0.02)	0.09	(0.02)	-0.11	(0.02)
Belgium	0.03	(0.02)	-0.22	(0.02)	0.01	(0.01)	-0.14	(0.02)	-0.07	(0.02)
Canada	0.11	(0.01)	0.32	(0.02)	-0.15	(0.01)	0.27	(0.02)	0.21	(0.01)
Czech Republic	-0.03	(0.02)	-0.24	(0.02)	0.05	(0.02)	-0.03	(0.02)	0.14	(0.02)
Denmark	-0.17	(0.02)	0.04	(0.01)	-0.15	(0.02)	-0.08	(0.02)	-0.08	(0.03)
Finland	-0.24	(0.02)	-0.21	(0.02)	-0.16	(0.01)	0.07	(0.02)	0.03	(0.02)
France	0.20	(0.02)	-0.07	(0.02)	-0.01	(0.02)	-0.11	(0.02)	-0.06	(0.02)
Germany	0.19	(0.02)	-0.07	(0.02)	0.12	(0.02)	0.26	(0.02)	0.07	(0.02)
Greece	0.19	(0.02)	0.08	(0.02)	0.27	(0.02)	0.04	(0.02)	-0.13	(0.02)
Hungary	-0.07	(0.01)	-0.07	(0.02)	0.32	(0.02)	-0.21	(0.02)	-0.06	(0.01)
Iceland	-0.14	(0.02)	0.09	(0.02)	-0.21	(0.02)	0.10	(0.02)	0.14	(0.02)
Ireland	-0.14	(0.02)	0.15	(0.02)	-0.43	(0.02)	-0.13	(0.02)	0.01	(0.02)
Italy	0.18	(0.01)	0.12	(0.01)	0.26	(0.01)	0.16	(0.01)	-0.20	(0.01)
Japan	-0.13	(0.02)	-0.43	(0.03)	-0.62	(0.02)	-0.87	(0.02)	-0.53	(0.02)
Korea	-0.24	(0.02)	-0.26	(0.02)	-0.19	(0.02)	-0.71	(0.02)	-0.22	(0.02)
Luxembourg	0.14	(0.02)	-0.14	(0.02)	0.11	(0.01)	0.24	(0.02)	-0.13	(0.02)
Mexico	0.76	(0.01)	0.54	(0.01)	0.73	(0.02)	0.53	(0.01)	0.09	(0.02)
Netherlands	-0.35	(0.02)	-0.22	(0.02)	-0.26	(0.02)	-0.33	(0.02)	0.03	(0.02)
New Zealand	-0.09	(0.02)	0.18	(0.02)	-0.26	(0.02)	-0.05	(0.02)	-0.01	(0.02)
Norway	-0.03	(0.03)	-0.16	(0.02)	-0.11	(0.02)	0.05	(0.02)	0.12	(0.02)
Poland	0.06	(0.02)	0.16	(0.02)	0.64	(0.01)	0.08	(0.02)	0.26	(0.02)
Portugal	0.16	(0.02)	0.47	(0.02)	0.45	(0.02)	0.31	(0.02)	0.20	(0.02)
Slovak Republic	-0.11	(0.02)	-0.19	(0.02)	0.23	(0.02)	0.15	(0.02)	0.11	(0.02)
Spain	-0.18	(0.01)	0.06	(0.02)	-0.14	(0.02)	-0.01	(0.01)	-0.07	(0.02)
Sweden	-0.13	(0.03)	-0.05	(0.02)	-0.41	(0.02)	0.01	(0.02)	-0.07	(0.03)
Switzerland	0.00	(0.02)	-0.25	(0.02)	0.03	(0.02)	0.10	(0.01)	-0.19	(0.02)
Turkey	0.22	(0.02)	0.34	(0.02)	0.57	(0.02)	0.15	(0.03)	0.02	(0.03)
United Kingdom	-0.01	(0.02)	0.18	(0.02)	-0.35	(0.02)	0.02	(0.01)	0.19	(0.02)
United States	0.03	(0.02)	0.29	(0.02)	-0.09	(0.02)	0.21	(0.02)	0.22	(0.02)
OECD average	**0.00**	**(0.00)**	**0.01**	**(0.00)**	**-0.00**	**(0.00)**	**0.00**	**(0.00)**	**0.00**	**(0.00)**
Partners										
Argentina	0.22	(0.02)	0.44	(0.02)	0.43	(0.03)	0.27	(0.03)	-0.05	(0.02)
Azerbaijan	0.60	(0.03)	0.55	(0.02)	1.22	(0.02)	0.65	(0.03)	-0.46	(0.03)
Brazil	0.51	(0.02)	0.48	(0.01)	0.53	(0.02)	0.36	(0.02)	-0.05	(0.02)
Bulgaria	0.18	(0.02)	0.36	(0.02)	0.78	(0.02)	0.37	(0.02)	-0.04	(0.03)
Chile	0.36	(0.02)	0.52	(0.03)	0.49	(0.02)	0.18	(0.02)	0.06	(0.02)
Colombia	1.15	(0.02)	0.65	(0.02)	1.00	(0.02)	0.75	(0.02)	0.09	(0.02)
Croatia	0.17	(0.02)	0.05	(0.03)	0.36	(0.01)	-0.03	(0.02)	0.14	(0.02)
Estonia	0.19	(0.01)	0.06	(0.01)	0.40	(0.01)	0.11	(0.02)	0.03	(0.02)
Hong Kong-China	0.19	(0.01)	0.16	(0.02)	0.26	(0.02)	-0.25	(0.02)	0.06	(0.02)
Indonesia	0.56	(0.02)	0.76	(0.02)	0.57	(0.02)	0.16	(0.03)	-0.70	(0.02)
Israel	-0.21	(0.03)	-0.37	(0.03)	0.13	(0.02)	0.27	(0.02)	0.02	(0.03)
Jordan	0.67	(0.02)	0.80	(0.02)	0.97	(0.02)	0.74	(0.02)	0.21	(0.02)
Kyrgyzstan	0.91	(0.01)	0.84	(0.02)	1.33	(0.02)	0.69	(0.02)	-0.15	(0.02)
Latvia	0.16	(0.02)	0.01	(0.02)	0.25	(0.02)	0.03	(0.02)	-0.02	(0.02)
Lithuania	0.35	(0.01)	0.37	(0.01)	0.26	(0.02)	-0.24	(0.02)	0.01	(0.02)
Macao-China	0.10	(0.01)	0.39	(0.02)	0.27	(0.01)	-0.11	(0.02)	-0.11	(0.02)
Montenegro	0.42	(0.02)	0.45	(0.02)	0.75	(0.01)	0.49	(0.01)	-0.02	(0.02)
Romania	0.38	(0.02)	0.40	(0.02)	0.64	(0.02)	0.34	(0.02)	-0.35	(0.02)
Russian Federation	0.28	(0.02)	0.21	(0.02)	0.56	(0.03)	0.16	(0.02)	-0.01	(0.03)
Serbia	0.26	(0.02)	0.11	(0.02)	0.54	(0.02)	0.24	(0.02)	0.05	(0.02)
Slovenia	0.03	(0.02)	0.06	(0.02)	0.43	(0.01)	0.22	(0.01)	-0.10	(0.01)
Chinese Taipei	0.09	(0.02)	0.27	(0.01)	0.40	(0.01)	-0.40	(0.02)	0.18	(0.02)
Thailand	0.79	(0.02)	0.72	(0.01)	1.10	(0.01)	0.69	(0.01)	0.06	(0.02)
Tunisia	0.77	(0.02)	0.84	(0.02)	1.11	(0.01)	0.64	(0.02)	-0.11	(0.02)
Uruguay	0.25	(0.02)	0.19	(0.02)	0.15	(0.02)	0.35	(0.02)	0.13	(0.02)

[Part 2/2]
Table A4.5 Country means of student approaches to learning

		Information in science related careers		School preparation for science careers		Share of students who took general science compulsory courses this or last year		The average number of compulsory courses in general science, physics, biology and chemistry*		Average number of science regular hours	
		Mean	S.E.	Mean	S.E.	% of students	S.E.	Mean	S.E.	Mean	S.E.
OECD	Australia	0.17	(0.01)	0.19	(0.02)	84.8	(0.7)	3.13	(0.06)	3.18	(0.03)
	Austria	-0.10	(0.02)	-0.24	(0.03)	a	a	3.36	(0.06)	2.41	(0.06)
	Belgium	-0.23	(0.01)	-0.12	(0.02)	61.4	(1.2)	3.53	(0.06)	2.56	(0.04)
	Canada	0.28	(0.01)	0.33	(0.01)	91.1	(0.3)	3.29	(0.03)	3.79	(0.03)
	Czech Republic	-0.10	(0.02)	-0.18	(0.03)	62.2	(0.9)	5.99	(0.08)	2.79	(0.06)
	Denmark	-0.10	(0.02)	-0.04	(0.02)	16.4	(0.7)	5.19	(0.04)	3.19	(0.04)
	Finland	0.13	(0.01)	0.17	(0.01)	88.0	(0.8)	7.01	(0.05)	3.09	(0.04)
	France	0.00	(0.02)	0.07	(0.03)	a	a	5.32	(0.03)	2.78	(0.05)
	Germany	0.02	(0.02)	0.11	(0.02)	71.8	(1.0)	5.84	(0.05)	2.97	(0.05)
	Greece	0.33	(0.02)	-0.13	(0.02)	a	a	4.00	(0.04)	3.10	(0.05)
	Hungary	-0.03	(0.01)	0.04	(0.02)	a	a	4.71	(0.05)	2.47	(0.04)
	Iceland	-0.06	(0.01)	0.05	(0.02)	91.8	(0.4)	5.96	(0.04)	2.95	(0.02)
	Ireland	0.00	(0.02)	0.19	(0.02)	64.7	(2.4)	0.83	(0.03)	2.52	(0.04)
	Italy	0.07	(0.01)	-0.09	(0.02)	73.5	(1.1)	3.74	(0.06)	2.81	(0.05)
	Japan	-0.39	(0.02)	-0.52	(0.02)	100.0	v	3.33	(0.05)	2.69	(0.05)
	Korea	-0.33	(0.02)	-0.27	(0.02)	96.1	(0.4)	1.82	(0.01)	3.54	(0.06)
	Luxembourg	-0.10	(0.01)	-0.11	(0.02)	a	a	3.76	(0.02)	2.29	(0.02)
	Mexico	-0.44	(0.02)	0.48	(0.02)	38.7	(0.7)	2.59	(0.04)	2.96	(0.03)
	Netherlands	-0.35	(0.02)	-0.24	(0.01)	72.7	(0.9)	4.59	(0.07)	2.12	(0.04)
	New Zealand	0.14	(0.02)	0.21	(0.02)	93.3	(0.5)	3.48	(0.07)	3.97	(0.04)
	Norway	-0.11	(0.02)	-0.31	(0.02)	100.0	v	2.00	v	2.63	(0.03)
	Poland	0.31	(0.02)	0.03	(0.02)	a	a	6.00	v	2.68	(0.04)
	Portugal	0.40	(0.02)	0.22	(0.01)	95.5	(0.5)	3.93	(0.05)	3.02	(0.04)
	Slovak Republic	-0.05	(0.02)	-0.14	(0.03)	a	a	4.88	(0.05)	2.36	(0.07)
	Spain	0.01	(0.01)	0.07	(0.01)	88.2	(0.5)	5.14	(0.04)	3.00	(0.04)
	Sweden	-0.13	(0.02)	-0.07	(0.02)	58.9	(1.2)	4.64	(0.08)	2.80	(0.03)
	Switzerland	0.04	(0.01)	0.02	(0.02)	83.1	(0.8)	4.66	(0.06)	2.32	(0.04)
	Turkey	0.27	(0.03)	-0.14	(0.03)	75.5	(0.9)	4.08	(0.05)	2.68	(0.08)
	United Kingdom	0.00	(0.02)	0.21	(0.02)	71.2	(0.8)	3.17	(0.04)	4.14	(0.03)
	United States	0.35	(0.02)	0.25	(0.02)	80.9	(0.9)	2.98	(0.04)	3.38	(0.05)
	OECD average	**0.00**	**(0.00)**	**0.00**	**(0.00)**	**76.52**	**(0.15)**	**4.10**	**(0.01)**	**2.91**	**(0.01)**
Partners	Argentina	-0.49	(0.03)	0.12	(0.02)	21.3	(1.1)	1.28	(0.06)	2.21	(0.06)
	Azerbaijan	0.36	(0.02)	0.65	(0.02)	a	a	3.58	(0.07)	2.73	(0.05)
	Brazil	0.33	(0.02)	0.16	(0.02)	11.6	(0.7)	0.70	(0.04)	2.18	(0.03)
	Bulgaria	0.25	(0.02)	0.40	(0.02)	a	a	4.70	(0.05)	2.52	(0.07)
	Chile	0.26	(0.02)	0.22	(0.03)	59.2	(1.0)	4.69	(0.10)	2.26	(0.05)
	Colombia	-0.02	(0.03)	0.51	(0.03)	17.4	(1.0)	1.00	(0.05)	3.41	(0.10)
	Croatia	0.02	(0.01)	0.18	(0.02)	a	a	4.35	(0.06)	1.99	(0.04)
	Estonia	-0.01	(0.02)	0.28	(0.02)	50.4	(0.9)	5.18	(0.06)	3.15	(0.04)
	Hong Kong-China	0.23	(0.01)	-0.13	(0.02)	59.2	(1.6)	3.64	(0.07)	2.88	(0.05)
	Indonesia	0.34	(0.03)	0.33	(0.03)	90.4	(0.6)	5.38	(0.06)	3.11	(0.07)
	Israel	0.20	(0.03)	-0.08	(0.03)	70.0	(1.0)	3.68	(0.07)	2.35	(0.05)
	Jordan	0.44	(0.02)	0.50	(0.02)	56.1	(1.8)	4.84	(0.09)	3.09	(0.05)
	Kyrgyzstan	0.30	(0.02)	0.64	(0.02)	68.3	(1.0)	4.57	(0.07)	2.00	(0.06)
	Latvia	0.05	(0.02)	0.22	(0.01)	78.4	(0.8)	6.60	(0.05)	2.78	(0.05)
	Lithuania	0.23	(0.01)	0.43	(0.02)	a	a	4.71	(0.04)	2.65	(0.04)
	Macao-China	-0.12	(0.01)	-0.17	(0.01)	43.2	(0.8)	3.23	(0.04)	3.51	(0.03)
	Montenegro	-0.03	(0.01)	0.34	(0.02)	82.5	(0.6)	6.07	(0.03)	2.71	(0.03)
	Romania	0.06	(0.02)	0.40	(0.03)	39.6	(1.1)	3.09	(0.11)	2.18	(0.07)
	Russian Federation	0.39	(0.02)	0.30	(0.02)	3.4	(0.9)	5.96	(0.02)	3.49	(0.06)
	Serbia	0.13	(0.01)	0.15	(0.02)	a	a	4.83	(0.04)	2.74	(0.05)
	Slovenia	0.03	(0.01)	0.07	(0.01)	66.6	(0.8)	6.23	(0.02)	2.71	(0.03)
	Chinese Taipei	0.06	(0.01)	0.26	(0.02)	43.4	(1.0)	4.26	(0.07)	2.81	(0.05)
	Thailand	0.26	(0.02)	0.63	(0.01)	91.4	(0.5)	4.42	(0.07)	3.66	(0.03)
	Tunisia	0.41	(0.02)	0.55	(0.02)	72.5	(0.9)	3.69	(0.05)	2.52	(0.04)
	Uruguay	-0.23	(0.02)	0.09	(0.02)	46.2	(0.9)	3.59	(0.07)	2.33	(0.04)

Note: * The number of additional courses was calculated treating missing values as zeroes.
a - The category does not apply in the country concerned. Data are therefore missing.
v - There is no variation in this indicator so the standard errors were not calculated.

Table A4.6 School policies, descriptive statistics

		Share of students in private schools*		Share of students in schools which compete for students with other schools		Share of students in schools who select students based on academic record		Index of science promotion activities		Index of school's educational resources and student performance in science	
		% of students	S.E.	% of students	S.E.	% of students	S.E.	Mean	S.E.	Mean	S.E.
OECD	Australia	w	w	93.6	(1.1)	9.4	(1.8)	0.41	(0.04)	0.41	(0.05)
	Austria	9.3	(2.2)	64.4	(3.5)	65.4	(2.1)	-0.38	(0.07)	0.36	(0.08)
	Belgium	w	w	90.7	(2.0)	25.7	(2.6)	-0.22	(0.05)	-0.04	(0.06)
	Canada	7.2	(0.6)	76.8	(2.3)	10.6	(1.2)	0.41	(0.04)	0.09	(0.05)
	Czech Republic	6.5	(2.7)	85.9	(2.5)	42.2	(3.2)	0.46	(0.06)	-0.08	(0.06)
	Denmark	20.0	(2.7)	77.5	(3.3)	4.0	(1.5)	-0.82	(0.07)	-0.09	(0.06)
	Finland	3.0	(1.2)	56.0	(3.7)	4.3	(1.9)	-0.60	(0.06)	-0.23	(0.06)
	France	w	w	w	w	w	w	w	w	w	w
	Germany	5.6	(1.7)	82.8	(2.6)	38.7	(3.8)	-0.10	(0.05)	0.11	(0.07)
	Greece	5.2	(1.2)	59.8	(3.4)	4.5	(1.7)	-0.42	(0.06)	-0.03	(0.08)
	Hungary	15.7	(3.2)	75.7	(3.6)	64.5	(3.8)	0.62	(0.06)	0.20	(0.07)
	Iceland	1.1	(0.1)	27.8	(0.2)	1.1	(0.0)	-0.71	0.00	0.20	0.00
	Ireland	60.1	(1.2)	83.5	(2.7)	2.5	(1.2)	0.12	(0.08)	-0.32	(0.07)
	Italy	3.8	(0.7)	80.8	(2.5)	7.0	(1.7)	0.01	(0.04)	0.18	(0.05)
	Japan	31.1	(1.3)	89.6	(2.2)	86.4	(2.5)	-1.15	(0.07)	0.45	(0.07)
	Korea	46.4	(3.9)	84.4	(3.0)	59.1	(4.0)	0.54	(0.07)	-0.19	(0.06)
	Luxembourg	14.5	(0.1)	66.8	(0.1)	41.6	(0.1)	0.15	0.00	0.26	0.00
	Mexico	14.8	(2.1)	84.3	(2.0)	38.0	(2.8)	-0.03	(0.04)	-0.86	(0.06)
	Netherlands	67.7	(4.3)	89.6	(2.1)	65.4	(3.9)	-0.50	(0.08)	0.26	(0.07)
	New Zealand	5.8	(0.3)	89.2	(2.1)	9.4	(2.1)	0.51	(0.06)	0.31	(0.06)
	Norway	1.9	(0.9)	34.3	(3.6)	0.0	(0.0)	-0.50	(0.05)	-0.44	(0.05)
	Poland	1.6	(0.1)	64.9	(3.5)	13.5	(2.5)	0.58	(0.04)	-0.09	(0.07)
	Portugal	10.2	(1.3)	72.8	(3.9)	6.7	(2.1)	0.66	(0.06)	-0.38	(0.06)
	Slovak Republic	7.7	(1.9)	91.4	(2.1)	46.5	(2.6)	0.70	(0.05)	-0.54	(0.05)
	Spain	35.5	(0.9)	79.8	(2.2)	3.0	(0.9)	0.19	(0.06)	-0.02	(0.06)
	Sweden	8.4	(0.8)	62.9	(3.7)	1.9	(0.7)	-0.49	(0.07)	0.04	(0.06)
	Switzerland	4.9	(0.6)	41.6	(2.7)	51.2	(2.5)	-0.25	(0.04)	0.67	(0.06)
	Turkey	2.3	(1.4)	68.4	(3.9)	29.1	(3.5)	-0.16	(0.08)	-0.84	(0.08)
	United Kingdom	7.1	(0.7)	92.3	(1.5)	10.0	(1.3)	0.41	(0.06)	0.27	(0.08)
	United States	7.7	(1.0)	74.1	(3.1)	8.0	(1.9)	0.47	(0.08)	0.29	(0.08)
	OECD average	**15.00**	**(0.31)**	**73.85**	**(0.50)**	**25.85**	**(0.42)**	**-0.00**	**(0.01)**	**-0.00**	**(0.01)**
Partners	Argentina	34.3	(3.8)	80.8	(3.4)	7.1	(2.1)	0.11	(0.07)	-0.54	(0.08)
	Azerbaijan	0.9	(0.4)	m	m	17.3	(3.1)	0.27	(0.07)	-1.37	(0.05)
	Brazil	13.5	(1.2)	67.3	(2.4)	8.0	(1.6)	0.24	(0.04)	-0.97	(0.06)
	Bulgaria	m	m	84.9	(3.2)	83.9	(2.7)	0.03	(0.06)	-0.58	(0.05)
	Chile	55.3	(2.1)	80.9	(3.3)	32.6	(3.7)	-0.27	(0.12)	-0.63	(0.09)
	Colombia	18.9	(2.6)	75.8	(5.0)	19.8	(3.4)	0.82	(0.08)	-1.17	(0.07)
	Croatia	1.4	(1.0)	77.0	(3.5)	90.6	(1.9)	0.15	(0.08)	-0.55	(0.06)
	Estonia	1.9	(0.9)	78.6	(2.6)	44.4	(3.4)	0.90	(0.04)	-0.28	(0.05)
	Hong Kong-China	92.5	(0.2)	98.8	(0.9)	82.8	(3.2)	0.92	(0.06)	0.35	(0.08)
	Indonesia	39.9	(3.5)	94.8	(1.4)	62.9	(4.4)	-0.04	(0.09)	-1.63	(0.09)
	Israel	29.9	(3.6)	82.8	(3.1)	35.7	(4.5)	0.20	(0.09)	0.07	(0.09)
	Jordan	19.9	(1.6)	55.8	(3.9)	27.0	(3.4)	0.88	(0.07)	-0.74	(0.07)
	Kyrgyzstan	1.4	(0.7)	64.9	(2.9)	22.7	(3.2)	0.76	(0.05)	-2.32	(0.06)
	Latvia	0.0	v	95.9	(1.6)	17.6	(2.4)	0.19	(0.03)	-0.54	(0.04)
	Lithuania	0.7	(0.7)	72.7	(2.9)	11.1	(2.3)	1.19	(0.04)	-0.39	(0.05)
	Macao-China	96.2	(0.0)	89.4	(0.1)	66.4	(0.1)	0.45	0.00	0.06	0.00
	Montenegro	0.2	(0.0)	98.5	(0.1)	66.8	(0.2)	0.34	0.00	-1.26	0.00
	Romania	0.0	v	54.8	(5.4)	61.6	(4.2)	0.77	(0.08)	-0.74	(0.07)
	Russian Federation	0.0	v	68.0	(4.3)	10.9	(2.1)	1.19	(0.05)	-1.18	(0.04)
	Serbia	0.6	(0.7)	72.9	(3.6)	91.4	(2.1)	0.31	(0.07)	-0.69	(0.05)
	Slovenia	2.3	(0.0)	52.4	(0.5)	38.2	(0.2)	1.15	0.00	0.22	(0.01)
	Chinese Taipei	35.1	(2.4)	93.7	(2.1)	52.8	(3.1)	0.77	(0.06)	0.59	(0.12)
	Thailand	16.5	(0.7)	88.3	(2.9)	43.5	(4.0)	1.34	(0.06)	-0.67	(0.07)
	Tunisia	2.3	(1.0)	51.1	(5.1)	23.6	(3.6)	0.36	(0.08)	-0.69	(0.05)
	Uruguay	14.8	(0.8)	47.9	(2.9)	9.0	(1.7)	-0.01	(0.05)	-0.72	(0.07)

Note: * missing information was coded as zero so this column contains the share of students in private schools among all students tested in PISA.
m - Data are not available. These data were collected but subsequently removed from the publication for technical reasons.
w - Data have been withdrawn at the request of the country concerned.
v - There is no variation in this indicator so the standard errors were not calculated.

[Part 1/2]
Table A4.7 Odds ratios for the background model used in Chapter 3

		ESCS		School average ESCS		Indicator for students with an immigrant background		Indicator for students speaking a different language than the language of the test		Indicator for female students		Indicator for students in 7th grade		Indicator for students in 8th grade		Indicator for students in 9th grade		Indicator for students in 10th grade	
		Ratio	S.E.	Ratio	S.E.	Ratio	S.E.	Ratio	S.E.	Ratio	S.E.	Ratio	S.E.	Ratio	S.E.	Ratio	S.E.	Ratio	S.E.
OECD	Australia	1.89	(0.16)	2.43	(0.22)	1.06	(0.15)	0.98	(0.19)	0.85	(0.10)	1.00	(0.00)	0.00	(1.35)	0.44	(0.28)	m	m
	Austria	1.12	(0.26)	18.38	(0.40)	0.46	(0.51)	0.32	(0.63)	0.57	(0.19)	0.00	(1.44)	0.13	(1.09)	0.62	(0.20)	m	m
	Belgium	1.26	(0.21)	16.16	(0.25)	0.52	(0.24)	1.80	(0.18)	0.60	(0.19)	0.00	(1.40)	0.00	(7.58)	0.18	(0.21)	m	m
	Canada	1.61	(0.15)	1.80	(0.16)	0.97	(0.19)	0.69	(0.23)	0.79	(0.11)	0.00	(2.44)	0.00	(6.95)	0.38	(0.18)	m	m
	Czech Republic	1.60	(0.35)	12.16	(0.39)	1.17	(0.60)	0.63	(0.66)	0.72	(0.18)	0.00	(1.09)	0.07	(1.42)	0.85	(0.19)	m	m
	Denmark	1.76	(0.24)	2.20	(0.31)	0.47	(0.45)	0.65	(0.60)	0.63	(0.19)	0.00	(1.29)	0.21	(0.38)	m	m	1.24	(0.77)
	Finland	1.74	(0.18)	1.08	(0.35)	0.13	(1.29)	0.98	(0.81)	0.91	(0.17)	0.00	(0.93)	0.59	(0.25)	m	m	m	m
	France	0.92	(0.28)	9.87	(0.46)	0.91	(0.32)	0.56	(0.49)	0.53	(0.22)	0.00	(3.13)	0.00	(8.07)	0.20	(0.29)	m	m
	Germany	1.14	(0.31)	16.25	(0.35)	0.64	(0.40)	0.33	(0.48)	0.66	(0.25)	0.00	(0.28)	0.42	(0.40)	m	m	2.67	(0.21)
	Greece	1.73	(0.22)	3.01	(0.24)	1.13	(0.36)	0.45	(0.95)	1.09	(0.20)	0.00	(0.33)	0.00	(0.24)	0.35	(0.73)	m	m
	Hungary	1.58	(0.36)	14.70	(0.28)	1.38	(0.89)	0.00	(0.96)	0.44	(0.27)	0.00	(0.74)	0.00	(8.61)	m	m	1.89	(0.21)
	Iceland	1.79	(0.21)	0.83	(0.24)	0.43	(1.19)	0.47	(1.01)	1.04	(0.19)	a	a	a	a	0.00	(0.37)	m	m
	Ireland	1.79	(0.23)	2.91	(0.31)	1.63	(0.44)	0.38	(0.65)	0.96	(0.16)	0.00	(1.75)	0.32	(0.99)	m	m	1.81	(0.21)
	Italy	1.66	(0.18)	6.28	(0.16)	1.07	(0.28)	0.83	(0.15)	0.60	(0.12)	0.00	(0.64)	0.12	(1.55)	0.41	(0.17)	m	m
	Japan	1.35	(0.26)	15.19	(0.38)	0.94	(1.01)	0.00	(7.44)	0.80	(0.19)	a	a	a	a	a	a	m	m
	Korea	1.03	(0.19)	7.44	(0.27)	c	c	c	c	0.84	(0.17)	a	a	a	a	0.00	(1.22)	m	m
	Luxembourg	1.16	(0.19)	4.00	(0.25)	0.33	(0.21)	2.71	(0.83)	0.53	(0.20)	0.00	(1.21)	0.53	(0.36)	m	m	3.66	(0.22)
	Mexico	1.15	(0.17)	1.76	(0.16)	0.09	(0.70)	0.74	(0.52)	0.61	(0.12)	0.15	(1.43)	0.12	(0.61)	0.31	(0.22)	m	m
	Netherlands	1.05	(0.28)	46.68	(0.48)	0.33	(0.46)	1.26	(0.55)	0.67	(0.21)	0.00	(1.21)	0.07	(0.81)	0.35	(0.26)	m	m
	New Zealand	1.61	(0.18)	3.13	(0.20)	0.97	(0.32)	0.91	(0.38)	0.96	(0.18)	a	a	a	a	0.00	(1.44)	0.36	(0.49)
	Norway	1.71	(0.24)	1.66	(0.31)	1.01	(0.38)	0.57	(0.49)	1.06	(0.16)	a	a	a	a	0.03	(6.68)	m	m
	Poland	2.14	(0.21)	0.85	(0.26)	0.00	(1.18)	1.13	(1.05)	0.71	(0.12)	0.00	(1.20)	0.00	(6.16)	m	m	191.78	(7.46)
	Portugal	1.45	(0.24)	1.32	(0.21)	0.00	(9.10)	0.06	(7.32)	0.51	(0.17)	0.00	(8.20)	0.02	(0.70)	0.15	(0.24)	m	m
	Slovak Republic	1.95	(0.35)	5.98	(0.34)	0.00	(0.54)	0.81	(0.27)	0.80	(0.19)	0.00	(0.54)	0.00	(0.41)	0.73	(0.20)	m	m
	Spain	1.53	(0.24)	1.58	(0.21)	0.41	(0.42)	0.73	(0.19)	0.61	(0.17)	0.00	(1.07)	0.02	(0.59)	0.13	(0.22)	m	m
	Sweden	1.69	(0.21)	1.79	(0.29)	0.38	(0.46)	0.70	(0.45)	0.80	(0.19)	a	a	0.01	(6.03)	m	m	1.15	(0.82)
	Switzerland	1.27	(0.21)	5.99	(0.25)	0.35	(0.26)	0.66	(0.30)	0.82	(0.16)	0.10	(1.12)	0.28	(0.22)	m	m	1.38	(0.21)
	Turkey	1.54	(0.28)	5.46	(0.28)	0.05	(6.53)	1.12	(0.48)	1.13	(0.21)	6.61	(0.76)	2.10	(0.67)	1.95	(0.20)	m	m
	United Kingdom	2.64	(0.23)	1.74	(0.29)	0.94	(0.36)	0.59	(0.43)	0.70	(0.15)	a	a	a	a	a	a	0.78	(0.32)
	United States	1.93	(0.19)	1.58	(0.24)	1.08	(0.28)	0.51	(0.31)	0.64	(0.16)	0.00	(1.47)	0.00	(1.49)	0.37	(0.36)	m	m
	OECD average	**1.52**	**(0.04)**	**4.02**	**(0.05)**	**0.18**	**(0.39)**	**0.50**	**(0.64)**	**0.73**	**(0.03)**	**0.00**	**(0.34)**	**0.01**	**(0.61)**	**0.15**	**(0.23)**	**1.31**	**(0.25)**
Partners	Argentina	1.39	(0.21)	3.71	(0.28)	1.58	(0.49)	0.00	(7.43)	0.83	(0.23)	0.00	(0.82)	0.18	(0.44)	0.31	(0.34)	m	m
	Azerbaijan	1.29	(0.26)	0.84	(0.32)	0.66	(0.84)	2.27	(0.39)	1.30	(0.16)	0.56	(1.00)	1.17	(0.37)	m	m	1.39	(0.19)
	Brazil	1.63	(0.24)	1.42	(0.31)	0.36	(0.65)	0.42	(2.42)	0.55	(0.18)	0.11	(0.52)	0.28	(0.26)	m	m	2.09	(0.19)
	Bulgaria	2.11	(0.32)	6.92	(0.39)	0.00	(6.05)	0.56	(0.36)	0.95	(0.24)	0.00	(1.35)	0.03	(7.33)	m	m	1.35	(0.23)
	Chile	1.07	(0.33)	3.14	(0.34)	0.00	(1.59)	1.20	(1.51)	0.50	(0.20)	0.00	(1.56)	0.00	(8.52)	0.23	(0.32)	m	m
	Colombia	1.44	(0.32)	1.09	(0.36)	0.00	(1.54)	0.00	(1.63)	0.50	(0.24)	0.15	(0.54)	0.21	(0.41)	0.60	(0.31)	m	m
	Croatia	1.32	(0.23)	8.17	(0.29)	0.78	(0.23)	0.41	(0.80)	0.72	(0.19)	a	a	0.00	(1.37)	m	m	1.46	(0.18)
	Estonia	1.51	(0.27)	1.36	(0.43)	0.30	(0.30)	1.16	(0.57)	0.87	(0.17)	0.19	(1.06)	0.43	(0.21)	m	m	2.83	(0.61)
	Hong Kong-China	1.22	(0.20)	7.10	(0.39)	1.50	(0.16)	0.59	(0.33)	0.59	(0.18)	0.03	(1.02)	0.21	(0.34)	0.49	(0.23)	m	m
	Indonesia	0.95	(0.23)	2.91	(0.38)	0.00	(0.36)	1.97	(0.30)	0.66	(0.23)	0.00	(0.56)	0.31	(0.37)	0.50	(0.27)	m	m
	Israel	1.48	(0.17)	3.00	(0.29)	1.10	(0.26)	1.25	(0.25)	0.63	(0.20)	a	a	0.00	(5.98)	0.66	(0.26)	m	m
	Jordan	1.35	(0.15)	1.21	(0.21)	1.63	(0.17)	0.83	(0.52)	2.00	(0.22)	0.00	(0.39)	0.73	(0.17)	0.14	(0.64)	m	m
	Kyrgyzstan	1.05	(0.14)	3.49	(0.32)	1.44	(0.52)	0.61	(0.36)	1.11	(0.16)	0.59	(1.90)	1.00	(0.22)	m	m	1.09	(0.18)
	Latvia	2.51	(0.33)	2.01	(0.25)	0.77	(0.43)	0.79	(0.44)	0.96	(0.22)	0.00	(7.52)	0.36	(0.32)	m	m	2.74	(0.72)
	Lithuania	3.18	(0.26)	2.33	(0.24)	1.69	(0.59)	0.55	(0.59)	0.96	(0.18)	0.00	(6.16)	0.51	(0.31)	m	m	1.19	(0.33)
	Macao-China	1.37	(0.20)	1.56	(0.23)	1.32	(0.22)	2.29	(0.74)	0.57	(0.19)	0.05	(0.58)	0.13	(0.22)	0.33	(0.15)	m	m
	Montenegro	1.54	(0.24)	5.07	(0.23)	2.19	(0.31)	0.83	(0.19)	0.94	(0.16)	a	a	0.00	(0.79)	m	m	2.18	(0.23)
	Romania	2.80	(0.41)	5.47	(0.38)	c	c	0.69	(0.62)	0.81	(0.30)	0.00	(0.61)	1.00	(0.56)	m	m	1.82	(0.51)
	Russian Federation	1.31	(0.28)	1.32	(0.26)	1.05	(0.28)	0.54	(0.37)	0.82	(0.17)	0.00	(1.05)	0.42	(0.26)	0.63	(0.18)	m	m
	Serbia	1.34	(0.21)	6.70	(0.36)	1.02	(0.27)	1.23	(0.58)	0.85	(0.19)	0.00	(1.58)	1.34	(1.43)	m	m	0.03	(6.71)
	Slovenia	1.17	(0.30)	39.16	(0.41)	0.54	(0.32)	0.46	(0.50)	0.76	(0.22)	a	a	0.00	(2.23)	0.00	(8.66)	m	m
	Chinese Taipei	1.17	(0.18)	17.12	(0.39)	0.37	(0.90)	1.13	(0.15)	0.63	(0.15)	a	a	0.00	(1.41)	0.68	(0.23)	m	m
	Thailand	1.50	(0.29)	2.05	(0.21)	0.00	(1.18)	1.42	(0.17)	1.12	(0.16)	0.00	(1.19)	0.72	(1.10)	0.46	(0.22)	m	m
	Tunisia	1.14	(0.16)	1.36	(0.20)	0.00	(7.23)	3.26	(0.55)	0.59	(0.17)	0.02	(0.64)	0.07	(0.35)	0.26	(0.23)	m	m
	Uruguay	1.42	(0.22)	1.60	(0.23)	0.01	(7.97)	0.83	(0.92)	0.81	(0.21)	0.12	(0.73)	0.07	(0.65)	0.30	(0.33)	m	m

[Part 2/2]
Table A4.7 Odds ratios for the background model used in Chapter 3

		Indicator for students in 11th grade		Indicator for students in 12th grade		Indicator for students in 13th grade		Indicator for students in 14th grade		Indicator for observations with imputed information on grade		Indicator for observations with imputed information on migrant background		Indicator for observations with imputed information on language spoken at home		Constant	
		Ratio	S.E.	Ratio	S.E.	Ratio	S.E.	Ratio	S.E.	Ratio	S.E.	Ratio	S.E.	Ratio	S.E.	Ratio	S.E.
OECD	Australia	1.72	(0.11)	0.00	(1.18)	a	a	a	a	a	a	0.40	(0.52)	0.33	(0.76)	0.37	(0.13)
	Austria	a	a	a	a	a	a	a	a	a	a	0.00	(6.78)	0.00	(7.48)	0.49	(0.21)
	Belgium	1.50	(1.07)	a	a	a	a	a	a	0.00	(1.47)	0.35	(1.14)	0.62	(0.34)	0.44	(0.19)
	Canada	3.15	(0.39)	a	a	a	a	a	a	a	a	0.61	(0.40)	0.31	(0.66)	0.43	(0.11)
	Czech Republic	a	a	a	a	a	a	a	a	a	a	4.59	(1.37)	0.23	(1.01)	0.50	(0.32)
	Denmark	3.63	(0.73)	a	a	a	a	a	a	a	a	0.04	(6.46)	0.53	(0.52)	0.46	(0.19)
	Finland	a	a	a	a	a	a	a	a	a	a	0.25	(1.20)	0.38	(1.15)	0.47	(0.18)
	France	1.39	(1.05)	a	a	a	a	a	a	a	a	0.39	(0.97)	0.23	(1.14)	0.75	(0.34)
	Germany	a	(0.73)	a	a	a	a	a	a	0.70	(1.02)	1.55	(0.64)	0.57	(0.50)	0.15	(0.28)
	Greece	1.27	(0.20)	a	a	a	a	a	a	a	a	0.51	(1.24)	0.95	(0.38)	0.65	(0.25)
	Hungary	a	a	a	a	a	a	a	a	a	a	0.00	(8.77)	1.70	(0.90)	0.88	(0.44)
	Iceland	6.32	(1.32)	a	a	a	a	a	a	a	a	0.43	(1.22)	0.00	(0.26)	0.35	(0.17)
	Ireland	2.00	(0.15)	a	a	a	a	a	a	a	a	0.03	(6.60)	0.00	(7.64)	0.39	(0.21)
	Italy	0.74	(0.59)	a	a	a	a	a	a	a	a	0.20	(0.60)	0.38	(0.23)	1.17	(0.21)
	Japan	a	a	a	a	a	a	a	a	a	a	0.00	(0.93)	0.50	(0.53)	0.59	(0.28)
	Korea	2.40	(0.61)	a	a	a	a	a	a	a	a	0.26	(0.94)	0.94	(0.84)	0.46	(0.19)
	Luxembourg	a	a	a	a	a	a	a	a	a	a	0.04	(6.53)	0.31	(1.11)	0.15	(0.82)
	Mexico	0.67	(0.22)	0.50	(0.43)	a	a	a	a	0.47	(0.40)	0.47	(0.48)	0.82	(1.02)	1.65	(0.40)
	Netherlands	a	(15.58)	a	a	a	a	a	a	a	a	0.27	(1.36)	1.29	(0.87)	0.27	(0.26)
	New Zealand			1.44	(0.42)	a	a	a	a	a	a	0.44	(1.21)	0.20	(0.69)	0.39	(0.16)
	Norway	a	a	a	a	a	a	a	a	a	a	0.00	(7.64)	0.25	(1.08)	0.27	(0.17)
	Poland	a	a	a	a	a	a	a	a	a	a	0.16	(1.04)	0.98	(0.70)	0.69	(0.23)
	Portugal	a	(10.46)	a	a	a	a	a	a	0.00	(6.90)	0.00	(1.91)	0.60	(0.63)	2.92	(0.41)
	Slovak Republic	a	a	a	a	a	a	a	a	a	a	0.03	(7.12)	0.00	(8.75)	1.00	(0.38)
	Spain	a	a	a	a	a	a	a	a	a	a	0.27	(0.68)	0.49	(0.47)	1.82	(0.32)
	Sweden	a	a	a	a	a	a	a	a	a	a	0.00	(7.87)	0.30	(0.94)	0.43	(0.18)
	Switzerland	a	(11.57)	a	a	a	a	a	a	a	a	0.31	(0.71)	0.23	(0.52)	0.50	(0.22)
	Turkey	1.96	(0.48)	a	a	a	a	a	a	a	a	0.18	(1.21)	3.07	(1.27)	5.96	(0.70)
	United Kingdom			1.67	(0.35)	a	a	a	a	a		0.98	(0.45)	0.28	(0.93)	0.49	(0.17)
	United States	1.52	(0.20)	0.00	(10.41)	a	a	a	a	0.00	(1.48)	0.38	(0.79)	0.09	(1.12)	0.52	(0.20)
	OECD average	**9.83**	**(0.74)**	**0.49**	**(0.35)**	**a**	**a**	**a**	**a**	**0.23**	**(0.24)**	**0.05**	**(0.70)**	**0.17**	**(0.48)**	**0.58**	**(0.06)**
Partners	Argentina	0.83	(0.57)	1.28	(0.97)	a	a	a	a	0.60	(1.96)	0.67	(1.26)	0.52	(1.13)	1.84	(0.45)
	Azerbaijan	3.55	(1.07)	0.00	(1.60)	0.02	(6.49)	1.00	(0.00)	a	a	0.35	(0.42)	0.76	(0.68)	0.37	(0.47)
	Brazil	0.40	(1.44)	a	a	a	a	a	a	a	a	0.05	(2.36)	2.89	(1.11)	2.57	(0.58)
	Bulgaria	0.00	(1.57)	a	a	a	a	a	a	a	a	0.39	(0.82)	0.85	(1.05)	1.06	(0.44)
	Chile	2.15	(0.28)	a	a	a	a	a	a	a	a	0.17	(1.19)	2.57	(0.75)	1.32	(0.55)
	Colombia	1.90	(0.26)	a	a	a	a	a	a	a	a	0.32	(0.90)	2.30	(0.88)	1.29	(0.88)
	Croatia	a	a	a	a	a	a	a	a	a	a	0.01	(6.64)	1.65	(0.90)	0.63	(0.21)
	Estonia	a	a	a	a	a	a	a	a	a	a	0.01	(6.53)	0.00	(6.25)	0.61	(0.23)
	Hong Kong-China	a	a	a	a	a	a	a	a	a	a	0.59	(0.97)	0.02	(6.19)	3.85	(0.45)
	Indonesia	1.04	(0.60)	a	a	a	a	a	a	a	a	0.08	(2.41)	1.99	(0.68)	1.93	(0.74)
	Israel	a	(14.44)	a	a	a	a	a	a	a	a	0.58	(0.40)	0.35	(0.54)	0.35	(0.19)
	Jordan	a	a	a	a	a	a	a	a	a	a	0.18	(0.81)	0.66	(0.79)	0.32	(0.32)
	Kyrgyzstan	a	a	a	a	a	a	a	a	a	a	0.38	(0.54)	0.52	(0.60)	0.93	(0.31)
	Latvia	a	a	a	a	a	a	a	a	0.54	(2.41)	0.28	(0.78)	0.41	(0.99)	1.06	(0.34)
	Lithuania	a	a	a	a	a	a	a	a	0.00	(0.85)	0.46	(0.74)	0.19	(1.21)	0.90	(0.29)
	Macao-China	1.51	(0.95)	a	a	a	a	a	a	a	a	0.70	(0.76)	1.00	(0.00)	1.21	(0.89)
	Montenegro	a	a	a	a	a	a	a	a	a	a	0.55	(0.86)	0.81	(0.26)	0.57	(0.24)
	Romania	a	a	a	a	a	a	a	a	a	a	0.00	(0.66)	1.00	(0.00)	2.32	(0.47)
	Russian Federation	2.76	(0.75)	a	a	a	a	a	a	a	a	0.62	(1.41)	0.00	(1.05)	0.58	(0.27)
	Serbia	a	a	a	a	a	a	a	a	a	a	0.00	(7.81)	0.00	(8.37)	0.65	(0.25)
	Slovenia	3.18	(0.41)	a	a	a	a	a	a	a	a	0.17	(1.47)	0.31	(1.14)	0.26	(0.26)
	Chinese Taipei	0.01	(7.70)	a	a	a	a	a	a	a	a	0.14	(1.04)	0.30	(0.54)	1.46	(0.26)
	Thailand	1.25	(0.37)	a	a	a	a	a	a	a	a	0.38	(0.67)	0.99	(0.55)	2.54	(0.78)
	Tunisia	1.90	(0.39)	a	a	a	a	a	a	a	a	0.55	(0.78)	0.79	(0.47)	2.37	(0.49)
	Uruguay	1.14	(0.41)	a	a	a	a	a	a	a	a	1.45	(0.59)	0.41	(0.72)	1.17	(0.38)

[Part 1/4]

Table A4.8 Regression coefficients for the background model used in Chapter 4

		The indicator for disadvantaged students		ESCS		ESCS squared		School mean ESCS		School mean ESCS squared	
		Coef.	S.E.	Coef.	S.E.	Coef.	S.E.	Coef.	S.E.	Coef.	S.E.
OECD	Australia	1.63	(3.47)	28.02	(2.12)	-2.83	(1.30)	53.69	(6.37)	6.41	(8.36)
	Austria	2.55	(5.05)	7.04	(3.00)	-2.85	(1.30)	105.33	(8.12)	-4.11	(10.50)
	Belgium	-1.73	(2.76)	11.67	(1.57)	-0.43	(0.67)	78.30	(5.46)	-2.03	(7.04)
	Canada	-2.15	(3.10)	19.71	(1.98)	-2.22	(1.04)	36.78	(8.99)	1.44	(8.46)
	Czech Republic	-2.16	(4.32)	15.03	(2.71)	-2.04	(1.43)	108.17	(7.58)	16.43	(8.48)
	Denmark	-1.20	(4.85)	25.13	(2.58)	2.09	(1.28)	37.84	(8.44)	-8.38	(10.62)
	Finland	1.07	(4.92)	26.48	(3.16)	2.21	(1.52)	-0.75	(10.45)	26.00	(12.55)
	France	-7.75	(4.23)	12.24	(2.23)	1.89	(1.51)	60.59	(5.64)	-16.79	(7.67)
	Germany	-3.41	(3.81)	5.24	(2.31)	0.64	(0.86)	102.75	(5.67)	-14.57	(6.79)
	Greece	0.99	(4.51)	15.81	(2.14)	-1.67	(1.48)	49.13	(4.71)	-11.37	(5.75)
	Hungary	1.72	(4.31)	4.96	(1.92)	-1.31	(1.17)	83.70	(5.92)	4.81	(6.30)
	Iceland	-1.30	(6.21)	28.56	(4.91)	-1.14	(1.72)	-28.09	(14.43)	17.39	(10.56)
	Ireland	1.31	(4.84)	27.75	(2.75)	-0.97	(1.35)	46.43	(5.33)	-19.11	(7.22)
	Italy	-2.91	(3.69)	4.71	(1.62)	-3.04	(0.90)	73.52	(4.88)	-3.66	(6.86)
	Japan	-3.22	(5.17)	3.52	(3.59)	-4.54	(2.37)	126.48	(9.46)	-23.78	(20.14)
	Korea	1.87	(4.50)	9.80	(2.60)	2.19	(1.46)	83.59	(8.66)	-10.71	(12.72)
	Luxembourg	-10.96	(3.81)	9.73	(2.22)	-1.16	(0.80)	56.80	(2.54)	-3.44	(4.04)
	Mexico	-3.00	(4.38)	6.44	(1.11)	1.12	(0.67)	40.36	(2.71)	6.81	(1.49)
	Netherlands	-5.48	(4.46)	3.46	(2.42)	1.58	(1.24)	115.95	(8.10)	-3.26	(10.67)
	New Zealand	0.81	(5.05)	38.08	(2.87)	2.91	(1.56)	53.97	(5.98)	-8.12	(9.25)
	Norway	-6.44	(4.68)	26.21	(3.26)	-3.05	(1.51)	16.29	(18.50)	18.48	(14.46)
	Poland	-0.12	(3.96)	31.70	(1.97)	0.22	(1.19)	24.92	(6.00)	23.14	(7.25)
	Portugal	0.24	(4.08)	11.14	(1.55)	1.42	(0.76)	11.92	(2.92)	-0.01	(2.08)
	Slovak Republic	-8.02	(4.51)	14.62	(2.64)	-1.58	(1.65)	71.59	(5.42)	23.30	(6.08)
	Spain	2.39	(4.16)	12.39	(1.92)	-2.77	(1.07)	16.66	(2.75)	2.48	(3.63)
	Sweden	-3.14	(5.07)	26.97	(3.57)	-0.51	(1.44)	34.98	(12.60)	-5.86	(17.83)
	Switzerland	-1.04	(3.29)	15.26	(2.16)	1.26	(1.16)	68.21	(6.03)	-2.55	(9.01)
	Turkey	4.53	(4.41)	14.52	(2.61)	2.01	(1.23)	82.14	(10.50)	9.43	(4.72)
	United Kingdom	2.94	(4.56)	33.57	(2.69)	-2.87	(1.61)	50.91	(6.20)	32.92	(9.94)
	United States	0.17	(5.07)	28.01	(2.66)	4.01	(1.26)	40.32	(4.50)	3.97	(7.46)
	OECD average	**-1.39**	**(0.81)**	**17.26**	**(0.48)**	**-0.38**	**(0.24)**	**56.75**	**(1.45)**	**1.84**	**(1.74)**
Partners	Argentina	-6.49	(7.09)	11.77	(2.59)	1.06	(1.37)	44.80	(8.74)	4.05	(5.95)
	Azerbaijan	7.36	(3.97)	8.10	(1.51)	-0.21	(0.88)	20.14	(3.49)	14.51	(4.63)
	Brazil	8.44	(4.49)	7.42	(1.84)	-0.65	(0.87)	63.28	(4.97)	14.70	(2.38)
	Bulgaria	-1.52	(4.33)	10.49	(2.12)	-2.14	(1.43)	90.44	(6.04)	21.72	(5.36)
	Chile	-9.43	(5.48)	8.01	(1.91)	1.61	(0.90)	46.93	(3.74)	3.78	(3.05)
	Colombia	2.75	(5.96)	8.86	(2.65)	0.85	(1.15)	37.53	(4.30)	10.56	(3.07)
	Croatia	-2.33	(3.86)	11.62	(2.00)	-0.94	(1.27)	81.35	(6.30)	12.23	(12.06)
	Estonia	4.07	(4.91)	19.06	(2.76)	3.73	(1.91)	28.73	(7.38)	27.51	(9.05)
	Hong Kong-China	6.66	(4.73)	6.57	(3.12)	-0.03	(1.12)	30.28	(18.24)	-37.17	(18.20)
	Indonesia	4.54	(3.60)	3.30	(2.13)	0.01	(0.79)	62.12	(15.03)	8.26	(5.61)
	Israel	-14.52	(5.95)	18.71	(3.26)	3.71	(1.57)	63.19	(12.77)	-12.27	(15.89)
	Jordan	-4.75	(3.76)	19.78	(2.29)	2.77	(0.68)	36.35	(6.78)	12.20	(3.67)
	Kyrgyzstan	6.33	(4.18)	8.45	(2.43)	0.21	(1.07)	90.51	(12.39)	12.18	(12.83)
	Latvia	8.31	(5.46)	19.33	(2.69)	-1.25	(2.12)	29.99	(6.37)	2.07	(9.66)
	Lithuania	9.51	(5.11)	25.79	(2.65)	-5.41	(1.77)	39.86	(5.00)	32.47	(8.49)
	Macao-China	-6.21	(4.68)	2.16	(2.64)	-0.25	(1.29)	-4.12	(7.60)	-11.14	(4.81)
	Montenegro	5.57	(4.54)	11.75	(2.50)	-2.21	(1.46)	69.30	(3.45)	42.71	(7.33)
	Romania	6.08	(5.51)	13.21	(4.03)	-1.16	(1.26)	73.59	(6.46)	14.70	(4.08)
	Russian Federation	-2.75	(4.91)	14.62	(2.66)	-0.13	(1.81)	46.20	(7.02)	37.53	(9.11)
	Serbia	-0.69	(4.40)	10.56	(1.86)	-2.15	(1.21)	74.94	(4.98)	3.57	(8.99)
	Slovenia	-2.14	(5.00)	1.28	(2.83)	1.10	(1.81)	123.20	(4.84)	20.25	(9.08)
	Chinese Taipei	3.24	(3.76)	14.68	(1.89)	1.99	(1.59)	112.57	(7.35)	7.45	(13.59)
	Thailand	5.63	(4.45)	13.93	(1.84)	1.77	(1.10)	58.27	(5.77)	10.09	(2.72)
	Tunisia	7.60	(3.94)	5.83	(1.82)	0.25	(0.59)	27.78	(10.10)	7.84	(3.51)
	Uruguay	2.19	(5.73)	13.76	(1.84)	1.76	(0.86)	27.94	(3.42)	7.48	(2.85)

[Part 2/4]
Table A4.8 Regression coefficients for the background model used in Chapter 4

		Indicator for students with an immigrant background		Indicator for students speaking a different language than the language of the test		Indicator for female students		Indicator for students in 7th grade		Indicator for students in 8th grade	
		Coef.	S.E.	Coef.	S.E.	Coef.	S.E.	Coef.	S.E.	Coef.	S.E.
OECD	Australia	-0.23	(3.44)	-16.03	(5.08)	-3.80	(2.42)	a	a	-124.37	(28.82)
	Austria	-31.02	(6.33)	-22.18	(7.90)	-15.66	(3.93)	-113.48	(36.37)	-55.41	(8.61)
	Belgium	-18.28	(4.67)	8.01	(3.31)	-11.90	(2.33)	-131.40	(18.25)	-100.95	(5.97)
	Canada	-11.58	(4.34)	-15.58	(4.15)	-8.25	(2.07)	-165.33	(43.24)	-99.16	(8.20)
	Czech Republic	-15.87	(11.04)	-25.65	(12.97)	-12.25	(4.57)	-102.30	(17.23)	-87.70	(10.04)
	Denmark	-30.98	(8.20)	-29.39	(8.24)	-12.90	(2.86)	-122.30	(28.64)	-51.30	(4.36)
	Finland	-42.36	(16.56)	-40.32	(15.58)	0.84	(2.85)	-77.55	(24.24)	-32.45	(4.20)
	France	-16.31	(5.91)	-10.30	(8.29)	-12.66	(2.78)	-154.04	(60.97)	-99.44	(8.61)
	Germany	-24.95	(5.65)	-22.34	(5.35)	-15.74	(2.33)	-75.00	(11.59)	-41.28	(3.39)
	Greece	6.53	(8.35)	-15.24	(9.88)	5.95	(3.75)	-130.53	(29.85)	-76.53	(27.20)
	Hungary	-11.42	(9.66)	-13.45	(16.67)	-20.87	(3.09)	-53.56	(10.32)	-23.54	(9.54)
	Iceland	-26.55	(15.30)	-44.08	(14.70)	5.84	(3.10)	a	a	a	a
	Ireland	8.11	(7.56)	-44.23	(10.16)	-3.57	(3.34)	-160.06	(29.69)	-62.43	(8.52)
	Italy	-22.01	(6.72)	0.32	(3.53)	-13.85	(2.82)	-115.73	(28.73)	-60.31	(17.35)
	Japan	32.25	(18.37)	-114.57	(22.06)	-4.51	(5.07)	a	a	a	a
	Korea	82.62	(27.78)	-24.81	(33.46)	2.32	(3.98)	a	a	a	a
	Luxembourg	-31.81	(3.53)	-12.40	(4.86)	-10.59	(2.13)	-40.99	(19.84)	-12.04	(3.69)
	Mexico	-47.71	(6.63)	-18.05	(10.07)	-13.38	(1.69)	-60.75	(6.28)	-65.61	(4.93)
	Netherlands	-14.01	(7.84)	-12.97	(6.23)	-13.65	(2.60)	-146.81	(32.18)	-64.50	(8.45)
	New Zealand	-7.18	(4.12)	-31.85	(5.91)	-1.05	(3.77)	a	a	a	a
	Norway	-13.92	(9.03)	-32.83	(8.93)	2.51	(3.09)	a	a	a	a
	Poland	-27.29	(53.28)	-4.78	(17.26)	-5.29	(2.43)	-119.09	(17.01)	-91.45	(7.16)
	Portugal	-23.32	(5.92)	-1.89	(7.84)	-15.22	(2.32)	-151.37	(4.69)	-108.71	(3.95)
	Slovak Republic	-26.39	(20.52)	-18.82	(6.93)	-10.67	(3.41)	-81.08	(20.59)	-89.04	(11.37)
	Spain	-25.40	(5.03)	-13.47	(3.37)	-15.13	(1.80)	-228.48	(33.73)	-122.63	(3.74)
	Sweden	-24.42	(8.04)	-25.88	(7.99)	-1.65	(2.83)	a	a	-68.56	(8.32)
	Switzerland	-42.47	(4.20)	-28.74	(4.79)	-11.89	(2.27)	-80.63	(12.81)	-45.29	(3.20)
	Turkey	-3.48	(9.78)	3.11	(9.71)	4.31	(3.46)	1.71	(21.42)	-2.44	(18.80)
	United Kingdom	-5.43	(5.38)	-23.47	(7.92)	-8.50	(2.47)	a	a	a	a
	United States	-7.94	(5.77)	-19.70	(6.19)	-7.48	(2.84)	-91.00	(10.44)	-99.95	(13.41)
	OECD average	**-14.09**	**(2.58)**	**-22.39**	**(2.10)**	**-7.62**	**(0.56)**	**-79.99**	**(4.20)**	**-56.17**	**(1.93)**
Partners	Argentina	4.86	(7.18)	-62.41	(26.24)	0.95	(4.16)	-142.96	(24.51)	-92.11	(6.98)
	Azerbaijan	-7.45	(6.37)	10.21	(4.34)	7.50	(2.03)	-6.52	(12.09)	-4.45	(4.57)
	Brazil	-16.54	(6.57)	10.92	(15.01)	-14.63	(2.12)	-67.08	(4.10)	-48.51	(4.10)
	Bulgaria	-35.99	(34.86)	-22.60	(6.20)	1.82	(4.02)	3.25	(22.28)	-21.78	(12.58)
	Chile	-40.95	(14.75)	-1.02	(18.23)	-22.82	(3.34)	-92.87	(14.09)	-88.61	(9.07)
	Colombia	-50.50	(26.36)	6.77	(16.63)	-16.40	(3.29)	-83.66	(8.92)	-59.33	(5.86)
	Croatia	-9.67	(4.18)	-19.17	(13.30)	-9.35	(3.42)	a	a	-84.22	(16.20)
	Estonia	-30.83	(5.12)	-11.63	(6.55)	-2.33	(2.70)	-92.05	(9.54)	-31.72	(3.28)
	Hong Kong-China	22.55	(3.48)	-27.36	(14.24)	-18.10	(3.66)	-106.14	(9.38)	-72.25	(6.37)
	Indonesia	-61.97	(10.16)	14.63	(6.60)	-15.94	(5.21)	-120.35	(39.63)	-42.81	(7.19)
	Israel	9.59	(5.10)	-0.10	(6.64)	-1.25	(5.05)	-78.31	(22.64)	-42.06	(36.65)
	Jordan	10.84	(3.80)	-9.27	(7.52)	28.13	(3.83)	-118.08	(18.09)	-100.23	(10.88)
	Kyrgyzstan	21.20	(9.26)	-16.49	(3.96)	4.41	(2.48)	-59.77	(28.89)	-15.93	(5.59)
	Latvia	-9.95	(5.38)	-22.90	(6.02)	-0.03	(2.83)	-99.74	(13.05)	-47.99	(4.25)
	Lithuania	-0.07	(10.88)	-22.39	(9.60)	2.28	(2.73)	-104.61	(13.28)	-43.37	(6.15)
	Macao-China	17.66	(2.52)	16.05	(14.38)	-14.46	(2.49)	-126.58	(5.65)	-79.63	(3.02)
	Montenegro	12.48	(5.18)	-5.65	(2.85)	-2.83	(2.44)	a	a	-86.93	(13.42)
	Romania	41.54	(34.06)	-15.19	(8.44)	-4.36	(2.58)	-67.47	(23.92)	-5.21	(11.97)
	Russian Federation	-7.34	(4.66)	-41.04	(7.09)	-5.71	(2.51)	-83.77	(20.22)	-56.36	(6.14)
	Serbia	-0.07	(3.64)	18.31	(11.70)	-5.95	(3.12)	-110.07	(28.88)	-17.64	(17.67)
	Slovenia	-20.76	(5.21)	-28.26	(6.58)	-9.82	(2.24)	a	a	-29.56	(28.75)
	Chinese Taipei	-51.08	(11.75)	-9.09	(4.16)	-8.52	(3.74)	a	a	23.19	(18.03)
	Thailand	-60.16	(21.50)	9.44	(2.96)	8.40	(2.70)	-141.93	(57.58)	-50.62	(16.49)
	Tunisia	-19.42	(9.46)	-11.50	(5.97)	-8.98	(2.76)	-119.43	(5.24)	-86.97	(3.84)
	Uruguay	4.38	(26.90)	0.05	(9.27)	-8.97	(3.88)	-110.48	(7.54)	-95.69	(6.36)

Note:
a - The category does not apply in the country concerned. Data are therefore missing.

[Part 3/4]
Table A4.8 Regression coefficients for the background model used in Chapter 4

		Indicator for students in 9th grade		Indicator for students in 10th grade		Indicator for students in 11th grade		Indicator for students in 12th grade		Indicator for students in 13th grade	
		Coef.	S.E.	Coef.	S.E.	Coef.	S.E.	Coef.	S.E.	Coef.	S.E.
OECD	Australia	-42.40	(3.57)	reference category		28.01	(3.31)	71.97	(32.76)	a	a
	Austria	-24.36	(3.25)	reference category		112.95	(27.36)	a	a	a	a
	Belgium	-62.69	(2.70)	reference category		43.26	(7.16)	a	a	a	a
	Canada	-35.02	(3.55)	reference category		35.09	(9.18)	90.86	(34.55)	a	a
	Czech Republic	-17.71	(6.29)	reference category		a	a	a	a	a	a
	Denmark	reference category		10.31	(13.97)	53.84	(14.10)	a	a	a	a
	Finland	reference category		-0.44	(12.79)	a	a	a	a	a	a
	France	-64.34	(6.37)	reference category		49.06	(9.22)	101.70	(47.95)	a	a
	Germany	reference category		40.07	(2.45)	87.66	(16.08)	a	a	a	a
	Greece	-34.37	(14.97)	reference category		18.35	(4.12)	a	a	a	a
	Hungary	reference category		22.72	(2.27)	4.88	(43.15)	a	a	a	a
	Iceland	-63.20	(28.04)	reference category		123.59	(17.80)	a	a	a	a
	Ireland	reference category		26.26	(3.89)	27.93	(3.78)	a	a	a	a
	Italy	-41.72	(3.69)	reference category		-1.42	(5.83)	a	a	a	a
	Japan	a	a	reference category		a	a	a	a	a	a
	Korea	-62.48	(19.97)	reference category		41.93	(10.99)	a	a	a	a
	Luxembourg	reference category		53.06	(2.65)	114.74	(30.13)	a	a	a	a
	Mexico	-36.98	(3.34)	reference category		-6.15	(2.80)	-13.93	(5.15)	a	a
	Netherlands	-39.18	(3.43)	reference category		54.82	(14.51)	156.88	(25.80)	a	a
	New Zealand	-51.83	(86.28)	-42.63	(6.52)	reference category		41.27	(7.30)	112.63	(27.43)
	Norway	-59.13	(21.17)	reference category		61.79	(25.53)	a	a	a	a
	Poland	reference category		44.46	(12.72)	a	a	a	a	a	a
	Portugal	-61.62	(3.17)	reference category		28.43	(26.42)	a	a	a	a
	Slovak Republic	-17.52	(5.20)	reference category		a	a	a	a	a	a
	Spain	-74.38	(2.58)	reference category		184.75	(52.51)	a	a	a	a
	Sweden	reference category		36.81	(13.08)	a	a	a	a	a	a
	Switzerland	reference category		19.23	(5.73)	18.20	(21.26)	-8.99	(32.45)	a	a
	Turkey	23.75	(4.93)	reference category		26.98	(6.64)	a	a	a	a
	United Kingdom	-211.21	(55.62)	-21.02	(8.73)	reference category		38.73	(8.27)	a	a
	United States	-60.56	(4.94)	reference category		14.99	(3.97)	8.06	(39.68)	a	a
	OECD average	**-34.56**	**(3.75)**	**6.30**	**(0.99)**	**37.46**	**(3.26)**	**16.22**	**(2.98)**	**a**	**a**
Partners	Argentina	-53.88	(5.69)	reference category		5.51	(7.86)	53.29	(21.22)	a	a
	Azerbaijan	reference category		7.77	(2.94)	34.17	(11.95)	-43.86	(18.07)	-19.43	(8.23)
	Brazil	reference category		30.32	(3.57)	17.78	(16.06)	a	a	a	a
	Bulgaria	reference category		18.89	(3.68)	-34.57	(42.57)	a	a	a	a
	Chile	-51.23	(3.30)	reference category		14.65	(4.36)	a	a	a	a
	Colombia	-32.07	(4.32)	reference category		24.25	(5.08)	a	a	a	a
	Croatia	reference category		20.63	(2.72)	a	a	a	a	a	a
	Estonia	reference category		36.41	(7.23)	a	a	a	a	a	a
	Hong Kong-China	-36.42	(3.83)	reference category		-8.69	(24.49)	a	a	a	a
	Indonesia	-27.28	(7.03)	reference category		2.75	(6.05)	a	a	a	a
	Israel	-20.26	(6.25)	reference category		60.02	(36.67)	a	a	a	a
	Jordan	-65.00	(5.55)	reference category		a	a	a	a	a	a
	Kyrgyzstan	reference category		9.59	(3.99)	18.14	(16.83)	a	a	a	a
	Latvia	reference category		53.36	(7.69)	60.38	(39.73)	a	a	a	a
	Lithuania	reference category		31.21	(5.02)	137.80	(33.20)	a	a	a	a
	Macao-China	-46.00	(3.17)	reference category		12.14	(9.91)	a	a	a	a
	Montenegro	reference category		19.45	(3.34)	a	a	a	a	a	a
	Romania	reference category		41.28	(9.08)	a	a	a	a	a	a
	Russian Federation	-30.69	(3.06)	reference category		31.79	(12.92)	a	a	a	a
	Serbia	reference category		11.39	(9.24)	a	a	a	a	a	a
	Slovenia	-17.36	(22.94)	reference category		30.33	(6.17)	a	a	a	a
	Chinese Taipei	-6.98	(5.20)	reference category		37.27	(25.39)	a	a	a	a
	Thailand	-25.99	(3.03)	reference category		26.34	(5.12)	a	a	a	a
	Tunisia	-57.71	(4.73)	reference category		26.54	(5.86)	a	a	a	a
	Uruguay	-57.74	(5.23)	reference category		19.42	(4.81)	a	a	a	a

Note: Reference category consists of students in the modal grade of each country. The coefficients for other grades reflect the difference in performance between students in this grade and students in the modal grade. These results cannot be compared across countries as modal grades can differ between countries.

[Part 4/4]
Table A4.8 Regression coefficients for the background model used in Chapter 4

		Indicator for students in 14th grade		Indicator for observations with imputed information on grade		Indicator for observations with imputed information on migrant background		Indicator for observations with imputed information on language spoken at home		Constant		Number of observations included
		Coef.	S.E.	Coef.	S.E.	Coef.	S.E.	Coef.	S.E.	Coef.	S.E.	N
OECD	Australia	a	a	a	a	-54.47	(8.22)	-74.03	(10.74)	515.12	(3.08)	13995
	Austria	a	a	a	a	-41.84	(16.35)	-39.60	(6.22)	521.40	(4.30)	4914
	Belgium	a	a	-71.23	(42.31)	-39.68	(11.33)	-22.94	(3.34)	530.16	(3.14)	8777
	Canada	a	a	a	a	-45.52	(7.85)	-59.94	(7.81)	533.98	(3.05)	22136
	Czech Republic	a	a	a	a	-37.89	(19.74)	-42.42	(9.44)	527.83	(6.60)	5903
	Denmark	a	a	a	a	-22.12	(18.70)	-24.51	(8.47)	494.63	(3.83)	4496
	Finland	a	a	a	a	-78.70	(15.45)	-43.73	(11.46)	557.51	(3.35)	4697
	France	a	a	a	a	-31.62	(11.36)	-24.65	(13.33)	545.75	(4.90)	4606
	Germany	a	a	9.45	(12.64)	-23.98	(7.49)	-30.33	(4.49)	501.98	(4.13)	4686
	Greece	a	a	-23.84	(26.34)	-41.37	(10.99)	-0.17	(6.08)	488.18	(4.09)	4862
	Hungary	a	a	a	a	-21.20	(10.37)	-0.21	(12.14)	517.54	(2.92)	4474
	Iceland	a	a	a	a	-77.01	(14.82)	-75.29	(15.91)	480.73	(6.16)	3745
	Ireland	a	a	a	a	-28.05	(12.20)	-42.09	(17.45)	509.44	(3.83)	4501
	Italy	a	a	a	a	-36.93	(7.03)	-36.86	(3.50)	506.90	(2.80)	21683
	Japan	a	a	a	a	-79.51	(59.54)	-25.17	(6.67)	544.07	(4.92)	5862
	Korea	a	a	a	a	-72.58	(14.38)	-25.36	(12.41)	523.65	(3.79)	5168
	Luxembourg	a	a	a	a	-59.80	(9.36)	-48.23	(5.62)	502.63	(5.89)	4488
	Mexico	a	a	-21.87	(12.27)	-34.84	(4.31)	-28.06	(16.06)	471.82	(2.71)	30877
	Netherlands	a	a	a	a	-34.49	(9.99)	-14.42	(9.49)	526.44	(4.36)	4838
	New Zealand	a	a	a	a	-41.49	(13.17)	-81.11	(8.42)	531.05	(4.25)	4727
	Norway	a	a	a	a	-65.75	(16.00)	-55.08	(10.33)	473.57	(6.74)	4602
	Poland	a	a	a	a	-64.81	(10.48)	6.93	(11.98)	516.26	(3.01)	5520
	Portugal	a	a	-112.40	(13.73)	-45.05	(10.67)	-17.65	(6.10)	540.44	(2.66)	5091
	Slovak Republic	a	a	a	a	-28.71	(10.08)	-47.55	(10.70)	516.24	(4.11)	4723
	Spain	a	a	a	a	-26.42	(11.36)	-36.49	(7.15)	545.01	(3.02)	19499
	Sweden	a	a	a	a	-72.17	(12.93)	-42.90	(15.49)	500.30	(3.50)	4392
	Switzerland	a	a	a	a	-67.28	(7.41)	-53.32	(6.85)	531.76	(2.52)	12136
	Turkey	a	a	a	a	-38.39	(7.62)	4.79	(14.16)	510.29	(8.61)	4934
	United Kingdom	a	a	a	a	-33.13	(9.16)	-63.19	(12.68)	503.44	(3.24)	12806
	United States	a	a	-51.99	(38.99)	-41.41	(8.84)	-34.62	(8.81)	490.11	(4.15)	5568
	OECD average	**a**	**a**	**-9.06**	**(2.24)**	**-46.21**	**(2.91)**	**-35.94**	**(1.91)**	**515.27**	**(0.80)**	
Partners	Argentina	-50.14	(27.17)	-74.58	(39.48)	-9.71	(17.89)	-33.49	(12.15)	448.71	(5.14)	4292
	Azerbaijan	a	a	a	a	-16.19	(3.72)	-15.27	(4.90)	378.46	(3.63)	5150
	Brazil	a	a	a	a	-43.06	(7.28)	-0.57	(13.03)	461.90	(3.69)	9208
	Bulgaria	a	a	a	a	-21.78	(8.74)	-44.09	(16.18)	448.53	(4.70)	4396
	Chile	a	a	a	a	-33.10	(9.44)	1.48	(16.39)	495.63	(4.53)	5128
	Colombia	a	a	a	a	-51.98	(9.10)	21.26	(11.99)	439.35	(5.15)	4453
	Croatia	a	a	a	a	-49.49	(12.13)	-4.89	(9.63)	504.94	(4.15)	5205
	Estonia	a	a	a	a	-53.48	(9.16)	-57.93	(12.12)	533.71	(3.49)	4853
	Hong Kong-China	a	a	a	a	-29.37	(16.68)	-57.22	(15.52)	610.96	(6.92)	4614
	Indonesia	a	a	a	a	-33.61	(8.83)	11.60	(8.81)	483.35	(11.87)	10633
	Israel	a	a	a	a	-55.51	(7.47)	-47.04	(9.38)	450.50	(6.06)	4344
	Jordan	a	a	a	a	-64.83	(8.27)	-62.71	(8.82)	438.52	(4.58)	6489
	Kyrgyzstan	a	a	a	a	-39.12	(7.05)	-31.26	(6.95)	379.08	(5.22)	5882
	Latvia	a	a	34.66	(30.25)	-43.33	(10.29)	-44.89	(10.70)	501.39	(3.62)	4691
	Lithuania	a	a	-121.06	(21.87)	-30.04	(10.69)	-50.63	(11.99)	484.28	(3.25)	4721
	Macao-China	a	a	a	a	-29.41	(10.02)	-13.16	(18.22)	544.17	(13.67)	4746
	Montenegro	a	a	a	a	-17.84	(8.01)	-5.99	(4.75)	408.54	(2.78)	4408
	Romania	a	a	a	a	-0.12	(28.67)	-63.78	(58.44)	445.60	(5.26)	5110
	Russian Federation	a	a	a	a	-55.32	(14.17)	-62.88	(24.18)	501.74	(4.12)	5785
	Serbia	a	a	a	a	-26.80	(10.99)	-61.98	(30.68)	452.27	(3.99)	4786
	Slovenia	a	a	a	a	-30.89	(10.89)	-57.11	(8.63)	506.96	(2.38)	6554
	Chinese Taipei	a	a	a	a	-56.36	(8.48)	-48.56	(5.64)	580.11	(5.05)	8794
	Thailand	a	a	a	a	-34.95	(5.77)	-12.60	(6.29)	489.89	(3.32)	6172
	Tunisia	a	a	a	a	-18.15	(8.56)	-7.89	(4.81)	450.99	(6.23)	4627
	Uruguay	a	a	a	a	-14.50	(6.86)	-3.64	(6.60)	471.52	(4.63)	4790

Note:
a - The category does not apply in the country concerned. Data are therefore missing.

Table A4.9 **Percentage of students with missing information on the socio-economic status in the original PISA sample by country**

		Percentage of students with no information on the ESCS index %
OECD	Australia	1.2
	Austria	0.3
	Belgium	0.9
	Canada	2.3
	Czech Republic	0.5
	Denmark	0.8
	Finland	0.4
	France	2.3
	Germany	4.2
	Greece	0.2
	Hungary	0.4
	Iceland	1.2
	Ireland	1.8
	Italy	0.4
	Japan	1.5
	Korea	0.2
	Luxembourg	1.7
	Mexico	0.3
	Netherlands	0.7
	New Zealand	2.0
	Norway	1.9
	Poland	0.5
	Portugal	0.4
	Slovak Republic	0.2
	Spain	0.5
	Sweden	1.1
	Switzerland	0.5
	Turkey	0.2
	United Kingdom	2.6
	United States	0.8
	OECD average	**1.1**
Partners	Argentina	1.1
	Azerbaijan	0.7
	Brazil	0.9
	Bulgaria	2.3
	Chile	2.0
	Chinese Taipei	0.2
	Colombia	0.6
	Croatia	0.2
	Estonia	0.2
	Hong Kong-China	0.7
	Indonesia	0.1
	Israel	5.2
	Jordan	0.3
	Kyrgyzstan	0.4
	Latvia	0.6
	Liechtenstein	0.6
	Lithuania	0.5
	Macao-China	0.3
	Montenegro	1.1
	Qatar	4.8
	Romania	0.2
	Russian Federation	0.2
	Serbia	0.3
	Slovenia	0.6
	Thailand	0.3
	Tunisia	0.3
	Uruguay	1.0

[Part 1/2] Table A4.10 **Share of students with missing information on a variable** (Percentage of observations in the analytical sample)

		General interest in science	Instrumental motivation to learn science	Participation in science related activities	Self-concept	Self-efficacy	Information in science related careers	School preparation for science careers	Share of students who attended general science compulsory courses
		%	%	%	%	%	%	%	%
OECD	Australia	16.5	0.3	0.2	16.6	0.2	0.9	0.8	1.6
	Austria	13.2	0.1	0.2	13.0	0.7	1.7	1.5	2.5
	Belgium	15.6	0.5	0.2	14.8	2.3	2.7	2.9	2.4
	Canada	19.5	0.3	0.3	18.6	0.3	0.6	0.5	1.1
	Czech Republic	3.0	0.1	0.8	2.9	2.1	2.4	2.4	2.5
	Denmark	6.9	1.0	0.6	6.3	0.9	1.9	1.3	3.8
	Finland	1.0	0.4	0.1	1.2	0.3	0.7	0.6	1.0
	France	3.3	0.6	0.7	3.3	0.2	1.6	1.5	1.8
	Germany	4.2	0.4	0.2	4.0	3.2	3.3	3.6	3.7
	Greece	1.3	0.2	0.2	1.1	0.2	0.6	0.4	0.5
	Hungary	1.3	0.1	0.1	1.2	0.3	0.2	0.1	0.4
	Iceland	5.5	0.4	0.4	5.2	0.2	0.7	0.8	1.2
	Ireland	13.3	0.7	0.2	12.7	0.3	1.1	1.0	2.2
	Italy	9.7	0.5	0.2	9.7	0.4	0.8	0.8	1.3
	Japan	1.0	0.1	0.2	1.0	0.1	0.4	0.3	0.0
	Korea	0.3	0.3	0.1	0.2	0.1	0.1	0.1	0.3
	Luxembourg	2.7	0.4	0.4	3.1	0.6	1.0	1.1	1.6
	Mexico	4.7	0.2	0.1	3.8	0.1	0.5	0.5	2.0
	Netherlands	12.3	0.2	0.2	12.3	2.1	2.3	2.3	2.3
	New Zealand	8.9	0.1	0.1	9.0	0.2	0.7	0.5	0.6
	Norway	4.2	0.9	0.6	4.2	0.8	2.0	2.4	0.0
	Poland	0.5	0.1	0.0	0.7	0.2	0.4	0.4	0.0
	Portugal	21.3	0.4	0.1	21.1	0.2	0.4	0.5	1.0
	Slovak Republic	1.8	0.2	0.2	1.4	1.1	1.3	1.2	1.1
	Spain	1.6	0.3	0.2	1.6	0.2	0.4	0.7	0.6
	Sweden	3.3	0.4	0.1	3.2	0.5	1.1	1.0	1.7
	Switzerland	10.6	0.4	0.2	9.8	0.3	0.6	0.7	1.1
	Turkey	2.1	0.3	0.2	2.9	0.3	0.6	0.5	1.4
	United Kingdom	2.4	0.3	0.2	3.0	0.3	0.7	0.7	1.8
	United States	2.0	0.9	0.9	2.0	0.9	1.3	1.3	1.9
	OECD average	**6.5**	**0.4**	**0.3**	**6.3**	**0.7**	**1.1**	**1.1**	**1.4**
Partners	Argentina	8.1	0.9	0.8	7.6	0.8	2.7	2.2	5.6
	Azerbaijan	8.9	2.0	2.2	9.0	2.7	5.6	4.5	7.4
	Brazil	5.9	0.5	0.5	6.0	0.5	2.0	1.6	3.5
	Bulgaria	4.2	1.1	0.9	4.1	3.0	2.4	2.3	2.8
	Chile	4.8	0.1	0.3	5.1	0.2	1.1	0.9	2.4
	Colombia	3.4	0.3	0.3	3.6	0.2	0.7	0.6	1.7
	Croatia	14.3	0.4	0.8	12.7	0.2	0.5	0.6	1.1
	Estonia	0.9	0.2	0.2	0.8	0.1	0.3	0.1	1.0
	Hong Kong-China	19.7	0.1	0.0	19.8	0.0	0.1	0.1	9.1
	Indonesia	3.4	0.5	0.5	3.5	0.6	1.2	0.9	1.8
	Israel	9.8	2.6	1.6	7.6	2.7	6.4	4.9	6.3
	Jordan	1.7	0.5	0.4	1.8	0.5	0.8	0.8	1.2
	Kyrgyzstan	9.9	1.2	1.2	10.2	1.2	3.8	3.0	7.3
	Latvia	0.8	0.1	0.1	0.9	0.2	0.3	0.3	0.8
	Lithuania	1.1	0.4	0.2	1.1	0.3	0.3	0.3	1.0
	Macao-China	38.3	0.1	0.1	38.3	0.1	0.3	0.2	1.5
	Montenegro	4.3	0.6	0.4	3.4	1.5	1.6	1.3	2.6
	Romania	1.4	0.2	0.2	1.0	0.3	0.7	0.4	0.5
	Russian Federation	2.6	0.2	0.2	2.6	0.3	0.6	0.4	0.2
	Serbia	5.3	0.3	0.3	5.2	0.6	0.8	0.8	1.2
	Slovenia	9.6	0.6	0.3	9.5	3.3	4.4	3.9	4.2
	Chinese Taipei	0.4	0.1	0.1	0.4	0.1	0.2	0.2	0.4
	Thailand	0.5	0.3	0.4	0.4	0.4	0.3	0.2	0.4
	Tunisia	8.0	0.9	0.5	9.7	0.5	2.1	1.8	4.6
	Uruguay	12.5	1.0	0.7	12.6	0.8	3.2	4.1	9.4

Table A4.10 [Part 2/2] Share of students with missing information on a variable (Percentage of observations in the analytical sample)

	The number of science regular hours	The number of compulsory courses in general science, physics, biology and chemistry*	Students in private schools*	Students in schools which compete for students	Students in schools which select based on academic record	Index of school activities to promote the learning of science	Index of the quality of school educational resources
	%	%	%	%	%	%	%
OECD							
Australia	2.2	1.6	w	0.7	0.9	0.3	0.0
Austria	4.3	a	0.0	1.1	2.4	2.6	0.0
Belgium	5.1	2.4	w	1.3	2.4	1.3	1.3
Canada	4.2	1.1	0.0	5.9	3.9	3.7	3.6
Czech Republic	3.3	2.5	0.0	4.3	3.7	2.5	4.8
Denmark	2.4	3.8	0.0	16.9	18.2	16.9	17.0
Finland	1.4	1.0	0.0	1.1	1.4	0.0	0.0
France	2.9	a	w	w	w	w	w
Germany	5.9	3.7	0.0	4.6	7.0	4.2	4.2
Greece	2.2	a	0.0	2.7	3.6	0.7	1.4
Hungary	2.1	a	0.0	2.1	4.1	2.4	2.1
Iceland	1.5	1.2	0.0	5.0	6.0	4.1	3.6
Ireland	2.1	2.2	0.0	1.9	3.2	1.9	2.5
Italy	2.5	1.3	0.0	3.1	4.2	2.8	2.5
Japan	0.6	0.0	0.0	1.1	0.8	0.0	0.0
Korea	1.3	0.3	0.0	0.7	2.2	0.0	0.0
Luxembourg	3.8	a	0.0	0.0	0.0	0.3	0.0
Mexico	3.2	2.0	0.0	3.6	2.2	3.3	1.5
Netherlands	8.4	2.3	0.0	0.8	0.8	0.2	0.2
New Zealand	1.5	0.6	0.0	5.3	4.5	4.5	5.6
Norway	2.7	0.0	0.0	2.5	5.4	1.9	1.9
Poland	1.3	a	0.0	2.4	0.7	0.7	0.7
Portugal	3.0	1.0	0.0	1.7	2.3	0.0	0.0
Slovak Republic	2.5	a	0.0	0.7	1.9	0.7	0.0
Spain	2.4	0.6	0.0	1.3	1.4	0.7	1.0
Sweden	1.8	1.7	0.0	0.1	2.0	0.0	0.0
Switzerland	2.5	1.1	0.0	1.9	2.0	0.5	1.6
Turkey	2.4	1.4	0.0	1.4	0.0	0.7	1.6
United Kingdom	1.8	1.8	0.0	7.2	7.6	7.2	7.2
United States	4.1	1.9	0.0	3.0	2.3	2.7	2.3
OECD average	**2.8**	**1.5**	**0.0**	**2.9**	**3.3**	**2.3**	**2.3**
Partners							
Argentina	7.2	a	0.0	5.0	2.4	2.6	1.5
Azerbaijan	10.3	7.4	0.0	m	5.7	0.1	1.7
Brazil	6.1	a	0.0	2.8	3.3	1.2	1.3
Bulgaria	5.8	2.8	m	0.6	1.4	3.1	0.8
Chile	3.5	2.4	0.0	2.5	2.9	4.1	2.2
Colombia	3.4	a	0.0	3.7	1.2	0.5	0.5
Croatia	4.1	1.1	0.0	0.0	0.0	0.0	0.0
Estonia	1.3	1.0	0.0	0.7	0.0	0.0	0.0
Hong Kong-China	1.3	9.1	0.0	0.0	0.0	0.0	0.0
Indonesia	2.0	1.8	0.0	4.7	2.4	0.8	0.6
Israel	9.9	6.3	0.0	11.0	7.5	6.6	2.3
Jordan	4.4	1.2	0.0	4.4	0.5	0.0	0.5
Kyrgyzstan	12.0	7.3	0.0	1.6	3.9	0.0	0.6
Latvia	1.6	a	0.0	1.9	1.1	0.0	0.0
Lithuania	1.6	1.0	0.0	0.0	0.0	0.4	0.6
Macao-China	0.9	1.5	0.0	0.0	0.0	0.0	0.0
Montenegro	5.2	2.6	0.0	0.1	0.0	0.0	0.0
Romania	1.9	0.5	0.0	3.3	1.5	0.0	0.0
Russian Federation	2.2	a	0.0	0.4	1.1	0.7	0.0
Serbia	3.0	1.2	0.0	2.0	1.4	0.7	0.0
Slovenia	6.1	4.2	0.0	1.1	2.1	1.1	0.8
Chinese Taipei	2.4	0.4	0.0	0.0	1.3	0.0	0.4
Thailand	0.5	0.4	0.0	2.1	0.0	0.0	0.0
Tunisia	5.2	4.6	0.0	2.7	2.1	2.0	1.3
Uruguay	7.4	9.4	0.0	3.4	3.2	1.1	2.8

Table A4.11 Weighted percentage of resilient students and comparison group

		Resilient		Disadvantaged low achievers (DLA)	
		Percentage of students	S.E.	Percentage of students	S.E.
OECD	Australia	6.4	(0.3)	15.6	(0.6)
	Austria	6.2	(0.5)	16.3	(1.1)
	Belgium	5.2	(0.3)	18.0	(0.8)
	Canada	7.0	(0.3)	15.1	(0.6)
	Czech Republic	5.4	(0.4)	16.3	(0.9)
	Denmark	6.1	(0.4)	16.1	(1.0)
	Finland	7.5	(0.4)	15.0	(0.6)
	France	4.5	(0.4)	18.2	(1.2)
	Germany	5.0	(0.4)	17.2	(1.2)
	Greece	5.8	(0.5)	16.6	(1.1)
	Hungary	5.0	(0.4)	17.6	(1.0)
	Iceland	7.1	(0.5)	14.6	(0.5)
	Ireland	6.3	(0.4)	15.9	(1.0)
	Italy	6.3	(0.4)	15.8	(0.5)
	Japan	6.9	(0.5)	15.5	(1.0)
	Korea	7.2	(0.5)	14.6	(0.8)
	Luxembourg	4.5	(0.3)	18.9	(0.5)
	Mexico	5.1	(0.3)	16.4	(1.2)
	Netherlands	6.0	(0.4)	16.7	(1.0)
	New Zealand	6.0	(0.4)	16.8	(0.8)
	Norway	6.7	(0.5)	15.2	(0.8)
	Poland	6.3	(0.4)	16.0	(0.7)
	Portugal	5.8	(0.5)	16.3	(1.1)
	Slovak Republic	5.8	(0.4)	17.1	(0.9)
	Spain	6.0	(0.3)	16.0	(0.8)
	Sweden	6.6	(0.5)	15.6	(0.8)
	Switzerland	5.3	(0.3)	16.8	(0.8)
	Turkey	6.4	(0.5)	14.4	(1.0)
	United Kingdom	5.8	(0.3)	16.1	(0.7)
	United States	5.2	(0.4)	17.0	(1.4)
	OECD average	**6.0**	**(0.1)**	**16.3**	**(0.2)**
Partners	Argentina	4.6	(0.4)	16.9	(1.6)
	Azerbaijan	8.7	(1.0)	13.0	(0.9)
	Brazil	5.7	(0.5)	15.1	(0.8)
	Bulgaria	4.6	(0.4)	17.9	(1.6)
	Chile	4.5	(0.4)	17.6	(1.6)
	Colombia	6.2	(0.7)	14.9	(1.2)
	Croatia	6.3	(0.4)	15.7	(0.8)
	Estonia	7.1	(0.6)	14.7	(0.8)
	Hong Kong-China	7.6	(0.5)	14.7	(0.8)
	Indonesia	6.9	(0.7)	14.2	(1.3)
	Israel	5.4	(0.5)	16.2	(0.9)
	Jordan	5.8	(0.4)	15.6	(0.8)
	Kyrgyzstan	7.4	(0.6)	13.4	(0.9)
	Latvia	7.1	(0.5)	15.2	(1.1)
	Lithuania	5.9	(0.4)	16.1	(0.7)
	Macao-China	8.5	(0.5)	13.1	(0.6)
	Montenegro	7.6	(0.4)	14.8	(0.6)
	Romania	5.9	(0.8)	16.2	(1.5)
	Russian Federation	7.0	(0.6)	14.8	(1.1)
	Serbia	6.1	(0.5)	15.8	(1.1)
	Slovenia	5.2	(0.4)	16.9	(0.5)
	Chinese Taipei	6.4	(0.4)	16.1	(1.2)
	Thailand	6.4	(0.5)	14.3	(0.8)
	Tunisia	7.2	(0.6)	13.3	(0.9)
	Uruguay	5.3	(0.5)	16.6	(0.9)

ANNEX A5: TECHNICAL NOTES

This annex provides additional information on the characteristics of students and schools analysed in the report and on the statistical approaches used. The annex presents the definitions and methods used to construct groups of disadvantaged and resilient students as well as results obtained from robustness checks that were conducted to ensure that results discussed in the report are not dependent on methods of analysis. The annex then provides descriptive information on the student and school characteristics used in the report. Finally, the regression models applied in Chapters 3 and 4 are discussed, giving detailed descriptions of the background model, missing data imputation, the logistic regression used in Chapter 3 and the linear regression applied in Chapter 4.

GROUP IDENTIFICATION PROCEDURE FOR THIS REPORT

Central to the analytic strategy of this report is the identification of several key student groups. The report takes two distinct approaches in this regard. One is to produce results which can be meaningfully compared across countries. The other one is to define groups of students which can be analysed within each country and which takes into account a country's context. While the cross-country comparable definition gives a hint on how successful different systems are in helping disadvantaged students performing at the top, this definition is less useful for within-country analysis as in some cases the number of resilient students is too small. For example, with the internationally comparable definition we have less than 1% of resilient students in some partner countries and economies. With such small samples, any analytical attempts cannot produce reliable results. In fact, one of the PISA quality requirements is not to publish results based on samples representing less than 3% of the population (or 30 students or less than 5 schools). Thus, another definition was developed which defines resilient students using performance levels relative to the context of each country. With this definition, it makes little sense to compare percentages of resilient students across countries as students defined as resilient importantly differ in their performance levels. However, this definition can be used to compare countries in how individual or school factors affect performance of disadvantaged students within each country. This way, important insights into how countries deal with relatively disadvantaged students can be obtained. The report uses this definition, more details are discussed below. After that, this section discusses the construction of internationally comparable measure of the share of resilient students, also refered in the report as internationally successful disadvantaged students. The section provides a graphical representation of how these definitions differ in practice using examples from two countries (Australia and Argentina).

The main group identification strategy: the relative within-country definition

Within each country, students were separated into three performance categories – low, middle and high achievers – and into three socio-economic groups – low, middle and high socio-economic background. These two sets of categories were combined to identify disadvantaged low achievers and resilient students. The implementation of the identification strategy described above was complicated by the fact that PISA provides five plausible values of performance rather than one single performance measure. A second issue was the need to ensure that students were split into equal sized groups according to their socio-economic background using the PISA index of economic, social and cultural status (ESCS).

The report defines students as low achievers if their assessment score is below the 33rd percentile of the score distribution in the country where they were assessed and as high achievers when their score is above the 67th percentile. As noted above, PISA provides five plausible values of science performance rather than one single measure. The five plausible values are a representation of the range of abilities that a student might reasonably have (OECD, 2007). Instead of directly estimating a student's ability PISA estimates a probability distribution for each student's ability. From the distribution obtained, five values were randomly selected. Consequently, each student was assigned to an achievement group (low, middle or high achiever) for each of the five plausible values.

Students were also assigned to one of three groups (or tertiles) using their values on the index of socio-economic background using the same criteria as for science assessment scores: one group of disadvantaged students (*i.e.* the bottom third) and two groups of non-disadvantaged students (*i.e.* the middle and top thirds). As noted below, in Chapter 4, the middle and top thirds are combined and referred to as "non-disadvantaged students". The use of a simple cut-point procedure to allocate students into the tertiles would have resulted in uneven group sizes across countries (*e.g.* the bottom group could have comprised 32.4% of students in country A but 33.2% of students in country B). In other words, if this simple procedure had been used, the definition of disadvantaged students would not have been consistent across countries, potentially introducing a source of error in the results. This problem arises because the distribution of the index of socio-economic background is not sufficiently continuous to prevent the grouping of students at the two cut-points. (The distribution of the five plausible values does not cause this problem.) To achieve equal group sizes across countries, it was necessary to randomly distribute students with values equal to one of the two cut-points into the two adjacent groups (*i.e.* low or middle for students with values at the 33rd percentile; middle or high for students with values equal to the 67th percentile).

Rather than simply assigning all of these students to one of these groups, the report used a random subsampling process to ensure equal groups for low, middle and high socio-economic background students across all countries. The following procedure was adopted: first a "pseudo" random number with a normal distribution with mean 0 and standard deviation of 1 was generated and then this random number was multiplied by 0.01 and added to the value of the index of socio-economic background (which has mean 0 and standard deviation 1 in the sample of students from OECD countries, weighting countries equally). The resulting distribution was sufficiently continuous for the cut-point procedure to be used to create equal groups across countries. This random allocation of a small portion of a point to each student's socio-economic index value added an error component to the standard error, however, which was accounted for using the plausible values approach by computing a set of five plausible socio-economic background group assignments for each student.

After assigning students to groups for both science achievement and socio-economic background, the five plausible group assignments for science achievement were combined with the five plausible group assignments for socio-economic background (*e.g.* combining the first science achievement group assignment with the first socio-economic background group assignment, combining the second science achievement group assignment with the second socio-economic background group assignment, etc.). This process resulted in five new grouping variables each with nine values (envision a 3x3 matrix: bottom third of socio-economic background and bottom third of performance, bottom third of socio-economic background and middle third of performance, bottom third of socio-economic background and top third of performance, etc).

The report identifies students as resilient if they belong to the bottom third of the socio-economic background distribution in the country where they took the assessment and to the top third in terms of science performance. The report identifies students as disadvantaged low achievers if they belong to the bottom third of socio-economic disadvantage and their science achievement scores place them in the bottom third of the achievement distribution in the country where they took the assessment. In the analyses the framework to identify resilient students and disadvantaged low achievers just described was applied to the five new grouping variables. This resulted in five plausible resilient student groups and five plausible disadvantaged low achievers groups in each country.

Internationally comparable definition of student groups

For the internationally comparable definition of resilient students, within each country students were defined as disadvantaged and non-disadvantaged relatively to distribution of socio-economic background in this country. This is identical to the method discussed above for the within-country relative definition, so the group of disadvantaged students is defined in the same way, the one on the bottom third of the distribution. However, performance level categories were defined in a more internationally comparable fashion. Performance thresholds were calculated by regressing student performance on their socio-economic background, more precisely, on the PISA index of economic, social and cultural status (with its square term to allow for non-linearities). Student performance levels were then defined by dividing regression residuals into equal thirds. In other words, students were divided into groups of successful, average, and low-performers, by looking at their performance in comparison to peers sharing similar socio-economic background across countries. The analysis was conducted on the pooled sample of students from all countries, so performance was compared among students from all countries (weighting countries equally). Students were defined as resilient or internationally successful disadvantaged students, if they were disadvantaged students who perform in the top third of students from all countries after accounting for socio-economic background. Similarly, a disadvantaged student whose performance after accounting for socio-economic background lies in the lowest third was defined as a disadvantaged low achiever. Shares of students in these two groups were then compared across countries to study where disadvantaged students are more likely to be among top performing students sharing a similar socio-economic background from all countries.

Difference between an internationally comparable and the within-country relative definition of resilient students

Figure A1 below compares graphically two methods of identifying resilient and disadvantaged low-achieving students. The graph uses data from two countries which are first in alphabetical order among PISA participants. These are Argentina and Australia, which noticeably differ in socio-economic background of their students as well as in their science performance. On the top panel, the definition valid for within-country comparisons is presented, while in the bottom panel the internationally comparable definition is displayed. The horizontal axis represents student socio-economic background and the vertical axis represents student performance in science. The blue solid line reflects a positive relation between socio-economic background and science performance on a pooled sample of students from all participating countries. The vertical solid black line delimits disadvantaged and non-disadvantaged students in each country. Now, in the top panel two dashed horizontal lines divide student sample into equal thirds according to their level of science performance relatively to performance distribution in each country. Green points are showing disadvantaged students who are among the top third of performers in each country, while red points are showing disadvantaged students who are among the bottom third of performers in each country. These are resilient and disadvantaged low-achieving students, respectively, according to the within-country comparable definition used throughout the report. Performance levels in these groups differ between countries (graphs in all panels are on the same scale to allow easy comparisons). While within this definition the shares of resilient students in the two countries are similar, resilient students in Argentina have on average much lower science scores than resilient students in Australia.

In the bottom panel, student performance is compared across all countries after taking into account student socio-economic background. Two dashed and positively sloped lines go in parallel to the thick blue line reflecting the international relation between socio-economic background and science performance (based on all countries, equally weighted). These lines cut into thirds student population tested in PISA according to how well student perform in science after accounting for their socio-economic background. Technically speaking, these lines cut into equal thirds the residuals from regression of science performance scores on the PISA index of economic, social, and cultural status and its squared term. In other words, these residuals reflect how much student gain in performance when comparing to their peers in an international sample who have exactly the same level of socio-economic background. Within this definition, green points are showing disadvantaged students who are among the top third of performers in the international sample, while red points are showing disadvantaged students who are among the bottom third of performers in an international sample, with the effect of socio-economic background on performance already accounted for. These are internationally successful disadvantaged students and and disadvantaged low-achieving students, respectively, according to the internationally comparable definition used in the second chapter of the report to make cross-country comparisons. In this case, disadvantaged students in Argentina have on average much lower socio-economic status, but they rarely perform at the top third even after taking into account the cross-national effect of socio-economic background on science performance. In internationally comparable terms, the share of resilient students is much lower in Argentina than in Australia.

Figure A5.1

Within-country relative definition of resilient and disadvantaged students in comparison to the internationally comparable definition.

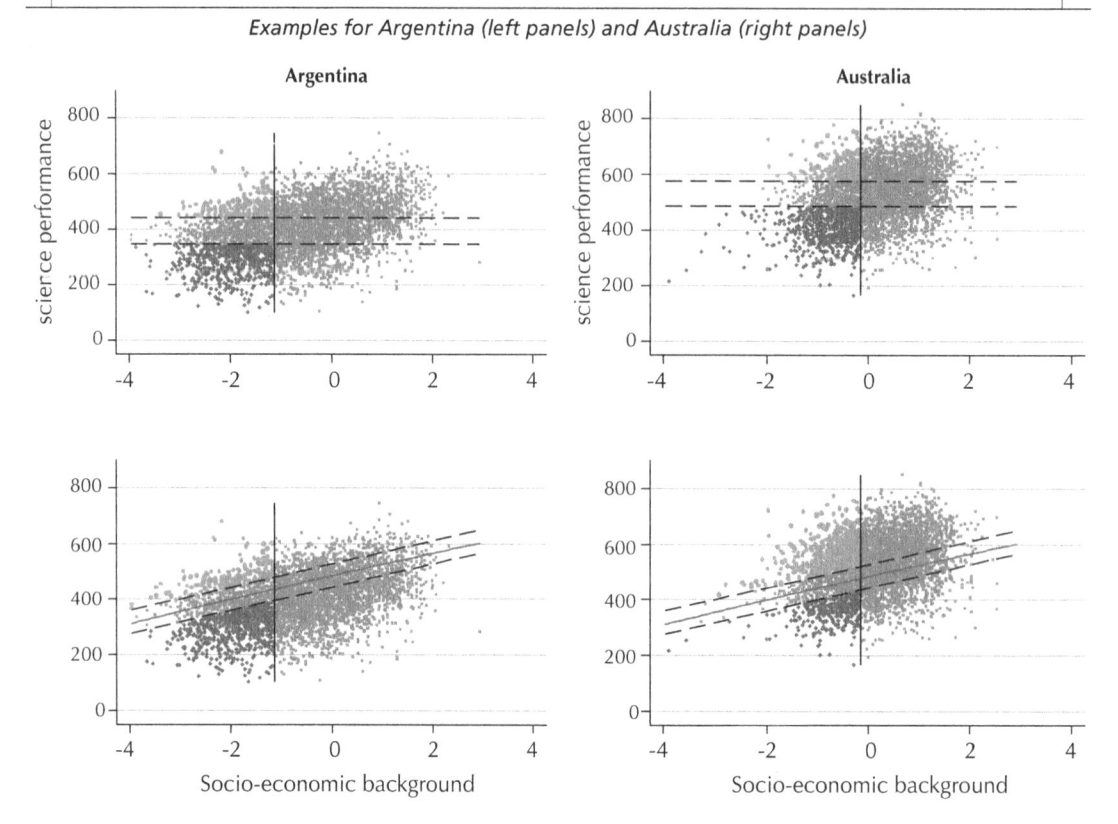

Examples for Argentina (left panels) and Australia (right panels)

Further details on the analysis with groups of disadvantaged and non-disadvantaged students

Analyses presented in the report were conducted using the methodology described in the OECD analysis manual: for each plausible group variable, the required statistic and its respective sampling variance were computed using the final and 80 replicate weights; then the five estimates and their respective sampling variances were averaged; the imputation variance was computed; and the sampling variance and the imputation variance were combined to obtain the final error variance.

For Chapter 4, where performance scores were not used to define groups, repeating analysis five times for different performance thresholds was less important and only one identifier of socio-economic group was used. In this chapter two categories of students were compared: disadvantaged and non-disadvantaged students. Chapter 4 defines disadvantaged students as those who have values in the bottom third of their country's distribution of the socio-economic background index and non-disadvantaged students as those who have middle or top third values in the socio-economic background index. The final analysis was conducted with five plausible values and replicate weights fully accounting for measurement error in student scores and for complex survey design.

ROBUSTNESS CHECKS FOR THE GROUP IDENTIFICATION PROCEDURES

Comparing student and parents responses

Throughout the report the PISA index of economic, social and cultural status was used to identify disadvantaged students. This index is constructed from student reports of household possessions as well as their parents' occupation and education attainment. There is a possibility that student reports of their parents' occupation and education attainment are inaccurate and thus introduce error into the PISA measure of socio-economic background. This possible measurement error could result in the exclusion of some disadvantaged students from the sample while some non-disadvantaged students are included. Here, the analysis makes use of the available parent survey data to conduct a robustness check of the identification of disadvantaged students. The results revealed no evidence across countries that students with low socio-economic background index values are any more or less likely to accurately state their parents' occupation and education than students with high socio-economic background index values. (See Tables A1 and A2.) Therefore, while this analysis does not rule out the presence of measurement error in the socio-economic background index, results suggest that measurement error is not a larger concern in identifying disadvantaged students than it is when identifying advantaged students.

The strategy used was to compare parent-reported occupation and educational attainment with the information provided by the student. Specifically, the analysis compares responses to two variables used in the construction of the socio-economic background index – highest occupational status of the parents (HISEI) and highest educational level of the parents (HISCED). The analysis calculates two statistics – the percentage of parent-student pairs with perfect agreement and the average disagreement between the parent and student responses – for students overall and by socio-economic background tertile.[1] It is possible to carry out this analysis in the 15 countries in which the parent survey was administered.

There are several limitations to this approach. First, ideally the analysis would create a socio-economic background index based on parent responses and compare this to the student-reported index, but this is not possible as parents were not asked the questions about household possessions which were asked of students. Therefore, it is not possible to assess the extent to which the observed disagreement between student and parent responses would result in movement across socio-economic background tertiles, changing which students are labelled as disadvantaged. Second, the parent survey was only administered in ten OECD countries and five partner countries and economies. These are not necessarily representative of the 55 countries analysed in this report. Third, the rate of non-response to the parent survey varies considerably across these 15 countries. High non-response rates increase the likelihood that the students with parent data are not representative of the students from that country. Although these limitations severely limit the report's ability to assess how robust the identification of disadvantaged students is to measurement error, this analysis does provide useable insights into the presence and scope of possible measurement error arising from the student reports.

There are three key findings that flow from this analysis. First, as expected, missing data from students is a larger problem among students with the lowest socio-economic background. In some cases, the rate of missing data was 20 percentage points higher among students with low socio-economic background than among students with high socio-economic background. Consequently, this analysis does a better job of assessing measurement error among high socio-economic background students than low socio-economic background students. Second, more students accurately indicate their parents' education than their parents' occupation. Overall, between 52% (Germany) and 86% (Turkey) of students with complete data correctly report their parents' education. Between 33% (Korea) and 99% (Bulgaria) of students with complete data correctly report their parents' occupation.[2] While these numbers suggest large measurement error in some countries (e.g., for parental occupation in Korea) and small measurement error in others (e.g., for parental occupation in Bulgaria), the analysis can not assess whether, or the degree to which, this disparity leads to student movement across socio-economic background tertiles. Finally, socio-economically disadvantaged students are no more or less accurate in their reports of parental occupation and education than students with a more advantaged socio-economic background. With respect to parental occupational status, socio-economically disadvantaged students have the highest rate of perfect agreement in eight countries. Socio-economically advantaged student have the highest rate in six countries and students with a middle socio-economic background index have the highest rate in one country. With respect to parental educational attainment, socio-economically disadvantaged students have the highest rate of agreement in six countries and socio-economically advantaged students have the highest rate in the other nine countries.

Socio-economic background-matched sample of resilient students and disadvantaged low achievers

Results presented in Chapter 2 indicate that resilient students and disadvantaged low achievers differ with respect to their average socio-economic background. Results presented in Chapter 3 reveal significant differences in approaches to learning and hours spent and courses taken between resilient students and disadvantaged low achievers. There is a concern that these differences across the two groups of students could be an artefact of underlying differences across the two groups in terms of average socio-economic background. Each resilient student was therefore matched on socio-economic background to two disadvantaged low achievers who are the same gender to check for potential bias introduced by differences in the socio-economic background means of resilient and disadvantaged low achievers. Each disadvantaged low achiever can be a match for more than one resilient student. The analysis then re-estimated the difference-in-means tests on the three variables: *i)* general interest in science, *ii)* self-concept and *iii)* time spent in regular science lessons.

Results suggest that findings reported in Chapter 3 are robust to group mean differences in socio-economic background (see Table A4.3). For all three variables, there is only a handful of countries where the group mean differences between disadvantaged low achievers and resilient students change substantially compared to the group means from the full sample and when they do, the change in mean differences is small – usually no greater than an increase/decrease of 10 percentage points or 10% of a standard deviation. There are no patterns across the three variables with respect to which group means increased or decreased. Additionally in only a few countries did the disadvantaged low achievers-resilient group mean differences lose or gain statistical significance in the matched sample compared to the full sample. Changes in the significance of group mean differences are reported below:

General interest in science: The estimate for one country gains significance while the others remain unchanged.

Science self-concept: The estimate in one country gains significance while the difference in another loses significance.

Time spent learning science in regular science lessons: Across the three categories – no time, up to four hours and more than four hours each week – a total of five estimates are no longer significant and one gains significance.

Alternative definitions

As previous analyses of PISA data have revealed, the relationship between socio-economic background and achievement is non-linear (OECD, 2007). There is a possibility that non-linearities may be driving the identification of resilient students and thus findings presented in the report. For example, if the cut-points are just above a kink point in some countries and just below a kink point in other countries, the across-country differences in the size of the student groups could be driven primarily by the location of these kink points. The results could be problematic if they are an artefact of these kink points. The purpose of this robustness check is not to determine the location of these kink points, but rather to determine how robust the findings are to an alternative definition of resilience.

The alternative definition analysed keeps the socio-economic background cut-point for disadvantaged students (*i.e.* those with values in the bottom third of their country's distribution) but applies a more conservative set of cut-points for science achievement. Low achievers are now those students with scores below the 30th percentile while high achievers have to have scores above the 70th percentile. This analysis re-estimated the difference-in-means tests for the same three variables as are used in the matched sample robustness check: *i*) general interest in science, *ii*) self-concept and *iii*) time spent in regular science lessons.

The results show that Chapter 3 findings are robust to more conservative definitions of low and high achievers (see Table A.4). The estimates of disadvantaged low achievers-resilient group mean differences using the alternative definition are usually within 5 percentage points or 10% of a standard deviation unit of the original estimate. The group mean estimates for resilient students drove these changes as the group mean estimates for disadvantaged low achievers changed very little (*i.e.* less than one one-hundredth). Differences between the original results and those derived from the alternative definition are larger for the science self-concept variable suggesting greater sensitivity to the cut-points used in the student group identification procedure. There is little change with respect to which disadvantaged low achievers-resilient group mean differences are significant though more self-concept estimates changed significance than changed in the other variables; specifically:

General interest in science: No estimates lost significance, in one country.

Science self-concept: The estimates in two countries lost significance.

Time spent learning science in school in regular lessons: Across the three categories – no time, up to four hours and more than four hours each week – there were practically no changes of significance.

DESCRIPTION OF VARIABLES ANALYSED IN THE REPORT

The report focuses on disadvantaged students and factors affecting their performance. In the report, several student and school characteristics are related to student science scores. These characteristics are measured through indices constructed from student responses or responses provided by school principals in the background questionnaires accompanying the student cognitive test. This section describes questions used to create indices and gives details on how they were constructed. Student-level indices describing approaches to learning, hours spent and courses taken and school-level indices summarising school characteristics are described separately.

Student approaches to learning

This report uses seven distinct indices reflecting student approaches to learning. The indices were scaled with IRT models using student questionnaire items and were standardised to have mean 0 and standard deviation 1 on average in OECD countries, weighting countries equally. Details on scaling and estimates of indices reliability are given in Chapter 16 of the PISA 2006 Technical Report (OECD, 2009). Information on

ANNEX A5: TECHNICAL NOTES

background questionnaire questions from which indices were constructed is provided below. The motivation for using these indices and their interpretation is discussed in the main text of the report.

General interest in science. Students reported how much interest they have in learning about eight science topics: physics, chemistry, the biology of plants, human biology, astronomy, geology, ways scientists design experiments and what is required for scientific explanations. Students provided responses on the ordinal scale using the following categories: "High interest", "Medium interest", "Low interest" and "No interest". The IRT model was then used to estimate an index, which is called INTSCIE in the PISA dataset. Higher values of this index correspond with higher interest in science topics.

Box A5.1. General interest in science

Q21 – How much interest do you have in learning about the following ‹broad science› topics?

(Please tick only one box in each row)

	High interest	Medium interest	Low interest	No interest
a) Topics in physics	☐₁	☐₂	☐₃	☐₄
b) Topics in chemistry	☐₁	☐₂	☐₃	☐₄
c) The biology of plants	☐₁	☐₂	☐₃	☐₄
d) Human biology	☐₁	☐₂	☐₃	☐₄
e) Topics in astronomy	☐₁	☐₂	☐₃	☐₄
f) Topics in geology	☐₁	☐₂	☐₃	☐₄
g) Ways scientists design experiments	☐₁	☐₂	☐₃	☐₄
h) What is required for scientific explanations	☐₁	☐₂	☐₃	☐₄

Instrumental motivation to learn science. Students reported on how much they agree with five statements describing the importance and usefulness of science learning to them, for example, "I study school science because I know it is useful for me" (all statements are given in the box below). The IRT model was then used to construct an index summarising these responses, which is named INSTSCIE in the PISA dataset. Higher values of this index correspond with higher instrumental motivation to learn science.

Box A5.2. Instrumental motivation to learn science

Q35 – How much do you agree with the statements below?

(Please tick only one box in each row)

	Strongly agree	Agree	Disagree	Strongly disagree
a) Making an effort in my ‹school science› subject(s) is worth it because this will help me in the work I want to do later on	☐₁	☐₂	☐₃	☐₄
b) What I learn in my ‹school science› subject(s) is important for me because I need this for what I want to study later on	☐₁	☐₂	☐₃	☐₄
c) I study ‹school science› because I know it is useful for me	☐₁	☐₂	☐₃	☐₄
d) Studying my ‹school science› subject(s) is worthwhile for me because what I learn will improve my career prospects	☐₁	☐₂	☐₃	☐₄
e) I will learn many things in my ‹school science› subject(s) that will help me get a job	☐₁	☐₂	☐₃	☐₄

© OECD 2011 Against the Odds: Disadvantaged Students Who Succeed in School

ANNEX A5: TECHNICAL NOTES

Participation in science-related activities. Students reported on how often they are involved in activities related to science. More precisely, students indicated how often they watch TV programmes about science, borrow or buy books about science, visit web sites about science, listen to radio programmes about advances in science, read magazines or science articles in newspapers and attend a science club. Students responded using four categories: "Very often", "Regularly", "Sometimes" and "Never or hardly ever". These responses were then used to estimate the index using the IRT model. The index is called SCIEACT in the PISA dataset. Higher values of this index correspond with higher participation in science-related activities.

Box A5.3. Participation in science-related activities

Q19 – How often do you do these things?

(Please tick only one box in each row)

	Very often	Regularly	Sometimes	Never or hardly ever
a) Watch TV programmes about ‹broad science›	☐₁	☐₂	☐₃	☐₄
b) Borrow or buy books on ‹broad science› topics	☐₁	☐₂	☐₃	☐₄
c) Visit web sites about ‹broad science› topics	☐₁	☐₂	☐₃	☐₄
d) Listen to radio programmes about advances in ‹broad science›	☐₁	☐₂	☐₃	☐₄
e) Read ‹broad science› magazines or science articles in newspapers	☐₁	☐₂	☐₃	☐₄
f) Attend a ‹science club›	☐₁	☐₂	☐₃	☐₄

Self–efficacy. Students assessed how easy it would be for them to perform different science-related tasks. Eight tasks were listed in the question and students assessed them using four categories: "I could do it easily", "I could do this with a bit of effort", "I would struggle to do this on my own" and "I couldn't do this". The tasks included describing the role of antibiotics in the treatment of disease and interpreting the scientific information provided in the labelling of food items. Exact wording of the eight tasks and the associated question is provided below. Based on these responses an index was constructed using the IRT model. The index is named SCIEEFF in the PISA dataset. Higher values of this index reflect higher student confidence in performing science-related tasks.

ANNEX A5: TECHNICAL NOTES

Box A5.4. Self-efficacy

Q17 – How easy do you think it would be for you to perform the following tasks on your own?

(Please tick only one box in each row)

	I could do this easily	I could do this with a bit of effort	I would struggle to do this on my own	I couldn't do this
a) Recognise the science question that underlies a newspaper report on a health issue	☐₁	☐₂	☐₃	☐₄
b) Explain why earthquakes occur more frequently in some areas than in others	☐₁	☐₂	☐₃	☐₄
c) Describe the role of antibiotics in the treatment of disease	☐₁	☐₂	☐₃	☐₄
d) Identify the science question associated with the disposal of garbage	☐₁	☐₂	☐₃	☐₄
e) Predict how changes to an environment will affect the survival of certain species	☐₁	☐₂	☐₃	☐₄
f) Interpret the scientific information provided on the labelling of food items	☐₁	☐₂	☐₃	☐₄
g) Discuss how new evidence can lead you to change your understanding about the possibility of life on Mars	☐₁	☐₂	☐₃	☐₄
h) Identify the better of two explanations for the formation of acid rain	☐₁	☐₂	☐₃	☐₄

Self-concept. Students assessed how difficult it is for them to learn science. They were asked how much they agree with six statements including "I learn science topics quickly" and "I can easily understand new ideas in school science". Responses were given using four categories: "Strongly agree", "Agree", "Disagree" and "Strongly disagree". Exact wording of the question and the possible responses is provided below. The scale was estimated using the IRT model and named SCSCIE in the PISA dataset. Higher values of this index indicate higher self-concept in science.

Box A5.5. Self-concept

Q37 – How much do you agree with the statements below?
The following question asks about your experience in learning ‹school science› topics.

(Please tick only one box in each row)

	Strongly agree	Agree	Disagree	Strongly disagree
a) Learning advanced ‹school science› topics would be easy for me	☐₁	☐₂	☐₃	☐₄
b) I can usually give good answers to ‹test questions› on ‹school science› topics	☐₁	☐₂	☐₃	☐₄
c) I learn ‹school science› topics quickly	☐₁	☐₂	☐₃	☐₄
d) ‹School science› topics are easy for me	☐₁	☐₂	☐₃	☐₄
e) When I am being taught ‹school science›, I can understand the concepts very well	☐₁	☐₂	☐₃	☐₄
f) I can easily understand new ideas in ‹school science›	☐₁	☐₂	☐₃	☐₄

ANNEX A5: TECHNICAL NOTES

School preparation for science careers. Students gave their perception of the usefulness of schooling as preparation for science-related careers. Four statements were assessed by students using four possible responses: "Strongly agree", "Agree", "Disagree" and "Strongly disagree". Exact wording of the question including the four statements is provided below. The responses were inverted and scaled using the IRT model so that higher values of this index indicate higher levels of agreement with usefulness of schooling as preparation for science-related careers. This index is called CARPREP in the PISA dataset.

Box A5.6. School preparation for science careers

Q27 – How much do you agree with the statements below?

(Please tick only one box in each row)

	Strongly agree	Agree	Disagree	Strongly disagree
a) The subjects available at my school provide students with the basic skills and knowledge for a ‹science-related career›	☐₁	☐₂	☐₃	☐₄
b) The ‹school science› subjects at my school provide students with the basic skills and knowledge for many different careers	☐₁	☐₂	☐₃	☐₄
c) The subjects I study provide me with the basic skills and knowledge for a ‹science-related career›	☐₁	☐₂	☐₃	☐₄
d) My teachers equip me with the basic skills and knowledge I need for a ‹science-related career›	☐₁	☐₂	☐₃	☐₄

Information on science-related careers. Students reported their perceptions of how informed they believed themselves to be about science-related careers. More precisely, students assessed how informed they were about four different topics using four response categories: "Very well informed", "Fairly informed", "Not well informed" and "Not informed at all". Exact wording of the question including the four topics is provided below. Responses were inverted and scaled using the IRT model so higher values of this index correspond with students believing they have better information about science-related careers. The index is called CARINFO in the PISA dataset.

Box A5.7. Information on science–related careers

Q28 – How informed are you about these topics?

(Please tick only one box in each row)

	Very well informed	Fairly informed	Not well informed	Not informed at all
a) ‹Science-related careers› that are available in the job market	☐₁	☐₂	☐₃	☐₄
b) Where to find information about ‹science-related careers›	☐₁	☐₂	☐₃	☐₄
c) The steps students need to take if they want a ‹science-related career›	☐₁	☐₂	☐₃	☐₄
d) Employers or companies that hire people to work in ‹science-related careers›	☐₁	☐₂	☐₃	☐₄

ANNEX A5: TECHNICAL NOTES

Hours spent and courses taken to learn science

The report uses three measures to describe hours spent and courses taken to learn science. These measures focus on science, because in 2006 PISA focused on this domain. The variables on courses tackle attendance and number of course. The time variable measures the amount of time spent learning science at school through regular lessons.

Attendance in compulsory science courses at school

Students reported whether they attended compulsory science courses this year or last year. Four different courses were listed in the question, *i.e.* general science, biology, physics and chemistry, and students reported whether these courses were taken last year or this year by ticking one of two options: "yes" and "no". Two distinct variables were constructed from these responses. The index of student attendance at a compulsory course in general science is an indicator variable, *i.e.* it only takes two values at the student level, either 0 or 1. The index takes the value of 1 if the student reports having taken a compulsory course in general science this year or last year. The second measure is the number of compulsory science courses the student reports taking over the two year period (this year or last) regardless of whether the courses were general science or on a specific science topic. As four courses were listed and students were asked about the last two years, the values of the index run from zero to a maximum of eight courses attended. The exact wording of the question is given in Box A.8 below. In the international PISA dataset, the variables used to construct this measure were ST33Q11, ST33Q12, ST33Q31, ST33Q32, ST33Q51, ST33Q52, ST33Q71 and ST33Q72.

There are two issues worth remembering when interpreting results using these variables. For students who responded to at least one category, missing responses were recoded to zero (that is, they were regarded as not attending courses for which they had not ticked a response). This means that a response was coded as missing only if a student did not tick any of the compulsory science courses this or last year. This approach holds when missing responses were given by students who only made an effort to give answers when these were positive, a plausible assumption. Otherwise, a student attending a physics course who ticked "yes" for physics, but did not make an effort to tick "no" for other courses, would have been coded as not having attended a single course. In any case, the recoding of missing values to zero mainly related to responses provided for general science courses. One can plausibly expect that students who attended specific science courses did not attend the general science courses, so a missing response for the latter can be plausibly coded as zero. While different interpretations are possible, these changes affected less than 5% of students in the case of general science courses and less than 0.1% for specific science courses. These changes also have negligible impact on the values of these variables, changing the average of students taking general science courses by no more than 2% and usually by less than 1% in most countries. Thus, the recoding of missing responses to zero allowed the sample size to be maintained while not changing values of the analysed variables in an important way.

The second issue is related to recoding of the attendance variables after data collection. In some countries, student responses were replaced by one value in the PISA datasets. This is the case in countries where all students are taking general science courses, or the opposite, none of them have this possibility. For these countries, the indicator of taking a compulsory general science course is 0 or 1 for all students. In this situation, the variable was not related to performance as there is no variation within a country. For some countries, the values for specific science courses were also recoded to one value. In these countries, all students attend courses in physics, biology or chemistry, because that is required by the curriculum, or they do not attend any of them. Countries like Ireland, Korea, Norway and Poland have no variation in the number of compulsory courses taken in biology, physics and chemistry and the only variation in the overall index is because of variability in the indicator of general science courses. While these issues are reflected in the means and variation of these indicators by country, they had no impact on the analysis presented in the report which concentrates on within-country differences. In other words, indices that take one value for all students in the country were not related to performance. That is reflected by a letter "v" in the result tables.

> **Box A5.8. Attendance in compulsory science courses at school**
>
> Q33 – Did you or do you take any of the courses listed below?
> <Instructions for students who do not study science>
>
> (Please tick as many boxes as apply in each row)
>
> | | Last year Yes | Last year No | This year Yes | This year No |
> |---|---|---|---|---|
> | a) A compulsory <general science course> | □₁ | □₂ | □₁ | □₄ |
> | c) A compulsory biology course | □₁ | □₂ | □₁ | □₄ |
> | e) A compulsory physics course | □₁ | □₂ | □₁ | □₄ |
> | g) A compulsory chemistry course | □₁ | □₂ | □₁ | □₄ |

Number of regular science learning hours

Students were asked to report their science learning time. In this report the number of hours spent in regular science lessons was analysed. Students denoted their learning time by ticking one out of five possible categories: "No time", "Less than 2 hours a week", "2 or more but less than 4 hours a week", "4 or more but less than 6 hours a week" and "6 or more hours a week". These responses were recoded to 0, 1, 3, 5 and 6, respectively, creating an index with the actual number of hours spent in regular science lessons. As a robustness check other recoding schemes were also tried, producing almost identical results. The exact wording of the question is given in the box below. In the international PISA dataset, the variables used to construct this measure was ST31Q01.

> **Box A5.9. Number of regular science learning hours**
>
> Q31 – How much time do you typically spend per week studying the following subjects?
> For each subject, please indicate separately:
> • the time spent attending regular lessons at your school;
> • the time spent attending out-of-school-time lessons (at school, at home or somewhere else);
> • the time spent studying or doing homework by yourself.
> <An hour here refers to 60 minutes, not to a class period>
>
> (Please tick only one box in each row)
>
> | | No time | Less than 2 hours a week | 2 or more but less than 4 hours a week | 4 or more but less than 6 hours a week | 6 or more hours a week |
> |---|---|---|---|---|---|
> | a) Regular lessons in <school science> at my school | □₁ | □₂ | □₃ | □₄ | □₅ |

Learning environment at school

All variables focusing on the learning environment that students experience at school are the product of the answers school principals gave in the school questionnaire. These variables cover a wide range of issues, such as the management and funding of the school, admittance policies, and the quality and use of school resources to promote science learning. Detailed definitions of each of these variables follow.

Private school. School principals were asked to report whether their school was a private or a public organisation. The PISA school questionnaire defined as private those schools that are managed directly or indirectly by a non-governmental organisation such as a church, a trade union, a business or another private institution. Public schools on the other hand are managed directly or indirectly by a public education authority, a government agency, or a governing board appointed by government or elected by public franchise. Exact wording of the question is provided in the box below. The variable analysed in the report was coded as 1 for students in private schools and 0 for students in public schools. In the international PISA dataset, the variables used to construct this measure was SC02Q01.

Box A5.10. **Public and private schools**

Q2 – Is your school a public or a private school?

(Please tick only one box)

A public school (This is a school managed directly or indirectly by a public education authority, government agency, or governing board appointed by government or elected by public franchise.)	☐₁
A private school (This is a school managed directly or indirectly by a non-government organisation; e.g. a church, trade union, business, or other private institution.)	☐₂

School competition

The PISA school questionnaire gathered information on the schooling options available to parents when choosing a school for their children and the amount of competition between schools. School principals were asked to report the presence of other schools in the area that compete with their school for students. Exact wording of the question is provided in the box below. The indicator of school competition was coded as 1 if school principals reported that there was at least another school in the area competing with their school for students and 0 otherwise. In the international PISA dataset, the variables used to construct this measure was SC18Q01.

Box A5.11. **School competition**

Q18 – We are interested in the options parents have when choosing a school for their children. Which of the following statements best describes the schooling available to students in your location?

(Please tick only one box)

There are two or more other schools in this area that compete for our students	☐₁
There is one other school in this area that competes for our students	☐₂
There are no other schools in this area that compete for our students	☐₃

Academic selection in admission policies

School principals reported whether their school considered students' academic records when deciding on their admission to the school. Exact wording of the question is provided in the box below. The indicator for the presence of academic selection in admission policies was coded as 1 if school principals reported that students' academic records were considered as a prerequisite or a high priority in admission decisions and as 0 when school principals reported that academic records were either not considered or considered but were not a high priority factor. In the international PISA dataset, the variables used to construct this measure was SC19Q02.

ANNEX A5: TECHNICAL NOTES

Box A5.12. **Academic selection in student admission policies**

Q19 – How much consideration is given to the following factors when students are admitted to your school?

(Please tick one box in each row)

	Prerequisite	High priority	Considered	Not considered
a) Residence in a particular area	☐₁	☐₂	☐₃	☐₄
b) Student's academic record (including placement tests)	☐₁	☐₂	☐₃	☐₄
c) Recommendation of feeder schools	☐₁	☐₂	☐₃	☐₄
d) Parents' endorsement of the instructional or religious philosophy of the school	☐₁	☐₂	☐₃	☐₄
e) Student's need or desire for a special programme	☐₁	☐₂	☐₃	☐₄
f) Attendance of other family members at the school (past or present)	☐₁	☐₂	☐₃	☐₄

School activities to promote science learning

School principals were asked to report which activities that promote students' learning of science occurred at their school. Possible activities include: science clubs, science fairs, science competitions, extracurricular science projects and excursions and field trips. Responses on whether the school provided such activities were used to calculate an index of the availability of activities to promote science learning at the school level, using the IRT model. Exact wording of the question is provided in the box below. Higher values on this index reflect higher levels of school activities in promoting science learning. This index is called SCIPROM in the PISA dataset.

Box A5.13. **School activities to promote science learning**

Q20 – Is your school involved in any of the following activities to promote engagement with science among students in ‹national modal grade for 15-year-olds›?

(Please tick one box in each row)

	Yes	No
a) Science clubs	☐₁	☐₂
b) Science fairs	☐₁	☐₂
c) Science competitions	☐₁	☐₂
d) Extracurricular science projects (including research)	☐₁	☐₂
e) Excursions and field trips	☐₁	☐₂

School's educational resources

School principals were asked to report the extent to which they perceived that instruction at their school was hindered by the following seven factors: *i)* shortage or inadequacy of science laboratory equipment, *ii)* shortage or inadequacy of instructional materials, *iii)* shortage or inadequacy of computers for instruction, *iv)* lack or inadequacy of internet connectivity, *v)* shortage or inadequacy of computer software for instruction, *vi)* shortage or inadequacy of library materials and *vii)* shortage or inadequacy of audio-visual resources. Exact wording of the question is provided in the box below. The IRT model was used to construct from these responses an index representing the school's educational resources. The items were inverted before scaling and higher values on this index indicate better quality of educational resources. This index is named SCMATEDU in the PISA dataset.

Box A5.14. School's educational resources

Q14 – Is your school's capacity to provide instruction hindered by any of the following?

(Please tick one box in each row)

	Not at all	Very little	To some extent	A lot
a) A lack of qualified science teachers	☐₁	☐₂	☐₃	☐₄
b) A lack of qualified mathematics teachers	☐₁	☐₂	☐₃	☐₄
c) A lack of qualified <test language> teachers	☐₁	☐₂	☐₃	☐₄
d) A lack of qualified teachers of other subjects	☐₁	☐₂	☐₃	☐₄
e) A lack of laboratory technicians	☐₁	☐₂	☐₃	☐₄
f) A lack of other support personnel	☐₁	☐₂	☐₃	☐₄
g) Shortage or inadequacy of science laboratory equipment	☐₁	☐₂	☐₃	☐₄
h) Shortage or inadequacy of instructional materials (e.g. textbooks)	☐₁	☐₂	☐₃	☐₄
i) Shortage or inadequacy of computers for instruction	☐₁	☐₂	☐₃	☐₄
j) Lack or inadequacy of Internet connectivity	☐₁	☐₂	☐₃	☐₄
k) Shortage or inadequacy of computer software for instruction	☐₁	☐₂	☐₃	☐₄
l) Shortage or inadequacy of library materials	☐₁	☐₂	☐₃	☐₄
m) Shortage or inadequacy of audio-visual resources	☐₁	☐₂	☐₃	☐₄

REGRESSION ANALYSES

The background model

The report analyses associations between approaches to learning, hours spent on learning, number of courses taken, and school characteristics to the probability of becoming resilient (in Chapter 3) or to student science performance (in Chapter 4). These relationships were analysed using regression models, namely, logit regression in Chapter 3 and linear regression in Chapter 4. Interpretation of results depends on the background variables included in the regression model which should reflect important student and school characteristics that cannot be easily changed through additional school efforts or educational policy. Results from logit regressions in Chapter 3 and linear regressions in Chapter 4 suggest that the variables included in the background regression models analysed in the report reflect important characteristics of students and schools, explaining large part of the variance in student performance which can not be affected by policy. Nevertheless, relationships between student and school characteristics and performance presented in the context of this report should not be considered causal. Rather they paint a picture of overall associations between student and school characteristics on the one hand and student performance on the other.

Analyses reported in the report are based on a common set of background variables that are well-known correlates of student performance and reflect student or schools characteristics. Similar sets of background variables were used in previous PISA studies including *PISA 2006 Science Competencies For Tomorrow's World*, OECD (2007a), for example, see Chapter 5 on multilevel modelling, and several thematic reports arising from PISA 2006 data. Among individual characteristics, the background model includes student gender (coded as 1 for females and 0 for males), an indicator of students with an immigrant background (1 for those students, 0 for others) and an indicator for students who speak at home a language that is different from the language of the test (1 for those speaking different language at home, 0 for those who speak the same language). A set of indicators for the grade in which students are currently enrolled is added to each regression to enable consideration of differences in average performance across grades. The grade indicator for the modal grade in a country's PISA sample was omitted, creating a baseline category, so the coefficients for other indicators represent the difference in average performance in the grade they represent and the modal grade. These coefficients cannot be compared across countries because different baseline categories were used for different countries, but accounting for differences in student performance between grades was needed to limit the confounding impact on the analysed associations of different sampling designs or grade composition. Finally, the index of student socio-economic background was added to each regression. This is usually the most important control variable since it reflects differences in parental background and resources students can access at home.

Chapter 3 uses logistic regression models adjusting for various background variables and uses the results to assess the importance of different factors in determining the likelihood that disadvantaged students will exhibit academic resilience. The first model does not account for any student characteristics. The second model accounts for all student background characteristics (gender, immigrant background, language spoken, grade). The third model accounts for student background characteristics and school mean socio-economic background (school level mean of the socio-economic background index). In Chapter 4, all regressions control for students' individual socio-economic background as well as for the mean socio-economic background of a school students attend and its squared term to take account of possible non-linearities. Finally, a dummy variable indicating disadvantaged students (the lowest tertile of the socio-economic background distribution in each country) was added to the background model in regressions developed in Chapter 4. The interaction between the "disadvantaged student" indicator and indices used to characterise student approaches to learning and school characteristics identifies potential differences between disadvantaged and non-disadvantaged students in the association between such indices and performance.

Estimated coefficients for the background model developed for analyses conducted in Chapter 3 are presented in Table A.7, while those developed in the context of Chapter 4 are presented in Table A.8. Results presented in Table A.7 suggest that background characteristics, including socio-economic background and mean school socio-economic background, are not significantly related to the probability of being resilient in some countries. This finding is not surprising, since Chapter 3 employs data solely on disadvantaged students and therefore differences across students and schools in terms of socio-economic background are much smaller than they are in the full sample. Background variables are far more strongly related to student performance in results presented in Table A.8, where student socio-economic background and its school mean are generally associated with performance in all countries. Indicators for gender, immigrant background and language spoken at home are statistically significant in many countries. The student grade indicators are also usually significant and positive for higher grades confirming the expectation that students in higher grades typically outperform students who attend lower grades.

Imputation of missing data

The PISA index of economic, social and cultural status is a crucial variable in the report. For this reason, students with missing information on this index were excluded from the analysis. Fortunately, the number of students with no information on the socio-economic background index is very small in most PISA 2006 participating countries (see Table A.9 for information on the share of students with missing socio-economic background information by country). In line with other reports based on PISA data that rely heavily on the

ANNEX A5: TECHNICAL NOTES

use of the socio-economic background index, Qatar was excluded from all analyses because of reliability problems with the socio-economic background index in this country. On average approximately 1% of students in OECD countries had no socio-economic background information (the country with the largest number of missing values in terms of socio-economic background was Germany - 4%).

For other variables analysed in the report, missing data were handled using a variety of approaches chosen depending on the nature of the variable and the type of analysis being developed. For all variables used in the background model, the report adopted the simple approach of imputing missing data with school means (or country level means if no school mean was available) of the same variables. For variables which have only integer values (including 0/1 dummy indicators), the imputed means were rounded to the closest integer. Subsequently, a dummy variable for each of the background factors was constructed to denote observations with imputed values and was included as part of the background model. This way missing information for immigrant background, language spoken at home and enrolled grade were imputed. For gender, only four cases in the whole PISA sample had missing information and these were arbitrary replaced by a value of 0.

While in theory this simple imputation approach could give biased regression results, it is unlikely that it is the case for this report. First of all, only a small number of observations had missing values. In addition, as a robustness check, multiple imputation techniques were used to examine whether the use of computationally demanding but theoretically more valid approaches would lead to different conclusions. No meaningful difference in estimates was found when comparing estimates obtained using no imputation (casewise deletion), a mean-dummy approach imputation and multiple imputation. Consequently, the mean-dummy imputation approach was adopted since it is not computationally demanding, it maintains sample size unaltered and it yields results that are comparable to the ones obtained with other approaches.

Missing information was imputed for background characteristics only, not for student and school indices that are the focus of this report. That was done to preserve the original relationship between these indicators and performance. Table A.10 highlights that very few students have missing information on these indices (between 0% and 2% on average across OECD countries) with only two noticeable exceptions. On average as many as 6% of students have missing information on the indicators for *general interest in science* and *self-concept* and in some countries, the share of students with no information on these indices is relatively high (see Table A.10). The greater the share of students with missing information in a country is, the greater care should be taken in interpreting results since estimates may not properly represent relationships in the population to the extent that students with missing information and students with all information are not homogeneous.

Imputation of missing data for student indices was needed for the combined model presented in Chapter 3 and for models used in Chapter 4. In these models several indices are simultaneously introduced in the same regression, which exacerbates the problem of missing information and severely reduces the sample size. A mean-dummy imputation approach was consequently adopted in the estimation of these models: missing information on each index was replaced by the relevant school mean (or country mean whenever the school mean could not be computed) and a dummy variable indicating observations for which information was imputed was included in the combined model.

Details on the logistic model applied in Chapter 3

Logistic regression models presented in result tables for Chapter 3 were used to answer the following question: which factors are associated with the likelihood that a disadvantaged student will beat the odds? The dependent or outcome variable in these models is an indicator that takes value 1 when disadvantaged students are high performers in their countries (top third) in the PISA science assessment and value 0

ANNEX A5: TECHNICAL NOTES

when disadvantaged students are not high performers. Logistic regression models were estimated on all disadvantaged students – *i.e.* a third of the entire PISA student sample – since the question they aim to answer is whether particular approaches to learning are associated with the likelihood that disadvantaged students will be high performers in science. Missing data were imputed for background variables and for indices analysed in the combined model using the methods described above.

For each factor three models are presented: the first model represents the base model with no background variables included. The second model introduces individual level background variables while the third model introduces a further background variable at the school level: the mean socio-economic background of students sampled in PISA that attend the same school as the respondent (represented by mean socio-economic background). The mean school value of the socio-economic background index was calculated on the whole sample, including non-disadvantaged students if such students were present in a school.

For each model, Tables 3.1c to 3.15c present the odds ratios associated with a one unit increase in a particular factor and standard errors from the underlying logistic regression model. Odds ratios over one indicate that higher values of the factor analysed are associated with a greater likelihood that a disadvantaged student will be resilient, while odds ratios below one are suggestive of a negative relationship between the factor and resilience. By comparing estimates of the relationship between different factors and academic resilience obtained in the base, individual level and school level models, the chapter examines whether the relationship between approaches to learning and resilience is (partially) explained by differences in individual characteristics and the schools which students attend. Box A.15 describes in greater detail the logistic regression model framework and how results can be interpreted.

Box A5.15. **Understanding logistic regression and interpreting odds ratios**

Multiple linear regression is appropriate when outcome variables are continuous, as in the case of the measure of science achievement used in PISA. However, when the outcome variable is dichotomous, such as whether or not a student is resilient, a variant of multiple regression, called logistic regression, is appropriate. Logistic regression is also a useful policy device since it allows estimation of the probability that a certain outcome will occur (for example, that a disadvantaged student will be resilient) as a function of various characteristics of the student, such as age, gender, or family income, or characteristics of the school, such as mean socio-economic background. Because coefficients estimated within the logistic regression framework are not easily interpretable, the chapter reports odds ratios.

The logistic regression model presented in equation (1) below represents the extended model predicting the likelihood that a disadvantaged student *i* attending school *j* will beat the odds and earn a science test score in the top third of all scores within his/her country.

$$(1) \quad \Pr(resilient = 1)_{ij} = \frac{1}{1 + \exp(-z_{ij})}, \text{ where } z_{ij} = X_{ij}\beta + \alpha \bar{S}_j$$

The model predicts a student's probability of being resilient $\Pr(resilient = 1)_{ij}$ as a function of a matrix of student characteristics and approaches to learning (X_{ij}), and the mean socio-economic background at the school level ($\bar{S}_j$). By accounting for mean socio-economic background at the school level, models account for the effect of school characteristics on the probability a disadvantaged student will demonstrate resilience.

The odds of an event occurring is the ratio of the likelihood of that event occurring to the likelihood

ANNEX A5: TECHNICAL NOTES

> of that event not occurring and in the context of this report the event is "disadvantaged student beats the odds". If a student has an 80% chance of being resilient, then the odds of being resilient are [0.80 / (1-0.8)], which is 4.0 while an event with odds of 1.0 has an equal chance of occurring or not occurring. An odds ratio is simply the ratio of the odds for two different sets of circumstances. For example, the odds of an event for female and male students could be assessed and the ratio of the odds could be calculated. Odds ratios are interpreted in a fashion similar to multiple regression coefficients: they denote the ratio of the odds of an event occurring as a consequence of a one-unit change in the independent variable, compared to what it was previously, given all other independent variables in the model are held constant.
>
> Source: Adapted from Box 4.1, OECD, 2003b, pp. 36-7.

Details on the linear regression applied in Chapter 4

Chapter 4 uses linear regression to estimate average associations between performance and student approaches to learning, number of hours and courses taken, and learning environment at school. In addition, this chapter discusses the difference in these associations between disadvantaged and non-disadvantaged students. Regressions were estimated country by country for all students with non-missing values on the socio-economic background index, accounting for background characteristics as discussed above. Results for average associations for all students were estimated by adding the policy indices to the background model. Results for differences in the strength of associations across disadvantaged and non-disadvantaged students were estimated by adding an interaction term – the dummy variable denoting disadvantaged students times the index of interest – to the regression model employed to estimate average effects. In other words, in this regression model the slope coefficient of key indices was allowed to differ for disadvantaged and non-disadvantaged students. The coefficient for the interaction term represents the difference in the association between disadvantaged and non-disadvantaged students. Regression models were estimated using all five plausible values for student performance and accounting for the complex survey design of the PISA study by using balanced repeated replicate (BRR) weights. Thus, these results are representative for populations of 15-year-old students in each country.

Notes

1. Here the average of the absolute value of the differences is calculated.

2. The measure of agreement between the student and parent responses about parental education is positively inflated. This is because of differences in how the question was asked of students and parents. Students were given the full range of ISCED levels (1 through 6), but parents were only given levels 3A to 6. Thus, all parents who have education below level 3A are grouped together in one category on the parent survey. Consequently, the analysis cannot pick up disagreement between students and parents among these levels. For example, consider a case where the student indicates their parent has a level 2 education but in fact the parent has a level 3B education. Due to the structure of the parent survey, the analysis cannot pick up on this disagreement.

ORGANISATION FOR ECONOMIC CO-OPERATION AND DEVELOPMENT

The OECD is a unique forum where governments work together to address the economic, social and environmental challenges of globalisation. The OECD is also at the forefront of efforts to understand and to help governments respond to new developments and concerns, such as corporate governance, the information economy and the challenges of an ageing population. The Organisation provides a setting where governments can compare policy experiences, seek answers to common problems, identify good practice and work to co-ordinate domestic and international policies.

The OECD member countries are: Australia, Austria, Belgium, Canada, Chile, the Czech Republic, Denmark, Estonia, Finland, France, Germany, Greece, Hungary, Iceland, Ireland, Israel, Italy, Japan, Korea, Luxembourg, Mexico, the Netherlands, New Zealand, Norway, Poland, Portugal, the Slovak Republic, Slovenia, Spain, Sweden, Switzerland, Turkey, the United Kingdom and the United States. The European Commission takes part in the work of the OECD.

OECD Publishing disseminates widely the results of the Organisation's statistics gathering and research on economic, social and environmental issues, as well as the conventions, guidelines and standards agreed by its members.

OECD PUBLISHING, 2, rue André-Pascal, 75775 PARIS CEDEX 16
(98 2010 06 1 P) ISBN 978-92-64-08995-2 – No. 57867 2011